NEW ZEALAND
MOTORHOME & CAMPING ATLAS

Hema Maps *will get you there ...*

CONTENTS

LAKE PUKAKI — JEFF DREWITZ

KAYAKING, DOUBTFUL SOUND — JEFF DREWITZ

INTRODUCTION

Introduction	5
How to use this book	6
The quality of Kiwi camping	8
'Free camping'	9
A guide to considerate Kiwi camping	9
Travelling with a pet	9
Toilet hygiene	9
Drinking water	9
20 top things to do	10
25 must-see attractions	11
Te Araroa – The long pathway	11

NATIONAL PARKS MAPS

Te Urewera National Park	12
Tongariro National Park	13
Arthur's Pass National Park	14
Kahurangi National Park	15
Mount Aspiring National Park	16
Aoraki/Mt Cook & Westland Tai Poutini National Parks	17
Nelson Lakes National Park	18
Fiordland National Park	19

NORTH ISLAND CAMPING SITES

Northland Region (Camps 1-127) — Pages 20-27

SH1 – Wellsford to Whangarei	21
SH1 – Whangarei to Kawakawa	22
SH10 – SH1 to Awanui	24
SH1 – Awanui to Cape Reinga	25
SH1 – Awanui to Kawakawa	26
SH12 – SH1 to Dargaville	27
SH12 – Dargaville to SH1	27

Auckland Region (Camps 128-215) — Pages 28-34

Islands of the Hauraki Gulf	28
SH1 – Auckland to Wellsford	29
SH16 – Wellsford to Auckland	31
Auckland to Waitakere Regional Park	31
Auckland to SH25	32
SH1 – Auckland to SH2	33

Central North Region (Camps 216-661) — Pages 34-58

SH1 – From SH2 to Hamilton	34
SH3 – Hamilton to Te Kuiti	35
SH3 – Te Kuiti to New Plymouth	35
SH4 – Te Kuiti to Ohakune	37
SH1 – Waiouru to Taupo	38
SH2 – SH1 to Tauranga	40
SH25 Coromandel Peninsula – SH2 to Waihi	42
SH1 – Hamilton to Taupo	46
SH2 – Tauranga to Opotiki	48
SH30 – Whakatane to Rotorua	50
SH5 & SH38 – Rotorua to Wairoa	52
SH35 – Opotiki to Gisborne	54
SH2 – Opotiki to Wairoa	55
SH2 – Wairoa to Hastings	56

Lower North Region (Camps 662-840) — Pages 58-68

SH1 – Wellington to SH3	58
SH1 – From SH3 to Waiouru	60
SH2 – Wellington to Masterton	61
SH2 – Masterton to Dannevirke	63
SH2 – Dannevirke to Hastings	64
SH3 – Palmerston North to Wanganui	65
SH4 – Wanganui to Ohakune	66
SH3 – Wanganui to Hawera	66
SH45 – Hawera to New Plymouth	67
SH3 & SH43 – Hawera to Taumarunui	68

SOUTH ISLAND CAMPING SITES

Nelson & Marlborough Region (Camps 841-1007) — Pages 70-79

Queen Charlotte Drive – Picton to SH6	70
SH6 – Havelock to Richmond	72
SH60 – Richmond to Collingwood	74
SH6 – Richmond to Inangahua Junction (SH69)	77
SH1 & SH63 – Picton to St Arnaud via Blenheim	78

West Coast Region (Camps 1008-1085) — Pages 79-84

SH6 – Inangahua Junction (SH69) to Greymouth	79
SH67 – Westport to Karamea	80
SH7 – Reefton to Greymouth	81
SH6 – Greymouth to Franz Josef	81
SH6 – Franz Josef to Haast	83

Canterbury Region (Camps 1086-1279) — Pages 84-94

SH1 – Blenheim to Waipara (SH7)	84
SH7 – Waipara (SH1) to Reefton	86
SH1 – Christchurch to Waipara	87
SH73 – Christchurch to Greymouth	88
Banks Peninsula – Christchurch to Akaroa	90
SH1 – Christchurch to Ashburton	91
SH1 – Ashburton to Timaru	92
SH8 – Timaru to Twizel	93
SH1 – Timaru to Oamaru	94

Otago Region (Camps 1280-1450) — Pages 94-103

SH83 – SH1 to Omarama (SH8)	94
SH1 – Omaru to Palmerston	95
SH85 – Palmerston to Alexandra	96
SH1 – Palmerston to Dunedin	96
SH1 – Dunedin to Milton	97
SH92 – Milton to Invercargill	98
SH8 – Milton to Cromwell	99
SH8 – Cromwell to Omarama (SH83)	100
SH6 – Cromwell to Haast	101
SH6 & SH6A – Cromwell to Glenorchy	102

Fiordland & Southland Region (Camps 1451-1530) — Pages 103-108

SH6 – Queenstown to Invercargill	103
SH99 – Invercargill to Te Anau	105
SH94 – Te Anau to Milford Sound	106
Stewart Island / Rakiura	108

TASMAN VALLEY — JEFF DREWITZ
WHARARIKI BEACH, FAREWELL SPIT — JEFF DREWITZ
BLUE POOLS, MT ASPIRING NP — JEFF DREWITZ

MAPS

Key map		109
North Island travel time and distances		110
South Island travel time and distances		111
Motorhome Dump Stations		220
Index		222
Camping Sites Index		234
Maps legends		Inside back cover
Campsite legend		Flap inside back cover

NORTH ISLAND REGIONAL MAPS

Far North	map	1-2
Kauri Coast & Whangarei	map	3-4
Kaipara Harbour & Kowhai Coast	map	5-6
Auckland & Coromandel	map	7-8
Waikato	map	9-10
Central Waikato	map	11-12
Rotorua & Bay of Plenty	map	13-14
Eastern Bay of Plenty & East Cape	map	15-16
North Taranaki & Taumarunui	map	17-18
Taupo	map	19-20
Hawke's Bay & Gisborne	map	21-22
Taranaki and River Region	map	23-24
South Taranaki	map	25-26
Napier & Hastings	map	27-28
The Manawatu & Horowhenua	map	29-30
The Manawatu & Wairarapa	map	31-32
Wellington & South Wairarapa	map	33-34
Cook Strait	map	35
Great Barrier Island	map	36

SOUTH ISLAND REGIONAL MAPS

Nelson	map	37-38
Nelson & Marlborough	map	39-40
Buller & Tasman	map	41-42
Marlborough	map	43-44
Central West Coast	map	45-46
Kaikoura & Hurunui	map	47-48
Glacier Country	map	49-50
Arthur's Pass	map	51-52
Central Canterbury	map	53-54
Ashburton & Christchurch	map	55-56
Southern West Coast	map	57-58
Mackenzie Region	map	59-60
Timaru & Ashburton	map	61-62
Northern Fiordland	map	63-64
Queenstown, Wanaka & Central Otago	map	65-66
Southern Canterbury & Northern Otago	map	67-68
Central Fiordland	map	69-70
Southland & Central Otago	map	71-72
Central Otago & Dunedin	map	73-74
Southern Fiordland	map	75-76
Southland	map	77-78
Coastal Otago	map	79
Stewart Island	map	80

NORTH ISLAND CITY AND SUBURBS MAPS

Bay of Islands	map	81
Russell	map	82
Paihia	map	83
Whangarei CBD	map	84
Whangarei Suburbs	map	85
Kerikeri CBD	map	86
Auckland CBD	map	87
North Shore Suburbs	map	88
West Auckland Suburbs	map	89
East & South Auckland Suburbs	map	90
Hamilton CBD	map	91
Hamilton Suburbs	map	92
Tauranga CBD	map	93
Tauranga Suburbs	map	94
Rotorua CBD	map	95
Rotorua Suburbs	map	96
Taupo CBD	map	97
Taupo Suburbs	map	98
Gisborne CBD	map	99
Gisborne Suburbs	map	100
Napier CBD	map	101
Hastings CBD	map	102
Napier / Hastings Suburbs	map	103
Palmerston North CBD	map	104
Palmerston North Suburbs	map	105
New Plymouth CBD	map	106
New Plymouth Suburbs	map	107
Wanganui CBD	map	108
Wanganui Suburbs	map	109
Wellington Suburbs	map	110
Wellington CBD	map	112

SOUTH ISLAND CITY AND SUBURBS MAPS

Picton CBD	map	113
Picton Suburbs	map	114
Nelson CBD	map	115
Nelson Suburbs	map	116
Blenheim CBD	map	117
Greymouth CBD	map	118
Christchurch CBD	map	119
Christchurch Suburbs	map	120
Timaru CBD	map	121
Oamaru CBD	map	122
Dunedin CBD	map	123
Dunedin Suburbs	map	124
Queenstown CBD	map	125
Queenstown Suburbs	map	126
Invercargill CBD	map	127
Invercargill Suburbs	map	128

Ask any Kiwi about the perfect childhood holiday, and chances are there's sand, sea and a tent, caravan or motorhome involved. Many campers' first memories of the joys of the road are of their Dad's trusty station wagon pulling an old '60s or '70s caravan. Built to last, it was loaded to the hilt with sleeping bags and pillows, polystyrene surf boards, canvas tents and awning, and fold-away chairs. At Mum's feet was the family dog, and at Nana's, a picnic basket for the journey and a thermos of tea, and her 'picnic special' bacon and egg pie.

The resulting holidays were a feast of fond memories: the first fish ever caught, catching your first wave, rowing the dingy, finding your feet on skis, sun-warmed skin, refreshing waters, new friends, and toasting marshmallows and playing cards around the campfire. In the background there was the deafening clikkety-clack as wetas and crickets battled it out under the night sky. Mornings were filled frying freshly speared flounder caught on whittled manuka sticks, burying Dad in the sand, and completing great feats of engineering with a bucket and spade, before heading to the dairy with new friends, jandals sticking to the road's hot tar, to get a rolled ice cream almost as big as your head… ah, those were the days…

So really these days it is little wonder that you often get the urge to hit the road. Fortunately the New Zealand coastline still provides plenty of sheltered nooks and crannies where you can park up, and a host of well-located holiday parks and camping grounds to choose from which offer clean ablutions and a range of additional facilities.

Not only is New Zealand one of the most beautiful countries in the world, but it's one of the few places where such a huge array of natural treats are still so accessible to so many. Whilst some beachside camps have been carved up into private housing, others have been purchased by the New Zealand government and regional councils and conserved for posterity.

So welcome to the thoroughly updated fourth edition of the New Zealand Motorhome and Camping Atlas, a guide which celebrates all the wonderful places to camp that New Zealand has to offer. Inside you will find a wide range of places to stay, from informal camp sites offering basic facilities, through to fully serviced Motorhome and Caravan Parks offering everything you could possibly wish, plus all the information and mapping you will ever need to guide you on an extended road trip around New Zealand.

Happy Camping!

Donna Blaber

DOUBTFUL SOUND, FIORDLAND, SOUTH ISLAND
JEFF DREWITZ

6 Camping New Zealand

HOW TO USE THIS BOOK

Simply view the map section for the area(s) that you wish to travel to, and find the relevant numbers for the area that interests you. Then find the number in the listing of motorhome parks, campsites and rest areas for information about the site you have chosen.

CAMPSITES

All of the campsites detailed in this guide are grouped into the following broad categories:

 SERVICED CAMPSITE

These sites have regular (usually daily) servicing of toilets and showers, and they often also have a variety of other services that can make your camping a delight. Such sites are normally commercial and payment is required.

 MOTORHOME PARK/CARAVAN PARK

This classification includes sites offering a similar level of facilities to a serviced campsite, but are also suitable for campervans, and also includes designated freedom camping sites for self-contained motorhomes, which have no facilities. Read the notes for each site to see what conditions and facilities are available.

 MOTORHOME PARK/CARAVAN PARK WITH DUMP STATION

These sites are motorhome park/caravan parks that also provide dump stations.

 INFORMAL CAMPING

This classification covers a wide variety of Department of Conservation (DOC) or local authority domain camping grounds where servicing is perhaps less regular, and facilities are more limited. Such areas should in no means be regarded as second-rate camping compared to their commercial alternatives; indeed such simple camping is often the very essence of what 'real Kiwi camping' is about. The scenic location of many casual camping sites means they provide highly memorable camping.

 ROADSIDE REST AREA

There are roadside rest areas (including short term parking and picnic areas) everywhere in New Zealand; and they range from scruffy patches of gravel used by road maintenance crews to pretty spots with seating, tables and shade for weary travellers to rest. It is impossible to mark every roadside gravel patch, so to rate a mention in this guide, acceptable rest areas need at least one of the following: picnic table, barbecue or fireplace, toilet, shade or shelter, or a worthwhile view. These areas are generally not intended for overnight camping unless signposted.

SITE INFORMATION

The details for the sites will include the following symbols and information:

SITE NUMBERS

- **100** Serviced Campsite
- **101** Motorhome/Caravan Park
- **102** Motorhome/Caravan Park with Dumpstation
- **103** Informal Camping
- **104** Roadside Rest Area

This arbitrary number has been allocated to enable you to find each site on the location map (refer to the Hema Map reference), and conversely to find a site's details from the location map. The site numbers are colour-coded to relate to their campsite category (see below). To order these sites New Zealand's two islands have been divided into regions, with touring routes followed within each district.

CAMPSITE CATEGORY

- Serviced Campsite
- Motorhome/Caravan Park
- Motorhome/Caravan Park with Dumpstation
- Informal Camping
- Roadside Rest Area

Each campsite has been classified as either a serviced campsite, motorhome park/caravan park, motorhome park/caravan park with dump station, informal camping or roadside rest area (see above).

NAME & ADDRESS DETAILS

This includes only the key contact details such as standard phone and email addresses. Free-phone reservation numbers, prefixed by 0800 or 0508, are included where this service is available. Road directions to help you find the site are also included where relevant.

NOTES

This includes further handy information, for example about bookings and opening times, as well as comments about the site.

Camping New Zealand

SITE FACILITIES

 FEES APPLY

Payment will be required for camping at these sites, but rates aren't included as these are subject to constant change. Use the contact details of the camp to check the current rates. (See also the comments on 'Free Camping' page 9).

 TOILETS

Toilet usage is usually free in New Zealand, however quality and cleanliness levels can fluctuate widely (especially in more remote areas).

 WATER

Water is provided at these sites, and it is usually of a standard suitable for drinking. (At a few DOC camps only stream water is provided). Hema Maps accepts no liability or responsibility for determining water quality, but simply points out that standards in New Zealand are usually high. If you are in doubt about water quality, ask the locals, or take appropriate steps to sterilize the water. (See the later section on Drinking Water for more information).

 SHOWERS

Showers (usually hot) are provided here, although no judgment is made as to the quality. In some cases extra payment (usually 20c, 50c or $1) is needed to feed slot machines and shower times are generally limited to five to eight minutes. In general, it has become more common for commercial sites to charge for shower usage.

 LAUNDRY

This indicates that clothes washing facilities are provided. Most serviced camps supply coin-operated washing facilities, usually requiring $2 coins.

 KITCHEN FACILITIES

Most camps with kitchen facilities will also provide hotplates, ovens, microwaves, refrigerators, freezers, toasters and kettles (or alternative means for boiling water). Some go even further and provide utensils and cleaning materials. Barbecues are a common feature of most serviced camps, some campsites even provide a dedicated barbecue area with several barbecues in a courtyard area and/or beneath shelter.

 ELECTRICITY

This indicates that powered sites are available for campervans, RVs, caravans or even for campers in tents to use.

 CABINS

Cabins are available at these sites but no judgement is given on their quality. Holiday parks and camping grounds often offer small cabins for the use of campers. Rates are usually more expensive than for tent camping, but they are much cheaper than hotel or motel rates. Linen (sheets and towels) are not normally provided in such cabins and you are expected to provide your own sleeping gear. However, if needed, linen is usually available for an extra charge.

 SHOP

Usually campsite shops are well equipped to supply any essentials that you may have forgotten. However, standards vary considerably and you are advised to be as self-contained as possible.

 BOAT LAUNCH

This indicates that boat launching facilities are available, either within the camp or nearby.

SWIMMING POOL

A swimming pool is available to campers at this site.

THERMAL POOL

A mineral or thermal pool is available to campers at this site.

 DISABLED FACILITIES

Some campsites make a special mention of this feature. However, the provision of disabled facilities is now entrenched in NZ building codes and you can expect all modern serviced camps above two star ratings to have suitable facilities.

 WASTEWATER DISPOSAL FACILITIES

Most serviced campsites provide facilities to empty the toilet waste and 'grey water' from motorhomes and campervans. There will be a charge to use a dump station at a camping ground, unless you are staying there. (Under no circumstances is it acceptable to dispose of wastewater in rubbish disposal facilities or into the environment - see the later section on Free Camping).

 PETS ALLOWED

Although pets are permitted at these sites conditions may apply. Many serviced motor camps and holiday parks will welcome a well-behaved pet, but in general there is widespread caution surrounding the issue of pets in camps. There are many campsites that clearly request 'No Pets'. This includes the Department of Conservation national parks, and most regional parks, where dogs and cats can kill native bird populations and nesting birds.

We strongly recommend that you leave your pet behind when you go on a camping holiday unless you have secured permission in advance to bring your pet to your chosen campsites.

 SCENIC

This indicates that this site has particular scenic advantages or is close to scenic viewpoints.

 WALKS

There are some interesting walking opportunities located in the area surrounding this site.

GPS COORDINATES

GPS technology is becoming more widespread, particularly in rental vehicles, so latitudes and longitudes have been included to assist you in locating your chosen campsite. (Your position can be displayed as either Eastings and Northings or Latitude and Longitude on your GPS unit).

Please be aware that to provide an accurate GPS reading the receiver must be able to 'see' at least three or four of the satellites and be clear of buildings or thick vegetation. The accuracy of the information listed here could possibly have been affected by these variables. As with any other method of navigation, you should not rely solely on your GPS.

HEMA ATLAS MAP REFERENCE

All of the sites listed in this book are shown in the Hema Maps' New Zealand Atlas pages that are included in this book. Simply use the reference, along with the address details, to find the site on the relevant Hema Atlas page.

CHANGE IS CERTAIN

While every attempt was made to ensure that the information contained in this book was accurate at the time of publication, the management and ownership of camps is constantly changing, and no responsibility is accepted by the publisher for any decisions or actions taken on the basis of information contained in this publication.

UPDATES

Campsite standards and services are always subject to change, and new facilities and services open up as old ones close down. The publisher welcomes information and suggestions for corrections and/or feedback. If you find any information has changed or you know of other suitable campsites for inclusion in this guide, please write or email and let us know so we can update the information in subsequent editions. [Hema Maps, PO Box 4365, Eight Mile Plains, Qld 4113 Australia or email manager@hemamaps.com.au

THE QUALITY OF KIWI CAMPING

THE EXPERIENCE OF CAMPING is often seen as an opportunity to 'get back to basics'; a chance to strip away the complications of civilization and escape to the 'simple life.' The only problem is that many of us cannot escape without the essentials of life, such as hairdryers, televisions, radios, microwaves, refrigerators, and hot and cold water on tap. It is these 'essentials' that serviced or commercial campsites are often expected to provide. Thus your enjoyment of campsites can be very much driven by your needs.

New Zealand camping grounds are generally of a very high standard. However, standards do vary as owners or managers come and go. What was a good camp a year ago, may no longer be so. Likewise what was once a poor camp can be improved by new and energetic management.

This guide is based on the standards that we found in camps at the time of print.

QUALMARK

The Qualmark symbol goes a long way in defining the 'quality' of camping and accommodation in New Zealand. While it is an excellent system, its major limitation is that camps are charged an annual fee for a Qualmark assessment and not all camps are willing or able to pay for such a privilege. Thus, many DOC camps as well as those run by regional councils, local bodies and smaller family-run or whanau-managed campsites are not Qualmark assessed. However, this lack of assessment is often no indication of their quality or charm.

It should also be noted that the Qualmark assessment does not take into account the scenic quality of the camp's location. So a beachside DOC or whanau-managed camp might only achieve a one star rating for its facilities of toilets and cold water. However, the scenery and peacefulness of the experience can more than compensate for such a low rating.

The Qualmark system of ratings defines quality as follows:

RATING	DEFINITION
★	Acceptable – meets customers' minimum requirements
★★	Good – exceeds customers' minimum quality standards
★★★	Very good – good to very good quality facilities and services
★★★★	Excellent – consistently achieves high quality levels
★★★★★	Exceptional – among the best in NZ

The vast majority of serviced campsites and holiday parks throughout New Zealand are the equivalent of a two star Qualmark rating or better.

OTHER ASSOCIATIONS

In addition to the Qualmark system, there are serviced camping grounds that form associations with the intention of improving standards, and work together to optimise service, marketing and business opportunities. Key amongst these groups are Top 10 Holiday Parks, Holiday Accommodation Parks of NZ (HAPNZ), and Family Parks.

TOP 10 HOLIDAY PARKS

To be a member of this group, campsites need to be independently assessed by Qualmark at a standard of four stars or better. Top 10 Holiday Parks tend to be managed extremely well, and offer excellent service. The only downside to these excellent camps is that due to their popularity they can get a little crowded, and prices tend to be higher than other more simple options. For further information visit www.top10.co.nz.

HOLIDAY ACCOMMODATION PARKS OF NZ (HAPNZ)

This association offers a more diverse range of quality. Parks under this scheme are generally operate to good or very good standards – i.e. three star or more. For further information visit www.holidayparks.co.nz.

FAMILY PARKS

Family Parks also offers a range of quality however parks operating under the group must have a minimum rating of three stars by Qualmark. The parks are neat and well presented, with clean and serviceable amenities. A range of accommodation must also be provided including powered and non-powered sites, plus on-site caravans or cabins. For further information visit www.familyparks.co.nz.

NZ MOTOR CARAVAN ASSOCIATION (NZMCA)

As you travel the roads in New Zealand you will notice many caravans, motorhomes, campervans and buses displaying a small red 'wing' logo. These travellers are members of the New Zealand Motor Caravan Association (NZMCA).

Membership of NZMCA is strongly recommended for those who anticipate being on the road for a while. The NZMCA offers a wide range of discounts and special offers. In addition, members of the NZMCA offer 'Park over Properties' (POPs) for the exclusive use of fellow members. These overnight camping areas are spread throughout New Zealand, but they are not depicted in this book as they are intended for the exclusive use of club members. If you want to find out more about POPs or how to utilize them you must be a member of NZMCA. For more information visit the website www.nzmca.org.nz or ph (09) 298 5466.

KAYAKING IN DOUBTFUL SOUND, FIORDLAND NP, SOUTH ISLAND — JEFF DREWITZ

LARCH FOREST IN AUTUMN, SKIPPERS CANYON, SOUTH ISLAND — JEFF DREWITZ

FREE CAMPING

IT ALL SEEMS SO SIMPLE, just roll up to a quiet campsite, pitch your tent, sit around the evening campfire telling yarns – and the next day, move on and find another idyllic location. The reality is that such 'free camping' is seldom so free: who mows the grass and tidies up the rubbish? For reasons such as these the New Zealand government and local authorities do not permit overnight camping outside of designated and approved areas. Where it is permitted, 'free camping' is usually limited to self-contained vehicles.

These days true 'Freedom camping' is less common in New Zealand than it was 10 years ago. In fact, new laws have been introduced which have allowed councils throughout New Zealand and the Department of Conservation (DOC) to designate areas within their regions as camping areas, prohibited places, and sites where camping is restricted to self-contained vehicles only. Automatic fines of $200 will be given to people camping illegally and court-imposed fines of up to $10,000 punish those caught dumping sewage.

While freedom camping is an important part of the Kiwi lifestyle and the NZ tourism industry, the numbers of campers has risen dramatically over the past decade and the new laws go a long way in protecting NZ's iconic scenery and environment.

To avoid any confusion, this atlas does not attempt to define areas for 'free camping' unless they have been designated so by the appropriate authorities.

A GUIDE TO CONSIDERATE KIWI CAMPING

- Park your vehicle, or pitch your tent, with safety in mind. Consider the possibilities of overnight strong winds, flooding (streams can rise very quickly) and fire as well as security.
- Keep your campsite clean and tidy, and try to leave it even tidier than when you found it.
- Dispose of all your wastewater in dump stations only, and dispose of rubbish in a sanitary and approved manner.
- Avoid causing visual or sound pollution. For example, use generators and stereos etc only at appropriate times during the day, and don't hang washing in places that may offend others.
- Observe all local fire restrictions and when appropriate use only existing fireplaces and/or portable BBQs.
- Ensure your vehicle is roadworthy and meets all relevant regulations.
- Be a considerate and safe driver, and obey road safety rules. If travelling slowly or sightseeing, keep an eye on your rear vision mirror and pull over to let others pass.
- Comply with local animal control bylaws. Preferably either leave your pets at home or in care, but if you must travel with them, keep your pets under control and pick up after them.
- Respect restrictions for length of stay. If asked to move on, do so graciously.
- Water, power, waste disposal, and road and ground maintenance all cost money. Be prepared to pay a reasonable contribution or donation to keep such facilities available.

TRAVELLING WITH A PET

The following points are general guides to follow if you do decide to travel with your pet:

- Not all camping grounds welcome pets - if in doubt ring and check before you arrive. Pets are banned from most Department of Conservation areas.
- A current hydatids certificate should be carried.
- Parvovirus inoculation certificates may be required in some areas.
- Pets should be exercised out of the camp area twice a day or more.
- Pets should be supervised and under control at all times.
- Pets should not be left unattended while owners are absent.
- Always clean up after your pet – many local authorities have substantial fines for inappropriate littering.

TOILET HYGIENE

The disposal of human waste into natural waters is not only dangerous to our health, it is culturally insensitive to the Maori culture.

To protect your own health and the environment while travelling in New Zealand:

- Always use the public toilets provided.
- Dispose of all caravan and campervan toilet wastes in appropriate and approved facilities. Dump stations are clearly signposted throughout New Zealand; if in doubt as to the local dump station's location, call into a service station or local i-Site Visitor Centre.
- When tramping in remote areas, bury your toilet waste at least 100m from picnic areas, campsites and waterways, and at least 15cm deep.

DRINKING WATER

While the majority of water found in New Zealand rivers was once pure and drinkable, it is now relatively common to see signs warning "this water is not suitable for drinking". The parasite Giardia has been found in some New Zealand lakes, rivers and streams, and it can cause severe diarrhoea. Giardia lives in the intestine of mammals and can be spread when toilet waste is not buried or is buried close to a stream, lake or well.

Despite this relatively new threat, water suited for drinking is readily available throughout New Zealand via most public taps, or you may prefer to purchase bottled water. If in doubt, ask the locals if the water is safe for drinking.

Water taken from streams and rivers can be made safe by:

- Boiling for three minutes.
- Adding iodine solution or chlorine bleach (available from most pharmacies).
- Filtering water through a suitable Giardia-rated filter (available from most outdoor equipment shops).

KNIGHTS POINT, WEST COAST, SOUTH ISLAND — JEFF DREWITZ

20 TOP THINGS TO DO

1 GREAT WALKS

There are six DOC Great Walks in the South Island: Abel Tasman Coast Track, Heaphy Track, Kepler Track, Milford Track, Rakiura Track and Routeburn Track. The North Island has three DOC Great Walks: Waikaremoana, Tongariro Northern Circuit and Whanganui Journey (a canoe trip).

2 SKI

The South Island has numerous skiing areas, including several near Queenstown and Lake Wanaka. The North Island has three skifields: Whakapapa, Turoa and Maunganui. The season in New Zealand generally runs between mid June and October.

3 FOLLOW WINE TRAILS

The Hawke's Bay region is the North Island's largest wine producing area; other major areas include Waiheke Island, West Auckland, Warkworth/Matakana, Gisborne and Martinborough. The South Island's largest wine producing region is Marlborough, and Central Otago, Nelson and Waipara are other booming areas.

4 CRUISE

In Auckland or Paihia you can charter a yacht or join a boat cruise around local islands. A highlight from Russell or Paihia is the cruise out to the Hole in the Rock. Cruising is also a good way to experience the waterways of Fiordland and Marlborough Sounds.

5 SEE WILDLIFE

Live kiwi displays can be seen throughout New Zealand including at the Auckland Zoo, the Kiwi Encounter at Rainbow Springs in Rotorua, Mt Bruce National Wildlife Centre, the National Kiwi Centre in Hokitika, and at the Orana Wildlife Park in Christchurch. The South Island's West Coast offers tours to see New Zealand's only white heron nesting site, and both coasts offer the chance to see colonies of both blue and yellow-eyed penguins. Spy upon fur seals at Cape Foulwind or along the Catlins Coast, and see the world's only mainland colony of Northern Royal albatross at Taiaroa Head on the Otago Peninsula.

6 SAMPLE LOCAL PRODUCE

Te Puke is New Zealand's kiwifruit 'capital'. Sample mussels and oysters on Coromandel Peninsula, tuatua at Ninety Mile Beach, kumara at Dargaville, honey just south of Warkworth, bacon in Pokeno, cheese in Eltham and Oamaru, and sun-ripened fruits from orchards in Hawke's Bay and Central Otago. Delicious crayfish are a highlight of any visit to Kaikoura, Greenshell mussels are a tasty treat in Havelock, and internationally-famous oysters can be found in Bluff. And don't forget to stock up on NZ's best preserves at Barker's in Geraldine.

7 SCENIC FLIGHTS

A scenic flight is a great way to see New Zealand's more remote scenery, like the sounds of Fiordland, and the glaciers of the Southern Alps. It's also a good way to see Australasia's highest mountain and the southern hemisphere's longest glacier located in Mt Cook National Park.

8 ADVENTURE ACTIVITIES

New Zealand is a wonderful country to experience a mind-numbing array of adventure activities from sky diving, bungy jumping, jet boating, mountain biking, and bridge climbing, through to kayaking, skiing, white-water rafting, four-wheel driving, diving, gliding and hot-air ballooning.

9 BUSHWALKS AND TRAMPS

Tramp in the Waipoua Forest, the Waitakere and Hunua Ranges, Whakarewarewa Forest, Tongariro and Whanganui national parks, and the Tararua Ranges in the North Island. Good hikes in the South Island include those found in the Abel Tasman, Kahurangi, Rakiura and Fiordland national parks.

10 THE TRANZALPINE TRAIN JOURNEY

This spectacular four hour journey winds through the breathtaking scenery of Arthurs Pass, en route to the west coast township of Greymouth from the eastern city of Christchurch.

11 GEOTHERMAL PHENOMENON, HOT POOLS AND SPRINGS

Rotorua and Taupo offer numerous geothermal parks, while hot pool complexes can be found at Rotorua, Taupo, Te Aroha, and Kaikohe, and also at Waiwera, Miranda and Parakai near Auckland. In the South Island seek out the spa townships of Hanmer Springs and Maruia Springs in the Lewis Pass.

12 SHOP

Auckland, Wellington and Dunedin offer a good range of designer shopping, and smaller cities offer artworks, gourmet food products and quality knitwear. On the West Coast of the South Island, good quality jade (greenstone) jewellery and carving are brilliant souvenirs.

13 FISH

Trout can be caught at in most fresh water lakes and rivers throughout the North and South Islands. For big game-fishing head to Tutukaka, Whangaroa Harbour, or the Bay of Islands. Salmon can be snared on most South Island rivers and lakes, including the Rakaia River, a world renowned salmon fishing area.

14 EXPERIENCE MAORI CULTURE

Cultural experiences can be found throughout New Zealand including those located at Waitangi, Auckland, Rotorua and Christchurch. There are numerous historic pa sites and marae to see throughout NZ, particularly around the North Island's East Coast.

15 BUNGY JUMP

Bungy jump off the Auckland Harbour Bridge, at Rotorua's Agrodome, or over the Waikato River in Taupo. Numerous jumps can be found in and around Queenstown, including the 134m high Nevis Highwire, Australasia's highest.

16 SURF

On the rough west coast, board surfers enjoy the breaks of Taranaki, Raglan, Piha, Muriwai and Ahipara. Highly recommended surfing venues on the east coast include: Castle Point, Gisborne, Mt Maunganui, Whangamata, Mangawhai Heads, Waipu Cove and Sandy Bay.

17 CAVE

The Waitomo region has extensive cave systems and caves can also be found throughout the nation at key sites including the Waipu Caves, Kawiti Caves, and Te Anau Caves. New Zealand's deepest cave, Nettlebed, is located in the South Island's Kahurangi National Park.

18 GOLF

Premium golf experiences are offered at Kauri Cliffs in Northland, Gulf Harbour north of Auckland, Wairakei near Taupo, and Terrace Downs near Christchurch. To tackle some of New Zealand's toughest holes, head to Clearwater Resort in Christchurch.

19 SCENIC DRIVES

To see the best of New Zealand's scenery, follow designated tourist routes such as the North Island's Twin Coast Discovery Highway, Thermal Explorer Highway and Pacific Coast Highway. In the South Island the Southern Scenic Route, Alpine Pacific Triangle, and Inland Scenic Route offer stunning scenery.

20 MOUNTAIN BIKE RIDES

Mountain bike tracks abound, from sites located at Woodhill and Waiheke Island in Auckland, the Whakarewarewa Forest in Rotorua, through to the Central Otago Rail Trail, and Queen Charlotte Walkway in the south.

25 MUST-SEE ATTRACTIONS

LORD OF THE RINGS MOVIE-SET LOCATIONS
(Throughout this atlas major filming locations are shown with a symbol).

CAPE REINGA LIGHTHOUSE (1 A1)
The meeting point of the Tasman Sea and the Pacific Ocean.

KERIKERI'S OLD BUILDINGS (4 A8)
New Zealand's oldest stone building (1833) and New Zealand's oldest house (1822).

POOR KNIGHTS ISLANDS MARINE RESERVE (4 E13)
One of the world's finest dive locations.

AUCKLAND (7 D4)
View the Sky Tower, Kelly Tarlton's Antarctic Encounter and Underwater World, and Waiheke and Rangitoto Islands.

CATHEDRAL COVE AND THE COROMANDEL PENINSULA (8 D13)
For beautiful beaches perfect for swimming, fishing and boating.

WAITOMO CAVES (11 H5)
To see glow-worm caverns and to try caving, abseiling and black-water rafting activities.

MOUNT TARAWERA (13 H6)
See the excavated dwellings of the Buried Village, near Rotorua.

ROTORUA (13 G4)
For colourful geothermal attractions, including hot springs, mud pools and geysers.

CRUISE TO WHITE ISLAND (14 E11)
Take a cruise from Whakatane to walk upon New Zealand's most active volcano.

LAKE TAUPO AREA (19 E4)
Explore this mammoth lake, its wild trout fishery, and geothermal areas.

MOUNT TARANAKI (23 D5)
See New Zealand's 'most climbed mountain' at 2517m.

TONGARIRO NATIONAL PARK (26 A12)
Ski at Whakapapa or Turoa, hike the Tongariro Crossing, and tramp up live volcanoes.

PANCAKE ROCKS

MOUNT TARANAKI PHOTO: DESTINATION LAKE TAUPO

WELLINGTON (33 F1)
Don't miss the highlights of New Zealand's capital: Te Papa Museum, the Embassy Theatre, Wellington Cable Car, Carter Observatory, and the Wellington Botanical Gardens.

MARLBOROUGH REGION (40)
Visit wineries and kayak or cruise the Sounds.

PANCAKE ROCKS BLOWHOLES (45 B5)
Explore spectacular limestone rocks and blowholes.

FRANZ JOSEF (49 G6) & FOX (49 H4) GLACIERS
Experience massive rivers of ice on foot or by helicopter.

MT COOK NATIONAL PARK (59 A7)
View the Tasman Glacier and Aoraki Mt Cook, Australasia's highest mountain at 3754m.

LAKE TEKAPO (60 D10)
Marvel at the vividness of this turquoise-blue glacial lake.

CHRISTCHURCH (56 D10)
Stroll through Hagley Park, punt on the Avon River, and visit the International Antarctic Centre.

DUNEDIN (74 H11)
Admire the city's wealth of Victorian and Edwardian architecture, and visit Larnach Castle, the Royal Albatross Centre, Penguin Place, and take a ride on Taieri Gorge Railway.

CURIO BAY (78 H11)
Photograph this fossilised forest in the Catlins, dating back from the Jurassic age.

INVERCARGILL'S QUEENS PARK (127 A3)
Meander around this 80ha CBD park, which comes complete with a golf course, the Southland Museum and Art Gallery, an aviary, and rose garden.

QUEENSTOWN (65 H4) AND WANAKA (66 D8)
The Adventure Capital: ride the gondola, cruise the lake on the TSS Earnslaw, discover the wine trails of Central Otago, take a scenic flight, hike in Mount Aspiring National Park, and visit Puzzling World.

MILFORD SOUND (63 C7)
Cruise, kayak or dive at Milford Sound and see the Bowen and Stirling Falls, Mitre Peak, and spy upon bottlenose dolphins, fur seals, and Fiordland crested penguins.

TE ARAROA
The Long Pathway

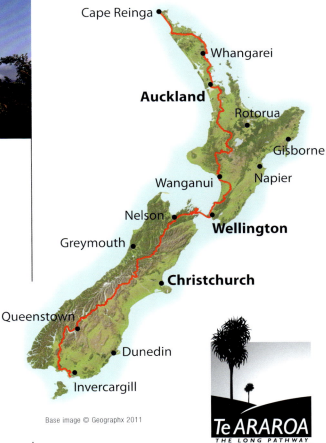

Base image © Geographx 2011

A 3,000 KILOMETRE LONG WALKING TRACK running from Cape Reinga to Bluff is nearly completed. Named Te Araroa, which means the Long Pathway, it was created by the Te Araroa Trust in consultation with local authorities and Department of Conservation (DOC) conservancies, by linking existing walking tracks with new routes.

Much of Te Araroa's route crosses countryside and coast that is legally walkable, for example on road reserve that has been surveyed off but not built on, or coastline, or down rivers where canoes are recommended, or across DOC land that is not tracked. Some of the tracks, for example the routes through the Tararua and Richmond Ranges, should only be attempted by experienced trampers. At major rivers, it's up to individual trampers whether they decide to cross and how they go about it. Te Araroa Trust recommends that any trampers who attempt remote tracks or significant river crossings should first consult with the local area office of DOC so they are fully aware of hazards. For safety, trampers must always fill out intentions forms at every hut and shelter they pass, even if they don't overnight there. Trampers should also take advantage of mountain safety and river crossing courses; for more information regarding courses visit www.mountainsafety.org.nz.

Te Araroa Trust intends to open all sections of the track by December 2011; for the latest track developments and trail maps visit www.teararoa.org.nz.

Te Urewera National Park

SITUATED BETWEEN ROTORUA AND GISBORNE, the remote and rugged Te Urewera National Park contains the largest forested wilderness remaining in the North Island. State Highway 38 links Wairoa on the East Coast with Murupara in the Central North, through the wilderness playgrounds of Te Urewera National Park past Lake Waikaremoana, one of the North Island's most scenic lakes.

The Park is popular with hunters and encompasses Lake Waikaremoana, which is known for its great walking tracks and trout fishing. Although much of the Park is remote and inaccessible, there are several well-maintained and clearly signposted walking tracks, with viewpoints and ridges that provide great photographic opportunities. The three- to four-day Lake Waikaremoana Great Walk follows the lake's shore for most of its 46km length. A moderately easy tramp, this Great Walk provides ample opportunities for swimming and fishing. There are five huts and five camping areas provided along the walk – bookings are essential for both huts and campsites.

Aniwaniwa, on the shores of Lake Waikaremoana, has a comprehensive visitor's centre and fully-serviced Department of Conservation motorcamp. Permits are available from the visitor centre for hunting introduced animals, including deer and pigs.

For centuries Te Urewera has been home to the Tuhoe people, dubbed the 'Children of the Mist' as it is believed they are the offspring of Hine-puhohu-rangi the celestial mist maiden.

See maps 14, 20 and 21 for touring maps.

LAKE WAIKAREMOANA

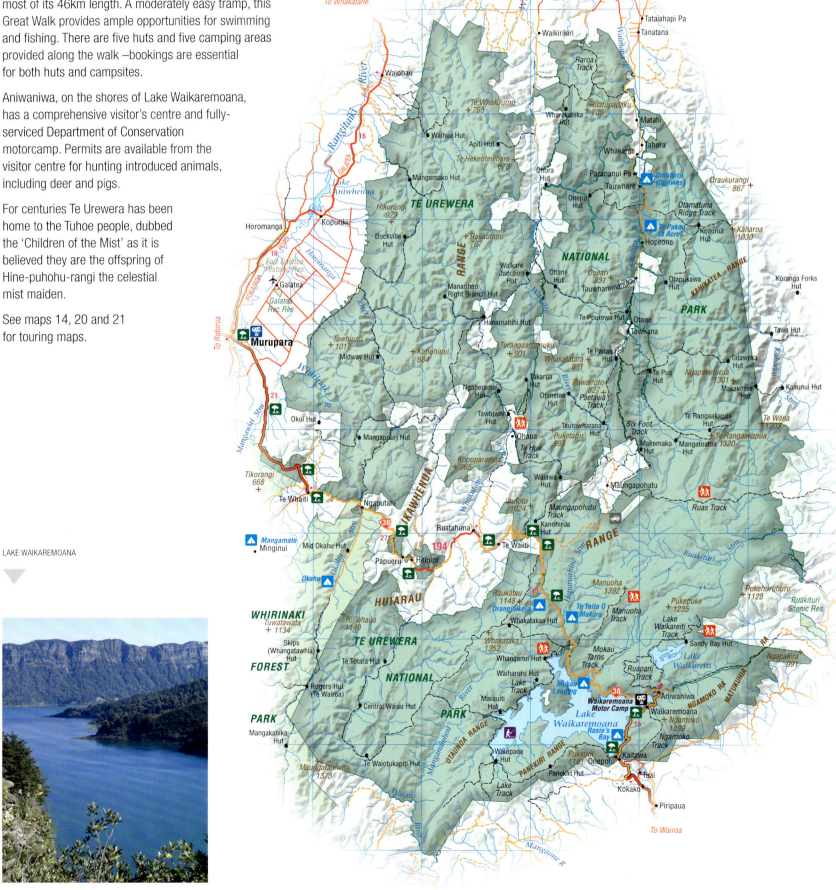

Tongariro National Park

CONTAINING BOTH ACTIVE AND EXTINCT VOLCANOES, Tongariro National Park is New Zealand's oldest national park and a World Heritage area. In Peter Jackson's Lord of the Rings films, the Park's dramatic landscape was the setting for Mordor and Mount Ngauruhoe made an appearance as Mount Doom.

Forming the Park's heart are the active volcanoes: Mt Tongariro with its red, raw craters; the charred cinder cone of Mt Ngaruhoe; and majestic Mt Ruapehu's snowy crown and sinister crater lake. Scenic flights provide excellent views of the mountains' diverse peaks.

The cream of the Park's hikes is the 17km Tongariro Crossing, which provides an opportunity to experience some of the most scenic volcanically active areas. There is the option to climb to the summit of Mt Ngauruhoe or Mt Tongariro en route. It is not a round trip so transport must be arranged at one end, or you can catch a shuttle bus from Turangi, Whakapapa Village or National Park Village.

During the summer, guided walks take you to NZ's largest active volcanic crater lake at Mt Ruapehu's summit, or you can 'self-hike' the Skyline Walk, a one-and-a-half-hour round trip, or the dramatic Meads Wall Walk. Other popular walks include the Tama Lakes and Taranaki Falls.

In winter, snow falls in the park and Mt Ruapehu has three skifields: Whakapapa, Turoa and Tukino.

See maps 18, 19, 26 and 27 for touring maps.

EMERALD LAKES

MANGATEPOPO VALLEY, TONGARIRO CROSSING

Arthur's Pass National Park

TRAMPERS AND CLIMBERS FLOCK TO ARTHUR'S PASS National Park for its amazing ridges, screes, deep valleys, waterfalls, glaciers and gorges. Sitting right in the heart of the national park, Arthur's Pass village has basic facilities and several accommodation options. The excellent DOC headquarters has detailed maps of all the tracks in the area and enthusiastic trampers can enquire here about overnight trips. There's also a small museum, which gives some historical background, and an old Cobb and Co coach on display. Nearby, at the Alpine Chapel, you can gain great views of the Avalanche Creek Waterfall.

Since Arthur Dobson surveyed the pass in 1864, it has been a popular route linking Westland and Christchurch. Skiers, trampers and climbers have been frequenting the region since the railway was completed in the early 1920s. During the summer experienced climbers flock to Arthur's Pass to climb nearby mountains including Mt Rolleston, Mt Murchison and Mt Franklin. In winter the park is transformed by snow, making it popular with skiers and climbers.

Make sure you stop at the lookout point above the pass to see the native mountain parrots called keas and gain excellent views before heading downhill to Otira.

See maps 45, 46, 51 and 52 for touring maps.

WAIMAKARIRI VALLEY

Kahurangi National Park

THE VAST KAHURANGI NATIONAL PARK is a 400,000 hectare wilderness of native forest and nikau palms that is a haven for adventure activities. The park contains New Zealand's deepest cave: Nettlebed.

Many tracks cross this isolated park, including the Heaphy Great Walk and the Wangapeka Track. It takes four to six days to complete this Great Walk, and DOC provides seven huts and six campsites. Many a hiker emerges from the national park reporting sightings of great spotted kiwi, short and long tailed bats, and giant land snails. The quiet township of Karamea is both the beginning and the end point of the Heaphy Track.

The beginning of the Heaphy Track provides one of the region's nicest short walks. A suspension bridge crosses the Kohaihai River accessing a 40-minute side-loop that winds through an amazing nikau palm grove where these beautiful palms thrust their smooth, ringed trunks from the pure white sands of a lagoon.

See maps 37, 38 and 42 for touring maps.

SUSPENSION BRIDGE, HEAPHY TRACK

Mount Aspiring National Park

PART OF TE WAHIPOUNAMU, the Southwest New Zealand World Heritage Area, Mount Aspiring National Park has many scenic walks including the Cascade Saddle Route and Rees-Dart Track, a moderately difficult four to five day tramp along the Rees and Dart rivers. Stunning mountain scenery, alpine landscapes and the Dart Glacier are all seen en route. It is also possible to climb Mount Aspiring (Tititea), but peaks such as these and the glaciers are best explored with experienced guides from a reputable trekking and climbing company.

The Routeburn Great Walk journeys through Mount Aspiring National Park and down over Harris Saddle into the Fiordland National Park. The 32km track takes two to three days to complete, and four huts and two campsites are provided along the way.

From Wanaka, SH6 follows the northern shores of Lake Wanaka towards Makarora before the incredibly scenic drive heads through Mount Aspiring National Park then hugs the Haast River into the small settlement of Haast, on the west coast. Be sure to stop at the Gates of Haast to see the river tumbling down over massive boulders.

See maps 57, 58, 64 and 65 for touring maps.

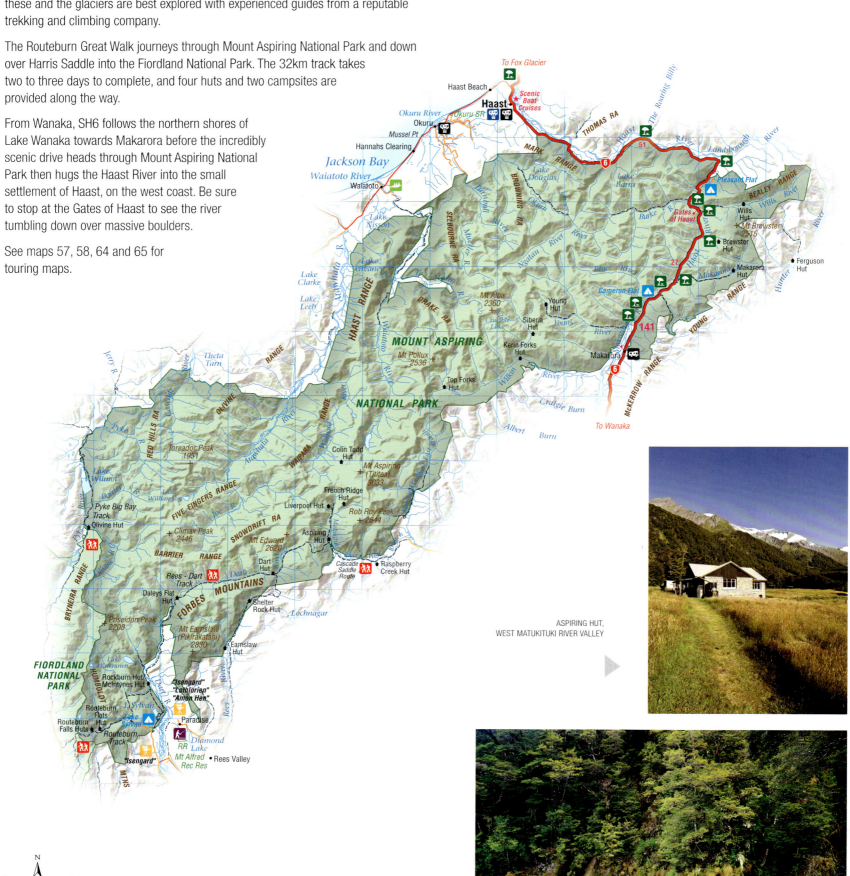

ASPIRING HUT, WEST MATUKITUKI RIVER VALLEY

BLUE POOLS ON THE MAKARORA RIVER

Aoraki/Mt Cook & Westland Tai Poutini National Park

THE INCREDIBLY SCENIC DRIVE TO MT COOK via SH80 skirts the shores of Lake Pukaki beneath the textured slopes of the Ben Ohau Range. The tiny alpine village of Mount Cook is an ideal base from which to explore the Aoraki/Mt Cook National Park, which boasts Australasia's highest mountain (Mt Cook) and the rumbling Tasman Glacier, the Southern Hemisphere's longest frozen river of ice.

During the winter heli-skiing is a popular pastime and various companies provide options for guided tours. Skiers can also land on the 27km-long Tasman Glacier in a ski plane. Heli-hiking on Mt Dark's rugged ridges and wide open basins is available year round.

In the summer visitors can enjoy 4WD journeys, rock climbing and hiking or an informative cruise on Tasman Glacier Lake, beneath the terminus of the glacier. There are a number of good family walks that leave from the village, including the Bowen Bush Walk, Glencoe Walk, Kea Point and Hooker Valley Track. The Blue Lakes to the Tasman Glacier viewpoint track offers stunning views of the glacier's lunar-like landscape. If you're looking to conquer Aoraki/Mt Cook (3754m) or Mt Tasman (3498m), Alpine Guides can lead you to either summit. Those tackling longer hikes should check in at the DOC Visitors' Centre for a weather update, as conditions can change fast, no matter what the season.

The Westland Tai Poutini National Park encompasses the Fox and Franz Josef glaciers, whose icy tongues are surrounded by rainforest. To really experience these massive rivers of ice, take a guided tour or take a helicopter ride for a bird's-eye view.

From Franz Josef it's a short drive to the glacier's car park. To gain a good view of the Franz Josef Glacier hike to Sentinel Rock (around 10 minutes) or hike the 3km Glacier Valley Walk to the terminal face (around an hour and a half return). You can join a guided tour and hike up the face of the glacier to explore stunning blue ice on the world's steepest and fastest-flowing commercially guided glacier.

Helicopter flights and guided walks of the Fox Glacier are also on offer and it takes around five minutes' hiking from the car park to gain a view of the glacier or 30 minutes to get close to the terminal face.

See maps 49, 50, 59 and 60 for touring maps.

TERMINAL FACE OF THE FOX GLACIER

Nelson Lakes National Park

ST ARNAUD, RIGHT AT THE DOORSTEP OF NELSON LAKES NATIONAL PARK, provides a great base for trampers exploring the park's various tracks including the four-to-seven-day Travers-Sabine Circuit. The two- to three-day hike to Lake Angelus, a stunning alpine pond, is also popular. There are also several excellent day hikes, including the Lake Rotoiti Circuit, Mount Robert loop track, St Arnaud Range track, and Whisky Falls track. A commercial water-taxi service on the lake whisks hikers to and from various points or provides cruises of the lake on demand. The latest weather report, maps, hut tickets and hunting permits are available from the DOC visitor centre in St Arnaud.

Located on the lake edge, the Rotoiti Nature Recovery Project is an important conservation site. The Bellbird and Honeydew tracks provide an insight into this work and honeydew nectar can be seen literally dripping from the beech trees.

Hunting in the region is encouraged by DOC and other activities visitors can enjoy include ice-skating, gold panning and mountaineering. There is a small ski club field at Mount Robert, but it can only be accessed by a 1.5 to 2 hour walk. Both Lake Rotoiti and Lake Rotoroa are good for trout fishing, and water-skiing is permitted on Rotoiti.

The wild Buller River, which begins its journey from Lake Rotoiti and flows through Murchison to meet the sea at Westport, is popular with both white-water rafters, white-water kayakers and anglers.

See maps 42, 46 and 47 for touring maps.

BUSHLINE HUT ABOVE LAKE ROTOITI

BLACK SWANS ON LAKE ROTOROA

Fiordland National Park

MOST VISITORS TRAVEL TO FIORDLAND NATIONAL PARK TO SEE MILFORD SOUND, but the journey to get there is equally inspiring with lots of wild waterfalls, forested valleys, granite peaks, crystal-clear lakes and friendly townships, like Te Anau and Manapouri, where activities are bountiful. Milford Sound lies within Te Wahipounamu, Southwest New Zealand World Heritage Area, and is totally encompassed by the Fiordland and Mount Aspiring National Parks.

To really experience Milford Sound, a cruise or kayaking trip is essential. Boat trips travel the length of the fiord and take one to two hours. There's the chance to see bottlenose dolphins, fur seals and Fiordland crested penguins, and diving is excellent here where deepwater species, including black corals, are visible at a much shallower depth. Even if you can't dive, you can still explore underwater attractions by visiting the Milford Deep Underwater Observatory.

Some people choose to reach the Sound by hiking the Milford Track, New Zealand's most popular Great Walk. The 54km track takes five days to complete and three huts are provided for overnight stays. Bookings (months in advance) are essential for both independent and guided walkers as numbers are limited.

Fiordland has a wealth of other Great Walks and hiking tracks. The 60km Kepler Track traverses lake edges, beech forest, alpine summits and a glacial valley over three to four days. The 32km Routeburn Track leads from the forested valleys of the Fiordland National Park up over Harris Saddle into Mount Aspiring National Park over two to three days. It is not a circuit so you'll need to consider transport at either end.

Further south, Lake Manapouri provides the launching point for visits to Doubtful Sound. Cruise or kayak the winding arms of this ice-carved fiord and its ever-changing panorama of waterfalls, beech forest and wildlife. Lake Manapouri and Lake Hauroko both provide access to the Dusky Track to Dusky Sound, an 84km track averaging ten days to complete. The Tuatapere Hump Ridge Track is a three-day hike providing a slice of the Fiordland experience.

See maps 63, 64, 69, 70, 75, and 76 for touring maps.

LAKE MARIAN, SOUTH-WEST OF HOLLYFORD

NORTH ISLAND CAMPING SITES

Northland Region (Camps 1-127)	**Pages 21-28**
SH1 – Wellsford to Whangarei	21
SH1 – Whangarei to Kawakawa	22
SH10 – SH1 to Awanui	24
SH1 – Awanui to Cape Reinga	25
SH1 – Awanui to Kawakawa	26
SH12 – SH1 to Dargaville	27
SH12 – Dargaville to SH1	27
Auckland Region (Camps 128-215)	**Pages 28-34**
Islands of the Hauraki Gulf	28
SH1 – Auckland to Wellsford	29
SH16 – Wellsford to Auckland	31
Auckland to Waitakere Regional Park	31
Auckland to SH25	32
SH1 – Auckland to SH2	33
Central North Region (Camps 216-661)	**Pages 34-58**
SH1 – From SH2 to Hamilton	34
SH3 – Hamilton to Te Kuiti	35
SH3 – Te Kuiti to New Plymouth	35
SH4 – Te Kuiti to Ohakune	37
SH1 – Waiouru to Taupo	38
SH2 – SH1 to Tauranga	40
SH25 Coromandel Peninsula – SH2 to Waihi	42
SH1 – Hamilton to Taupo	46
SH2 – Tauranga to Opotiki	48
SH30 – Whakatane to Rotorua	50
SH5 & SH38 – Rotorua to Wairoa	52
SH35 – Opotiki to Gisborne	53
SH2 – Opotiki to Wairoa	55
SH2 – Wairoa to Hastings	56
Lower North Region (Camps 662-840)	**Pages 58-68**
SH1 – Wellington to SH3	58
SH1 – From SH3 to Waiouru	60
SH2 – Wellington to Masterton	61
SH2 – Masterton to Dannevirke	63
SH2 – Dannevirke to Hastings	64
SH3 – Palmerston North to Wanganui	65
SH4 – Wanganui to Ohakune	66
SH3 – Wanganui to Hawera	66
SH45 – Hawera to New Plymouth	67
SH3 & SH43 – Hawera to Taumarunui	68

BAY OF PLENTY SUNRISE — JEFF DREWITZ

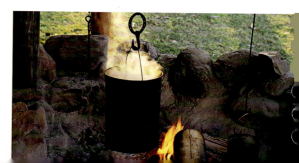

NORTHLAND REGION

MATAURI BAY PHOTO: DESTINATION NORTHLAND

SH1 — WELLSFORD TO WHANGAREI	21
SH1 — WHANGAREI TO KAWAKAWA	22
SH10 — SH1 TO AWANUI	24
SH1 — AWANUI TO CAPE REINGA	25
SH1 — AWANUI TO KAWAKAWA	26
SH12 — SH1 TO DARGAVILLE	27
SH12 — DARGAVILLE TO SH1	27

SH1 WELLSFORD TO WHANGAREI

1 Roadside Rest Area
Alongside SH1 N of Wellsford
36.237705S 174.511456E   Hema Atlas Map Ref 6 D8

2 Kaiwaka North Roadside Rest Area
SH1 N of Kaiwaka
36.159019S 174.441985E   Hema Atlas Map Ref 6 B8

3 Riverside Holiday Park
41 Black Swamp Road, Mangawhai
Ph (09) 431 4825 Fax (09) 431 4825
riverside.goodlife@xtra.co.nz www.riversideholidaypark.co.nz
36.131106S 174.584883E   Hema Atlas Map Ref 6 B9

4 Mangawhai Heads Motor Camp
2 Mangawhai Heads Rd, Off Cove Rd:
beachside at Mangawhai Heads
Ph/Fax (09) 431 4675
Popular waterfront location has a huge camp on the waterfront with good shelter. Children's playground.
36.086196S 174.58836E   Hema Atlas Map Ref 6 B9

5 Waipu Cove Roadside Rest Area
Off Cove Rd: S end of Waipu Beach
Waterside picnic spot is a popular beach with good surfing.
36.029697S 174.507135E   Hema Atlas Map Ref 6 A8

6 Camp Waipu Cove
Cove Rd, Waipu Cove: signposted from Beach Rd
Ph (09) 432 0410 info@campwaipucove.com
Fax (09) 432 0412 www.campwaipucove.com
A huge camp right on the beach at this very popular spot.
36.02769S 174.504865E   Hema Atlas Map Ref 6 A8

7 Waipu Cove Cottages & Camping
685 Cove Rd, Waipu: Signposted from Beach Rd
Ph (09) 432 0851 covecottages@xtra.co.nz
www.waipucovecottages.co.nz
Compact and immaculate. Playground, recreation room, free boats, free BBQs.
36.023038S 174.498441E   Hema Atlas Map Ref 6 A8

8 Uretiti Fatigue Stop
SH1 S of Ruakaka
35.935763S 174.455693E   Hema Atlas Map Ref 4 J13

9 Uretiti
Adjoining SH1 at Uretiti: 34km S of Whangarei
DOC Whangarei Area Office Ph (09) 470 3304
whangareiao@doc.govt.nz
Self registration applies; cold showers only. Beachside, but pretty exposed.
35.933662S 174.460081E   Hema Atlas Map Ref 4 J13

10 Ruakaka Reserve Motor Camp
21 Beach Rd, Ruakaka: signposted from SH1
Ph (09) 432 7590 Fax (09) 432 7284
ruakaka@ihug.co.nz www.motorcamp.co.nz
A large and popular camp right on the beach with plenty of shelter and access to the nearby estuary. Bird Sanctuary, wildlife. Internet access.
35.905591S 174.453473E   Hema Atlas Map Ref 4 J13

11 Lookout Hill Roadside Rest Area
SH1 S of Whangarei
Table, day use only.
35.768634S 174.309522E   Hema Atlas Map Ref 85 D1, 4 G11

12 Tarewa Park Roadside Rest Area
Otaika Rd, SH1 Whangarei
Toilets, table, day use only.
35.738425S 174.310047E   Hema Atlas Map Ref 85 C1, 4 G11

13 Alpha Motel & Holiday Park
34 Tarewa Rd: adjoining SH1, S of Whangarei
Ph (09) 438 6600 info@alphaholidaypark.co.nz
Fax (09) 438 6601 www.alphaholidaypark.co.nz
Pets on approval. Shop limited. Internet access.
35.732509S 174.314639E   Hema Atlas Map Ref 84 D2, 85 C1, 4 G11

14 Beach Road Rest Area
Beach Road boat ramp (SW), Whangarei
Toilets, table, day use only
35.774744S 174.359172E   Hema Atlas Map Ref 85 D3, 4 G12

15 Roadside Rest Area
Whangarei Heads Rd, Waikaraka on Whangarei Harbour
Waterside picnic spot.
35.764306S 174.391023E   Hema Atlas Map Ref 4 G12

North Island Camping Sites — Northland Region

16 Roadside Rest Area
Devonshire Park, Whangarei Heads Rd
Waterside picnic spot.
35.780112S 174.415066E   Hema Atlas Map Ref 4 G12

17 Blue Heron Holiday Park
85 Scott Rd; signposted from the Whangarei Heads Rd
Ph (09) 436 2293 stay@blueheron.co.nz
Fax (09) 436 3013 www.blueheron.co.nz
Small but scenic waterside spot. Free wifi.
35.783898S 174.419402E   Hema Atlas Map Ref 4 G12

18 McLeod Bay Roadside Rest Area
Whangarei Heads Road, Whangarei
Toilets, table, day use only.
35.812769S 174.503908E   Hema Atlas Map Ref 4 H13

19 Treasure Island
Pataua Bay, off Whangarei Heads Rd
Ph (09) 436 2390 treasure@xtra.co.nz www.treasureislandnz.co.nz
Huge park-like grounds with dual waterfront access: open sea or estuary.
35.717228S 174.530513E   Hema Atlas Map Ref 4 G13

SH1 WHANGAREI TO KAWAKAWA

20 Whangarei Top 10 Holiday Park
24 Mair St, Whangarei: signposted from SH1 on the N side of Whangarei city centre
Ph 0800 455 488 (09) 437 6856
stay@whangareitop10.co.nz www.whangareitop10.co.nz
Wooded location next to stream and scenic reserve. Internet access.
35.711352S 174.328139E   Hema Atlas Map Ref 85 B2, 4 G11

21 Kamo Springs Holiday Park
55 Great North Road. Adjoining SH1, approx 7km N of Whangarei
Ph/Fax (09) 435 1208 kamosprings@xtra.co.nz
www.kamosprings.co.nz
Mineral pool.
35.668016S 174.29768E   Hema Atlas Map Ref 85 A1, 4 F11

22 Roadside Rest Area
Whangarei Falls Scenic Reserve, off Ngunguru Rd
35.68442S 174.334686E   Hema Atlas Map Ref 85 A2, 4 F12

23 Hikurangi Roadside Rest Area
SH1 S of Hikurangi
35.603952S 174.282326E   Hema Atlas Map Ref 4 E11

24 Roadside Rest Area
SH1 N of Hikurangi
35.585816S 174.28294E   Hema Atlas Map Ref 4 E11

25 Roadside Rest Area
SH1 S of Kensington, Whangarei
35.712866S 174.316403E   Hema Atlas Map Ref 85 B2

26 Roadside Rest Area
SH1 S of Kensington, Whangarei
35.717777S 174.315536E   Hema Atlas Map Ref 85 B2

27 Maunu Hill Roadside Rest Area
SH14 Horahora, W of Whangerei
35.734889S 174.288173E   Hema Atlas Map Ref 85 C1

28 Whangarei Falls Holiday Park & Backpackers
12 Ngunguru Rd, Glenbervie, Whangarei
Ph/Fax (09) 437 0609 www.whangareifalls.co.nz
book@whangariefalls.co.nz
Also caters for backpackers. Wireless internet, outdoor spa pool.
35.683086S 174.336331E   Hema Atlas Map Ref 85 A2, 4 F12

29 Roadside Rest Area
Roadside S of Tutukaka, off Ngunguru Rd
35.620199S 174.515575E   Hema Atlas Map Ref 4 F13

30 Tutukaka Holiday Park
Matapouri Rd, Tutukaka: at the N end of Tutukaka township
Ph/Fax (09) 434 3938 tutukakaholidaypark@gmail.com
www.tutukaka-holidaypark.co.nz
Short walk to Tutukaka's marinas and wharf from this clean and tidy camp. Internet access.
35.608911S 174.523359E   Hema Atlas Map Ref 4 E13

31 Roadside Rest Area
Whale Bay, off Matapouri Rd
Waterside picnic spot.
35.562194S 174.498001E   Hema Atlas Map Ref 4 E13

32 Roadside Rest Area
Woolleys Bay, off Matapouri Rd
Waterside picnic spot.
35.562086S 174.491066E   Hema Atlas Map Ref 4 E13

33 Roadside Rest Area
Sandy Bay, off Matapouri Rd
Waterside picnic spot.
35.55685S 174.47471E   Hema Atlas Map Ref 4 E13

34 Whananaki North Motel & Holiday Park
Whananaki North Rd: signposted on entering Whananaki
Ph/Fax (09) 433 8896 whananaki@igrin.co.nz www.whananakiholiday.co.nz
Has self-contained units and motel units.
35.513413S 174.454111E   Hema Atlas Map Ref 4 D13

Northland Region — North Island Camping Sites 23

35 — Otamure Beach
Beachside at Otamure on Whananaki North Rd,
just 2km from Whananaki
DOC Whangarei Area Office Ph (09) 470 3304
whangareiao@doc.govt.nz
*Self registration applies; cold showers only.
Beachside in a beautiful location.*

35.491655S 174.464165E Hema Atlas Map Ref 4 D13

36 — Waikahoa Bay, Mimiwhangata Coastal Park
Mimiwhangata Coastal Park, 48km NE of Whangarei
DOC Whangarei Area Office Ph (09) 470 3304
whangareiao@doc.govt.nz
Closed June 1 to October 31; bookings required for peak season; cold showers only. No campervan access. 5 min walk to campground

35.442383S 174.412006E Hema Atlas Map Ref 4 D12

37 — Oakura Motels & Holiday Park
Te Kapua St, Oakura Bay: off Russell Rd
Ph/Fax (09) 433 6803 oakuramotelsandhp@xtra.co.nz
Sheltered site is just back from the beach.

35.39059S 174.343808E Hema Atlas Map Ref 4 C12

38 — Whangaruru Beachfront Camp
Ohawini Road, just N of the Oakura township
Ph (09) 433 6806
Beachside, and just a stone's throw from Oakura.

35.379887S 174.343838E Hema Atlas Map Ref 4 C12

39 — Bland Bay Reserve
Whangaruru North Head Rd, Bland Bay

35.348535S 174.35858E Hema Atlas Map Ref 4 B12

40 — Bland Bay Motor Camp
Whangaruru North Head Rd, Bland Bay
Ph (09) 433 6759 Fax (09) 433 6727
A caretaker may collect koha or fees if they are in attendance.

35.346258S 174.354252E Hema Atlas Map Ref 4 B12

41 — Puriri Bay, Whangaruru Scenic Reserve
Whangaruru North Head Rd, 30km SE of Russell;
signposted from Bland Bay
DOC Whangarei Area Office
Ph (09) 470 3304 whangareiao@doc.govt.nz
Bookings required in peak season; foot access only July 1 - November 30; casual camping self registration applies; cold showers only. Simple camping in a lovely environment, difficult to choose between this and the nearby Bland Bay option.

35.364S 174.360271E Hema Atlas Map Ref 4 C12

42 — Kawakawa Roadside Rest Area
SH1, just N of Queen St, Kawakawa
35.380265S 174.07169E Hema Atlas Map Ref 4 C9

43 — Roadside Rest Area & picnic area
Rawhiti Beach, off Russell Rd
Local Iwi allow some simple camping, but make sure you ask permission, and be prepared to pay some koha.
35.236446S 174.259429E Hema Atlas Map Ref 4 A11

44 — Orongo Bay Holiday Park
5960 Russell Rd, approx 2km S of Russell
Ph/Fax (09) 403 7704 stay@russellaccommodation.co.nz
www.orongobayholidaypark.co.nz
Native forest setting in a kiwi and weka protection zone. Sheltered valley that's handy to boat ramps.

35.281857S 174.14729E Hema Atlas Map Ref 81 B3, 4 B10

45 — Russell Top 10 Holiday Park
1 James St, off Longbeach Rd, Russell:
signposted to the N of Russell town centre
Ph (09) 403 7826 russelltop10@xtra.co.nz www.russelltop10.co.nz
Only 800m from Russell town centre. Children's playground. Internet access.

35.25911S 174.124881E Hema Atlas Map Ref 82 A5, 81 A3, 4 B10

46 — Sunset Bay
Southern coast of Urupukapuka Island
DOC Bay of Islands Area Office Ph (09) 407 0300
bayofislandsbooking@doc.govt.nz
Bookings required, cold showers only

35.220386S 174.235034E Hema Atlas Map Ref 4 A11

47 — Urupukapuka Bay
Eastern shores of Urupukapuka Island
DOC Bay of Islands Area Office Ph (09) 407 0300
bayofislandsbooking@doc.govt.nz
Bookings required, cold showers only

35.217453S 174.238142E Hema Atlas Map Ref 4 A11

48 — Cable Bay
Southern shores of Urupukapuka Island
DOC Bay of Islands Area Office Ph (09) 407 0300
bayofislandsbooking@doc.govt.nz
Bookings required, cold showers only

35.226452S 174.234852E Hema Atlas Map Ref 4 A11

49 — Beachside Holiday Park
1290 SH11, Paihia, 3km S of Paihia
Ph (09) 402 7678 Fax (09) 402 6678 info@beachsideholiday.co.nz
www.beachsideholiday.co.nz
Compact and beachside.

35.303506S 174.101596E Hema Atlas Map Ref 81 C2, 4 B10

50 — Roadside Rest Area
Paihia
Several waterside picnic spots in this area.
35.27866S 174.086823E Hema Atlas Map Ref 83 C4, 81 B2, 4 B9

51 — Te Haumi Rest Area
SH11 (Paihia Rd, N side of bridge)
35.297438S 174.099109E Hema Atlas Map Ref 4 B10, 81 B2

North Island Camping Sites — Northland Region

52 Waitangi Holiday Park
21 Tahuna Rd, Waitangi: just off the Waitangi Rd, N of Paihia
Ph (09) 402 7866 waitangiholidaypark@xtra.co.nz
www.waitangiholidaypark.no.nz
Handy camp close to the beach and adjoining the Waitangi River estuary for canoeing.
35.275779S 174.077906E Hema Atlas Map Ref 81 B1, 4 B9

53 Bay of Islands RV Park
251 Puketona Road, Haruru
Ph (09) 946 8252 murray-thelma-finch@hotmail.com
Limited facilities but ideal for self-contained vehicles. Cassette dump station.
35.283658S 174.061217E Hema Atlas Map Ref 4 B9

54 Twin Pines Tourist Park
340 Puketona Rd, 3km N of Paihia
Ph/Fax (09) 402 7322 enquiries@twinpines.co.nz
www.twinpines.co.nz
Three camps share the banks of the Waitangi River below the Haruru Falls. Internet access.
35.279887S 174.052643E Hema Atlas Map Ref 81 B1, 4 B9

55 Haruru Falls Resort
Off Puketona Rd, 3km N of Paihia: bottom of Old Wharf Road.
Ph (09) 402 7525 resort@harurufalls.co.nz www.harurufalls.co.nz
Three camps share the banks of the Waitangi River below the Haruru Falls. Restaurant, bar, conference facilities. Internet access.
35.279011S 174.054541E Hema Atlas Map Ref 81 B1, 4 B9

56 Falls Motel & Waterfront Campground
Cnr Puketona Rd and Old Wharf Rd, 3km N of Paihia
Ph (09) 402 7816, 0800 111 090 Fax (09) 402 8541
bookings@falls.co.nz www.falls.co.nz
Three camps share the banks of the Waitangi River below the Haruru Falls. Tour bookings. Kayaks for hire. Internet access.
35.280014S 174.053435E Hema Atlas Map Ref 81 B1, 4 B9

57 Bay of Islands Holiday Park (Lily-Pond)
678 Puketona Rd, Paihia, 5km N of Paihia. SH11.
Ph (09) 402 7646 bayofislandsholidaypark@xtra.co.nz
www.bayofislandsholidaypark.co.nz Fax (09) 402 7604
Huge park-like grounds with ample shade right next to the Waitangi River. Children's playground. Tours. Pets by arrangement. Internet access.
35.290294S 174.018462E Hema Atlas Map Ref 4 B9

SH10 – SH1 TO AWANUI

58 Wagon Train RV Park
1265 SH10, Kerikeri
Ph (09) 407 7889 Fax (09) 407 9956
enquiries@rvparknz.com www.rvparknz.com
Qualmark four star. Internet & Wifi facilities.
35.26755S 173.939363E Hema Atlas Map Ref 4 B8

59 Hideaway Lodge
111 Wiroa Rd, Kerikeri
Ph (09) 407 9773 Fax (09) 407 9793 skedgwell@xtra.co.nz
Backpackers lodge, internet access.
35.258962S 173.922126E Hema Atlas Map Ref 4 B8

60 Gibby's Place
331 Kerikeri Rd, Kerikeri: 500m S of Kerikeri village centre
Ph (09) 407 9024 gibbysplace@xtra.co.nz www.gibbysplace.co.nz
35.232944S 173.94463E Hema Atlas Map Ref 86 C1, 4 A8

61 Kerikeri Top 10 Holiday Park
Aranga Drive, Kerikeri: 800m S of Kerikeri village centre
Ph 0800 272 642 (09) 407 9326 Fax (09) 407 9897
www.kerikeritop10.co.nz mail@kerikeritop10.co.nz
Backpacker accommodation, internet. Qualmark four star plus.
35.229334S 173.943025E Hema Atlas Map Ref 86 C1, 4 A8

62 Pagoda Lodge
81 Pa Road, Kerikeri: signposted from Kerikeri village centre
Ph (09) 407 8617 info@pagoda.co.nz www.pagoda.co.nz
Powered sites and furnished safari tents in a tranquil setting. Grounds are stunning, fabulous facilities. Bikes and kayaks for hire.
35.221404S 173.964578E Hema Atlas Map Ref 86 B3, 4 A8

63 Rainbow Falls Scenic Reserve Rest Area
Signposted from N access road to Kerikeri
Walking, swimming.
35.214206S 173.944229E Hema Atlas Map Ref 86 B1, 4 A8

64 Kerikeri River Rest Area
SH10, S of Waipapa
35.217694S 173.92057E Hema Atlas Map Ref 4 A8

65 Kerikeri Stone House DOC Reserve
Just N of the Stone House, Kerikeri
Walking, swimming.
35.216385S 173.96315E Hema Atlas Map Ref 86 B2, 4 A8

66 Matauri Bay Holiday Park Ltd
Beach Rd, Matauri Bay
Ph/Fax (09) 405 0525 matauribayhp@actrix.co.nz www.matauribay.co.nz/camp.html
Surfing, diving. Dust from the gravel access road. Pets welcome in off-peak period.
35.029152S 173.914791E Hema Atlas Map Ref 2 H12

67 Roadside Rest Area
Te Ngaere Bay: along the scenic coastal route
Waterside picnic spot.
35.021705S 173.866325E Hema Atlas Map Ref 2 H12

68 Roadside Rest Area
SH10, W of Kaeo
35.098892S 173.776081E Hema Atlas Map Ref 2 J11

Northland Region

North Island Camping Sites 25

69 Roadside Rest Area
SH10, E of Kaeo
35.124644S 173.873141E   Hema Atlas Map Ref 2 J11

70 Tauranga Bay Holiday Park
Tauranga Bay Beach: a 3km diversion from the coastal scenic route.
Ph/Fax (09) 405 0436   holiday@igrin.co.nz   www.taurangabay.co.nz
Traditional NZ beach campsite. Pets OK off-peak.
35.006127S 173.785577E   Hema Atlas Map Ref 2 H11

71 Whangaroa Harbour Holiday Park
Whangaroa Harbour, along the coastal scenic route:
6km N of SH10.
Ph (09) 405 0306
Fishing. Right next to the harbour in a sheltered valley.
35.063389S 173.743428E   Hema Atlas Map Ref 2 H10

72 Taupo Bay Holiday Park
1070 Taupo Bay Rd: 10km from SH10,
signposted 10km S of Mangonui.
Ph (09) 406 0315   Fax (09) 406 0318   taupobay@value.net.nz
Fishing, surfing, swimming. A sheltered spot where volcano-formed cliffs and landforms make an impressive backdrop. Pets by arrangement. Greywater disposal facility available.
34.990722S 173.708755E   Hema Atlas Map Ref 2 G10

73 Roadside Rest Area
Beachside at Taupo Bay, along Taupo Bay Rd: 10km from SH10
Nice beachside reserve with waterside picnic area.
34.990058S 173.70908E   Hema Atlas Map Ref 2 G10

74 Hihi Beach Holiday Camp
58 Hihi Beach Rd, Hihi: 5km from SH10,
signposted 5km SE of Mangonui
Ph/Fax (09) 406 0307   hihicamp@xtra.co.nz   www.hihicamp.co.nz
Fishing, boating. Fish smokehouse on-site and dinghy hire. Wireless internet access.
34.969442S 173.538797E   Hema Atlas Map Ref 2 G9

75 Roadside Rest Area
Adjacent SH10 at Coopers Beach
Waterside picnic spot.
34.990659S 173.512505E   Hema Atlas Map Ref 2 G8

76 Roadside Rest Area
SH10, W of Mangonui towards Coopers Beach
34.990712S 173.522398E   Hema Atlas Map Ref 2 H8

77 Roadside Rest Area
Adjacent SH10 at Cable Bay
Waterside picnic spot.
34.990863S 173.483904E   Hema Atlas Map Ref 2 G8

78 Roadside Rest Area
SH10 between Cable Bay and Taipa
34.989947S 173.479617E   Hema Atlas Map Ref 2 H8

79 Tokerau Beach Motor Camp
13 Melissa Rd, Tokerau Beach, Karikari Peninsula
Ph/Fax (09) 408 7150
*Sheltered grounds right on Tokerau Beach with reasonable rates. Shop operates during Christmas period.
No pets during peak season 15/12 - 15/1.*
34.888719S 173.36909E   Hema Atlas Map Ref 1 F7

80 Whatuwhiwhi Top 10 Holiday Park
17 Whatuwhiwhi Rd, off Inland Rd, Whatuwhiwhi, Karikari Peninsula
Ph 0800 142 444   whatuwhiwhi@xtra.co.nz   Fax (09) 408 7502
www.whatuwhiwhitop10.co.nz
Fishing, boating. A sheltered valley with its own small bay: 4 star camping. Close to winery and golf club. Qualmark four star plus.
34.874164S 173.389486E   Hema Atlas Map Ref 2 F7

81 Maitai Bay
Off Karikari Peninsula Rd, follow the signs to Maitai Bay:
25km NE of Kaitaia
Kaitaia DOC Office, Ph (09) 408 6014
Self registration applies; cold showers only. Fishing, diving.
34.828765S 173.406398E   Hema Atlas Map Ref 2 F7

82 Norfolk Motel & Campervan Park
29 SH10: 500m E of Awanui on SH10
Ph/Fax (09) 406 7515   norfolkmotel@xtra.co.nz
www.norfolkmotel.co.nz
Motel offering a sheltered rear paddock for campervans. Wireless internet.
35.046379S 173.258779E   Hema Atlas Map Ref 1 H6

SH1 — AWANUI TO CAPE REINGA

83 Roadside Rest Area
Off SH1 alongside Lake Ngatu, near Waipapakauri
Waterside picnic spot is a popular spot for boating.
35.026618S 173.198629E   Hema Atlas Map Ref 1 H5

84 The Park Top 10, Ninety Mile Beach
6 Matai St, Awanui, 5km W of SH1 at Waipapakauri Ramp: signposted diversion
Ph (09) 406 7298   ninetymilebeach@xtra.co.nz
www.ninetymilebeach.co.nz
Handy access to Ninety Mile Beach and a popular base for local anglers. Internet.
35.038361S 173.171843E   Hema Atlas Map Ref 1 H5

85 Wagener Holiday Park
(Houhara Heads Motor Camp)
3km E of SH1 at Houhora Heads, S of Pukenui: signposted diversion
Ph/Fax (09) 409 8564   wagenerpark@xtra.co.nz
www.northlandholiday.co.nz
Beautiful sheltered spot well worth the short diversion. This camp is popular with families, boaters and anglers. Bus wash on site.
34.824158S 173.148137E   Hema Atlas Map Ref 1 F5

North Island Camping Sites

Northland Region

HOUHORA HARBOUR PHOTO: DESTINATION NORTHLAND

86 Pukenui Holiday Park
34 Lamb Rd, Pukenui: signposted W of SH1 at the centre of Pukenui
Ph (09) 409 8803 Fax (09) 409 8802 pukenuiholidays@xtra.co.nz
www.northland-camping.co.nz
Free showers.

34.817157S 173.115682E Hema Atlas Map Ref 1 F5

87 Rarawa
Rarawa Beach Rd; signposted E of SH1 N of Pukenui
Kaitaia DOC Office, Ph (09) 408 6014
Casual camping self registration applies; cold showers only. Beautiful beachside location, but the entrance sign is a little confusing - take the right fork for camping.

34.726145S 173.082933E Hema Atlas Map Ref 1 E4

88 Waitiki Holiday Park
Far North Road, SH1 at Waitiki Landing
Ph (09) 409 7508 waitiki.landing@xtra.co.nz
Small, functional camp that's the closest serviced camp to Cape Reinga. Internet access.

34.517423S 172.83979E Hema Atlas Map Ref 1 B2

89 Kapowairua (Spirits Bay), Te Paki Recreation Reserve
Spirits Bay Rd, 16km from Waitiki Landing on SH1
Kaitaia DOC Office, Ph (09) 408 6014
Cold showers only.

34.428124S 172.863366E Hema Atlas Map Ref 1 A2

90 Tapotupotu
On Far North Rd: signposted from SH1 just S of Cape Reinga, a 3km diversion.
Kaitaia DOC Office, Ph (09) 408 6014
Casual camping self registration applies; cold showers only. Don't leave Cape Reinga without visiting the white sands of this magic bay.

34.437052S 172.715869E Hema Atlas Map Ref 1 A1

91 Cape Reinga Roadside Rest Area
Cape Reinga
Iconic and well worth the journey.

34.428837S 172.680977E Hema Atlas Map Ref 1 A1

SH1— AWANUI TO KAWAKAWA

92 Ahipara Holiday Park
164-170 Takahe Rd, Ahipara, signposted from Ahipara
Ph 0800 888 988 camp@ahipara.co.nz Fax (09) 409 2118
www.ahiparamotorcamp.co.nz
Nice location, just 800m from Ninety Mile Beach, under the shade of pine trees. Surf, quad bike, trek, fish, ride. Wireless internet access.

35.160159S 173.159557E Hema Atlas Map Ref 1 J5

93 Te Kohania Camping Ground
Beachside at the end of Ahipara Bay
A caretaker may collect koha or fees if they are in attendance. Right on the coast at the favoured surf spot on this beach.

35.178516S 173.119332E Hema Atlas Map Ref 1 J5

94 Roadside Rest Area
Summit of the Mangamuka Saddle at 390m: along SH1
35.189619S 173.455975E Hema Atlas Map Ref 2 K8

95 Forest View Rest Area
SH1, W of Mangamuka
35.18683S 173.471158E Hema Atlas Map Ref 2 K8

96 Roadside Rest Area
Mangamuka Gorge Scenic Reserve alongside SH1
Waterside picnic area is a nice swimming spot.

35.193859S 173.482471E Hema Atlas Map Ref 2 K8

97 Raetea North Side
Along SH1: north side of Raetea Range, beyond concrete ford
DOC Kaitaia Area Office Ph (09) 408 6014
Drinking water is from a stream.

35.169161S 173.434113E Hema Atlas Map Ref 2 K8

98 The Tree House
168 West Coast Rd, Kohukohu, W of the Rawene Ferry's northern landing point
Ph (09) 405 5855 Fax (09) 405 5857 www.treehouse.co.nz
Internet access.

35.372189S 173.510495E Hema Atlas Map Ref 3 C4

99 Forest Pools, Puketi Forest
Forest Road, Puketi Forest
DOC Bay of Islands Area Office Ph (09) 407 0300
bayofislandsbooking@doc.govt.nz
Camping only permitted overnight; drinking water is from a stream.

35.278292S 173.684572E Hema Atlas Map Ref 3 B6

100 Puketi Recreation Area
Waiare Rd, Puketi Forest: 20km NE of Okaihau
DOC Bay of Islands Area Office Ph (09) 407 0300
bayofislandsbooking@doc.govt.nz
Cold showers only; firewood provided.

35.249302S 173.76409E Hema Atlas Map Ref 3 A7

Northland Region

SH12 — SH1 TO DARGAVILLE

101 Rawene Holiday Park
1 Marmon St West, Rawene: signposted from Rawene Rd, off SH12
Ph (09) 405 7720
Hillside camp with nice views of the Hokianga. Pets by arrangement.
35.402377S 173.504705E   Hema Atlas Map Ref 3 C4

102 Opononi Beach Holiday Park
43 SH12 at Opononi
Ph/Fax (09) 405 8791 harrybarlow@xtra.co.nz
Opposite the magic beaches lining this part of the Hokianga.
35.508771S 173.390337E   Hema Atlas Map Ref 3 D3

103 Roadside Rest Area
Along SH12 S of Opononi: several sites
Camping is not allowed but there are several picnic spots right next to the white sand beaches of the Hokianga Harbour.
35.514488S 173.388791E   Hema Atlas Map Ref 3 D3

104 Taheke Rest Area
SH12, W of Kaikohe, E of Taheke
35.46059S 173.693818E   Hema Atlas Map Ref 3 C7

105 Roadside Rest Area
Taheke Rd, Kaikohe, just W of Orrs Rd
35.411466S 173.792962E   Hema Atlas Map Ref 3 D6

106 Roadside Rest Area
SH12, midway between Opononi and Omapere
35.51955S 173.387668E   Hema Atlas Map Ref 3 D3

107 Roadside Rest Area
Arai-Te-Uru Recreation Reserve: signposted 800m from SH12
Nice views over Hokianga Harbour and beach walks from this reserve - but no camping.
35.537834S 173.372176E   Hema Atlas Map Ref 3 D3

108 Roadside Rest Area
Pakia Hill, SH12: overlooking the entrance to the Hokianga Harbour
Best approached from the S. This viewpoint provides memorable views of the famed Hokianga Harbour.
35.540994S 173.387101E   Hema Atlas Map Ref 3 E3

109 Tane Mahuta Reserve and Rest Area
Adjacent SH12, Waipoua Forest
Take a short walk to view Tane Mahuta ('Lord of the Forest') - a revered kauri tree 4.4m in diameter, and thought to be 2000 years old.
35.600401S 173.528107E   Hema Atlas Map Ref 3 E4

110 Waipoua Forest Campsite
Waipoua River Rd, Waipoua Forest: signposted W of SH12
Now managed by Te Iwi O Te Roroa Ph (09) 439 6445
Self registration applies. Sheltered forest setting next to a nice stream.
35.650836S 173.551747E   Hema Atlas Map Ref 3 F5

111 Trounson Kauri Park
Donnellys Crossing Loop Rd: 40km N of Dargaville
DOC Kauri Coast Area Office Ph (09) 439 3450
kauricoastareaoffice@doc.govt.nz
Self registration applies; closed Easter to Labour Weekend. Located in a pretty valley with a stream.
35.720335S 173.651483E   Hema Atlas Map Ref 3 G5

112 Kauri Coast Top 10 Holiday Park
Trounson Park Rd: signposted to the E of SH12, S of Waipoua Forest Park
Ph/Fax (09) 439 0621, 0800 807 200 kauricoast.top10@xtra.co.nz
www.kauricoasttop10.co.nz
Sheltered valley alongside a pretty swimming hole. Qualmark four star plus. Pets by arrangement. Internet access.
35.75004S 173.673862E   Hema Atlas Map Ref 3 G6

113 Pine Beach Campground, Kaiiwi Lakes
End of Campground Rd, off Kai Iwi Lakes Rd, Taharoa Domain
Ph (09) 439 4757 lakes@kaipara.govt.nz www.kaipara.govt.nz
Cold showers only, bookings required.
35.809401S 173.662578E   Hema Atlas Map Ref 3 H6

114 Promenade Point Campground, Kaiiwi Lakes
Off Kai Iwi Lakes Rd, Taharoa Domain
Kauri Coast Information Centre, Dargaville
lakes@kaipara.govt.nz www.kaipara.govt.nz
A caretaker may collect koha or fees if they are in attendance. White sand beaches line this freshwater lake. Bookings required.
35.804979S 173.637491E   Hema Atlas Map Ref 3 H5

115 Baylys Beach Holiday Park
22 Seaview Rd, Bayleys Beach: 10km W of Dargaville
Ph/Fax (09) 439 6349 motorcamp@baylysbeach.co.nz
www.baylysbeach.co.nz
Just up the road from a nice West Coast beach. Wireless internet.
35.950354S 173.74737E   Hema Atlas Map Ref 3 J6

SH12 – DARGAVILLE TO SH1

116 Dargaville Holiday Park
10 Onslow St, Dargaville: signposted from SH12 E of Dargaville town centre
Ph 0800 114 441 dargholidaypark@slingshot.co.nz
www.kauriparks.co.nz
Neat and tidy with good facilities. Internet access. Pets by arrangement.
35.933722S 173.877364E   Hema Atlas Map Ref 3 J7

117 Dargaville Campervan Park & Cabins
18 Gladstone St, Dargaville: signposted from Dargaville town centre
Ph/Fax (09) 439 8479 rayglen@xtra.co.nz
Handy to the town centre with railway carriages converted to cabins with ensuites.
35.939092S 173.87162E   Hema Atlas Map Ref 3 J7

North Island Camping Sites

Auckland Region

118 Roadside Rest Area
Near the town centre at Dargaville
Waterside picnic area.
35.944475S 173.861517E   Hema Atlas Map Ref 3 J7

119 Dargaville North Rest Area
SH12, N of Murdoch St, Dargaville
35.950724S 173.864783E   Hema Atlas Map Ref 3 J7

120 Roadside Rest Area
Grey St before the bridge, Dargaville
35.935728S 173.881621E   Hema Atlas Map Ref 3 J7

121 Kellys Bay Reserve
Follow Pouto Rd off SH12 to Kellys Bay
Ph (09) 439 4204
36.248205S 174.100378E   Hema Atlas Map Ref 5 D4

122 Pouto Point Motor Camp
Follow Pouto Rd off SH12 to Pouto Point
Ph (09) 439 0199
Backpackers accommodation. Pets by arrangement.
36.362496S 174.180342E   Hema Atlas Map Ref 5 E5

123 Roadside Rest Area
Adjacent SH12, S of Dargaville
Waterside picnic area.
36.070205S 173.972496E   Hema Atlas Map Ref 5 B3

124 Matakohe Top 10 Holiday Park
Church Rd, Matakohe: follow the signs to the Matakohe Kauri Museum
Ph 0800 431 6431   matakoheholidaypark@xtra.co.nz
www.matakohetop10.co.nz
Compact, rural environment next door to the Kauri Museum. Facilities can get a little pressured at peak times. Children's playground, internet. Qualmark four star.
36.134009S 174.189061E   Hema Atlas Map Ref 5 B5

125 Pahi Beach Motor Camp
Beachside at Pahi Beach: 7km from SH12
Ph/Fax (09) 431 7322
Worthwhile deviation to see old buildings in a pretty harbourside location.
36.156899S 174.228305E   Hema Atlas Map Ref 5 B6

126 Roadside Rest Area
SH12, W of Paparoa
36.099907S 174.235382E   Hema Atlas Map Ref 5 B6

127 Paparoa Motor Camp
17 Pahi Rd, Paparoa, Cnr SH12 & Pahi Rd, Paparoa
Ph/Fax (09) 431 6515   paparoamotorcamp@xtra.co.nz
Conveniently located camp. Internet. Shops and walks all within walking distance.
36.107096S 174.22862E   Hema Atlas Map Ref 5 B6

AUCKLAND REGION

AUCKLAND CITY

ISLANDS OF THE HAURAKI GULF	28
SH1 — AUCKLAND TO WELLSFORD	29
SH16 — WELLSFORD TO AUCKLAND	31
AUCKLAND TO WAITAKERE RANGES REGIONAL PARK	31
AUCKLAND TO SH25	32
SH1 — AUCKLAND TO SH2	33

ISLANDS OF THE HAURAKI GULF

128 Home Bay
Motutapu Island, east coast (boat access only)
DOC Auckland Visitor Centre Ph (09) 379 6476
aucklandvc@doc.govt.nz
36.767996S 174.927859E   Hema Atlas Map Ref 7 C6

129 Motuihe
Motuihe Wharf, Wharf Bay, Motuihe Island (boat access only)
DOC Auckland Visitor Centre Ph (09) 379 6476
aucklandvc@doc.govt.nz
Bookings required for boat access: Ph (09) 307 8005
36.804471S 174.934584E   Hema Atlas Map Ref 90 B6, 7 D6

130 Whakanewha Regional Park
Waiheke Island
Auckland Council Ph (09) 301 0101
regionalparks@aucklandcouncil.govt.nz   www.aucklandcouncil.govt.nz
Bookings essential all year; recycling bins; outdoor shower.
36.830626S 175.068978E   Hema Atlas Map Ref 7 D7

131 Medlands Beach
S end of Medlands Beach, Great Barrier Island (car ferry access)
DOC Auckland Visitor Centre Ph (09) 379 6476
aucklandvc@doc.govt.nz
Bookings essential all year; cold showers; serviced Dec 1 to end Feb.
36.271017S 175.504275E   Hema Atlas Map Ref 36 E5

132 Awana Beach
Awana estuary, Great Barrier Island east coast (car ferry access)
DOC Auckland Visitor Centre Ph (09) 379 6476
aucklandvc@doc.govt.nz
Bookings essential all year; cold showers; serviced Dec 1 to end Feb.
36.20944S 175.47776E   Hema Atlas Map Ref 36 D5

Auckland Region

North Island Camping Sites

29

133 Harataonga
Kaitoke/Port Fitzroy Rd, Great Barrier Island (car ferry access)
DOC Auckland Visitor Centre Ph (09) 379 6476
aucklandvc@doc.govt.nz
Bookings essential all year; cold showers; serviced Dec 1 to end Feb.

36.171779S 175.479426E   Hema Atlas Map Ref 36 D5

134 Akapoua Bay
Port Fitzroy DOC Headquarters, Great Barrier Island (car ferry access)
DOC Auckland Visitor Centre Ph (09) 379 6476
aucklandvc@doc.govt.nz
Bookings essential all year; cold showers; serviced Dec 1 to end Feb.

36.171944S 175.363237E   Hema Atlas Map Ref 36 D4

135 The Green
Whangaparapara Harbour, Great Barrier Island
DOC Auckland Visitor Centre Ph (09) 379 6476
aucklandvc@doc.govt.nz
Bookings essential all year; serviced Dec 1 to end of Feb.

36.236544S 175.398267E   Hema Atlas Map Ref 36 E4

136 Whangapoua
Edge of estuary at Okiwi, Great Barrier Island (car ferry access)
DOC Auckland Visitor Centre Ph (09) 379 6476
aucklandvc@doc.govt.nz
Bookings essential all year; cold showers; serviced Dec 1 to end Feb.

36.145127S 175.421824E   Hema Atlas Map Ref 36 C4

SH1 – AUCKLAND TO WELLSFORD

137 Auckland North Shore Motels & Holiday Park
52 Northcote Rd, Takapuna: 500m W of SH1
Ph (09) 418 2578 Fax (09) 480 0435 info@nsmotels.co.nz
www.top1.co.nz
Nice camp, children's playground, internet. Qualmark four star. Spa pool.

36.793576S 174.746351E   Hema Atlas Map Ref 88 J4, 90 A4, 7 D4

138 Takapuna Beach Holiday Park
22 The Promenade, Takapuna: signposted from Hurstmere Rd,
at the N end of Takapuna town centre
Ph/Fax (09) 489 7909 takabeach@xtra.co.nz
www.takapunabeachholidaypark.co.nz
Prime waterfront location, yet only a short stroll to the cafes of Takapuna. Be warned, it can get a tad crowded. Internet access.

36.784027S 174.775698E   Hema Atlas Map Ref 88 H5, 90 A4, 7 D4

139 Roadside Rest Area
Milford Beach Marina
Waterside picnic area.

36.768038S 174.765841E   Hema Atlas Map Ref 88 H4, 7 C4

140 Roadside Rest Area
Milford Beach Reserve
Waterside picnic area.

36.766113S 174.766376E   Hema Atlas Map Ref 88 H4, 7 C4

141 Roadside Rest Area
Castor Bay Beach Reserve
Waterside picnic area.

36.755422S 174.764868E   Hema Atlas Map Ref 88 G4, 7 C4

142 Roadside Rest Area
Mairangi Bay Beach Reserve
Waterside picnic area.

36.738115S 174.756001E   Hema Atlas Map Ref 88 G4, 7 C4

143 Roadside Rest Area
Browns Bay Beach Reserve: along the coastal route, follow the signs to Browns Bay town centre
Waterside picnic area.

36.716802S 174.749277E   Hema Atlas Map Ref 88 F4, 7 C4

144 Shakespear Regional Park
Whangaparoa Peninsula: road's end, a 20km diversion from the Hibiscus Coast route
Auckland Council Ph (09) 301 0101
regionalparks@aucklandcouncil.govt.nz www.aucklandcouncil.govt.nz
Bookings essential all year.

36.614124S 174.830101E   Hema Atlas Map Ref 88 B6, 7 B5

145 Pinewoods Motor Park
23 Marie Ave, Red Beach: Follow the signs to Red Beach from Hibiscus Highway
Ph (09) 426 4526 office@pinewoods.co.nz www.pinewoods.co.nz
Compact, sheltered and just a short walk from beach. On-site gym. Internet access. Qualmark four star.

36.602031S 174.706093E   Hema Atlas Map Ref 88 B3, 7 B4

146 Orewa Beach Top 10 Holiday Park
265 Hibiscus Coast Highway: beachside at the S end of Orewa Beach
Ph (09) 426 5832 Fax (09) 426 7883 obhpark@rodney.govt.nz
www.orewabeachtop10.co.nz
Fabulous beachside location with sheltered estuary safe swimming. Can get crowded due to popularity. Internet. Qualmark 4 star.

36.596528S 174.699335E   Hema Atlas Map Ref 88 A3, 7 A4

147 Roadside Rest Area
Moana Reserve: waterfront at Orewa
Waterside picnic area.

36.591408S 174.698724E   Hema Atlas Map Ref 88 A3, 7 A4

148 Roadside Rest Area
SH17, N side of the bridge over Orewa River

36.599174S 174.697944E   Hema Atlas Map Ref 88 A3, 7 A4

North Island Camping Sites — Auckland Region

149 — Roadside Rest Area
Hatfields Beach, adjoining SH1
Waterside picnic area.

36.56511S 174.694285E   Hema Atlas Map Ref 7 A4

150 — Orewa Lookout Rest Area
SH17 between Orewa and Hatfields Beach
36.573435S 174.69216E   Hema Atlas Map Ref 7 A4

151 — Waiwera Holiday Park
37 Waiwera Place, Waiwera: signposted from SH1 at Waiwera
Ph (09) 426 5270 camp@waiwera.co.nz
www.waiwera.co.nz/waiwera-accommodation
Compact camp, close to beach and hot pools. Internet.

36.547512S 174.707087E   Hema Atlas Map Ref 7 A4

152 — Wenderholm Regional Park
Alongside SH1 N of Hatfields Beach
Auckland Council Ph (09) 301 0101
regionalparks@aucklandcouncil.govt.nz www.aucklandcouncil.govt.nz
Bookings essential all year: self-contained caravans and motorhomes can stay in designated carparks for up to two nights (limited numbers). Features a lovely tree-lined bay.

36.534172S 174.705219E   Hema Atlas Map Ref 7 A4

153 — Mahurangi Regional Park
Sullivans Bay: Signposted E of SH1, S of Warkworth
Auckland Council Ph (09) 301 0101
regionalparks@aucklandcouncil.govt.nz www.aucklandcouncil.govt.nz
Bookings essential all year: self-contained caravans and motorhomes can stay in designated car parks for up to two nights (limited numbers). Peaceful but simple camping.

36.509246S 174.720756E   Hema Atlas Map Ref 6 F10

154 — Roadside Rest Area
Kowhai Park: N end of Warkworth on SH1
 36.39626S 174.660373E   Hema Atlas Map Ref 6 E10

155 — Moirs Hill Walkway Rest Area
SH1, S of Warkworth
Access on left for north-bound traffic.
36.453244S 174.652541E   Hema Atlas Map Ref 6 F9

156 — Roadside Rest Area
SH1, S of Warkworth
Access on left for south-bound traffic.
36.456947S 174.652673E   Hema Atlas Map Ref 6 F9

157 — Sheepworld Caravan Park
Alongside SH1 4km N of Warkworth
Ph/Fax (09) 425 9962 sheepworld@maxnet.co.nz
www.sheepworldcaravanpark.co.nz
A slick sheep-related sales outlet, with cafe and camp. Pets by arrangement.

36.37088S 174.629023E   Hema Atlas Map Ref 6 E9

158 — Roadside Rest Area
SH1 N of Warkworth
36.350115S 174.573972E   Hema Atlas Map Ref 6 E9

159 — Motuora Island
Motuora Island, east coast (boat access only):
6km E of Mahurangi Harbour
DOC Auckland Visitor Centre Ph (09) 379 6476
aucklandvc@doc.govt.nz
Bookings required for boat access: Ph 0274 928 586; cold showers only.

36.505386S 174.789806E   Hema Atlas Map Ref 6 F11

160 — Martins Bay Holiday Park
287 Martins Bay Rd, Warkworth. Follow signs to Snells Beach from Warkworth then follow signs to Martins Bay
Ph (09) 425 5655 Fax (09) 425 5618 mbhpark@rodney.govt.nz
www.martinsbayholidaypark.co.nz
Beachside and sheltered amongst Pohutakawas. Children's playground.

36.449229S 174.762604E   Hema Atlas Map Ref 6 F10

161 — Roadside Rest Area
Martins Bay, signposted from Warkworth
36.450476S 174.763459E   Hema Atlas Map Ref 6 F10

162 — Scandrett Regional Park
Signposted from Warkworth
Auckland Council Ph (09) 301 0101
regionalparks@aucklandcouncil.govt.nz www.aucklandcouncil.govt.nz
Bookings essential all year: permit required for self-contained caravans and motorhomes for overnight (limited numbers).

36.440277S 174.759676E   Hema Atlas Map Ref 6 F10

163 — Roadside Rest Area
Sandspit
Waterside picnic area.

36.392923S 174.727641E   Hema Atlas Map Ref 6 E10

164 — Sandspit Holiday Park
1334 Sandspit Rd, Beachside at Sandspit: Signposted from Warkworth
Ph/Fax (09) 425 8610 sandspit@xtra.co.nz
www.sandspitholidaypark.co.nz
Fabulous collection of old buildings make a unique backdrop to this camp. Popular with anglers and boat owners. Qualmark 4 star.

36.393557S 174.727821E   Hema Atlas Map Ref 6 E10

165 — Tawharanui Regional Park
13km deviation from the Leigh-Warkworth Rd: very well signposted
Auckland Council Ph (09) 301 0101
regionalparks@aucklandcouncil.govt.nz www.aucklandcouncil.govt.nz
Bookings essential all year (especially popular in the summer months): self-contained caravans and motorhomes can stay in designated carparks for up to three nights (limited numbers). Beautiful camping and surfing beach with lots of walks. No dogs. Access to disabled toilets is across grass.

36.367788S 174.829251E   Hema Atlas Map Ref 6 E11

166 — Whangateau Holiday Park
559 Leigh Rd, Whangateau
Ph (09) 422 6305 Fax (09) 422 6686 whpark@rodney.govt.nz
www.whangateauholidaypark.co.nz
Waterside, but a bit exposed to sun and heat. Qualmark 4 star plus. Environmental Bronze. Kayaks for hire, large children's playground.

36.314943S 174.764956E   Hema Atlas Map Ref 6 D10

Auckland Region

North Island Camping Sites

167 Goat Island Camping & Accommodation
Goat Island Marine Reserve: A short deviation from the Leigh-Pakiri Rd: follow the signs
Ph (09) 422 6185 goatiscamp@xtra.co.nz
www.goatislandcamping.co.nz
A short walk to Marine Reserve for excellent diving and snorkelling.
36.270635S 174.79502E Hema Atlas Map Ref 6 D11

168 Roadside Rest Area
Okakari Point Scenic Reserve, Cape Rodney
Popular point for access to nearby Marine Reserve. A glass-bottom boat operates from here, so bring your snorkel and flippers.
36.270975S 174.794809E Hema Atlas Map Ref 6 D11

169 Pakiri Beach Holiday Park
261 Pakiri River Rd, Pakiri: follow signs to Pakiri from either Wellsford or Leigh
Ph/Fax (09) 422 6199 pakiri@khh.co.nz www.pakiriholidaypark.co.nz
Extremely well-managed beachside camp with great facilities.
36.245509S 174.72242E Hema Atlas Map Ref 6 D10

SH16 — WELLSFORD TO AUCKLAND

170 Roadside Rest Area
Alongside SH16: scenic lookout 208m above sea level
36.35164S 174.471406E Hema Atlas Map Ref 6 E8

171 Roadside Rest Area
Omeru Reserve, alongside SH16
36.558679S 174.475118E Hema Atlas Map Ref 6 E8

172 Roadside Rest Area
SH16, S of Kaupakapaka
36.622722S 174.502232E Hema Atlas Map Ref 6 H8

173 Paradise Springs Motor Camp
150 Parkhurst Rd, Parakai SH16
Ph (09) 420 8998 Fax (09) 420 8909 info@parakaisprings.com
www.parakaisprings.com
Located next to a major thermal pool complex for swimming and soothing those aches. A simple camp equivalent to a 2-3 star rating.
36.66046S 174.43359E Hema Atlas Map Ref 5 H7

174 Roadside Rest Area
Shelly Beach Rd, Helensville
Waterside picnic area.
36.569461S 174.378671E Hema Atlas Map Ref 5 G7

175 Shelly Beach Camping Ground
Shelly Beach Rd, Helensville
Ph (09) 420 2595 www.rodney.govt.nz
Swimming, fishing. Harbourside location with a white shell beach.
36.568115S 174.37709E Hema Atlas Map Ref 5 G7

176 Muriwai Beach Motor Camp
Beachfront at Muriwai: in Muriwai Regional Park
Ph (09) 411 9262 info@muriwaimotorcamp.co.nz
www.muriwaimotorcamp.co.nz
Surfing, angling. Sheltered tree-clad site right next to this rugged West Coast beach.
36.827835S 174.427314E Hema Atlas Map Ref 7 D1

177 Glen Esk Road
Waitakere Ranges Regional Park
Auckland Council Ph (09) 301 0101
regionalparks@aucklandcouncil.govt.nz www.aucklandcouncil.govt.nz
Bookings essential all year.
36.952521S 174.478748E Hema Atlas Map Ref 7 E2

178 Piha Domain Motor Camp
21 Seaview Rd, Piha
Ph (09) 812 8815 pihacamp@xtra.co.nz
www.pihabeach.co.nz/piha-camp.htm
Surfing, angling. Pretty beachside spot with no cabins, but some caravans available. Pets by arrangement.
36.953939S 174.472554E Hema Atlas Map Ref 7 E2

179 Roadside Rest Area
S of Piha
36.962333S 174.473707E Hema Atlas Map Ref 7 F2

180 Log Jam Road
Waitakere Ranges Regional Park
Auckland Council Ph (09) 301 0101
regionalparks@aucklandcouncil.govt.nz www.aucklandcouncil.govt.nz
Bookings essential all year.
36.96808S 174.474594E Hema Atlas Map Ref 7 F2

AUCKLAND TO WAITAKERE RANGES REGIONAL PARK

181 Roadside Rest Area
Waikowhai Park: alongside Route 15, SW of Auckland
36.93356S 174.735096E Hema Atlas Map Ref 89 D3, 7 E4

182 Avondale Motor Park
46 Bollard Ave, Avondale: signposted from New North Rd, S of Mt Albert township
Ph 0800 100 542 Fax (09) 828 4433
avondalemotorpark@xtra.co.nz www.aucklandmotorpark.co.nz
Clean and compact site that makes a good base for entering/leaving Auckland from the West and exploring areas such as Titirangi, Piha and Murawai. Qualmark 4 star. Internet access.
36.897684S 174.707367E Hema Atlas Map Ref 89 C3, 7 E4

183 Roadside Rest Area
Craigavon Park: alongside Route 15, SW Auckland
36.928518S 174.690452E Hema Atlas Map Ref 89 D3, 7 E4

184 Roadside Rest Area
Rahui Kahika Reserve: alongside Route 15, Titirangi
36.932691S 174.665665E Hema Atlas Map Ref 89 D2, 7 E3

North Island Camping Sites — Auckland Region

185 Roadside Rest Area
Huia Rd, Titirangi
36.948998S 174.641748E   Hema Atlas Map Ref 89 D2, 7 E3

186 Arataki Visitors Centre
Waitakere Ranges Regional Park: alongside Scenic Route 24 between Titirangi & Waiatarua
Auckland Council Ph (09) 301 0101
regionalparks@aucklandcouncil.govt.nz www.aucklandcouncil.govt.nz
Overnight for certified self-contained motorhomes allowed, max 2 nights.

36.944513S 174.60781E   Hema Atlas Map Ref 89 D2, 7 E3

187 Roadside Rest Area
Huia Rd, Mill Bay, Waitakere Regional Park
Several picnic spots in this vicinity.
36.990865S 174.604943E   Hema Atlas Map Ref 89 E2, 7 F3

188 Roadside Rest Area
Beachfront along Huia Rd, Huia Bay, Waitakere Ranges Regional Park

36.999428S 174.57045E   Hema Atlas Map Ref 89 E1, 7 F3

189 Huia – Karamatura Valley and Barn Paddock Campgrounds
Huia Rd, 2km past Huia Bay, Waitakere Ranges Regional Park
Auckland Council Ph (09) 301 0101
regionalparks@aucklandcouncil.govt.nz www.aucklandcouncil.govt.nz
Bookings essential all year. Simple camping in a rural environment, handy to the Manukau Harbour. Max. 7 nights stay.

37.004318S 174.562017E   Hema Atlas Map Ref 89 E1, 7 F2

AUCKLAND TO SH25

190 Roadside Rest Area
Okahu Bay Reserve, Tamaki Drive
Waterside picnic area.

36.850947S 174.816703E   Hema Atlas Map Ref 90 C5, 7 D5

191 Roadside Rest Area
Mission Bay, Tamaki Drive
Waterside picnic area with iconic views of Rangitoto Island.

36.848009S 174.832516E   Hema Atlas Map Ref 90 B5, 7 D5

192 Remuera Motor Lodge & Inner City Camping Ground
16 Minto Rd, Remuera: signposted SW of Remuera Rd, S of Remuera township
Ph 0508 244 244   (09) 524 5126   remlodge@ihug.co.nz
www.remueramotorlodge.co.nz
Small, compact site in a suprisingly quiet wooded valley only a stone's throw from the cafes of Remuera Rd. Wireless internet.

36.881751S 174.812091E   Hema Atlas Map Ref 90 C5, 7 E5

193 Omana Regional Park
Signposted near Beachlands on the Whitford to Clevedon coastal road (Whitford Maraetai Coast Road)
Auckland Council Ph (09) 301 0101
regionalparks@aucklandcouncil.govt.nz www.aucklandcouncil.govt.nz
Bookings essential all year, cold outdoor shower, boat ramp Omana Beach. Campervans can stay up to 3 nights. Access to disabled toilets is across grass.

36.879974S 175.018928E   Hema Atlas Map Ref 7 E7

194 Maraetai Beach Reserve
Alongside Whitford to Clevedon coastal road

36.881693S 175.04807E   Hema Atlas Map Ref 7 E7

195 Roadside Rest Area
Kawakawa Bay, on the Clevedon to Kaiaua road
Waterside picnic area.

36.948646S 175.165317E   Hema Atlas Map Ref 8 E8

196 Orere Point Top 10 Holiday Park
2 Orere Point Rd, Orere Point: on the Clevedon to Kaiaua road
Ph 0800 391 905 Ph/Fax (09) 292 2774 orerepoint@xtra.co.nz
www.orerepointholidaypark.co.nz
Boating, fishing. Pretty location, just back from the beach. Wireless internet. Pets by arrangement. Qualmark four star.

36.960791S 175.243313E   Hema Atlas Map Ref 8 F9

197 Roadside Rest Area
Orere Point on the Clevedon to Kaiaua road
Waterside picnic area.

36.957742S 175.245872E   Hema Atlas Map Ref 8 F9

198 Tapapakanga Regional Park (Sea View & Beachfront Campgrounds)
On the Clevedon to Miranda Coast road
Auckland Council Ph (09) 301 0101
parks@aucklandcouncil.govt.nz www.aucklandcouncil.govt.nz
Bookings essential all year. Kaparanui Stream and Tapakanga Stream Campsites - self-contained motorhomes only, max. 7 nights.

36.973567S 175.254632E   Hema Atlas Map Ref 8 F9

199 Waharau Regional Park (Blackberry Flats & Tainui)
On the Clevedon to Miranda Coast road
Auckland Council Ph (09) 301 0101
regionalparks@aucklandcouncil.govt.nz www.aucklandcouncil.govt.nz
Closed in winter if boggy. Stay up to 7 nights. Tainui is open 21 Feb - 30 Nov. Self-contained motorhomes max. 3 nights in carpark. Powered sites only avilable at Tainui Campground.

37.038749S 175.293993E   Hema Atlas Map Ref 8 F9

200 Roadside Rest Area
On the Clevedon to Miranda Coast road
Waterside picnic area.

37.037652S 175.296292E   Hema Atlas Map Ref 8 G9

Auckland Region — North Island Camping Sites

201 Kaiaua Motor Camp
1204 East Coast Road, Kaiaua
Ph (09) 232 2712 camp@ecoquest.co.nz
Not open all year - phone to confirm.

37.087821S 175.301875E — Hema Atlas Map Ref 8 G9

202 Upper Mangatawhiri Campground
Hunua Ranges Regional Park
Auckland Council Ph (09) 301 0101
regionalparks@aucklandcouncil.govt.nz www.aucklandcouncil.govt.nz

Bookings essential all year, water must be boiled, steep road can be difficult for caravan access. Max. 7 nights. Campervans can stay if ground hard enough.

37.089012S 175.154609E — Hema Atlas Map Ref 8 G8

203 Lower Mangatawhiri Campground
Hunua Range Regional Park
Auckland Council Ph (09) 301 0101
regionalparks@aucklandcouncil.govt.nz www.aucklandcouncil.govt.nz

Bookings essential all year, water is stream water and must be boiled. 7km walk to campsite from Upper Mangatawhiri.

37.121501S 175.167262E — Hema Atlas Map Ref 8 G8

204 Piggotts Campground
Hunua Ranges Regional Park
Auckland Council Ph (09) 301 0101
regionalparks@aucklandcouncil.govt.nz www.aucklandcouncil.govt.nz

Bookings essential all year, water is stream water and must be boiled. Max. 7 nights. It is a 5km walk to this campsite.

37.080934S 175.196824E — Hema Atlas Map Ref 8 G8

205 Rays Rest Roadside Rest Area
On the Clevedon to Miranda Coast road
37.151116S 175.307154E — Hema Atlas Map Ref 8 H9

206 Miranda Holiday Park
595 Front Miranda Rd, Waitakaruru
Ph (07) 867 3205 mirandaholidaypark@xtra.co.nz
www.mirandaholidaypark.co.nz

New luxury spa-bath apartments, tennis courts. Right next to the Miranda Hot Thermal Pools. Wireless internet.

37.207431S 175.333562E — Hema Atlas Map Ref 8 H9

SH1 — AUCKLAND TO SH2

207 Ambury Regional Park
Ambury Rd, Manukau: follow SH20 taking the Mangere Bridge offramp, Ambury Park is signposted from here
Auckland Council Ph (09) 301 0101
regionalparks@aucklandcouncil.govt.nz www.aucklandcouncil.govt.nz

Bookings essential all year. Simple camping in a picturesque rural location, yet only 30 min from downtown Auckland, and 15 min from the airport. Self-contained motorhomes may stay overnight in the carpark, max. 7 nights stay.

36.946285S 174.758811E — Hema Atlas Map Ref 90 D4, 7 E4

208 Manukau Top 10 Holiday Park
902 Great South Rd, Manukau: take the Manukau exit from SH1, head S on Great Sth Rd from Manukau city centre and Rainbow's End, 1.5km S of Manukau Shopping Centre
Ph (09) 266 8016 www.manukautop10.co.nz
Fax (09) 268 4209 info@manukautop10.co.nz

A suprisingly peaceful, small camp handy to S Auckland and Manukau City Centre. An ideal base for campers returning their hire vehicles to the nearby Auckland airport. Internet. Qualmark four star. Pets by arrangement.

37.00776S 174.890223E — Hema Atlas Map Ref 90 E5, 7 F5

209 South Auckland Caravan Park
25 Ararimu Rd, Ramarama: signposted from the Ramarama exit SH1, S of Auckland
Ph (09) 294 8903 Fax (09) 294 7903 sacp@ihug.co.nz

A rural setting, handy to South Auckland. Store opposite, swimming pool summer only, dogs to be kept in van.

37.143879S 174.962714E — Hema Atlas Map Ref 7 H6

210 Clarks Beach Holiday Park
226 Torkar Rd, Clarks Beach, Auckland: signposted from the town centre at Clarks Beach, exit SH1 at Papakura, and follow signs to Kingseat and Waiau Pa
Ph (09) 232 1685 cbhp@ihug.co.nz www.cbhp.co.nz

Opposite a tree-lined waterside recreational area, with boat launching and picnicking facilities. Also handy to a golf course. It's a little hard to find, but a nice spot south of Auckland. Dogs by prior arrangement in tent, power sites only. Internet access.

37.140734S 174.690467E — Hema Atlas Map Ref 7 H4

211 Roadside Rest Area
Torkar Rd, Clarks Beach: signposted from the town centre at Clarks Beach, exit SH1 at Papakura, and follow signs to Kingseat and Waiau Pa
Waterside picnic area.

37.137159S 174.692793E — Hema Atlas Map Ref 7 G4

212 Sandspit Motor Camp
15 Rangiwhea Rd, Waiuku: signposted N of Waiuku town centre
Ph/Fax (09) 235 9913 sandspitmotor@xtra.co.nz
This has a nice location, next to a waterfront reserve.

37.233981S 174.726931E — Hema Atlas Map Ref 7 J4

213 Awhitu Regional Park (Brook Homestead and Peninsula Campground)
Awhitu Regional Park, Auckland Council Ph (09) 301 0101
regionalparks@aucklandcouncil.govt.nz www.aucklandcouncil.govt.nz
Permits essential all year, max. 7 nights stay.

37.108766S 174.652766E — Hema Atlas Map Ref 7 G3

214 Big Bay Motor Camp
271 Big Bay Rd, Awhitu: follow signs to Manukau Heads from Waiuku then to Big Bay
Ph (09) 235 1132 bigbay@ihug.co.nz www.bigbaymotorcamp.co.nz
Simple and compact site, 100m from a pretty beach. Pets by arrangement.

37.044489S 174.640964E — Hema Atlas Map Ref 7 F3

North Island Camping Sites

Central North Region

215 Orua Bay Beach Motor Camp & Accommodation

294 Orua Bay Rd: on Awhutu Peninsula, 38km N of Waiubu
Ph (09) 235 1129 oruabay@ihug.co.nz www.oruabay.co.nz

A clean and quiet camp in a magic location, I'm amazed that more Aucklanders have not discovered this spot, less than two hours from Auckland (depending on the traffic!).

37.048624S 174.61133E   Hema Atlas Map Ref 7 F3

CENTRAL NORTH REGION

WHITE ISLAND   PHOTO: TOURISM ROTORUA

SH1 — FROM SH2 TO HAMILTON	34
SH3 — HAMILTON TO TE KUITI	35
SH3 — TE KUITI TO NEW PLYMOUTH	35
SH4 — TE KUITI TO OHAKUNE	37
SH1 — WAIOURU TO TAUPO	38
SH2 — SH1 TO TAURANGA	40
SH25 COROMANDEL PENINSULA — SH2 TO WAIHI	42
SH1 — HAMILTON TO TAUPO	46
SH2 — TAURANGA TO OPOTIKI	48
SH30 — WHAKATANE TO ROTORUA	50
SH5 & SH38 — ROTORUA TO WAIROA	52
SH35 — OPOTIKI TO GISBORNE	53
SH2 — OPOTIKI TO WAIROA	55
SH2 — WAIROA TO HASTINGS	56

SH1 — FROM SH2 TO HAMILTON

216 Roadside Rest Area

Les Batton Reserve, Port Waikato Rd, W of Tauranganui: beside the Waikato River
Riverside swimming and boating opportunities.

37.295223S 174.946608E   Hema Atlas Map Ref 9 D3

217 Wayside Road Roadside Rest Area

Off SH1, N of Te Kauwhata turnoff
37.40087S 175.118042E   Hema Atlas Map Ref 9 E4

218 Riverhaven Roadside Rest Area

SH1, N of Huntly
37.541183S 175.158346E   Hema Atlas Map Ref 9 G5

219 Boat Ramp Roadside Rest Area

SH1, N of Huntly
37.549231S 175.15849E   Hema Atlas Map Ref 9 G5

220 Ngaruawahia Roadside Rest Area

SH1, S of Jordan St, Ngaruawahia
37.670317S 175.150515E   Hema Atlas Map Ref 9 J5

221 Riverwalk Way Roadside Rest Area

SH39 by the river, Ngaruawahia
37.678284S 175.153591E   Hema Atlas Map Ref 9 J5

222 Halfway Hill Roadside Rest Area

SH1, S of Horotiu
37.723022S 175.217197E   Hema Atlas Map Ref 9 J5

223 Port Waikato Holiday Park

115B Maunsell Rd, Port Waikato
Ph (09) 232 9857 Fax (09) 232 9802
info@portwaikatoholidaypark.co.nz www.portwaikatoholidaypark.co.nz
Laidback little community with old-style Kiwi batches. Qualmark three star plus.

37.392026S 174.722554E   Hema Atlas Map Ref 9 E1

224 Waingaro Hot Springs Caravan Park & Hot Pools

Alongside Waingaro Rd, at Waingaro
Ph/Fax (07) 825 4761 waingaro.hot.springs@clear.net.nz
www.waingarohotsprings.co.nz
A peaceful rural location - a great place to unwind.

37.691492S 174.999932E   Hema Atlas Map Ref 9 J3

225 Raglan Kopua Holiday Park

Marine Parade, Raglan: well signposted from the town centre, just off the road to the surf beaches
Ph (07) 825 8283 stay@raglanholidaypark.co.nz
www.raglanholidaypark.co.nz
A huge camp beside the estuary for boating and swimming, yet just a short walk across a bridge to the town centre. Qualmark four star.

37.802568S 174.862988E   Hema Atlas Map Ref 11 C3

226 Wainui Beach Reserve

Off Wainui Rd, S of Raglan
Access point to the great Raglan surf beach.

37.818442S 174.831874E   Hema Atlas Map Ref 11 C3

227 Four Brothers Roadside Rest Area

SH23, Four Brothers Scenic Reserve
37.825985S 175.076995E   Hema Atlas Map Ref 11 C5

228 Puti Bluffs Rest Area

SH31, 300m W of Puti Bluffs
38.052633S 174.858274E   Hema Atlas Map Ref 11 F3

229 Lookout Rest Area

SH31, 2km W of Te Rauamoa
38.074274S 175.018433E   Hema Atlas Map Ref 11 F4

Central North Region — North Island Camping Sites

230 Solscape Eco Retreat
611 Wainui Rd. Follow Wainui Rd S from Raglan towards Manu Bay: roadside on the way to Whale Bay
Ph (07) 825 8268 info@solscape.co.nz www.solscape.co.nz
A small peaceful location on a hill overlooking the famous Raglan surf break. Provides 3 powered campervan sites. Internet. Solar power & heating. Natural spring.
37.825465S 174.820757E Hema Atlas Map Ref 11 C2

231 Hamilton City Holiday Park
14 Ruakura Rd, Claudelands: from Hamilton Centre cross the Claudelands Bridge and follow signs to the Waikato University
Ph (07) 855 8255 hchp@xtra.co.nz www.hamiltoncityholidaypark.co.nz
Close to the city centre, in spacious park-like grounds. Qualmark three star plus.
37.780776S 175.299733E Hema Atlas Map Ref 92 E4, 11 C7

SH3 – HAMILTON TO TE KUITI

232 Roadrunner Motel and Holiday Park
141 Bond Rd, Te Awamutu
Ph (07) 871 7420 Fax (07) 871 6664 road.runner@xtra.co.nz
www.roadrunneraccommodation.co.nz
38.005544S 175.328907E Hema Atlas Map Ref 11 E7

233 Roadside Rest Area
Alongside SH3
38.123167S 175.328821E Hema Atlas Map Ref 11 F7

234 Otorohanga Holiday Park
20 Huiputea Drive, Otorohanga: signposted at N end of Otorohanga
Ph (07) 873 7253 Fax (07) 873 7256
billie@kiwiholidaypark.co.nz www.kiwiholidaypark.co.nz
Facilities include a fitness centre. Wireless internet.
38.187018S 175.213893E Hema Atlas Map Ref 11 G6

235 Camp Kiwi
Domain Drive, Otorohanga: follow signs to the Kiwi House
Ph (07) 873 7391
Casual Camping - a caretaker may collect koha or fees if they are in attendance. Compact, neat and tidy.
38.180354S 175.212379E Hema Atlas Map Ref 11 G6

236 Kawhia Beachside S-Cape/Kawhia Harbourview Cottages
225 Pouewe St, Kawhia: signposted alongside the main road at the entrance to Kawhia
Ph (07) 871 0727 kawhiabeachsidescape@xtra.co.nz
Fax (07) 871 0217 www.kawhiabeachsidescape.co.nz
Boating, angling, pets by arrangement.
38.060956S 174.827337E Hema Atlas Map Ref 11 F3

237 Forest View Motor Camp
232 Waiwera St, Kawhia: follow signs to the boat ramp from town centre
Ph/Fax (07) 871 0858
Boating, angling.
38.066149S 174.818663E Hema Atlas Map Ref 11 F2

238 Kawhia Camping Ground
73 Moko St, Kawhia: follow signs to the boat ramp from the town centre
Ph (07) 871 0863 Fax (07) 871 0859
kawhiacampingground@xtra.co.nz www.kawhiacampingground.co.nz
Boating, angling, thermal pools nearby. Kayaks for hire.
38.069681S 174.814784E Hema Atlas Map Ref 11 F2

239 Roadside Rest Area
Alongside SH2 S of Otorohanga
38.233888S 175.189265E Hema Atlas Map Ref 11 H6

240 Waitomo Top 10 Holiday Park
Follow the signs to Waitomo Caves from SH3: campsite is almost opposite Waitomo's Information Centre and Caves Museum, 800m from Waitomo Caves
Ph 0508 498 666, (07) 878 7639
stay@waitomopark.co.nz www.waitomopark.co.nz
Small, compact, neat and tidy as well as very convenient location. Internet. Spa pool. Qualmark four star plus.
38.260224S 175.109829E Hema Atlas Map Ref 11 H5

SH3 — TE KUITI TO NEW PLYMOUTH

241 Roadside Rest Area
Overlooking Te Kuiti from SH3 S of the township
38.348545S 175.166173E Hema Atlas Map Ref 11 J6

242 Kopaki Rest Area
SH4, 400m N of Kopaki Rd
38.503747S 175.204521E Hema Atlas Map Ref 18 B10

243 Hiwi Hills Rest Area
SH4, 100m N of the Ohura River Bridge
38.653218S 175.207908E Hema Atlas Map Ref 18 C10

244 Waimiha/Ongarue Rest Area
SH4, 200m S of Waimiha Rd
38.727972S 175.259848E Hema Atlas Map Ref 18 D10

245 Okahukura Rest Area
SH4, 600m S of Okahukura Rd
38.800215S 175.22087E Hema Atlas Map Ref 18 E10

246 Roadside Rest Area
Alongside SH3 at the N end of Piopio
38.465437S 175.018989E Hema Atlas Map Ref 18 A8

247 Roadside Rest Area
Alongside SH3 at Paemako Scenic Reserve
38.498505S 174.941004E Hema Atlas Map Ref 17 B7

248 Mangaotaki Rest Area
SH3, 300m N of Mangaotaki Bridge
38.517093S 174.910906E Hema Atlas Map Ref 17 B7

249 Awakino Bridges (Ladies Mile) Rest Area
SH3, E of Awakino
38.666442S 174.649354E Hema Atlas Map Ref 17 C5

North Island Camping Sites — Central North Region

250 Seaview Holiday Park
5270 SH3, N of Mokau
Ph/Fax (06) 752 9708 0800 478 786 seaviewhp@xtra.conz
*Compact, neat and tidy site on an interesting stretch of coast.
Pets by arrangement.*
38.67744S 174.618077E   Hema Atlas Map Ref 17 D5

251 Roadside Rest Area
Alongside SH3 and the Mohakatino River
38.699295S 174.621146E   Hema Atlas Map Ref 17 D5

252 Tainui Scenic Reserve
SH3, S of Awakino
38.687313S 174.618761E   Hema Atlas Map Ref 17 D5

253 Whitebait Inn Cabins & Motor Camp
Alongside SH3 in the centre of Mokau
Enquiries to the Whitebait Inn Ph (06) 752 9713
*Compact, and close to the town centre with access to nearby
river and beaches.*
38.698955S 174.62074E   Hema Atlas Map Ref 17 D5

254 Tainui Wetere Domain
SH3, S of Mokau
38.708364S 174.621391E   Hema Atlas Map Ref 17 D5

255 Mohakatino Rest Area
SH3 Mohakatino, S of Mokau
38.729874S 174.615261E   Hema Atlas Map Ref 17 D5

256 Roadside Rest Area
Beachside SH3, S of Mokau
38.75792S 174.605052E   Hema Atlas Map Ref 17 D4

257 Roadside Rest Area
Alongside SH3 at the Rapuni Stream bridge
38.800104S 174.592806E   Hema Atlas Map Ref 17 E4

258 Roadside Rest Area
Alongside SH3 at Tongaporutu
38.814253S 174.593057E   Hema Atlas Map Ref 17 E4

259 Roadside Rest Area
Three Sisters Reserve: a 800m deviation from SH3 at the S end of
Tongaporutu bridge
38.819596S 174.597163E   Hema Atlas Map Ref 17 E4

260 Roadside Rest Area
Alongside SH3 at the summit of Mt Messenger (192m)
38.895707S 174.59886E   Hema Atlas Map Ref 17 F4

261 Roadside Rest Area
Beachside at Wai-iti Beach: a 4km deviation from SH3
38.922053S 174.475481E   Hema Atlas Map Ref 17 F3

262 Wai-iti Beach Retreat
30 Beach Rd, Wai-iti Beach, Urenui
Ph (06) 752 3726 info@wai-itibeach.co.nz www.wai-itibeach.co.nz
Licensed cafe, 6 hole golf, tennis court (bring own equipment).
38.924844S 174.474002E   Hema Atlas Map Ref 17 F3

263 Urenui Beach Camp Ground
148 Beach Rd, Urenui: a 2km deviation signposted from SH3 at Urenui
Ph/Fax (06) 752 3838 urenuibeachcamp@xtra.co.nz
www.urenuibeachcamp.co.nz
*A large camp that's handy to both a nearby beach and estuary and
adjoining a golf course.*
38.990755S 174.392833E   Hema Atlas Map Ref 17 G3

264 Onaero Bay Holiday Park
Beachside, a short diversion from SH3 at Onaero, 10km N of Waitara
Ph (06) 752 3643 Fax (06) 752 3645 onaerobay@xtra.co.nz
Whitebaiting in season. Pets, seasonal, by arrangement.
38.996428S 174.365658E   Hema Atlas Map Ref 17 G2

265 Roadside Rest Area
Waitara Marine Park, Waitara
38.989579S 174.219655E   Hema Atlas Map Ref 17 G1

266 Mangorei Road Information Area
SH3, just S of junction with Mangorei Rd
39.093773S 174.105604E   Hema Atlas Map Ref 23 B5

267 Waiongana Hill Roadside Rest Area
SH3A, S of Waiongana, N of Inglewood
39.116978S 174.215589E   Hema Atlas Map Ref 23 B6

268 Tariki Subway Roadside Rest Area
SH3, S of Norfolk
39.214301S 174.234723E   Hema Atlas Map Ref 23 C6

269 Marine Park Motor Camp
Centennial Ave, Waitara: follow signs from Waitara town centre
to Beach Reserve & Domain
Ph (06) 754 7121
*Huge park-like grounds next to the beach and a favoured rivermouth
fishing spot.*
38.989938S 174.225181E   Hema Atlas Map Ref 17 G1

270 Sentry Hill Motel & Roadhouse
56 Mountain Rd, New Plymouth: N end of SH3A New Plymouth bypass
Ph (06) 752 0696 sentryhill@infogen.net.nz www.sentryhill.co.nz
Motel units, bar, restaurant. Tents are not recommended, but are allowed.
39.025878S 174.195568E   Hema Atlas Map Ref 23 A6

271 Airport Information Roadside Rest Area
SH3, E of New Plymouth
39.029576S 174.167408E   Hema Atlas Map Ref 23 A6

272 Fitzroy Beach Holiday Park
Beach St, New Plymouth: signposted N of SH3,
E of New Plymouth at Fitzroy
Ph/Fax (06) 758 2870 fitzroybeach@xtra.co.nz
*Right on the beach at a favoured surf spot and linked to the city centre
by the fabulous coastal walkway. Two dump stations on-site.*
39.044675S 174.099322E   Hema Atlas Map Ref 107 A5, 23 B5

Central North Region — North Island Camping Sites

273 New Plymouth Top 10 Holiday Park
29 Princes St, Fitzroy: signposted N of SH3 E of New Plymouth
Ph/Fax (06) 758 2566 info@nptop10.co.nz www.nptop10.co.nz
Sheltered, clean and tidy site just a 7 minute walk to the beach. Children's playground. Internet. Pets by arrangement. Qualmark four star. Grass and concrete park sites. Spa and sauna.
39.046509S 174.107631E   Hema Atlas Map Ref 107 A5, 23 B5

SH4 — TE KUITI TO OHAKUNE

274 Piriaka Lookout Rest Area 4.10
SH 4, west of Manunui on Taumarunui road
www.horizons.govt.nz/getting-people-places/planning-and-road-safety/feeling-tired-while-driving-pull-over-and-take-a-break
Picnic table, set beside the highway, overlooking the Whanganui River. Can be noisy with road and rail noise.
38.884108S 175.309272E   Hema Atlas Map Ref 18 F10

275 Taumarunui Holiday Park
SH4, South Taumarunui: 3km S of Taumarunui
Ph (07) 895 9345, 0800 473 281 taumarunuiholidaypark@xtra.co.nz
www.taumarunuiholidaypark.co.nz
Neat and tidy in a nice sheltered setting. Train spotters will enjoy the location. Qualmark three star. Internet access.
38.882537S 175.306806E   Hema Atlas Map Ref 18 F11

276 Roadside Rest Area
Ohinetonga Scenic Reserve, off SH4
38.995353S 175.378494E   Hema Atlas Map Ref 18 G11

277 Owhango Rest Area 4.9
South of Owhango on SH4
www.horizons.govt.nz/getting-people-places/planning-and-road-safety/feeling-tired-while-driving-pull-over-and-take-a-break
Grassed area with tables and shade, but carpark is right at highway edge.
38.99775S 175.377631E   Hema Atlas Map Ref 18 G11

278 Poukaria
Access from the Whanganui River only 35.5km downstream from Taumarunui
DOC Whanganui Area Office Ph (06) 349 2100
WhanganuiArea@doc.govt.nz
Campsite is free between 1 May and September 30; hut and camp ticket required if completing Whanganui Journey between 1 Oct and 30 April.
38.991769S 175.119939E   Hema Atlas Map Ref 18 G9

279 Maharanui
Access from the Whanganui River only 53km downstream from Taumarunui
DOC Whanganui Area Office Ph (06) 349 2100
WhanganuiArea@doc.govt.nz
Campsite is free between 1 May and September 30; hut and camp ticket required if completing Whanganui Journey between 1 Oct and 30 April.
39.071364S 175.046192E   Hema Atlas Map Ref 18 H8

280 Mangapapa
Access from the Whanganui River only 68km downstream from Taumarunui
DOC Whanganui Area Office Ph (06) 349 2100
WhanganuiArea@doc.govt.nz
Campsite is free between 1 May and September 30; hut and camp ticket required if completing Whanganui Journey between 1 Oct and 30 April.
39.128997S 174.998172E   Hema Atlas Map Ref 18 J8

281 Ohauora
Access from the Whanganui River only 83km downstream from Taumarunui
DOC Whanganui Area Office Ph (06) 349 2100
WhanganuiArea@doc.govt.nz
Campsite is free between 1 May and September 30; hut and camp ticket required if completing Whanganui Journey between 1 Oct and 30 April.
39.171197S 174.958856E   Hema Atlas Map Ref 17 J7

282 John Coull
Access from the Whanganui River only 95.5km downstream from Taumarunui
DOC Whanganui Area Office Ph (06) 349 2100
WhanganuiArea@doc.govt.nz
Campsite is free between 1 May and September 30; hut and camp ticket required if completing Whanganui Journey between 1 Oct and 30 April.
39.233194S 174.913172E   Hema Atlas Map Ref 25 A7

283 Mangawaiiti
Access from the Whanganui River only 105km downstream from Taumarunui
DOC Whanganui Area Office Ph (06) 349 2100
WhanganuiArea@doc.govt.nz
Campsite is free between 1 May and September 30; hut and camp ticket required if completing Whanganui Journey between 1 Oct and 30 April.
39.285603S 174.90535E   Hema Atlas Map Ref 25 A7

284 Mangapurua
Access from the Whanganui River only 114km downstream from Taumarunui
DOC Whanganui Area Office Ph (06) 349 2100
WhanganuiArea@doc.govt.nz
Campsite is free between 1 May and September 30; hut and camp ticket required if completing Whanganui Journey between 1 Oct and 30 April.
39.281839S 174.966697E   Hema Atlas Map Ref 25 A7

285 Tieke Kainga
Access from the Whanganui River only 124km downstream from Taumarunui
DOC Whanganui Area Office Ph (06) 349 2100
WhanganuiArea@doc.govt.nz
Campsite is free between 1 May and September 30; hut and camp ticket required if completing Whanganui Journey between 1 Oct and 30 April.
39.337233S 174.993825E   Hema Atlas Map Ref 26 B8

North Island Camping Sites — Central North Region

286 Ngaporo
Access from the Whanganui River only 136km downstream from Taumarunui
DOC Whanganui Area Office Ph (06) 349 2100
WhanganuiArea@doc.govt.nz
Campsite is free between 1 May and September 30; hut and camp ticket required if completing Whanganui Journey between 1 Oct and 30 April.

39.424781S 175.037067E   Hema Atlas Map Ref 26 C8

287 Whakahoro
End of Oio Rd, off SH4 at Owhango
DOC Whanganui Area Office Ph (06) 349 2100
WhanganuiArea@doc.govt.nz
Free for drive-in campers, hut and camp ticket required if completing Whanganui Journey.

39.109133S 175.070752E   Hema Atlas Map Ref 18 H9

288 Mangahuia
Off SH47: 6km from National Park township
DOC Ohakune Visitor Centre Ph (06) 385 8427 ohakunevc@doc.govt.nz
Self registration system. Handy for a great variety of walks and sightseeing.

39.179145S 175.468445E   Hema Atlas Map Ref 18 J12

289 Discovery Lodge
Whakapapa, SHWY 47. Along SH47:
1km SW of junction of SH47 & SH48
Ph (07) 892 2744 info@discovery.net.nz www.discovery.net.nz
Good location, with restaurant, bar, internet.

39.16752S 175.481747E   Hema Atlas Map Ref 18 J12

290 Whakapapa Holiday Park
SH48 adjacent Whakapapa Visitor Centre, Whakapapa Village, Tongariro National Park
DOC Whakapapa Visitor Centre
Ph (07) 892 3729 whakapapavc@doc.govt.nz;
Bookings Ph (07) 892 3897 whakapapaholpark@xtra.co.nz
Compact, sheltered and handy to Whakapapa Village with skiing and walking opportunities as the seasons allow.

39.200408S 175.538294E   Hema Atlas Map Ref 18 J12

291 Makatote Gorge Rest Area 4.8
South of Waikune on SH4
www.horizons.govt.nz/getting-people-places/planning-and-road-safety/feeling-tired-while-driving-pull-over-and-take-a-break
Table, shade, grassed area, on the edge of the highway.
39.219697S 175.400625E   Hema Atlas Map Ref 26 A11

292 Last Spike Obelisk Rest Area 4.7
Adjacent SH4, S of National Park
Set above the road, right beside the railway. There is a monument to NZ's main trunk railway as a feat of engineering. Picnic table.
39.275701S 175.389214E   Hema Atlas Map Ref 26 A11

293 Horopito Rest Area 4.6
North of Horopito on SH4
www.horizons.govt.nz/getting-people-places/planning-and-road-safety/feeling-tired-while-driving-pull-over-and-take-a-break
Picnic table, set behind a small island of trees. Gravel surface.
39.312286S 175.388389E   Hema Atlas Map Ref 26 B11

294 Mangaturuturu Roadside Rest Area
SH4, N of Horopito
39.311858S 175.38871E   Hema Atlas Map Ref 26 B11

295 Roadside Rest Area
SH49, just N of Okahune
39.414346S 175.397145E   Hema Atlas Map Ref 26 C11

296 Ohakune Top 10 Holiday Park
5 Moore St, Ohakune: signposted S of SH49, W side of village
Ph (06) 385 8561 info@ohakune.net.nz www.ohakune.net.nz
Neat and tidy site right next to a bush reserve. Qualmark four star plus. Herb gardens and bike hire. Wireless internet. Spa pool.

39.41764S 175.39513E   Hema Atlas Map Ref 26 C11

297 Mangawhero
Ohakune Mountain Rd: 2km from Ohakune
DOC Ohakune Visitor Centre Ph (06) 385 8427 ohakunevc@doc.govt.nz
Self registration system. Handy to a wide range of mountain activities.

39.391402S 175.431492E   Hema Atlas Map Ref 26 C11

SH1 — WAIOURU TO TAUPO

298 Roadside Rest Area
Adjacent SH49 W of Waiouru, at the Tangiwai Disaster Memorial

39.465932S 175.576213E   Hema Atlas Map Ref 26 C13

299 Roadside Rest Area
Alongside SH1 (Desert Rd): summit is 1077m above sea level
39.309492S 175.73703E   Hema Atlas Map Ref 26 B14

300 Moawhango Lookout
SH1, N of Waiouru
39.386292S 175.708703E   Hema Atlas Map Ref 27 C2

301 Roadside Rest Area
W of SH1 (Desert Rd): beside Oturere Stream
39.182668S 175.757971E   Hema Atlas Map Ref 19 J2

302 Kaimanawa Road
15km south of Turangi, turn off SH1 along Kaimanawa Rd
DOC Tongariro National Park Visitor Centre Ph (07) 892 3729
tongarirovc@doc.govt.nz
Drinking water from a stream.

39.137118S 175.830515E   Hema Atlas Map Ref 19 J3

303 Urchin
15km south of Turangi, turn off SH1 along Kaimanawa Rd, 3km south of Kaimanawa Road camp.
DOC Tongariro National Park Visitor Centre Ph (07) 892 3729
tongarirovc@doc.govt.nz

39.153817S 175.823057E   Hema Atlas Map Ref 19 J3

Central North Region
North Island Camping Sites

304 Tongariro Family Holiday Park
On SH47: Near junction of SH47 and SH46, S of Turangi
Ph (07) 386 8062 Fax (07) 386 7659 www.thp.co.nz info@thp.co.nz
Adequate site with good cabins for skiing and camping bases. Alpine crossing transport. Spa pool.
39.046038S 175.603981E   Hema Atlas Map Ref 19 H1

305 Pokaka Mill
Off SH47, at the end of Pukehinau Rd.
DOC Tongariro National Park Visitor Centre Ph (07) 892 3729
tongarirovc@doc.govt.nz
Rough gravel road, 4WD recommended.
39.043529S 175.510967E   Hema Atlas Map Ref 18 H12

306 Lake View Rest Area
Adjacent SH47
38.990974S 175.763245E   Hema Atlas Map Ref 19 G2

307 Oasis Motel & Caravan Park
426 State Hwy 41, Toraanu. SH41 at Tokaanu
Ph (07) 386 8569 oasismotelstokaanu@xtra.co.nz
www.oasismotel.co.nz
Wireless internet.
38.971489S 175.770459E   Hema Atlas Map Ref 19 G2

308 Roadside Rest Area
100m off SH41, W of Tokaanu
38.950745S 175.73796E   Hema Atlas Map Ref 19 G2

309 Club Habitat
25 Ohuanga Rd, Turangi
Ph (07) 386 7492 info@clubhabitat.co.nz
Backpacker thru to motel rooms.
38.990599S 175.807234E   Hema Atlas Map Ref 19 G3

310 Parklands Motor Lodge
Cnr SH1 & Arahori St, Turangi: opposite the Shell petrol station
Ph (07) 386 7515, 0800 456 284 info@parklandsmotorlodge.co.nz
www.parklandsmotorlodge.co.nz
A handy trout fishing base. Restaurant on site. Wireless internet. Sauna, spa, tennis court.
38.991394S 175.81101E   Hema Atlas Map Ref 19 G3

311 Turangi Holiday Park
13 Te Reiti Tamara Grove, Turangi
Ph/Fax (07) 386 8754 turangihp@xtra.co.nz
A former single man's work camp: it's my choice of a budget base in Turangi. Suitable for school camps & groups. Internet. 96 cabins. Pets by arrangement.
38.992726S 175.802889E   Hema Atlas Map Ref 19 G3

312 Rest Area
Adjoining SH1 at Turangi: N end of township, by the river
38.986997S 175.817374E   Hema Atlas Map Ref 19 G3

313 Motuoapa Motor Camp
13 Parekarangaranga St, Motuoapa: signposted from SH1
Ph/Fax (07) 386 7162 motuoapamotorcamp@xtra.co.nz
Lakeside, but it can get crowded and there is not a lot of shade. Basic store, more a cafe.
38.93285S 175.87105E   Hema Atlas Map Ref 19 G3

314 Parikarangaranga Scenic Reserve
SH1, S of Motuoapa
38.934575S 175.8715E   Hema Atlas Map Ref 19 G3

315 Roadside Rest Area
Lakeside adjacent to SH1 and Lake Taupo
38.894959S 175.947613E   Hema Atlas Map Ref 19 F4

316 Mission Bay Reserve
SH1, S of Motutere
38.891239S 175.95013E   Hema Atlas Map Ref 19 F4

317 Mission Bay Rest Area
SH1, E of Tauranga Taupo
38.905774S 175.927256E   Hema Atlas Map Ref 19 F4

318 Motutere Bay Holiday Park
Lakeside at Motutere: adjacent to SH1 and Lake Taupo
Ph/Fax (07) 386 8963
Hard to get a better lakeside spot: plenty of shade, good swimming, boating and fishing.
38.887627S 175.957823E   Hema Atlas Map Ref 19 F4

319 Waipehu Reserve & Picnic Area
Lakeside adjacent to SH1 and Lake Taupo
38.8868S 175.963944E   Hema Atlas Map Ref 19 F4

320 Halletts Bay Picnic Area
Lakeside adjacent to SH1 and Lake Taupo
38.866255S 176.007869E   Hema Atlas Map Ref 19 F5

321 Hinemaiaia Scenic Reserve Access
SH1, N of Hatepe
38.854704S 176.020151E   Hema Atlas Map Ref 19 F5

322 Hinemaiaia River Access
SH1, N of Hatepe
38.853882S 176.021802E   Hema Atlas Map Ref 19 F5

323 Windsor Lodge Motel & Caravan Park
147 SH1 Waitahanui, Taupo 3378. Lakeside at Waitahanui: adjacent to SH1 and Lake Taupo
Ph (07) 378 6271 windsor.lodge@xtra.co.nz Fax (07) 378 6246
www.windsorlodge.co.nz
A favoured trout fishing spot. Pets by arrangement.
38.790874S 176.076779E   Hema Atlas Map Ref 19 E5

324 Lakeside Rest Area
Lakeside at Waitahanui: adjacent to SH1 and Lake Taupo
38.773287S 176.076375E   Hema Atlas Map Ref 19 E5

North Island Camping Sites

Central North Region

325 Roadside Rest Area
SH1, N of Waitahanui
38.775778S 176.07656E
Hema Atlas Map Ref 19 E5

326 Roadside Rest Area
SH1, N of Waitahanui
38.777315S 176.07679E
Hema Atlas Map Ref 19 E5

327 Opepe Historic Graves Carpark
SH5, E of Taupo
38.766988S 176.217733E
Hema Atlas Map Ref 19 E6

328 5 Mile Bay Rest Area
Lakeside adjacent to SH1 and Lake Taupo
38.738308S 176.070938E
Hema Atlas Map Ref 98 D4, 19 E5

329 Roadside Rest Area
SH1, S of Rainbow Point
38.721566S 176.079391E
Hema Atlas Map Ref 98 C4, 19 D5

330 Taupo De Bretts Spa Resort
259 Napier Taupo Hwy (SH5): from SH1 follow Lake Terrace for 2.5km then turn onto SH5 for 1km
Ph (07) 378 8559 www.taupodebretts.com info@taupodebretts.com
Well-established grounds with a long and proud tradition as a spa resort. Qualmark four star plus. Internet.
38.703928S 176.099562E
Hema Atlas Map Ref 98 B5, 19 D5

331 Taupo All Seasons Holiday Park
16 Rangatira St, Taupo: signposted from Spa Rd
Ph (07) 378 4272 reservations@taupoallseasons.co.nz
Fax (07) 378 1272 www.taupoallseasons.co.nz
Qualmark four star. Wireless internet. Family bathrooms.
38.683463S 176.088745E
Hema Atlas Map Ref 98 B4, 19 D5

332 Great Lake Holiday Park
406 Acacia Bay Rd, Taupo: signposted from SH5 N of Taupo
Ph (07) 378 5159 gtlake@xtra.co.nz www.greatlake.co.nz
Spa pool, playground, internet.
38.691351S 176.046115E
Hema Atlas Map Ref 98 B3, 19 D5

333 Lake Taupo Top 10 Holiday Resort
28 Centennial Drive, Taupo: signposted off Spa Rd
Ph (07) 378 6860 0800 332 121 office@taupotop10.co.nz
www.taupotop10.co.nz
New facilities and rated Qualmark five star. It has all the trimmings, and the Taupo Aquatic Centre just a short walk away. Wireless internet. Underfloor heating in communal areas. Adventure playground.
38.675091S 176.098629E
Hema Atlas Map Ref 98 A5, 19 D5

SH2 — SH1 TO TAURANGA

334 Roadside Rest Area
N side of SH2 E of Maramarua
37.276484S 175.288204E
Hema Atlas Map Ref 9 D6

335 Roadside Rest Area
SH2, E of Mangatarata
37.290341S 175.37814E
Hema Atlas Map Ref 9 D7

336 Roadside Rest Area
SH2, E of Ngatea
37.272332S 175.521234E
Hema Atlas Map Ref 10 D8

337 Roadside Rest Area
SH27, N of Kaihere
37.359518S 175.418239E
Hema Atlas Map Ref 9 E7

338 Roadside Rest Area
Along SH26 S of Paeroa
37.50764S 175.69695E
Hema Atlas Map Ref 10 G9

339 Roadside Rest Area
Normanby Rd (SH2), S of Te Aroha Rd, Paeroa
37.383304S 175.674965E
Hema Atlas Map Ref 10 E9

340 Roadside Rest Area
Normanby Rd (SH2), S of Russell St, Paeroa
37.386708S 175.679666E
Hema Atlas Map Ref 10 E9

341 Passing Bay
SH2, E of Karangahake
37.419542S 175.739817E
Hema Atlas Map Ref 10 F10

342 Roadside Rest Area
SH2, E of Karangahake
37.41673S 175.755593E
Hema Atlas Map Ref 10 F10

343 Roadside Rest Area
Kenrick St (SH26), W edge of Te Aroha
37.547511S 175.705632E
Hema Atlas Map Ref 10 G9

344 Te Aroha Holiday Park
217 Stanley Rd, Te Aroha: signposted 3km SW of Te Aroha on SH 26
Ph (07) 884 9567 marta@xtra.co.nz
www.tearohaholidaypark.co.nz
Sheltered park-like grounds make this site a good base from which to explore the hot pools. Mineral baths on-site, free WIFI.
37.566215S 175.719423E
Hema Atlas Map Ref 10 G10

345 Roadside Rest Area
SH26, NE of Morrinsville
37.591413S 175.646485E
Hema Atlas Map Ref 10 H9

346 Roadside Rest Area
SH26, SW of Tatauanui
37.643044S 175.560959E
Hema Atlas Map Ref 10 H8

347 Roadside Rest Area
SH26, SW of Morrinsville
37.683488S 175.472716E
Hema Atlas Map Ref 10 J7

348 Truck stop
SH1B, E of Gordonton
37.671628S 175.308664E
Hema Atlas Map Ref 9 J6

Central North Region — North Island Camping Sites

349 Roadside Rest Area
SH27: NW of Matamata or W of Morrinsville
37.652111S 175.654192E   Hema Atlas Map Ref 10 H9

350 Dickey Flat
At the end of Dickey Flat Rd, Kaimai-Mamaku Conservation Park:
10km SW of Waihi, off SH2
DOC Tauranga Area Office (07) 578 7677
taurangainfo@doc.govt.nz
Drinking water is from a stream.
37.43884S 175.747757E   Hema Atlas Map Ref 10 F10

351 Waihi Motor Camp
6 Waitete Rd, Waihi: signposted on SH2 W of the town
Ph (07) 863 7654 gloria@waihimotorcamp.co.nz
www.waihimotorcamp.co.nz
A sheltered little valley, not too far from the town, or gold mine. Internet access.
37.388659S 175.825557E   Hema Atlas Map Ref 10 F10

352 Roadside Rest Area
On the outskirts of Waihi
37.392464S 175.833396E   Hema Atlas Map Ref 10 F11

353 Roadside Rest Area
SH25, S of Whiritoa
37.304273S 175.891454E   Hema Atlas Map Ref 10 E11

354 Beach Haven Holiday Camp
21 Leo St, Waihi Beach: follow signs to Waihi Beach from SH2
Ph/Fax (07) 863 5505 beachhavenwaihi@xtra.co.nz
37.40307S 175.938919E   Hema Atlas Map Ref 10 F12

355 Waihi Beach Top 10 Holiday Park
15 Beach Rd, Waihi Beach: follow signs to Waihi Beach from SH2
Ph (07) 863 5504 Fax (07) 863 5515 info@waihibeach.com
www.waihibeach.com
A great location: nestled into the bush, yet right in the heart of the 'old town' and right on the beach. Internet, heated pool, gym, sauna, indoor playground. Qualmark five star. Two dump stations.
37.398087S 175.937041E   Hema Atlas Map Ref 10 F12

356 Sea Air Motel & Holiday Park
Emerton Rd, off Waihi Beach Rd:
follow signs to Waihi Beach from SH2
Ph (07) 863 5655 www.seaair.co.nz
More a motel than a campground.
37.431456S 175.955764E   Hema Atlas Map Ref 10 F12

357 Athenree Hot Springs & Holiday Park
1 Athenree Rd, Athenree: 4km NE of SH2
Ph/Fax (07) 863 5600 hotsprings@xtra.co.nz
www.athenreehotsprings.co.nz
Across the road from a sheltered estuary. Fishing and boating options abound from this award-winning and friendly little camp. Wireless internet. Free use of mineral hot pools for guests. Qualmark 4 star plus.
37.448429S 175.966715E   Hema Atlas Map Ref 10 F12

358 Bowentown Beach Holiday Park
510 Seaforth Rd, Bowentown:
Southern end of Waihi Beach and NE of SH2
Ph/Fax (07) 863 5381 info@bowentown.co.nz www.bowentown.co.nz
Internet, WIFI. Qualmark four star plus. Bike and kayak hire.
37.463642S 175.986736E   Hema Atlas Map Ref 10 F12

359 Beachfront Reserve Picnic Area
Bowentown: S of Waihi Beach and NE of SH2
Well worth a picnic here if you decide not to stay at the nearby Bowentown Holiday Park.
37.465641S 175.98544E   Hema Atlas Map Ref 10 F12

360 Athenree Lavender Holiday Park
1254 SH2: about 13km S of Waihi in the Athenree Forest Gorge
Ph/Fax (07) 549 4812
Sheltered spot handy to stream with nice swimming holes.
37.457364S 175.924636E   Hema Atlas Map Ref 10 F11

361 Roadside Rest Area
Adjacent SH2: E of turnoff to Athenree
37.461018S 175.933092E   Hema Atlas Map Ref 10 F12

362 Roadside Rest Area
SH2, S of Waihi
37.455909S 175.896957E   Hema Atlas Map Ref 10 F11

363 Roadside Rest Area
Adjacent SH2: E of Katikati
37.563416S 175.913381E   Hema Atlas Map Ref 10 G11

364 Katikati Naturist Park
149 Wharawhara Rd, Katikati: not signposted from SH2
Ph 0800 456 7567 www.katikati-naturist-park.co.nz
'Clothes free' site. Internet. Sauna, mini golf, petanque.
37.573267S 175.892353E   Hema Atlas Map Ref 10 G11

365 Sapphire Springs Motor Camp
274 Hot Springs Rd, Katikati: signposted from SH2 at Katikati
Ph (07) 549 0768 Fax (07) 549 1697 sapphire.springs@xtra.co.nz
www.sapphiresprings.net.nz
A peaceful, rural and bush-clad alternative to the coastal crowds.
37.588408S 175.881429E   Hema Atlas Map Ref 10 H11

366 Omokoroa Thermal Holiday Park
165 Omokoroa Beach Rd, Omokoroa Beach: a 4km deviation NE of SH2
Ph (07) 548 0857 stay@omokoroa.co.nz www.omokoroa.co.nz
Neat and tidy site that is handy to the estuary. Internet access.
37.641713S 176.039175E   Hema Atlas Map Ref 10 H12

367 Accommodation at Te Puna
Cnr Minden Rd and Auckland Waihi Rd, Te Puna
Ph (07) 552 5621 info@accommodationtepuna.co.nz
www.accommodationtepuna.co.nz
Wireless internet.
37.696307S 176.072372E   Hema Atlas Map Ref 10 J13

North Island Camping Sites — Central North Region

368 — Roadside Rest Area
Adjacent SH2 on the S bank of the Wairoa River: visible from the bridge
Swimming, picnicking, canoeing.
37.699562S 176.094197E — Hema Atlas Map Ref 94 C1, 10 J13

369 — Roadside Rest Area
SH2, N of Hairini, Tauranga South
37.714208S 176.165204E — Hema Atlas Map Ref 94 C2, 13 B3

370 — Tauranga Tourist Park
9 Mayfair St, Tauranga:
signposted W from SH2 N of the Waimapu Estuary
Ph/Fax (07) 578 3323 info@taurangatouristpark.co.nz
www.taurangatouristpark.co.nz
Clean and tidy site that's very handy to Tauranga's city centre. Wireless internet, book exchange.
37.711392S 176.16449E — Hema Atlas Map Ref 94 C2, 10 J13

371 — Silver Birch Family Holiday Park
101 Turret Rd, Tauranga:
adjacent SH2 on the N shore of Waimapu Estuary
Ph/Fax (07) 578 4603 www.silverbirch.co.nz
Neat site on the water's edge. Internet.
37.715415S 176.164571E — Hema Atlas Map Ref 94 C2, 10 J13

372 — Fernland Spa Thermal Mineral Springs
250 Cambridge Rd, Bethlehem, Tauranga
Ph/Fax (07) 578 3081 www.fernlandspa.co.nz
Features a bushwalk to downtown Tauranga.
37.706308S 176.124104E — Hema Atlas Map Ref 94 C1, 10 J13

373 — Sanctuary Point
140 SH29, Tauranga: SW of intersection with SH2
Ph (07) 544 0700 info@sanctuarypoint.co.nz
www.sanctuarypoint.co.nz
More modern facilities than the other Tauranga options, and more spacious, but you pay extra for the thermal pools.
37.730859S 176.156499E — Hema Atlas Map Ref 94 D2, 10 J13

374 — Welcome Bay Hot Pools & Campground
R409 Welcome Bay Rd, RD 5, Tauranga
Ph/Fax (07) 544 2327 wbhp@xtra.co.nz
Dogs only by prior arrangement.
37.724431S 176.209677E — Hema Atlas Map Ref 94 D3, 13 B4

SH25 COROMANDEL PENINSULA — SH2 TO WAIHI

375 — Roadside Rest Area
Kauaeranga Valley, SE of Thames
37.162964S 175.612381E — Hema Atlas Map Ref 8 H12

376 — Walking Track Car Park
SH25A, E of Kopu
37.143414S 175.659229E — Hema Atlas Map Ref 10 C9

377 — Kaitarakiri Walking Track
SH25A, E of Kopu
37.148925S 175.673125E — Hema Atlas Map Ref 10 C9

378 — Roadside Rest Area
SH25A, E of Kopu
37.148893S 175.68016E — Hema Atlas Map Ref 10 C9

379 — Trestle View
Follow the Kauaeranga Valley Rd from Thames for 14km to the new visitor centre, camp is 9km north beside river.
DOC Kauaeranga Visitor Centre Ph (07) 867 9080
kauaerangavc@doc.govt.nz
Drinking water from a stream.
37.066696S 175.667378E — Hema Atlas Map Ref 8 G12

380 — Totara Flat
Approx. 15km along Kauaeranga Valley Rd, opposite the Education camp.
DOC Kauaeranga Visitor Centre Ph (07) 867 9080
kauaerangavc@doc.govt.nz
Drinking water from a stream.
37.07103S 175.662197E — Hema Atlas Map Ref 8 G12

381 — Wainora
Approx. 15km along Kauaeranga Valley Rd, next to the Education camp.
DOC Kauaeranga Visitor Centre Ph (07) 867 9080
kauaerangavc@doc.govt.nz
Drinking water from a stream; open Oct (Labour w'end) to end April.
37.072151S 175.65685E — Hema Atlas Map Ref 8 G12

382 — Catleys
Follow the Kauaeranga Valley Rd from Thames for 8km to the new visitor centre, camp is 6km north beside river.
DOC Kauaeranga Visitor Centre Ph (07) 867 9080
kauaerangavc@doc.govt.nz
Drinking water from a stream; open Oct (Labour w'end) to end April.
37.076441S 175.656155E — Hema Atlas Map Ref 8 G12

383 — Booms Flat
Follow the Kauaeranga Valley Rd from Thames for 8km to the new visitor centre, camp is 6km north beside river.
DOC Kauaeranga Visitor Centre Ph (07) 867 9080
kauaerangavc@doc.govt.nz
Dogs permitted on a leash; open Oct (Labour w'end) to end April.
37.079172S 175.650508E — Hema Atlas Map Ref 8 G12

384 — Whangaiterenga
Follow the Kauaeranga Valley Rd from Thames for 14km to the new visitor centre, camp is 5km north beside river.
DOC Kauaeranga Visitor Centre Ph (07) 867 9080
kauaerangavc@doc.govt.nz
Drinking water from a stream; open Oct (Labour w'end) to end April.
37.083943S 175.645149E — Hema Atlas Map Ref 8 G12

Central North Region — North Island Camping Sites

385 Hotoritori
Follow the Kauaeranga Valley Rd from Thames for 8km to the new visitor centre, camp is 3km north beside river.
DOC Kauaeranga Visitor Centre Ph (07) 867 9080
kauaerangavc@doc.govt.nz
Dogs permitted on a leash; Drinking water from a stream.
37.100162S 175.634172E   Hema Atlas Map Ref 8 G12

386 Shag Stream
Follow the Kauaeranga Valley Rd from Thames for 8km to the new visitor centre, camp is opposite, beside river.
DOC Kauaeranga Visitor Centre Ph (07) 867 9080
kauaerangavc@doc.govt.nz
Open Oct-April, check dates. Drinking water from a stream.
37.123295S 175.625887E   Hema Atlas Map Ref 8 H12

387 Kauaeranga Christian Camp
304 Kauaeranga Valley Road. Kauaeranga SE of Thames: take the turnoff to Parawai S of Thames
Ph (07) 868 8348 Fax (07) 868 5047 www.kvcc.org.nz
For group bookings. Four caravan sites available. Quiet rural location that's streamside for swimming.
37.154949S 175.59072E   Hema Atlas Map Ref 8 H11

388 Kuranui Bay Reserve
SH25, N of Thames North
37.124139S 175.531794E   Hema Atlas Map Ref 8 G11

389 Roadside Rest Area
SH25, N of Thames
Many similar picnic and rest areas along this coast north to Wilson Bay.
37.116067S 175.524501E   Hema Atlas Map Ref 8 G11

390 Dickson Holiday Park
Victoria St, Tararu: turnoff S of Tararu
Ph (07) 868 7308   thames@vacationz.co.nz   www.dicksonpark.co.nz
Sheltered valley location set in a reserve established in 1869. This camp includes a butterfly house and orchid garden. Internet. Free bikes.
37.111318S 175.523582E   Hema Atlas Map Ref 8 G11

391 Te Puru Holiday Park
473 Thames Coast Rd, Te Puru
Ph (07) 868 2879 Fax (07) 868 2875 tepuruholidaypark@xtra.co.nz
www.tepuruholidaypark.co.nz
Very small and low key park with only 5 casual cabins and 5 casual tent/motorhome sites. There is a boat ramp 500m away.
37.045425S 175.52134E   Hema Atlas Map Ref 8 G11

392 Waiomu Domain Rest Area
Seaside along SH25 at Waiomu
37.028405S 175.517419E   Hema Atlas Map Ref 8 G11

393 Tapu Creek Campervan Park
285 Tapu-Coroglen Rd: turnoff from SH25 at Tapu, 2.5km down Tapu-Coroglen Rd
Ph (07) 868 4560   mail@tapucreek.co.nz   www.tapucreek.co.nz
Swimming stream nearby.
36.980492S 175.532214E   Hema Atlas Map Ref 8 F11

394 Tapu Camp
723 Thames Coast Rd: SH25 at Tapu
Ph (07) 868 4837   tapumotorcamp@xtra.co.nz
Very popular beachfront location. It can get a tad crowded, but to many that is the charm.
36.983502S 175.501187E   Hema Atlas Map Ref 8 F11

395 Roadside Rest Area
SH25 at Waikawau: S of the stream
Waterside picnic area.
36.939921S 175.471334E   Hema Atlas Map Ref 8 E11

396 Te Mata Reserve
Thames Coast Rd (SH25) S of Te Mata
36.970697S 175.496391E   Hema Atlas Map Ref 8 F11

397 Roadside Rest Area
Thames Coast Rd (SH25) N of Te Mata
36.945916S 175.475466E   Hema Atlas Map Ref 8 F11

398 Tapu Reserve Entrance
Thames Coast Rd (SH25) N of Tapu
36.981685S 175.500263E   Hema Atlas Map Ref 8 F11

399 Tapu Reserve
Thames Coast Rd (SH25) S of Tapu
36.987693S 175.501821E   Hema Atlas Map Ref 8 F11

400 Roadside Rest Area
SH25 at Wilson's Bay
Waterside picnic area.
36.885393S 175.426341E   Hema Atlas Map Ref 8 E10

401 Tidewater Tourist Park
270 Tiki Rd, Coromandel: just S of Coromandel township
Ph (07) 866 8888   tidewatercoromandel@gmail.com
www.tidewater.co.nz
Although this is more a motel than a campground there's a small grassed area available if needed. Sauna.
36.762291S 175.498939E   Hema Atlas Map Ref 8 D11

402 Tui Lodge
60b Whangapoua Rd, Coromandel: about 800m E of Coromandel township
Ph (07) 866 8237   tuilodge@paradise.net.nz
More suited to camping than motorhomes, but it's a lovely spot favoured by backpackers, cyclists and motorcyclists. Internet access.
36.761252S 175.506994E   Hema Atlas Map Ref 8 C11

44 North Island Camping Sites — Central North Region

403 Coromandel Motels & Holiday Park
636 Rings Rd, Coromandel: main road, N of Coromandel
Ph (07) 866 8830 enquiries@coromandelholidaypark.co.nz
www.coromandelholidaypark.co.nz

Neat and tidy site, and the closest camp to Coromandel township. Pets allowed by arrangement. Internet - WIFI, backpacker dorms. Mountain bike hire.

36.756164S 175.501201E Hema Atlas Map Ref 8 C11

404 Long Bay Motor Camp
3200 Long Bay Rd, Long Bay: signposted from the centre of Coromandel
Ph (07) 866 8720 lbmccoromandel@xtra.co.nz

A magic location, ideal for anglers and swimmers. Boat and kayak hire.

36.745702S 175.477127E Hema Atlas Map Ref 8 C11

405 Shelly Beach Top 10 Holiday Park
243 Colville Rd: N of Coromandel township
Ph (07) 866 8988 Ph/Fax 0800 424 655 shelly@world-net.co.nz
www.shellybeachcoromandel.co.nz

Well-managed camp in a nice waterfront location. Internet. Qualmark four star plus.

36.735038S 175.483027E Hema Atlas Map Ref 8 C11

406 Oamaru Bay Motor Camp
440 Colville Rd: N of Coromandel township
Ph/Fax (07) 866 8735 oamarubayholidaypark@xtra.co.nz

A beautiful spot, just across the road from the beach. Small dogs only.

36.731857S 175.469731E Hema Atlas Map Ref 8 C11

407 Papa Aroha Holiday park
Beachside on Colville Rd, Papa Aroha
Ph/Fax (07) 866 8818 fish@papaaroha.co.nz www.papaaroha.co.nz

Another beautiful beachside spot, but it can get a bit crowded. Kayak hire, water taxi.

36.701011S 175.431906E Hema Atlas Map Ref 8 C10

408 Anglers Lodge Motels & Holiday Park
1446 Colville Rd, Amodeo Bay: 17km N of Coromandel town.
Ph (07) 866 8584 Fax (07) 866 7352 info@anglers.co.nz www.anglers.co.nz

Very good facilities, just opposite a rocky beach and handy to good fishing. Qualmark equivalent of at least four stars, and such quality is relatively rare on this coast. Spa pools, sea views.

36.672601S 175.442264E Hema Atlas Map Ref 8 B10

409 Colville Farm Holidays
2140 Colville Rd, Just S of Colville township
Ph/Fax (07) 866 6820 whitestar@colville.org.nz www.colvillefarmholidays.co.nz

Simple camping in a rural location, and horse treks are available. Backpacker accommodation available.

36.648597S 175.482122E Hema Atlas Map Ref 8 B11

410 Colville Bay Motel & Motor Camp
Wharf Rd, Colville
Ph/Fax (07) 866 6814 colvillemotel@xtra.co.nz
www.colvillebaymotel.co.nz

Spa pool.

36.62925S 175.467288E Hema Atlas Map Ref 8 B11

411 Colville Bay Roadside Rest Area
N of Colville

Waterside picnic area.

36.624567S 175.472132E Hema Atlas Map Ref 8 B11

412 Otautu Bay Motor Camps
257 Port Jackson Rd, Colville. Bayside at Otautu
Ph (07) 866 6801

Beautiful beachside location, with several spots to choose from.

36.611782S 175.446501E Hema Atlas Map Ref 8 B10

413 Fantail Bay
Off Port Jackson Rd en route to Port Jackson: 44km N of Coromandel
DOC Kauaeranga Visitor Centre Ph (07) 867 9080
kauaerangavc@doc.govt.nz

Self registration system; cold showers only; fishing, diving, swimming. Sheltered pohutakawa-clad valley leading to a sheltered stony beach.

36.525036S 175.328185E Hema Atlas Map Ref 8 A9

414 Port Jackson
Beachside at Port Jackson: 58km N of Coromandel
DOC Kauaeranga Visitor Centre Ph (07) 867 9080
kauaerangavc@doc.govt.nz

Self registration system; cold showers only. More open camping than Fantail Bay, but located right on the beachfront. A tranquil spot.

36.481769S 175.345509E Hema Atlas Map Ref 8 A9

415 Fletcher Bay
Off Fletcher Bay Rd: 53km N of Coromandel
DOC Kauaeranga Visitor Centre Ph (07) 867 9080
kauaerangavc@doc.govt.nz

Cold showers only.

36.47653S 175.391102E Hema Atlas Map Ref 8 A10

416 Stony Bay
Stony Bay Rd, off Port Charles Rd: 45km N of Coromandel
DOC Kauaeranga Visitor Centre Ph (07) 867 9080
kauaerangavc@doc.govt.nz

Cold showers only.

36.512256S 175.422662E Hema Atlas Map Ref 8 A10

417 Waikawau Bay
Off Waikawau Beach Rd: 36km N of Coromandel
DOC Kauaeranga Visitor Centre Ph (07) 867 9080
kauaerangavc@doc.govt.nz

Bookings required for December & January: Ph (07) 866 1106; Cold showers only.

36.605868S 175.537005E Hema Atlas Map Ref 8 B11

Central North Region

North Island Camping Sites

418 Kaipawa Trig Lookout
SH25, E of Coromandel
36.748722S 175.537529E
Hema Atlas Map Ref 8 C11

419 Kuaotunu Motor Camp
33 Bluff Rd, Kuaotunu West: signposted from SH25, W end of Kuaotunu Bay
Ph (07) 866 5628 kuaotunucamp@xtra.co.nz
www.kuaotunumotorcamp.co.nz
A nice spot opposite the very pretty beach, and backing onto a small stream. Boat wash & storage. Kayaks for hire.
36.728224S 175.704411E
Hema Atlas Map Ref 8 C13

420 Roadside Rest Area
Alongside Kuaotunu Bay
36.726239S 175.710997E
Hema Atlas Map Ref 8 C13

421 Roadside Rest Area
Alongside Kuaotunu Bay
Waterside picnic area.
36.724843S 175.714575E
Hema Atlas Map Ref 8 C13

422 Roadside Rest Area
Alongside Kuaotunu Bay
36.724364S 175.719199E
Hema Atlas Map Ref 8 C13

423 Roadside Rest Area
Alongside Kuaotunu Bay
36.722719S 175.727104E
Hema Atlas Map Ref 8 C13

424 Roadside Rest Area
Blackjack Rd, just N of Kuaotunu
Waterside picnic area.
36.721461S 175.729879E
Hema Atlas Map Ref 8 C13

425 Otama Beach Reserve Picnic Area
Signposted from Kuaotunu: 10km via gravel road
Overnight camping not allowed.
36.706618S 175.765169E
Hema Atlas Map Ref 8 C13

426 Otama Beach Camp
400 Blackjack Rd: signposted from Kuaotunu: 10km via gravel road
Ph (07) 866 2872 dean.glen@gmail.com www.otamabeachcamp.co.nz
Opposite a beautiful beach this farmer's property offers simple and sheltered camping.
36.709848S 175.751734E
Hema Atlas Map Ref 8 C13

427 Roadside Rest Area
Alongside SH25: S of Kuaotunu
36.751846S 175.728288E
Hema Atlas Map Ref 8 C13

428 Roadside Rest Area
Alongside SH25: N of Whitianga
36.797181S 175.723473E
Hema Atlas Map Ref 8 D13

429 Whitianga Campground & Beach Motel & Cabins
6 Bongard Rd, Whitianga: signposted from SH25 N end of Mercury Bay, about 1.2km from Whitianga
Ph (07) 866 5834 beachmotel@xtra.co.nz
www.whitiangacampground.co.nz
A sheltered valley a mere stone's throw from the beach.
36.812362S 175.698168E
Hema Atlas Map Ref 8 D13

430 Mercury Bay Motor Camp & Holiday Park
121 Albert St, Whitianga: signposted from S end of Whitianga town centre
Ph/Fax (07) 866 5579 mercurybayholidaypark@xtra.co.nz
www.mercurybayholidaypark.co.nz
Handy to boat launching and the town centre. Internet access.
36.837385S 175.703292E
Hema Atlas Map Ref 8 D13

431 Harbourside Holiday Park
135 Albert St, Whitianga: signposted from S end of Whitianga town centre
Ph/Fax (07) 866 5746 info@harboursidewhitianga.co.nz
www.harboursidewhitianga.co.nz
Handy to boat launching and the town centre. Spa pool. Free dinghy hire.
36.838482S 175.70266E
Hema Atlas Map Ref 8 D13

432 Mill Creek Bird & Campervan Park
365 Mill Creek Rd, Whitianga
Ph (07) 866 0166 p.park@farmside.co.nz
www.bird-and-animal-park.co.nz
There is a boat ramp in town. Free entry into Bird Park. Pets by arrangement only.
36.899424S 175.637174E
Hema Atlas Map Ref 8 E12

433 Riverglen Holiday Park
Tapu Coroglen Rd, Coroglen: off SH25, 3.6km up Tapu Coroglen Rd, turn off next to the Coroglen Tavern.
Ph (07) 866 3130 www.whitianga.co.nz/riverglen riverglen@xtra.co.nz
Swimming, trout fishing, lodge available for functions. Pets by arrangement.
36.924321S 175.690943E
Hema Atlas Map Ref 8 E13

434 Seabreeze Holiday Park
1043 Tairua/Whitianga Rd, Whenuakite
Ph (07) 866 3050 Fax (07) 866 3827
info@seabreezetouristpark.co.nz www.seabreezetouristpark.co.nz
Pets by arrangement only. Internet access. Free bikes.
36.915641S 175.778855E
Hema Atlas Map Ref 8 E13

435 Shakespeare's Scenic Reserve
Off Purangi Rd, from SH25: signposted NW of Cooks Beach
36.830981S 175.729068E
Hema Atlas Map Ref 8 D13

436 Flaxmill Bay Hideaway
1031 Purangi Rd, Flaxmill Bay
Ph (07) 866 2386 Fax (07) 866 2389 www.flaxmillbay.co.nz
36.833057S 175.724293E
Hema Atlas Map Ref 8 D13

North Island Camping Sites — Central North Region

437 Hahei Holiday Resort
41 Harsant Ave. Approximately 14km N of SH25 from Whenuakite; signposted from Hahei town centre
Ph (07) 866 3889 info@haheiholidays.co.nz www.haheiholidays.co.nz
Fishing, swimming, boating, 500m of beach on-site.
Beautiful beachside location. Make sure you do the one hour walk to Cathedral Cove. Wireless internet.
36.84097S 175.808419E Hema Atlas Map Ref 8 D14

438 Hot Water Beach Holiday Park
790 Hot Water Beach Road, Hot Water Beach, Whitianga
Ph (07) 866 3116 Fax (07) 866 3106
info@hotwaterbeachholidaypark.co.nz
www.hotwaterbeachholidaypark.com
Hire spades to dig your own spa in the sand at Hot Water Beach.
36.890381S 175.820375E Hema Atlas Map Ref 8 E14

439 Kauri Grove Lookout & Scenic Reserve
Alongside SH25 N of Tairua
36.966231S 175.823329E Hema Atlas Map Ref 8 F14

440 Kauri Grove Track/Lynch Stream Coast Track
Alongside SH25 N of Tairua
36.955034S 175.816438E Hema Atlas Map Ref 8 F14

441 Twin Kauri Walking Track
Alongside SH25 N of Tairua
36.978979S 175.841914E Hema Atlas Map Ref 8 F14

442 Roadside Rest Area
Off Ocean Beach Rd, Tairua
Waterside picnic area.
36.98902S 175.855626E Hema Atlas Map Ref 8 F14

443 The Glade Holiday Park
58 Vista Paku, Pauanui; signposted from Pauanui town centre
Ph (07) 864 8559 info@pauanui-glade.co.nz Fax (07) 864 7158
www.pauanui glade.co.nz
37.013245S 175.860087E Hema Atlas Map Ref 8 G14

444 Info/Rest Area
SH25, S of Hikuai, just S of junction with Whangamata Rd
37.090513S 175.780276E Hema Atlas Map Ref 8 G13

445 Upper Entrance Rest Area
Whangamata Rd between Hikuai and Wharekawa
37.101747S 175.800459E Hema Atlas Map Ref 8 G13

446 Roadside Rest Area
Pauanui
37.028161S 175.871547E Hema Atlas Map Ref 8 G14

447 Broken Hills
4km off SH25, on Hikaui/Puketui Rd
DOC Kauaeranga Visitor Centre Ph (07) 867 9080
kauaerangavc@doc.govt.nz
Swimming, fishing, walking; self registration system;
Drinking water is from a stream.
37.105489S 175.738382E Hema Atlas Map Ref 8 G13

448 Opoutere Coastal Camping
460 Ohui Road: 5km NE of SH25 at Opoutere: follow Opoutere Rd off SH25, signposted at the end of the tarseal
Ph/Fax (07) 865 9152 info@opouterebeach.co.nz
www.opouterebeach.co.nz
Simple camping with easy access to a good surfing beach, backing onto a peaceful estuary and surrounded by DOC wildlife reserves. Closed in winter months.
37.101919S 175.878915E Hema Atlas Map Ref 8 G14

449 Whangamata Motor Camp
104 Barbara Ave, Whangamata: signposted from the town centre
Ph (07) 865 9128 adbrien@xtra.co.nz
The handiest to the town centre and the beach, but it is busy.
Pets by arrangement; winter only.
37.207514S 175.873038E Hema Atlas Map Ref 8 H14

450 Settlers Motor Camp
101 Leander Rd, Whangamata: signposted from Port Rd, just S of the township
Ph/Fax (07) 865 8181 settlersmotorcamp@xtra.net.nz
37.210848S 175.870024E Hema Atlas Map Ref 8 J14

451 Wentworth
Off SH25 S of Whangamata
DOC Kauaeranga Visitor Centre Ph (07) 867 9080
kauaerangavc@doc.govt.nz
Self registration system. A rural alternative to the crowds of Whangamata, yet still handy to the beach. Only dogs permitted, must be on leash at all times, phone manager in advance Ph (07) 865 7032. Cold showers.
37.246828S 175.818169E Hema Atlas Map Ref 8 J14

SH1 — HAMILTON TO TAUPO

452 Roadside Rest Area
Hamilton Gardens: riverside from SH1 E of the town centre
37.802322S 175.305861E Hema Atlas Map Ref 92 G4, 11 C7

453 Roadside Rest Area
Morrinsville Rd (SH26) N of Silverdale Rd, Hamilton
37.795594S 175.333852E Hema Atlas Map Ref 92 F6, 11 C7

454 Tamahere Wayside Stop
SH1 from Hamilton, near Tamahere
37.813689S 175.340912E Hema Atlas Map Ref 92 G6, 11 C7

455 Airport Road Rest Area
SW from Tamahere, S of Hamilton
37.841239S 175.3485E Hema Atlas Map Ref 92 H6, 11 C7

Central North Region — North Island Camping Sites

456 Cambridge Motor Park
32 Scott St, Leamington: signposted from SH1 E of Cambridge across the river at Leamington
Ph/Fax (07) 827 5649   cambridgemotorpark@actrix.net.nz
www.cambridgemotorpark.co.nz
Huge park-like grounds adjoining a public domain. Internet access.
37.905879S 175.478746E   Hema Atlas Map Ref 12 D8

457 Roadside Rest Area
Cambridge Rd, W of Vogel St, Hamilton
37.889717S 175.455283E   Hema Atlas Map Ref 12 D8

458 Roadside Rest Area
Adjacent SH1 and Lake Karapiro
Lakeside picnic area.
37.923878S 175.540643E   Hema Atlas Map Ref 12 D9

459 Lake Karapiro Camping & Pursuits Centre
601 Maungatautari Road, Cambridge: adjacent Lake Karapiro
Ph (07) 827 4178   karapiro@xtra.co.nz   www.lakekarapiro.co.nz
Handy to the Lake Karapiro rowing venue.
37.929664S 175.539636E   Hema Atlas Map Ref 12 D9

460 Roadside Rest Area
Adjacent SH1 and Lake Karapiro
Lakeside picnic area.
37.946821S 175.594655E   Hema Atlas Map Ref 12 E9

461 Roadside Rest Area
Adjacent SH1 and Lake Karapiro
Lakeside picnic area.
37.947968S 175.607655E   Hema Atlas Map Ref 12 E9

462 Roadside Rest Area
Alongside Maungatauri Rd and Lake Karapiro
Lakeside picnic area.
37.948192S 175.653519E   Hema Atlas Map Ref 12 E10

463 Roadside Rest Area
Adjacent SH27
37.942912S 175.756185E   Hema Atlas Map Ref 12 E11

464 Opal Hot Springs & Holiday Park
257 Okauia Springs Rd, Okauia: SH27 5km NE of Matamata, follow the signs to the Tower Museum and carry on another 2km
Ph (07) 888 8198   Fax (07) 888 5813   info@opalhotsprings.co.nz
www.opalhotsprings.com
Adjacent to 18-hole golf course.
37.787999S 175.838474E   Hema Atlas Map Ref 12 C11

465 Rapurapu Reserve
Rapurapu Rd, off SH24, E of Matamata
37.884725S 175.88613E   Hema Atlas Map Ref 12 D12

466 Roadside Rest Area
SH24, E of Matamata
37.873584S 175.927121E   Hema Atlas Map Ref 12 D12

467 Kaimai Watering Hole Rest Area
SH24, E of Matamata
37.871355S 175.929633E   Hema Atlas Map Ref 12 D12

468 Fitzgerald Glade
SH5, E of Tapapa, E of Tirau
38.000532S 175.889286E   Hema Atlas Map Ref 12 E12

469 Roadside Rest Area
SH1, between Putaruru and Tokoroa
38.13229S 175.824813E   Hema Atlas Map Ref 12 G11

470 Kea Motel & Holiday Park
SH1: N end of Putaruru
Ph/Fax (07) 882 1590   keamotel@xtra.co.nz   www.keamotel.co.nz
Basically an add-on to the motel but useful. Internet access.
38.046446S 175.781405E   Hema Atlas Map Ref 12 F11

471 Tokoroa Motor Camp
22 Sloss Rd, Tokoroa: N end of Tokoroa, signposted from SH1
Ph (07) 886 6642   tokoroa.camp@orcon.net.nz
www.tokoroamotorcamp.co.nz
Pets by arrangement.
38.215632S 175.875004E   Hema Atlas Map Ref 12 H12

472 Lake Access and Rest Areas (2)
SH30, Lake Whakamaru
38.419616S 175.909322E   Hema Atlas Map Ref 19 A4

473 Jim Currie Reserve
SH1, near Kinleith turnoff
38.279067S 175.903511E   Hema Atlas Map Ref 12 H12

474 Roadside Rest Area
SH1, W of Lake Atiamuri
38.378601S 176.001901E   Hema Atlas Map Ref 12 J13

475 Dunham Point Reserve
Along SH30, Dunham Point, Lake Whakamaru: signposted W of SH30 & SH1 intersection
Overnight camping allowed for certified self-contained motorhomes. Shelter and shade in a picturesque lakeside location.
38.423667S 175.894722E   Hema Atlas Map Ref 19 A4

476 Whakamaru Recreation Reserve
Ongaroto Rd (SH30), N side of Lake Whakamaru
Overnight camping for self-contained motorhomes. Plus camping max. 2 nights at Ski Club S of Lake.
38.423521S 175.817962E   Hema Atlas Map Ref 19 A3

477 Waipapa Road Rest Area
Waipapa Rd: beside Lake Arapuni
38.29528S 175.67962E   Hema Atlas Map Ref 12 J10

478 Landing Road
East of Kihikihi via Arapuni Rd, turn right into Landing Rd, follow to end at the river
DOC Maniapoto Area Office   Ph (07) 878 1050
maniapotoao@doc.govt.nz
Swimming, fishing.
38.166239S 175.657669E   Hema Atlas Map Ref 12 G10

48 North Island Camping Sites — Central North Region

479 Roadside Rest Area
Whakamaru Rd (SH29), near the dam N of Whakamaru
38.420552S 175.80318E — Hema Atlas Map Ref 19 A3

480 Piropiro
Off SH4, on the Waimiha-Mangapehi Rd. Turn east at Waimiha, follow Ongarue Stream Rd into Kokomiko Rd.
DOC Maniapoto Area Office Ph (07) 878 1050
maniapotoao@doc.govt.nz
Drinking water is from a stream.
38.633788S 175.464172E — Hema Atlas Map Ref 18 C12

481 Ngaherenga
Off SH30, adjacent to Pureora Forest Park Headquarters
DOC Maniapoto Area Office Ph (07) 878 1050
maniapotoao@doc.govt.nz
Drinking water is from a stream.
38.511268S 175.562329E — Hema Atlas Map Ref 18 B13

482 Kakaho
Link Rd from Pureora Forest Park Headquarters; or Kakaho Rd from SH32
DOC Maniapoto Area Office Ph (07) 878 1050
maniapotoao@doc.govt.nz
Drinking water is from a stream.
38.567942S 175.717884E — Hema Atlas Map Ref 19 C2

483 Roadside Rest Area
SH32, S of turnoff to Whanganui Bay
Scenic views.
38.803971S 175.689916E — Hema Atlas Map Ref 19 E2

484 Wairakei Thermal Valley
On SH1, signposted from SH5 at Wairakei, on your left before the SH1 and SH5 intersection: 8.5km NE from Taupo
Ph (07) 374 8004 johnrichards@wave.co.nz
thermalvalley@clear.net.nz
Pets by arrangement.
38.62518S 176.08995E — Hema Atlas Map Ref 19 C5

485 Huka Falls Scenic Reserve
Follow signs from SH5 N of Taupo to Huka Falls
A short walk to view these pretty falls.
38.64794S 176.087545E — Hema Atlas Map Ref 19 D6

486 Reids Farm Recreation Reserve
Follow signs from SH5 N of Taupo to Huka Falls: camp adjoins the Huka Falls Rd and the river
Ph (07) 376 0617
Overnight camping allowed. Simple camping in a magnificent setting, and the swimming pools are magnificent. Boil stream water before drinking.
38.65647S 176.086105E — Hema Atlas Map Ref 19 D5

SH2 — TAURANGA TO OPOTIKI

487 Mt Maunganui Beachside Holiday Park
1 Adams Ave, Mt Maunganui: beachfront right under the Mt Mauao
Ph 0800 682 3224 info@mountbeachside.co.nz
www.mountbeachside.co.nz
A great base for boating, fishing, surfing or walking Mauao.
37.631714S 176.176364E — Hema Atlas Map Ref 94 A3, 13 A4

488 Cosy Corner Holiday Park
40 Ocean Beach Rd, Mt Maunganui
Ph (07) 575 5899 Fax (07) 575 5670 stay@cosycorner.co.nz
www.cosycorner.co.nz
Just opposite the beach, and handy to Mt Maunganui although big rigs may struggle with the entrance. Internet. Wireless internet.
37.657455S 176.210871E — Hema Atlas Map Ref 94 B3, 13 B4

489 Golden Grove Holiday Park
73 Girven Rd, Mt Maunganui
Ph (07) 575 5821 www.golden-grove.co.nz
A very neat and tidy 'newish' camp that's handy to the beach. Qualmark four star. Internet.
37.672953S 176.230472E — Hema Atlas Map Ref 94 B4, 13 B4

490 Beach Grove Holiday Park
386 Papamoa Beach Rd, Papamoa
Ph (07) 572 1337 beachgrove@xtra.co.nz www.beachgrove.co.nz
New facilities in a neat and tidy park, although it's quite suburban.
37.69051S 176.26718E — Hema Atlas Map Ref 94 C5, 13 B4

491 Papamoa Beach Top 10 Holiday Resort
535 Papamoa Beach Rd, Papamoa
Ph (07) 572 0816 Fax (07) 572 0841 www.papamoabeach.co.nz
A beautiful camp in a magic location, and the Qualmark four star plus rating makes it a nice treat.
37.696422S 176.284138E — Hema Atlas Map Ref 94 C5, 13 B5

492 Papamoa Village Park
267 Parton Rd, Papamoa
Ph (07) 542 1890 Fax (07) 542 3159 villagepark@callplus.net.nz
Neat and tidy in park-like grounds. Internet. Pets by arrangement, with vaccination certificate.
37.711052S 176.31277E — Hema Atlas Map Ref 94 D5, 13 B5

493 Pacific Park Christian Holiday Camp
1110 Papamoa Beach Rd, Papamoa
Ph (07) 542 0018 office@ppchc.co.nz Fax (07) 542 1312
www.pacificpark.co.nz
Across the road from beach, hot pool, mini golf. Alcohol and smoke-free. There is a boat ramp 2km away.
37.714136S 176.332792E — Hema Atlas Map Ref 94 C6, 13 B5

Central North Region — North Island Camping Sites

494 Te Puke Holiday Park
SH2: W of Te Puke
Ph/Fax (07) 573 9866
Sheltered, but close to a very busy road.
37.772595S 176.308032E   Hema Atlas Map Ref 13 C5

495 Donovan Park Entrance
Jellicoe St (SH2) just W of Cameron St, Te Puke
37.782075S 176.317586E   Hema Atlas Map Ref 13 C5

496 Beach Holiday Park
Town Point Rd, Maketu: off SH2 at Little Waihi: at the shopping centre
Ph (07) 533 2165 Fax (07) 533 2135
maketu@maketubeachholidaypark.com
www.maketubeachholidaypark.com
The location is magic but this camp is being overtaken by motel units and cabins, so it is better suited to campervans than camping. Internet.
37.754473S 176.457112E   Hema Atlas Map Ref 13 C6

497 Bledisloe Holiday Park
Off SH2 at Little Waihi
Ph (07) 533 2157 info@bledisloeholiday.co.nz
www.bledisloeholiday.co.nz
37.759373S 176.478206E   Hema Atlas Map Ref 13 C6

498 Maketu Hilltop Holiday Park
195 Arawa Ave, Maketu
Ph (07) 533 2222 Fax (07) 533 2209
stay@maketuholidaypark.co.nz www.maketuholidaypark.co.nz
Although this is the most distant camp from the area's beaches this is compensated for by it being so good. Internet.
37.768482S 176.462345E   Hema Atlas Map Ref 13 C6

499 Paengaroa Motor Lodge
84 SH33: 1km S of the SH33/SH2 intersection
Ph (07) 533 1170 Fax (07) 533 1698 paengaroa.motels@xtra.co.nz
37.811033S 176.407591E   Hema Atlas Map Ref 13 C6

500 Pukehina Motor Camp
26 Costello Cres, Pukehina
Ph (07) 533 3600
Compact and tidy with a few permanents.
37.790461S 176.528012E   Hema Atlas Map Ref 13 C7

501 Beachfront Reserve
Beachside on SH2 near Waitahanui Stream
37.834055S 176.607966E   Hema Atlas Map Ref 13 D7

502 Roadside Rest Area
SH2, E of Pukehina
37.825014S 176.58572E   Hema Atlas Map Ref 13 D7

503 Paengaroa Domain Entrance
SH33, N of Sunset Drive, Paengaroa
37.823229S 176.411169E   Hema Atlas Map Ref 13 D6

504 Pikowai Reserve Camping Ground
Shoreside SH2 at Pikowai
Whakatane District Council Ph (07) 306 0500
Self registration system. Beachside with plenty of shelter and shade.
37.857421S 176.667208E   Hema Atlas Map Ref 14 D8

505 Roadside Rest Area
SH2, S of Pikowai
37.863058S 176.681865E   Hema Atlas Map Ref 14 D8

506 Roadside Rest Area
SH2, S of Pikowai
37.871958S 176.709122E   Hema Atlas Map Ref 14 D8

507 Murphy's Holiday Camp
174 SH2, Matata: Shoreside on SH2 W of Matata
Ph (07) 322 2136 Fax (07) 322 2419
This cosy beachside camp is actually quite big and popular. Pets by arrangement.
37.877685S 176.726762E   Hema Atlas Map Ref 14 D8

508 Matata Recreation Reserve
Arawa St, Matata: Alongside SH2 at Matata
Rangitaiki Visitor Centre Ph (07) 366 1080 www.rangitaikivc.doc.govt.nz
Simple overnight camping in a great spot and it's cheap too.
37.886478S 176.760613E   Hema Atlas Map Ref 14 D9

509 Te Pakau (Eight Acre)
Waimana Valley, Te Urewera National Park
DOC Te Urewera NP Visitor Centre Ph (06) 837 3803
teureweravc@doc.govt.nz
Drinking water from a stream. Phone Te Urewera Visitor Centre re access.
38.347951S 177.120984E   Hema Atlas Map Ref 14 H12

510 Omahuru (Ogilvies)
Waimana Valley, off SH2 and then Matahi Valley Rd, 18km from Waimana. DOC Te Urewera NP Visitor Centre
Ph (06) 837 3803 teureweravc@doc.govt.nz
Drinking water from a stream.
38.312692S 177.120291E   Hema Atlas Map Ref 14 J12

511 Ohiwa Family Holiday Park
Ohiwa Harbour Road, Ohiwa: signposted as a 5km diversion W from SH2
Ph (07) 315 4741 Fax (07) 315 4601 www.ohiwaholidays.co.nz
All the benefits of Ohope, but without the crowds. By reclaiming coastal erosion, this holiday park has won several environmental awards. Qualmark four star. Kayak hire.
37.989695S 177.161447E   Hema Atlas Map Ref 14 F12

512 Roadside Rest Area
Waiotahi Beach Rd (SH2), W of Opotiki
Several roadside and seaside rest areas east of this vicinity along the beautiful pohutakawa-clad coastline.
37.994132S 177.203039E   Hema Atlas Map Ref 14 F13

North Island Camping Sites

Central North Region

513 Roadside Rest Area
Waiotahi Beach Rd (SH2), W of Opotiki
Several seaside rest areas along this coastline.
37.991849S 177.227942E   Hema Atlas Map Ref 14 F13

514 Island View Family Holiday Park
8 Appleton Rd, Waiotahi Beach: W of Opotiki
Ph/Fax (07) 315 7519 info@islandviewholiday.co.nz
www.islandviewholiday.co.nz
Close to a pretty beach and good fishing.
37.99242S 177.242468E   Hema Atlas Map Ref 14 F13

515 Opotiki Holiday Park
39 Potts Ave, Opotiki: signposted from the city centre
Ph/Fax (07) 315 6050 www.opotikiholidaypark.co.nz
The closest camp to the city centre yet pretty quiet, clean and tidy. Internet.
38.00223S 177.282971E   Hema Atlas Map Ref 14 F13

SH30 – WHAKATANE TO ROTORUA

516 Whakatane Holiday Park
McGarvey Rd, Whakatane:
signposted from SH30 at W end of Whakatane
Ph (07) 308 8694 Fax (07) 308 2070 whak@xtra.co.nz
www.whakataneholidaypark.co.nz
Close to the beach set in park-like grounds this is a big camp and the handiest to the centre of Whakatane. Internet.
37.949095S 176.985622E   Hema Atlas Map Ref 14 E11

517 Thornton Beach Holiday Park
163 Thornton Beach Rd, Thornton: W of Whakatane
Ph/Fax (07) 304 8296 www.thorntonbeach.co.nz
Beachside and handy to the river mouth for boating and fishing. Wireless internet. Brand new ablution blocks.
37.909575S 176.876528E   Hema Atlas Map Ref 14 E10

518 Roadside Rest Area
Thornton Beach Reserve, Thornton: NW of Whakatane
37.911448S 176.876086E   Hema Atlas Map Ref 14 E10

519 Roadside Rest Area
SH2, E of Awakeri, just S of White Pine Bush
38.012285S 176.948269E   Hema Atlas Map Ref 14 F10

520 Ohope Beach Top 10 Holiday Park
367 Harbour Rd: E of Ohope township, E of Whakatane
Ph 0800 264 673 Fax (07) 312 6353 www.ohopebeach.co.nz
Beachside for swimming, surfing and fishing, and boat launching nearby. Internet, tennis court, mini golf. Qualmark four star. Surf & Sand Conference Park (next door) offers campsites from Christmas Day to Feb 6.
37.982526S 177.112451E   Hema Atlas Map Ref 14 E12

521 Ohope Beach Picnic Areas
W end of Ohope Beach: E of Whakatane
There are several reserves in this vicinity with toilets and cold water showers for beach goers. No camping allowed.
37.980206S 177.112428E   Hema Atlas Map Ref 14 F12

522 Roadside Rest Area
SH2, S of Taneatua
38.106282S 177.043164E   Hema Atlas Map Ref 14 G11

523 Awakeri Hot Springs
Beside SH30: 15km SW of Whakatane
Ph (07) 304 9117 Fax (07) 304 9290 awakeri.springs@xtra.co.nz
www.awakerisprings.co.nz
A peaceful, bush-clad setting with hot springs.
38.005834S 176.861456E   Hema Atlas Map Ref 14 F9

524 Matahi Spit Reserve
At the E end of Lake Rotoma: signposted off SH30
38.065531S 176.601067E   Hema Atlas Map Ref 13 F7

525 Roadside Rest Area
SH34, S of Islington St, centre of Kawerau, opposite the netball courts
38.084414S 176.700347E   Hema Atlas Map Ref 14 F8

526 Roadside Rest Area
Beside Lake Rotoma & SH30
38.051981S 176.570956E   Hema Atlas Map Ref 13 F7

527 Rotoma Holiday Park
8 Manawahe Rd: off SH30, signposted from SH30 at Lake Rotoma
Ph/Fax (07) 362 0815 rotomaholidaypark@xtra.co.nz
www.rotomahp.wordpress.com
Soda water mineral pools nearby.
38.042187S 176.545854E   Hema Atlas Map Ref 13 F7

528 Roadside Rest Area
Beside Lake Rotoiti and SH30
38.036353S 176.513814E   Hema Atlas Map Ref 13 F6

529 Roadside Rest Area
Beside Lake Rotoiti and SH30
38.031037S 176.486573E   Hema Atlas Map Ref 13 F6

530 Roadside Rest Area
Beside Lake Rotoiti and SH30
38.042759S 176.487102E   Hema Atlas Map Ref 13 F6

531 Emery Store Entry
SH 30, W of Rotoiti Forest
38.055658S 176.463224E   Hema Atlas Map Ref 13 F6

532 Roadside Rest Area
Beside Lake Rotoiti and SH30
38.05717S 176.430405E   Hema Atlas Map Ref 13 F6

Central North Region — North Island Camping Sites

533 All Seasons Holiday Park
50-58 Lee Rd, Hannah's Bay: signposted off SH30 near the airport
Ph (07) 345 6240 Fax (07) 345 6241
allseasonsrotorua@xtra.co.nz www.allseasonsrotorua.co.nz
Three hectare parkland, 100m from Lake Rotorua. Internet access. Spa pool. Bikes and kayaks for hire.
38.117301S 176.306954E Hema Atlas Map Ref 96 B5, 13 G5

534 Holdens Bay Top 10 Holiday Park
7 Stonebridge Park, Holdens Bay: signposted off SH30 near the airport
Ph 0800 148 884 Fax (07) 345 5126
accommodation@holdensbay.co.nz www.holdensbay.co.nz
Sparkling new amenities. Spa pools. Wireless internet.
38.122031S 176.307449E Hema Atlas Map Ref 96 B5, 13 G4

535 Redwood Holiday Park
5 Tarawera Rd: signposted at Blue Lake, turnoff SH30
Ph/Fax (07) 345 9380 reservations@redwoodpark.co.nz
www.redwoodparkrotorua.co.nz
Although it's near a major road there's good walking to be had nearby. Internet, spa.
38.14827S 176.277247E Hema Atlas Map Ref 96 C4, 13 G4

536 Blue Lake Top 10 Holiday Park
723 Tarawera Rd: follow signs to Blue Lake
Ph (07) 362 8120, 0800 808 292 Fax (07) 362 8600
www.bluelaketop10.co.nz
Swimming, fishing, boating and walking opportunities abound in this very tranquil setting. It's hard to believe you are so close to Rotorua. Internet. Qualmark four star plus. Spa pool.
38.185727S 176.332447E Hema Atlas Map Ref 13 G5

537 Lake Okareka
Northern shores of Lake Okareka off Miller Road
DOC www.doc.govt.nz or Tourism Rotorua Information Centre
Ph (07) 348 5179
info@rotoruaNZ.com
Fishing, kayaking.
38.162122S 176.360467E Hema Atlas Map Ref 13 G5

538 Lake Tarawera Outlet
Eastern shore of Lake Tarawera (boat access); vehicle access via Kawerau requires a permit from Fletcher Challenge Forest Information Centre in Rotorua
DOC www.doc.govt.nz or Tourism Rotorua Ph (07) 348 5179
info@rotoruaNZ.com
38.184677S 176.503018E Hema Atlas Map Ref 13 H6

539 Hot Water Beach
Te Rata Bay, Lake Tarawera (boat access only)
DOC www.doc.govt.nz or Tourism Rotorua Ph (07) 348 5179
info@rotoruaNZ.com
38.244048S 176.433768E Hema Atlas Map Ref 13 H6

540 Rotorua Thermal Holiday Park
463 Old Taupo Rd, Rotorua: S end near junction with SH5
Ph (07) 346 3140 Fax (07) 346 1324
info@rotoruathermal.co.nz www.rotoruathermal.co.nz
Lovely location: one of the most impressive in Rotorua. Qualmark four star. Internet.
38.163708S 176.244969E Hema Atlas Map Ref 96 D3, 13 G4

541 Rotorua Top 10 Holiday Park
1495 Pukuatua St, Rotorua: several blocks from the city centre
Ph 0800 223 267 stay@rotoruatop10.co.nz www.rotoruatop10.co.nz
Handiest to the centre of Rotorua. Internet. Qualmark four star plus.
38.136515S 176.240498E Hema Atlas Map Ref 96 C3, 13 G4

542 Cosy Cottage International Holiday Park
67 Whittaker Rd, Rotorua: lakeside N of Rotorua city centre, signposted from SH5
Ph 0800 22 24 24 stay@cosycottage.co.nz www.cosycottage.co.nz
Bike hire. Wireless internet.
38.125351S 176.242845E Hema Atlas Map Ref 96 B3, 13 G4

543 Willowhaven Holiday Park
31 Beaumonts Rd: lakeside N of Rotorua, signposted from SH5 at Ngongotaha
Ph (07) 357 4092 Fax (07) 357 5078 info@willowhaven.co.nz
www.willowhaven.co.nz
Kayaks and dinghies for hire.
38.084334S 176.218079E Hema Atlas Map Ref 13 F4

544 Rotorua Family Holiday Park
22 Beaumonts Rd, Rotorua
Ph/Fax (07) 357 4289 stay@rotoruafamilypark.co.nz
www.rotoruafamilypark.co.nz
Close to boat ramp and Lake Rotorua. Spa pool. Kayaks and bikes for hire. Wireless internet.
38.084054S 176.216523E Hema Atlas Map Ref 13 F4

545 Waiteti Trout Stream Holiday Park
14 Okona Cres, Ngongotaha, Rotorua: signposted N of Rotorua on lake loop road
Ph (07) 357 5255 stay@waiteti.com www.waiteti.com
Sheltered, quiet location handy to a fishing stream. Pets by arrangement. Spa pool. Free kayaks and dinghies. Internet.
38.071898S 176.212143E Hema Atlas Map Ref 13 F4

546 Roadside Rest Area
Hamurana Springs Recreation Reserve, Hamurana: N side of Lake Rotorua
38.034433S 176.256103E Hema Atlas Map Ref 13 F4

547 Tarukenga Rest Area
SH5, W of Ngongotaha
38.072511S 176.173623E Hema Atlas Map Ref 13 F3

548 Roadside Rest Area
SH33, N of Lake Rotoiti near Okere Falls
38.035115S 176.336751E Hema Atlas Map Ref 13 F5

52 North Island Camping Sites — Central North Region

549 Summit Rest Area
SH33, E of Okere Falls
38.012534S 176.362437E
Hema Atlas Map Ref 13 F5

550 Roadside Rest Area
SH33, between Tokerau and Paengaroa
37.949009S 176.371016E
Hema Atlas Map Ref 13 E5

551 Lake Rotoiti Holiday Park
103 Okere Rd, Okere Falls R.D.4 Rotorua: off SH33, N of Okere Falls
Ph (07) 362 4860 lakerotoiti@xtra.co.nz
www.lakerotoitiholidaypark.co.nz

Good canoeing and rafting to be had on the Okere Falls, and the nearby fishing is also very good. Book for private functions. Water slide. Kayaks and dinghies.

38.022237S 176.350953E
Hema Atlas Map Ref 13 F5

SH5 & SH38 — ROTORUA TO WAIROA

552 Roadside Rest Area
SH5, S of Rotorua
38.18048S 176.25035E
Hema Atlas Map Ref 13 G4

553 Taahunaatara Rest Area
SH30, S of Rotorua
38.305089S 176.130446E
Hema Atlas Map Ref 13 J3

554 Maungaongaonga Scenic Reserve
Just S of junction of SH5 & SH38
A pretty stopping point.

38.315808S 176.374905E
Hema Atlas Map Ref 13 J5

555 Tumunui
SH5, S of Rotorua
38.230469S 176.297769E
Hema Atlas Map Ref 13 H4

556 Waikite Valley Thermal Pools
Follow signs to the Waikite Valley from SH5: 29km from Rotorua
Ph/Fax (07) 333 1861 thermalpools@xtra.co.nz www.hotpools.co.nz

A pretty rural location for these thermal pools, well away from the Rotorua crowds and well worth checking out. Campers have unlimited access to pools.

38.327161S 176.302781E
Hema Atlas Map Ref 13 J4

557 Golden Springs Motel, Holiday Park & Restaurant
4085 SH 5, Golden Springs: midway Rotorua/Taupo
Ph/Fax (07) 333 8280 www.goldenspringsholidaypark.co.nz
golden-springs@farmside.co.nz

Pets by arrangement only. There is a boat ramp 2km down the road. Motel, chalet and tourist flats. Restaurant.

38.46955S 176.307642E
Hema Atlas Map Ref 19 B7

558 Mihi Bridge Rest Area
SH5, E of Mihi
38.483701S 176.291377E
Hema Atlas Map Ref 19 C7

559 Tahorakuri Forest Roadside Rest Area
SH5, E of Wairakei
38.567701S 176.225978E
Hema Atlas Map Ref 19 C7

560 Guy Roe Reserve (Homestead Arm)
Guy Roe Reserve, on Brett Rd alongside Lake Rerewhakaaitu: follow signs from SH38 to Mt Tarawera
Rotorua District Council Parks & Recreation Ph (07) 348 4199

Lakeside for swimming, fishing and boating and handy to Rotorua yet peaceful. Dogs must be on leash at all times. Max. 2 nights stay.

38.30233S 176.479254E
Hema Atlas Map Ref 13 J6

561 Rerewhakaaitu - Ashpit Road (Ash Pit Bay)
Rerewhakaaitu Rd off SH38, then follow Ash Pit Rd, alongside Lake Rerewhakaaitu: 29km SE of Rotorua
DOC Rotorua Lakes Area Office Ph (07) 349 7400
rotorualakesao@doc.govt.nz www.doc.govt.nz
or Tourism Rotorua Ph (07) 348 5179 info@rotoruaNZ.co.nz

Self registration applies. Dogs must be on leash at all times.

38.277614S 176.508797E
Hema Atlas Map Ref 13 J6

562 Rerewhakaaitu - Brett Road (Awaatua Bay)
Rerewhakaaitu Rd off SH38, then follow Brett Rd, alongside Lake Rerewhakaaitu: 29km SE of Rotorua
DOC Rotorua Lakes Area Office Ph (07) 349 7400
rotorualakesao@doc.govt.nz www.doc.govt.nz
or Tourism Rotorua Ph (07) 348 5179 info@rotoruaNZ.co.nz

Self registration applies. Dogs must be on leash at all times.

38.277614S 176.508797E
Hema Atlas Map Ref 13 J6

563 Rangitaiki Bridge Roadside Rest Area
Main Rd, Murapara: alongside the river, adjacent to the SE abutment of the bridge.
38.458678S 176.699016E
Hema Atlas Map Ref 20 B11

564 Mangawhiri Bridge Roadside Rest Area
Te Urewera Rainforest Route, Te Whaiti Road, 5km south of the Te Whaiti Rd / Whirinaki Rd intersection
38.586361S 176.781406E
Hema Atlas Map Ref 20 B11

565 Goudies Road Rest Area
SH38, NW of Murupara
38.401272S 176.50426E
Hema Atlas Map Ref 20 A9

566 Roadside Rest Area
Alongside road to Lake Waikaremoana
Nice riverside spot.

38.566859S 176.773061E
Hema Atlas Map Ref 20 C11

567 Te Whaiti Roadside Rest Area
Te Urewera Rainforest Route, Te Whaiti Rd / Minginui Rd, SE corner of intersection
38.586283S 176.781311E
Hema Atlas Map Ref 20 C11

Central North Region — North Island Camping Sites 53

568 Mangamate
Minginui Rd off SH38: 90km SE of Rotorua
Hawkes Bay Regional Visitor Centre (06) 834 3111
hawkesbayvc@doc.govt.nz
Drinking water is from a stream; Dogs permitted, must be on leash at all times.

38.621084S 176.731836E Hema Atlas Map Ref 20 D11

569 Sanctuary
From Minginui Rd turn off into Sanctuary Rd and follow to the end.
Hawkes Bay Regional Visitor Centre (06) 834 3111
hawkesbayvc@doc.govt.nz
Drinking water is from a stream.

38.658236S 176.726158E Hema Atlas Map Ref 20 D11

570 Okahu Roadend
Okahu Rd, off SH38: 105km SE of Rotorua
Hawkes Bay Regional Visitor Centre (06) 834 3111
hawkesbayvc@doc.govt.nz
Drinking water is from stream; Dogs permitted, must be on leash at all times.

38.676401S 176.810246E Hema Atlas Map Ref 20 D12

571 Ruatahuna Road Rest Area
Te Urewera Rainforest Route, at the Tarapounamu Summit, 13km SE of Ruatahuna Rd / Minginui Rd intersection
38.614458S 176.874625E Hema Atlas Map Ref 20 C12

572 Mimiha Roadside Rest Area
Te Urewera Rainforest Route, Ruatahuna Road at Mimiha, 22km SE of Ruatanhuna Rd / Minginui Rd intersection, or 7km NW of Ruatahuna / Sister Annie Rd intersection
38.641022S 176.895697E Hema Atlas Map Ref 20 D12

573 Roadside Rest Area
Mano-o-rongo Stream
38.62396S 176.967997E Hema Atlas Map Ref 20 D13

574 Huiarau Summit Roadside Rest Area
Waikaremoana Road, 15km E of Waikaermoana Rd / Sister Annie Rd intersection
38.884108S 175.309272E Hema Atlas Map Ref 20 C14

575 Roadside Rest Area
Roadside Rest Area for Whakataka Hut Track
38.63264S 177.032066E Hema Atlas Map Ref 20 D14

576 Orangihikoia, Te Urewera National Park
SH38, north of Lake Waikaremoana: roadside at Orangihikoia Stream
DOC Te Urewera Visitor Centre Ph (06) 837 3803
teureweravc@doc.govt.nz
Drinking water is from a stream.

38.668231S 177.041294E Hema Atlas Map Ref 20 D14, 21 D2

577 Te Taita O Makora, Te Urewera National Park
Adjacent SH38, N of Waikaremoana
DOC Te Urewera Visitor Centre Ph (06) 837 3803
teureweravc@doc.govt.nz
Drinking water is from a stream.

38.685851S 177.058937E Hema Atlas Map Ref 20 D14, 21 D2

578 Mokau Landing, Te Urewera National Park
At Lake Waikaremoana, adjacent SH38: N of Waikaremoana
DOC Te Urewera Visitor Centre Ph (06) 837 3803
teureweravc@doc.govt.nz
Swimming, boating, tramping, fishing.

38.732971S 177.089739E Hema Atlas Map Ref 20 E14, 21 E2

579 Waikaremoana Motor Camp, Te Urewera National Park
Home Bay at Lake Waikaremoana, adjacent SH38
DOC Te Urewera Visitor Centre Ph (06) 837 3803
teureweravc@doc.govt.nz Bookings Ph (06) 837 3826
Swimming, boating, tramping, fishing.

38.753212S 177.155446E Hema Atlas Map Ref 21 E2

580 Whaitiri Point Rest Area
Roadside at Lake Waikaremoana (SH38)
38.755971S 177.151639E Hema Atlas Map Ref 21 E2

581 Rosie Bay
Lake Waikaremoana, SH38, 10km south of Te Urewera Visitor Centre
DOC Te Urewera Visitor Centre Ph (06) 837 3803
teureweravc@doc.govt.nz
Drinking water is from stream.

38.785846S 177.130892E Hema Atlas Map Ref 21 E2

582 Onepoto Caves Walk Rest Area
Alongside road to Lake Waikaremoana (SH38)
38.798433S 177.1234E Hema Atlas Map Ref 21 F2

583 Tiniroto Lakes and Community Centre Campground
Tiniroto Rd (SH36), Tiniroto: 36km N of SH38
Lake Falls Hotel Ph (06) 863 7019
Basic camping using facilities in community hall.

38.774107S 177.566415E Hema Atlas Map Ref 21 E6

584 Donneraille Park
Along Tiniroto Rd, N of Tiniroto: off SH38 from S or SH2 from N
Gisborne District Council 'Freedom Camping' Ph (06) 867 2049
www.gdc.govt.nz/freedom-camping-permit-request
Overnight Freedom Camping is permitted from Labour weekend to Easter; Permit required - see website for full 'Freedom Camping' details. Overnight tent camping permitted, with own chemical toilet.

38.733654S 177.585975E Hema Atlas Map Ref 21 E6

585 Glen Innis Farmstay
3558 Tiniroto Rd, Hangaroa
Ph (06) 863 7127 Fax (06) 863 7126 j-mcdonald@clear.net.nz
Backpacker accommodation available. Pets by arrangement.

38.709105S 177.61671E Hema Atlas Map Ref 21 E7

North Island Camping Sites — Central North Region

SH35 — OPOTIKI TO GISBORNE

586 Tirohanga Beach Motor Camp
SH35 (Pacific Coast Highway), Tirohanga: E of Opotiki
Ph/Fax (07) 315 7942 tmcamp@xtra.co.nz
www.tirohangabeachmotorcamp.co.nz
My pick for the Opotiki area. Pets by arrangement.

37.98876S 177.349894E — Hema Atlas Map Ref 15 F3

587 Opape Motor Camp
7 Opape Rd, Opape: along SH35 NE of Opotiki
Ph (07) 315 8175 opape.mc@gmail.com
Simple camping in East Coast style.

37.980262S 177.419946E — Hema Atlas Map Ref 15 F3

588 Hawai Bay Camping Ground
SH35, Hawai, NE edge of town
Ph (07) 315 6308
A caretaker may collect fees if they are in attendance.
Just across the road from nice swimming and fishing.

37.921013S 177.530507E — Hema Atlas Map Ref 15 E4

589 Te Kaha Holiday Park
SH35, Te Kaha
Ph/Fax (07) 325 2894 tekahahp@xtra.co.nz
www.tekahaholidaypark.co.nz
Pets by arrangement. Kayak and bike hire.

37.732064S 177.689582E — Hema Atlas Map Ref 15 C6

590 Maungaroa Station
Maungaroa Access Rd, Te Kaha
Ph (07) 325 2727 Fax (07) 325 2776
maungaroa@xtra.co.nz www.maungaroa.co.nz
Lodge accommodation available for 12 people. Horse treks.
Pets by arrangement.

37.752817S 177.787921E — Hema Atlas Map Ref 15 C7

591 Roadside Rest Area
Adjacent SH35, Maraetai Bay

37.726276S 177.694375E — Hema Atlas Map Ref 15 C6

592 Waikawa Point Roadside Rest Area
Adjacent SH35, Waikawa Pt
Day use only, camping no longer permitted.
37.682593S 177.730009E — Hema Atlas Map Ref 15 B6

593 Maraehako Camping Ground
SH35, Maraehako: just N of Whanarua Bay
The essence of East Coast camping with simple amenities and beachside with fishing, swimming and canoeing options. A local Maori family choose to share this magic bay with you, please respect their generosity.

37.674246S 177.803618E — Hema Atlas Map Ref 15 B7

594 Waihau Bay Holiday Park
SH35, NE of Waihau Bay: next to the Kowhai Café
Ph (07) 325 3844 waihaubay@clear.net.nz
The beach is just a stroll across the road, and boat launching is nearby.

37.61544S 177.907375E — Hema Atlas Map Ref 16 B8

595 Te Araroa Holiday Park
SH35, Te Araroa: W of the township
Ph/Fax (06) 864 4873 bill.martin@xtra.co.nz
Nice, quiet and sheltered site even boasting its own movie theatre.

37.606063S 178.314203E — Hema Atlas Map Ref 16 B11

596 Roadside Rest Area
SH35: at turnoff to Ruatoria
37.903261S 178.297996E — Hema Atlas Map Ref 16 E11

597 Waipiro Bay
Kopuaroa Rd from N off SH35 or
Waipiro Rd from S off SH35: Waipiro Bay
Gisborne District Council 'Freedom Camping' Ph (06) 867 2049
www.gdc.govt.nz/freedom-camping-permit-request
Freedom Camping is permitted from Labour weekend to Easter;
Permit required - see website for full 'Freedom Camping' details

38.019371S 178.334661E — Hema Atlas Map Ref 16 G11

598 Roadside Rest Area
Adjacent SH35: 7.5km S of Te Puia Springs
38.113034S 178.294155E — Hema Atlas Map Ref 16 H11

599 Tokomaru Bay
3 areas available for freedom camping: northern end of the bay on Beach Rd, middle of the bay on Mere St, southern end of the bay on Waiotu Rd. www.gdc.govt.nz/freedom-camping
Good fishing and surfing, care required when swimming.

38.135347S 178.315972E — Hema Atlas Map Ref 16 H11

600 Waterfront Rest Area
Adjacent SH35: Tokomaru Bay
38.124655S 178.318314E — Hema Atlas Map Ref 16 H11

601 Mayfair Camping Ground and Cabins
Waitangi St, Tokomaru Bay
Ph/Fax (06) 864 5843
Convenient location near shops and town centre.

38.128845S 178.315574E — Hema Atlas Map Ref 16 H11

602 Anaura Bay Motor Camp
Anaura Bay Rd: take Anaura turnoff from SH35 N of Tolaga Bay
Ph/Fax (06) 862 6380 anaura@farmside.co.nz
Beautiful location right on the beachfront. Fishing, boating and swimming opportunities abound. Eftpos available.

38.24764S 178.316341E — Hema Atlas Map Ref 16 J11

Central North Region — North Island Camping Sites

603 Anaura Bay, Waipare Scenic Reserve
Anaura Rd off SH35: 85km N of Gisborne between Tokomaru Bay and Tolaga Bay
DOC Te Urewera Visitor Centre Ph (06) 837 3803
teureweravc@doc.govt.nz
Closed from Easter to Labour Weekend (Oct); boil any water you collect from stream; maximum stay is 3 weeks; only one dog per site.
38.23304S 178.308328E   Hema Atlas Map Ref 16 J11

604 Kaiaua Beach
Kaiaua Rd, 10km from SH35: signposted about 5km N of Tolaga Bay
Gisborne District Council 'Freedom Camping' Ph (06) 867 2049
www.gdc.govt.nz/freedom-camping-permit-request
Overnight/Freedom Camping is permitted from Labour weekend to Easter; Permit required - see website for full 'Freedom Camping' details.
38.311844S 178.323254E   Hema Atlas Map Ref 22 A13

605 Blue Waters
Tolaga Bay. At the northern end of the bay at the end of Ferneaux St.
Gisborne District Council 'Freedom Camping' Ph (06) 867 2049
www.gdc.govt.nz/freedom-camping-permit-request
Overnight/Freedom Camping is permitted from Labour weekend to Easter; Permit required - see website for full 'Freedom Camping' details. Excellent fishing and swimming. Freedom camping area for self-contained vehicles, starts 9/9 till Easter.
38.362236S 178.305814E   Hema Atlas Map Ref 22 A13

606 Roadside Rest Area
N side of Uawa River SH35 Bridge
Swimming opportunities here.
38.374535S 178.296314E   Hema Atlas Map Ref 22 A13

607 Tolaga Bay Holiday Park
167 Wharf Rd: Just off SH35 2km S of Tolaga Bay township: beside the historic wharf
Ph/Fax (06) 862 6716 tolagabayholidaypark@msn.com
www.holidayparks.co.nz/tolaga
Sheltered beach front location. Store open Christmas to January.
38.382444S 178.316402E   Hema Atlas Map Ref 22 B13

608 Loisel's Beach, Waihau Bay
Waihau Rd, Waihau Beach: off SH35, about 13km S of Tolaga Bay
Gisborne District Council 'Freedom Camping' Ph (06) 867 2049
www.gdc.govt.nz/freedom-camping-permit-request
Freedom Camping is permitted from Labour weekend to Easter; Permit required - see website for full 'Freedom Camping' details.
38.446033S 178.302144E   Hema Atlas Map Ref 22 B13

609 Pouawa Beach
Alongside SH35: right next to the beach
Gisborne District Council 'Freedom Camping' Ph (06) 867 2049
www.gdc.govt.nz/freedom-camping-permit-request
Freedom Camping is permitted from Labour weekend to Easter; Permit required - see website for full 'Freedom Camping' details.
38.615913S 178.177736E   Hema Atlas Map Ref 22 D12

610 Turihaua Beach
Alongside SH35: right next to the beach
Gisborne District Council 'Freedom Camping' Ph (06) 867 2049
www.gdc.govt.nz/freedom-camping-permit-request
Freedom Camping is permitted from Labour weekend to Easter; Permit required - see website for full 'Freedom Camping' details.
38.63017S 178.158555E   Hema Atlas Map Ref 22 D11

611 Turihaua Point
Alongside SH35: right next to the beach
Gisborne District Council 'Freedom Camping' Ph (06) 867 2049
www.gdc.govt.nz/freedom-camping-permit-request
Freedom Camping is permitted from Labour weekend to Easter; Permit required - see website for full 'Freedom Camping' details.
38.63017S 178.158555E   Hema Atlas Map Ref 22 D11

612 Tatapouri By the Sea
516 Whangara Rd: Alongside SH35, Tatapouri
Ph (06) 868 3269 Fax (06) 868 3270 info@tatapouri.com
www.tatapouri.co.nz
38.646478S 178.144916E   Hema Atlas Map Ref 22 D11

613 Makorori Beach Rest Area
Alongside SH35, Makorori Beach
38.650369S 178.126062E   Hema Atlas Map Ref 22 D11

614 Roadside Rest Area
Okitu Beach, just N of Gisborne
38.671015S 178.090367E   Hema Atlas Map Ref 100 C6, 22 E11

615 Waikanae Beach Holiday Park
Grey St, Gisborne: signposted from city centre
Ph (06) 867 5634 info@waikanaebeachtop10.co.nz
www.waikanaebeachtop10.co.nz
Well run, neat and tidy camp right on the beach and the closest to Gisborne city centre. Also close to boat launching, fun parks and the Aquatic Centre.
38.670619S 178.017783E   Hema Atlas Map Ref 99 C2, 100 C3, 22 E10

616 Boulders
Turn off SH2, south of Opotiki and into Otara Rd. Follow to Te Waiti then turn left and follow for 4km.
DOC Te Urewera NP Visitor Centre Ph (06) 837 3803
teureweravc@doc.govt.nz
Drinking water is from stream.
38.12398S 177.392277E   Hema Atlas Map Ref 15 G3

SH2 — OPOTIKI TO WAIROA

617 Roadside Rest Area
Alongside SH2 and the Waioeka River, Waioeka Gorge Scenic Reserve
38.146614S 177.271842E   Hema Atlas Map Ref 15 G2

618 Roadside Rest Area
Alongside SH2 and the Waioeka River, Waioeka Gorge Scenic Reserve
38.280562S 177.350551E   Hema Atlas Map Ref 15 J2

619 Manganuku Roadside Rest Area
Alongside SH2 and the Waioeka River, Waioeka Gorge Scenic Reserve
38.291948S 177.38511E   Hema Atlas Map Ref 15 J3

North Island Camping Sites — Central North Region

620 Manganuku
Adjacent SH2, Waioeka Gorge, Waioeka Gorge Scenic Reserve
DOC Opotiki Area Office Ph (07) 315 1001 opotiki-ao@doc.govt.nz
Self registration system; fishing, walking. Drinking water is from stream.

38.290824S 177.385286E Hema Atlas Map Ref 15 J3

621 Whitikau
Takaputahi Rd (access rd unsealed): Motu Rd off SH2 at Matawai
DOC Opotiki Area Office Ph (07) 315 1001 opotiki-ao@doc.govt.nz
Drinking water is from a stream.

38.119804S 177.588781E Hema Atlas Map Ref 15 G5

622 Roadside Rest Areas
On either side of the road, Waioeka Gorge Scenic Reserve
38.340462S 177.425742E Hema Atlas Map Ref 21 A5

623 Roadside Rest Area
SH2: Papatu Scenic Reserve
38.413703S 177.560812E Hema Atlas Map Ref 21 A6

624 Roadside Rest Area
SH2, Otoko Walkway Reserve
38.462721S 177.731419E Hema Atlas Map Ref 22 B8

625 Roadside Rest Area
SH2: near Ormond
Shade plus nice vistas of vineyards.
38.4897S 177.904948E Hema Atlas Map Ref 22 B9

626 Gisborne Showgrounds Park Motorcamp
20 Main Rd, Makaraka: W of Gisborne on SH2
Ph/Fax (06) 867 529 camp@gisborneshow.co.nz
www.gisborneshow.co.nz

38.650776S 177.982973E Hema Atlas Map Ref 100 A2, 22 D10

627 Morere Hot Springs Camping Ground
SH2: opposite the Morere Hot Pools, halfway between Wairoa & Gisborne.
Ph (06) 837 8792 morere@xtra.co.nz
Sheltered spot next to a lovely bathing stream, with the hot pools just across the road. Native trees and birds.

38.984949S 177.790751E Hema Atlas Map Ref 22 H8

628 Roadside Rest Area
Along Nuhaka Opoutama Rd: S off SH2 towards Mahia Peninsula
Overnight camping is not allowed.

39.067098S 177.798992E Hema Atlas Map Ref 22 J8

629 Roadside Rest Area
Along Nuhaka Opoutama Rd: S off SH2 towards Mahia Peninsula
Overnight camping is not allowed.
39.064619S 177.831052E Hema Atlas Map Ref 22 J8

630 Mahia Beach Motels & Holiday Park
43 Moana Dr, Mahia Beach
Ph (06) 837 5830 mahia.beach.motels@xtra.co.nz
Beachside spot with beautiful bathing and fishing just across the road, and boat launching facilities close by.

39.080323S 177.873651E Hema Atlas Map Ref 22 J9

SH2 — WAIROA TO HASTINGS

631 Riverside Motor Camp
19 Marine Parade, Wairoa: signposted S of bridge
Ph (06) 838 6301 riversidemotorcamp@vodaphone.net.nz
Rated Qualmark four stars this park is a little gem. The river provides good swimming and boating. Powered sites have water and greywater drain on-site. Easy for big rigs.

39.032384S 177.415176E Hema Atlas Map Ref 21 H5

632 Roadside Rest Area
Beside Wairoa River, S of Wairoa
39.040424S 177.386275E Hema Atlas Map Ref 21 H4

633 Roadside Rest Area
Adjoining SH2 & the Mohaka River
Great views of the viaducts and river.
39.073628S 177.127958E Hema Atlas Map Ref 21 J2

634 Waikare River Mouth
Waikare Rd: from SH2 at Putorino turn onto Waikare Rd, then follow the unsealed road for approximately 20min to the road end
DOC Hawke's Bay Regional Visitor Centre Ph (06) 834 3111
hawkesbayvc@doc.govt.nz
Fishing, swimming, boating.

39.164547S 177.080352E Hema Atlas Map Ref 28 A13

635 Roadside Rest Area
Adjacent SH2 & Lake Tutira
39.21704S 176.889343E Hema Atlas Map Ref 28 A12

636 Roadside Rest Area
SH5, N of Te Pohue
38.981555S 176.534073E Hema Atlas Map Ref 28 A10

637 Lake Tutira, Hawke's Bay
Adjacent SH2, Tutira
DOC Hawke's Bay Regional Visitor Centre Ph (06) 834 3111
hawkesbayvc@doc.govt.nz
Fishing, swimming, boating (no motorised craft). Fee by donation.

39.233308S 176.892761E Hema Atlas Map Ref 28 A12

638 Roadside Rest Area
Adjacent SH2, White Pine Bush Scenic Reserve
39.290332S 176.879273E Hema Atlas Map Ref 28 B12

639 Waipatiki Beach Farm Park
498 Waipatiki Rd, Waipatiki Beach: Tangoio Rd off SH2, then Waipatiki Rd
Ph (06) 836 6075 waipatiki@xtra.co.nz
Fax (06) 836 6051 www.waipatikibeachfarmpark.co.nz
Horses allowed with prior arrangement.

39.297559S 176.971055E Hema Atlas Map Ref 28 B13

640 Eskdale Caravan Park
Yule Rd, Eskdale: signposted 4km N from SH5 and SH2 intersection
Ph (06) 836 6864
Very peaceful, shaded and sheltered spot on the banks of the Esk River, yet only 20 minutes from Napier town centre.

39.390269S 176.836796E Hema Atlas Map Ref 28 C12

Central North Region — North Island Camping Sites

641 Glenfalls, Mohaka River
From SH5 turn into Waitara Rd, follow the unsealed road for approximately 10min
DOC Hawke's Bay Regional Visitor Centre Ph (06) 834 3111
hawkesbayvc@doc.govt.nz
Drinking water is from a stream; fishing, swimming, canoeing, rafting; Dogs permitted.
39.143451S 176.672082E — Hema Atlas Map Ref 20 J10

642 Everetts, Mohaka River
From SH5 turn into Waitara Rd, follow the unsealed road for approximately 20min, turn into Auroa Rd & follow to sign
DOC Hawke's Bay Regional Visitor Centre Ph (06) 834 3111
hawkesbayvc@doc.govt.nz
Drinking water is from a stream; fishing, swimming, canoeing, rafting. Not suitable for caravans or motorhomes.
39.087141S 176.705259E — Hema Atlas Map Ref 20 J11

643 Mangatutu Hot Springs, Kaweka Forest Park
From Puketitiri Rd turn right into Pakaututu Rd then left into Makahu Rd, follow to the road end (access road unsealed with river ford)
DOC Hawke's Bay Regional Visitor Centre Ph (06) 834 3111
hawkesbayvc@doc.govt.nz
Drinking water is from a stream; fishing, swimming, tramping, hunting, rafting.
39.18435S 176.454529E — Hema Atlas Map Ref 28 A8

644 Clements Clearing, Kaimanawa Forest Park
27km east of Taupo turn right off SH5 into Taharua Rd and follow for 9.5km, then turn right into Clements Mill Rd.
DOC Tongariro NP Visitor Centre Ph (07) 892 3729
tongarirovc@doc.govt.nz
Drinking water is from a stream; Be aware of fire bans.
38.947456S 176.18447E — Hema Atlas Map Ref 19 G6

645 Clements Roadend, Kaimanawa Forest Park
27km east of Taupo turn right off SH5 into Taharua Rd and follow for 9.5km, then turn right into Clements Mill Rd. 21km to end.
DOC Tongariro NP Visitor Centre Ph (07) 892 3729
tongarirovc@doc.govt.nz
Be aware of fire bans.
38.989425S 176.140605E — Hema Atlas Map Ref 19 G6

646 Army Road, Kaimanawa Forest Park
27km east of Taupo turn right off SH5 into Taharua Rd and follow for 9.5km, then turn right into Clements Mill Rd.
On Clements & Army Rd. 12.5km from start of Clements Rd.
DOC Tongariro NP Visitor Centre Ph (07) 892 3729
tongarirovc@doc.govt.nz
Be aware of fire bans.
38.967979S 176.154809E — Hema Atlas Map Ref 19 G6

647 Kakapo, Kaimanawa Forest Park
27km east of Taupo turn right off SH5 into Taharua Rd and follow for 9.5km, then turn right into Clements Mill Rd.
10km from start of Clements Road.
DOC Tongariro NP Visitor Centre Ph (07) 892 3729
tongarirovc@doc.govt.nz
Drinking water is from a stream; Be aware of fire bans.
38.953988S 176.174251E — Hema Atlas Map Ref 19 G6

648 Te Iringa, Kaimanawa Forest Park
4km from start of Clements Road.
DOC Tongariro NP Visitor Centre Ph (07) 892 3729
tongarirovc@doc.govt.nz
Be aware of fire bans.
38.957197S 176.22056E — Hema Atlas Map Ref 19 G6

649 Bay View Snapper Holiday Park
10 Gill Rd, Bay View: between the beach & SH2, N of Napier
Ph (06) 836 7084 or 0800 287 275 info@snapperpark.co.nz
www.snapperpark.co.nz
Qualmark four star rated park in a sheltered, water's edge location.
39.430886S 176.873475E — Hema Atlas Map Ref 28 C12

650 Bay View Van Park
3 Onehunga Rd, Bay View, Napier. Cnr SH2 & Onehunga Rd, Bay View: N of Napier
Ph/Fax (06) 836 6064 bayviewvanpark@paradise.net.nz
www.bayviewvanpark.co.nz
The park has brand new facilities catering to motorhomes, campervans and caravans. Limited camping sites. Pets by arrangement. Qualmark four star plus. Wireless internet.
39.437125S 176.869713E — Hema Atlas Map Ref 28 D12

651 Affordable Westshore Holiday Park
88 Meeanee Quay, Westshore Napier: signposted off SH2 N of Napier
Ph/Fax (06) 835 9456 westshoreholiday@xtra.co.nz
www.westshoreholidaypark.co.nz
Neat and tidy park close to the beach and an inlet with a wildlife reserve.
39.475593S 176.878134E — Hema Atlas Map Ref 103 B1, 28 D12

652 Kennedy Park Top 10 Resort
11 Storkey St, Napier: signposted from SH2 & SH50 S of Napier
Ph 0800 457 275 info@kennedypark.co.nz www.kennedypark.co.nz
Set in park-like grounds and handy to Napier centre, this park is rated four star plus by Qualmark. Internet.
39.504107S 176.899867E — Hema Atlas Map Ref 103 B1, 28 D12

653 Roadside Rest Area
Several rest areas N of this vicinity between SH2 and the beachfront
This site at the mouth of the Ngaruroro River is favoured by anglers.
39.564028S 176.9228E — Hema Atlas Map Ref 103 A3, 28 E12

654 Clive Motor Camp & Chalets
31 Farndon Rd, Clive: signposted from SH2, N of Clive River
Ph (06) 870 0609 clivemotorcamp@xtra.co.nz
39.580946S 176.911331E — Hema Atlas Map Ref 103 A4, 28 E12

North Island Camping Sites — Lower North Region

655 Clifton Road Reserve
Clifton Rd: beachside en route to Clifton
Freedom Camping for certified self-contained motorhomes, overnight.

39.618777S 176.960064E   Hema Atlas Map Ref 103 A5, 28 F13

656 Te Awanga Holiday Park
52 Kuku Street, Te Awanga: signposted N from Clifton Rd
Ph/Fax (06) 875 0334   teawangaholidaypark@yahoo.co.nz
Right next to the beach for swimming and surfing.

39.633413S 176.986111E   Hema Atlas Map Ref 28 F13

657 Clifton Beach Reserve Motor Camp
495 Clifton Rd, Clifton
Ph (06) 875 0265   cliftoncamp@xtra.co.nz   www.cliftonbeach.co.nz
Magic location, and you can walk to the gannet colony.

39.63865S 176.9989E   Hema Atlas Map Ref 28 F13

658 Hastings Top 10 Holiday Park
610 Windsor Ave, Hastings: signposted off Heretunga St,
en route to Havelock North
Freephone 0508 427 846   info@hastingstop10.co.nz
www.hastingstop10.co.nz

Top 10's usual high standard (four star plus Qualmark rating) and handy to Splash Planet and a picturesque park.

39.648866S 176.860877E   Hema Atlas Map Ref 103 C5, 28 F12

659 Arataki Motels & Holiday Park
139 Arataki Rd, Havelock North: hard to find from the S but signposted from the Napier to Havelock Rd
Ph/Fax (06) 877 7479   arataki.motel.holiday.park@xtra.co.nz
www.aratakimotelandholidaypark.co.nz
The Arataki Honey Centre is just up the road.

39.659771S 176.901354E   Hema Atlas Map Ref 103 B6, 28 F12

660 Ocean Beach Camping Ground
87 Ocean Beach Rd, Ocean Beach: off Waimarama Rd from Havelock North
Ph (06) 874 7814
A caretaker may collect fees if they are in attendance. Handy to a great beach for surfing and fishing.

39.743556S 177.009386E   Hema Atlas Map Ref 28 G13

661 Waimarama Seaside Resort
30 Harper Rd, Waimarama: visible from the main road as you enter Waimarama
Ph (06) 874 6813   Fax (06) 874 6516   ruth.bright@xtra.co.nz
www.escapetowaimaramabeach.co.nz
Handy to a magic beach.

39.816995S 176.990982E   Hema Atlas Map Ref 28 H13

LOWER NORTH REGION

KAPITI ISLAND   PHOTO: CENTRE STAGE

SH1 – WELLINGTON TO SH3	58
SH1 – FROM SH3 TO WAIOURU	60
SH2 – WELLINGTON TO MASTERTON	61
SH2 – MASTERTON TO DANNEVIRKE	63
SH2 – DANNEVIRKE TO HASTINGS	64
SH3 – PALMERSTON NORTH TO WANGANUI	65
SH4 – WANGANUI TO OHAKUNE	66
SH3 – WANGANUI TO HAWERA	66
SH45 – HAWERA TO NEW PLYMOUTH	67
SH3 & SH43 – HAWERA TO TAUMARUNUI	68

SH1 — WELLINGTON TO SH3

662 Wahine Bay
Breaker Bay Rd, Breaker Bay, Wellington
Picturesque parking and picnicking just kilometres from central Wellington and the ferries.

41.342487S 174.820344E   Hema Atlas Map Ref 110 E2, 33 F2

663 Karaka & Scorching Bay Reserves
Karaka Bay Rd, Seatoun Bays, Wellington
Picturesque parking and picnicking just kilometres from central Wellington and the ferries.

41.296871S 174.833176E   Hema Atlas Map Ref 110 E2, 33 F2

664 Picnic Reserves
Shelly Bay Road & Massey Rd, Maupuia, Wellington
Picturesque parking and picnicking just kilometres from central Wellington and the ferries.

41.297453S 174.820497E   Hema Atlas Map Ref 110 E2, 33 F2

665 Capital Gateway Motor Inn
1 Newlands Rd, Newlands, Wellington
Ph (04) 478 7812 or 0800 422 748   Fax (04) 478 1342
capitalgateway@xtra.co.nz   www.capitalgateway.co.nz
10 min drive to Inter Island Ferry Terminal. It's suitable for campervans and big rigs but not for tent camping.

41.231069S 174.810714E   Hema Atlas Map Ref 110 C2, 33 E2

666 Camp Elsdon
18 Raiha St, Porirua: 23km NW of Wellington, off SH1
Ph (04) 237 8987   camp_elsdon@xtra.co.nz   www.campelsdon.co.nz
Functional but not suited to big rigs. Pets by arrangement.

41.137196S 174.827789E   Hema Atlas Map Ref 110 B2, 33 D2

Lower North Region

North Island Camping Sites

667 Aotea Camping Ground
3 Whitford Brown Ave, Porirua:
follow signs NW of Porirua from the Titahi Bay Road
Ph (04) 235 9599 info@aoteacamping.co.nz www.aoteacamping.co.nz
Free local phone calls.
41.120658S 174.867373E   Hema Atlas Map Ref 110 B3, 33 D2

668 Roadside Rest Area
Paremata Rd (SH58), E of Paremata
41.105985S 174.890316E   Hema Atlas Map Ref 33 D2

669 Roadside Rest Area
Paremata Rd (SH58), N of Whitby on Porirua Harbour
41.10609S 174.882166E   Hema Atlas Map Ref 33 D2

670 Motukaraka Point Reserve
East of SH1 at Plimmerton on minor road linking to SH58
Sheltered site with nice views of Pauatahanui Inlet.
41.091982S 174.898793E   Hema Atlas Map Ref 33 C2

671 Roadside Rest Area
SH1, N of Pukerua Bay
41.03017S 174.89733E   Hema Atlas Map Ref 33 C2

672 Roadside Rest Area
SH1, N of Pukerua Bay
Several beachside rest areas.
41.022897S 174.907003E   Hema Atlas Map Ref 33 C3

673 Roadside Rest Area
SH1, N of Pukerua Bay
Several beachside rest areas.
41.021568S 174.909513E   Hema Atlas Map Ref 33 C3

674 Roadside Rest Area
SH1, S of Paekakariki
Several beachside rest areas.
40.997474S 174.942845E   Hema Atlas Map Ref 33 B3

675 Roadside Rest Area
SH1, N of Pukerua Bay
41.00427S 174.930807E   Hema Atlas Map Ref 33 B3

676 Paekakariki Holiday Park
180 Wellington Rd, Paekakariki: signposted W of SH1
Ph (04) 292 8292 Fax (04) 292 8292 bookings@paekakarikiholidaypark.co.nz www.paekakarikiholidaypark.co.nz
This gem of a camp is a nice surprise. It's located within QE2 park with nice walks to the beach, good facilities and plenty of space. Internet.
40.975299S 174.961615E   Hema Atlas Map Ref 33 B3

677 Roadside Rest Area
QE2 Park, Paekakariki: signposted W of SH1
40.973568S 174.961889E   Hema Atlas Map Ref 33 B3

678 Lindale Motor Park
Ventnor Drive, Paraparaumu: SH1, 3km N of Paraparaumu
Ph/Fax (04) 298 8046 lindalemotorpark@xtra.co.nz
Pets by arrangement.
40.907423S 175.017814E   Hema Atlas Map Ref 33 A3

679 Kapiti Holiday Resort
16 Beach Haven Place, Paraparaumu Beach
Ph/Fax (04) 233 1965 prestige.caravans@xtra.co.nz
www.prestigecaravans.co.nz
40.882374S 174.988127E   Hema Atlas Map Ref 33 A3

680 El Rancho
25 Kauri Rd, Waikanae: signposted W of SH1
Ph (04) 902 6287 Fax (04) 902 6289
bookings@elrancho.co.nz www.elrancho.co.nz
Caretaker will collect fees. This site welcomes all. It has good facilites in park-like surrounds and is extremely peaceful. Café on-site. Alcohol-free site.
40.8757S 175.025612E   Hema Atlas Map Ref 33 A4

681 Otaki Forks
14km E of Otaki, on Otaki Gorge Rd, Tararua Forest Park
DOC Wellington Visitor Centre Ph (04) 384 7770
wellingtonvc@doc.govt.nz
Fire ban applies all year. Dogs permitted.
40.880927S 175.222753E   Hema Atlas Map Ref 33 A5

682 Bridge Lodge
3 Otaki Gorge Rd, Otaki:
signposted off SH1 just S of the Otaki River bridge
Ph (06) 364 6667 www.bridgelodge.co.nz
Handy to Tararua Forest Park, and located beside a nice river.
40.774543S 175.144598E   Hema Atlas Map Ref 29 J4

683 Roadside Rest Area
Alongside SH1: S of Otaki
40.773183S 175.144282E   Hema Atlas Map Ref 29 J4

684 Byron's Resort
20 Tasman Rd, Otaki Beach: signposted W of SH1 at Otaki
Ph (06) 364 8121, 0800 800 122 Fax (06) 364 8119
www.byronsresort.co.nz
Nice camp that's tidy and sheltered. On-site restaurant. Spa pool. Internet.
40.740061S 175.117273E   Hema Atlas Map Ref 29 J3

685 Roadside Rest Area
Otaki Beach: W of SH1
Waterside picnic area.
40.738885S 175.114734E   Hema Atlas Map Ref 29 H3

686 Roadside Rest Area
Alongside SH1: approx 2km N of Otaki
40.740917S 175.179049E   Hema Atlas Map Ref 29 H4

60 North Island Camping Sites — Lower North Region

687 Waikawa
9km north of Otaki, on North Manakau Rd, Tararua Forest Park
DOC DOC Wellington Visitor Centre Ph (04) 384 7770
wellingtonvc@doc.govt.nz
Drinking water is from a stream.
40.720884S 175.247121E   Hema Atlas Map Ref 29 H5

688 Tatum Park
820-850 State Hwy 1, Manakau, Levin. W side of SH1:
midway between Levin & Otaki
Ph (06) 362 6799 bookings@tatumpark.co.nz
Fax (06) 362 6502 www.tatumpark.co.nz
Great facilities in a sheltered location that is handy to Wellington. This former Boy Scouts' camp is now available to all. Pets by arrangement.
40.695108S 175.229396E   Hema Atlas Map Ref 29 H4

689 Levin Motorcamp
38 Parker Ave, Levin: signposted from SH57 & SH1
Ph (06) 368 3549 levin.motor.camp@xtra.co.nz
www.levinmotorcamp.co.nz
Pets by arrangment. Qualmark four star. Wireless internet.
40.630046S 175.289818E   Hema Atlas Map Ref 29 G5

690 Roadside Rest Area
E of SH1: on N edge of Levin
40.6145S 175.294978E   Hema Atlas Map Ref 29 G5

691 Roadside Rest Area
SH57: S of Shannon
40.577016S 175.377533E   Hema Atlas Map Ref 29 G6

692 Makerua Rest Area
SH57, N of Makerua
40.508912S 175.473287E   Hema Atlas Map Ref 29 F6

693 Hydrabad Holiday Park
Forest Rd, Waitarere Beach: signposted on entry into the township
Ph (06) 368 4941 hydrabad@paradise.net.nz
www.waitarerebeachcamps.co.nz
Neat and tidy park. Pets by arrangement.
40.553822S 175.204762E   Hema Atlas Map Ref 29 G4

694 Waitarere Beach Motor Camp
133 Park Ave, Waitarere Beach
Ph (06) 368 8732 hydrabad@paradise.net.nz
www.waitarerebeachcamps.co.nz
Next to the beach. Pets by arrangement.
40.547258S 175.199303E   Hema Atlas Map Ref 29 F4

695 Roadside Rest Area
SH1: on the S bank of the Manawatu River
40.517067S 175.276521E   Hema Atlas Map Ref 29 F5

696 Foxton Beach Motor Camp
1 Holben Parade, Foxton Beach: off SH1 at Foxton
Ph/Fax (06) 363 8211 foxtonbeachmotorcamp@yahoo.co.nz
This site is handy to the beach, with a children's playground and tennis courts. Petanque court. Pets by arrangement.
40.465132S 175.222577E   Hema Atlas Map Ref 29 F4

697 Foxton North Roadside Rest Area
SH1: N of Foxton. On the right as you enter Foxton from the N. Access just off Victoria St.
Picnic tables, no trees.
40.465114S 175.288528E   Hema Atlas Map Ref 29 E5

698 Foxton Straights Roadside Rest Area
SH1: N of Foxton.
Right beside the highway, so can be noisy. Local information board, tables, shade.
40.419383S 175.305376E   Hema Atlas Map Ref 29 E5

699 Himatangi Beach Holiday Park
30 Koputara Rd, Himatangi Beach: off SH1 at Himatangi
Ph (06) 329 9575 info@himatangibeachholidaypark.co.nz
Fax (06) 329 9576 www.himatangibeachholidaypark.co.nz
Pets by arrangement. New cabins, upgraded bathrooms.
40.369494S 175.234132E   Hema Atlas Map Ref 29 D4

700 Himatangi North Roadside Rest Area
Adjacent SH1: N of SH56 intersection
Small rest area close to the highway, can be noisy. Nice views across grassy paddocks, handful of chickens call it home. Table, shade.
40.339705S 175.337668E   Hema Atlas Map Ref 29 D5

SH1 – FROM SH3 TO WAIOURU

701 Marton Motor Camp
Maunder St, Marton: off Signal St, signposted at N end of town
Ph (06) 327 8590
A caretaker may collect fees if they are in attendance. A nice little spot with established trees in sheltered location next to the town's gardens.
40.066215S 175.377617E   Hema Atlas Map Ref 29 A6

702 Hunterville Rest Area 1.7
South of Hunterville on SH1
www.horizons.govt.nz/getting-people-places/planning-and-road-safety/feeling-tired-while-driving-pull-over-and-take-a-break
Large park-like rest area on the northern edge of Hunterville, just by the monument to the Huntaway dog. Lots of room, plenty of shade trees.
39.9361S 175.569103E   Hema Atlas Map Ref 26 J12

703 Roadside Rest Area
Adjacent SH1, Queens Park, Hunterville: E of SH1 at N end of Hunterville
Shade, shelter and picnic tables - it's a nice spot right next to SH1 and handy to Hunterville's restaurants and cafes.
39.934344S 175.569624E   Hema Atlas Map Ref 26 J13

704 Vinegar Hill (Putai Ngahere Reserve)
Putai Ngahere Reserve: near junction of SH1 & SH54
39.934399S 175.641103E   Hema Atlas Map Ref 27 J1

Lower North Region — North Island Camping Sites

705 Vinegar Hill Rest Area 54.1
South of Vinegar Hill on SH3
www.horizons.govt.nz/getting-people-places/planning-and-road-safety/feeling-tired-while-driving-pull-over-and-take-a-break

Large free-camping spot right beside the Rangitikei River. Plenty of room, but road is rutted and uneven. Some secluded areas, be aware of personal security.

39.934339S 175.641369E   Hema Atlas Map Ref 27 J1

706 Ohingaiti Rest Area 1.6
North of Vinegar Hill on SH1
www.horizons.govt.nz/getting-people-places/planning-and-road-safety/feeling-tired-while-driving-pull-over-and-take-a-break

A new rest area with views up to the railway viaduct overhead. No facilities.

39.871233S 175.681442E   Hema Atlas Map Ref 26 H13

707 Roadside Rest Area
Makohine Viaduct, W of SH1
39.871246S 175.681428E   Hema Atlas Map Ref 27 H1

708 Roadside Rest Area
Just N of Makohine Viaduct, E of SH1
Splendid views of the Rangitikei River.
39.868477S 175.69457E   Hema Atlas Map Ref 27 H2

709 Mangaweka South Rest Area 1.5
South of Mangaweka on SH1
www.horizons.govt.nz/getting-people-places/planning-and-road-safety/feeling-tired-while-driving-pull-over-and-take-a-break

Set above Mangaweka with expansive and truly impressive views over the Rangitikei River. Picnic table.

39.827928S 175.781506E   Hema Atlas Map Ref 27 G2

710 Mangaweka Campgrounds
Ruahine Rd, Mangaweka. 1km E of SH1, Mangaweka Mangaweka Adventure Company
Ph/Fax (06) 382 5744 info@mangaweka.co.nz www.mangaweka.co.nz

Sheltered and tranquil spot in a magic location with boating, canoeing, rafting and swimming options nearby.

39.809693S 175.807137E   Hema Atlas Map Ref 27 G3

711 Kawhatau
Follow the Kauaeranga Valley Rd from Thames for 8km to the new visitor centre, camp is 3km north beside river.
DOC Whanganui Area Office Ph (06) 349 2100
WhanganuiArea@doc.govt.nz

39.787192S 176.044312E   Hema Atlas Map Ref 27 G5

712 Mangaweka North Roadside Rest Area
Adjacent SH1: N of Mangaweka & S of Taihape.
Easier access when travelling south.

At the top of the hill, with amazing views. Plaque here dedicated to the engineering expertise required to complete SH1. Picnic tables.

39.767817S 175.800316E   Hema Atlas Map Ref 27 G2

713 Roadside Rest Area
Adjacent SH1: approximately 8km S of Taihape
Picnic tables and shade, separated from the highway by a garden.
39.746554S 175.835394E   Hema Atlas Map Ref 27 G3

714 Taihape Riverview Holiday Park
Old Abattoir Rd, Taihape: 3km N of Taihape off SH1
Ph/Fax (06) 388 0718 taihape.riverview.holidaypark@xtra.co.nz

Don't be put off by the industrial area nearby. Pets by arrangement.

39.659388S 175.785536E   Hema Atlas Map Ref 27 F2

715 Hautapu River Bridge Rest Area 1.2
North of Turangarere on SH1
www.horizons.govt.nz/getting-people-places/planning-and-road-safety/feeling-tired-while-driving-pull-over-and-take-a-break

Picnic table, set back slightly from the road, tucked in behind trees.
39.579992S 175.722472E   Hema Atlas Map Ref 26 E14

716 Roadside Rest Area
Titoki Point, S of Waiouru: E of SH1
Picnic table in picturesque setting, with trees and a stream.
39.543136S 175.683704E   Hema Atlas Map Ref 27 D2

717 Roadside Rest Area
Rangitikei River Bridge Reserve, Taihape-Napier Road
Waterside picnic area.
39.486302S 176.035167E   Hema Atlas Map Ref 27 D5

718 Roadside Rest Area
Taruarau River Bridge Reserve, Taihape-Napier Road
Waterside picnic area.
39.434048S 176.225473E   Hema Atlas Map Ref 27 C6

719 Kuripapango (Ox Bow)
Kaweka Forest Park 1 hour 45 min south of Napier. From SH2 west of Dannevirke follow Maharahara Rd, then Kumeti Rd and follow to end.
DOC Hawkes Bay Visitor Centre Ph (06) 834 3111
hawkesbayvc@doc.govt.nz

Drinking water is from a stream; fishing, rafting.

39.38609S 176.332108E   Hema Atlas Map Ref 27 C7

720 Lawrence, Kaweka Forest Park
From Napier-Taihape Rd turn into Lawrence Rd, follow to the road end (access rd unsealed)
DOC Hawkes Bay Visitor Centre Ph (06) 834 3111
hawkesbayvc@doc.govt.nz

Drinking water is from a stream; tramping, fishing, swimming, 4WD access to campsite.

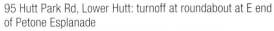

39.371298S 176.438745E   Hema Atlas Map Ref 28 C8

SH2 — WELLINGTON TO MASTERTON

721 Wellington Top 10 Holiday Park
95 Hutt Park Rd, Lower Hutt: turnoff at roundabout at E end of Petone Esplanade
Ph (04) 568 5913 or 0800 488 872 info@huttpark.co.nz
www.huttpark.co.nz

Handy to both Wellington and the Hutt Valley and an ideal spot to await, or recover from, a Cook Strait ferry crossing. Internet. Qualmark four star plus. Internet access.

41.235781S 174.910267E   Hema Atlas Map Ref 110 D3, 33 E3

North Island Camping Sites — Lower North Region

722 Catchpool Valley, Rimutaka Forest Park
Coast Rd, 10km S of Wainuiomata
DOC Wellington Conservation Information Centre
Ph (04) 472 7356 wellingtonvc@doc.govt.nz

Gates open 8am – 8pm summer & 8am – 6pm winter; Dogs permitted on a leash. A pretty setting with a safe stream for paddling yet only one hour from downtown Wellington.

41.351972S 174.923074E   Hema Atlas Map Ref 33 F3

723 Graces Stream
12km south of Wainuiomata, off SH2 via Hutt Valley
DOC Wellington Visitor Centre Ph (04) 384 7770
wellingtonvc@doc.govt.nz

Drinking water from a stream. Gates open summer 8am - 8pm; winter 8am - 6pm

41.348392S 174.926928E   Hema Atlas Map Ref 33 F3

724 Corner Creek
45 minutes from Featherston, along Western Lake Road
DOC Wellington Visitor Centre Ph (04) 384 7770
wellingtonvc@doc.govt.nz

Dogs permitted, must be on leash at all times.

41.373658S 175.03885E   Hema Atlas Map Ref 33 G4

725 Roadside Rest Area
SH2: S of Upper Hutt, alongside the Hutt River
41.119893S 175.043089E   Hema Atlas Map Ref 111 B5, 33 D4

726 Harcourt Holiday Park
43 Akatarawa Rd, Upper Hutt: 4km N of Upper Hutt, signposted from SH2
Ph (04) 526 7400 Fax (04) 526 7401
harcourtholidaypark@xtra.co.nz www.harcourtholidaypark.co.nz

Plenty of shade and shelter, and adjoining a major park with established trees and gardens. Qualmark four star. Playground and toddler's pool. Internet.

41.100745S 175.093008E   Hema Atlas Map Ref 33 C4

727 Rimutaka Summit Rest Area
SH2, Rimutaka Forest Park: 555m above sea level

41.114737S 175.23198E   Hema Atlas Map Ref 33 D5

728 Roadside Rest Area
SH2: E side of Rimutakas, near Featherston
41.113519S 175.312031E   Hema Atlas Map Ref 33 D6

729 Bucks Road
15 min from Featherston, via Wakefield St, Underhill Rd then Bucks Rd to end.
DOC Wellington Visitor Centre Ph (04) 384 7770
wellingtonvc@doc.govt.nz

Lock your car and take valuables with you.
Drinking water is from a stream; Dogs permitted

41.065148S 175.353355E   Hema Atlas Map Ref 33 C6

730 Roadside Rest Area
SH53: alongside Ruamahanga River, NW of Martinborough
Swimming and picnicking spot.
41.201972S 175.442758E   Hema Atlas Map Ref 34 E7

731 Martinborough Village Camping
10 Dublin St West. Cnr Princes & Dublin Sts, Martinborough: signposted from SH53 on E side of town
Ph (06) 306 8946 www.martinboroughcamping.com

A caretaker may collect fees if they are in attendance. Located right beside Martinborough's swimming pool. Bike hire. Qualmark four star. Internet.

41.216053S 175.451884E   Hema Atlas Map Ref 33 E7

732 Lake Ferry Holiday Park
25-39 Lake Ferry Rd
Ph (06) 307 7873 lakeferry@wise.net.nz
www.lakeferryholidaypark.co.nz

Situated on the shores of Lake Onoke with swimming and boating at your back door.

41.390911S 175.145066E   Hema Atlas Map Ref 33 G4

733 Putangirua Pinnacles
Whatarangi Rd, Putangirua Pinnacles Scenic Reserve: off Lake Ferry Rd
DOC Wellington Visitor Centre Ph (04) 384 7770
wellingtonvc@doc.govt.nz

Dogs permitted on a leash.

41.449841S 175.224598E   Hema Atlas Map Ref 33 G5

734 Roadside Rest Area
W of SH2, S end of Greytown
Nice sheltered garden for a picnic.

41.089557S 175.450124E   Hema Atlas Map Ref 33 C7

735 Greytown Camp Ground
Memorial Park, Kuratawhiti St, Greytown: W of SH2, N end of town
Ph (06) 304 9837

41.075971S 175.459007E   Hema Atlas Map Ref 34 C7

736 Waiohine Gorge, Tararua Forest Park
Waiohine Gorge Rd, Tararua Forest Park: Swamp Rd off SH2, then Moffats Rd, then Josephs Rd, then Waiohine Gorge Rd; 18km NW of Greytown
DOC Wellington Visitor Centre Ph (04) 384 7770
wellingtonvc@doc.govt.nz

Dogs permitted on a leash; Drinking water is from a stream.

40.996316S 175.390542E   Hema Atlas Map Ref 33 B7

737 Carterton Holiday Park
198 Belvedere Rd, Carterton: W of SH2, N end of town
Ph (06) 379 8267 cartertonholidaypark@contact.net.nz
www.cartertondc.co.nz/caravanpark

Qualmark four star plus.

41.019156S 175.522795E   Hema Atlas Map Ref 34 C8

738 Holdsworth, Tararua Forest Park
Mt Holdsworth Rd, Tararua Forest Park: Norfolk Rd off SH2 at Waingawa, then left into Mt Holdsworth Rd; 15km W of Masterton
DOC Wellington Visitor Centre Ph (04) 384 7770
wellingtonvc@doc.govt.nz

Dogs permitted on a leash.

40.907115S 175.481147E   Hema Atlas Map Ref 34 B7

Lower North Region — North Island Camping Sites 63

739 Mawley Park Motor Camp
15 Oxford St, Masterton: N of bridge W of SH2 at N end of town
Ph/Fax (06) 378 6454 jclarke@contact.net.nz
A popular camp that is nice and handy to a major swimming complex, QE2 Park, gardens and play areas.
40.944241S 175.667444E Hema Atlas Map Ref 34 B9

740 Castlepoint Holiday Park & Motels
Jetty Rd, Castlepoint: follow Masterton Castlepoint Rd from Masterton to Castlepoint; beachside E of main road at N end of Castlepoint
Ph (06) 372 6705 holiday@castlepoint.co.nz www.castlepoint.co.nz
Simple camping in a stunning beachside location, with surfing, boating, swimming and fishing at your doorstep. Playground. Internet.
40.895528S 176.218457E Hema Atlas Map Ref 34 A13

SH2 – MASTERTON TO DANNEVIRKE

741 Roadside Rest Area
W of SH2: N of Masterton
40.848855S 175.634973E Hema Atlas Map Ref 34 A9

742 Roadside Rest Area
E of SH2: N of Masterton
40.826597S 175.625843E Hema Atlas Map Ref 34 A9

743 Kiriwhakapapa, Tararua Forest Park
End of Kiriwhakapapa Rd, Tararua Forest Park:
turn off SH2 16km N of Masterton
DOC Wellington Visitor Centre Ph (04) 384 7770
wellingtonvc@doc.govt.nz
Dogs permitted on a leash; Drinking water is from a stream.
40.80826S 175.545974E Hema Atlas Map Ref 34 A8

744 Miller's Reserve Roadside Rest Area
W of SH2: N of Mt Bruce National Wildlife Centre, 8.5km S of Eketahuna
40.705816S 175.655757E Hema Atlas Map Ref 31 H2

745 Eketahuna Camping
Stout St, Eketahuna: off SH2 at Bridge St, into Stanley St, into Stout St
Ph (06) 375 8587
A caretaker may collect fees if they are in attendance.
A simple, but nice, camp in a lovely riverside location.
40.651835S 175.703132E Hema Atlas Map Ref 31 H2

746 Alfredton Domain Rest Area
Alfredton Rd (SH52), Alfredton: E of SH2 at Eketahuna
Alfredton Domain Board Ph (06) 375 8440
40.682654S 175.857591E Hema Atlas Map Ref 31 H4

747 Ekatahuna North Roadside Rest Area
Adjacent SH2: N of Eketahuna
A pretty rest area with tables, plenty of shade and a stream at the northern end.
40.566868S 175.737587E Hema Atlas Map Ref 31 G3

748 Pahiatua South Rest Area 2.4
South of Pahiatua on SH2
www.horizons.govt.nz/getting-people-places/planning-and-road-safety/feeling-tired-while-driving-pull-over-and-take-a-break
Memorial and information board offer intersting local history. Table, shade, entry when travelling south.
40.473383S 175.821081E Hema Atlas Map Ref 31 F3

749 Carnival Park Campground
Glasgow St, Pahiatua: Halls Rd off SH2, then turn left into Glasgow St; 1km W of SH2 at S end of Pahiatua
Ph/Fax (06) 376 6340
An unexpected gem set in five acres of park.
40.460401S 175.827575E Hema Atlas Map Ref 31 F3

750 Woodville Domain Camping Area
Signposted from SH2 at N end of town, E of SH2
A bit public and austere, but very cheap.
40.339219S 175.868651E Hema Atlas Map Ref 31 D4

751 Ashhurst Domain
Napier Road, Ashhurst. Ashhurst Domain, Ashhurst: cnr of SH3 and Cambridge Ave
Ph (06) 326 8203
A caretaker may collect fees if they are in attendance.
40.299347S 175.753204E Hema Atlas Map Ref 31 D3

752 Totara Reserve/Camp Rangi Woods
Pohangina Valley East Rd, Totara Reserve
Ph (06) 326 9310
40.120607S 175.852063E Hema Atlas Map Ref 31 B4

753 Piripiri
Turn off SH3 at Ashhurst, follow the Pohangina Valley East Road, campsite is on the left just before the bridge
DOC Whanganui Area Office Ph (06) 349 2100
WhanganuiArea@doc.govt.nz
Drinking water from a stream.
40.052417S 175.937411E Hema Atlas Map Ref 30 A11

754 Roadside Rest Area
Adjacent SH2, S side: 2km N of Woodville
40.338408S 175.892798E Hema Atlas Map Ref 31 D4

755 Pull Off Area
SH3, W of Woodville
Several Pull Off areas along this stretch.
40.309303S 175.775764E Hema Atlas Map Ref 31 D3

756 Pull Off Area
SH3, W of Woodville
Several Pull Off areas along this stretch.
40.318085S 175.800527E Hema Atlas Map Ref 31 D3

757 Barneys Point Rest Area
SH3, W of Woodville
40.317889S 175.814848E Hema Atlas Map Ref 31 D3

North Island Camping Sites — Lower North Region

758 — Pull Off Areas (2)
SH3, W of Woodville
Several Pull Off areas along this stretch.
40.324819S 175.816599E — Hema Atlas Map Ref 31 D3

759 — Kumeti, Ruahine Forest Park
From SH2 west of Dannevirke turn into Umatoaroa Rd, then left into Top Grass Rd, then right into Tamaki West Rd, follow to the road end
DOC Hawkes Bay Regional Visitor Centre Ph (06) 834 3111
hawkesbayvc@doc.govt.nz
Drinking water is from a stream; tramping.
40.173357S 175.978869E — Hema Atlas Map Ref 31 B5

760 — Dannevirke Holiday Park
29 George St, Dannevirke: signposted at N end of town, E of SH2
Ph/Fax (06) 374 7625 dannevirkeholidaypark@xtra.co.nz
Simple, but nice, park set in sheltered park-like grounds next to a scenic reserve with lots of ducks and wildlife for the children.
40.207889S 176.11068E — Hema Atlas Map Ref 31 C6

761 — Akitio Beach Camping Ground
The Esplanade, Akitio Beach: Weber Rd from Dannevirke, then Route 52 to Waione, then River Rd to Akitio; 1 hour east of Dannevirke
Ph (06) 374 3450 akitobeachstore@wizviz.net.nz
Small dogs permitted.
40.620887S 176.414746E — Hema Atlas Map Ref 32 G8

762 — Herbertville Motor Camp
15 Seaview Rd, Herbertville: Weber Rd from Dannevirke, then Route 52 from Weber to Wimbledon, then Herbertville Rd to Herbertville; 68km east of Dannevirke
Ph (06) 374 3446 herbertvillecamp@xtra.co.nz
40.490724S 176.558699E — Hema Atlas Map Ref 32 F10

SH2 — DANNEVIRKE TO HASTINGS

763 — Wahi Pai Reserve North Entrance
SH2, N of Dannevirke
40.186141S 176.12152E — Hema Atlas Map Ref 31 C6

764 — Roadside Rest Area
E of SH2: N of Dannevirke
40.164759S 176.140069E — Hema Atlas Map Ref 31 B6

765 — Norsewood South Rest Area 2.1
South of Norsewood on SH2
www.horizons.govt.nz/getting-people-places/planning-and-road-safety/feeling-tired-while-driving-pull-over-and-take-a-break
Alongside SH2, with farmland at its edges. Lots of trees. Picnic table.
40.164861S 176.140247E — Hema Atlas Map Ref 31 B7

766 — Roadside Rest Area With Camping
ANZAC Park, adjacent SH2 4km N of Norsewood
Casual camping allowed. Shaded & sheltered, with access to a pretty stream.
40.056018S 176.223815E — Hema Atlas Map Ref 31 A7

767 — Roadside Rest Area
Adjoining SH2: W of Waipukurau
39.982933S 176.477784E — Hema Atlas Map Ref 32 A9

768 — Waipukurau Holiday Park
River Tce, Waipukurau: adjoining SH2, N end of town, next to Tukituki River
Ph (06) 858 8184 ypukholidaypark@xtra.co.nz
39.991904S 176.557277E — Hema Atlas Map Ref 32 A10

769 — Beach Road Holiday Park
566 Beach Rd, Porangahau Beach:
Porangahau Rd from SH2 at Waipukurau
Ph/Fax (06) 855 5281
40.299817S 176.65617E — Hema Atlas Map Ref 32 D11

770 — Te Paerahi Beach
Cnr Te Paerahi St & Puketauhinu Pl, Porangahau:
Porangahau Rd from SH2 at Waipukurau
Central Hawke's Bay District Council 'Freedom Camping' (06) 857 8060
www.chbdc.govt.nz/freedom-camping
Check website or phone, as camps may be closed. If permitted, campers must notify the Council's Bylaw Officer of their name, address and contact telephone number as well as their intended camp spot and length of stay.
40.300669S 176.666119E — Hema Atlas Map Ref 32 D11

771 — Blackhead Beach Camping Ground
McHardy Pl, Blackhead Beach: from Waipukurau take Farm Rd, then Motere Rd, then Long Range Rd; or from Waipawa take Pourerere Rd, then Long Range Rd
Ph (06) 857 7335
Pets by arrangement – cats only, no dogs.
40.171703S 176.825956E — Hema Atlas Map Ref 32 C12

772 — River's Edge Holiday Park
Harker St, Waipawa: adjoining SH2, S end of town
Ph (06) 857 8976 paddy.mccloskey@paradise.net.nz
www.riversedgeholidaypark.co.nz
Next to Waipawa's Centennial Swimming Pool and the Waipawa River.
39.945414S 176.589318E — Hema Atlas Map Ref 28 J9

773 — Pourerere Beach
Pourerere Rd, Pourerere Beach: take Pourerere Rd from Waipawa
Central Hawke's Bay District Council 'Freedom Camping' (06) 857 8060
www.chbdc.govt.nz/freedom-camping
Check website or phone, as camps may be closed. Where signposted – permit required. Campers must notify the Council's Bylaw Officer of their name, address and contact telephone number as well as their intended camp spot and length of stay. Fee applies 17 Dec to 6 Feb.
40.099567S 176.868954E — Hema Atlas Map Ref 32 B13

774 — Aramoana Beach
S from Pourerere: take Pourerere Rd from Waipawa
Central Hawke's Bay District Council 'Freedom Camping' (06) 857 8060
www.chbdc.govt.nz/freedom-camping
Check website or phone, as camps may be closed. Fully self-contained motorhomes only at signposted area S end of car park.
40.149892S 176.845869E — Hema Atlas Map Ref 32 B12

Lower North Region — North Island Camping Sites

775 Kairakau Beach
N end of Beach Rd, Kairakau Beach: from Waipawa take Pourerere Rd, then River Rd, then Elsthorpe Rd then Kairakau Rd
Central Hawke's Bay District Council 'Freedom Camping' (06) 857 8060
www.chbdc.govt.nz/freedom-camping

Check website or phone, as camps may be closed. Fully self-contained motorhomes only, in area signposted. No other camping permitted.

39.941774S 176.929604E   Hema Atlas Map Ref 28 J12

SH3 — PALMERSTON NORTH TO WANGANUI

776 Palmerston North Holiday Park
133 Dittmer Drive, Palmerston North: signposted off Fitzherbert St East
Ph/Fax (06) 358 0349 www.holidayparks.co.nz/palmerstonnorth

Close to the aquatic centre for swimming, Victoria Esplanade Gardens and the Manawatu River. Wireless internet.

40.37172S 175.609039E   Hema Atlas Map Ref 105 C3, 30 E8

777 Feilding Holiday Park
5 Arnott St, Feilding: N side of Feilding, signposted off Kimbolton Rd
Ph/Fax (06) 323 5623 info@feildingholidaypark.co.nz www.feildingholidaypark.co.nz

Sheltered park in well-established grounds.

40.209075S 175.591386E   Hema Atlas Map Ref 29 C7

778 Memorial Lookout Rest Area 3.4
South of Sanson on SH3
www.horizons.govt.nz/getting-people-places/planning-and-road-safety/feeling-tired-while-driving-pull-over-and-take-a-break

Picnic table and amazing views in every direction.
40.240144S 175.487781E   Hema Atlas Map Ref 29 C6

779 Cheltenham Rest Area 54.3
South of Cheltenham on SH54
www.horizons.govt.nz/getting-people-places/planning-and-road-safety/feeling-tired-while-driving-pull-over-and-take-a-break

A pretty rest area with little bridges to a fenced off area (no dogs allowed) of gardens, picnic tables and the local War Memorial.
40.138806S 175.660756E   Hema Atlas Map Ref 30 B8

780 Stormy Point Lookout Rest Area 54.2
North of Waituna West on SH54
www.horizons.govt.nz/getting-people-places/planning-and-road-safety/feeling-tired-while-driving-pull-over-and-take-a-break

Not signposted as a rest area, but the panoramic view and viewing platform are worth a stop.
40.004517S 175.640167E   Hema Atlas Map Ref 30 A8

781 Bridge Motor Lodge
2 Bridge St, Bulls: E end of Bulls
Ph (06) 322 0894 bullsmotel@infogen.net.nz

Sheltered riverside location. Small dogs by arrangement.

40.184739S 175.387209E   Hema Atlas Map Ref 29 B6

782 Bulls by Rangitikei River Bridge Rest Area 3.3
South of Bulls on SH3
www.horizons.govt.nz/getting-people-places/planning-and-road-safety/feeling-tired-while-driving-pull-over-and-take-a-break

Tables, shade, but right on the roadside and can be very noisy. A short walk to Rangitikei River can be muddy.
40.184744S 175.386942E   Hema Atlas Map Ref 29 B6

783 Duddings Lake Motorcamp
1525 Bulls/Turakina Hwy (SH3): signposted approx 19km W of Bulls
Ph/Fax (06) 327 8127 duddingslake@clear.net.nz

A fabulous location for a family break with good facilities and sheltered with its own small lake. On-site caravans.

40.099568S 175.282512E   Hema Atlas Map Ref 29 A5

784 Turakina Rest Area 3.2
S of Turakina on SH3, just S of Wanganui Rd to Marton.
Picnic table and shade, set away from roadside, with pleasant views over farmland.
40.057965S 175.218798E   Hema Atlas Map Ref 29 A4

785 Koitiata Camping Ground
Beach Rd, Koitiata: signposted S of SH3, E of Turakina Valley Rd intersection
Custodian (06) 327 3770

A caretaker may collect fees if they are in attendance. Compact, clean and tidy spot with access to the beach across the road. 8 powered sites and lots of unpowered sites. Internet.

40.071018S 175.139766E   Hema Atlas Map Ref 29 A4

786 Whangaehu Hill Rest Area 3.1
SH3, N of Whangaehu, S of Wanganui
www.horizons.govt.nz/getting-people-places/planning-and-road-safety/feeling-tired-while-driving-pull-over-and-take-a-break

Picnic table, back from the road, shade from a single pine tree.
39.998403S 175.16865E   Hema Atlas Map Ref 26 J9

787 Wiritoa Lake Reserve Rest Area
Kaitake Rd: signposted approx 6km E of Wanganui off SH3
Lakeside picnic spot, with opportunities for boating, swimming and canoeing.

39.972105S 175.090503E   Hema Atlas Map Ref 26 J8

788 Scoutlands
316 Kaitake Rd: further along from the Wiritoa Lake Reserve
Ph (06) 348 8618
Lakeside camping spot, that is sheltered and quiet, yet close to Wanganui.

39.977307S 175.0846E   Hema Atlas Map Ref 26 J8

789 Putiki Rest Area
SH3, S of Wikitoria Drive, Putiki
www.horizons.govt.nz/getting-people-places/planning-and-road-safety/feeling-tired-while-driving-pull-over-and-take-a-break
39.949856S 175.053678E   Hema Atlas Map Ref 26 J8, 109 D4

790 Bignell St Motel & Caravan Park
86 Bignell St, Wanganui: follow the signs to Castlecliff from SH3, at E side of Wanganui
Ph 0800 244 635 Fax (06) 344 2011

Budget camping and long-stay permanent accommodation. Pets by arrangement.

39.946159S 175.018187E   Hema Atlas Map Ref 109 D3, 26 J8

North Island Camping Sites — Lower North Region

791 Avro Motel & Caravan Park
36 Alma Rd, Wanganui: S of the racecourse
Ph (06) 345 5279 bookings@wanganuiaccommodation.co.nz
www.wanganuiaccommodation.co.nz

The handiest to the city centre. Each powered site has its own toilet and shower, which is a nice touch. Internet.

39.939374S 175.031587E Hema Atlas Map Ref 109 C3, 26 J8

792 Castlecliff Seaside Holiday Park
1A Rangiora St, Castlecliff: signposted S of Wanganui off SH3 at Eastern entrance to Wanganui
Ph (06) 344 2227, 0800 254 947 tokiwipark@xtra.co.nz
www.castlecliffholidaypark.co.nz

Seaside 'Wanganui style': you have to go through an industrial area to get there, but the camp is good and tidy. Spa, sauna, internet. Pets by arrangement.

39.937495S 174.978673E Hema Atlas Map Ref 109 C1, 25 J7

SH4 — WANGANUI TO OHAKUNE

793 Whanganui River Top 10 Holiday Park
460 Somme Pde, Upper Aramoho, Wanganui: just follow the W bank of the river inland 5km
Ph (06) 343 8402, 0800 27 26 64 wrivertop10@xtra.co.nz
www.wrivertop10.co.nz

Sheltered and shady park backing onto the river for swimming and boating. Internet. Qualmark four star plus. Spa. Kayak and jetski hire.

39.895072S 175.088894E Hema Atlas Map Ref 109 A6, 26 H8

794 Roadside Rest Area
Riverbank Rd on S side of Whanganui River, opposite Kaimatira Rd
39.897228S 175.090315E Hema Atlas Map Ref 109 A6, 26 H8

795 Roadside Rest Area
Adjacent Whanganui River Rd at the summit of Aromoana: about 2km N of SH4

Extensive views of the Whanganui River Valley from this point.

39.829044S 175.138302E Hema Atlas Map Ref 26 G9

796 Aberfeldy Hill North Side Rest Area
SH4, NE of Wanganui
39.788061S 175.242802E Hema Atlas Map Ref 26 G10

797 Roadside Rest Area
Adjacent Whanganui River Rd: about 23km N of SH4
39.727907S 175.139629E Hema Atlas Map Ref 26 F9

798 Kauika Campsite
Adjacent Whanganui River Rd: about 45km N of SH4 or 16km S of Pipiriki
Caretaker, Winiata Tapa Ph (06) 342 8762

39.585157S 175.109475E Hema Atlas Map Ref 26 E9

799 Jerusalem Rest Area
Adjacent Whanganui River Rd, Jerusalem: about 50km N of SH4 or 11km S of Pipiriki
39.553836S 175.079607E Hema Atlas Map Ref 26 D8

800 Pipiriki Rest Area
Adjacent Whanganui River Rd, Pipiriki: about 25km from SH4 at Raetihi
39.478767S 175.043314E Hema Atlas Map Ref 26 C8

801 Raetihi North Roadside Rest Area
SH4, N of Raetihi
39.424489S 175.281821E Hema Atlas Map Ref 26 C10

802 Raetihi Holiday Park
10 Parapara Rd, Raetihi
Ph 0800 408 888 or (06) 385 4176 info@raetihiholidaypark.com
Fax (06) 385 4176 www.raetihiholidaypark.com

Clean and functional. Wireless internet. Pets by arrangement.

39.430397S 175.282424E Hema Atlas Map Ref 26 C10

803 Raetihi South Roadside Rest Area
SH4, S of Raetihi
www.horizons.govt.nz/getting-people-places/planning-and-road-safety/feeling-tired-while-driving-pull-over-and-take-a-break

Table, shade, tucked away from the road, beside the cemetery.

39.432971S 175.282977E Hema Atlas Map Ref 26 C10

804 Ore Ore Rest Area 4.4
North of Ore Ore on SH4
www.horizons.govt.nz/getting-people-places/planning-and-road-safety/feeling-tired-while-driving-pull-over-and-take-a-break

Tables set behind grassed island of trees, pleasant views over adjacent farmland.

39.505742S 175.289992E Hema Atlas Map Ref 26 D10

805 Raukawa Falls Rest Area 4.3
South of Ore Ore on SH4
www.horizons.govt.nz/getting-people-places/planning-and-road-safety/feeling-tired-while-driving-pull-over-and-take-a-break

Just off the highway with a view of the falls a few metres away. No facilities.

39.626072S 175.314934E Hema Atlas Map Ref 26 E10

806 Raukawa Falls & YMCA Raukawa
Adventure Centre Parapara SH4, Kakatahi
Ph (06) 349 0197 ymca@ymcawanganui.co.nz

39.631731S 175.31513E Hema Atlas Map Ref 26 E10

SH3 — WANGANUI TO HAWERA

807 Mowhanau Holiday Park
Kai Iwi Beach: 5km S of SH3 from just W of Kai Iwi
Ph/Fax (06) 342 9658 bookings@campmowhanau.co.nz

Just back from the beach, in a very pretty setting.

39.882843S 174.90514E Hema Atlas Map Ref 25 H7

808 Ashley Park Campground
Adjacent SH3: 15 min N of Wanganui
Ph (06) 346 5917 info@ashleypark.co.nz Fax (06) 346 5821
www.ashleypark.co.nz

The owner will collect fees. Suprisingly nice farmstay accommodation for campers and mobile campers.

39.809129S 174.763837E Hema Atlas Map Ref 25 G6

Lower North Region — North Island Camping Sites

809 Wai-inu Beach Camp
Nukumaru Parade, Waitotara Beach: signposted from SH3, follow Waiinu Beach Rd from Waitotara
Ph 0800 111 322

A donation is encouraged. Right beside the beach, but could be a tad exposed if it is windy. Maximum stay 50 days.

39.864693S 174.746154E   Hema Atlas Map Ref 25 H5

810 Waverley Beach Domain
Waverley Beach Rd: 9km S of SH3 at Waverley
Ph 0800 111 323
Pay at the library in town.

39.832066S 174.635034E   Hema Atlas Map Ref 25 G4

811 Carlyle Beach Motor Camp
9 Beach Rd, Patea: signposted at the E end of Patea at the top of the hill; 1km S of Patea where the Patea River meets the sea
Ph (06) 273 8620
Nice mix of ocean beach, river and forest.

39.769206S 174.48763E   Hema Atlas Map Ref 25 G3

812 Patea Dam
End of Ball Road, just north of Patea
South Taranaki District Council Ph 0800 111 323
Excellent bushwalks, hot showers, NZ's longest man-made lake.

39.545428S 174.572636E   Hema Atlas Map Ref 25 F3

813 Roadside Rest Area
Adjacent SH3: about 17km W of Patea
39.641945S 174.377231E   Hema Atlas Map Ref 25 E2

814 Birch Park Rest Area
SH3, W of Maxwell
39.823669S 174.841583E   Hema Atlas Map Ref 25 G6

SH45 — HAWERA TO NEW PLYMOUTH

815 Ohawe Beach Motor Camp
Rangatapu Rd, Ohawe: 9km S of SH45
Ph (06) 278 6939

A caretaker may collect koha or fees if they are in attendance. Simple beachside camping.

39.586056S 174.1957E   Hema Atlas Map Ref 23 H6

816 Kaupokonui Beach Motorcamp
Lower Glenn Road, Kaupokonui: S of SH45 just E of Kaupokonui
Ph (06) 274 8577

Simple camping at a quiet beachside haven, with good fishing and surfing at your door step. It's one of the best spots south of Mt Taranaki.

39.566075S 174.061991E   Hema Atlas Map Ref 23 G5

817 Opunake Beach Holiday Park
Beach Rd, Opunake: signposted from the centre of Opunake
Ph/Fax (06) 761 7525 or 0800 758 009
opunakebeach@xtra.co.nz www.opunakebeachnz.co.nz

Well worth checking out because it is right next to the beach with playgrounds for the children, and not far from good surf. Qualmark four star plus. Internet.

39.45747S 173.857399E   Hema Atlas Map Ref 23 F3

818 Roadside Rest Area
South Rd (SH45), N of Eltham Rd, Opunake
39.456842S 173.866995E   Hema Atlas Map Ref 23 F3

819 Roadside Rest Area
Adjacent SH45 at Pungarehu: near the Cape Egmont & Parihaka turnoffs
39.2853S 173.806971E   Hema Atlas Map Ref 23 D3

820 Roadside Rest Area
Seaside at the end of Cape Road: W of SH45 from Pungarehu
39.276864S 173.752473E   Hema Atlas Map Ref 23 D2

821 Lucys Gully Rest Area
SH45, N of Tataraimaka
39.145534S 173.935117E   Hema Atlas Map Ref 23 C4

WELLINGTON SOUTH COAST

PHOTO: POSITIVELY WELLINGTON TOURISM

North Island Camping Sites — Lower North Region

822 — Oakura Beach Holiday Park
2 Jans Tce, Oakura: signposted N of SH45, 15km S of New Plymouth
Ph (06) 752 7861 oakurabeachcamp@internet.co.nz
www.oakurabeach.com
Surfside camping at this favoured surf haunt. Qualmark four star.
39.11698S 173.945492E   Hema Atlas Map Ref 23 B4

823 — Belt Road Seaside Holiday Park
2 Belt Rd, New Plymouth: signposted N of SH45, W of city centre
Ph (06) 758 0228 or 0800 804 204 enquiries@beltroad.co.nz
www.beltroad.co.nz
Although this is the closest camp to the town centre, it's beachside and you feel miles away. The coastal walkway makes the walk to town a pleasure. Internet
39.057953S 174.054609E   Hema Atlas Map Ref 107 B3, 23 B5

SH3 & SH43 — HAWERA TO TAUMARUNUI

824 — King Edward Park Motor Camp
70 Waihi Road, Adjacent SH3: N of Hawera
South Taranaki i-site Ph/Fax (06) 278 8544 or 0800 111 323
A handy base from which to visit the nearby Tawhiti Museum. Pets by arrangement.
39.583864S 174.270735E   Hema Atlas Map Ref 25 E2

825 — Normanby Rest Area
SH3, Normanby, N of Hawera
39.535289S 174.273462E   Hema Atlas Map Ref 23 G6

826 — Te Ngutu-O-Te Manu Historic Reserve Campground
914 Ahipaipa Road, Okaiawa
Ph South Taranaki District Council 0800 111 323
Very basic campsite in historic setting. Relaxing, plenty of birdlife. Max. 2 nights.
39.487997S 174.184386E   Hema Atlas Map Ref 23 F6

827 — Ngaere Overbridge Rest Area
SH3, S of Stratford
39.373513S 174.298164E   Hema Atlas Map Ref 23 E7

828 — Stratford Top Town Holiday Park
10 Page St, Stratford: W of SH3 signposted S of the town centre
Ph/Fax (06) 765 6440 stratfordholpark@hotmail.com
www.stratfordtoptownholidaypark.co.nz
Shaded and sheltered site in spacious grounds. Handy to Stratford's parks and swimming pool. Internet. Qualmark four star. Internet, spa pool, mountain bike hire.
39.343582S 174.277986E   Hema Atlas Map Ref 25 B1

829 — Douglas Domain Rest Area
SH43, W of Douglas
39.306532S 174.463433E   Hema Atlas Map Ref 24 E8

830 — Roadside Rest Area
SH43 (Forgotten World Hwy): E of Stratford
Hilltop views of Mt Egmont (Mt Taranaki).
39.28918S 174.504971E   Hema Atlas Map Ref 25 A3

831 — Te Wera Valley Lodge
SH43 (Forgotten World Hwy): E of Stratford
Ph (06) 762 3859 teweracamp@xtra.co.nz
Simple sheltered camping.
39.22984S 174.596397E   Hema Atlas Map Ref 25 A4

832 — Roadside Rest Area
SH43, E of Douglas
39.176835S 174.630383E   Hema Atlas Map Ref 24 D9

833 — Whangamomona Saddle Rest Area
SH43, E of Douglas
39.155061S 174.699759E   Hema Atlas Map Ref 24 C11

834 — Whangamomona
SH43 (Forgotten World Hwy): 64km from SH3 at Stratford; campsite occupies the old school grounds, 500m S of the township, signposted by the hotel
Ph (06) 762 5881
39.148526S 174.740042E   Hema Atlas Map Ref 17 J6

835 — Back Country Accommodation
7225 SH43: midway between Stratford & Taumarunui on the Forgotten World Hwy.
Ph/Fax (06) 762 5858 bacountry@bigfrog.co.nz
www.backcountryaccommodation.kiwiweb.net.nz
Small hilltop B&B campsite with impressive views.
39.066215S 174.798153E   Hema Atlas Map Ref 17 H6

836 — Roadside Rest Area
SH43 at the Tangarakau River Bridge: Morgans Grave, Tangarakau Scenic Reserve
Take the walk to some nice swimming holes.
38.978244S 174.833333E   Hema Atlas Map Ref 17 G6

837 — Nevans Lookout Rest Area
SH43, W of Taumarunui
38.919576S 174.975209E   Hema Atlas Map Ref 18 F8

838 — Ohinepane
SH43 (Whanganui River Rd): 21km from Taumarunui
DOC Whanganui Area Office Ph (06) 349 2100
WhanganuiArea@doc.govt.nz
Free for drive-in campers, hut and camp ticket required if completing Whanganui Journey.
38.952416S 175.148229E   Hema Atlas Map Ref 18 G9

839 — Otunui Stream Rest Area
SH43, SW of Taumarunui
38.939263S 175.152566E   Hema Atlas Map Ref 18 G9

840 — Roadside Rest Area
SH43 (Wanganui River Rd): alongside the Whanganui River
38.919148S 175.227622E   Hema Atlas Map Ref 13 F10

SOUTH ISLAND CAMPING SITES

Nelson & Marlborough Region
  (Camps 841-1007) — **Pages 70-79**
Queen Charlotte Drive - Picton to SH6	70
SH6 – Havelock to Richmond	72
SH60 – Richmond to Collingwood	74
SH6 – Richmond to Inangahua Junction (SH69)	77
SH1 & SH63 – Picton to St Arnaud via Blenheim	78

West Coast Region (Camps 1008-1085) — **Pages 79-84**
SH6 – Inangahua Junction (SH69) to Greymouth	79
SH67 – Westport to Karamea	80
SH7 – Reefton to Greymouth	81
SH6 – Greymouth to Franz Josef	81
SH6 – Franz Josef to Haast	83

Canterbury Region (Camps 1086-1279) — **Pages 84-94**
SH1 – Blenheim to Waipara (SH7)	84
SH7 – Waipara (SH1) to Reefton	86
SH1 – Christchurch to Waipara	87
SH73 – Christchurch to Greymouth	88
Banks Peninsula – Christchurch to Akaroa	90
SH1 – Christchurch to Ashburton	91
SH1 – Ashburton to Timaru	92
SH8 – Timaru to Twizel	93
SH1 – Timaru to Oamaru	94

Otago Region (Camps 1280-1450) — **Pages 94-103**
SH83 – SH1 to Omarama (SH8)	94
SH1 – Omaru to Palmerston	95
SH85 – Palmerston to Alexandra	96
SH1 – Palmerston to Dunedin	96
SH1 – Dunedin to Milton	97
SH92 – Milton to Invercargill	98
SH8 – Milton to Cromwell	99
SH8 – Cromwell to Omarama (SH83)	100
SH6 – Cromwell to Haast	101
SH6 & SH6A – Cromwell to Glenorchy	102

Fiordland & Southland Region
  (Camps 1451-1530) — **Pages 103-108**
SH6 – Queenstown to Invercargill	103
SH99 – Invercargill to Te Anau	105
SH94 – Te Anau to Milford Sound	106
Stewart Island / Rakiura	108

HOLLYFORD RIVE, FIORDLAND — *JEFF DREWITZ*

HOOKER VALLEY TRAIL, AORAKI/MT COOK NATIONAL PARK — *JEFF DREWITZ*

DESTINATION LAKE TAUPO

NELSON AND MARLBOROUGH REGION

PICTON, MARLBOROUGH SOUNDS.   PHOTO: DONNA BLABER

QUEEN CHARLOTTE DRIVE - PICTON TO SH6	70
SH6 – HAVELOCK TO RICHMOND	72
SH60 – RICHMOND TO COLLINGWOOD	74
SH6 – RICHMOND TO INANGAHUA JUNCTION (SH69)	77
SH1 & SH63 – PICTON TO ST ARNAUD VIA BLENHEIM	78

QUEEN CHARLOTTE DRIVE — PICTON TO SH6

841 **Picton Campervan Park**
42 Kent St, Picton: signposted en route between ferry terminals and SH1
Ph (03) 573 8875 Fax (03) 973 8872 picton.cvpark@xtra.co.nz
www.pictoncampervanpark.co.nz

The handiest camp to the town centre and ferry terminals. Qualmark 4 star plus. Internet.

41.295785S 174.001157E   Hema Atlas Map Ref 40 G10, 113 D2, 114 C3

842 **Picton Top 10 Holiday Park**
78 Waikawa Rd, Picton: follow the signs towards Waikawa Bay from Picton town centre
Ph (03) 573 7212 Reservations 0800 277 444
enquiries@pictontop10.co.nz www.pictontop10.co.nz

Clean, quiet and sheltered. Qualmark 5 star rating. Handy to boat launching facilities and the marina. Internet. Spa pool, kids' paddling pool and playground.

41.289013S 174.014883E   Hema Atlas Map Ref 40 G10, 113 B5, 114 C3

843 **Alexanders Holiday Park**
Canterbury St, Picton
Ph/Fax (03) 573 6378 0800 474 286 alexanders.picton@xtra.co.nz
Pets by arrangement. Internet.

41.298566S 174.005454E   Hema Atlas Map Ref 40 H10, 113 D3, 114 D3

844 **Bob's Bay Roadside Rest Area**
Off Waikawa Road, NE of Picton

This is a car park area with a track at the end of Shelly Beach which leads to Bob's Bay. It takes 30 minutes to hike one-way.

41.274504S 174.019632E   Hema Atlas Map Ref 40 G10, 114 B4

845 **Parklands Marina Holiday Park**
10 Beach Rd, Waikawa Bay, Picton
Ph/Fax (03) 573 6343 parktostay@xtra.co.nz www.parktostay.co.nz

Handy to boat launching facilities. Adventure playground. Wireless internet.

41.271982S 174.031873E   Hema Atlas Map Ref 40 G10, 114 B4,

846 **Waikawa Bay Holiday Park**
5 Waimarama St, Waikawa Bay
Ph (03) 573 7434 hiyah@ihug.co.nz
Handy to boat launching facilities.

41.270665S 174.04122E   Hema Atlas Map Ref 40 G10 ,114 B5

847 **Whatamango Bay, Queen Charlotte Sound**
Port Underwood Rd, Queen Charlotte Sound: off SH6, N of Renwick
www.doc.govt.nz or Picton Visitor Information Centre
Ph (03) 520 3113 picton@i-site.org

41.268812S 174.074803E   Hema Atlas Map Ref 40 G11

848 **Governors Bay Scenic Reserve**
Seaside, on Queen Charlotte Drive: W of Picton

41.26854S 173.968558E   Hema Atlas Map Ref 40 G10, 114 A1

849 **Ngakuna Bay Rest Area**
Seaside, on Queen Charlotte Drive: W of Picton

A harbourside rest area at the west end of town.

41.273207S 173.962147E   Hema Atlas Map Ref 40 G10

850 **Momorangi Bay Holiday Park, Queen Charlotte Sound**
Momorangi Bay, Grove Arm, Queen Charlotte Sound (road and boat access) www.doc.govt.nz or Picton Visitor Information Centre
Ph (03) 520 3113 picton@i-site.org
Bookings Ph (03) 573 7865

41.271155S 173.940637E   Hema Atlas Map Ref 40 G9

851 **Aussie Bay, Queen Charlotte Sound**
Near Momorangi Bay, on Queen Charlotte Drive (road and boat access)
www.doc.govt.nz or Picton Visitor Information Centre
Ph (03) 520 3113 picton@i-site.org
Beautiful spot.

41.273112S 173.928938E   Hema Atlas Map Ref 40 G9

852 **Roadside Rest Area**
Anakiwa, start of the Queen Charlotte Walkway: off Queen Charlotte Drive

41.264049S 173.920461E   Hema Atlas Map Ref 40 G9

853 **Davies Bay**
Iwituaroa Scenic Reserve. Grove Arm, Queen Charlotte Sound (boat access or walk in from Queen Charlotte Track)
Picton Visitor Information Centre Ph (03) 520 3113
picton@I-site.org www.doc.govt.nz

41.252442S 173.940433E   Hema Atlas Map Ref 40 G9

Nelson and Marlborough Region — South Island Camping Sites

854 Putanui Point
Putanui Point, Pelorus Sound (boat access only)
DOC Nelson Regional Visitor Centre Ph (03) 546 9339
nelsonvc@doc.govt.nz
41.221478S 173.868428E Hema Atlas Map Ref 40 G9

855 Smiths Farm Holiday Park
Queen Charlotte Drive: 13km E of Havelock
Ph/Fax (03) 574 2806 cbfaulls@xtra.co.nz www.smithsfarm.co.nz
Tidy and clean. Internet.
41.289646S 173.887199E Hema Atlas Map Ref 40 G9

856 Roadside Rest Area
Seaside, on Queen Charlotte Drive: E of Havelock
41.288307S 173.813639E Hema Atlas Map Ref 40 G8

857 Cullen Point Lookout
Seaside, on Queen Charlotte Drive: E of Havelock
41.268698S 173.784975E Hema Atlas Map Ref 40 G8

858 Havelock Motor Camp
24 Inglis St, Havelock: NE of SH6
Ph (03) 574 2339 havelock.mc@xtra.co.nz Fax (03) 574 2335
www.havelockmotorcamp.co.nz
Conveniently located between the town and boat harbour. Pets by arrangement. Adjacent to tennis courts, swimming pool and playground.
41.278834S 173.768393E Hema Atlas Map Ref 40 G8

859 Chartridge Park
Adjacent SH6: 7km S of Havelock
Ph/Fax (03) 574 2129
41.338151S 173.766081E Hema Atlas Map Ref 40 H8

860 Moetapu Bay, Pelorus Sound
Moutapu Bay, Mahau Sound (road and boat access)
DOC Nelson Regional Visitor Centre Ph (03) 546 9339
nelsonvc@doc.govt.nz
41.259627S 173.854924E Hema Atlas Map Ref 40 G9

861 Double Bay
Mahau Sound
Ph (03) 520 7400
www.marlborough.govt.nz/Recreation/Parks-and-Reserves/Camping
Designated camping area for fully self-contained vehicles.
No toilets. Maximum of two nights in any calendar month.
41.257S 173.869E Hema Atlas Map Ref 40 G9

862 Ohingaroa Bay
Mahau Sound
Ph (03) 520 7400
www.marlborough.govt.nz/Recreation/Parks-and-Reserves/Camping
Designated camping area for fully self-contained vehicles. No toilets. Maximum of two nights in any calendar month.
41.248S 173.8839E Hema Atlas Map Ref 40 G9

863 Roadside Rest Area
Ohingaroa DOC Reserve, Mahau Sound: N of Queen Charlotte Drive
41.246768S 173.885266E Hema Atlas Map Ref 40 G9

864 Mistletoe Bay
Kenepuru Rd, Picton
Ph/Fax (03) 573 4048
www.mistletoebay.co.nz stay@mistletoebay.co.nz
Situated right on Queen Charlotte Track. The road is very bendy and not really suitable for motorhomes. Backpackers welcome.
41.221455S 173.972615E Hema Atlas Map Ref 40 G10

865 Cowshed Bay, Pelorus Sound
Portage Rd, Kenepuru Sound (road and boat access)
DOC Nelson Regional Visitor Centre Ph (03) 546 9339
nelsonvc@doc.govt.nz
A small waterside camp spot that is more suitable for campers and small vans. Big rigs and caravans could find this road tricky.
41.199811S 174.187886E Hema Atlas Map Ref 40 G10

866 Kumutoto Bay
Kumutoto Bay Scenic Reserve. Queen Charlotte Sound (boat access only)
Picton Visitor Information Centre Ph (03) 520 3113
picton@I-site.org www.doc.govt.nz
Drinking water from a stream.
41.205381S 174.069742E Hema Atlas Map Ref 40 G10

867 Black Rock
Kumutoto Bay Scenic Reserve. Queen Charlotte Track (access from Queen Charlotte Track only)
Picton Visitor Information Centre Ph (03) 520 3113
picton@I-site.org www.doc.govt.nz
41.192933S 174.064261E Hema Atlas Map Ref 40 F10

868 Bay of Many Coves
Bay of Many Coves Scenic Reserve. Queen Charlotte Track (access from Queen Charlotte Track only)
Picton Visitor Information Centre Ph (03) 520 3113
picton@I-site.org www.doc.govt.nz
41.171706S 174.141836E Hema Atlas Map Ref 40 F11

869 Ngaruru Bay
Arapawa Island Scenic Reserve. Ngaruru Bay, Tory Channel (boat access only)
DOC Nelson Regional Visitor Centre Ph (03) 546 9339
nelsonvc@doc.govt.nz
Drinking water from a stream.
41.227375S 174.214425E Hema Atlas Map Ref 40 G12

870 Wharehunga Bay
Wharehunga Bay, Queen Charlotte Sound.
Northern side of Arapawa Island (boat access only)
DOC Nelson Regional Visitor Centre Ph (03) 546 9339
nelsonvc@doc.govt.nz
41.179714S 174.291042E Hema Atlas Map Ref 40 F12

871 Picnic Bay, Pelorus Sound
Picnic Bay, Kenepuru Sound (road and boat access)
DOC Nelson Regional Visitor Centre Ph (03) 546 9339
nelsonvc@doc.govt.nz
41.193077S 174.04588E Hema Atlas Map Ref 40 F10

South Island Camping Sites — Nelson and Marlborough Region

872 Nikau Cove, Pelorus Sound
Picnic Bay, Kenepuru Sound (road and boat access)
DOC Nelson Regional Visitor Centre Ph (03) 546 9339
nelsonvc@doc.govt.nz
41.193934S 174.050663E Hema Atlas Map Ref 40 F10

873 Ratimera Bay, Queen Charlotte Sound
Ratimera Bay, Queen Charlotte Sound (boat access only)
www.doc.govt.nz or Picton Visitor Information Centre
Ph (03) 520 3113 picton@i-site.org
41.203259S 174.112821E Hema Atlas Map Ref 40 G11

874 Kenepuru Head, Pelorus Sound
Kenepuru Sound Rd: head of Kenepuru Sound (road and boat access)
DOC Nelson Regional Visitor Centre Ph (03) 546 9339
nelsonvc@doc.govt.nz
Access not suited to big rigs and caravans. Dogs allowed, permit required.
41.170796S 174.117041E Hema Atlas Map Ref 40 F11

875 Ohauparuparu Bay
Kenepuru Sound
Ph (03) 520 7400
www.marlborough.govt.nz/Recreation/Parks-and-Reserves/Camping
*Designated camping area for fully self-contained vehicles.
No toilets. Maximum of two nights in any calendar month.*
41.1705S 174.0894E Hema Atlas Map Ref 40 F11

876 Ferndale, Pelorus Sound
Kenepuru Sound (boat access only)
DOC Nelson Regional Visitor Centre Ph (03) 546 9339
nelsonvc@doc.govt.nz
41.187418S 173.971994E Hema Atlas Map Ref 40 F10

877 Waimaru, Pelorus Sound
Kenepuru Sound Rd, Waimaru Bay, Outer Pelorus Sound
(road and boat access)
DOC Nelson Regional Visitor Centre Ph (03) 546 9339
nelsonvc@doc.govt.nz
Access not suited to big rigs and caravans.
41.070737S 174.023994E Hema Atlas Map Ref 40 E10

878 Camp Bay, Queen Charlotte Sound
Endeavour Inlet, Queen Charlotte Sound (access via Queen Charlotte
Walkway and boat only) www.doc.govt.nz or
Picton Visitor Information Centre Ph (03) 520 3113 picton@i-site.org
41.128517S 174.150519E Hema Atlas Map Ref 40 F11

879 Schoolhouse Bay
Resolution Bay, Queen Charlotte Sound (boat access or
walk in from Queen Charlotte Track)
Picton Visitor Information Centre Ph (03) 520 3113
picton@I-site.org www.doc.govt.nz
41.113147S 174.218858E Hema Atlas Map Ref 40 F12

880 Cannibal Cove
Outer Queen Charlotte Sound (boat access only)
Picton Visitor Information Centre Ph (03) 520 3113
picton@I-site.org www.doc.govt.nz
Drinking water from a stream.
41.076558S 174.252133E Hema Atlas Map Ref 40 E12

881 Blumine Island
Blumine Island Scenic Reserve. Outer Queen Charlotte Sound
(boat access only)
Picton Visitor Information Centre Ph (03) 520 3113
picton@I-site.org www.doc.govt.nz
41.169533S 174.233622E Hema Atlas Map Ref 40 F12

SH6 — HAVELOCK TO RICHMOND

882 The Trout Hotel
SH6, Canvastown
Ph (03) 574 2888
41.291195S 173.66991E Hema Atlas Map Ref 39 G7

883 Pinedale Motor Camp
820 Wakamarina Road, Canvastown: 9km S of SH6 from Canvastown
Ph (03) 574 2349 pinedale.motor.camp@xtra.co.nz
41.347899S 173.637251E Hema Atlas Map Ref 39 H7

884 Butchers Flat, Mt Richmond Conservation Park
End of Waikamarina Rd, Waikamarina Valley: off SH6 at Canvastown
DOC Nelson Regional Visitor Centre Ph (03) 546 9339
nelsonvc@doc.govt.nz
Dogs allowed, permit required.
41.375898S 173.594015E Hema Atlas Map Ref 39 H6

885 Pelorus Bridge
Adjacent SH6: 19km NW of Havelock www.doc.govt.nz or
Picton Visitor Information Centre Ph (03) 520 3113
picton@i-site.org Bookings
Ph (03) 571 6019
*This site has magic swimming holes and walks, but remember
to bring the insect repellant.*
41.299022S 173.571972E Hema Atlas Map Ref 39 H6

886 Roadside Rest Area
Alfred Stream, adjacent SH6: at S end of Rai Valley township
41.231896S 173.581323E Hema Atlas Map Ref 39 G6

887 Totara Flat Picnic Area
SH6 between Blenheim and Nelson, just downstream from
the Pelorus Bridge.
*Deep swimming hole with slow-moving water and a grassy picnic area.
Day use only.*
41.301347S 173.577657E Hema Atlas Map Ref 39 H6

Nelson and Marlborough Region   South Island Camping Sites   73

888 Roadside Rest Area
Carluke DOC Reserve, off SH6
Ph (03) 520 3113 picton@i-site.org
No camping allowed.
41.21589S 173.592344E   Hema Atlas Map Ref 39 G6

889 Roadside Rest Area
Brown River Picnic Area, SH6: at the turnoff to Tennyson Inlet
41.218882S 173.586856E   Hema Atlas Map Ref 39 G6

890 Roadside Rest Area
Tennyson Inlet DOC Reserve: 43km NE of Rai Valley
Ph (03) 520 3113 picton@i-site.org
This route is not suited to caravans and big rigs.
41.138735S 173.73014E   Hema Atlas Map Ref 40 F8

891 Harvey Bay, Pelorus Sound
Harvey Bay, Tennyson Inlet: 43km NE of Rai Valley
DOC Nelson Regional Visitor Centre Ph (03) 546 9339
nelsonvc@doc.govt.nz
This peaceful spot is located in a sheltered valley and set back from the water. Not recommended for big rigs and caravans.
41.120453S 173.74272E   Hema Atlas Map Ref 40 E8

892 Nydia
Nydia Bay, Pelorus Sound (boat access or walk in from Nydia Track)
DOC Nelson Regional Visitor Centre Ph (03) 546 9339
nelsonvc@doc.govt.nz
41.150061S 173.781703E   Hema Atlas Map Ref 40 F8

893 Pipi Beach
Hikapau Reach, Pelorus Sound (boat access only)
DOC Nelson Regional Visitor Centre Ph (03) 546 9339
nelsonvc@doc.govt.nz
41.175022S 173.863061E   Hema Atlas Map Ref 40 F9

894 Kauauroa Bay, Pelorus Sound
Outer Pelorus Sound (boat access only)
DOC Nelson Regional Visitor Centre Ph (03) 546 9339
nelsonvc@doc.govt.nz
Stream water only.
41.039092S 173.969166E   Hema Atlas Map Ref 40 E10

895 Okiwi Bay Holiday Park and Lodge
Okiwi Bay: 22km N of Rai Valley, Ronga Rd N from SH6
Ph (03) 576 5006 Fax (03) 576 5005 info@okiwi.co.nz
www.okiwi.co.nz
This is a nice small camp, but it has limited facilities (three toilets and three showers) so it could get crowded at peak holiday times.
41.11211S 173.654852E   Hema Atlas Map Ref 39 E7

896 Elaine Bay, Pelorus Sound
French Pass Rd, Elaine Bay, Tennyson Inlet (road and boat access)
DOC Nelson Regional Visitor Centre Ph (03) 546 9339
nelsonvc@doc.govt.nz
41.053503S 173.76787E   Hema Atlas Map Ref 40 E8

897 Tawa Bay
Tawa Bay, Tennyson Inlet (boat access only)
DOC Nelson Regional Visitor Centre Ph (03) 546 9339
nelsonvc@doc.govt.nz
41.0714S 173.824803E   Hema Atlas Map Ref 40 E8

898 Waiona Bay, Pelorus Sound
Outer Pelorus Sound (boat access only)
DOC Nelson Regional Visitor Centre Ph (03) 546 9339
nelsonvc@doc.govt.nz
Stream water only.
41.002749S 173.874674E   Hema Atlas Map Ref 40 D9

899 French Pass, Pelorus Sound
Road end of Croiselles/French Pass Rd, French Pass (road and boat access)
DOC Nelson Regional Visitor Centre Ph (03) 546 9339
nelsonvc@doc.govt.nz
40.92751S 173.843911E   Hema Atlas Map Ref 40 C9

900 Lucky Bay, Rangitoto Kite tonga/D'Urville Island
Lucky Bay, East Coast D'Urville Island (boat access only)
DOC Nelson Regional Visitor Centre Ph (03) 546 9339
nelsonvc@doc.govt.nz
Stream water only.
40.890363S 173.861576E   Hema Atlas Map Ref 40 C9

901 Penguin Bay, Rangitoto Kite tonga/D'Urville Island
Penguin Bay, East Coast D'Urville Island (boat access only)
DOC Nelson Regional Visitor Centre Ph (03) 546 9339
nelsonvc@doc.govt.nz
Stream water only.
40.84448S 173.907594E   Hema Atlas Map Ref 40 B9

902 Mill Arm, Rangitoto Kite tonga/D'Urville Island
Mill Arm, Greville Harbour, D'Urville Island (boat access only)
DOC Nelson Regional Visitor Centre Ph (03) 546 9339
nelsonvc@doc.govt.nz
Stream water only.
40.839589S 173.84086E   Hema Atlas Map Ref 40 B9

903 Moawhitu
D'Urville Island Scenic Reserve (boat access only)
DOC Nelson Regional Visitor Centre Ph (03) 546 9339
nelsonvc@doc.govt.nz
40.810206S 173.804447E   Hema Atlas Map Ref 40 B8

904 South Arm, Rangitoto Kite tonga/D'Urville Island
South Arm, Port Hardy, D'Urville Island (boat access only)
DOC Nelson Regional Visitor Centre Ph (03) 546 9339
nelsonvc@doc.govt.nz
Stream water only.
40.807428S 173.86591E   Hema Atlas Map Ref 40 B9

South Island Camping Sites

Nelson and Marlborough Region

905 Roadside Rest Area
Collins Valley Picnic Area, adjacent SH6: NW of Rai Valley
41.180802S 173.559179E   Hema Atlas Map Ref 39 F6

906 Roadside Rest Area
Adjacent SH6, alongside the Collins River: NW of Rai Valley
41.161832S 173.524836E   Hema Atlas Map Ref 39 F6

907 Roadside Rest Area
Adjacent SH6, Graham Stream: NW of Rai Valley
41.185294S 173.486275E   Hema Atlas Map Ref 39 F6

908 Roadside Rest Area
Adjacent SH6, Hira Forest: NE of Nelson
41.22753S 173.40826E   Hema Atlas Map Ref 39 G5

909 Cable Bay Holiday Park
800 Cable Bay Rd, Cable Bay: 9km N of SH6, 23km E of Nelson.
Turn off at Happy Valley sign; 8km to Cable Bay.
Ph (03) 545 0443 cablebayfarm@scorch.co.nz
www.cablebayfarm.co.nz
Small, sheltered, seaside camp, with good fishing and walking, yet only 23km from Nelson. Pets by arrangement.
41.16169S 173.412578E   Hema Atlas Map Ref 39 F5

910 Roadside Rest Area
Cable Bay: 9km N of SH6, 23km E of Nelson
41.160439S 173.413718E   Hema Atlas Map Ref 39 F5

911 Roadside Rest Area
Nelson Botanic Gardens, Nelson
41.274237S 173.295225E   Hema Atlas Map Ref 115 C6, 116 A5, 39 G4

912 Maitai Valley Motor Camp
472 Maitai Valley Rd, Nelson: 8km SE of the city centre
Ph/Fax (03) 548 7729 maitaivalleymc@xtra.co.nz www.mvmc.co.nz
Sheltered and spacious camp set in native bush and adjoining a swimming stream - yet only eight minutes drive from downtown Nelson.
41.290122S 173.324989E   Hema Atlas Map Ref 116 B6, 39 G4

913 Brook Valley Holiday Park
600 Brook St, Brook Valley
Ph (03) 548 0399 Fax (03) 548 7582 www.brookholidaypark.co.nz
stay@brookholidaypark.co.nz
41.311781S 173.292567E   Hema Atlas Map Ref 116 C5, 39 H4

914 Nelson City Holiday Park & Motels
230 Vanguard St, Nelson: S of Nelson city centre, head S on Rutherford St and into Waimea Rd
Ph (03) 548 1445 Fax (03) 548 2670 info@nelsonholidaypark.co.nz
Reservations 0800 77 88 98 www.nelsonholidaypark.co.nz
The handiest camp to the city centre. Internet.
41.284921S 173.268577E   Hema Atlas Map Ref 116 B4, 39 G4

915 Tahuna Beach Holiday Park
70 Beach Rd, Tahunanui: signposted at the W end of Rocks Rd, where it meets Tahunanui Beach
Ph (03) 548 5159 tahuna@tahunabeach.co.nz
www.tahunabeachholidaypark.co.nz
A huge and popular camp handy to the city, yet right on the beach. Wireless internet. Qualmark four star. Three playgrounds.
41.283587S 173.241745E   Hema Atlas Map Ref 39 G3, 116 B4

SH60 — RICHMOND TO COLLINGWOOD

916 Richmond Top 10 Holiday Park
29 Gladstone Rd (SH6), Richmond: 1km S of Richmond
Ph 0800 250 218 (03) 544 5218 stay@nelsontop10.co.nz
www.nelsontop10.co.nz
Internet. Qualmark four and a half stars.
41.339634S 173.177508E   Hema Atlas Map Ref 39 H3, 116 D2

917 Club Waimea, Waimea Town & Country Club
345 Queen St, Richmond: just W of the SH6 intersection with Queen St
Ph (03) 543 9179 reception@clubwaimea.co.nz
www.clubwaimea.co.nz
Bookings essential. Long term rates available.
41.335602S 173.179376E   Hema Atlas Map Ref 39 H3, 116 C2

918 Greenwood Park
Cnr Landsdowne Rd & Appleby Highway, Appleby
Ph (03) 544 4685 or 0800 473 369 greenwood.park@xtra.co.nz
www.greenwoodholidaypark.co.nz
Handy to seasonal fruit picking opportunities.
41.315179S 173.134871E   Hema Atlas Map Ref 39 H3, 116 C1

919 Roadside Rest Area
SH60: W of the Appleby Bridge on the Waimea River
This spot provides nice swimming and picnic opportunities.
41.308674S 173.128354E   Hema Atlas Map Ref 39 H3, 116 B1

920 Roadside Rest Area
SH6, SW of Richmond
41.427843S 172.99188E   Hema Atlas Map Ref 39 J2

921 Mapua Leisure Park
33 Toru St, Mapua: follow the signs to the centre of Mapua from SH60
Ph (03) 540 2666 booking@mapualeisurepark.co.nz
www.mapualeisurepark.co.nz
Magic sheltered setting with 'clothes optional' bathing for those who dare in February and March. Tennis courts, volleyball, kayak hire.
41.251677S 173.103429E   Hema Atlas Map Ref 39 G2

922 Roadside Rest Area
Several spots adjacent SH60 at Ruby Bay: W of Motueka, N of Richmond
41.228757S 173.083669E   Hema Atlas Map Ref 39 G2

Nelson and Marlborough Region — South Island Camping Sites — 75

923 McKee Recreation Reserve
Seaside at the W end of Ruby Bay: signposted from SH60
Tasman District Council
A caretaker may collect fees if they are in attendance.
Great seaside location for cheap and simple camping.
41.214503S 173.084048E   Hema Atlas Map Ref 39 G2

924 Tasman Motor Camp
55 Aporo Road, Ruby Bay
Ph/Fax (03) 540 2542 tasmancamping@xtra.co.nz
Popular camp handy to fruit picking seasonal work (Feb-Apr) opportunities. Internet.
41.21438S 173.076328E   Hema Atlas Map Ref 39 G2

925 Kina Beach Camping Ground
Cliff Rd, Kina
Phone: (03) 526 6161 / 027 491 0562
41.184534S 173.064635E   Hema Atlas Map 38 H10, Ref 39 F2

926 Helme Holiday Park
201 Kina Peninsula Rd, Kina Beach: 13km S of Motueka,
off King Beach Rd.
Ph/Fax (03) 526 6848 info@helmeholiday.co.nz
www.helmeholiday.co.nz
41.166908S 173.046345E   Hema Atlas Map Ref 39 F2

927 Fernwood Holiday Park
519 High St Sth, Motueka
Ph/Fax (03) 528 7488 or 0800 528 7488
gary@fernwoodholidaypark.co.nz www.fernwoodholidaypark.co.nz
Handy to the centre of Motueka, and a good base for seasonal fruit picking opportunities. Internet. Aviary on site.
41.134633S 173.008877E   Hema Atlas Map Ref 39 F2

928 Marchwood Park
62 Marchwood Park Road, Motueka
Ph (03) 528 8840
41.119165S 172.989223E   Hema Atlas Map Ref 39 E2

929 Motueka Top 10 Holiday Park (Fearons Bush)
10 Fearon St, Motueka: signposted E of Motueka's Main St,
at the N end of town
Ph (03) 528 7189 Fax (03) 528 7182 Reservations 0800 66 8835
info@motuekatop10.co.nz www.motuekatop10.co.nz
A well-managed camp that is very spacious and sheltered. Qualmark four star. Wireless internet, jumping pillow, spa pool, close to restaurants, shops. Bikes for hire.
41.104348S 173.013353E   Hema Atlas Map Ref 39 E2

930 Roadside Rest Area
Adjacent SH60, Motueka: NW side of the Motueka River Bridge
41.091286S 173.00691E   Hema Atlas Map Ref 39 E2

931 Riwaka Domain Rest Area
SH6, NW of Riwaka
41.06519S 172.984941E   Hema Atlas Map Ref 39 E1

932 Roadside Rest Area
Little Kaiteriteri: E of Kaiteriteri
A beautiful beach that is now sadly rather overshadowed by expensive subdivisions.
41.042487S 173.018104E   Hema Atlas Map Ref 39 E2

933 Kaiteriteri Beach Motor Camp
Sandy Bay Rd, Kaiteriteri: off SH60 N of Motueka
Ph (03) 527 8010 kaiteritericamp@xtra.co.nz
www.kaiteriteribeach.co.nz
A big bustling camp right on one of the prettiest beaches in NZ, and a great base from which to explore the Abel Tasman Park. Internet. Qualmark four star.
41.036664S 173.017187E   Hema Atlas Map Ref 39 E2

934 Marahau Beach Camp
9 Franklin St, Marahau: signposted from the main
road at Marahau. Turn off SH60.
Ph (03) 527 8176, 0800 80 8018 Fax (03) 527 8176
info@abeltasmancentre.co.nz www.abeltasmancentre.co.nz
Another handy base from which to explore the Abel Tasman Park. Pets OK in low season.
41.004938S 173.009458E   Hema Atlas Map Ref 39 D2

935 The Barn, Cabins, Camping & Backpackers
14 Harvey Road, RD2, Marahau
Ph (03) 527 8043 info@barn.co.nz www.barn.co.nz
40.994816S 173.003181E   Hema Atlas Map Ref 38 F10

936 Old McDonald's Farm & Holiday Park
Harvey Rd, Marahau
Ph (03) 527 8288 Fax (03) 527 8289
www.oldmacs.co.nz info@oldmacs.co.nz
Pets only allowed in off-season. There is a boat ramp 1km away. River swimming. Wireless internet.
40.992447S 173.00063E   Hema Atlas Map Ref 38 F9

937 Roadside Rest Area
Abel Tasman National Park, Marahau: NE of SH60
41.00415S 173.009279E   Hema Atlas Map Ref 38 F10

938 Roadside Rest Area
Abel Tasman National Park, beachside reserve: NE of SH60
40.997026S 173.004924E   Hema Atlas Map Ref 38 F10

939 Roadside Rest Area
Hawkes Lookout, Takaka Hill, SH60
41.023621S 172.907744E   Hema Atlas Map Ref 38 F9

940 Canaan Downs
From SH60 on the Tanaka Hill Rd turn off at Canaan Rd
and follow it 11km to the end.
DOC Nelson Regional Visitor Centre Ph (03) 546 9339
nelsonvc@doc.govt.nz
40.942989S 172.892221E   Hema Atlas Map Ref 38 F9

941 Paddys Lookout Rest Area
SH60, E of Takaka Hill
41.02422S 172.879409E   Hema Atlas Map Ref 38 F9

South Island Camping Sites

Nelson and Marlborough Region

942 Roadside Rest Area
Takaka Hilltop Walkway, SH60
41.030826S 172.866496E   Hema Atlas Map Ref 38 G8

943 Rocky Angle Rest Area
SH60, just W of Takaka Hill
41.034683S 172.854632E   Hema Atlas Map Ref 38 G8

944 Cobb River, Kahurangi National Park
Kahurangi National Park
DOC Nelson Regional Visitor Centre Ph (03) 546 9339
nelsonvc@doc.govt.nz
Stream water only.
41.128832S 172.615185E   Hema Atlas Map Ref 37 H6

945 Roadside Rest Area
Lindsay Bridge Reserve, Takaka River: SH60
40.987992S 172.820564E   Hema Atlas Map Ref 38 F8

946 Roadside Rest Area
Paynes Ford Scenic Reserve: SH60
40.883069S 172.810885E   Hema Atlas Map Ref 38 E8

947 Hangdog Camp
1900 Takaka Valley Highway, Takaka
Ph (03) 525 85311 www.hangdogcamp.co.nz
Basic campsite in pretty setting. No rubbish service.
40.882072S 172.813056E   Hema Atlas Map Ref 38 E8

948 Takaka Camping Ground
56 Motupipi St, Takaka: signposted on the Takaka to Pohara Rd, from the S end of Takaka main street
Ph (03) 525 7300 www.holidayparks.co.nz/takakacaravan
Handy to the centre of Takaka. Pets by prior arrangement.
40.858115S 172.81049E   Hema Atlas Map Ref 38 E8

949 Pohara Beach Top 10 Holiday Park
Abel Tasman Dr, Pohara: 11km from SH60 at Takaka
Ph 0800 764 272, (03) 525 9500 pohara@xtra.co.nz
www.poharabeach.com
Beachside and handy to some nice cafes, with the town of Takaka down the road and the Abel Tasman National Park at your back door. Internet. Qualmark four star.
40.833211S 172.884991E   Hema Atlas Map Ref 38 D8

950 Roadside Rest Area
Pohara Beach Reserve: 11km from SH60 at Takaka
40.832533S 172.885928E   Hema Atlas Map Ref 38 D8

951 Roadside Rest Area
Tarakohe Beach Reserve, Abel Tasman Dr: off SH60 at Takaka
40.821865S 172.902527E   Hema Atlas Map Ref 38 D9

952 Roadside Rest Area
Tata Beach Reserve, Abel Tasman Dr: off SH60 at Takaka
40.811974S 172.916102E   Hema Atlas Map Ref 38 D9

953 Totaranui, Abel Tasman National Park
Totaranui Beach, Abel Tasman National Park:
signposted about 32km from Takaka
DOC Nelson Regional Visitor Centre Ph (03) 546 9339
nelsonvc@doc.govt.nz Bookings Ph (03) 528 8083
Cold shower only. A nice beach base to explore the Abel Tasman National Park. The road is not recommended for caravans, trailers or big rigs.
40.822435S 173.0041E   Hema Atlas Map Ref 38 D9

954 Roadside Rest Area
SH60: just S of the Pupu Springs turnoff
40.831552S 172.79249E   Hema Atlas Map Ref 38 D8

955 Roadside Rest Area
Patons Rock Reserve: 2km N of SH60, NW of Takaka
40.787723S 172.761461E   Hema Atlas Map Ref 38 D8

956 Golden Bay Holiday Park
99 Tukurua Beach: signposted N of SH60
Ph (03) 525 9742 goldenbay.holiday@xtra.co.nz
www.goldenbayholidaypark.co.nz
With its own beach, this sheltered camp is one of the best in the Bay. Wireless internet.
40.733907S 172.700753E   Hema Atlas Map Ref 37 C7

957 Collingwood Motor Camp
William St, Collingwood: at the W end of Collingwood's main street
Ph (03) 524 8149 langmuir.clan@xtra.co.nz
A caretaker may collect fees if they are in attendance. Simple camping in a small waterfont location that's handy to the town.
40.675494S 172.681877E   Hema Atlas Map Ref 37 C7

958 Farewell Gardens Motor Camp & Holiday Accommodation
57 Seddon St, Puponga, Golden Bay: Adjacent SH60,
Port Puponga: 22km N of Collingwood
Ph (03) 524 8445 Fax (03) 524 8445
farewellgardens@clear.net.nz www.farewellgardens.co.nz
Closest camp to Cape Farewell and Farewell Spit. Motorcamp, self and semi-self contained units, caravans, power and tent sites. Opposite beach. Kitchens, BBQ, TV/dining room.
40.525866S 172.733199E   Hema Atlas Map Ref 37 A7

959 Roadside Rest Area
Seddon St Reserve, Port Puponga: 22km N of Collingwood
40.525629S 172.735828E   Hema Atlas Map Ref 37 A7

960 Whariariki Beach Holiday Park
End of Whariariki Road, Whariariki Beach, Golden Bay
Ph (03) 524 8507 stay@whariariki.co.nz
www.whariarikibeachholidaypark.co.nz
40.508742S 172.6852E   Hema Atlas Map Ref 37 A7

Nelson and Marlborough Region — South Island Camping Sites

961 Roadside Rest Area
Whariki Beach Reserve: N of Port Puponga
40.509446S 172.685364E   Hema Atlas Map Ref 37 A7

SH6 — RICHMOND TO INANGAHUA JUNCTION (SH69)

962 Quinney's Bush Camp and Caravan Park
SH6, Motupiko: S of Richmond
Ph (03) 522 4249 quinneysbush@xtra.co.nz www.quinneysbush.co.nz
A fabulous riverside camp, and ideal if you are travelling with children as there is quite a lot to entertain them.
41.458047S 172.814732E   Hema Atlas Map Ref 42 C13

963 Tapawera Settle
19 Tadmor Valley Rd, Tapawera: signposted from the Motueka Valley Hwy, at the N end of town
Ph/Fax (03) 522 4334 www.settle.co.nz camping@settle.co.nz
Small but friendly with hot bubble-jet spa. Wireless internet.
41.38659S 172.821384E   Hema Atlas Map Ref 42 B13

964 Siberia Flat, Kahurangi National Park
Wangapeka Valley, Kahurangi National Park
DOC Nelson Regional Visitor Centre Ph (03) 546 9339
nelsonvc@doc.govt.nz
Stream water only.
41.441942S 172.58395E   Hema Atlas Map Ref 42 C11

965 Courthouse Flat, Kahurangi National Park
Wangapeka Valley, Kahurangi National Park: adjoins historic goldfield
DOC Nelson Regional Visitor Centre Ph (03) 546 9339
nelsonvc@doc.govt.nz
Stream water only.
41.467849S 172.567564E   Hema Atlas Map Ref 42 C11

966 Roadside Rest Area
McLeans Recreational Reserve, Motueka Valley Hwy: adjacent the Motueka River
Riverside picnic and swimming spot. Self-contained motorhomes only, 1 night.
41.288811S 172.807187E   Hema Atlas Map Ref 42 A13

967 Te Ora Farm
146 Graham Valley Rd, Pokororo
Ph (03) 526 8783
41.204227S 172.832022E   Hema Atlas Map Ref 42 A13, 38 J8

968 Roadside Rest Area
SH6, N of Kawatiri
41.590948S 172.764113E   Hema Atlas Map Ref 42 E13

969 Kawatiri Junction, Kahurangi National Park
Riverside at the intersection of SH63 & SH6
DOC Nelson Lakes Visitor Centre Ph (03) 521 1806
nelsonlakesvc@doc.govt.nz
Nice short walks from this spot. Stream water only.
41.693533S 172.617727E   Hema Atlas Map Ref 42 F11

970 Roadside Rest Area
SH6: SE of Gowanbridge
41.711681S 172.553647E   Hema Atlas Map Ref 42 F11

971 Roadside Rest Area
Gowan Bridge Reserve, SH6
St Arnaud DOC Visitor Information Centre Ph (03) 521 1806
starnaudao@doc.govt.nz
41.713314S 172.561067E   Hema Atlas Map Ref 42 F11

972 Lake Rotoroa, Nelson Lakes National Park
Lake Rotoroa: signposted E of SH6 about 5km S of the Kawatiri intersection
DOC Nelson Lakes Visitor Centre Ph (03) 521 1806
nelsonlakesvc@doc.govt.nz
Magic spot with good walks and fishing.
41.795827S 172.597203E   Hema Atlas Map Ref 42 G11

973 Roadside Rest Area
SH6: W of Gowanbridge
41.698623S 172.503361E   Hema Atlas Map Ref 42 F10

974 Owen River Recreation Reserve
Beside the Owen River Hotel on SH6: 20km N of Murchison
Ph (03) 532 9273 (Owen River Hotel)
Casual Camping - a caretaker may collect fees - if they are in attendance. Enquiries to the Owen River Hotel.
41.686604S 172.450779E   Hema Atlas Map Ref 42 F10

975 Murchison Motorhome Park
2595 Kawatiri-Murchison Hwy (SH6), Murchison (8 kms north of Murchison)
Ph (03) 523 9666 info@murchisonmotorhomepark.co.nz
www.murchisonmotorhomepark.co.nz
Brand new facilities featuring a log fire and underfloor heating!
41.757102S 172.391452E   Hema Atlas Map Ref 42 F10

976 Roadside Rest Area
SH6: S of Owen River
41.743998S 172.397516E   Hema Atlas Map Ref 42 F10

977 Roadside Rest Area
Mangles River Bridge, SH6: N of Murchison
41.786721S 172.368885E   Hema Atlas Map Ref 42 G9

978 Riverview Holiday Park
Riverview Road, Murchison: N end of Murchison township, signposted from SH6
Ph/Fax (03) 523 9591 riverviewhp@xtra.co.nz
Great riverside base for rafting and canoeing in a parklike setting.
41.794628S 172.339425E   Hema Atlas Map Ref 42 G9

South Island Camping Sites — Nelson and Marlborough Region

979 Kiwi Park Motels & Holiday Park
170 Fairfax St, Murchison: signposted S of Murchison, signposted from Murchison town centre. Turn between supermarket & hotel, on right 800m along Fairfax St.
Ph (03) 523 9248, 0800 22 80 80 kiwipark@xtra.co.nz
Fax (03) 523 9241 www.kiwipark.co.nz

Modern facilities in a compact rural location. Animal park. Mountain bikes, gold pans, fishing gear to hire. Pets by arrangement. Qualmark 4 star plus.

41.809542S 172.324896E   Hema Atlas Map Ref 42 G9

980 Maruia Falls Roadside Rest Area
SH65, S of Ariki, approx 6km S of the intersection with SH6
Nice waterfall views.

41.858961S 172.252846E   Hema Atlas Map Ref 42 H8

981 Roadside Rest Area
SH6, Upper Buller Gorge Rd, E of Newton Flat. River access
41.775468S 172.180818E   Hema Atlas Map Ref 42 G8

982 Flat Ford Rest Area
SH6, Upper Buller Gorge Road
41.778295S 172.132481E   Hema Atlas Map Ref 41 G7

983 Eight Mile Rest Area
SH6, Upper Buller Gorge Road
41.787609S 172.11752E   Hema Atlas Map Ref 41 G7

984 Monument Lookout Rest Area
SH6, Upper Buller Gorge Road
41.808689S 172.095005E   Hema Atlas Map Ref 41 G7

985 Arnold Park Rest Area
SH6, Upper Buller Gorge Road
41.81278S 172.057544E   Hema Atlas Map Ref 41 G7

986 Lyell
SH6, Upper Buller Gorge: 10km NE of Inangahua
www.doc.govt.nz or Reefton Visitor Centre Ph (03) 732 8391
reefton@i-site.org
Dogs must be on leash at all times.

41.796389S 172.048993E   Hema Atlas Map Ref 41 G6

SH1 & SH63 — PICTON TO ST ARNAUD VIA BLENHEIM

987 Collins Memorial Reserve
Mt Pleasant, on SH1 S of Picton

Self-contained motorhomes only, max 2 nights.
41.339639S 173.963267E   Hema Atlas Map Ref 40 H10

988 Robin Hood Bay
Turn of SH1 at Tuamarine, 8km north of Blenheim, into Hunter Rd, drive east to Rarangi Beach Rd, turn left into Port Underwood Rd. Follow to campsite.
DOC Nelson Regional Visitor Centre Ph (03) 546 9339
nelsonvc@doc.govt.nz
Steam water only.

41.358806S 174.070365E   Hema Atlas Map Ref 40 H11

989 Whites Bay
Port Underwood Rd, Rarangi: at Pukatea Stream www.doc.govt.nz or Picton Visitor Information Centre Ph (03) 520 3113 picton@i-site.org

A beautiful secluded seaside spot with simple camping: the gates close at night. It's a very pleasant place to use as a base to explore Blenheim, or await the ferry.

41.382377S 174.057323E   Hema Atlas Map Ref 40 J10

990 Rarangi
Turn of SH1 at Tuamarine, 8km N of Blenheim, into Hunter Rd, drive east to Rarangi Beach Rd, turn left into Port Underwood Rd. Follow coast to Rarangi, S of Whites Bay.
DOC Nelson Regional Visitor Centre Ph (03) 546 9339
nelsonvc@doc.govt.nz

41.392732S 174.04713E   Hema Atlas Map Ref 40 J10

991 Wairau Incident Rest Area
SH1, Tuamarina, between Pioneer Place and highway
41.428653S 173.960621E   Hema Atlas Map Ref 44 B11

992 Spring Creek Holiday Park
1199 Rapaura Rd: near intersection with SH1
Ph (03) 570 5893 www.springcreekhp.co.nz
Fax (03) 5705 889 pennym@springcreekhp.co.nz

Close to the many vineyards along Rapaura Rd. Internet.

41.457855S 173.955345E   Hema Atlas Map Ref 44 B10

993 Roadside Rest Area
SH1, N of Blenheim, towards Grovetown
41.491726S 173.964571E   Hema Atlas Map Ref 44 C11

994 Blenheim Backpackers and Motorcamp
27 Budge Street, Blenheim
Ph/Fax (03) 578 7419 bbpackers@xtra.co.nz
www.blenheimbackpackers.co.nz

Located next door to 24-hour petrol station.

41.503237S 173.961751E   Hema Atlas Map Ref 44 C10, 117 A5

995 Blenheim Top 10 Holiday Park
78 Grove Rd (SH1), Blenheim: just N of Blenheim
Ph (03) 578 3667, 0800 26 86 66 blenheimtop10@xtra.co.nz
www.blenheimtop10.co.nz

A Qualmark four star-rated Top 10 park that's handy to the centre of Blenheim and not far from the ferries. Internet.

41.50141S 173.961527E   Hema Atlas Map Ref 44 C11

996 Riverlands Roadhouse
State Highway 1, Riverlands
Ph (03) 577 9130 Fax (03) 577 9131
kenlond@riverlandsroadhouse.co.nz

This is a truck stop which also accommodates motorhomes. No tent sites.

41.538255S 174.025906E   Hema Atlas Map Ref 44 C11

997 Sutherland Stream Picnic Area
Wither Hills Farm Park, Redwood Street, Blenheim

41.544058S 173.96304E   Hema Atlas Map Ref 44 C10

West Coast Region

South Island Camping Sites 79

998 Taylor Dam Rest Area
Taylor Pass Road, Blenheim

41.572771S 173.929438E   Hema Atlas Map Ref 44 D10

999 Onamalutu

Onamalutu Rd (nth bank of Wairau Flats): take Northbank Rd off SH6, N of Renwick www.doc.govt.nz or Picton Visitor Information Centre
Ph (03) 520 3113 picton@i-site.org

41.45841S 173.706606E   Hema Atlas Map Ref 40 J8 44 C9

1000 Mill Flat

Pine Valley: 22km up Northbank Rd, NW of Blenheim (4WD only)
www.doc.govt.nz or Picton Visitor Information Centre
Ph (03) 520 3113 picton@i-site.org
Stream water only. Dogs must be on leash at all times.

41.514617S 173.524909E   Hema Atlas Map Ref 43 C7

1001 Wairau Valley Tavern

SH63, Wairau Valley
Wairau Valley Tavern Ph (03) 572 2878
Flat grassed area adjacent to pub. No kitchen but meals available at pub.

41.563693S 173.532207E   Hema Atlas Map Ref 43 C7

1002 Kowhai Point

Adjacent SH63, Wash Bridge, Wairau River
DOC Nelson Lakes Visitor Centre Ph (03) 521 1806
nelsonlakesvc@doc.govt.nz
Stream water only.

41.711717S 173.112677E   Hema Atlas Map Ref 43 E3

1003 Coldwater

Turn off SH63 east of St Arnaud. Follow road beside Wairau River for 46km to Coldwater Stream. Or drive from Hanmer Springs via Hanmer-Rainbow Road.
DOC Nelson Lakes Visitor Centre Ph (03) 521 1806
nelsonlakesvc@doc.govt.nz
Isolated campsite. High clearance 4WD required. Toll road from St Arnaud. Stream water only.

42.062757S 172.922519E   Hema Atlas Map Ref 43 J2

1004 Lake Tennyson

Turn off SH63 east of St Arnaud. Follow road beside Wairau River Rd until it meets the Clarence River. Accessible from Hanmer Springs via Hanmer-Rainbow Road.
DOC Nelson Lakes Visitor Centre Ph (03) 521 1806
nelsonlakesvc@doc.govt.nz
Isolated campsite. 2WD from Hanmer, 4WD from St Arnaud, open Dec to March. Stream water only.

42.211585S 172.739833E   Hema Atlas Map Ref 47 C4

1005 Kerr Bay, Nelson Lakes National Park

Eastern Bay of Lake Rotoiti, St Arnaud: off SH63
DOC Nelson Lakes Visitor Centre Ph (03) 521 1806
nelsonlakesvc@doc.govt.nz
Laundry is open during summer only.

41.806136S 172.844444E   Hema Atlas Map Ref 42 G13

1006 West Bay, Nelson Lakes National Park

Signposted 2km W of St Arnaud: off SH63
DOC Nelson Lakes Visitor Centre Ph (03) 521 1806
nelsonlakesvc@doc.govt.nz
Open mid Dec-March and over Easter. Bookings required during peak Christmas holiday period. Cold showers only.

41.797995S 172.827297E   Hema Atlas Map Ref 43 F1

1007 Roadside Rest Area
Glenhope Reserve, SH63: S of junction with SH6
41.699007S 172.621987E   Hema Atlas Map Ref 42 F11

WEST COAST REGION

LAKE MATHESON REFLECTIONS   PHOTO: TOURISM WEST COAST

SH6 – INANGAHUA JUNCTION (SH69) TO GREYMOUTH	79
SH67 – WESTPORT TO KARAMEA	80
SH7 – REEFTON TO GREYMOUTH	81
SH6 – GREYMOUTH TO FRANZ JOSEF	81
SH6 – FRANZ JOSEF TO HAAST	83

SH6 — INANGAHUA JUNCTION (SH69) TO GREYMOUTH

1008 Roadside Rest Area
Kilkenny Lookout: adjacent SH6 and the Buller River
41.863528S 171.781405E   Hema Atlas Map Ref 41 H4

1009 Ohikanui Rest Area
SH6, W of Tiroroa
41.845817S 171.71358E   Hema Atlas Map Ref 41 H4

1010 Roadside Rest Area
SH6: E of Westport
41.835736S 171.676301E   Hema Atlas Map Ref 41 G4

1011 Jack's Gasthof, Camping & Accommodation, Bar & Pizzeria

Adjacent SH6, Little Beach: 23 km S of Westport
Ph (03) 789 6501 Jack.schubert@xtra.co.nz www.jacksgasthof.co.nz
A pretty and peaceful setting.

41.887204S 171.470377E   Hema Atlas Map Ref 41 H2

South Island Camping Sites

West Coast Region

1012 Charleston Motor Camp
4 Darkies Terrace Rd, Charleston: signposted next to Charleston Hotel
Ph (03) 789 6773 cmcamp@xtra.co.nz
41.907756S 171.438415E   Hema Atlas Map Ref 41 H1

1013 Roadside Rest Area
Irimahuwheri scenic viewpoint, SH6: S of Charleston
Magic coastal views: on a clear day you can even see Mt Cook to the south.
42.076135S 171.35515E   Hema Atlas Map Ref 45 A5

1014 Roadside Rest Area
Pororari River Walkway, SH6: N of Punakaiki
42.106993S 171.339438E   Hema Atlas Map Ref 45 B5

1015 Punakaiki Beach Camp
Owen St, Punakaiki: off SH6, at N end of Punakaiki township
Ph (03) 731 1894 beachcamp@xtra.co.nz Fax (03) 731 1897
With the pounding sea at your doorstep this site is a great base to explore the walks and Punakaiki rocks.
42.106486S 171.336466E   Hema Atlas Map Ref 45 B5

1016 Punakaiki Bridge Rest Area
SH6, Punakaiki River Bridge S of Punakaiki
42.12376S 171.332567E   Hema Atlas Map Ref 45 B5

1017 Bakers Creek Rest Areas (2)
Beach Rd (SH6), S of Barrytown
42.274484S 171.300936E   Hema Atlas Map Ref 45 D4

1018 Roadside Rest Area
W of SH6: S of Punakaiki, at Thirteen Mile Creek
42.302558S 171.284164E   Hema Atlas Map Ref 45 D4

1019 Roadside Rest Area
Adjacent SH6: S of Punakaiki
42.329451S 171.264748E   Hema Atlas Map Ref 45 D4

1020 Roadside Rest Area
Strongman Mine Memorial, W of SH6: N of Rapahoe
42.349841S 171.256303E   Hema Atlas Map Ref 45 D4

1021 Rapahoe Beach Motor Camp
10 Hawken St, Rapahoe: signposted W of SH6 at Rapahoe
Ph/Fax (03) 762 7025, 0508 465 432 rapahoebeach@actrix.co.nz
www.rapahoebeach.co.nz
Beachside spot that is 'budget' but charming. Wireless internet.
42.372108S 171.242738E   Hema Atlas Map Ref 45 E4

SH67 — WESTPORT TO KARAMEA

1022 Roadside Rest Area
SH67: on the N side of the Buller River Bridge at the S entrance to Westport
41.765024S 171.597636E   Hema Atlas Map Ref 41 G3

1023 Bazil's Hostel
54-56 Russell Street, Westport
Ph (03) 789 6410 Fax (03) 789 6240 info@bazils.com
www.bazils.com
41.754053S 171.599398E   Hema Atlas Map Ref 41 G3

1024 Westport Holiday Park & Motel
31-37 Domett St, Westport: signposted from the main street
Ph (03) 789 7043 westportholidaypark@xtra.co.nz
www.westportholidaypark.co.nz
Sheltered camping spot in park-like grounds that's handy to the centre of Westport. Mini golf course, internet.
41.752207S 171.611693E   Hema Atlas Map Ref 41 G3

1025 Seal Colony Top 10 Holiday Park
Marine Parade, Carters Beach: signposted on SH67A to Cape Foulwind
Ph (03) 789 8002 Reservations 0508 937 876
www.top10westport.co.nz
Beachside spot in a pretty location that's handy to parks, playgrounds and a nice cafe. Wireless internet. Qualmark four star plus. Bikes for hire.
41.74966S 171.555409E   Hema Atlas Map Ref 41 G2

1026 Seddonville Holiday Park
108 Gladstone St, Seddonville: 4km inland from SH67
Ph (03) 782 1314
Simple camping in an old school.
41.555829S 171.991418E   Hema Atlas Map Ref 41 D6

1027 Gentle Annie Point Camp & Cafe
A 2km diversion from SH67
A beautiful base from which to explore Seddonville, surf or fish.
41.522953S 171.942079E   Hema Atlas Map Ref 41 D6

1028 Little Wanganui Hotel & Camping Ground
SH67, Little Wanganui
Ph (03) 782 6752
Traditional West Coast camping, by arrangement. New ablution blocks.
41.37587S 172.075175E   Hema Atlas Map Ref 41 B7

1029 Karamea Holiday Park
67 Maori Point Rd, Karamea: 3km S of Karamea township
Ph (03) 782 6758 info@karamea.com www.karamea.com
Nice sheltered camping on an estuary south of Karamea.
41.25891S 172.106494E   Hema Atlas Map Ref 41 A7

1030 Karamea Domain Camping Ground
Waverly St, Karamea: signposted W of Karamea township
Ph (03) 782 6069
This site is run by the local school.
41.248723S 172.116093E   Hema Atlas Map Ref 41 A7

West Coast Region — South Island Camping Sites

1031 Oparara Basin, Kahurangi National Park
Kahurangi National Park:
45 minute drive NE of Karamea www.doc.govt.nz or
Karamea Information & Resource Centre Ph (03) 7826 652
info@karameainfo.co.nz

World-class scenic treats await those daring to explore this beautiful valley but there is no camping in this vicinity, and the access road is not suited to big rigs and caravans.

41.151208S 172.190585E Hema Atlas Map Ref 37 H3

1032 Kohaihai, Kahurangi National Park
Kohaihai River mouth, Kahurangi National Park:
15km N of Karamea www.doc.govt.nz or
Karamea Information & Resource Centre Ph (03) 7826 652
info@karameainfo.co.nz

Simple, picturesque camping at the start/end of the Heaphy Track. Insect repellent is essential.

41.108894S 172.102371E Hema Atlas Map Ref 37 H2

SH7 — REEFTON TO GREYMOUTH

1033 Reefton Motor Camp
Ross St, Reefton: signposted off SH7 at E side of Reefton township
Ph (03) 732 8477 Fax (03) 732 8478 roa.reuben@xtra.co.nz

A caretaker may collect fees if they are in attendance. Simple camping that's handy to Reefton's town centre.

42.120117S 171.868995E Hema Atlas Map Ref 46 B9

1034 Roadside Rest Area
Tawhai Reserve, SH7: S of Reefton
42.145676S 171.814491E Hema Atlas Map Ref 46 B9

1035 Slab Hut Creek
Slab Creek Rd, off SH7:
a 2km diversion from SH7 approx 10km S of Reefton
www.doc.govt.nz or Reefton Visitor Centre
Ph (03) 732 8391 reefton@i-site.org

Nice streamside location with tame wekas. Stream water only.

42.151967S 171.789033E Hema Atlas Map Ref 46 B9

1036 Blackwater Creek Rest Area
SH7, N of Ikamatua
42.240707S 171.698897E Hema Atlas Map Ref 46 C8

1037 Ikamatua Holiday Park
218 Main Rd, Ikamatua: beside the Ikamatua Hotel
Ikamatua Hotel Ph (03) 732 3555

Traditional West Coast camping.

42.270771S 171.68533E Hema Atlas Map Ref 46 C8

1038 Nelson Creek Reserve
Nelson Creek: 5km E of SH7

A caretaker may collect fees or make a donation to the local hotel. Charming township with nice walks and a pleasant stream adjoining the campsite.

42.405074S 171.519224E Hema Atlas Map Ref 45 E6

1039 The Old Steam Engine Roadside Rest Area
E of SH7: NE of Stillwater
42.417881S 171.42432E Hema Atlas Map Ref 45 E5

1040 Lake Brunner Country Motel Holiday Park
2014 Arnold Valley Rd: about 2km NW of Moana
Ph (03) 738 0144 lakebrunnermotel@xtra.co.nz
Fax (03) 738 0143 www.lakebrunnermotel.co.nz

Modern facilities in a parklike setting adjoining a native bush reserve. Spa pool, chip and putt golf. Wireless internet.

42.561902S 171.47712E Hema Atlas Map Ref 45 G6

1041 Lake Brunner Motor Camp
86 Ahau St, Moana: signposted from the centre of Moana
Ph/Fax (03) 738 0600 lake.brunner@paradise.net.nz

Handy to the lake, boat ramp and town centre. Pets by arrangement, dogs must be on leash.

42.575005S 171.473249E Hema Atlas Map Ref 45 G6

SH6 — GREYMOUTH TO FRANZ JOSEF

1042 Central Motor Home Park
117-119 Tainui St, Greymouth: At rear of Challenge Station, just S of town centre
Ph (03) 768 4924 coastautos@xtra.co.nz

A caretaker may collect fees if they are in attendance. There's tarseal camping for campervans, and it's handy to the town centre.

42.452761S 171.209835E Hema Atlas Map Ref 45 E4, 118 B4

1043 Greymouth Seaside Top 10 Holiday Park
2 Chesterfield St, Greymouth: signposted W of SH6, S of town centre
Ph (03) 768 6618 Reservations 0800 867 104
info@top10greymouth.co.nz www.top10greymouth.co.nz

Well appointed and next to the beach. Internet. Qualmark four star plus. Spa pool.

42.467378S 171.187392E Hema Atlas Map Ref 45 F4

1044 South Beach Motel & Motor Park
318 Main South Rd, South Beach: W of SH6, 6km S of Greymouth
Ph (03) 762 6768 Reservations 0800 101 222
stay@southbeach.co.nz Fax (03) 762 6748 www.southbeach.co.nz

Internet. Pets by arrangement. Spa pool. Four dumpstations on site.

42.492532S 171.176241E Hema Atlas Map Ref 45 F3

1045 Sumner Road Rest Area
SH6, N of Gladstone
42.519701S 171.163468E Hema Atlas Map Ref 45 F3

1046 KJ's Accommodation & Camping
SH6: 50m W of Kumara Junction
Ph (03) 736 9558 kjsaccommodation@paradise.net.nz

Funky camping in the grounds of the old Kumara School.

42.583528S 171.128697E Hema Atlas Map Ref 45 G3

1047 Acre Creek Rest Area
SH6, SW of Kumara Junction
42.590508S 171.111199E Hema Atlas Map Ref 45 G3

South Island Camping Sites — West Coast Region

1048 Goldsborough
Stafford Dillmanstown Rd, Goldsborough Valley: 17km from Hokitika
Reefton Visitor Centre Ph (03) 732 8391 reefton@I-site.org
Dogs must be on leash at all times.
42.675448S 171.124304E Hema Atlas Map Ref 45 H3

1049 Beachwalk Motor Camp
8 Greyhound Rd: W of SH6, 6km N of Hokitika
Ph 0275 556 550, (03) 755 7251 kiwi.house@xtra.co.nz
www.jacquiegrantsplace.com
This site has near new facilities, and it's handy to Hokitika. Wireless internet.
42.674913S 171.014369E Hema Atlas Map Ref 45 H2

1050 Shining Star Beachfront Accommodation
16 Richards Dr, Hokitika: W of SH6, 1km N of Hokitika town centre
Ph (03) 755 8921, 0800 744 646 shining@xtra.co.nz
Fax (03) 755 8653 www.shiningstar.co.nz
This site has nice facilities and it's opposite glowworm caves. Qualmark four star plus. Wireless internet. Sauna, spa.
42.707965S 170.972877E Hema Atlas Map Ref 45 H2

1051 252 Beachside Motels & Holiday Park
252 Revell St, Hokitika: signposted W of the town centre
Ph (03) 755 8773 Reservations 0508 252 252
info@252beachside.co.nz www.252beachside.co.nz
Although this site is handy to the beach it is more suited to mobile homes. Spa pool.
42.707803S 170.971958E Hema Atlas Map Ref 45 H2

1052 Hokitika Holiday Park
242 Stafford St, Hokitika: signposted E of the town centre, near the dairy factory
Ph (03) 755 8172, 0800 465 436
holidaypark@hokitika.co.nz www.hokitikaholidaypark.co.nz
Older style camp, in sheltered and spacious grounds, in a quiet location. Qualmark three stars. Wireless internet.
42.72294S 170.978487E Hema Atlas Map Ref 45 H2

1053 Hans Bay-Lake Kaniere
Lake Kaniere Rd: 19km E of Hokitika
Reefton Visitor Centre Ph (03) 732 8391 reefton@I-site.org
42.808304S 171.154946E Hema Atlas Map Ref 45 J3

1054 Lake Mahinapua
E of SH6: 16km S of Hokitika
DOC Arthur's Pass Visitor Centre Ph (03) 318 9211
arthurspassvc@doc.govt.nz
A simple, scenic, lakeside camping spot that's close to Hokitika.
42.7953S 170.901035E Hema Atlas Map Ref 45 J1

1055 Ross Historic Goldfields Reserve
SH6: NE end of main street in Ross, 28km S of Hokitika
Interesting walks, goldpanning, and some lovely old buildings.
42.900693S 170.814916E Hema Atlas Map Ref 50 B11

1056 Roadside Rest Area
Fergusons Bush Scenic Reserve, adjacent SH6: approx 10km S of Ross
42.921398S 170.759967E Hema Atlas Map Ref 50 B10

1057 Pukekura Lodge (The Bushman's Centre)
Adjacent SH6, Pukekura: 22km S of Ross
Ph (03) 755 4144 pete&justine@pukekura.co.nz www.pukekura.co.nz
Funky camping with rustic West Coast hospitality; adjoining the 'road kill cafe' and bar. Heated pools, no swimming pool.
43.009904S 170.671256E Hema Atlas Map Ref 50 C10

1058 Lake Ianthe Matahi
Lake Ianthe. Adjacent SH6: 15km N Harihari
DOC Westland Tai Poutini National Park Visitor Centre
Ph (03) 752 0796 westlandpvc@doc.govt.nz
This is a beautiful spot but insect repellent is a must.
43.059525S 170.634368E Hema Atlas Map Ref 50 C9

1059 Harihari Motor Inn
Main Road, Harihari.
Ph 0800 833 026 hhmi@paradise.net.nz
Beachside, traditional West Coast camping.
43.149597S 170.560461E Hema Atlas Map Ref 50 D9

1060 Roadside Rest Area
E side of SH6, S end of Harihari
43.149373S 170.556042E Hema Atlas Map Ref 50 D9

1061 Roadside Rest Area
Whataroa Scenic Reserve, adjacent SH6
43.28516S 170.40182E Hema Atlas Map Ref 49 F7

1062 Okarito Camping Ground
Russell St, Okarito: a 14km diversion W of SH6
Ph (03) 753 4223
A caretaker may collect fees if they are in attendance. Simple camping in a very pretty part of the world.
43.222358S 170.163247E Hema Atlas Map Ref 49 E5

1063 Okarito Car Park
Okarito: 14km W of SH6
43.22435S 170.158333E Hema Atlas Map Ref 49 E5

1064 Otto/MacDonalds
Adjacent SH6: 15km N of Franz Josef
DOC Westland Tai Poutini National Park Visitor Centre
Ph (03) 752 0796 westlandpvc@doc.govt.nz
A peaceful and simple camping option less than 18km from the often crowded Franz Josef township.
43.297055S 170.224E Hema Atlas Map Ref 49 F6

1065 Roadside Rest Area
Lake Mapourika Reserve, SH6: 10km N of Franz Josef
DOC Westland Tai Poutini National Park Visitor Centre
Ph (03) 752 0796 westlandpvc@doc.govt.nz
43.329157S 170.214224E Hema Atlas Map Ref 49 F6

West Coast Region — South Island Camping Sites

SH6 — FRANZ JOSEF TO HAAST

1066 Franz Josef Mountain View Top 10 Holiday Park
2902 Franz Josef Hwy (SH6), Franz Josef:
1km N of the main township
Ph (03) 752 0735, 0800 467 897
bookings@mountain-view.co.nz www.mountain-view.co.nz
It pays to arrive early or book ahead, as accommodation can be scarce in this area. Internet. Qualmark five star. Internet Cafe, playground, spa pool.

43.372935S 170.181377E   Hema Atlas Map Ref 49 G6

1067 Rainforest Retreat & Holiday Park
46 Cron St, Franz Josef Glacier:
one block E of SH6 in the centre of Franz Josef
Ph 0800 873 346 or (03) 752 0220
comestay@rainforestretreat.co.nz www.rainforestholidaypark.co.nz
It pays to arrive early or book ahead, as accommodation can be scarce in this area. Internet, spa and sauna.

43.385484S 170.184174E   Hema Atlas Map Ref 49 G6

1068 Glacier Country Campervan Park
64 Cron St, Franz Josef
Ph (03) 752 0145
Set in rainforest across the road from Glacier Pools.

43.384858S 170.184775E   Hema Atlas Map Ref 49 G6

1069 Fox Glacier Lodge & Campervan Park
41 Sullivan Rd, Fox Glacier: signposted at the S end of Fox Glacier, E of SH6, opposite BP petrol station.
Ph (03) 751 0888 Fax (03) 751 0026 foxglacierlodge@xtra.co.nz
This lodge is in a handy, central location but it is only for caravans and campervans. Internet.

43.465768S 170.018013E   Hema Atlas Map Ref 49 H4

1070 Fox Glacier Viewpoint
E of SH6, Fox Glacier
There are scenic views of the glacier, and walks east of this point.

43.476698S 170.009985E   Hema Atlas Map Ref 49 H5

1071 Fox Glacier Holiday Park & Motels
Kerrs Rd, Fox Glacier: signposted W of Fox Glacier & SH6 on the Lake Matheson Rd, 800m from the town centre
Ph (03) 751 0821, 0800 154 366 Fax (03) 751 0813
info@fghp.co.nz www.foxglacierholidaypark.co.nz
It pays to arrive early or book ahead, as accommodation can be scarce in this area. Internet.

43.463924S 170.008178E   Hema Atlas Map Ref 49 H4

1072 Lake Matheson Roadside Rest Area
Lake Matheson: 3km W of Fox Glacier town centre
DOC Fox Glacier Visitor Information Centre Ph (03) 751 0807
westlandpvc@doc.govt.nz
This stop is a must for the famous mirror-lake views from Lake Matheson. It is stunning if the mountains are clear and there is no wind (a rare combination).

43.447543S 169.969279E   Hema Atlas Map Ref 49 H4

1073 Peak Lookout Roadside Rest Area
After the Lake Matheson turnoff on the Gillespies Beach Rd: W of SH6

43.451729S 169.914003E   Hema Atlas Map Ref 49 H4

1074 Gillespies Beach
N end of Gillespies Beach: 22km from Fox Glacier, a half hour drive along a twisting gravel drive west from the Lake Matheson turnoff
DOC South Westland - Weheka Area Office Ph (03) 751 0807
westlandpvc@doc.govt.nz
This is an interesting part of the world, with a seal colony nearby and nice views of the Alps.

43.41554S 169.820569E   Hema Atlas Map Ref 49 G3

1075 Roadside Rest Area
Westland National Park, SH6: the Copland Track starts from this point

43.574046S 169.808073E   Hema Atlas Map Ref 49 J3

1076 Roadside Rest Area
Bruce Bay Reserve, SH6
43.598362S 169.595119E   Hema Atlas Map Ref 58 A13

1077 South Westland Salmon Farm & Cafe Roadside Rest Area
SH6
43.710312S 169.499119E   Hema Atlas Map Ref 58 B12

1078 Lake Paringa
W of SH6, Lake Paringa, beside Jamie Ck: 40km N of Haast
DOC Haast Visitor Centre Ph (03) 750 0809 haastvc@doc.govt.nz
This is a pretty spot but insect repellent is essential. Stream water only.

43.721397S 169.410124E   Hema Atlas Map Ref 58 B12

1079 Roadside Rest Area
SH6: near the Haast-Paringa Track
DOC Haast Visitor Centre Ph (03) 750 0809 haastvc@doc.govt.nz
43.772174S 169.354817E   Hema Atlas Map Ref 58 C11

1080 Munro Beach Track Roadside Rest Area
SH6, near Lake Moeraki
43.717058S 169.269046E   Hema Atlas Map Ref 58 B11

1081 Roadside Rest Area
Knights Point Lookout, SH6: N of Haast

43.715249S 169.225475E   Hema Atlas Map Ref 58 B10

1082 Roadside Rest Area
Ships Creek Reserve, SH6: N of Haast
DOC Haast Visitor Centre Ph (03) 750 0809 haastvc@doc.govt.nz
There are interesting forest and coastal walk options from this point, but insect repellent is essential.

43.758304S 169.147479E   Hema Atlas Map Ref 58 B9

1083 Roadside Rest Area
N shore of the Haast River Bridge

43.85391S 169.054614E   Hema Atlas Map Ref 58 D9

South Island Camping Sites — Canterbury Region

1084 Haast Lodge
Marks Rd, Haast
Ph (03) 750 0703 info@haastlodge.com
Fax (03) 750 0718 www.haastlodge.com

This former warehouse, now providing backpacker accommodation, a caravan park and some camping, is functional but not pretty.

43.882204S 169.04413E   Hema Atlas Map Ref 58 D9

1085 Haast Beach Holiday Park
Jackson Bay Rd: 18km S of Haast River
Ph (03) 750 0860   Fax (03) 750 0862   haastpark@xtra.co.nz

This simple and functional park is very popular during the whitebaiting season.

43.908447S 168.900454E   Hema Atlas Map Ref 58 D8

CANTERBURY REGION

CANTERBURY REGION CHRISTCHURCH   PHOTO: CANTERBURY MARKETING

SH1 – BLENHEIM TO WAIPARA (SH7)	84
SH7 – WAIPARA (SH1) TO REEFTON	86
SH1 – CHRISTCHURCH TO WAIPARA	87
SH73 – CHRISTCHURCH TO GREYMOUTH	88
BANKS PENINSULA – CHRISTCHURCH TO AKAROA	90
SH1 – CHRISTCHURCH TO ASHBURTON	91
SH1 – ASHBURTON TO TIMARU	92
SH8 – TIMARU TO TWIZEL	93
SH1 – TIMARU TO OAMARU	93

SH1 — BLENHEIM TO WAIPARA (SH7)

1086 Awatere Motor Camp
Seddon Domain, Seymour Street, Seddon
Ph (03) 575 7285 awaterecom@xtra.co.nz

Council-run campsite.

41.672767S 174.071995E   Hema Atlas Map Ref 44 E11

1087 Blairich Bridge Rest Area and Camping Ground
Awatere Valley Road, Seddon
Ph (03) 520 7400
www.marlborough.govt.nz/Recreation/Parks-and-Reserves/Camping

Designated camping area for fully self-contained vehicles. Maximum of two nights in any calendar month.

41.690992S 173.932245E   Hema Atlas Map Ref 44 E10

1088 Awatere Rest Area
Adjacent SH1, S of Seddon
41.69653S 174.095043E   Hema Atlas Map Ref 44 E12

1089 Marfells Beach
Marfells Beach, Lake Grassmere: off SH1
www.doc.govt.nz or Picton Visitor Information Centre
Ph (03) 520 3113 picton@i-site.org

Boil all water before drinking.

41.725454S 174.205051E   Hema Atlas Map Ref 44 E13

1090 Elterwater Rest and Camping Area
State Highway 1, Ward
Ph (03) 520 7400 www.marlborough.govt.nz/Recreation/Parks-and-Reserves/Camping

Designated camping area for fully self-contained vehicles. Maximum of two nights in any calendar month.

41.794198S 174.147761E   Hema Atlas Map Ref 44 F12

1091 Roadside Rest Area
SH1, N of Clarence
42.05242S 173.958047E   Hema Atlas Map Ref 44 J10

1092 Waipapa Bay Camping Ground & Cray Shop
Adjacent SH1, 32km N of Kaikoura
Ph (03) 319 6340 waipapa.bay@xtra.co.nz

Simple camping with the opportunity to purchase or catch crayfish.

42.211183S 173.871018E   Hema Atlas Map Ref 48 C14

1093 Okiwi Bay
SH1, 28km north of Kaikoura
Picton Visitor Information Centre Ph (03) 520 3113
picton@i-site.org www.doc.govt.nz

Dogs permitted, must be on leash at all times.

42.216417S 173.859747E   Hema Atlas Map Ref 48 C14

1094 Mororimu Rest Area
Adjacent SH1, N of Kaikoura
42.216922S 173.865196E   Hema Atlas Map Ref 48 C14

1095 Roadside Rest Area
SH1, between Okiwi Bay and Half Moon Bay
42.234774S 173.845772E   Hema Atlas Map Ref 48 C13

1096 Ohau Point Lookout Rest Area
SH1, between Okiwi Bay and Half Moon Bay
42.24938S 173.825849E   Hema Atlas Map Ref 48 C13

1097 Roadside Rest Area
SH1, N of Rakautara
42.260782S 173.810533E   Hema Atlas Map Ref 48 C13

1098 Roadside Rest Area
Adjacent SH1, about 23km N of Kaikoura

You can purchase yummy cooked crayfish at this spot.

42.264356S 173.807662E   Hema Atlas Map Ref 48 C13

1099 Roadside Rest Area
Adjacent SH1, about 20km N of Kaikoura
42.276826S 173.783366E   Hema Atlas Map Ref 48 C13

Canterbury Region — South Island Camping Sites

1100 Puhi Puhi
Puhi Puhi Rd, off SH1 9km north of Kaikoura
Picton Visitor Information Centre Ph (03) 520 3113
picton@i-site.org www.doc.govt.nz
Drinking water from a stream.
42.270133S 173.737653E   Hema Atlas Map Ref 48 C13

1101 Alpine-Pacific Holiday Park
69 Beach Rd, Kaikoura: N of Kaikoura town centre
Ph/Fax (03) 319 6275 or 0800 692 322
www.alpine-pacific.co.nz info@alpine-pacific.co.nz
Spa pools, bike hire, wireless internet.
42.393048S 173.678636E   Hema Atlas Map Ref 48 E12

1102 Kaikoura Top 10 Holiday Park
34 Beach Rd, Kaikoura: N of Kaikoura town centre
Ph (03) 319 5362, 0800 36 36 38 kaikouratop10@ihug.co.nz
www.kaikouratop10.co.nz
This is Qualmark four star plus camping, and it even has a spa. The only negative is its close proximity to rail traffic. Internet. Pets allowed but must check by phone prior to arrival. Dump station for guest use only.
42.396101S 173.679704E   Hema Atlas Map Ref 48 E12

1103 A1 Kaikoura Motels & Holiday Park
9-15 Beach Rd, Kaikoura
Ph (03) 319 5999 Reservations 0800 605 999
kaikouramotel@xtra.co.nz www.a1kaikouramotel.co.nz
Closest campsite to Kaikoura centre, good facilities.
42.398445S 173.679695E   Hema Atlas Map Ref 48 E12

1104 Roadside Rest Area
SH1, SW of Kaikoura
42.417391S 173.630794E   Hema Atlas Map Ref 48 E12

1105 Kaikoura Peketa Beach Holiday Park
665 SH1, Peketa
Ph (03) 319 6299 beachfront@kaikourapeketabeach.co.nz
Fax (03) 319 7296 www.kaikourapeketabeach.co.nz
This park is right next to the beach for swimming and fishing. Pets welcome, except between Dec 22 and Jan 10. Dump station for guest use only.
42.427669S 173.594304E   Hema Atlas Map Ref 48 E11

1106 Roadside Rest Area
SH1, N of Goose Bay
42.467236S 173.538047E   Hema Atlas Map Ref 48 F11

1107 Kaikoura Coastal Campgrounds, Goose Bay
Adjacent SH1, 17km S of Kaikoura
Ph (03) 319 5348 goosebay@ihug.co.nz
A caretaker may collect fees if they are in attendance. Several coastal options are offered from this base stretching from Paia Point in the north to Omihi Bay and Boat Harbour in the south. No pets during peak holiday period, Dec 24-Jan 7.
42.478797S 173.528027E   Hema Atlas Map Ref 48 F11

1108 Roadside Rest Area
SH1, S of Goose Bay
Several rest areas along this coastline.
42.483943S 173.529081E   Hema Atlas Map Ref 48 F11

1109 Roadside Rest Area
SH1, S of Goose Bay
Several rest areas along this coastline.
42.501388S 173.513755E   Hema Atlas Map Ref 48 F11

1110 Roadside Rest Area
SH1, N of Oaro
42.506813S 173.508323E   Hema Atlas Map Ref 48 F11

1111 Roadside Rest Area
SH1, N of Oaro
42.510525S 173.507106E   Hema Atlas Map Ref 48 F11

1112 Roadside Rest Area
SH1, N of Hundalee
42.541922S 173.451553E   Hema Atlas Map Ref 48 F10

1113 Roadside Rest Area
SH1, N of Hundalee
42.568512S 173.441461E   Hema Atlas Map Ref 48 G10

1114 Roadside Rest Area
SH1, Hundalee
42.600357S 173.417579E   Hema Atlas Map Ref 48 G10

1115 The Staging Post
Hawkswood: off SH1
Ph (03) 319 2727 linda@stagingpost.co.nz www.stagingpost.co.nz
This is a pleasant farmstay environment, and a base for the Kaikoura Coast walking track. Pets by arrangement only. Camping open only Oct-April. Tennis court on-site.
42.651765S 173.32714E   Hema Atlas Map Ref 48 H9

1116 Roadside Rest Area
SH1, S of Parnassus, beside Waiau River
42.718228S 173.286783E   Hema Atlas Map Ref 48 H9

1117 Cheviot Motel & Holiday Park
44 Ward Road, Cheviot: W of town centre
Ph (03) 319 8607 info@cheviotmotel.co.nz www.cheviotmotel.co.nz
42.808516S 173.267563E   Hema Atlas Map Ref 48 J9

1118 Gore Bay & Buxton Campgrounds
Gore Bay: 8km SE of Cheviot
Ph (03) 319 8010 manukabay@xtra.co.nz www.gorebaycamp.co.nz
A caretaker may collect fees if they are in attendance. There are numerous camping options in a relatively sheltered bay adjoining a favoured surfing and swimming beach.
42.85436S 173.311897E   Hema Atlas Map Ref 54 A13

1119 Roadside Rest Area
SH1, S of Cheviot, beside Hurunui River
42.897695S 173.102666E   Hema Atlas Map Ref 54 A11

86 South Island Camping Sites — Canterbury Region

1120 Greta Valley Rest Area
SH1: 100m E
42.963468S 172.968167E — Hema Atlas Map Ref 54 B10

1121 Greta Valley Camping Ground
7 Valley Road, SH1: 800m E
Ph (03) 314 3340 Mobile 025 290 7061
A caretaker may collect fees if they are in attendance.
This spot is in a nice sheltered valley with the basics provided.
42.961618S 172.980005E — Hema Atlas Map Ref 54 B10

1122 Motunau Beach Camping Ground
Lyndsay Terrace, Motunau Beach
Camp fees are paid into an honesty box. $5 per night per family.
43.047027S 173.074805E — Hema Atlas Map Ref 54 C11

SH7 — WAIPARA (SH1) TO REEFTON

1123 Waipara Sleepers Motor Camp
200m from junction of SH1 & SH7, Waipara
Ph/Fax (03) 314 6003 waipara.sleepers@inet.net.nz
This camp is a bit funky, with the opportunity to bunk down in old railway wagons and free eggs supplied if the hens feel generous.
43.063757S 172.755004E — Hema Atlas Map Ref 54 C8

1124 Lake Taylor
Lake Sumner Rd: 74km NW of Amberley
DOC Arthur's Pass Visitor Centre Ph (03) 318 9211
arthurspassvc@doc.govt.nz
Stream water only. Dogs allowed.
42.777072S 172.250827E — Hema Atlas Map Ref 46 J12

1125 Loch Katrine
Lake Sumner Rd: 81km NW of Amberley (7km of 4WD-only track)
DOC Arthur's Pass Visitor Centre Ph (03) 318 9211
arthurspassvc@doc.govt.nz
Dogs allowed.
42.723743S 172.206857E — Hema Atlas Map Ref 46 H12

1126 Watters Cottage Rest Area
Adjacent SH70 (Inland Rd): N of junction with SH7
An opportunity to picnic in the grounds of an historic cobb cottage.
42.702299S 172.939111E — Hema Atlas Map Ref 47 H6

1127 Waiau Motor Camp
9 Highfield St, Waiau: signposted from SH70 (Inland Rd), W end of town
Ph (03) 315 6672 waiaumc@actrix.co.nz www.waiaumotorcamp.co.nz
Campers are permitted to use local school pool during summer months.
42.652561S 173.04055E — Hema Atlas Map Ref 47 H7

1128 Roadside Rest Area
Adjacent SH70 (Inland Rd): N of Waiau
42.586893S 173.099637E — Hema Atlas Map Ref 47 G7

1129 Mt Lyford Lodge
10 Mt Lyford Forrest Drive, Mt Lyford Skifield, SH70 (Inland Rd): 23km N of Waiau, 60km S of Kaikoura
Ph (03) 315 6446 enquiries@mtlyfordlodge.co.nz
www.mtlyfordlodge.co.nz
This lodge is a base for winter skiing and horse trekking. Spa pools.
42.507729S 173.153193E — Hema Atlas Map Ref 48 F8

1130 Hanmer River Rest Areas
Either side of SH7A alongside Hanmer River: just N of SH7
This is a nice riverside spot with some shelter from the wind and sun.
42.585752S 172.780693E — Hema Atlas Map Ref 47 G5

1131 Roadside Rest Area
SH7, SW of Hanmer Springs
42.578498S 172.747868E — Hema Atlas Map Ref 47 G4

1132 Roadside Rest Area
SH7, SW of Hanmer Springs
42.573302S 172.667002E — Hema Atlas Map Ref 47 G4

1133 Hanmer River Holiday Park
26 Medway Rd, Hanmer Springs
Ph (03) 315 7111 www.hanmerriverholidaypark.co.nz
stayhanmerriver@xtra.co.nz
Internet. Pets by prior arrangement.
42.578987S 172.790038E — Hema Atlas Map Ref 47 G5

1134 Hanmer Springs Forest Camp
243 Jollies Pass Rd, Hanmer Springs, off SH7A
Ph (03) 315 7202 hanmer.forest.camp.@xtra.co.nz
www.hanmerforestcamp.co.nz
42.518802S 172.857268E — Hema Atlas Map Ref 47 F5

1135 Hanmer Springs Alpine Holiday Apartments & Campground
9 Fowlers Lane, Hanmer Springs
Ph 0800 315 7478 or (03) 315 7478 Fax (03) 315 7248
alpineholidayapartments@xtra.co.nz www.alpine-apartments.co.nz
42.519615S 172.8535E — Hema Atlas Map Ref 47 F5

1136 Mountain View Top 10 Holiday Park
Main Rd, Hanmer Springs
Ph (03) 315 7113, 0800 90 45 45 mtview.hanmer@clear.net.nz
www.mountainviewtop10.co.nz
Although this park is the closest to the thermal pools, it can get a bit crowded. Internet. Bike hire.
42.527758S 172.829723E — Hema Atlas Map Ref 47 F5

1137 Pines Holiday Park
158 Argelins Rd, Hanmer Springs
Ph (03) 315 7152 reservations@pinesholidaypark.co.nz
www.pinesholidaypark.co.nz
Internet. Bike hire.
42.520521S 172.820387E — Hema Atlas Map Ref 47 F5

Canterbury Region

South Island Camping Sites

1138 Alpine Adventure Holiday Park
200 Jacks Pass Rd, Hanmer Springs: signposted from Hanmer Springs' main street. SH7A. Drive right to the end of Jacks Pass Road.
Ph (03) 315 7112 info@hanmerspringsaccommodation.co.nz
www.hanmerspringsaccommodation.co.nz

Although this park isn't as close to the town centre as the others it is set in 20 acres of park, spacious, sheltered and quiet, with all the facilities you need. Wireless internet, rope challenge, adventure playground, bike hire, free courtesy coach available.

42.508602S 172.814768E Hema Atlas Map Ref 47 F5

1139 Acheron Accommodation House
Molesworth - Acheron Rd, 26km from Hanmer
DOC Nelson Lakes Visitor Centre Ph (03) 521 1806
nelsonlakesvc@doc.govt.nz
Stream water only.
42.395737S 172.956639E Hema Atlas Map Ref 47 E6

1140 Molesworth Cobb Cottage
Molesworth - Acheron Rd, 122km from Blenheim
DOC Nelson Lakes Visitor Centre Ph (03) 521 1806
nelsonlakesvc@doc.govt.nz
Stream water only.
42.084801S 173.27009E Hema Atlas Map Ref 43 J5

1141 Horseshoe Creek Rest Area
Adjacent SH7, Lewis Pass
42.596149S 172.52399E Hema Atlas Map Ref 47 G3

1142 Hope River Rest Area
Adjacent SH7, Lewis Pass
42.588107S 172.450757E Hema Atlas Map Ref 47 G2

1143 Lake Sumner Forest Park Rest Area
800m from SH7, Lewis Pass
42.58408S 172.383256E Hema Atlas Map Ref 47 G1

1144 Roadside Rest Area
SH7, S of Boyle Village
42.557525S 172.350479E Hema Atlas Map Ref 47 F1

1145 St James Walkway Rest Area
Adjacent SH7, Lewis Pass
42.51555S 172.388686E Hema Atlas Map Ref 47 F1

1146 Riverside Rest Area
Adjacent SH7, Lewis Pass
42.493016S 172.387028E Hema Atlas Map Ref 47 F1

1147 Deer Hunters Flat
Adjacent SH7, Lewis Pass
42.470212S 172.395825E Hema Atlas Map Ref 47 F1

1148 Deer Valley
W of SH7: adjacent Lewis River
DOC Arthur's Pass Visitor Centre Ph (03) 318 9211
arthurspassvc@doc.govt.nz
Stream water only.
42.404781S 172.397279E Hema Atlas Map Ref 46 E13

1149 Maruia Springs Thermal Resort
SH7, 15km SE of Springs Junction (SH65)
Ph/Fax (03) 523 8840 info@maruiasprings.co.nz
www.maruiasprings.co.nz

Although this is really more accommodation, camping options and spots for caravans are available. The surrounding mountains, beech forests and tussocks combine to make this a unique thermal pool experience.

42.378941S 172.333366E Hema Atlas Map Ref 46 D13

1150 Rough Creek Rest Area
SH7, W of Maruia Springs
42.378968S 172.278052E Hema Atlas Map Ref 46 E12

1151 Roadside Rest Area
SH7, SE of Springs Junction (SH65)
42.35494S 172.242664E Hema Atlas Map Ref 46 D12

1152 Marble Hill
SH7, 7km E of Springs Junction (SH65)
www.doc.govt.nz or Reefton Visitor Centre Ph (03) 732 8391
reefton@i-site.org
Access to the Lake Daniells Track.
42.351601S 172.221336E Hema Atlas Map Ref 46 D12

1153 Roadside Rest Area
SH7, at E edge of Springs Junction (SH65)
42.334734S 172.182491E Hema Atlas Map Ref 46 D12

1154 Roadside Rest Area
SH7, SE of Reefton
42.196304S 171.93699E Hema Atlas Map Ref 46 C10

1155 Roadside Rest Area
Inangahua Swingbridge Reserve, SH7: SE of Reefton
42.188022S 171.938416E Hema Atlas Map Ref 46 B10

SH1 — CHRISTCHURCH TO WAIPARA

1156 Christchurch Top 10 Meadow Park Holiday Park
39 Meadow St, Papanui, Christchurch: signposted from Main Nth Rd, just N of Northlands shopping centre
Ph (03) 352 9176 stay@christchurchtop10.co.nz
www.christchurchtop10.co.nz

Wireless internet. Spa pool. Qualmark four star plus.

43.491048S 172.618107E Hema Atlas Map Ref 56 D9, 120 E4

1157 219 on Johns' Motel & Holiday Park
219 Johns Rd, Belfast: alongside SH1 Christchurch by-pass route S of Belfast
Ph (03) 323 8640 219 office@219onjohns.co.nz

Pets by arrangement, conditions apply.

43.453913S 172.605401E Hema Atlas Map Ref 56 C9, 120 D5

South Island Camping Sites — Canterbury Region

1158 North South Holiday Park
Cnr of Johns (SH1) & Sawyers Arms Rds, Harewood, Christchurch
Ph (03) 359 5993, 0800 567 765 Fax (03) 359 1257
info@northsouth.co.nz www.northsouth.co.nz
Handy to the Christchurch International Airport.
Tennis court, sauna, duck pond.
43.471017S 172.569846E Hema Atlas Map Ref 56 D9, 120 C5

1159 Spencer Beach Holiday Park
Heyders Rd, Spencerville, Christchurch. Off lower Styx Rd
into Heyders Rd, beside Spencer Park.
Ph (03) 329 8721 www.spencerbeachholidaypark.co.nz
spencerpark@xtra.co.nz
Pets by arrangement only (off season only). Internet. Spa pool.
Bikes, pedal go-carts, surfboards and fishing gear to hire.
43.430016S 172.704804E Hema Atlas Map Ref 56 C10, 120 G7

1160 Waimakariri River Rest Areas
On either bank of the River at major road crossings
Popular fishing and boating spots for the locals.
43.413703S 172.646863E Hema Atlas Map Ref 56 C10

1161 Riverlands Holiday Park
45 Doubledays Rd, Kaiapoi:
signposted from Old Main Rd 4km S of Kaiapoi
Ph/Fax (03) 327 5511 www.riverlandspark.co.nz
riverlandspark@xtra.co.nz
9-hole golf course; small dogs permitted.
43.401161S 172.658751E Hema Atlas Map Ref 56 C10

1162 Blue Skies
12 Williams St, Kaiapoi: adjacent old Main Rd, S of Kaiapoi
Ph (03) 327 8007 gary@blueskies.org.nz
Fax (03) 327 5210 www.blueskies.org.nz
A Boy Scouts camp that is open to the public; offering comprehensive
facilities, including abseiling. Swimming pool open summer only.
43.392885S 172.652584E Hema Atlas Map Ref 56 C10

1163 Kairaki Beach Motor Camp
Featherston Ave, Kairaki Beach: signposted from centre of Kaiapoi
Ph (03) 327 7335
The many permanent residents offer incredible 'home and garden' displays,
and there are opportunities for swimming and walking on the nearby beach.
43.38659S 172.704464E Hema Atlas Map Ref 56 C10

1164 Rangiora Holiday Park
337 Lehmans Rd, Rangiora: signposted off SH72 W of Rangiora,
opposite the Racecourse
Ph/Fax (03) 313 5759 rangioraholidaypark@hotmail.com
The very good facilities have attracted numerous permanent residents.
43.292487S 172.561431E Hema Atlas Map Ref 56 B9

1165 Rangiora Leigh Camp & Holiday Park
433 Dixons Rd, Loburn. 3km N of Rangiora.
Ph (03) 312 8872 Fax (03) 312 8272
Large peaceful campground, wide vehicle access. Pets by arrangement.
43.269625S 172.552551E Hema Atlas Map Ref 56 A9

1166 Pineacres Holiday Park
740 Main North Rd: N of Kaiapoi on SH1
Ph (03) 327 5022 pineacres@xtra.co.nz
Fax (03) 327 5029 www.pineacres.co.nz
43.350875S 172.664138E Hema Atlas Map Ref 56 B10

1167 Woodend Beach Holiday Park
14 Beach Rd, Woodend Beach; 4km E of SH1 at Woodend Beach:
follow the signs from SH1
Ph (03) 312 7643 woodendbeachhp@xtra.co.nz
www.woodendbeachholidaypark.co.nz
Next to a lovely beach. Store available weekends and holidays.
Bike hire, aviaries. Wireless internet.
43.336772S 172.704091E Hema Atlas Map Ref 56 B10

1168 Waikuku Beach Holiday Park
1 Domain Tce, Waikuku Beach; 5km E of SH1 at Waikuku:
follow the signs from SH1
Ph/Fax (03) 312 7600 arkiwi@hotmail.com
Neat facilities with swimming and walking at the nearby beach.
43.287319S 172.719233E Hema Atlas Map Ref 56 B10

1169 Leithfield Beach Motor Camp
18 Lucas Dr, Leithfield Beach: turn off SH1 at the Pukeko Junction Cafe
Ph/Fax (03) 314 8518
Right next to the beach. Children's paddling pool.
43.210301S 172.754641E Hema Atlas Map Ref 56 A11

1170 Delhaven Motels & Camping Ground
124 Carters Rd, Amberley: adjacent SH1 at S end of Amberley
Ph (03) 314 8550 amberleydelhavenmotel@xtra.co.nz
Pets by arrangement.
43.157333S 172.729871E Hema Atlas Map Ref 54 D8

1171 Amberley Beach Reserve
Amberley Beach: 4km E of SH1
A caretaker may collect fees if they are in attendance.
Simple, sheltered reserve that's handy to a nice beach.
43.174528S 172.777797E Hema Atlas Map Ref 54 D9

SH73 — CHRISTCHURCH TO GREYMOUTH

1172 Addington Accommodation Park
47-51 Whiteleigh Ave, Addington, Christchurch: follow signs
to Addington Park raceway
Ph (03) 338 9770 addacc@xtra.co.nz
43.542791S 172.605633E Hema Atlas Map Ref 56 D9, 120 D2

1173 Amber Holiday Park
308 Blenheim Rd, Upper Riccarton
Ph/Fax (03) 348 3327 www.amberpark.co.nz amberpark@xtra.co.nz
A little beauty - compact, neat and tidy.
Qualmark four star. Wireless internet.
43.538367S 172.582304E Hema Atlas Map Ref 56 D9, 120 D2

Canterbury Region
South Island Camping Sites

1174 Riccarton Park Holiday Park
19 Main Sth Rd, Church Corner, Upper Riccarton
Ph (03) 348 5690 www.riccartonparkholidaypark.co.nz
Fax (03) 348 3855 info@riccartonparkholidaypark.co.nz
Older in style, but neat and tidy.
43.532428S 172.569477E Hema Atlas Map Ref 56 D9, 120 C2

1175 Glentunnel Holiday Park
Homebush Rd, Glentunnel: signposted from SH77
Ph (03) 318 2868 glentunnelholidaypark@xtra.co.nz
Swimming in the adjoining Selwyn River. Internet. Pets by arrangement.
43.483469S 171.932848E Hema Atlas Map Ref 55 D4

1176 Roadside Rest Area
SH77, E of Mt Hutt, beside Rakaia River
43.527448S 171.673873E Hema Atlas Map Ref 55 D2

1177 Waimakariri River Rest Area
Adjacent SH72 (Waimakariri Gorge Rd): S side of river
Fishing, canoeing and boating options abound.
43.3609S 172.049826E Hema Atlas Map Ref 55 B5

1178 Rest Area
Adjacent SH72: S of Oxford
43.30209S 172.167974E Hema Atlas Map Ref 55 B6

1179 Ashley Gorge Holiday Park
697 Ashley Gorge Rd, Ashley Gorge: 9km N of Oxford
Ph (03) 312 4099 bh.norton@farmside.co.nz
Fax (03) 312 4926 www.ashleygorgeholidaypark.co.nz
Currently developing an area for guests to house pets during their stay.
43.230559S 172.227693E Hema Atlas Map Ref 55 A6

1180 Grey River
Cramptons Bush Rd at the Brodie Rd intersection,
20km west of Amberley
DOC Christchurch Visitor Centre Ph (03) 341 9113
christchurchvc@doc.govt.nz
Stream water only. Dogs on leash at all times.
43.148371S 172.527484E Hema Atlas Map Ref 53 D7

1181 Wooded Gully
Turn off SH73 at Waddington, follow road to Oxford,
then Ashley Gorge Rd to Hayland Rd.
DOC Christchurch Visitor Centre Ph (03) 341 9113
christchurchvc@doc.govt.nz
43.193222S 172.336173E Hema Atlas Map Ref 53 E5, 55 A7

1182 Kowai Pass Domain Camp
E end of Springfield: signposted from SH73
Ph (03) 318 4887
Sheltered spot with tennis courts; well worth checking out.
43.342859S 171.941839E Hema Atlas Map Ref 55 B4

1183 Roadside Rest Area
SH73, W of Springfield
43.33044S 171.821859E Hema Atlas Map Ref 55 B3

1184 Roadside Rest Area
SH73, W of Springfield
43.31068S 171.768704E Hema Atlas Map Ref 55 B3

1185 Lake Lyndon Rest Area
SH73, Lake Lyndon
43.293433S 171.709195E Hema Atlas Map Ref 55 B2

1186 Roadside Rest Area
SH73, S of Castle Hill Village
43.244092S 171.726411E Hema Atlas Map Ref 52 E9

1187 Cave Stream Scenic Reserve
SH73, N of Castle Hill Village
43.196571S 171.742045E Hema Atlas Map Ref 52 E9

1188 Craigieburn, Craigieburn Conservation Park
Adjacent SH73, Craigieburn Conservation Park
DOC Arthur's Pass Visitor Centre Ph (03) 318 9211
arthurspassvc@doc.govt.nz
Stream water only. Favoured for walking and mountain biking.
43.1512S 171.731111E Hema Atlas Map Ref 52 D9

1189 Lake Pearson (Moana Rua)
Adjacent SH73, Lake Pearson: halfway between Springfield
and Arthur's Pass
DOC Arthur's Pass Visitor Centre Ph (03) 318 9211
arthurspassvc@doc.govt.nz
Stream water only. Good for bird watching, fishing, photography.
43.091457S 171.780979E Hema Atlas Map Ref 52 C10

1190 Andrews Shelter, Arthur's Pass National Park
5km along Mt White Rd: off SH73
DOC Arthur's Pass Visitor Centre Ph (03) 318 9211
arthurspassvc@doc.govt.nz
Stream water only.
42.994208S 171.793141E Hema Atlas Map Ref 52 B10

1191 Hawdon Shelter, Arthur's Pass National Park
Lower Hawdon Valley, Arthurs Pass National Park
DOC Arthur's Pass Visitor Centre Ph (03) 318 9211
arthurspassvc@doc.govt.nz
Stream water only.
42.988211S 171.748762E Hema Atlas Map Ref 52 B9

LAKE PEARSON, ARTHUR'S PASS DISTRICT PHOTO: DONNA BLABER

South Island Camping Sites — Canterbury Region

1192 Klondyke Corner, Arthur's Pass National Park
Adjacent SH73, 8km S of Arthur's Pass
DOC Arthur's Pass Visitor Centre Ph (03) 318 9211
arthurspassvc@doc.govt.nz
Stream water only; no fires.

43.002361S 171.58908E   Hema Atlas Map Ref 52 B8

1193 Greyneys, Arthur's Pass National Park
Adjacent SH73, 5km E of Arthur's Pass
DOC Arthur's Pass Visitor Centre Ph (03) 318 9211
arthurspassvc@doc.govt.nz
Stream water only.

42.98187S 171.591322E   Hema Atlas Map Ref 52 B8

1194 Avalanche Creek (Arthur's Pass), Arthur's Pass National Park
Opposite the DOC Information Centre, Arthur's Pass
DOC Arthur's Pass Visitor Centre Ph (03) 318 9211
arthurspassvc@doc.govt.nz
Casual camping right next to the town (and rail yards).

42.941999S 171.562392E   Hema Atlas Map Ref 52 B8

1195 Roadside Rest Area
Temple Basin Skifield carpark: adjacent SH73, W of Arthur's Pass
42.912343S 171.55905E   Hema Atlas Map Ref 52 A8

1196 Viaduct Lookout Rest Area
SH73, N of Temple Basin carpark
42.898777S 171.559029E   Hema Atlas Map Ref 52 A8

1197 Peg Leg Hill Rest Area
SH73, S of Deaths Corner
42.894558S 171.559115E   Hema Atlas Map Ref 52 A8

1198 Roadside Rest Area
Deaths Corner, SH73: near the summit of Arthurs Pass (923m)
42.888155S 171.556367E   Hema Atlas Map Ref 52 A8

1199 Otira Viaduct Lookout
Adjacent SH73, N of Arthur's Pass
42.880872S 171.555439E   Hema Atlas Map Ref 52 A8

1200 Otira Hotel Campsite
Opposite Otira Hotel: adjacent SH73, Otira
Ph (03) 738 2890 chris.hennah@xtra.co.nz
Traditional West Coast camping, that is basic and best suited to campervans. No charge if you don't require power.

42.831147S 171.561163E   Hema Atlas Map Ref 52 A8

1201 Morrison Memorial Bridge
SH73, N of Otira
42.786412S 171.602887E   Hema Atlas Map Ref 45 J6

1202 Jacksons Retreat
Great Alpine Highway, SH73
Ph/Fax (03) 738 0474 jacksonsretreat@xtra.co.nz
www.jacksonsretreat.co.nz
Pets by prior arrangement.

42.744224S 171.511473E   Hema Atlas Map Ref 45 J6

1203 Roadside Rest Area
The Avenue Scenic Reserve, SH73: W of Jacksons
DOC Arthur's Pass Visitor Centre Ph (03) 318 9211
arthurspassvc@doc.govt.nz
42.743553S 171.505324E   Hema Atlas Map Ref 45 J7

1204 Roadside Rest Area
Adjacent SH73: W of Jacksons
42.738698S 171.430504E   Hema Atlas Map Ref 45 J6

1205 Roadside Rest Area
Okuku Scenic Reserve, SH73: W of Turiwhate
DOC Arthur's Pass Visitor Centre Ph (03) 318 9211
arthurspassvc@doc.govt.nz
42.715229S 171.24476E   Hema Atlas Map Ref 45 H4

BANKS PENINSULA — CHRISTCHURCH TO AKAROA

1206 All Seasons Holiday Park
5 Kidbrooke St, Woolston, Christchurch: signposted off Linwood Rd
Ph (03) 384 9490 Reservations 0800 500 232 Fax (03) 384 9843
stay@allseasonsholidaypark.co.nz www.allseasonsholidaypark.co.nz
Handy to Sumner Beach. Internet. Qualmark four star plus.

43.544506S 172.69272E   Hema Atlas Map Ref 120 G2, 56 D10

1207 South Brighton Motor Camp
59 Halsey St, South New Brighton, Christchurch: Find the pier at New Brighton, head south 3km and Halsey St is on your right.
Ph/Fax (03) 388 9844 www.southbrightonmotorcamp.co.nz
relax@southbrightonmotorcamp.co.nz
A typical beach camping ground, with walks and swimming opportunities, yet only 20 minutes from Christchurch city centre. Internet. Tranquil grounds with mature trees and sheltered sites. Mountain bike hire.

43.534285S 172.735844E   Hema Atlas Map Ref 56 D10, 120 H2

1208 Sumner Beach Reserve
Waterfront, Sumner, Christchurch

43.564568S 172.754329E   Hema Atlas Map Ref 56 E11, 120 H1

1209 Mt Cavendish Scenic Reserve
Summit Rd, Heathcote Valley, Christchurch
43.593681S 172.707903E   Hema Atlas Map Ref 56 E10

1210 Coronation Hill Reserve/Sign of the Kiwi Rest Area
Dyers Pass Rd, Christchurch
43.606262S 172.645275E   Hema Atlas Map Ref 56 E10

1211 Allendale Reserve
Governors Bay, Christchurch
43.640514S 172.649663E   Hema Atlas Map Ref 56 E10

Canterbury Region

1212 Charteris Bay Reserve
Marine Dr, Charteris Bay, Christchurch
43.645673S 172.709414E Hema Atlas Map Ref 56 F10

1213 Gebbies Pass Summit
Akaroa end of Summit Rd, Banks Peninsula
43.68923S 172.639164E Hema Atlas Map Ref 56 F10

1214 Roadside Rest Area
SH75, S of Hilltop
43.75297S 172.872789E Hema Atlas Map Ref 56 G11

1215 French Farm Rest Area
Wainui Main Rd, French Farm, Banks Peninsula: S of SH75
43.782097S 172.907605E Hema Atlas Map Ref 56 G12

1216 YMCA Wainui Park Campground
Wainui Valley Rd, Wainui, Banks Peninsula
Ph (03) 304 8460 wainui@ymcachch.org.nz Fax (03) 304 8784
www.ymcachch.org.nz/wainui/camping
Canoeing and highwire facilities. Bookings recommended.
43.813181S 172.893833E Hema Atlas Map Ref 56 G12

1217 Roadside Rest Area
SH75, W of Duvauchelle
43.759426S 172.913645E Hema Atlas Map Ref 56 G12

1218 Duvauchelle Bay Rest Area
SH75, Duvauchelle Bay, Banks Peninsula
43.750997S 172.927596E Hema Atlas Map Ref 56 G12

1219 Duvauchelle Holiday Park
Seafield Rd, Duvauchelle, Banks Peninsula: clearly visible from SH75
Ph (03) 304 5777 Fax (03) 304 5778
duvauchelleholidaypark@hotmail.com
Exposed but harbourside. DOC does not let dogs stay, but cats and birds are allowed.
43.753954S 172.941979E Hema Atlas Map Ref 56 G12

1220 Akaroa Top 10 Holiday Park
96 Morgan Rd, Akaroa, Banks Peninsula: signposted from main road into Akaroa, and from Akaroa Centre
Ph/Fax (03) 304 7471 akaroa.holidaypark@xtra.co.nz
www.akaroa-holidaypark.co.nz
Sheltered spot with charming views that's handy to Akaroa town centre. Internet. Qualmark four star.
43.796865S 172.9706E Hema Atlas Map Ref 56 G12

1221 Akaroa Domain Rest Area
Akaroa Domain, Akaroa, Banks Peninsula
43.800589S 172.967847E Hema Atlas Map Ref 56 G12

1222 Okains Bay Camping Ground
1162 Okains Bay Rd, Okains Bay, Banks Peninsula: 13km from Akaroa Rd, via Summit Rd
Ph (03) 304 8789 Fax (03) 340 8635
Caretaker on-site Aug-May. Honesty box system operates June-July. Take care on the twisty access road. Okains Bay museum is well worth a visit.
43.709351S 173.043643E Hema Atlas Map Ref 56 F13

SH1 — CHRISTCHURCH TO ASHBURTON

1223 Alpine View Holiday Park
650 Main South Rd (SH1), Templeton, Christchurch
Ph (03) 349 7666 alpine.view@xtra.co.nz
43.547476S 172.494849E Hema Atlas Map Ref 56 D8, 120 A2

1224 Roadside Rest Area
Adjacent SH1 at both ends of the Rakaia bridge
43.737207S 172.045498E Hema Atlas Map Ref 55 G5

1225 Rakaia River Holiday Park & Motels
Main South Rd (SH1), Rakaia: S end of Rakaia bridge
Ph/Fax (03) 302 7257 rrjackson@xtra.co.nz
www.rakaiariverholidaypark.co.nz
Situated next to a major salmon-fishing river. Wireless internet.
43.751826S 172.029253E Hema Atlas Map Ref 55 G5

1226 Rakaia Huts Camping Area
At N mouth of Rakaia River: 30km SE of SH1 Ashburton District Council 'Freedom Camping'
www.ashburtondc.govt.nz
A caretaker may collect fees if they are in attendance. Regarded as a favoured spot for keen salmon anglers.
43.888152S 172.240544E Hema Atlas Map Ref 55 H6

1227 Roadside Rest Area
Adjacent SH1, at intersection with Sommerton Rd:
S of Rakaia, N of Ashburton
43.836905S 171.850125E Hema Atlas Map Ref 55 H3

1228 Coronation Holiday Park
778 East St, Ashburton: adjacent SH1 at N end of Ashburton
Ph (03) 308 6603 info@coronationpark.co.nz Fax (03) 308 6606
www.coronationpark.co.nz
Spa pool. Wireless internet.
43.896225S 171.761276E Hema Atlas Map Ref 55 J3

1229 Roadside Rest Area
SH1: either end of the bridge at the S end of Ashburton
43.91128S 171.735943E Hema Atlas Map Ref 55 J2

1230 Methven Camping Grounds
Barkers Rd, Methven: SH77, N of Ashburton, S of Mount Hutt
Ph (03) 302 8005 Reservations 0800 122 695
methvennz@hotmail.com
Spacious parklike grounds.
43.629656S 171.650355E Hema Atlas Map Ref 52 J9, 55 E2

South Island Camping Sites — Canterbury Region

1231 Abisko Lodge & Apartment (& Campground)
74 Main St, Methven
accommodation@abisko.co.nz
Wireless internet. Spa pool, sauna.
43.635857S 171.647191E   Hema Atlas Map Ref 52 J9, 55 F2

1232 Pudding Hill Lodge
5259 Arundel Rakaia Gorge Rd. SH72 Pudding Hill: SW of Mount Hutt, NW of Methven. Take the gravel road between one-lane bridges.
Ph (03) 302 9627   www.puddinghilllodge.co.nz
info@puddinghilllodge.co.nz
Qualmark three star. Pets by prior arrangement.
43.587036S 171.529771E   Hema Atlas Map Ref 52 J8

1233 Mount Somers Holiday Park
Hoods Rd, Ashburton
Ph (03) 303 9719 Fax (03) 303 9797   www.mountsomers.co.nz
camp@mountsomers.co.nz
Pets by arrangement only.
43.705062S 171.397648E   Hema Atlas Map Ref 61 A5

SH1 — ASHBURTON TO TIMARU

1234 Ashburton Holiday Park
86 Moronan Rd, Tinwald: W from SH1, S of Tinwald township
Ph (03) 308 6805 Fax (03) 307 0115
office@ashburtonholidaypark.co.nz   www.ashburtonholidaypark.co.nz
Set in mature, parklike grounds, adjoining tennis courts and duck pond. Internet. Pets by arrangement.
43.925566S 171.70036E   Hema Atlas Map Ref 62 D8

1235 Rangitata Rest Area
SH1, NE of intersection with SH79
44.065679S 171.372871E   Hema Atlas Map Ref 61 E5

1236 Upper Orari Rest Area
SH79, E side of Orari River
44.04428S 171.273675E   Hema Atlas Map Ref 61 E5

1237 Grumpys Retreat N' Holiday Park
7 Keen Rd, Orari Bridge: 6km N of Geraldine
Ph 0800 478 679, (03) 693 7453   2grumpys@xtra.co.nz
www.grumpiesretreat.co.nz
Internet. Tennis courts. Pets by arrangement. Quiet and peaceful, sites for large and small vans.
44.04622S 171.262785E   Hema Atlas Map Ref 61 E5

1238 Arundel Bridge Reserve
S end of Arundel Bridge, SH72
43.973878S 171.297496E   Hema Atlas Map Ref 61 D5

1239 Peel Forest
Peel Forest: off SH72, 12km NW of Arundel
Arthur's Pass Visitor Centre (03) 318 9211   arthurspassvc@doc.govt.nz
43.890675S 171.266416E   Hema Atlas Map Ref 61 C5

1240 Orari Gorge
Yates Rd: 12km NW of Geraldine, via Tripp Settlement
Arthur's Pass Visitor Centre (03) 318 9211   arthurspassvc@doc.govt.nz
43.987791S 171.183065E   Hema Atlas Map Ref 61 E4

1241 Waihi Gorge
Waihi Gorge Rd: 14km NW of Geraldine, beside Waihi River
Arthur's Pass Visitor Centre (03) 318 9211   arthurspassvc@doc.govt.nz
44.002832S 171.155608E   Hema Atlas Map Ref 61 E4

1242 Geraldine Kiwi Holiday Park
39 Hislop St, Geraldine: signposted from SH72 & SH79 in town centre
Ph/Fax (03) 693 8147   info@geraldineholidaypark.co.nz
www.geraldineholidaypark.co.nz
Internet. Bike hire. Outdoor chess and petanque.
44.094181S 171.243739E   Hema Atlas Map Ref 61 F4

1243 Orari River Rest Area
SH1, NE of Orari
44.127636S 171.309119E   Hema Atlas Map Ref 61 H5

1244 Speechleys Bridge Rest Area
SH79, SE of Geraldine
44.117562S 171.208352E   Hema Atlas Map Ref 61 F4

1245 Winchester Motor Camp
Adjacent SH1, Winchester: S end of town
Ph (03) 615 7564
This is a council-run site which operates during summer Oct-April.
44.191795S 171.278177E   Hema Atlas Map Ref 61 G5

1246 Temuka Holiday Park
1 Fergusson Dr, Temuka: signposted E from Temuka town centre
Ph (03) 615 7241   temukaholidaypark@xtra.co.nz   Fax (03) 615 6554
www.temukaholidaypark.co.nz
An unexpected treat.
44.246793S 171.281293E   Hema Atlas Map Ref 61 G5

1247 Riverside Rest Area
Adjacent SH1, S of Temuka
44.261714S 171.27061E   Hema Atlas Map Ref 61 F5

1248 Timaru Top 10 Holiday Park
154A Selwyn St, Timaru: turn into Hobbs St, on N side of Pak'n-Save, drive 500m to intersection with Selwyn St.
Ph (03) 684 7690 Fax (03) 688 1004
topten@timaruholidaypark.co.nz   www.timaruholidaypark.co.nz
Just 1km from the beach and town centre. Qualmark four star plus. Pets by arrangement.
44.384149S 171.231734E   Hema Atlas Map Ref 61 J4

1249 Caroline Bay Beach Rest Area
Caroline Bay Park: signposted from Timaru town centre
44.390241S 171.252137E   Hema Atlas Map Ref 61 J5, 121 B2

Canterbury Region — South Island Camping Sites

1250 Glenmark Holiday Park
30 Beaconsfield Rd, Timaru: signposted from SH1 at S end of Timaru
Ph/Fax (03) 684 3682 glenmarkmotorcamp@xtra.co.nz
www.timarumotorcamp.co.nz
44.41775S 171.237315E Hema Atlas Map Ref 61 J4

SH8 — TIMARU TO TWIZEL

1251 Cave Rest Area
Adjacent SH8: 16km W of Pleasant Point, 29km S of Fairlie
44.309381S 170.953551E Hema Atlas Map Ref 61 H2

1252 Mt Nimrod
Back Line Rd: 32km SW of Timaru, via Motukaika
Arthur's Pass Visitor Centre Ph (03) 318 9211
arthurspassvc@doc.govt.nz
44.432607S 170.872057E Hema Atlas Map Ref 60 J13

1253 Rest Area
Adjacent SH8: S Fairlie
44.204914S 170.869051E Hema Atlas Map Ref 61 G2

1254 Fairlie Gateway Top 10 Holiday Park
10 Allandale Rd, Fairlie: SH79 signposted from the centre of Fairlie
Ph/Fax (03) 685 8375 or 0800 324 754 relax@fairlietop10.co.nz
www.fairlietop10.co.nz
Peaceful parklike surroundings. Qualmark four star.
44.097554S 170.832443E Hema Atlas Map Ref 61 F1

1255 Pioneer Park
Homebush Rd: 14km W of Geraldine, via Gudex/Middle Valley roads
Arthur's Pass Visitor Centre Ph (03) 318 9211
arthurspassvc@doc.govt.nz
Dogs allowed, must be on leash at all times.
44.141792S 170.960167E Hema Atlas Map Ref 61 F2

1256 Kakahu Rest Area
SH79, E of Beautiful Valley
44.123765S 171.082166E Hema Atlas Map Ref 61 F3

1257 Edwards Stream Rest Area
SH8, SE of Lake Tekapo
44.061874S 170.503359E Hema Atlas Map Ref 60 F10

1258 Lake Tekapo Holiday Park
Lakeside Dr, Lake Tekapo: Adjacent SH8, W end of Tekapo Village
Ph (03) 680 6825 or 0800 853 853 Fax (03) 680 6824
www.laketekapo-accommodation.co.nz
info@laketekapo-accommodation.co.nz
Lakefront boating and swimming opportunities in a picturesque and sheltered location.
44.000966S 170.464691E Hema Atlas Map Ref 60 E9

1259 Lake Pukaki Rest Area & Viewpoint
Adjacent SH8, S end of Lake Pukaki
Designated camping area for fully self-contained vehicles. Maximum one night in any calendar month.
44.190309S 170.141624E Hema Atlas Map Ref 59 G7

1260 Glentanner Park
Adjacent SH80: 15 min S of Mt Cook Village
Ph (03) 435 1855 or 0800 453 682 Fax (03) 435 1854
www.glentanner.co.nz info@glentanner.co.nz
This is a convenient base for alpine flights as it adjoins The Helicopter Line's airstrip. Pets permitted with staff approval. Internet. Licensed Cafe.
43.912105S 170.121261E Hema Atlas Map Ref 59 D6

1261 White Horse Hill
Adjacent SH80, Mt Cook Village
Christchurch Visitor Centre Ph (03) 341 9113
christchurchvc@doc.govt.nz
43.718035S 170.09407E Hema Atlas Map Ref 59 B6

1262 Bendrose Creek Rest Area
Adjacent SH8, just N of Twizel
44.252447S 170.116256E Hema Atlas Map Ref 59 H6

1263 Parklands Tourist Park
122 Mackenzie Dr, Twizel
Ph (03) 435 0507 parklands1@xtra.co.nz
Fax (03) 435 0544 www.parklandstwizel.co.nz
Pets only by prior arrangement in camping area (no pets allowed in cabins or units).
44.252472S 170.100249E Hema Atlas Map Ref 59 H6

1264 Lake Ruataniwha Holiday Park
Max Smith Dr, Twizel: about 4km S of Twizel, signposted from SH8 at S end of Twizel
Ph (03) 435 0613 holidaypark2000@xtra.co.nz
Handy to the South Island's best rowing venue, with fishing, boating and safe swimming at your back door.
44.272067S 170.068324E Hema Atlas Map Ref 59 H6

1265 Lake Ruataniwha Recreation Reserve
Adjacent SH8, S of Twizel
44.288638S 170.080304E Hema Atlas Map Ref 59 H6

1266 Lake Wairepo Rest Area
Adjacent SH8, S of Twizel
44.303373S 170.068645E Hema Atlas Map Ref 59 H6

1267 Lake Ohau and Lake Middleton Recreation Reserves
Lake Ohau Road. 17km NW of SH8: turn off SH8 13km S of Twizel
Ph (03) 434 8060 ext. 8658
A caretaker may collect fees if they are in attendance.
44.274118S 169.849195E Hema Atlas Map Ref 59 H4

1268 Roadside Rest Area
SH8, S of Twizel
44.381967S 169.997982E Hema Atlas Map Ref 59 J6

1269 Temple
Lake Ohau Rd: 18km N of Lake Ohau Alpine Village
Arthur's Pass Visitor Centre Ph (03) 318 9211
arthurspassvc@doc.govt.nz
Stream water only.
44.107267S 169.818265E Hema Atlas Map Ref 59 F4

SH1 — TIMARU TO OAMARU

1270 Otaio Gorge
Back Line Rd: 29km SW of Timaru, via Gordons Valley
Arthur's Pass Visitor Centre Ph (03) 318 9211
arthurspassvc@doc.govt.nz
44.52267S 170.928115E Hema Atlas Map Ref 68 B11

1271 St Andrews Recreation Reserve & Camping Ground
Adjacent SH1, S end of Saint Andrews Ph (03) 689 0000
Pay caretaker or use honesty system.
44.535831S 171.184768E Hema Atlas Map Ref 68 B13

1272 Victoria Park Camp & Cabins
Cnr Tennant & Naylor Sts, Waimate: at S end of Waimate
Ph (03) 689 8079 graeme@waimatedc.govt.nz
Good facilities in a parklike setting, and handy to the town centre.
44.73714S 171.038345E Hema Atlas Map Ref 68 D12

1273 Knottingley Park Motor Camp
Waihao Back Rd, Waimate: at S end of Waimate
Ph (03) 689 8079 graeme@waimatedc.govt.nz
Peaceful and reasonably priced with 'character' facilities in a magnificent 36ha forest park.
44.750231S 171.055083E Hema Atlas Map Ref 68 D12

1274 Kelcey's Bush Farmyard Holiday Park
677 Mill Rd: 12 km inland from Waimate. Off SH32.
Ph (03) 689 8057 Fax (03) 689 8091 kelceysbush@xtra.co.nz
www.kelseysbush.co.nz
An opportunity to get up close and personal with a range of NZ wildlife and farm animals in a pretty valley setting. Pets by arrangement.
44.704352S 170.974755E Hema Atlas Map Ref 68 C11

1275 Rest Area
SH82: S of Waimate, W of Glenavy
44.872078S 170.886577E Hema Atlas Map Ref 68 F11

1276 Waitaki River Rest Area
Adjacent SH1: at N end of Waitaki River bridge
44.923569S 171.101604E Hema Atlas Map Ref 68 F13

1277 Waitaki Waters Holiday Park
305 Kaik Rd, Waitaki: E off SH1, just S of the Waitaki River bridge
Ph/Fax (03) 431 3880 derek.chapple@mac.com
www.camping-oamaru.co.nz
Ideal for anglers seeking salmon and trout from the nearby Waitaki River. Internet.
44.945532S 171.131725E Hema Atlas Map Ref 68 F13

1278 Roadside Rest Area
SH1, S of Waitaki Bridge
44.960336S 171.081068E Hema Atlas Map Ref 68 F12

1279 Roadside Rest Area
SH1, S of Pukiuri
45.060197S 171.001122E Hema Atlas Map Ref 68 G12

OTAGO REGION

MOERAKI BEACH PHOTO: MICHELLE BIGNELL

SH83 — SH1 TO OMARAMA (SH8) 94
SH1 — OMARU TO PALMERSTON 95
SH85 — PALMERSTON TO ALEXANDRA 96
SH1 — PALMERSTON TO DUNEDIN 96
SH1 — DUNEDIN TO MILTON 97
SH92 — MILTON TO INVERCARGILL 98
SH8 — MILTON TO CROMWELL 99
SH8 — CROMWELL TO OMARAMA (SH83) 100
SH6 — CROMWELL TO HAAST 101
SH6 & SH6A — CROMWELL TO GLENORCHY 102

SH83 — SH1 TO OMARAMA (SH8)

1280 Dansey's Pass Holiday Park
276 Dansey's Pass Rd: 15km S of Duntroon, SH83
Ph (03) 431 2564 danseyspass@gmail.com Fax (03) 431 2560
www.danseyspassholidaypark.co.nz
A magic and tranquil spot, with opportunities for gold panning or swimming in the Maerewhenua River. It's also a convenient base from which to explore the Vanished World fossil trail. Pets by prior arrangement.
44.944914S 170.569447E Hema Atlas Map Ref 68 F8

1281 Kurow Holiday Park
76 Bledisloe St, Kurow: adjacent SH83 at NW end of Kurow
Ph (03) 436 0725 Fax (03) 436 0726
www.kurowholidaypark.co.nz
Located on the south bank of the Waitaki River, with freshwater swimming and fishing at your backdoor. Internet.
44.727045S 170.467496E Hema Atlas Map Ref 67 D7

1282 Hakataramea Rest Area
Adjacent SH82: N side of Waitaki R
44.727868S 170.479089E Hema Atlas Map Ref 68 D8

1283 Roadside Rest Area
SH83, Waitaki Dam Lookout
44.690299S 170.424503E Hema Atlas Map Ref 68 D7

1284 Roadside Rest Area
SH83, by dam wall at Aviemore
44.657705S 170.347158E Hema Atlas Map Ref 67 C6

Otago Region — South Island Camping Sites — 95

1285 — Fisherman's Bend, Lake Aviemore
N side of Lake Aviemore: off SH83
Ph (03) 689 8079 - Waimate District Council

Season is from October to April. Overnight tickets available from camp registration booths and camp supervisors. Numerous casual camping, boat launching, picnicking and fishing sites that are well worth exploring.

44.663699S 170.362535E   Hema Atlas Map Ref 67 C7

1286 — Roadside Rest Area
SH83, beside Lake Aviemore
44.635917S 170.287895E   Hema Atlas Map Ref 67 C6

1287 — Parsons Creek Recreation Reserve
Adjacent SH83: S side of Lake Aviemore

A caretaker may collect fees if they are in attendance. Lakeside swimming, fishing and boating opportunities.

44.617056S 170.240511E   Hema Atlas Map Ref 67 C6

1288 — Roadside Rest Area
SH83, S of Otematata
44.614445S 170.229536E   Hema Atlas Map Ref 67 C5

1289 — Otematata Holiday Park
East Rd, Otematata: S of SH83
Ph/Fax (03) 438 7826 otem.camp@xtra.co.nz

44.60623S 170.1949E   Hema Atlas Map Ref 67 C5

1290 — Benmore Dam Recreation Reserve
N of SH83 from Otematata

A caretaker may collect fees if they are in attendance. Follow this road for a scenic drive to Aviemore with plentiful lakeside camping, swimming, fishing and boating opportunities.

44.599432S 170.194279E   Hema Atlas Map Ref 67 C5

1291 — Loch Laird Recreation Reserve
Adjacent SH83 and Lake Benmore

A caretaker may collect fees if they are in attendance.

44.575148S 170.182446E   Hema Atlas Map Ref 67 B4

1292 — Sailors Cutting Recreation Reserve
Adjacent SH83 and Lake Benmore

A caretaker may collect fees if they are in attendance.

44.545491S 170.085906E   Hema Atlas Map Ref 67 B4

1293 — Lake Benmore Holiday Park
Adjacent SH83 and Lake Benmore: 8km E of Omarama.
8km east of Omarama beside Lake Benmore.
Ph/Fax (03) 438 9624 benmoreview@xtra.co.nz

Campers have access to the lake edge for boating, fishing and swimming. Each site even has its own personal toilet and shower!

44.522805S 170.053351E   Hema Atlas Map Ref 67 B4

SH1 — OMARU TO PALMERSTON

1294 — Oamaru Top 10 Holiday Park
30 Chelmer St, Oamaru: adjoining Oamaru's Botanic Gardens
Ph (03) 434 7666 Fax (03) 434 7662 oamarutop10@xtra.co.nz
www.oamarutop10.co.nz

Sheltered site with pretty walks. Qualmark four star.

45.097473S 170.956082E   Hema Atlas Map Ref 68 H11

1295 — Kakanui Camping Ground
Waianakarua Rd, 14km S of Oamaru on Coast Rd.
Around the corner from Maheno turnoff.
Ph 021 525 896 camping@kakanui.net www.kakanui.net

A relaxed and friendly camping ground. Good for fishing, surfing and looking for penguins.

45.185016S 170.891048E   Hema Atlas Map Ref 68 J11

1296 — All Day Bay Recreation Reserve
All Day Bay, Coast Rd: S of Kakanui

45.210947S 170.884137E   Hema Atlas Map Ref 68 J11

1297 — Glencoe Reserve
2km W of Herbert: off SH1
DOC Coastal Otago Area Office Ph (03) 477 0677

Dogs allowed.

45.228751S 170.758379E   Hema Atlas Map Ref 68 J10, 74 A13

1298 — Olive Grove Lodge and Holiday Park
Waianakarua: adjacent SH1, 25km S of Oamaru
Ph (03) 439 5830 www.olivebranch.co.nz info@olivebranch.co.nz

Relaxed rural ambiance with stream for bathing and/or swimming. Organic meals provided on request. Spa, sauna.

45.254758S 170.795412E   Hema Atlas Map Ref 68 J10, 74 A13

1299 — Moeraki Boulders Holiday Park
2 Carlisle St, Hampden: E of SH1, 35km S of Oamaru
Ph (03) 439 4439 info@moerakibouldersholidaypark.co.nz
www.moerakibouldersholidaypark.co.nz

Sheltered scenic beachside camp. Kayaks and bikes for rent. Wireless internet.

45.323407S 170.823155E   Hema Atlas Map Ref 74 B13

1300 — Moeraki Village Holiday Park
114 Haven St, Moeraki: E of SH1, 40km S of Oamaru
Ph/Fax (03) 439 4759 moerakivillageholidaypark@xtra.co.nz
www.moerakivillageholidaypark.co.nz

Scenic coastal fishing village with a great local seafood restaurant in Fleurs Cafe. Deluxe cabins and tourist flats with SkyTV. Pets must be on leash, owners must clean up after them.

45.360667S 170.852838E   Hema Atlas Map Ref 74 B14

1301 — Trotters Gorge
Approx 3km south of Moeraki, turn west off SH1 into Horse Range Rd
DOC Queenstown Regional Visitor Centre Ph (03) 442 7935
queenstownvc@doc.govt.nz

Stream water only.

45.404288S 170.781529E   Hema Atlas Map Ref 74 B13

South Island Camping Sites

Otago Region

1302 Roadside Rest Area
SH1, beachside near Katiki
45.400267S 170.838847E   Hema Atlas Map Ref 74 B14

1303 Roadside Rest Area
SH1, beachside N of Shag Point
45.452534S 170.808544E   Hema Atlas Map Ref 74 C13

SH85 — PALMERSTON TO ALEXANDRA

1304 Roadside Rest Area
Shag River swimming hole: adjacent SH1, NW of Palmerston
Favoured local swimming and picnic spot.
45.406013S 170.643327E   Hema Atlas Map Ref 74 B12

1305 Roadside Rest Area
Pigroot Creek, adjacent SH85: SE of Kyeburn
45.197023S 170.425301E   Hema Atlas Map Ref 67 J7

1306 Otago Central Rail Trail Memorial Rest Area
Adjacent SH87: S of Hyde, N of Middlemarch
45.354762S 170.233467E   Hema Atlas Map Ref 74 B9

1307 Dansey Pass Hotel
Dansey's Pass Rd: N of SH85 from Kyeburn
Dansey's Pass Rd is not recommended for bigger campers and buses: treat this road with respect.
44.987582S 170.285795E   Hema Atlas Map Ref 67 G6

1308 Ranfurly Holiday Park
3 Reade St, Ranfurly: signposted from the centre of Ranfurly
Reservations Ph 0800 726 6387 bookings@ranfurlyholidaypark.co.nz
Ph/Fax (03) 444 9144 www.ranfurlyholidaypark.co.nz
A convenient base for the Ranfurly to Middlemarch stage of the Otago Central Rail Trail. Pets by arrangement only. Internet.
45.131447S 170.102604E   Hema Atlas Map Ref 67 H5

1309 Larchview Holiday Park
8 Swimming Dam Rd, Naseby, Central Otago SH85:
signposted from Naseby centre
Ph (03) 444 9904 bookings@larchviewholidaypark.co.nz
www.larchviewholidaypark.co.nz
Set in a pretty former goldmining town, this camp is handy to mountainbiking trails and a dam for ice skating and curling in winter. Small pets by arrangement only. Bike, toboggan and wheat bag hire. Internet.
45.022286S 170.142433E   Hema Atlas Map Ref 67 G5

1310 Wedderburn Roadside Rest Area
SH85: rest Area for the Central Otago Rail Trail
45.030024S 170.010188E   Hema Atlas Map Ref 67 G4

1311 Roadside Rest Area
Hills Creek, adjacent SH85
44.944049S 169.912506E   Hema Atlas Map Ref 66 G14, 67 G3

1312 Blue Lake Recreation Reserve
St Bathans: a 10km diversion N of SH85
A beautiful picnic spot in an intriguing old gold town.
44.870004S 169.811292E   Hema Atlas Map Ref 66 F13, 67 F2

1313 St Bathans Domain
From SH85, northeast of Alexandra at Becks follow Loop Rd north until Fish Pond Rd.
DOC Queenstown Regional Visitor Centre Ph (03) 442 7935
queenstownvc@doc.govt.nz
44.867529S 169.79961E   Hema Atlas Map Ref 66 F13, 67 F2

1314 Homestead
From SH85, turn into the Ranfurly end of Loop Rd, follow for 6.5km. Turn into Hawkdun Run Rd and follow for 15km.
DOC Queenstown Regional Visitor Centre Ph (03) 442 7935
queenstownvc@doc.govt.nz
44.776909S 169.889713E   Hema Atlas Map Ref 66 E14, 67 E3

1315 Lauder Roadside Rest Area
SH85: Rest Area for the Central Otago Rail Trail
45.054157S 169.672692E   Hema Atlas Map Ref 66 H12, 67 H1

1316 Omakau Recreation Reserve Camping Ground
Signposted W off SH85 at the S end of Omakau. Lauder-Omakau Road.
Ph (03) 447 3814
A caretaker may collect fees or donations.
45.09953S 169.595709E   Hema Atlas Map Ref 66 H12

1317 Alexandra Tourist Park
31 Ngapara St, Alexandra: signposted off SH85, N of Alexandra
Ph (03) 448 8861 alex.touristpark@xtra.co.nz
Only 250m from the Central Otago Rail Trail.
45.242539S 169.395601E   Hema Atlas Map Ref 73 A2

1318 Alexandra Holiday Park
Manuherikia Rd, Alexandra: off SH85, N of Alexandra
Ph (03) 448 8297 alex.hol.park@xtra.co.nz Fax (03) 448 8294
www.alexandraholidaypark.com
A very popular camp with swimming in the adjoining river. Store open only Christmas/January. Internet.
45.2451S 169.403741E   Hema Atlas Map Ref 73 A2

SH1 — PALMERSTON TO DUNEDIN

1319 Waikouaiti Beach Motor Camp
186 Beach St, Waikouaiti: E from SH1, S edge of Waikouaiti township
Ph (03) 465 7432 cleghorns@xtra.co.nz
45.611532S 170.672928E   Hema Atlas Map Ref 74 E12

1320 Roadside Rest Area
SH1, western edge of Waikouaiti
45.605693S 170.650575E   Hema Atlas Map Ref 74 E12

1321 Roadside Rest Area
SH1, S of Merton
45.652935S 170.58466E   Hema Atlas Map Ref 74 E12

Otago Region — South Island Camping Sites

1322 Leith Valley Touring Park
103 Malvern St, Dunedin: off Duke St
Ph 0800 555 331 lvtpdun@xtra.co.nz Fax (03) 467 9502
www.leithvalleytouringpark.co.nz
Sauna. Pets by arrangement. Internet.
45.850737S 170.50358E   Hema Atlas Map Ref 74 G11, 124 D3

1323 3 Mile Hill Rest Area & View Point
Three Mile Hill Rd: follow Stuart St up the hills from the top of the Octagon
On the most scenic route from Dunedin to Outram and SH87 to Middlemarch. Extensive views of the Taieri Plains, yet only five minutes from Dunedin's city centre.
45.849803S 170.427892E   Hema Atlas Map Ref 74 G11, 124 F3,

1324 Vauxhall Reserve
Portobello Rd, Otago Peninsula
Day parking only.
45.884546S 170.525109E   Hema Atlas Map Ref 74 H11, 124 D4,

1325 Dunedin Holiday Park
41 Victoria Rd, St Kilda, Dunedin
Ph (03) 455 4690 Fax (03) 455 4691 office@dunedinholidaypark.co.nz
www.dunedinholidaypark.co.nz
Qualmark four star plus. Pets by arrangement. Internet.
45.905226S 170.514654E   Hema Atlas Map Ref 74 H11, 124 D5

1326 Macandrew Bay Rest Area & Reserve
Portobello Rd, Macandrew Bay, Otago Peninsula
Harbourside swimming and sunbathing adjoining Macandrew Bay village.
45.8689S 170.597326E   Hema Atlas Map Ref 74 H12, 124 B3

1327 Portobello Village Tourist Park
27 Hereweka St, Portobello: E from centre of Portobello village
Ph (03) 478 0359 portobellopark@xtra.co.nz www.portobellopark.co.nz
Peaceful and sheltered spot, yet only 500m from Portobello village. Qualmark four star. Pets by arrangement. Internet.
45.842798S 170.650879E   Hema Atlas Map Ref 74 G12, 124 A2

SH1 — DUNEDIN TO MILTON

1328 Aaron Lodge Top 10 Holiday Park
162 Kaikorai Valley Rd, Burnside, Dunedin:
3km from Dunedin City Centre
Ph (03) 476 4725 0800 879 227 stay@aaronlodge.co.nz
www.aaronlodge.co.nz www.aaronlodgetop10.co.nz
Qualmark four star plus.
45.868705S 170.474911E   Hema Atlas Map Ref 74 H11, 124 E3

1329 Mosgiel Motor Camp
221 Gordon Rd, Mosgiel
Ph (027) 489 5517
45.867865S 170.34581E   Hema Atlas Map Ref 74 H10, 124 J3

1330 Outram Glen Picnic Area
Taieri Gorge/Outram Glen Scenic Reserve:
turn N at the W end of the Taieri River Bridge just 1km N of Outram
A favourite summer swimming spot for local families.
45.85157S 170.238855E   Hema Atlas Map Ref 74 G9

1331 Blind Billy's Holiday Camp & Middlemarch Motels
Mold St, Middlemarch: signposted from the town centre
Ph (03) 464 3355 info@middlemarch-motels.co.nz
www.middlemarch-motels.co.nz
A handy base for the start/finish of the Otago Central Rail Trail. Pets by arrangement.
45.506607S 170.125572E   Hema Atlas Map Ref 74 D8

1332 Brighton Motor Camp & Boat Hire
1044 Brighton Rd, Brighton: 20km S of Dunedin on coastal route
Ph (03) 481 1404
Close to an attractive sheltered beach.
45.947866S 170.329808E   Hema Atlas Map Ref 74 H10, 124 J6

1333 Brighton Domain
Brighton Domain, Brighton: across the bridge at S end of township
Day use only.
45.947661S 170.334003E   Hema Atlas Map Ref 74 J10, 124 J6

1334 Taieri River Scenic Reserve (AKA Kaarston Park)
24km E of SH1 at Waihola or 40km S of Dunedin on coastal route
Favoured launching spot for coastal and river fishing.
46.056035S 170.19626E   Hema Atlas Map Ref 79 C7

1335 East Taieri Roadside Rest Area
SH1: 14km S of Dunedin, just S of turnoff to Dunedin Airport
Sheltered with picnic tables.
45.919753S 170.26236E   Hema Atlas Map Ref 74 H9

1336 Lake Waihola Holiday Park & Recreation Reserve
Waihola Domain, Waihola: W from SH1 in the centre of Waihola township
Ph (03) 417 8908 Fax (03) 417 8973
A favoured lakeside picnic spot that's popular for boating and jet skiing. Pets by arrangement. Disabled toilet only.
46.022129S 170.093337E   Hema Atlas Map Ref 79 B6

1337 Sinclair Wetlands Camp
854 Clarendon-Berwick Road, Berwick:
W from SH1 either N or S of Waihola
Ph (03) 486 2654
An eco-camp/lodge offering a small area for campervans and camping with an opportunity to explore the adjoining wildlife and wetlands reserve.
45.98469S 170.078338E   Hema Atlas Map Ref 79 B6

98 South Island Camping Sites — Otago Region

1338 Taylor Park Motor Camp
11 Park Road, Milton: at north end of town, next to the swimming centre
Ph (03) 417 8109
Enter campsite at Park Road entrance.
A caretaker may collect fees if they are in attendance.
46.112599S 169.967229E   Hema Atlas Map Ref 79 C5

SH92 — MILTON TO INVERCARGILL

1339 Roadside Rest Area
SH1, S of Milton
46.128607S 169.950314E   Hema Atlas Map Ref 79 D5

1340 Roadside Rest Area
250m S of SH1 & SH8 intersection
Sheltered with picnic tables.
46.130798S 169.919623E   Hema Atlas Map Ref 79 D5

1341 Roadside Rest Area
SH1, N of Balclutha. Left side of road when driving N
46.217049S 169.770771E   Hema Atlas Map Ref 79 E4

1342 Roadside Rest Area
SH1, N of Balclutha. Left side of road when driving N
46.221107S 169.770326E   Hema Atlas Map Ref 79 E4

1343 Balclutha Motor Camp
56 Charlotte St, Balclutha: signposted W of SH1 or Main St, Balclutha
Ph (03) 418 0088 balcluthacamp@xtra.co.nz
46.238523S 169.732961E   Hema Atlas Map Ref 79 E3

1344 Roadside Rest Area
SH1, W of Balclutha
46.242341S 169.655567E   Hema Atlas Map Ref 79 E3

1345 Roadside Rest Area
Cnr Clinton Hwy and Anzac St
46.201662S 169.380034E   Hema Atlas Map Ref 78 C12

1346 Roadside Rest Area
SH1, Pukerau
46.096242S 169.101806E   Hema Atlas Map Ref 78 B10

1347 Kaitangata Riverside Motor Camp
20 Water Street, Kaitangata
Ph (03) 413 9219 tsupa@kinect.co.nz
Pizzeria on-site. Shop and pub nearby.
46.286051S 169.844446E   Hema Atlas Map Ref 79 E4

1348 Kaka Point Camping Ground
34 Tarata St, Kaka Point: 14km from SH92, 7km S of Balclutha; 10km from SH92, 7km N of Owaka
Ph (03) 412 8801 Fax (03) 412 8803 kakapoint@hotmail.com
Freedom camping is not allowed on public reserves stretching sth from Kaka Point to Nugget Point. Pets by arrangement.
46.385724S 169.775393E   Hema Atlas Map Ref 79 G4

1349 Thomas's Lodge & Holiday Park
Cnr Clark And Ryley Street, Owaka
Ph (03) 415 8333 Fax (03) 415 8335 stay@thomascatlins.co.nz
Mountain bike and kayak hire available. Site closes during winter.
46.449038S 169.664527E   Hema Atlas Map Ref 79 G3

1350 Keswick Park Camping Ground
Pounawea Road, Pounawea: off SH92 at Owaka
Ph (03) 419 1110 pounawea@ihug.co.nz
46.471379S 169.693222E   Hema Atlas Map Ref 79 H3

1351 Pounawea Motor Camp
Park Lane, Pounawea: off SH92 at Owaka
Ph/Fax (03) 415 8483 pounawea.motor.camp@xtra.co.nz
46.475989S 169.693053E   Hema Atlas Map Ref 79 H3

1352 Newhaven Holiday Park
324 Newhaven Rd, Surat Bay
Ph (03) 415 8834 www.newhavenholiday.com
Fax (03) 415 8099 newhaven@ihug.co.nz
Located right on the beach. Pets allowed only in off-season by prior arrangement. There is a boat ramp 1km away. Internet.
46.473163S 169.716522E   Hema Atlas Map Ref 79 H3

1353 Catlins Woodstock Lodge & Camping Ground
348 Catlins Valley Rd: signposted W of main road, approx 10km S of Owaka
Ph/Fax (03) 415 8583 www.woodstocklodge.co.nz
Laidback rural surrounds with nearby trout stream. Pets by arrangement.
46.466142S 169.560773E   Hema Atlas Map Ref 78 E14, 79 G2

1354 Purakaunui Bay
Purakaunui Bay Scenic Reserve, Catlins Coast: E of SH92
DOC Coastal Otago Area Office Ph (03) 477 0677
Dogs allowed.
46.544199S 169.610959E   Hema Atlas Map Ref 79 H2

1355 Tawanui
Catlins Conservation Park: W of Papatowai Hwy (SH92)
DOC Coastal Otago Area Office Ph (03) 477 0677
Dogs allowed.
46.457247S 169.493139E   Hema Atlas Map Ref 78 E13, 79 G1

1356 Tautuku Beach Scenic Reserve
Adjacent SH92 (Southern Scenic Route): S of Papatowai
46.576134S 169.4537E   Hema Atlas Map Ref 79 J1

1357 McLean Falls Holiday Park
29 Rewcastle Rd, Chaslands, on the Southern Scenic Route at the McLean Falls turnoff.
Ph/Fax (03) 415 8551 paulbridson@yahoo.com www.catlinsnz.com
900 acre farm environment backing onto McLean Falls. Cafe and bar on-site. Pets by arrangement.
46.592043S 169.35732E   Hema Atlas Map Ref 78 G12

Otago Region — South Island Camping Sites

1358 Waikawa Recreation Reserve
Waikawa township
Freedom camping allowed overnight for self-contained units only. Nice facilities, grassed area, short walks, museum close by.
46.62221S 169.134107E Hema Atlas Map Ref 78 G11

1359 Curio Bay Holiday Park
601 Waikawa-Curio Bay Rd, Curio Bay: 13km S SH92, via Waikawa
Ph (03) 246 8897 curiobay@catlinscoaster.co.nz www.catlins.org.nz
900 acre farm environment backing onto McLean Falls. Cafe and bar on-site.
46.661533S 169.101345E Hema Atlas Map Ref 78 H11

1360 Wiers Beach Reserve
South from Haldane along Slope Point Rd, into Weirs Beach Rd
Freedom camping allowed for up to 28 days for self-contained units only. Grassed paddock.
46.655993S 169.030503E Hema Atlas Map Ref 78 H10

1361 Fortrose Domain
Moray Tce, Fortrose: 46km E of Invercargill
Freedom camping allowed for up to 2 days for self-contained units only. Basic facilities.
46.575486S 168.796895E Hema Atlas Map Ref 78 G8

1362 Fortrose Area B
Fortrose township, follow Boat Harbour Drive
Freedom camping allowed for up to 4 months for self-contained units only. No facilities. Used mainly by Whitebaiters.
46.585428S 168.802234E Hema Atlas Map Ref 78 G8

SH8 — MILTON TO CROMWELL

1363 Tokamariro River Picnic Area
SH8: eastern end of Manuka Gorge, NW of Milton
Sheltered spot with good trout fishing.
46.082534S 169.853939E Hema Atlas Map Ref 79 C4

1364 Manuka Gorge Tunnel Rest Area
SH8: midway through Manuka Gorge, NW of Milton
46.066888S 169.824811E Hema Atlas Map Ref 79 C4

1365 Lawrence Rest Area
SH8, Lawrence: E end of the town
45.919037S 169.69062E Hema Atlas Map Ref 79 A3

1366 Gold Park Motor Camp
Harrington St, Lawrence: signposted at either end of Lawrence township
Ph (03) 485 9850
Quiet, sheltered, rural location.
45.919946S 169.683797E Hema Atlas Map Ref 79 A3

1367 Lawrence Rest Area
SH8, Lawrence: W end of the town
45.913748S 169.678694E Hema Atlas Map Ref 79 A3

1368 Roadside Rest Area
SH8, between Lawrence and Beaumont
45.859432S 169.607443E Hema Atlas Map Ref 79 A2

1369 Black Gully Retreat
Highway 90, Tapanui
Ph (03) 204 2187
45.892602S 169.347634E Hema Atlas Map Ref 72 H13

1370 Roadside Rest Area
SH90, N of Tapanui
45.921135S 169.263135E Hema Atlas Map Ref 73 J1

1371 Tapanui Motor Camp
83 Northumberland St, Tapanui
Ph (03) 204 8212 www.tapanuimotorcamp.com
dave@tapanuimotorcamp.com
A very small low-key campground, mainly for hunters and fishermen. The manager allows use of his own laundry if needed.
45.943661S 169.26895E Hema Atlas Map Ref 72 J13

1372 Millers Flat Holiday Park
N of SH8 at Millers Flat: cross the Clutha River
Ph (03) 446 6877
A caretaker may collect fees if they are in attendance.
45.66161S 169.409052E Hema Atlas Map Ref 73 F3

1373 Ettrick Holiday Park
7 James St, Ettrick
Ph (03) 446 6600
Handy to seasonal fruit-picking work.
45.639442S 169.369814E Hema Atlas Map Ref 73 E2

1374 Roadside Rest Area
SH8, NW of Ettrick
45.633719S 169.362981E Hema Atlas Map Ref 73 E2

1375 Clutha River Rest Area
SH8: 2km E of Roxburgh, on the Clutha River
Picnic spot with fishing potential.
45.574968S 169.313142E Hema Atlas Map Ref 73 E2

1376 Roxburgh Rest Area
Adjacent SH8, Roxburgh: S end of town
45.545962S 169.313324E Hema Atlas Map Ref 73 D2

1377 Gorge Creek Miners Monument & Picnic Area
SH8: about 25km N Roxburgh, 15km S Alexandra
45.376254S 169.275404E Hema Atlas Map Ref 73 B1

1378 Butchers Dam Reserve
E of SH8: about 5km S Alexandra
Fishing and swimming at the dam.
45.290453S 169.341943E Hema Atlas Map Ref 73 B2

1379 Roadside Rest Area
SH8, Clyde: Otago Central Rail Trail start/finish
45.194177S 169.334836E Hema Atlas Map Ref 66 J10

South Island Camping Sites — Otago Region

1380 Clyde Holiday & Sporting Complex
10 Whitby St, Clyde: signposted in Clyde township, 1km S of SH8
Ph (03) 449 2713 crrc@ihug.co.nz
45.191891S 169.320347E   Hema Atlas Map Ref 66 J10

1381 Clyde Dam Recreation Reserve
Just off SH8, Lake Dunstan: N end of Clyde
Popular picnic and boating base.
45.174731S 169.309723E   Hema Atlas Map Ref 66 J10

1382 Champagne Creek Reserve
Adjacent SH8, Lake Dunstan: N of Clyde
45.129619S 169.317217E   Hema Atlas Map Ref 66 J10

1383 Nine Mile Creek Reserve
Adjacent SH8, Lake Dunstan: S of Cromwell
45.087251S 169.270802E   Hema Atlas Map Ref 66 H9

1384 Roadside Rest Area
Adjacent SH8, Lake Dunstan: S of Cromwell
45.051057S 169.214825E   Hema Atlas Map Ref 66 H9

1385 Cromwell Top 10 Holiday Park
1 Alpha St, Cromwell: off SH8 at E end of Cromwell
Ph (03) 445 0164 Reservations 0800 10 72 75
info@cromwellholidaypark.co.nz www.cromwellholidaypark.co.nz
Pets by arrangement. Qualmark four star plus. Spa. Internet.
45.039122S 169.2154E   Hema Atlas Map Ref 66 H9

1386 Cromwell Roadside Rest Area
SH8B beside Lake Dunstan
45.035959S 169.212791E   Hema Atlas Map Ref 66 H9

SH8 — CROMWELL TO OMARAMA (SH83)

1387 Roadside Rest Area
John Bulls Creek: W side of SH8 alongside Lake Dunstan
44.992079S 169.241918E   Hema Atlas Map Ref 66 G9

1388 Devils Creek Rest Area
Devils Creek: W side of SH8 alongside Lake Dunstan
44.982792S 169.252376E   Hema Atlas Map Ref 66 G9

1389 Bendigo Rest Area
Bendigo: W side of SH8 alongside Lake Dunstan
44.93811S 169.290581E   Hema Atlas Map Ref 66 G9

1390 Roadside Rest Area
Rocky Point: W side of SH8 alongside Lake Dunstan
44.932855S 169.300707E   Hema Atlas Map Ref 66 F9

1391 Roadside Rest Area
Bendigo: signposted E off SH8
The 'ghost town' of Logantown and some interesting old stone buildings, and mine shafts, are 3km up the hill from this spot - take care.
44.924845S 169.344443E   Hema Atlas Map Ref 66 F10

1392 Roadside Rest Area
SH8, just W of Tarras
44.836885S 169.411608E   Hema Atlas Map Ref 66 E10

1393 Roadside Rest Area
W side of SH8 in the Lindis Valley
A favourite local swimming and fishing hole.
44.717659S 169.50462E   Hema Atlas Map Ref 66 D11

1394 Roadside Rest Area & Scenic Viewpoint
Alongside SH8, near the summit of Lindis Pass (967m)
44.587977S 169.645512E   Hema Atlas Map Ref 66 B12

1395 Roadside Rest Area
W side of SH8, beside the Dalrachney Bridge & Dalrachney Station entrance
44.517978S 169.727412E   Hema Atlas Map Ref 66 B12

1396 Roadside Rest Area
W side of SH8, 17km SW from Omarama
Entrance to the Ahuriri Conservation Park and Dingleburn Valley.
44.497488S 169.759373E   Hema Atlas Map Ref 66 A13

1397 Omarama Top 10 Holiday Park
1 Omarama Ave, Omarama
Ph (03) 438 9875 or 0800 662 726 stay@omaramatop10.co.nz
www.omaramatop10.co.nz
Located in a ten acre park setting, and handy to world-class gliding facilities at Omarama Airport. There's also plentiful fishing in the nearby lakes and streams. Qualmark four star. Bike hire. Internet.
44.487505S 169.963763E   Hema Atlas Map Ref 67 A3

1398 Ahuriri Motels
SH83, Omarama
Ph (03) 438 9451 Fax (03) 438 9461 www.ahuririmotels.co.nz
ahuririmotels@xtra.co.nz
Also has a motel and backpacker lodge. There is a shop and boat ramp about 500m away in the town. Pets by arrangement.
44.490954S 169.973581E   Hema Atlas Map Ref 67 A3

1399 Ahuriri Bridge
Adjacent to a bridge on SH8, 3km north of Omarama
DOC Aoraki/Mt Cook National Park Visitor Centre Ph (03) 435 1186
mtcookvc@doc.govt.nz
Flooding can restrict access; Stream water only.
44.467934S 169.987986E   Hema Atlas Map Ref 67 A4

Otago Region — South Island Camping Sites

SH6 — CROMWELL TO HAAST

1400 The Chalets Holiday Park
102 Barry Ave, Cromwell: on road to Bannockburn, S of Cromwell
Ph (03) 445 1260 thechalets@xtra.co.nz www.thechalets.co.nz
Plenty of summer shade. Pets by arrangement. Internet.
45.048148S 169.195235E   Hema Atlas Map Ref 66 H8

1401 Cairnmuir Lakeside Reserve
Cairnmuir Rd: E of Bannockburn Rd, just N of Bannockburn
Ideal summer swimming and boating plus fishing.
45.085335S 169.175877E   Hema Atlas Map Ref 66 H8

1402 Cairnmuir Camping Ground
219 Cairnmuir Rd: E of Bannockburn Rd, just N of Bannockburn
Ph (03) 445 1956 cairnmuirmc@slingshot.co.nz
www.cromwell.org.nz/cairnmuir
Adjoining a lake that's great for boating and swimming.
45.084679S 169.179581E   Hema Atlas Map Ref 66 H8

1403 Bannockburn Domain Motorcamp
Signposted just past the Hotel in Bannockburn township
Ph (03) 445 0001
45.087182S 169.158876E   Hema Atlas Map Ref 66 H8

1404 Roadside Rest Area
E of SH6 on the SW edge of Lake Dunstan, just N of Cromwell
45.021664S 169.205767E   Hema Atlas Map Ref 66 H9

1405 Lowburn Rest Area
Lowburn: E of SH6
45.00812S 169.213214E   Hema Atlas Map Ref 66 G9

1406 Roadside Rest Area
SH6, S of Queensberry
44.852776S 169.316721E   Hema Atlas Map Ref 66 F9

1407 Luggate Cricket Club Camping Ground
W side of SH6, 800m N of Luggate
Sheltered and handy to Wanaka, with cheap rates.
44.747971S 169.268025E   Hema Atlas Map Ref 66 D9

1408 Wanaka Lakeview Holiday Park
212 Brownston St, Wanaka: signposted from the Lakeside, W of Wanaka township, W of Pembrook Park
Ph (03) 443 7883 info@wanakalakeview.co.nz
www.wanakalakeview.co.nz
Waterfront location close to the town centre. Internet.
44.701726S 169.126956E   Hema Atlas Map Ref 66 D8

1409 Roadside Rest Area
Beacon Point Reserve, Beacon Point Rd, Lake Wanaka
44.68912S 169.129868E   Hema Atlas Map Ref 66 D8

1410 Lake Outlet Holiday Park
197 Outlet Road, Wanaka. Off Aubury Rd. Signposted from SH6 intersection with Anderson Rd on the E edge of Wanaka township, and also from Aubrey Rd
Ph (03) 443 7478 info@lakeoutlet.co.nz Fax (03) 443 7471
www.outletcamp.co.nz
Simple camping adjoining the lake, and it's a favoured fishing area. Bookings are essential for busy periods, eg. Christmas to Easter. Pets by arrangement. Wireless internet.
44.665982S 169.152068E   Hema Atlas Map Ref 66 D8

1411 Roadside Rest Area
N side of the Mt Aspiring Rd at Roys Bay, Lake Wanaka
44.6982S 169.127906E   Hema Atlas Map Ref 66 D8

1412 Wanaka Top 10 Holiday Park
217 Mt Aspiring Rd, Wanaka: W of Wanaka township
Ph (03) 443 7360 plelow@xtra.co.nz Fax (03) 443 7354
www.nzsouth.co.nz/pleasantlodge
Qualmark four star. Internet.
44.69926S 169.100334E   Hema Atlas Map Ref 66 D8

1413 Aspiring Campervan Park
263 Studholme Rd Nth, Wanaka:
signposted S off the Mt Aspiring Rd, W of Wanaka township
Ph (03) 443 6603 or 0800 229 8439 Fax (03) 4439 9194
info@campervanpark.co.nz www.campervanpark.co.nz
This park has modern facilities, but is a purpose-built motorhome complex. Log fire, underfloor heating, drying room. Qualmark five star.
44.705077S 169.108651E   Hema Atlas Map Ref 66 D8

1414 Glendhu Bay Motor Camp
Lakeside at Glendhu Bay: 11km from Wanaka on the Mt Aspiring Rd
Ph (03) 443 7243 glendhucamp@xtra.co.nz
An iconic family-friendly lakeside holiday park. It's very popular so has a tendancy to be crowded throughout the Christmas/New Year/January period.
44.674395S 169.018788E   Hema Atlas Map Ref 65 D7

1415 Albert Town Tavern
20 Alison Avenue, Albert Town
Ph (03) 443 4545 Fax (03) 443 9539 alberttowntavern@xtra.co.nz
Self-contained vehicles are welcome to stay overnight in the tavern's car park.
44.683188S 169.189115E   Hema Atlas Map Ref 66 D8

1416 Lake Hawea Holiday Park
SW corner of Lake Hawea, Makarora Park Road, off SH6
Ph (03) 443 1767 office@haweaholidaypark.co.nz
www.haweaholidaypark.co.nz
During the less crowded, off-peak times this camp is an understated gem. Lakeside swimming, fishing and boating opportunities abound.
44.606406S 169.246733E   Hema Atlas Map Ref 66 C9

1417 Lake Hawea Lookout
Adjacent Lake Hawea & SH6, about halfway along the Lake
44.508853S 169.247389E   Hema Atlas Map Ref 66 B9

South Island Camping Sites

Otago Region

1418 Roadside Rest Area
SH6, SE of The Neck, 32km from Wanaka on Lake Hawea
44.443451S 169.200699E   Hema Atlas Map Ref 66 A8

1419 Kidds Bush Reserve
6km off SH6, at the 'Neck-: between Lakes Hawea and Wanaka, 32km from Wanaka
DOC Mt Aspiring Visitor Information Centre Ph (03) 443 7660 mtaspiringvc@doc.govt.nz
A pretty, sheltered and remote spot that's a favoured trout-fishing base.
44.44183S 169.262604E   Hema Atlas Map Ref 66 A9

1420 Roadside Rest Area
SH6, NW of The Neck, on Lake Wanaka
44.430916S 169.182878E   Hema Atlas Map Ref 66 A8

1421 Boundary Creek
Off SH6, head of Lake Wanaka: 32km from Wanaka & SE of Makarora
DOC Makarora Visitor Centre Ph (03) 443 8365 makaroravc@doc.govt.nz
A sheltered lakeside campsite in a pretty location.
44.352064S 169.168389E   Hema Atlas Map Ref 58 J10

1422 Makarora Wilderness Resort
Makarora, via Wanaka
Ph (03) 443 8372 info@makarora.co.nz www.makarora.co.nz
A pleasant base from which to explore this alpine area. Jet boats and planes can be hired to transport you to remote areas.
44.231421S 169.232229E   Hema Atlas Map Ref 58 H11

1423 Roadside Rest Area
SH6, N of Makarora
44.190767S 169.257444E   Hema Atlas Map Ref 58 H10

1424 Blue Pools Roadside Rest Area
SH6, NW of Makarora
DOC Makarora Visitor Centre Ph (03) 443 8365 makaroravc@doc.govt.nz
44.164556S 169.276739E   Hema Atlas Map Ref 58 G11

1425 Cameron Flat, Mount Aspiring National Park
SH6, 8km NW of Makarora
DOC Makarora Visitor Centre Ph (03) 443 8365 makaroravc@doc.govt.nz
44.156513S 169.294633E   Hema Atlas Map Ref 58 G11

1426 Cameron Creek Rest Area
SH6, SE of Haast Summit
44.155276S 169.301907E   Hema Atlas Map Ref 58 G11

1427 Davis Flat Roadside Rest Area
SH6, SE of Haast Summit
44.13373S 169.335693E   Hema Atlas Map Ref 58 G11

1428 Roadside Rest Area
SH6, Haast Pass
44.107579S 169.354556E   Hema Atlas Map Ref 58 F11

1429 Fantail Falls Roadside Rest Area
SH6, SE of Gates of Haast
44.077028S 169.386144E   Hema Atlas Map Ref 58 F12

1430 Gates of Haast Bridge
SH6, Gates of Haast
44.040923S 169.381632E   Hema Atlas Map Ref 58 F12

1431 Thunder Creek Falls & Forest Walk
SH6, 2km W of Gates of Haast
44.037157S 169.365816E   Hema Atlas Map Ref 58 F11

1432 Pleasant Flat
SH6, Pleasant Flat: 45km E of Haast
DOC Haast Visitor Centre Ph (03) 750 0809 haastvc@doc.govt.nz
44.012003S 169.381452E   Hema Atlas Map Ref 58 E12

1433 Clarkes Bluff
SH6, at the confluence of the Landsborough & Haast rivers
43.977392S 169.42284E   Hema Atlas Map Ref 58 E12

1434 Roaring Billy Falls Reserve
SH6, SE of Haast
43.939275S 169.285385E   Hema Atlas Map Ref 58 D11

SH6 & SH6A — CROMWELL TO GLENORCHY

1435 Roaring Meg Viewpoint and Picnic Area
Adjacent SH6 and Kawarau River
The picnic area is on the opposite side of the road, so take care with the traffic. If you are lucky you may see canoeists shooting the rapids here.
45.001319S 169.070589E   Hema Atlas Map Ref 66 G8

1436 Arrowtown 'Born of Gold' Holiday Park
12 Centennial Ave, Arrowtown
Ph (03) 442 1876 arrowtownpark@qldc.govt.nz Fax (03) 442 1421 www.arrowtownholidaypark.co.nz
Handy to the public swimming pool and only 600m from the town centre. New playground, tennis courts. Modern amenities with underfloor heating.
44.942991S 168.838417E   Hema Atlas Map Ref 65 G6

1437 Macetown
15km up the Arrow River from Arrowtown (4WD only with river crossings)
DOC Queenstown Visitor Centre Ph (03) 442 7935 queenstownvc@doc.govt.nz
Stream water only.
44.867417S 168.82079E   Hema Atlas Map Ref 65 F6

1438 Roadside Rest Area
SH6, near Lake Hayes
44.99518S 168.800239E   Hema Atlas Map Ref 65 G5

1439 Frankton Motor Camp
Yewlett Crescent, Frankton, Queenstown: signposted one block from Frankton roundabout
Ph (03) 442 2079 g.orourke@xtra.co.nz www.franktonmotorcamp.co.nz
Lakeside for fishing, swimming and boating. Wireless internet.
45.017584S 168.726468E   Hema Atlas Map Ref 65 H5, 126 A5

Fiordland & Southland Region — South Island Camping Sites

1440 Queenstown Lake View Holiday Park
4 Cemetery Road, Queenstown: follow signs to Gondola terminal from Queenstown town centre
Ph (03) 442 7252 or 0800 482 7352 holidaypark@qldc.govt.nz
www.holidaypark.net.nz
Only 150m from town centre. Wireless internet.
45.030432S 168.656493E Hema Atlas Map Ref 65 H4, 125 B2, 126 B2

1441 Queenstown Rest Area
Lakeside by Fernhill Rd roundabout. Follow signs from Queenstown centre towards Glenorchy
45.037725S 168.648631E Hema Atlas Map Ref 65 H4, 125 D1, 126 B2

1442 Queenstown Top 10 Holiday Park 'Creeksyde'
54 Robins Rd, Queenstown: signposted from roundabout near recreation reserve and fire station
Ph (03) 442 9447 or 0800 786 222 creeksyde@camp.co.nz
www.camp.co.nz
This environmentally certified park is 'clean and green', and handy to the town centre. Qualmark five star.
45.026001S 168.660304E Hema Atlas Map Ref 65 H4, 125 A2, 126 B2

1443 Shotover Top 10 Holiday Park
70 Arthurs Point Rd, Queenstown: adjacent the Queenstown to Arrowtown Rd, N of Arthurs Point, 1.5km S of the Coronet Peak Skifield turnoff.
Ph (03) 442 9306 Reservations 0800 462 267 Fax (03) 442 9307
stay@shotoverholidaypark.co.nz www.shotoverholidaypark.co.nz
Handy to the Coronet Peak and Shotover Jet attractions.
Located in a stunning alpine setting. Qualmark four star. Internet.
44.984759S 168.677577E Hema Atlas Map Ref 65 G4

1444 Skippers-Mt Aurum
Skippers Rd: 26km from Queenstown
DOC Queenstown Visitor Centre Ph (03) 442 7935
queenstownvc@doc.govt.nz
44.842997S 168.681413E Hema Atlas Map Ref 65 F4

1445 Moke Lake
Glenorchy Rd: about 12km W of Queenstown
DOC Queenstown Visitor Centre Ph (03) 442 7935
queenstownvc@doc.govt.nz
A world away from Queenstown, yet so close. Stream water only.
44.999615S 168.574008E Hema Atlas Map Ref 64 H14, 65 H4,

1446 Twelve Mile Delta
Glenorchy Rd: 11km from Queenstown, signposted on road to Glenorchy
DOC Queenstown Visitor Centre Ph (03) 442 7935
queenstownvc@doc.govt.nz
Dogs allowed.
45.068516S 168.547272E Hema Atlas Map Ref 64 H13, 65 H3

1447 Glenorchy Lakeside Reserve
Glenorchy Rd, Glenorchy
44.850301S 168.382017E Hema Atlas Map Ref 65 F2

1448 Glenorchy Holiday Park
Oban St, Glenorchy
Ph (03) 441 0303
Lakeside, and handy to the town centre.
44.851141S 168.38888E Hema Atlas Map Ref 65 F2

1449 Kinloch
Kinloch Rd: 24km from Glenorchy
DOC Queenstown Visitor Centre Ph (03) 442 7935
queenstownvc@doc.govt.nz
Lakeside for fishing and swimming. Stream water only.
44.843476S 168.351046E Hema Atlas Map Ref 64 F12, 65 F2

1450 Sylvan
Routeburn Rd, beside Routeburn River: 20km from Glenorchy
DOC Queenstown Visitor Centre Ph (03) 442 7935
queenstownvc@doc.govt.nz
Nice walking nearby. Stream water only.
44.72616S 168.315542E Hema Atlas Map Ref 64 E11, 65 E1

FIORDLAND AND SOUTHLAND REGION

ONE OF THE MANY WATERFALLS ALONG THE MILFORD TRACK. PHOTO: DESTINATION FIORDLAND

SH6 — QUEENSTOWN TO INVERCARGILL 103
SH99 — INVERCARGILL TO TE ANAU 105
SH94 — TE ANAU TO MILFORD SOUND 106
STEWART ISLAND / RAKIURA 108

SH6 — QUEENSTOWN TO INVERCARGILL

1451 Lakeside Rest Area
SH6, S end of Lake Wakatipu
Sheltered with picnic tables.
45.293783S 168.761301E Hema Atlas Map Ref 72 B8

1452 Lakeside South Rest Area
SH6, S end of Lake Wakatipu
45.312149S 168.754071E Hema Atlas Map Ref 72 B8

1453 Roadside Rest Area
SH6, just N of Kingston
45.333041S 168.729458E Hema Atlas Map Ref 72 B8

South Island Camping Sites
Fiordland & Southland Region

1454 Kingston Motels & Holiday Park
16 Kent St, Kingston
Ph/Fax (03) 248 8501/0800 807 836 Fax (03) 248 8509
www.kingstonmotels.co.nz
Fishing and walking nearby, as well as the Kingston Flyer for steamtrain enthusiasts.
45.338003S 168.722757E   Hema Atlas Map Ref 72 B8

1455 Kingston Flyer Southern Railway Terminal & Reserve
SH6, S of Kingston
45.4199S 168.674749E   Hema Atlas Map Ref 72 C8

1456 Kingston Flyer Northern Railway Terminal & Reserve
W of SH6 at Kingston
45.330064S 168.71218E   Hema Atlas Map Ref 72 B8

1457 Glenquoich Caravan Park
Avor Street, Athol
Ph (03) 248 8987, 0274 553 520
Open Oct - May, depending on weather. Pets by prior arrangement.
45.51334S 168.579614E   Hema Atlas Map Ref 71 D7

1458 Athol Roadside Rest Area
SH6, just W of Athol
45.509403S 168.571617E   Hema Atlas Map Ref 71 D7

1459 Roadside Rest Area
SH6, between Athol and Five Rivers
45.571669S 168.503537E   Hema Atlas Map Ref 71 E6

1460 Mossburn Country Park
333 Mossburn-Five Rivers Rd, Mossburn: just N of Mossburn
Ph (03) 248 6444 info@mossburncountrypark.co.nz
www.mossburncountrypark.co.nz
Peaceful rural holiday park, with farm animals.
45.653226S 168.269167E   Hema Atlas Map Ref 71 F5

1461 Mossburn Roadside Rest Area
SH94, Mossburn
45.6€7656S 168.233786E   Hema Atlas Map Ref 71 F4

1462 Roadside Rest Area
SH94, W of Mossburn
45.637S 168.17555E   Hema Atlas Map Ref 71 F4

1463 Roadside Rest Area
SH94, S of Manapouri Rd turnoff
45.524355S 167.810349E   Hema Atlas Map Ref 70 E12

1464 Roadside Rest Area
SH6, N of Lumsden
45.731512S 168.437316E   Hema Atlas Map Ref 71 G6

1465 Dipton Roadside Rest Area
SH6, just W of Dipton, beside the river
45.901619S 168.36365E   Hema Atlas Map Ref 71 J6

1466 Balfour Roadside Rest Area
SH94, just S of Balfour
45.839271S 168.599807E   Hema Atlas Map Ref 71 H7

1467 Riversdale Rest Area
SH94, main street of Riverdale, centre of town
45.901086S 168.742147E   Hema Atlas Map Ref 72 J8

1468 Waikaia Domain Motor Camp
Scotswood St, Waikaia
Ph (03) 202 7822
This camp is closed for winter (1st May to 1st October).
45.725446S 168.848589E   Hema Atlas Map Ref 72 F9

1469 Piano Flat
23km N of Waikaia: off SH94 at Riversdale
DOC Fiordland National Park Visitor Centre Ph (03) 249 7924
fiordlandvc@doc.govt.nz
Fees usually via self registration envelopes. Stream water only. Dogs allowed.
45.561276S 169.015259E   Hema Atlas Map Ref 72 E11

1470 Dolamore Park Scenic Reserve
No. 7 RD, Gore: off SH94
Ph (03) 209 0330 isoper@goredc.govt.nz
Administered by Gore District Council.
46.064446S 168.827347E   Hema Atlas Map Ref 78 A8

1471 Gore Motor Camp
35 Broughton St, Gore: W of SH1, S of town centre
Ph/Fax (03) 208 4919 gorecamp@xtra.co.nz
A little known gem that's well signposted.
Pets by arrangement in motorhomes.
46.109369S 168.934051E   Hema Atlas Map Ref 78 B9

1472 Wyndham Camping Ground
Cardigan Rd, Wyndham
Ph (03) 206 4825
Pets by arrangement.
46.323646S 168.853337E   Hema Atlas Map Ref 78 D9

AERIAL VIEW OF ALEXANDRA   PHOTO: TOURISM CENTRAL OTAGO

Fiordland & Southland Region — South Island Camping Sites

1473 Dunsdale Recreation Reserve
End of Whitehorse Road, off Dunsdale Valley Road, off SH 96
Freedom camping allowed for up to 3 days. Large grassed area.
46.134492S 168.599263E Hema Atlas Map Ref 77 B6

1474 Winton Golf Course & Camp
Sub Station Road, Winton
Ph (03) 236 8422
46.150697S 168.296981E Hema Atlas Map Ref 77 B4

1475 Roadside Rest Area
SH6, just N of Winton
46.128833S 168.324584E Hema Atlas Map Ref 77 E2

1476 McGregor Park
Nightcaps township beside the racecourse
Freedom camping allowed overnight for self-contained units only. No facilities. Grassed area.
45.966295S 168.026483E Hema Atlas Map Ref 77 A2

1477 Alec McKenzie Arboretum
Otautau, at the corner of the Riverton Otautau Road and Glenburn Road
Freedom camping allowed for up to 4 nights for self-contained units only. Grassed area. Basic facilities.
46.160379S 168.009015E Hema Atlas Map Ref 77 C2

1478 Thornbury Aparima Bridge
Off SH99, N of Thornbury, beside Aparima River
Freedom camping allowed for up to 28 days for self-contained units only. Banks of river, grassed area. Basic facilities.
46.285052S 168.084208E Hema Atlas Map Ref 77 D3

1479 Invercargill Top 10 Holiday Park (Gum Tree Farm)
77 McIvor Rd, Invercargill: E of SH6, 6km from Invercargill
Ph (03) 215 9032 or 0800 486 873 gumtreefarmmp@xtra.co.nz
www.invercargilltop10.co.nz
Qualmark four star. Internet.
46.364104S 168.356497E Hema Atlas Map Ref 77 E5

1480 Lorneville Holiday Park
352 Lorneville-Dacre Rd, Invercargill: E of SH6, 7km N of Invercargill, on SH6, 3.5km E on SH98
Ph (03) 235 8031 lornepark@xtra.co.nz Fax (03) 235 8035
www.lornevilleholidaypark.co.nz
Set on 17 acre working farm. Pets by arrangement.
46.348725S 168.391809E Hema Atlas Map Ref 77 E5

1481 Coachman's Inn Motor Lodge
705 Tay St, Invercargill
Ph (03) 217 6046, 0508 426 224 Fax (03) 217 6045
reservations@coachmans.co.nz www.coachmans.co.nz
Pets by prior arrangement.
46.406455S 168.393009E Hema Atlas Map Ref 77 E5, 128 A3,

1482 Amble on Inn Holiday Park
145 Chesney St, Invercargill: signposted E of Invercargill, enroute to Catlins
Ph (03) 216 5214 enquiries@ambleoninn.co.nz
Fax (03) 216 9683 www.ambleoninn.co.nz
A peaceful rural setting 5km from city centre. Pets by arrangement.
46.440724S 168.380908E Hema Atlas Map Ref 77 F5, 128 B5

1483 Bluff Camping Ground
Argyle Park, 11 Gregory St, Bluff: signposted S end of town, off Marine Pde
Ph (03) 212 8774, 027 626 2018 service@icc.govt.nz
46.604394S 168.351166E Hema Atlas Map Ref 77 G5

1484 Beach Road Motor Camp
375 Dunns Road, Otatara
Ph (03) 213 0400 info@beachroadholidaypark.co.nz
Fax (03) 216 3009 www.beachroadholidaypark.co.nz
Pets by arrangement only.
46.434742S 168.260191E Hema Atlas Map Ref 77 F4

SH99 — INVERCARGILL TO TE ANAU

1485 Longwood Holiday Park
43 Richard St, Riverton: follow signs S on W side of bridge
Ph (03) 234 8132 lex.wylie@xtra.co.nz
Pets by arrangement.
46.362447S 168.008027E Hema Atlas Map Ref 76 H14, 77 E2

1486 Riverton Rocks Scenic Reserve
The Rocks: SE of Riverton
46.383711S 168.032065E Hema Atlas Map Ref 77 E2

1487 Colac Bay/Oraka Township Camping Area
Colac Foreshore Road between the boatramp and shelter shed
Southland District Council Ph 0800 732 732
Freedom camping allowed for up to 2 days for self-contained units only.
46.379119S 167.884006E Hema Atlas Map Ref 76 H13

1488 Colac Bay Tavern & Camping Ground
15 Colac Bay Road, Colac Bay
Ph (03) 234 8399 dusty@dustezbakpakas.co.nz
www.dustezbakpakas.co.nz
Internet.
46.361053S 167.878264E Hema Atlas Map Ref 76 H13

1489 Colac Bay Boat Ramp
Colac Bay: 11km W Riverton
Freedom camping at W end of Colac Bay for self-contained vehicles for 2 nights max. Must display current self-containment certificate.
46.37673S 167.88273E Hema Atlas Map Ref 76 H13, 77 E1

South Island Camping Sites — Fiordland & Southland Region

1490 Monkey Island
S of Orepuki on SH99, take Frentz Rd, then Monkey Island Road
Freedom camping allowed for up to 28 days for self-contained units only. Popular Area, narrow road strip with view to Monkey Island. Basic facilities.
46.298745S 167.728373E — Hema Atlas Map Ref 76 G12

1491 Tuatapere Motel
73 Main St, Tuatapere
Ph (027) 222 2612 info@tuatapereaccommodation.co.nz
www.tuatapereaccommodation.co.nz
Spa and sauna. Internet.
46.135278S 167.688814E — Hema Atlas Map Ref 76 F12

1492 Last Light Lodge
6 Clifden Rd, Tuatapere: E of SH99 at N end of town
Ph (03) 226 6667
46.126562S 167.67495E — Hema Atlas Map Ref 76 E11

1493 Tuatapere Domain Reserve
Riverside spot off Elder Drive, Tuatapere
Ph (03) 226 6650
46.12514S 167.68429E — Hema Atlas Map Ref 76 E11

1494 Clifden Historic Bridge Reserve
14km N of Tuatapere on SH99
Riverside spot suited to fishing and swimming.
46.03075S 167.714207E — Hema Atlas Map Ref 76 D12

1495 Thicket Burn
Lake Hauroko Rd: 25km W of Clifden
DOC Fiordland National Park Visitor Centre Ph (03) 249 7924
fiordlandvc@doc.govt.nz
46.007955S 167.454901E — Hema Atlas Map Ref 76 D10

1496 Monowai
Lake Monowai road end
DOC Fiordland National Park Visitor Centre Ph (03) 249 7924
fiordlandvc@doc.govt.nz
45.812382S 167.521738E — Hema Atlas Map Ref 76 B10, 70 H10

1497 Manapouri Lakeside Reserve
Waterfront at Manapouri township
Swimming, fishing and boating options.
45.564569S 167.610779E — Hema Atlas Map Ref 70 E10

1498 Possum Lodge Motel & Holiday Park
13 Murrell Ave, Manapouri
Ph/Fax (03) 249 6623 www.possumlodge.co.nz
possumlodge@xtra.co.nz
Open summer only.
45.566855S 167.603974E — Hema Atlas Map Ref 70 E10

1499 Manapouri Motels & Holiday Park
50 Manapouri Te Anau Rd, Manapouri:
across the road from the lake, N end of Manapouri
Ph (03) 249 6624 manapourimotels@clear.net.nz
Fax (03) 249 6699 www.manapourimotels.co.nz
Charming in a budget way. Pets by prior arrangement.
45.55887S 167.621094E — Hema Atlas Map Ref 70 E10

1500 Whitestone Stream Bridge
Hillside Manapouri Road bridge over Whitestone Stream
Freedom camping allowed overnight for self-contained units only. No facilities.
45.527325S 167.755976E — Hema Atlas Map Ref 70 E12

SH94 — TE ANAU TO MILFORD SOUND

1501 Roadside Rest Area
SH94, S of Te Anau
45.460576S 167.788393E — Hema Atlas Map Ref 70 D12

1502 Te Anau Lakeview Holiday Park
Te Anau-Manapouri Rd, Te Anau
Ph (03) 249 7457 res@teanau.info www.teanau.info
Lakeside and walk to the town centre. Qualmark four star plus. Sauna, spa bath. Wireless internet.
45.426018S 167.718931E — Hema Atlas Map Ref 70 D11

1503 Te Anau Top 10 Holiday Park
128 Te Anau Tce, Te Anau: 200m W of town centre
Ph 0800 249 746 fivestar@teanautop10.co.nz Fax (03) 249 7262
www.teanautop10.co.nz
Everything you need in a compact, sheltered environment. Qualmark five star plus. Bike hire. Spa pool. Wireless internet.
45.414509S 167.708784E — Hema Atlas Map Ref 70 D11

1504 Te Anau Great Lakes Holiday Park
15 Luxmore Drive, Te Anau: W of Caltex Station
Ph (03) 249 8538 Reservations 0800 249 555 Fax (03) 249 8539
info@greatlakes.co.nz www.teanaugreatlakes.co.nz
Qualmark four star plus. Adventure playground. Scooter hire. Internet.
45.414404S 167.718789E — Hema Atlas Map Ref 70 D11

1505 Mavora Lakes
Off SH94: about 40km N of SH94
DOC Fiordland National Park Visitor Centre Ph (03) 249 7924
fiordlandvc@doc.govt.nz
Dogs allowed; fees usually via self registration envelopes.
45.274593S 168.172604E — Hema Atlas Map Ref 71 B4

1506 Fiordland Great Views Holiday Park
Milford Rd, Te Anau: 1.5km N of Te Anau. SH94.
Ph (03) 249 7059 fiordland.holiday.park@xtra.co.nz
www.fiordlandgreatviewsholidaypark.co.nz
Fitness centre, spa, sauna, vehicle storage. New toilets/showers. Spacious, sheltered and quiet. Internet. Qualmark four star plus. Pets by arrangement.
45.407969S 167.743324E — Hema Atlas Map Ref 70 C11

Fiordland & Southland Region — South Island Camping Sites — 107

1507 Henry Creek
Adjacent SH94 (Milford Rd): 25km N Te Anau
DOC Fiordland National Park Visitor Centre Ph (03) 249 7924
fiordlandvc@doc.govt.nz

Stream water only; fires not permitted.

45.232736S 167.811511E   Hema Atlas Map Ref 70 B12

1508 Fiordland National Park Lodge, Te Anau Downs
Adjacent SH94 (Milford Rd): 33km N of Te Anau
Ph (03) 249 7811, 0800 500 805
info@fiordlandnationalparklodge.co.nz   www.teanau-milfordsound.co.nz

Hotel, motel and backpackers accommodation. Only 600m from the Milford Track Great Walk departure point. Internet.

45.198691S 167.822157E   Hema Atlas Map Ref 70 A12

1509 Te Anau Downs Rest Area
Adjacent SH94 (Milford Rd): N Te Anau

45.192126S 167.827797E   Hema Atlas Map Ref 70 A12

1510 Roadside Rest Area
SH94, E of Te Anau Downs
45.198794S 167.854175E   Hema Atlas Map Ref 70 A12

1511 Walker Creek
Adjacent SH94 (Milford Rd): 49km N Te Anau
DOC Fiordland National Park Visitor Centre Ph (03) 249 7924
fiordlandvc@doc.govt.nz

Stream water only; fees usually via self registration envelopes.

45.100725S 167.968373E   Hema Atlas Map Ref 64 J9

1512 Totara
Adjacent SH94 (Milford Rd): 53km N Te Anau
DOC Fiordland National Park Visitor Centre Ph (03) 249 7924
fiordlandvc@doc.govt.nz

Stream water only; fees usually via self registration envelopes.

45.076398S 167.984542E   Hema Atlas Map Ref 64 J9

1513 Mackay Creek
Adjacent SH94 (Milford Rd): 53km N Te Anau
DOC Fiordland National Park Visitor Centre Ph (03) 249 7924
fiordlandvc@doc.govt.nz

Stream water only; fees usually via self registration envelopes.

45.070118S 167.990746E   Hema Atlas Map Ref 64 J9

1514 Mirror Lakes DOC Reserve
Adjacent SH94 (Milford Rd): N Te Anau

Well worth the walk to view the mirror reflections of adjacent mountains (providing there is no wind).

45.02859S 168.011083E   Hema Atlas Map Ref 64 H9

1515 Deer Flat
Adjacent SH94 (Milford Rd): 62km N Te Anau
DOC Fiordland National Park Visitor Centre Ph (03) 249 7924
fiordlandvc@doc.govt.nz

Stream water only; fees usually via self registration envelopes.

44.99879S 168.003169E   Hema Atlas Map Ref 64 H9

South Island Camping Sites — Fiordland & Southland Region

1516 Knobs Flat Rest Area
Adjacent SH94 (Milford Rd), Knobs Flat: 65km N Te Anau
Pretty much just a toilet stop for all the tourist buses that ply this route.

44.97454S 168.016932E   Hema Atlas Map Ref 64 H9

1517 Knobs Flat
SH 94: between Te Anau and Milford
Ph (03) 249 9122 Fax (03) 249 7077 www.knobsflat.co.nz
info@knobsflat.co.nz
Peaceful atmosphere where you can help make a difference in the local environment.

44.97751S 168.016805E   Hema Atlas Map Ref 64 H9

1518 Kiosk Creek
Adjacent SH94 (Milford Rd): 65km N Te Anau
DOC Fiordland National Park Visitor Centre Ph (03) 249 7924
fiordlandvc@doc.govt.nz
Stream water only; fees usually via self registration envelopes.

44.974162S 168.017926E   Hema Atlas Map Ref 64 H10

1519 Smithy Creek
Adjacent SH94 (Milford Rd): 67km N Te Anau
DOC Fiordland National Park Visitor Centre Ph (03) 249 7924
fiordlandvc@doc.govt.nz
Stream water only; fees usually via self registration envelopes.
44.957001S 168.019757E   Hema Atlas Map Ref 64 G9

1520 Upper Eglinton
Adjacent SH94 (Milford Rd): 71km N Te Anau
DOC Fiordland National Park Visitor Centre Ph (03) 249 7924
fiordlandvc@doc.govt.nz
Stream water only; fees usually via self registration envelopes.
44.928745S 168.030162E   Hema Atlas Map Ref 64 G9

1521 Cascade Creek
Adjacent SH94 (Milford Rd): 76km N Te Anau
DOC Fiordland National Park Visitor Centre Ph (03) 249 7924
fiordlandvc@doc.govt.nz
Stream water only: fees usually via self registration envelopes.
44.895339S 168.082904E   Hema Atlas Map Ref 64 G10

1522 Lake Gunn
Adjacent SH94 (Milford Rd): 78km N Te Anau
DOC Fiordland National Park Visitor Centre Ph (03) 249 7924
fiordlandvc@doc.govt.nz
Stream water only: fees usually via self registration envelopes.
44.858794S 168.100519E   Hema Atlas Map Ref 64 F10

1523 The Divide & Routeburn Track Base
Adjacent SH94 (Milford Rd): 89km N Te Anau
44.825047S 168.11693E   Hema Atlas Map Ref 64 F10

1524 Roadside Rest Area
SH94, N of Lake Gunn
44.809437S 168.107879E   Hema Atlas Map Ref 64 F10

1525 Roadside Rest Area
SH94, S of Homer Tunnel
44.795138S 168.021692E   Hema Atlas Map Ref 64 F9

1526 The Chasm
Adjacent SH94 (Milford Rd):
half way between the Homer Tunnel and Milford Sound
Spectacular viewing to appreciate just how water can wear rock in a climate like this.
44.721482S 167.95138E   Hema Atlas Map Ref 64 E8

1527 Milford Sound Lodge
94 Milford Sound Highway, Milford Sound:
on the S edge of Milford Sound township. SH94
Ph (03) 249 8071 bookings@milfordlodge.com www.milfordlodge.com

44.676631S 167.934251E   Hema Atlas Map Ref 64 D9

STEWART ISLAND / RAKIURA

1528 Maori Beach
Rakiura Track in Rakiura National Park, Stewart Island.
Halfway between Lee Bay and Port William Hut
Rakiura National Park Visitor Centre Ph (03) 219 0009
rakiuravc@doc.govt.nz
Part of the Great Walks.

46.856206S 168.088717E   Hema Atlas Map Ref 80 D5

1529 Port William
Rakiura Track in Rakiura National Park, Stewart Island.
Located 5mins from Port William Hut.
Rakiura National Park Visitor Centre Ph (03) 219 0009
rakiuravc@doc.govt.nz
Part of the Great Walks.

46.836117S 168.082578E   Hema Atlas Map Ref 80 D5

1530 Sawdust Bay
Rakiura Track in Rakiura National Park, Stewart Island.
Located 1.5hrs from North Arm
Rakiura National Park Visitor Centre Ph (03) 219 0009
rakiuravc@doc.govt.nz
Part of the Great Walks.

46.898981S 168.033686E   Hema Atlas Map Ref 80 E5

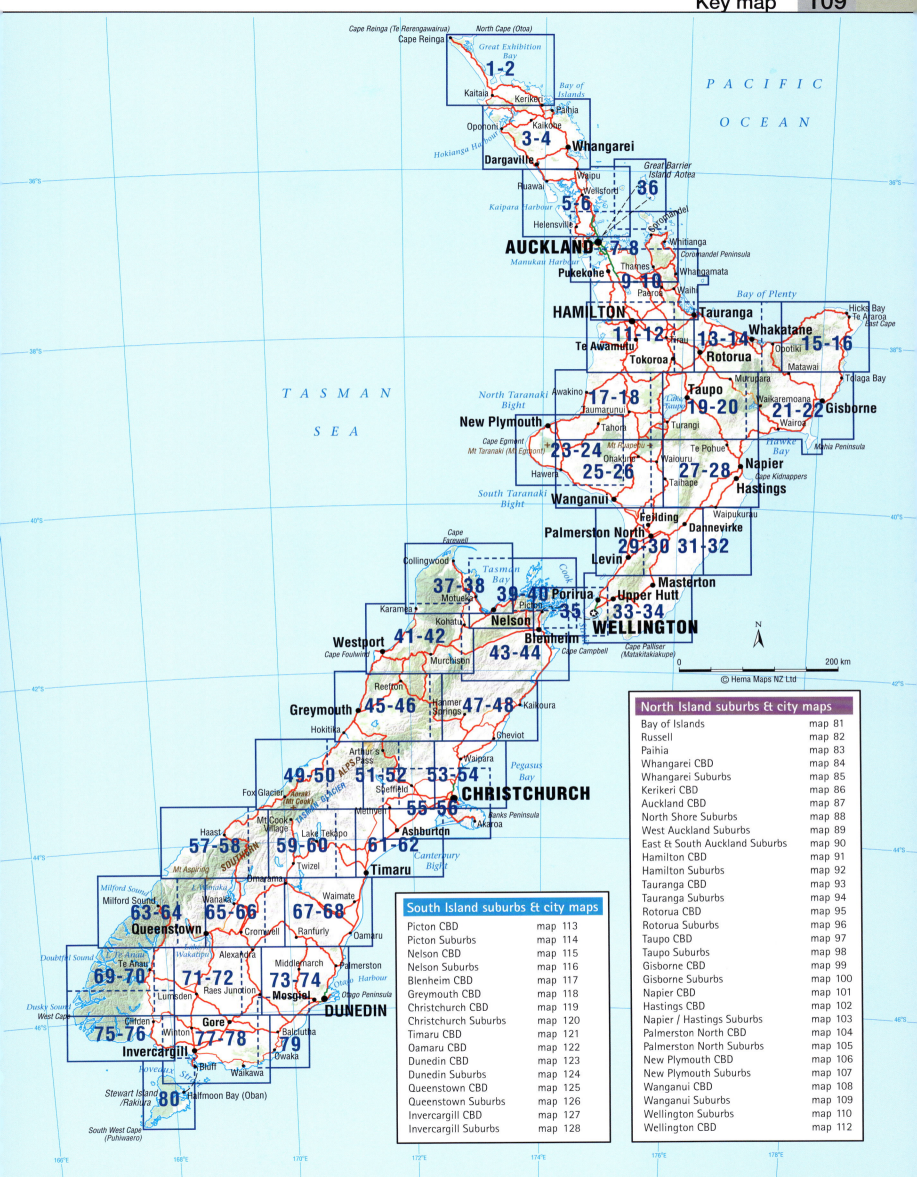

NORTH ISLAND Travel Times & Distances

NAPIER — DONNA BLABER

Distances are shown in kilometres and assume the most direct route on sealed roads where possible.
Travelling times are shown in hours & minutes and are calculated for a driver travelling at 80-100 km/hr on open stretches, with an allowance for rest stops.

From	Cape Reinga	Chateau Tongariro	Dargaville	Gisborne	Hamilton	Hicks Bay	Kaitaia	Masterton	Napier	New Plymouth	Paihia	Palmerston North	Rotorua	Taupo	Taumarunui	Tauranga	Thames	Waikaremoana	Waitomo Caves	Wanganui	Wellington	Whakatane	Whangarei
Auckland	444 / 8:15	342 / 5:35	182 / 3:05	496 / 8:20	124 / 1:55	500 / 9:05	321 / 6:00	626 / 9:20	424 / 6:35	365 / 6:20	237 / 4:15	521 / 7:40	235 / 3:50	282 / 4:05	284 / 4:45	201 / 3:20	115 / 1:50	390 / 7:50	198 / 3:10	457 / 8:00	652 / 9:15	295 / 4:55	166 / 3:00
Cape Reinga	•	786 / 13:50	290 / 5:25	940 / 16:35	568 / 10:10	944 / 17:20	112 / 2:15	1070 / 17:35	868 / 14:50	809 / 14:35	216 / 4:30	967 / 15:55	679 / 11:50	726 / 12:20	728 / 13:00	645 / 11:35	559 / 10:05	834 / 16:05	642 / 11:25	901 / 16:15	1096 / 17:30	739 / 13:10	267 / 5:15
Chateau Tongariro		•	524 / 8:40	431 / 6:55	218 / 3:40	468 / 8:25	663 / 11:35	314 / 4:50	234 / 4:00	251 / 4:20	579 / 9:50	207 / 3:10	178 / 2:50	94 / 1:30	58 / 0:50	250 / 3:45	311 / 4:40	283 / 6:05	158 / 2:45	138 / 2:45	338 / 4:15	263 / 4:25	508 / 8:20
Dargaville			•	678 / 11:25	306 / 5:00	682 / 12:10	178 / 3:10	808 / 12:25	606 / 9:40	547 / 9:25	126 / 2:20	705 / 10:45	417 / 6:40	464 / 7:10	466 / 7:50	383 / 6:25	297 / 4:55	572 / 10:55	380 / 6:15	639 / 11:05	834 / 12:20	477 / 8:00	55 / 1:05
Gisborne				•	385 / 6:30	176 / 3:40	817 / 14:20	452 / 6:45	221 / 3:25	582 / 10:25	733 / 12:35	397 / 6:05	337 / 4:50	446 / 5:25	291 / 7:20	500 / 5:00	167 / 7:05	435 / 2:55	469 / 7:30	534 / 7:15	201 / 8:15	662 / 3:25	290 / 11:20
Hamilton					•	389 / 7:15	445 / 7:55	504 / 7:25	298 / 4:40	241 / 4:25	361 / 6:10	397 / 5:45	111 / 1:40	158 / 2:10	160 / 2:50	109 / 1:55	110 / 1:50	266 / 5:55	72 / 1:15	326 / 6:05	528 / 7:30	196 / 3:05	290 / 4:55
Hicks Bay						•	821 / 15:05	628 / 10:25	397 / 7:55	586 / 11:10	737 / 13:20	573 / 9:45	278 / 5:35	362 / 6:55	450 / 8:50	295 / 5:45	406 / 7:50	343 / 6:35	439 / 8:15	582 / 10:40	710 / 11:55	205 / 4:10	666 / 12:05
Kaitaia							•	947 / 15:20	745 / 12:35	686 / 12:20	109 / 2:15	844 / 13:40	556 / 9:35	603 / 10:05	605 / 10:45	522 / 9:20	436 / 7:50	711 / 13:50	519 / 9:10	778 / 14:00	973 / 15:15	616 / 10:55	155 / 3:00
Masterton								•	231 / 3:20	341 / 5:15	863 / 13:35	107 / 1:40	430 / 6:35	346 / 5:15	342 / 6:05	502 / 7:40	563 / 8:25	413 / 6:30	442 / 8:00	179 / 2:50	100 / 1:50	515 / 8:00	792 / 12:20
Napier									•	410 / 6:15	661 / 10:50	176 / 2:40	224 / 3:50	140 / 2:30	252 / 4:25	296 / 4:55	357 / 5:40	182 / 3:10	309 / 5:05	248 / 3:50	313 / 4:50	309 / 5:15	590 / 9:35
New Plymouth										•	602 / 10:35	234 / 3:35	308 / 5:35	305 / 5:25	193 / 3:30	309 / 5:40	343 / 6:15	463 / 10:00	181 / 3:30	162 / 2:25	352 / 5:10	393 / 7:00	531 / 9:20
Paihia											•	760 / 11:55	472 / 7:50	519 / 8:20	521 / 9:00	438 / 7:35	352 / 6:05	627 / 12:05	435 / 7:25	694 / 12:15	889 / 13:30	532 / 9:10	71 / 1:15
Palmerston North												•	323 / 4:55	239 / 3:35	235 / 4:25	395 / 6:00	456 / 6:45	358 / 5:50	335 / 6:20	72 / 1:10	142 / 2:10	408 / 6:20	689 / 10:40
Rotorua													•	84 / 1:20	172 / 2:50	83 / 1:30	168 / 2:40	155 / 4:15	161 / 2:45	304 / 4:25	454 / 6:30	85 / 1:25	401 / 6:35
Taupo														•	112 / 1:55	156 / 2:25	217 / 3:10	189 / 4:35	169 / 2:35	220 / 3:05	370 / 5:10	169 / 2:45	448 / 7:05
Taumarunui															•	227 / 4:05	288 / 4:40	301 / 6:30	100 / 1:55	166 / 3:15	356 / 5:15	257 / 4:15	450 / 7:45
Tauranga																•	111 / 2:05	238 / 5:45	149 / 2:30	376 / 6:35	526 / 8:00	94 / 1:35	367 / 6:20
Thames																	•	323 / 6:55	173 / 3:05	425 / 6:55	587 / 8:20	205 / 3:40	281 / 4:50
Waikaremoana																		•	316 / 7:00	430 / 7:00	495 / 8:00	240 / 5:40	556 / 10:50
Waitomo Caves																			•	266 / 5:10	456 / 7:10	243 / 4:05	364 / 6:10
Wanganui																				•	190 / 2:45	389 / 5:10	623 / 10:00
Wellington																					•	539 / 7:55	818 / 12:15
Whakatane																						•	461 / 7:55
Whangarei																							•

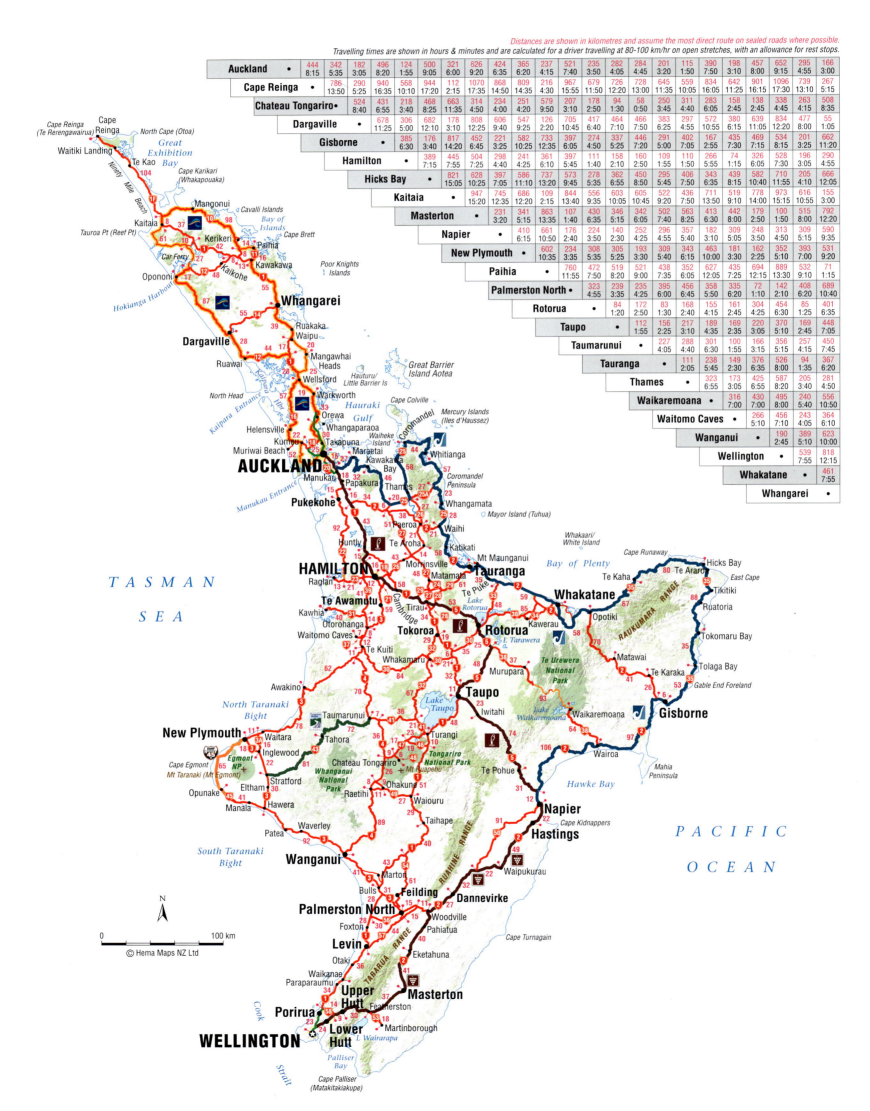

© Hema Maps NZ Ltd

SOUTH ISLAND Travel Times & Distances

LITTLE GREY RIVER NEAR REEFTON — JEFF DREWITZ

Distances are shown in kilometres and assume the most direct route on sealed roads where possible.
Travelling times are shown in hours & minutes and are calculated for a driver travelling at 80-100 km/hr on open stretches, with an allowance for rest stops.

648 11:35	88 1:25	300 4:40	260 4:00	95 1:30	799 11:40	139 2:20	227 3:20	836 12:55	380 5:30	233 3:30	643 9:20	202 2:55	507 9:45	223 5:10	547 9:50	181 2:00	346 6:50	193 3:00	923 16:45	470 6:40	232 3:25	772 11:10	379 5:45	558 8:40	• Alexandra
198 3:03	511 8:35	258 4:00	733 11:05	568 9:35	447 7:03	398 6:04	345 5:01	386 6:35	414 4:55	853 13:25	313 4:55	671 10:00	101 1:04	385 6:04	97 1:45	616 9:05	262 4:35	462 6:05	473 7:55	159 2:25	701 10:03	420 7:05	182 2:55	• Arthur's Pass
380 6:15	343 5:25	79 1:05	578 8:10	400 6:40	420 6:05	230 3:30	166 2:15	509 7:25	246 3:40	698 10:30	264 3:55	492 7:05	283 4:35	478 8:45	279 4:10	437 6:10	444 7:30	283 3:55	583 8:55	91 1:05	522 7:35	393 5:40		Ashburton
258 4:15	736 11:20	472 6:45	971 13:50	793 11:50	27 0:25	623 9:25	559 7:55	116 1:45	639 9:30	1091 15:15	129 1:50	885 12:45	363 5:50	647 10:45	323 5:05	830 11:50	524 8:45	676 9:35	247 4:35	311 13:15	915			Blenheim
885 13:35	325 5:10	443 6:30	190 2:55	220 3:30	942 13:40	376 5:45	356 5:20	1031 14:45	470 6:55	30 0:30	786 11:30	744 11:45	460 8:40	784 11:50	96 1:25	583 10:45	239 3:40	1105 16:30	613 8:40					• Bluff
330 5:10	434 6:30	170 2:10	669 9:15	491 7:15	338 5:00	321 4:35	257 3:20	427 6:15	337 4:55	789 11:35	182 2:50	583 8:10	260 4:05	544 8:55	256 4:10	374 7:15	501 6:55	324 5:00	7:50					Christchurch
311 5:20	841 15:10	662 10:00	1127 19:50	948 17:05	235 4:20	813 12:25	749 11:20	131 1:45	829 12:45	1247 21:55	376 6:00	1075 16:00	416 6:55	700 11:55	376 6:10	1020 15:05	577 9:50	866 12:50						• Collingwood
660 10:55	281 4:25	204 2:50	295 4:15	288 4:25	703 10:00	237 3:25	117 1:40	792 10:05	331 4:35	415 6:35	547 7:20	209 3:10	563 8:05	416 9:35	559 8:10	154 2:15	539 9:45							• Dunedin
302 5:25	264 5:25	532 8:10	536 10:00	371 7:15	551 9:10	371 7:20	491 9:05	490 8:25	465 12:20	656 9:30	530 10:15	545 2:55	161 2:05	123 3:40	201 8:50	483								• Fox Glacier
785 12:10	225 3:25	355 5:05	141 2:00	171 2:35	857 12:15	276 4:20	271 3:55	946 13:30	370 5:30	261 4:20	701 9:05	65 1:05	644 10:20	360 6:45	684 10:25									• Gore
101 1:45	465 9:05	355 5:20	737 13:40	572 10:55	350 5:30	495 8:10	442 6:55	289 4:35	511 8:55	857 16:00	329 6:15	746 11:20	40 0:45	324 5:40										• Greymouth
425 7:30	141 3:20	409 8:10	413 7:55	248 5:10	674 11:25	248 5:15	368 7:00	613 10:15	342 6:25	533 10:15	422 11:25	653 8:10	284 5:00											• Haast
141 2:30	425 8:20	359 5:15	697 12:55	532 10:10	390 6:15	499 8:05	446 6:50	325 5:25	515 8:15	817 15:15	369 6:35	706 11:15												• Hokitika
855 13:05	295 4:40	413 6:00	160 2:25	190 3:00	912 13:10	346 5:15	326 4:50	1001 14:15	440 6:25	280 4:05	756 11:00													• Invercargill
332 5:30	607 9:20	343 5:00	842 13:55	674 11:10	156 2:15	494 7:25	430 6:10	245 3:35	510 7:45	962 16:15														• Kaikoura
958 16:50	398 6:55	619 9:25	120 2:20	299 5:05	1118 18:25	455 7:45	532 8:15	1146 18:35	549 8:55															• Milford Sound
612 10:00	207 3:00	212 3:10	429 6:30	264 3:50	666 9:45	94 1:10	214 3:55	755 10:30																• Mount Cook
224 3:45	754 12:45	580 8:25	1026 16:15	861 13:30	104 2:10	739 9:55	675 9:35																	• Nelson
543 8:30	233 3:40	87 1:10	412 5:55	290 4:50	586 8:20	120 1:45																		• Oamaru
596 9:50	113 1:55	161 2:40	342 5:25	170 2:40	650 9:50																			• Omarama
285 4:40	763 11:45	499 7:10	998 16:05	830 13:20																				• Picton
673 12:30	113 1:50	331 5:35	179 2:45																					• Queenstown
838 14:30	278 4:35	499 7:05																						• Te Anau
456 7:20	274 4:35																							• Timaru
566 10:45																								• Wanaka
• Westport																								

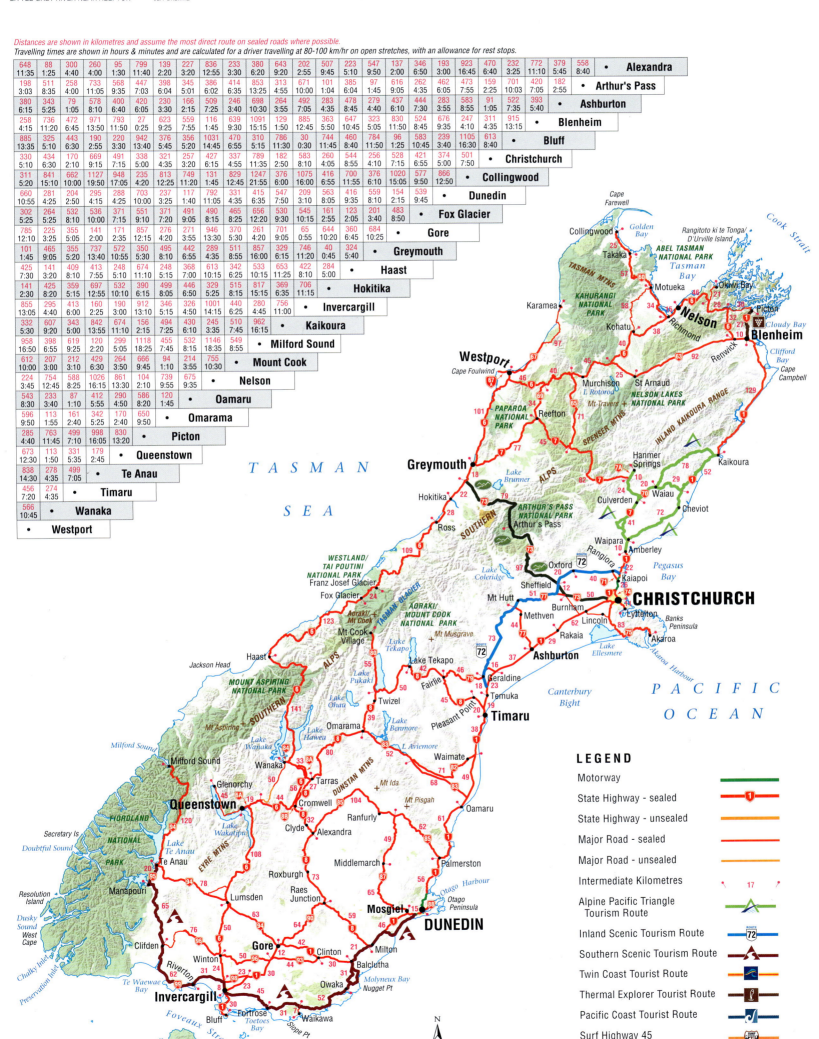

LEGEND

Motorway	
State Highway - sealed	
State Highway - unsealed	
Major Road - sealed	
Major Road - unsealed	
Intermediate Kilometres	
Alpine Pacific Triangle Tourism Route	
Inland Scenic Tourism Route	
Southern Scenic Tourism Route	
Twin Coast Tourist Route	
Thermal Explorer Tourist Route	
Pacific Coast Tourist Route	
Surf Highway 45	

Kauri Coast & Whangarei

MAP 5 — Kaipara Harbour & Kowhai Coast

North Island

MAP 9 Waikato

MAP 11 Central Waikato

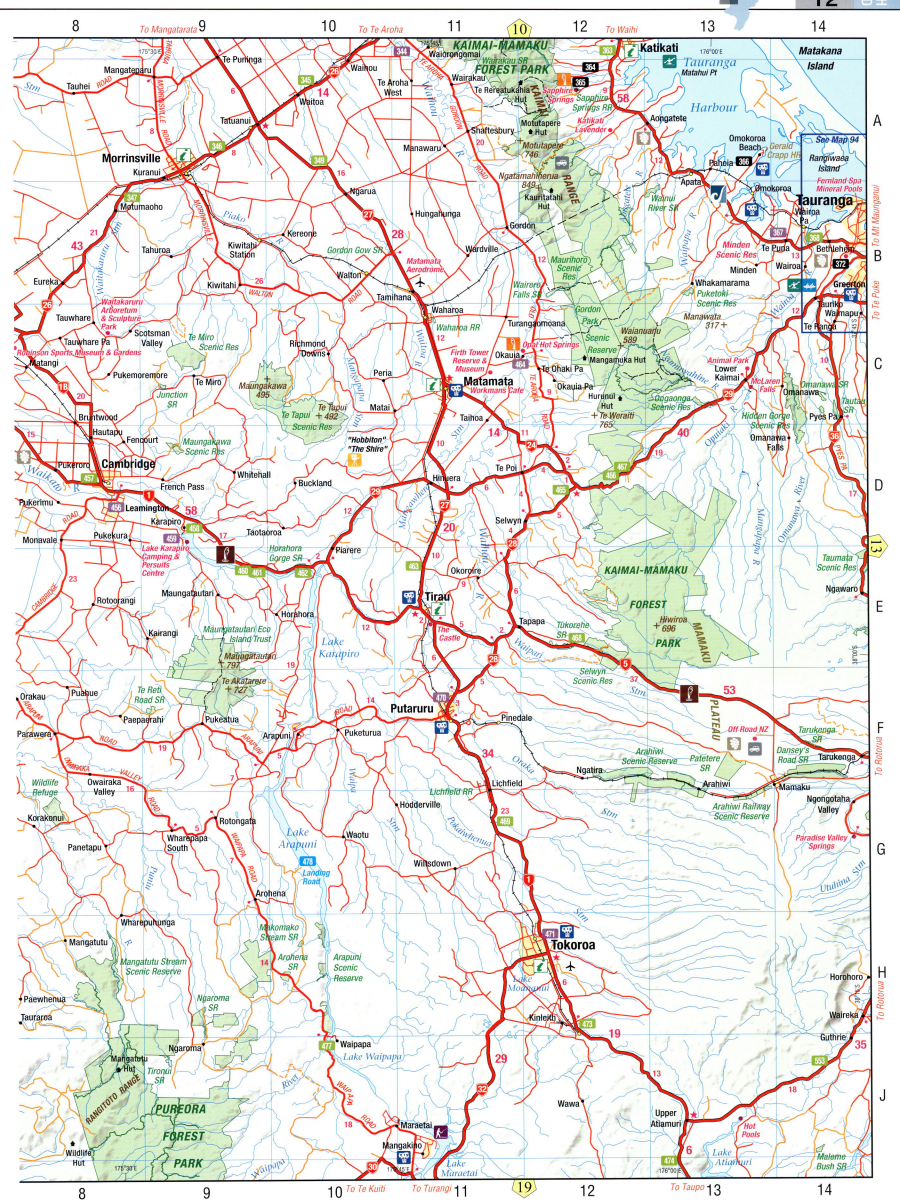

MAP 13 Rotorua & Bay of Plenty

MAP 15 Eastern Bay of Plenty & East Cape

MAP 16 NORTH ISLAND

MAP 17 — North Taranaki & Taumarunui

Taupo

MAP 19

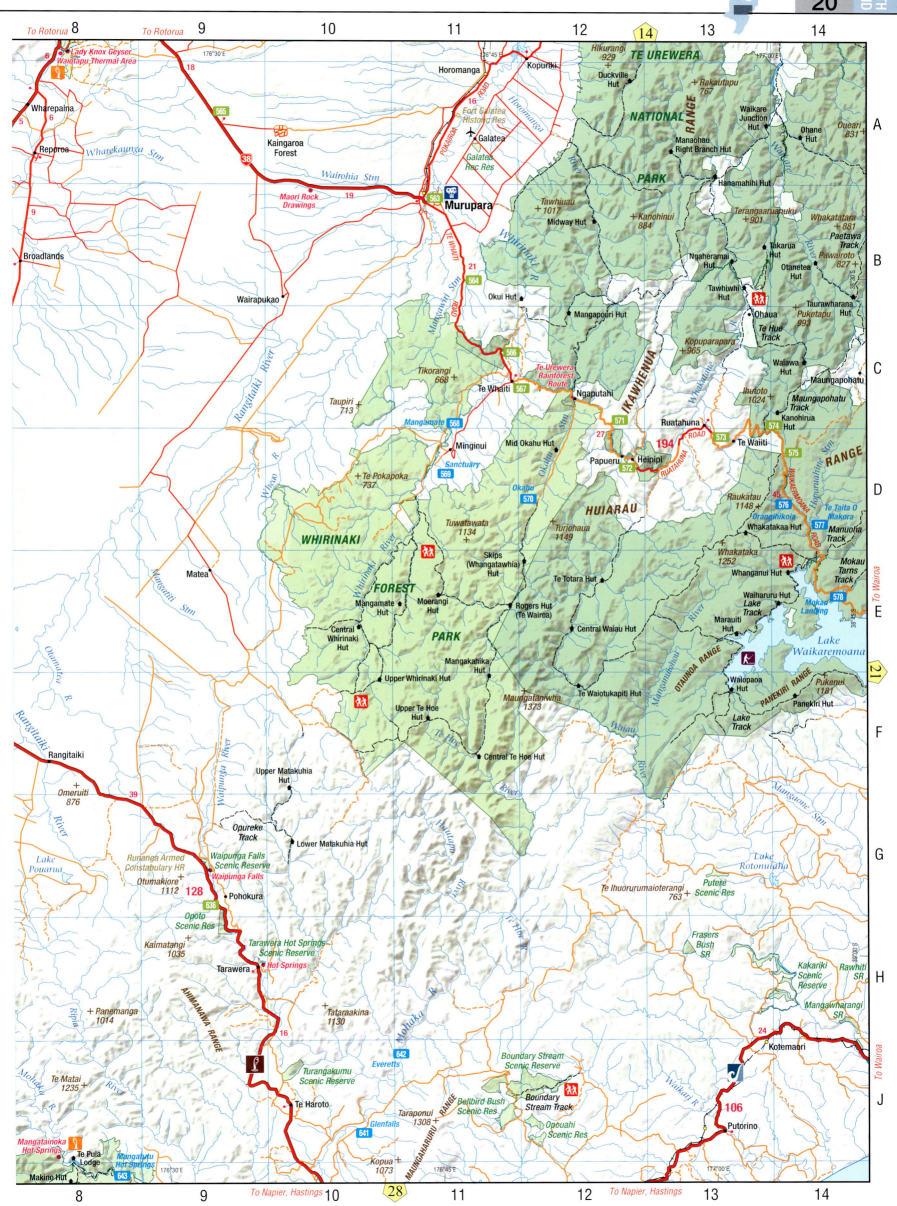

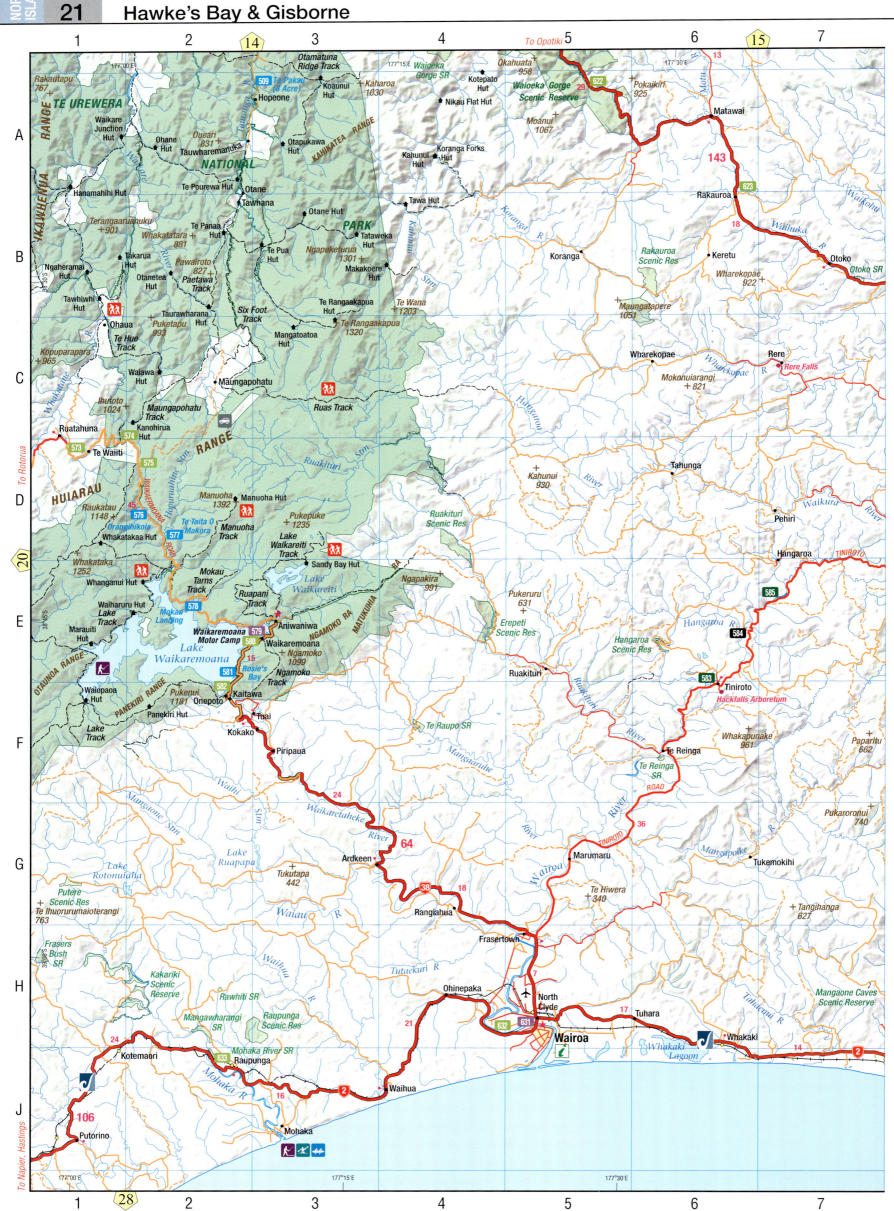

MAP 21 — Hawke's Bay & Gisborne

MAP 23 Taranaki & River Region

MAP 25 — South Taranaki

MAP 27: Napier & Hastings

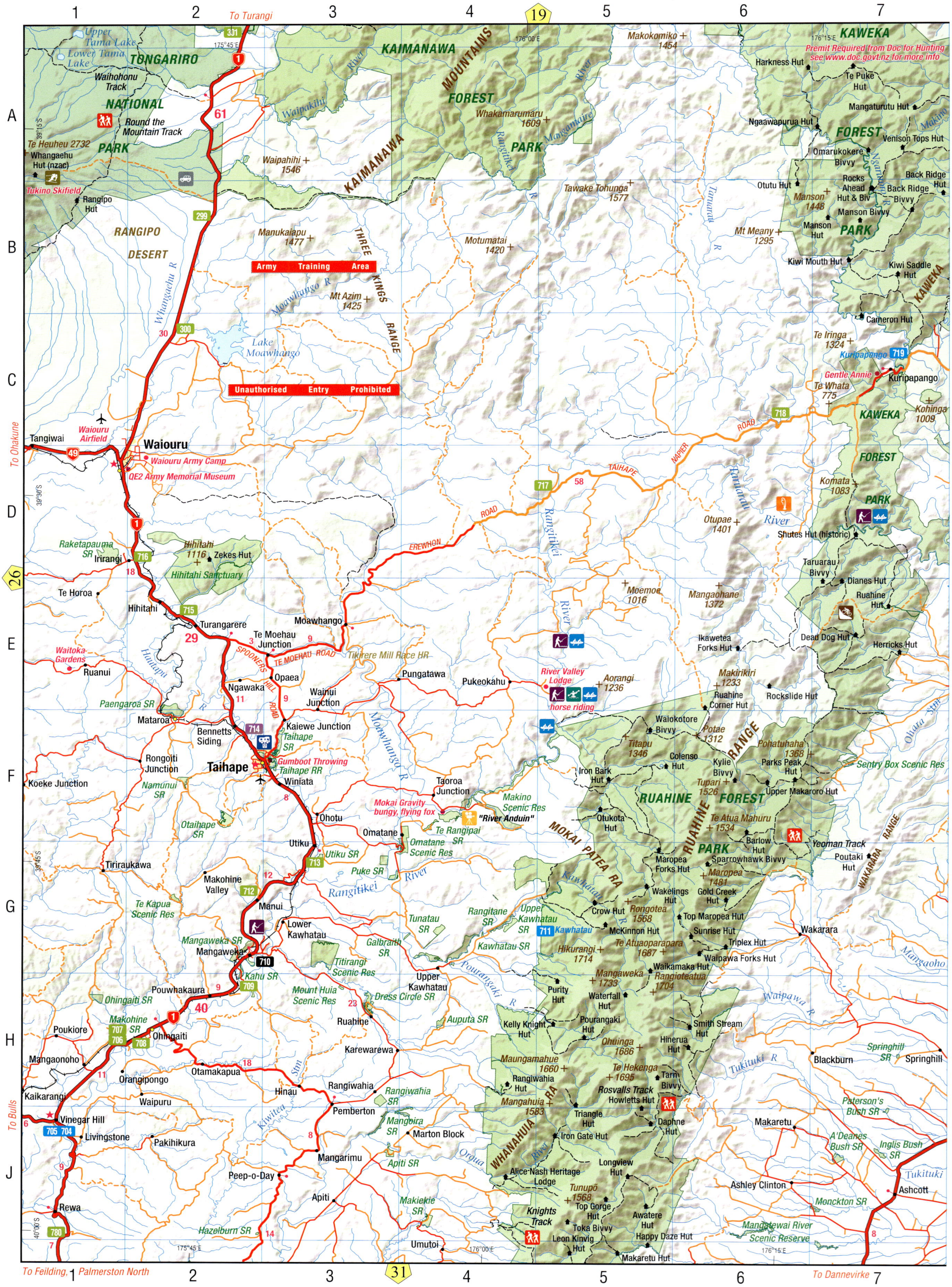

MAP 29 — Manawatu & Horowhenua

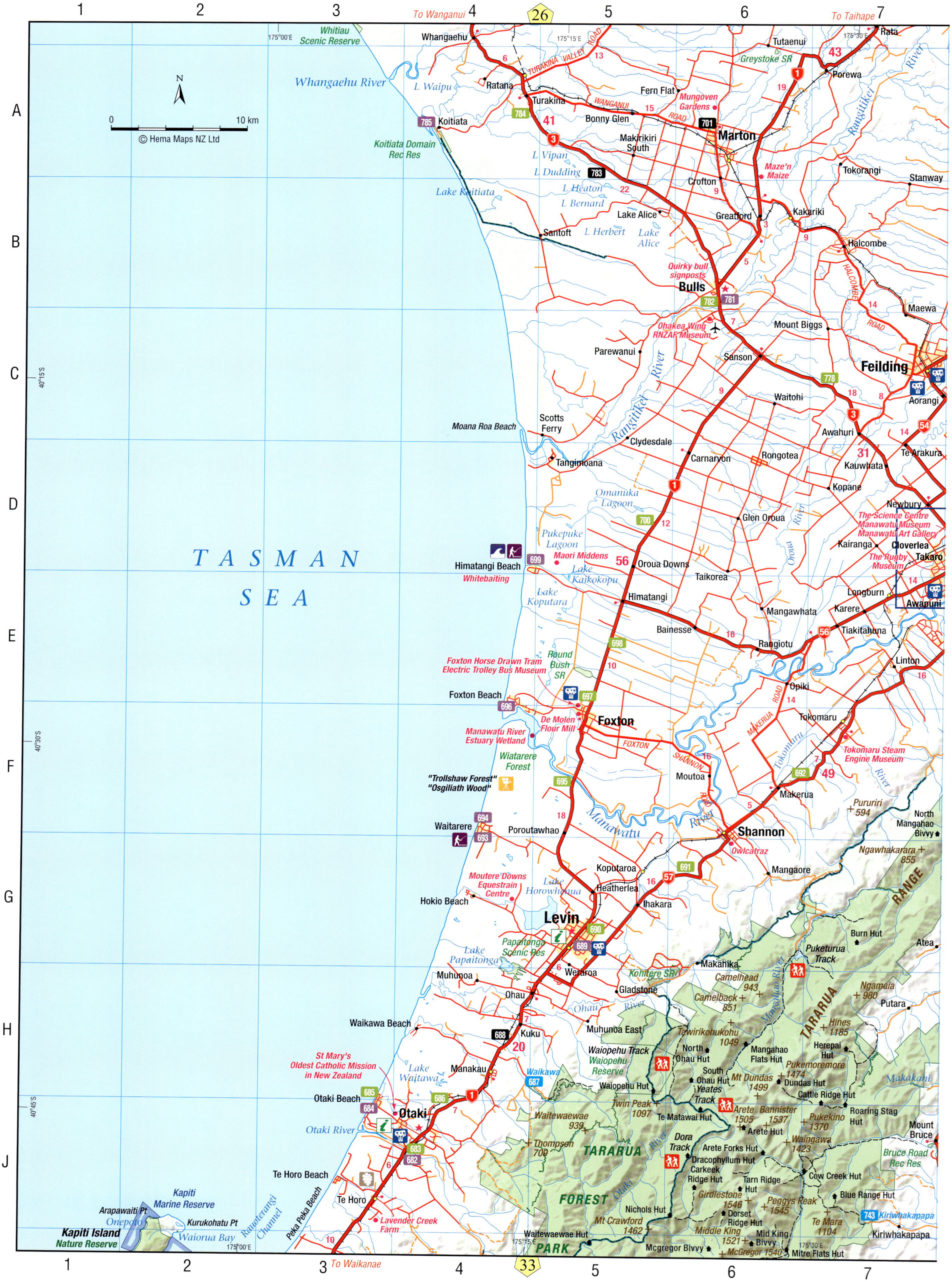

MAP 31 — Manawatu & Wairarapa

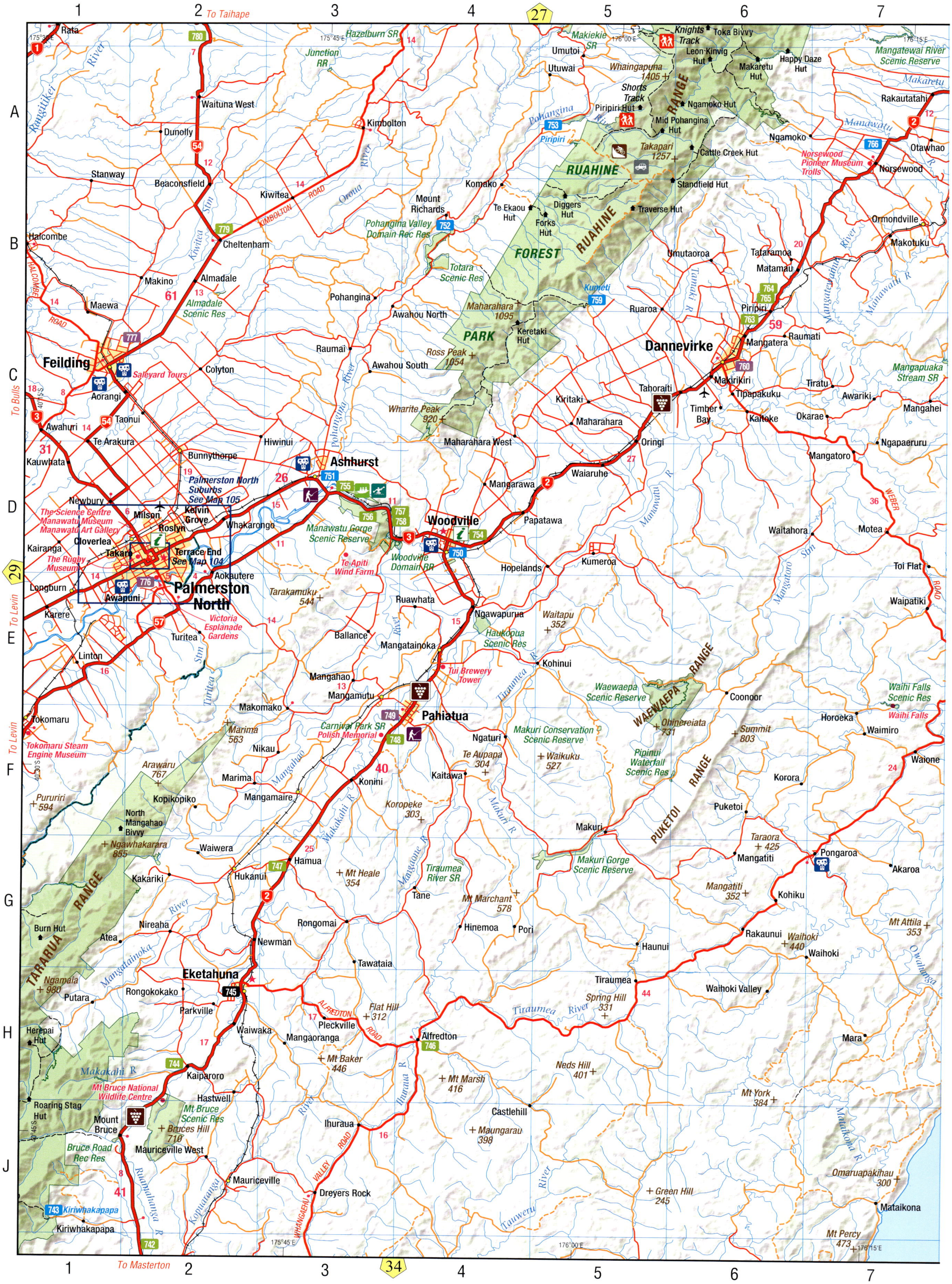

MAP 33 — Wellington & South Wairarapa

NORTH ISLAND

MAP 35 Cook Strait

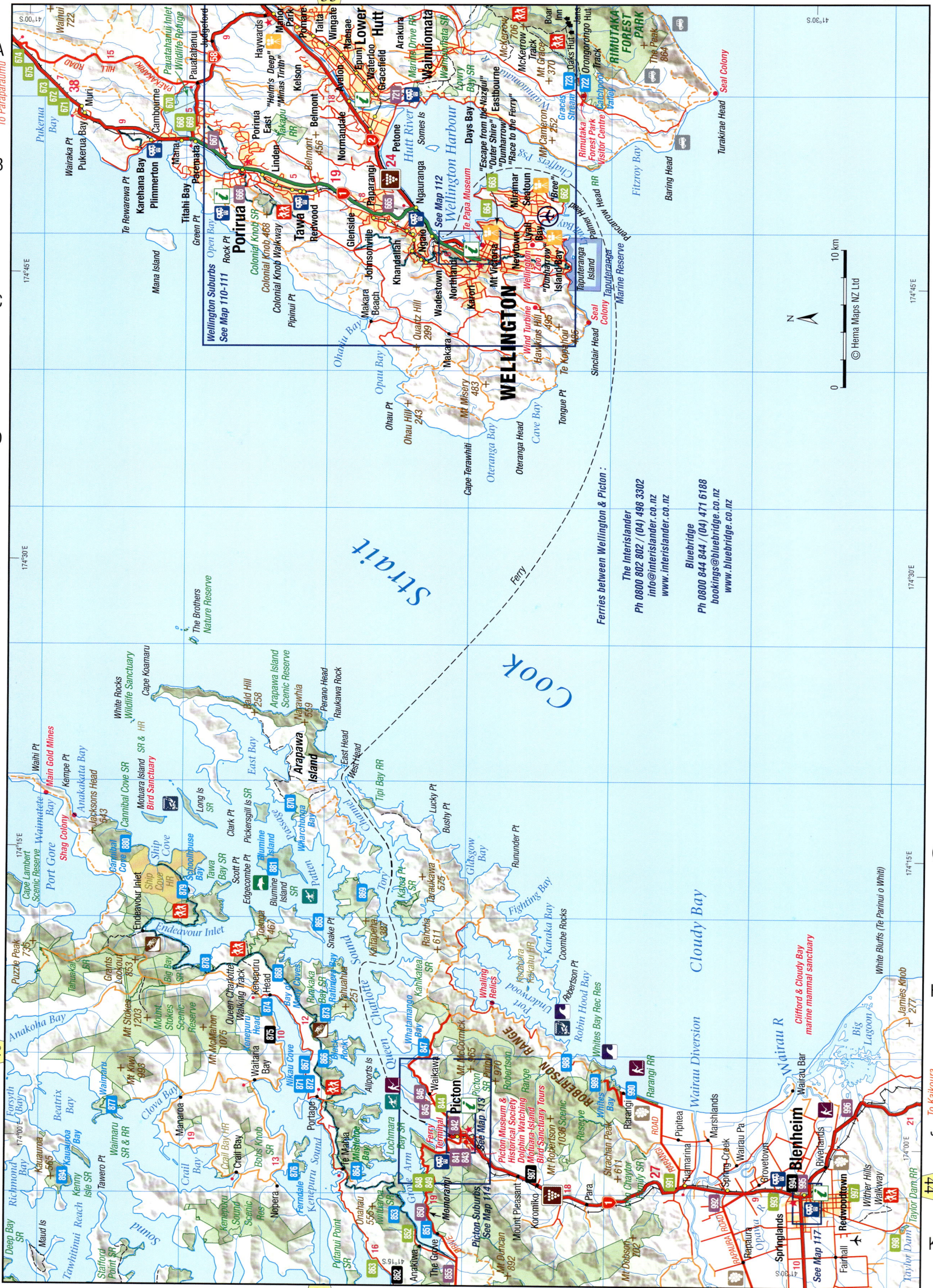

MAP 38 SOUTH ISLAND

MAP 39 Nelson & Marlborough

MAP 41 Buller & Tasman

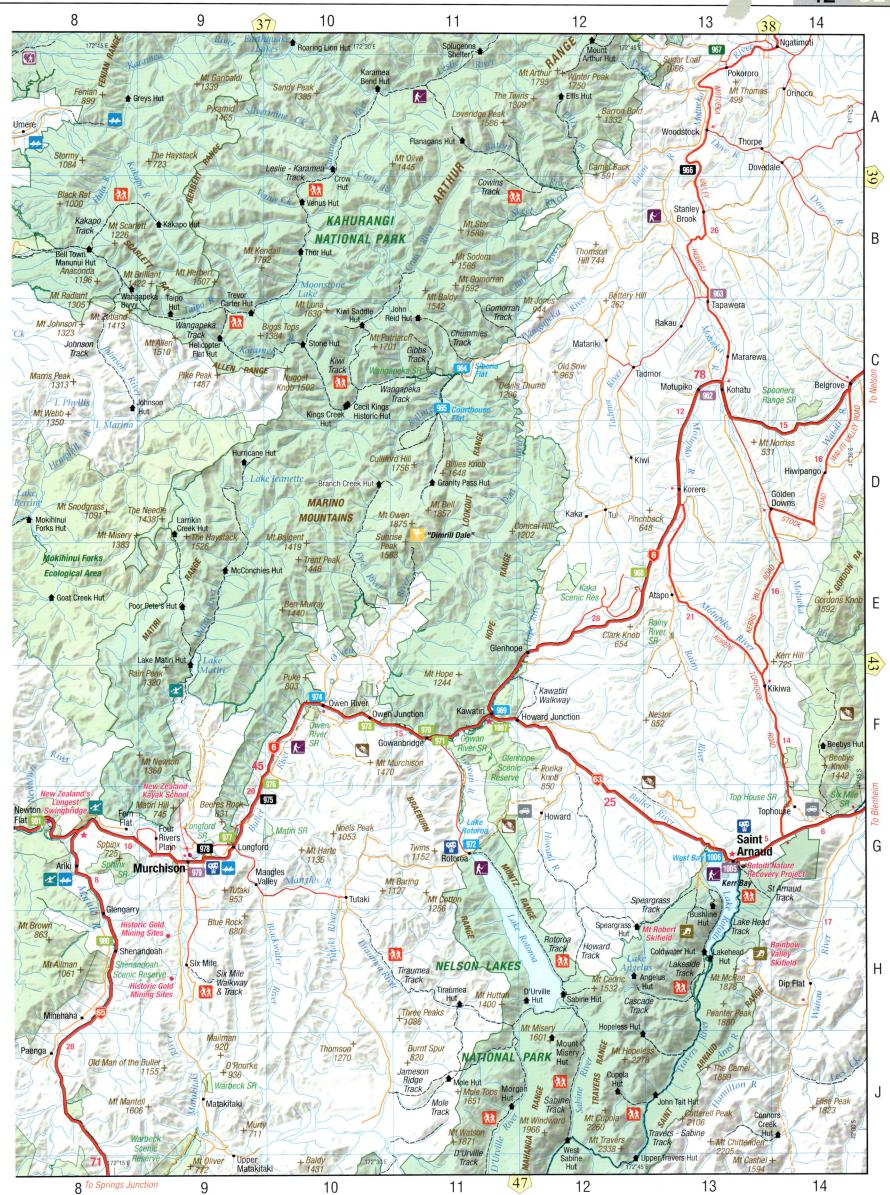

MAP 43 Marlborough

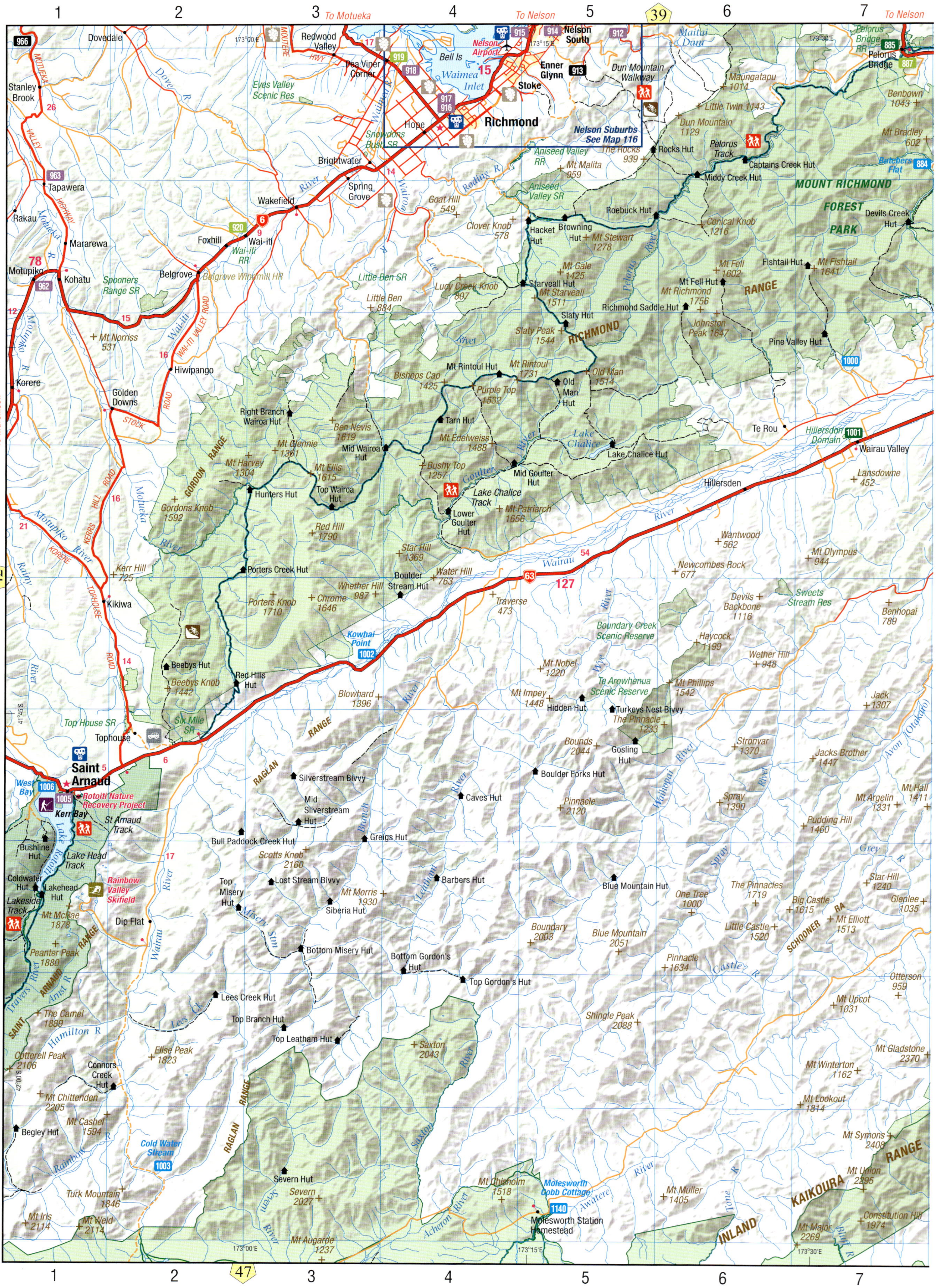

MAP 45 — Central West Coast
South Island

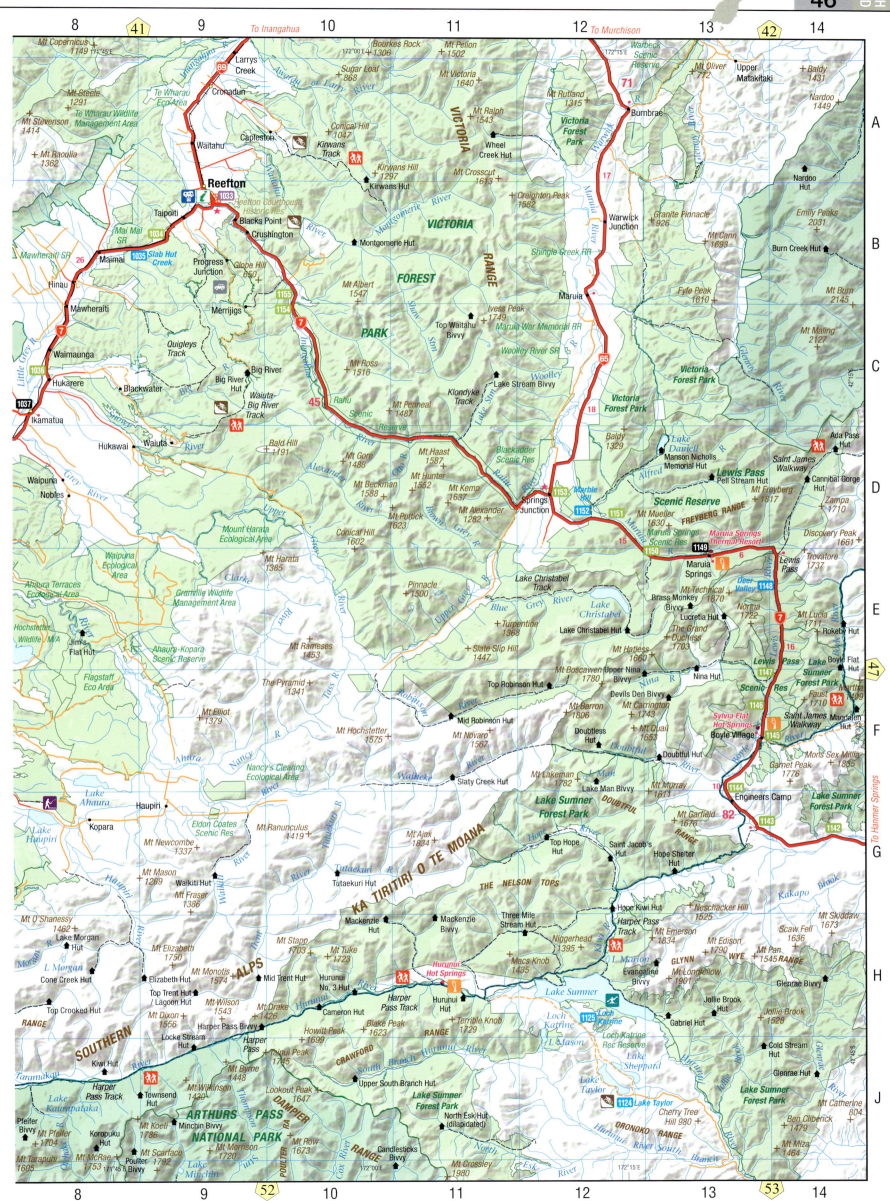

MAP 50 SOUTH ISLAND

MAP 51 Arthur's Pass

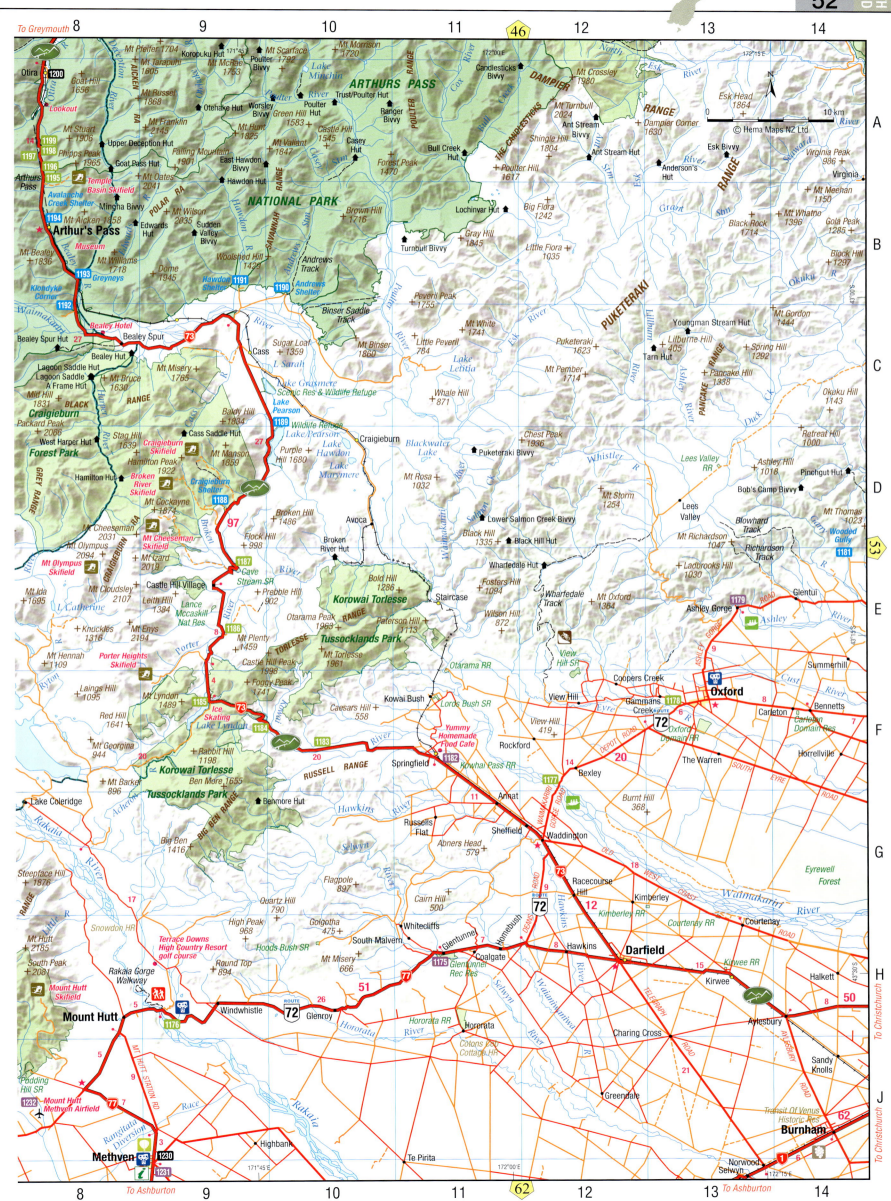

MAP 53 Central Canterbury

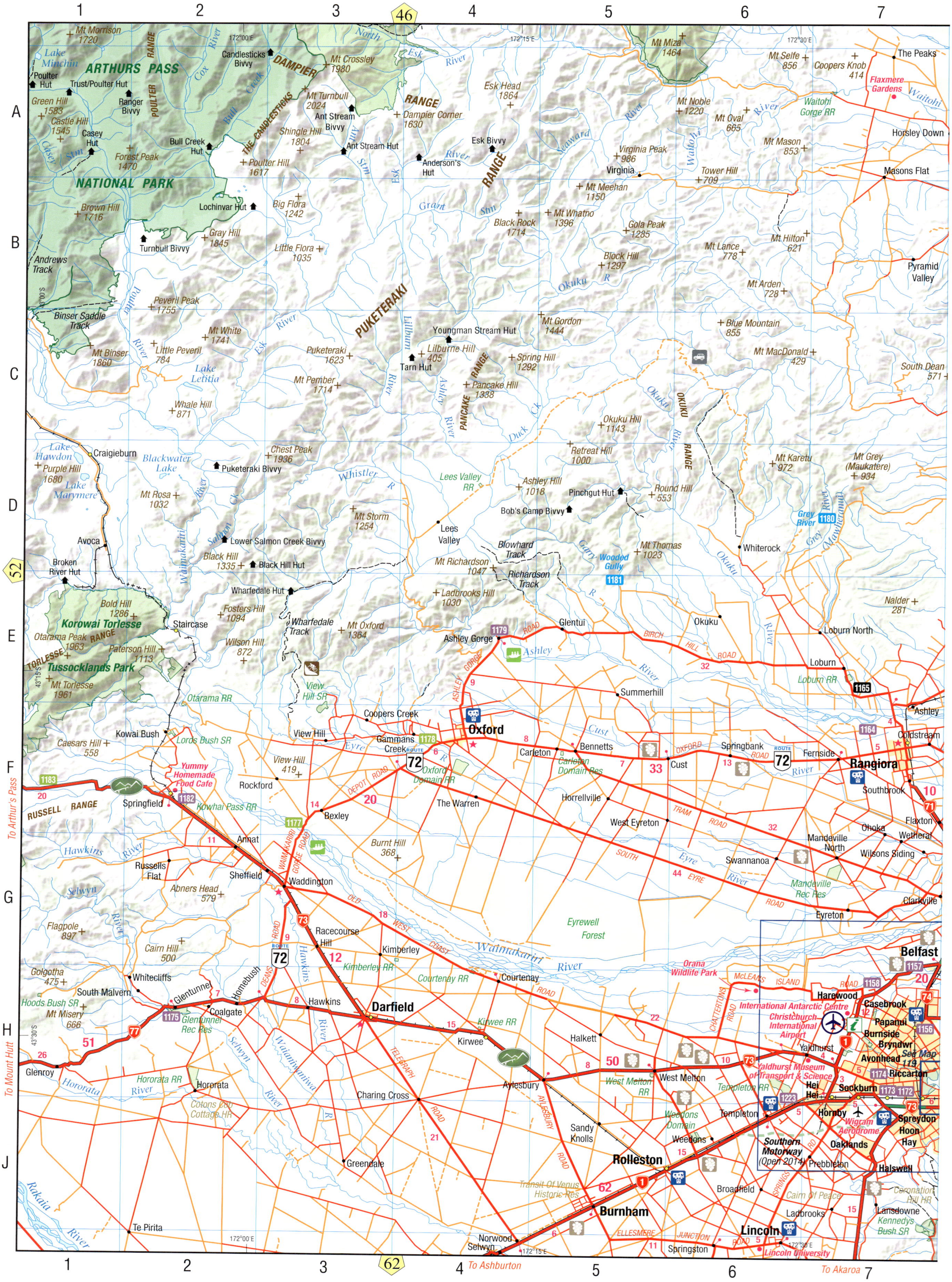

MAP 55 — Ashburton & Christchurch

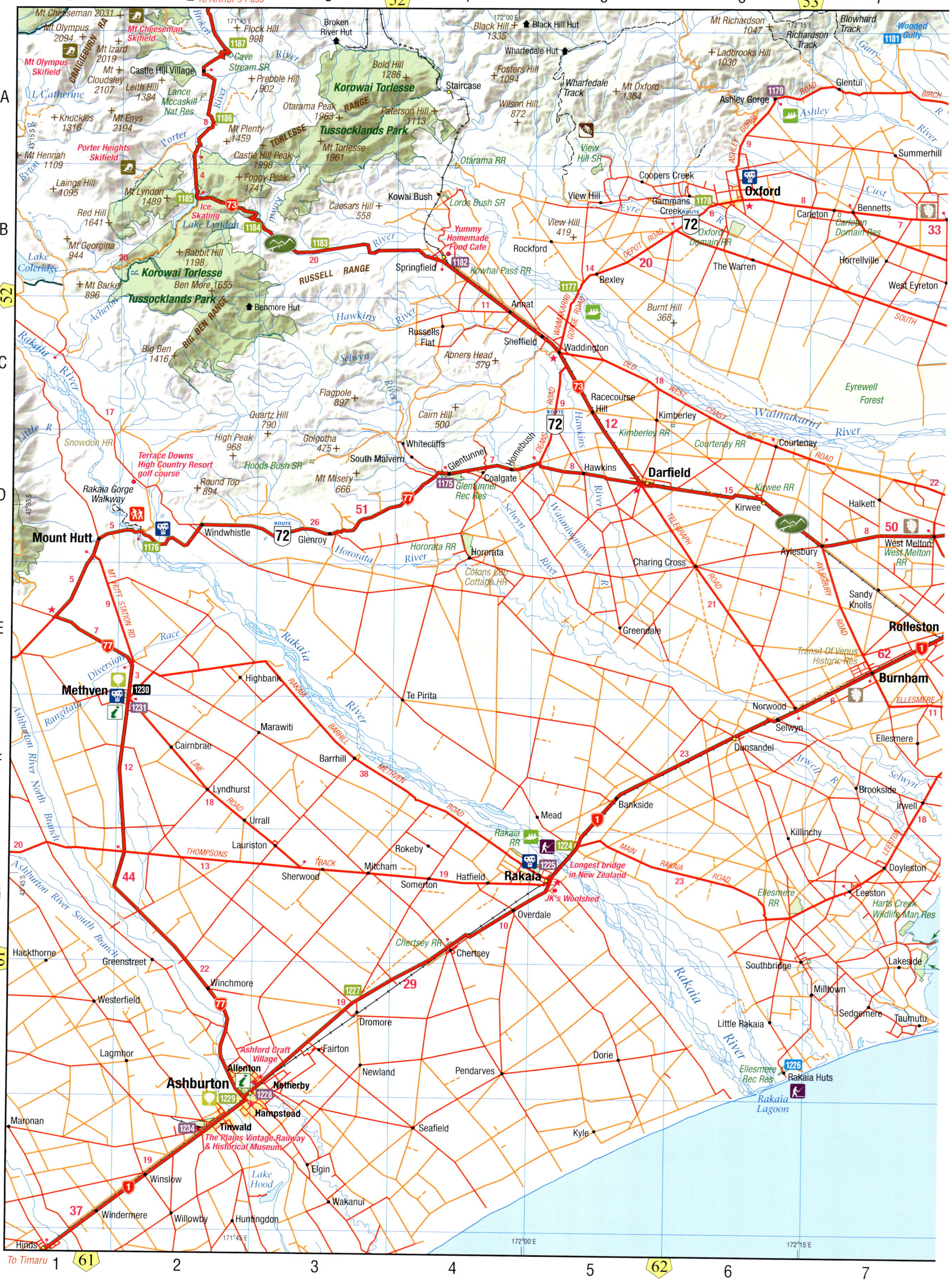

SOUTH ISLAND

MAP 56 SOUTH ISLAND

Southern West Coast

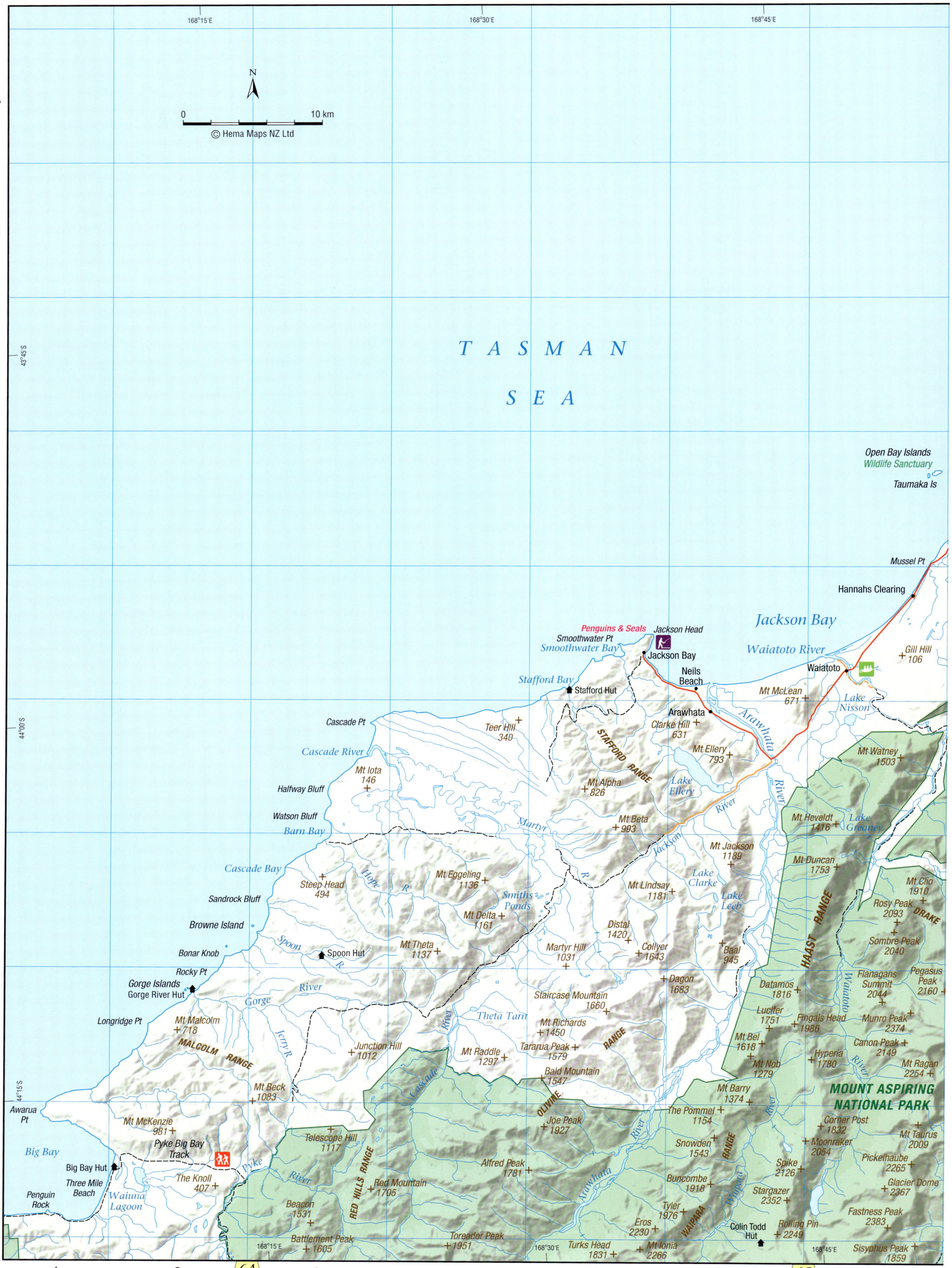
TASMAN SEA
0 10 km
© Hema Maps NZ Ltd
168°15'E
168°30'E
168°45'E
43°45'S
44°00'S
44°15'S
Open Bay Islands
Wildlife Sanctuary
Taumaka Is
Mussel Pt
Hannahs Clearing
Jackson Bay
Penguins & Seals
Jackson Head
Smoothwater Pt
Smoothwater Bay
Jackson Bay
Neils Beach
Waiatoto River
Waiatoto
Gill Hill 106
Stafford Bay
Stafford Hut
Mt McLean 671
Lake Nisson
Arawhata
Clarke Hill 631
Cascade Pt
Teer Hill 340
STAFFORD RANGE
Arawhata
Cascade River
Mt Ellery 793
Mt Watney 1503
Mt Iota 146
Halfway Bluff
Mt Alpha 826
Lake Ellery
River
Watson Bluff
Barn Bay
Martyr
Mt Beta 993
River
Mt Heveldt 1416
Lake Greaney
Jackson
Mt Jackson 1189
Cascade Bay
Hope
Mt Eggeling 1136
Mt Duncan 1753
Steep Head 494
R
Smiths Ponds
R
Mt Lindsay 1181
Lake Clarke
Mt Clio 1910
Sandrock Bluff
Lake Leeb
Rosy Peak 2093
DRAKE
Mt Delta 1161
HAAST RANGE
Browne Island
Distal 1420
Spoon
Sombre Peak 2040
Bonar Knob
Spoon Hut
Mt Theta 1137
Martyr Hill 1031
Collyer 1643
Baal 945
R
Rocky Pt
Gorge Islands
Gorge River Hut
River
Dagon 1683
Datamos 1816
Flanagans Summit 2044
Pegasus Peak 2160
Staircase Mountain 1660
Waiatoto
Gorge
Longridge Pt
Mt Malcolm 718
Theta Tarn
Lucifer 1751
Fingals Head 1986
Munro Peak 2374
River
Mt Richards 1450
MALCOLM RANGE
Jerry R
Mt Bel 1618
Canon Peak 2149
Tarapua Peak 1579
RANGE
Junction Hill 1012
Mt Raddle 1297
Hyperia 1780
River
Mt Nob 1279
Mt Ragan 2254
Cascade
Bald Mountain 1547
Mt Beck 1083
Mt Barry 1374
MOUNT ASPIRING NATIONAL PARK
Awarua Pt
OLIVINE
The Pommel 1154
River
Corner Post 1832
Mt McKenzie 981
Joe Peak 1927
Mt Taurus 2009
Telescope Hill 1117
River
Moonraker 2054
Big Bay
Pyke Big Bay Track
Snowden 1543
RANGE
Big Bay Hut
Pyke
Alfred Peak 1781
Pickelhaube 2265
RED HILLS RANGE
Spike 2126
The Knoll 407
River
Three Mile Beach
Red Mountain 1705
Arawhata
Buncombe 1918
Glacier Dome 2367
Penguin Rock
Waiuna Lagoon
Stargazer 2352
Beacon 1531
Tyler 1976
Waipara
Fastness Peak 2383
WAIPARA
Eros 2230
Colin Todd Hut
Rolling Pin 2249
Battlement Peak 1605
Toreador Peak 1951
Turks Head 1831
Mt Ionia 2266
Sisyphus Peak 1859
1 2 3 4 5 6 7
A B C D E F G H J

64
65

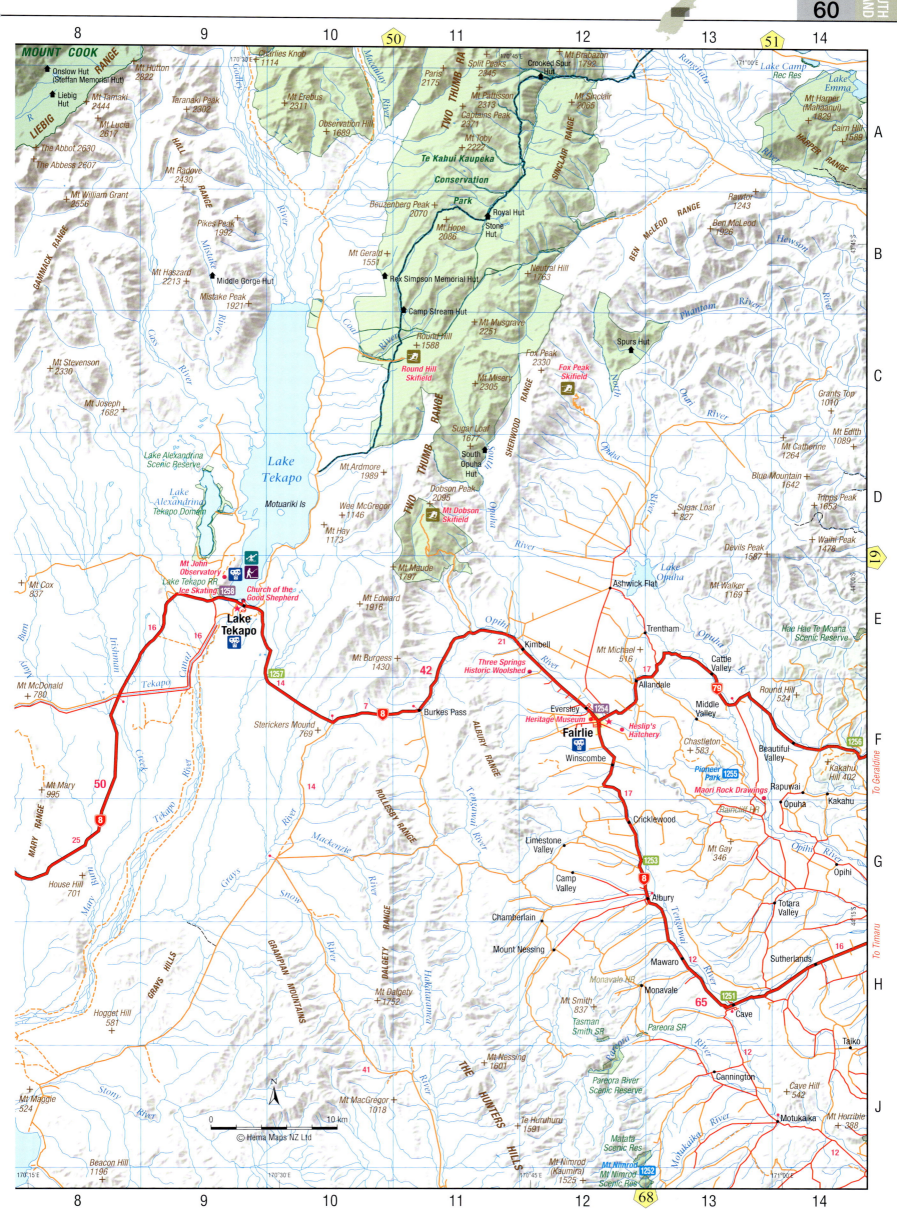

MAP 61: Timaru & Ashburton

SOUTH ISLAND

MAP 63 Northern Fiordland

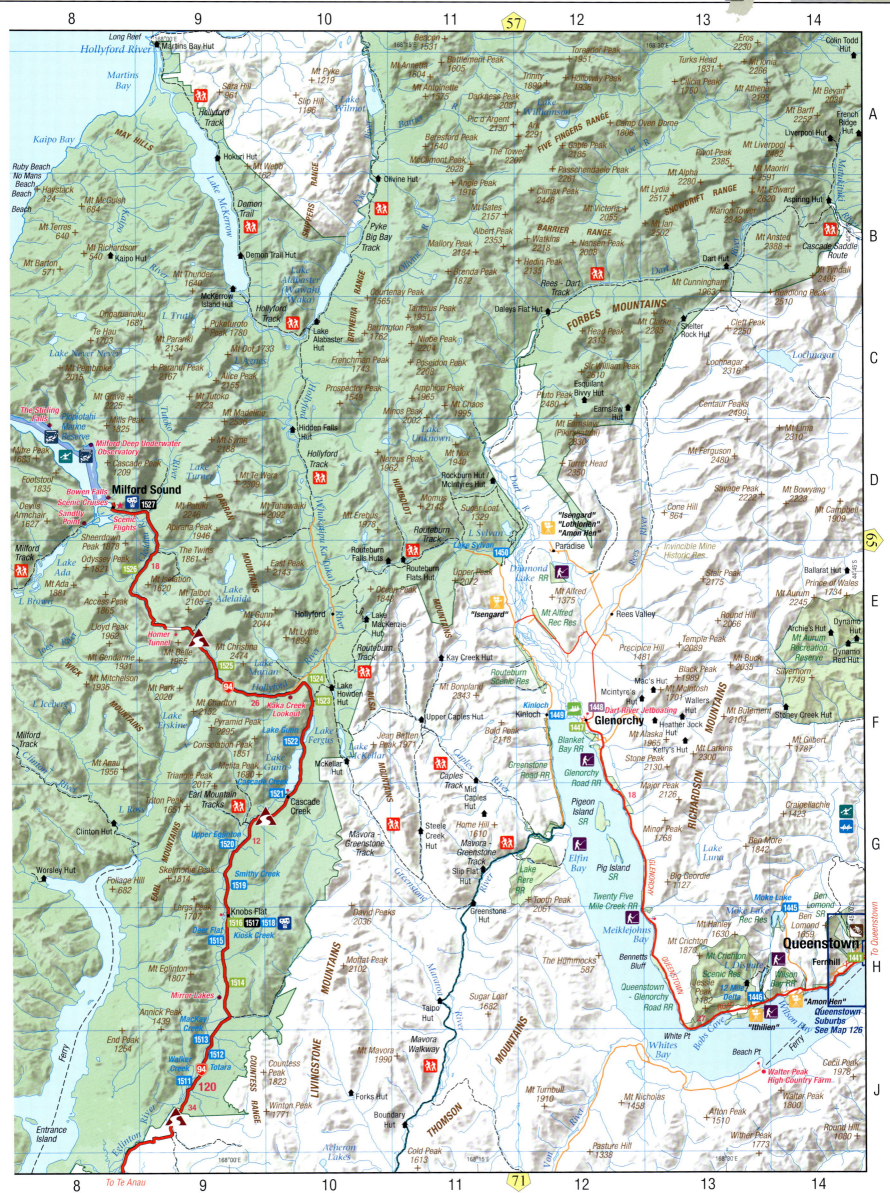

MAP 65 — Queenstown, Wanaka & Central Otago

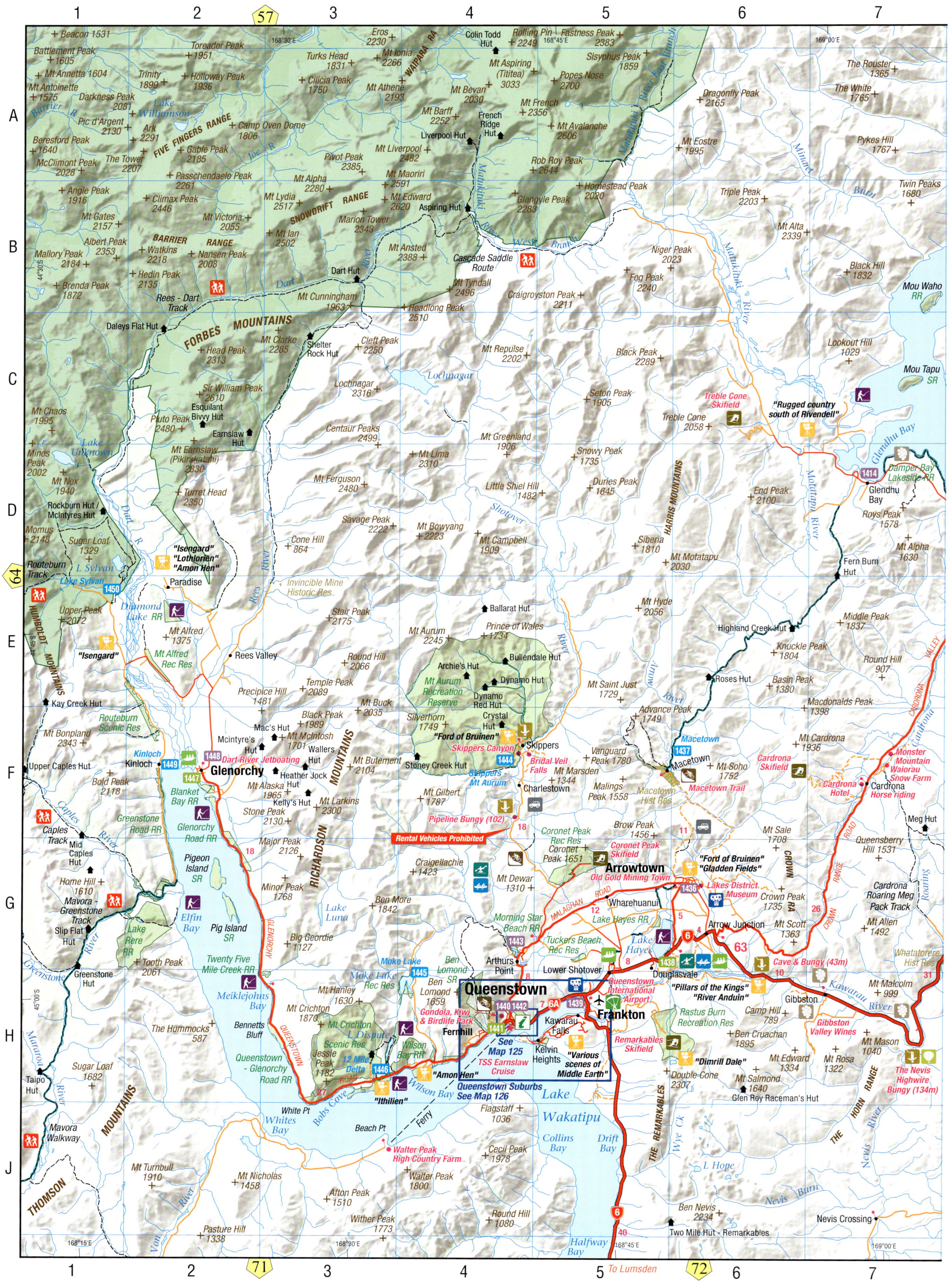

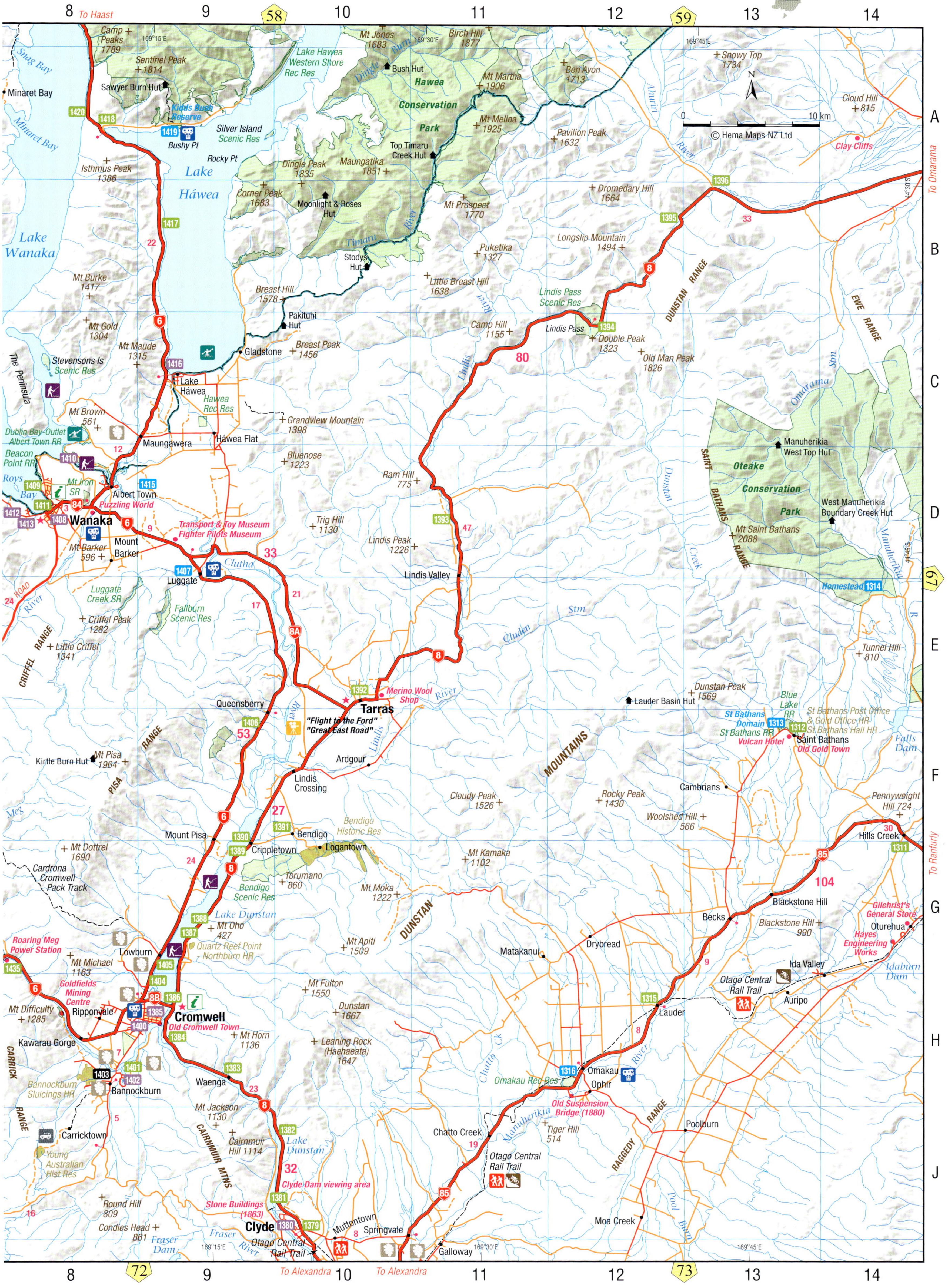

MAP 66 SOUTH ISLAND

MAP 67: Southern Canterbury & Northern Otago

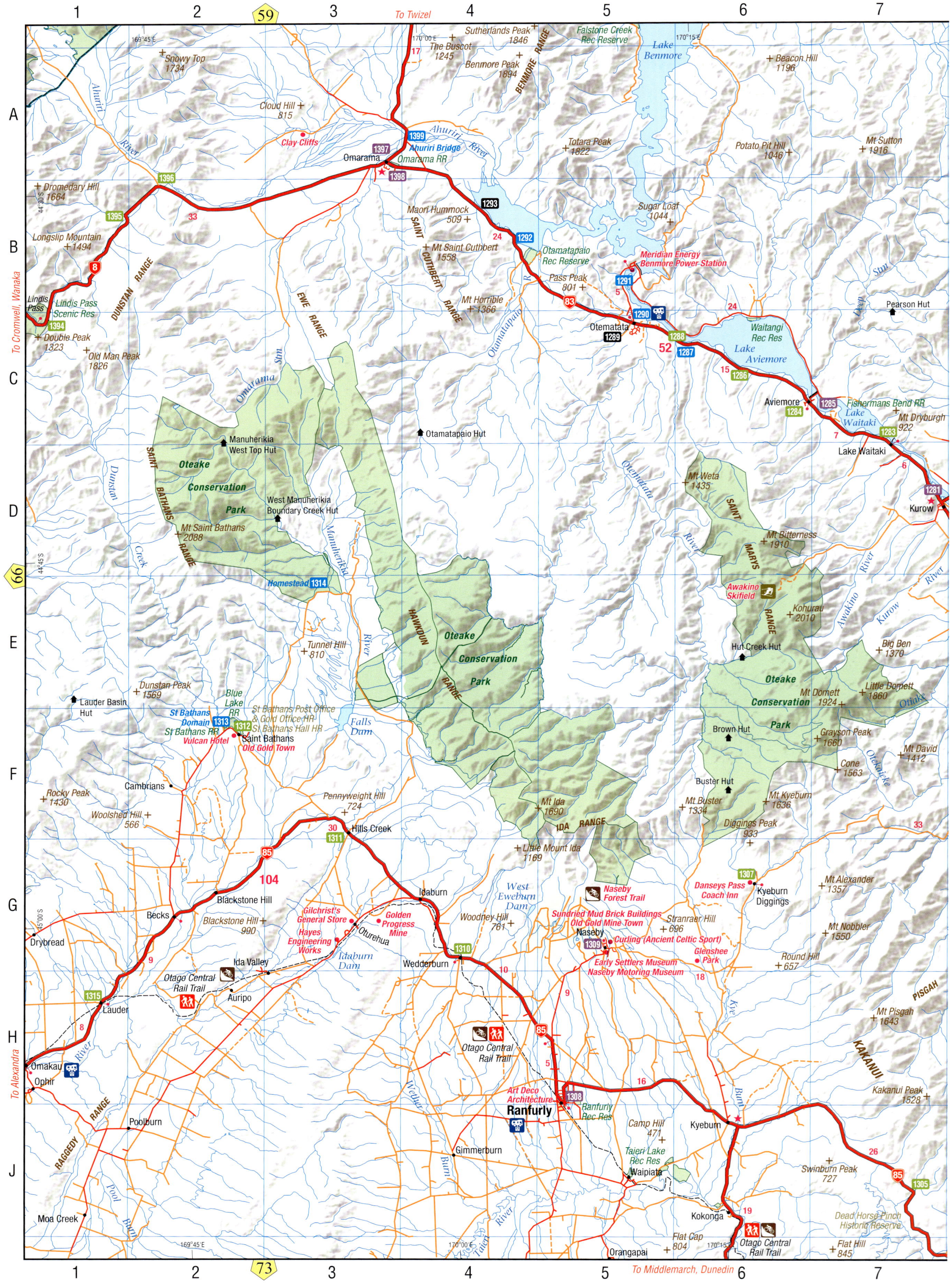

MAP 69 Central Fiordland

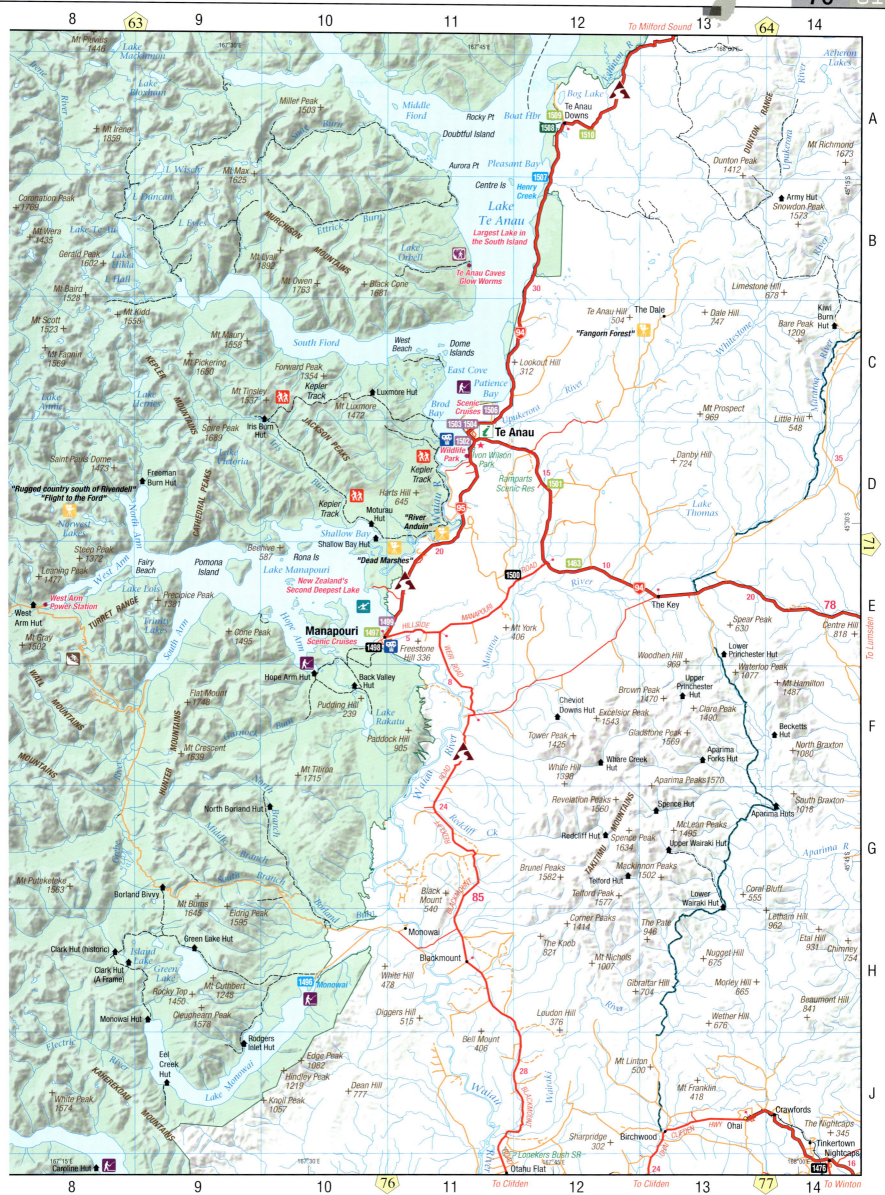

MAP 71 Southland & Central Otago

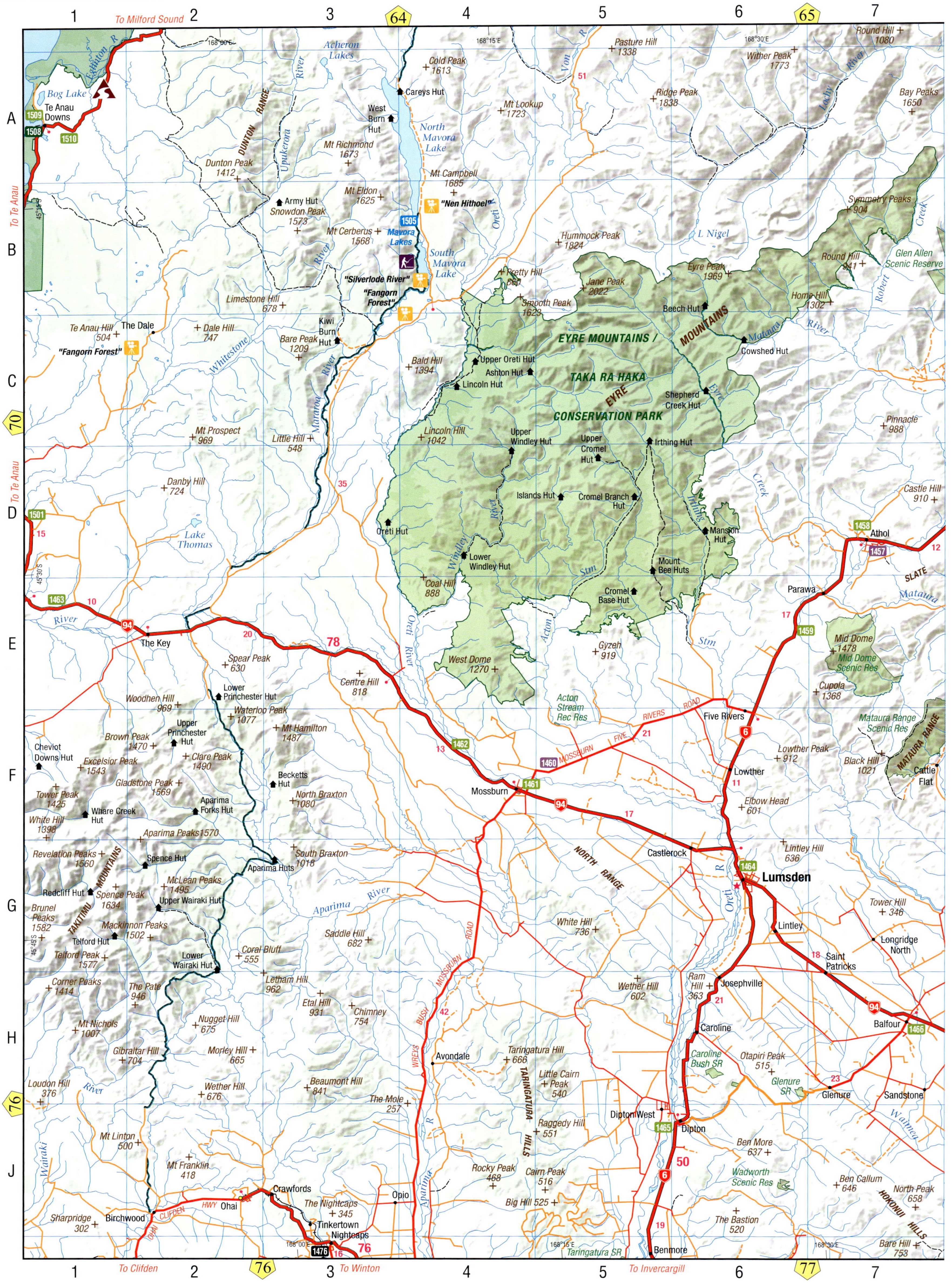

MAP 73 — Central Otago & Dunedin

SOUTH ISLAND

MAP 75 Southern Fiordland

MAP 77 Southland

MAP 79 Coastal Otago

City and Suburbs legend

Motorway	
Urban Route	
State Highway	
Ring Road	
Main Road	
Street	
Lane/Path	
Railway & Station	
City Tramway	
Road Tunnel	
Major Bridge/overpass	
Ferry Route	
Major Building	
Govt Building	
Accommodation	
Theatre/Cinema	
Shopping	
Mall/City Square	
School/Educational	
Park/Reserve	

Cemetery	
Hospital	
Postal Service	
Police Station	
Church	
One Way Street	
Place of Interest	Tui Brewery
Information Centre	
To Airport	
Alpine Pacific Triangle Tourist Route	
Inland Scenic Tourist Route	
Southern Scenic Tourist Route	
Twin Coast Tourist Route	
Thermal Explorer Tourist Route	
Pacific Coast Tourist Route	
Forgotten World Tourist Route	
Classic New Zealand Wine Trail	
The Great Alpine Highway	

Suburbs Legend

Motorway	
Motorway (proposed)	
Urban Ring Road	
State Highway/Number	
Main Rd/Regional Number	
Secondary Road	
Minor Road	
Railway and Station	Rolleston
Busway	
Park, Reserve, Golf Course	Harewood
Special Use	Hospital
Mountain	Mt Herbert
Ferry Route	
Tourist Point of Interest	Christchurch Gondola
Major Shopping Centre	The Palms Mall
Information Centre	

MAP 81 Bay of Islands — For touring map see map 4
MAP 82 Russell
MAP 83 Paihia (below)

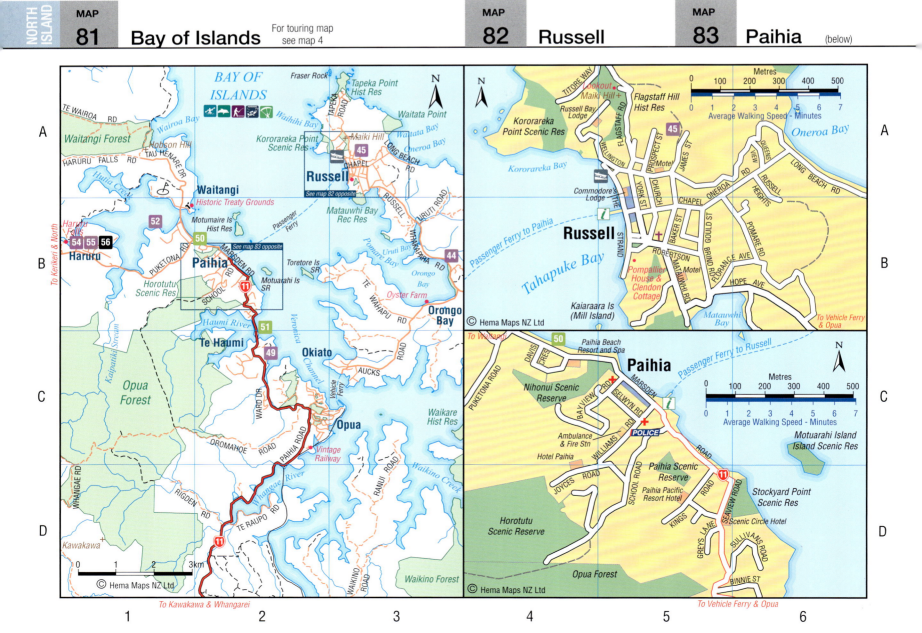

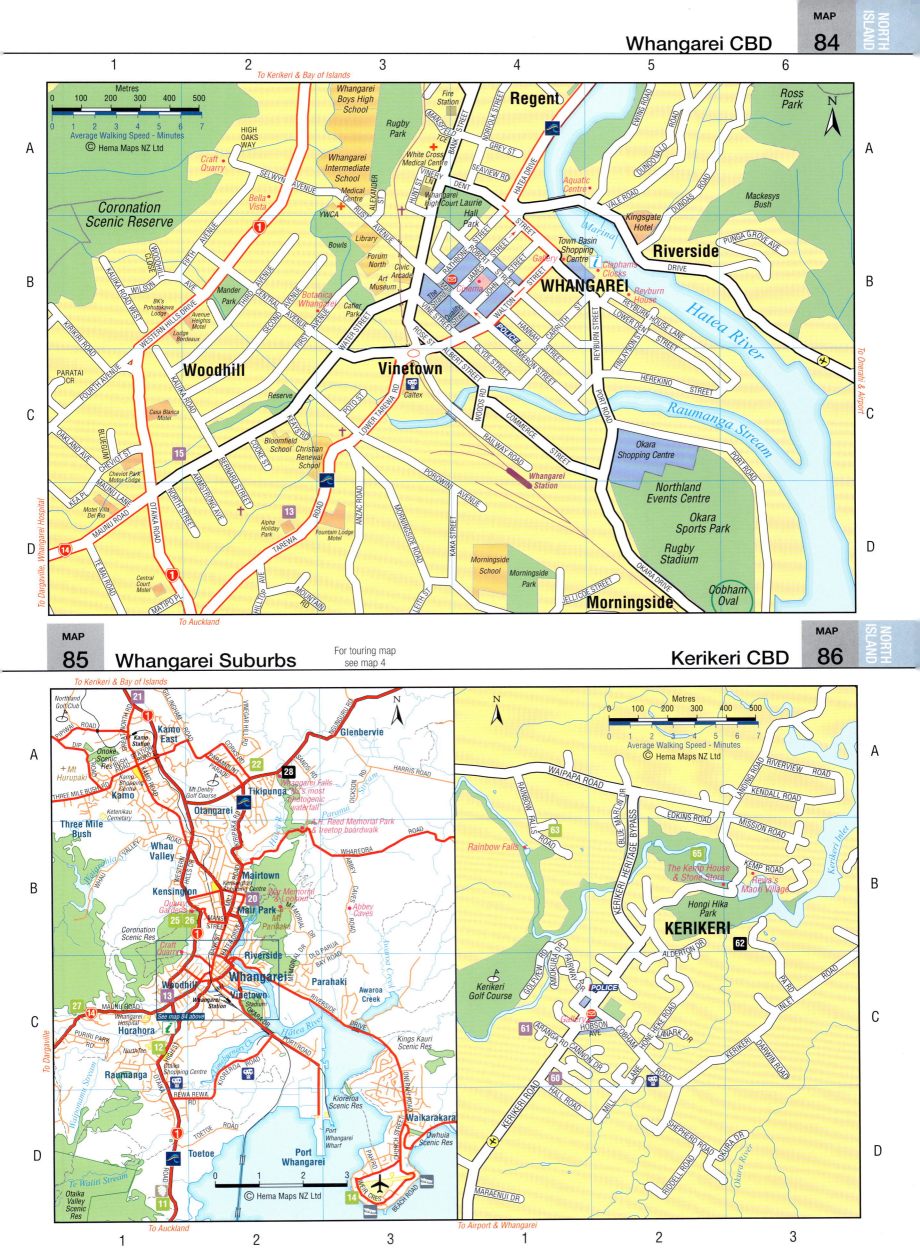

MAP 87 Auckland CBD

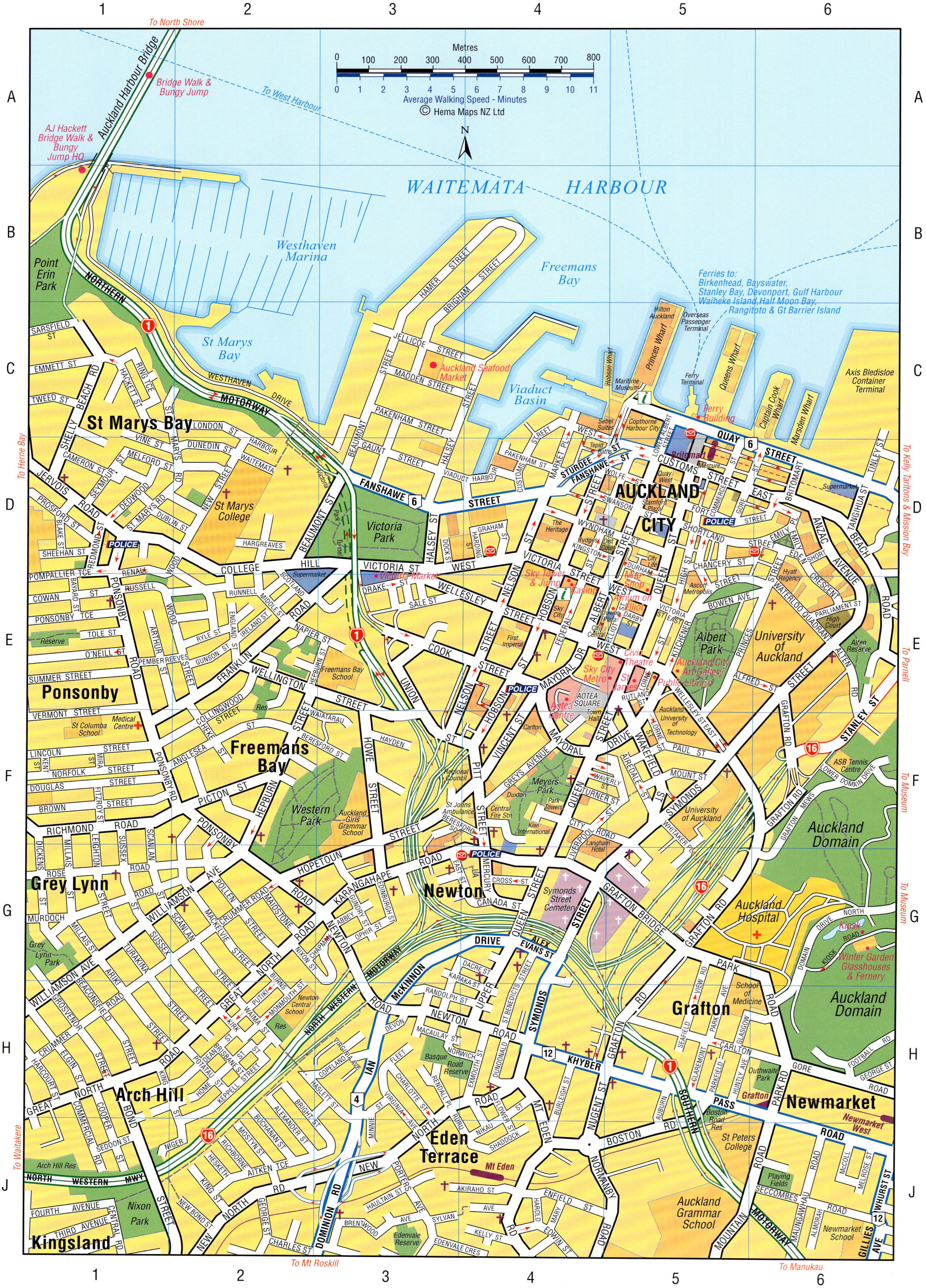

North Shore Suburbs

MAP 88 — NORTH ISLAND

MAP 89 West Auckland Suburbs

East & South Auckland Suburbs — Map 90

MAP 91 Hamilton CBD

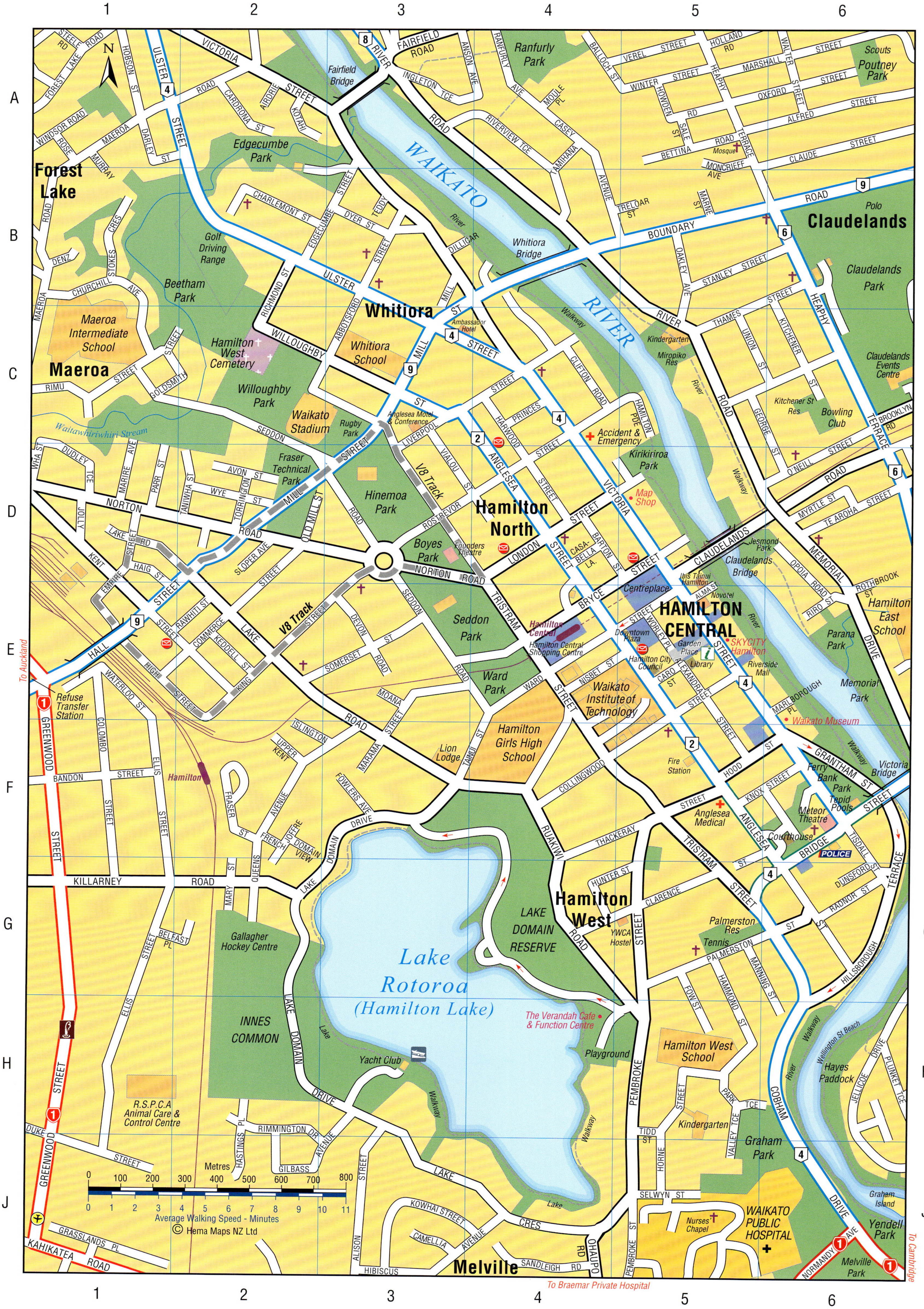

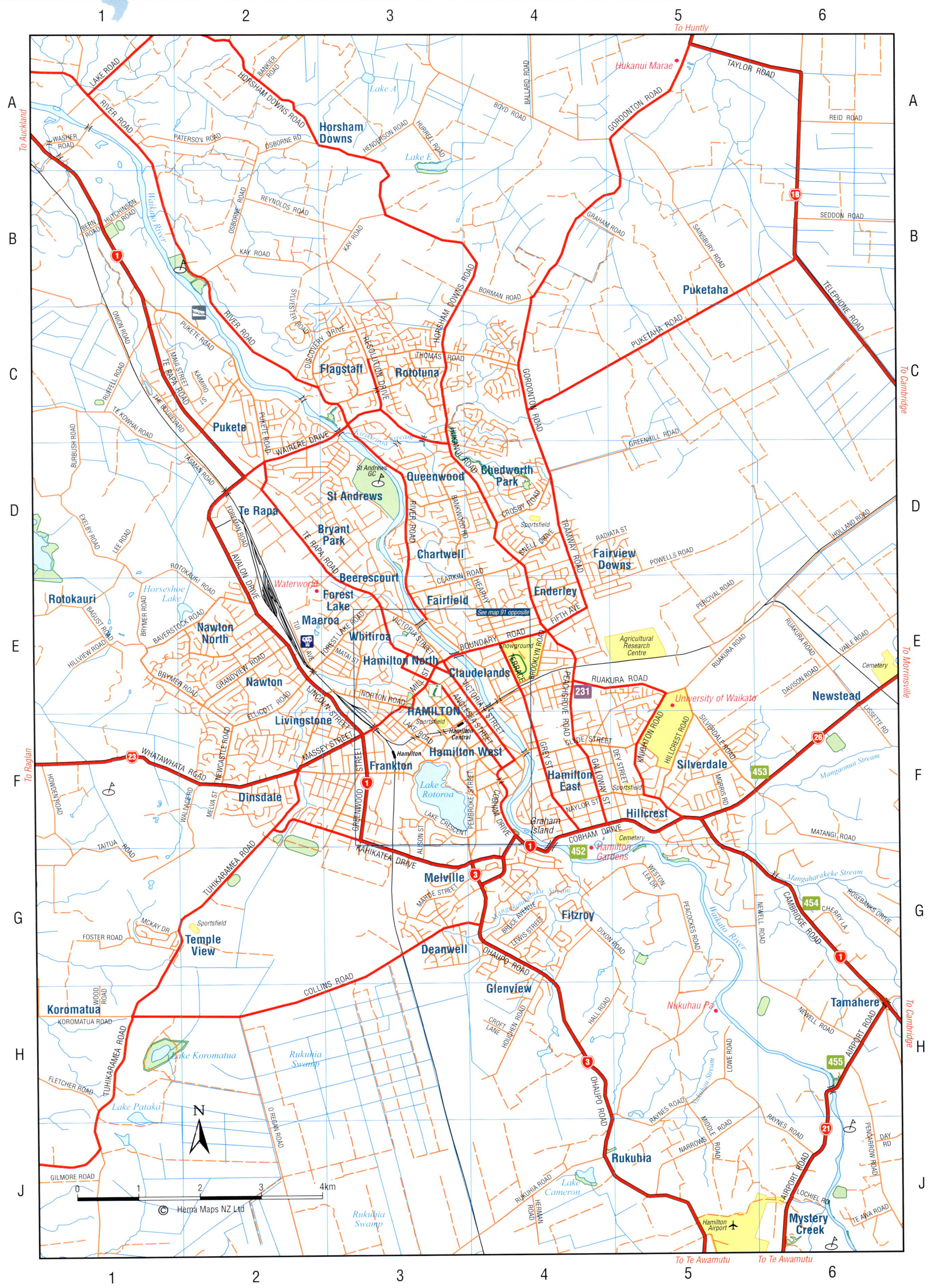

Hamilton Suburbs

MAP 92 — NORTH ISLAND

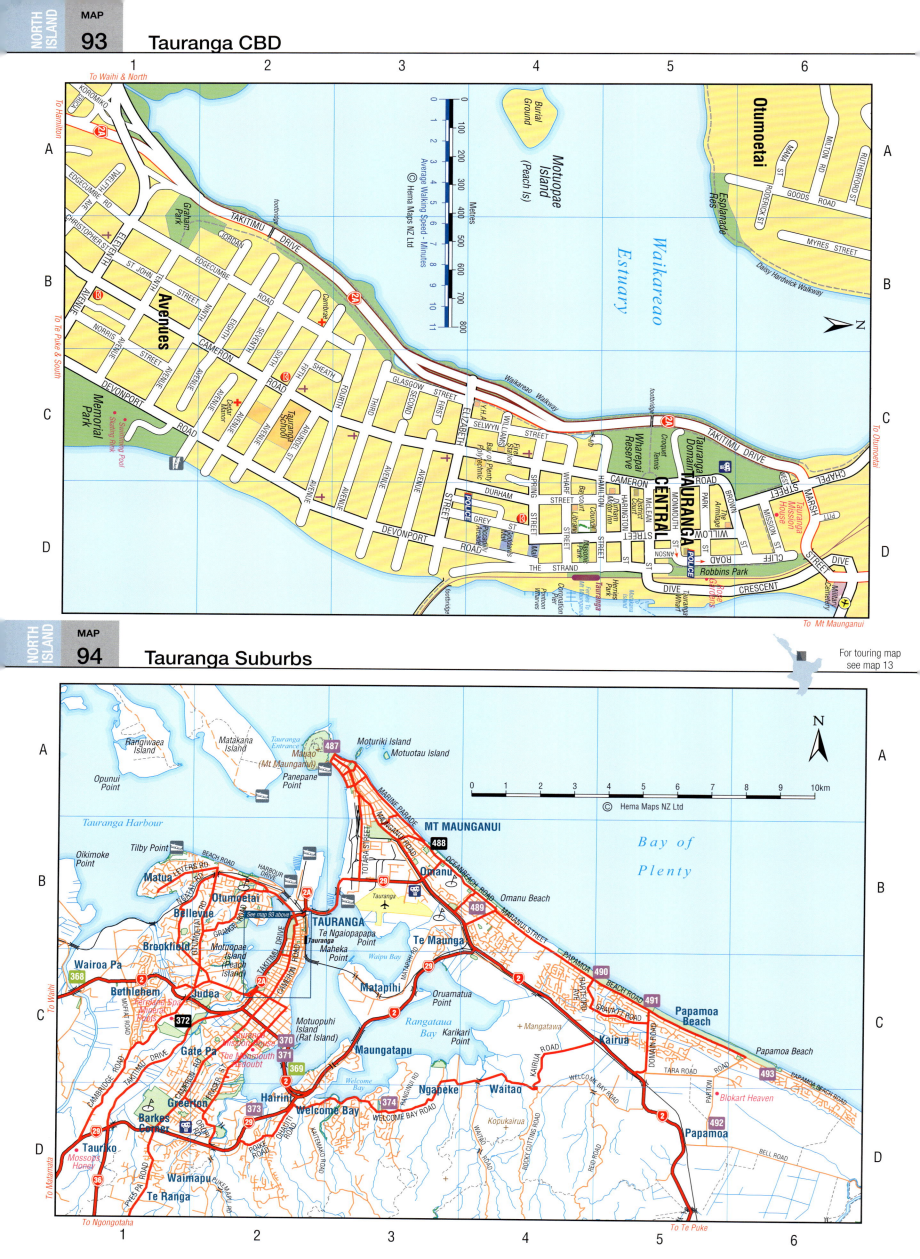

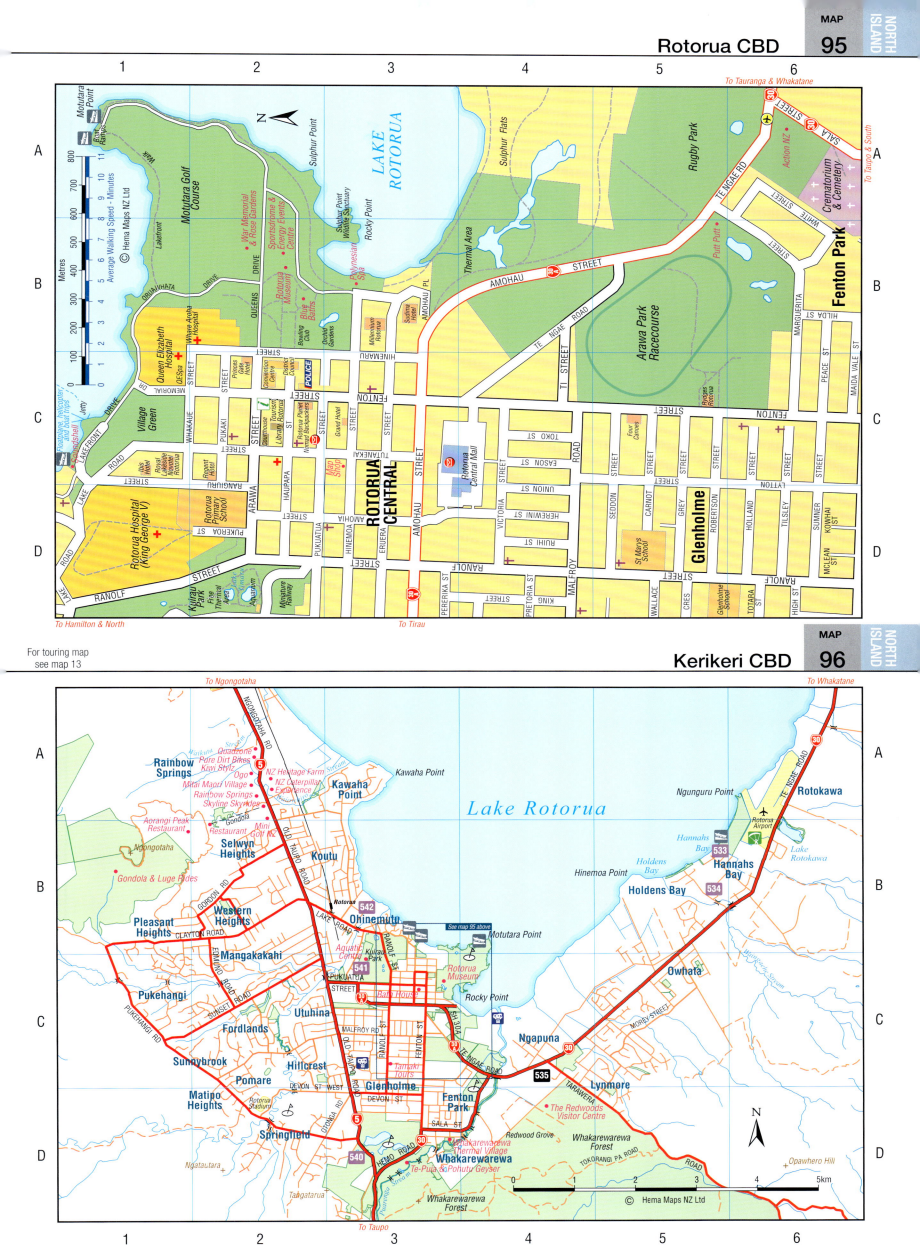

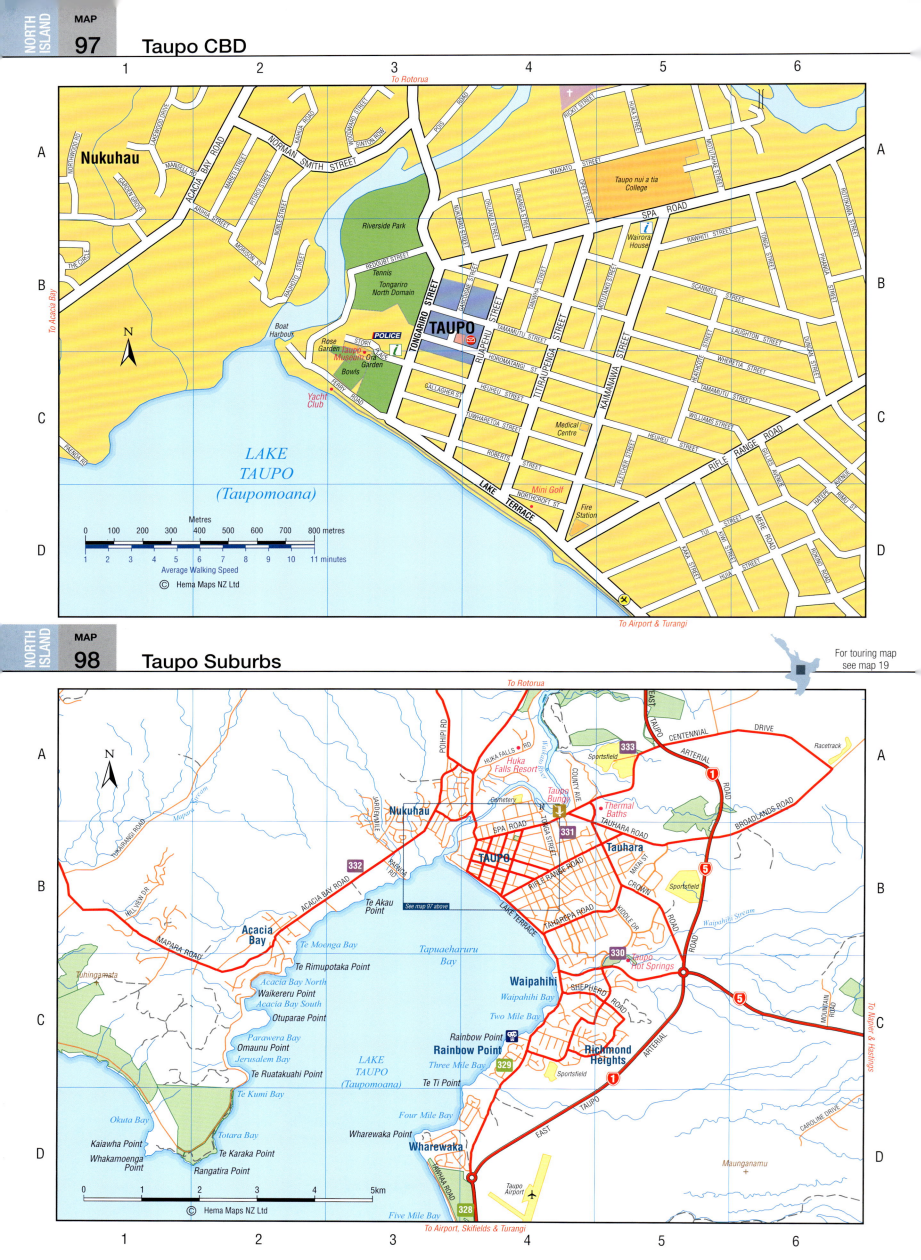

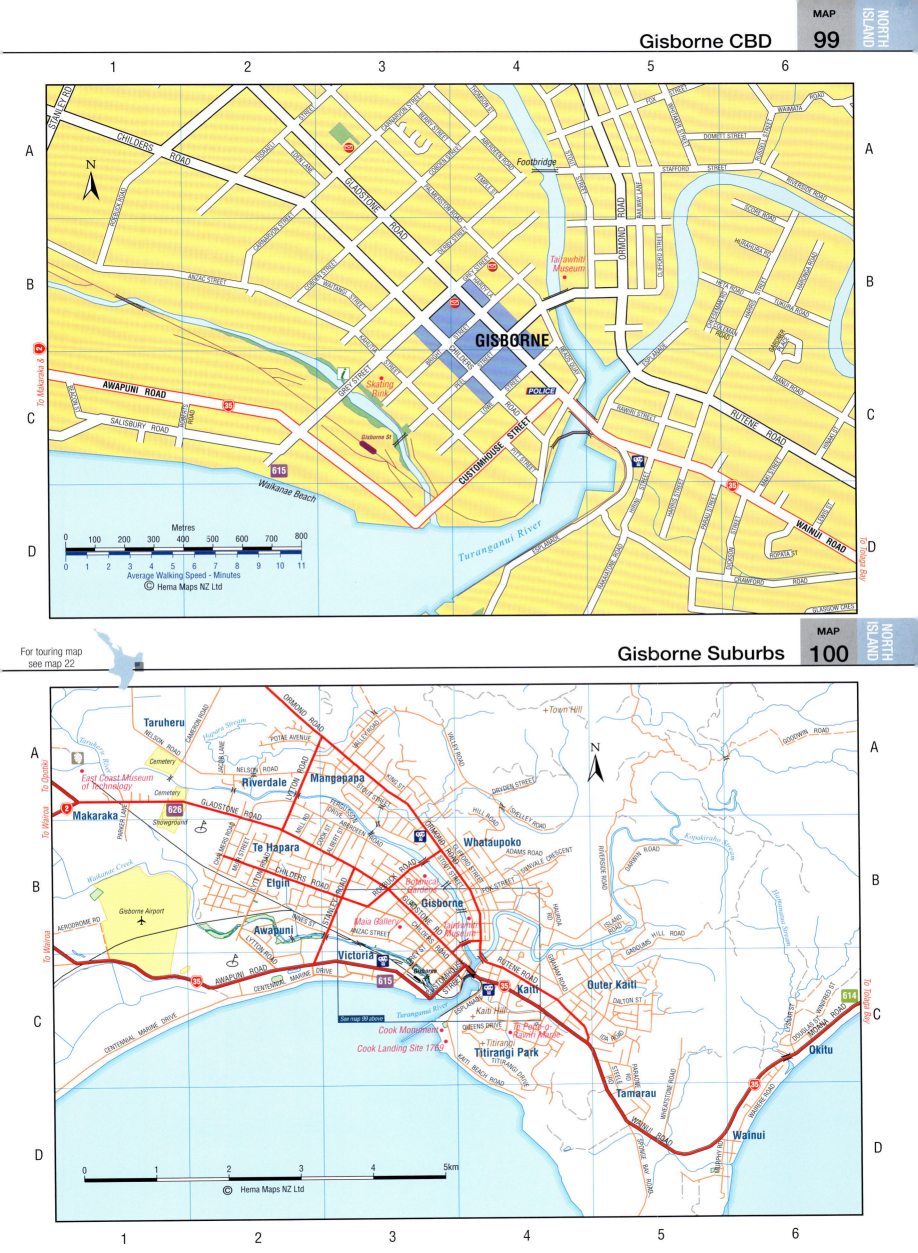

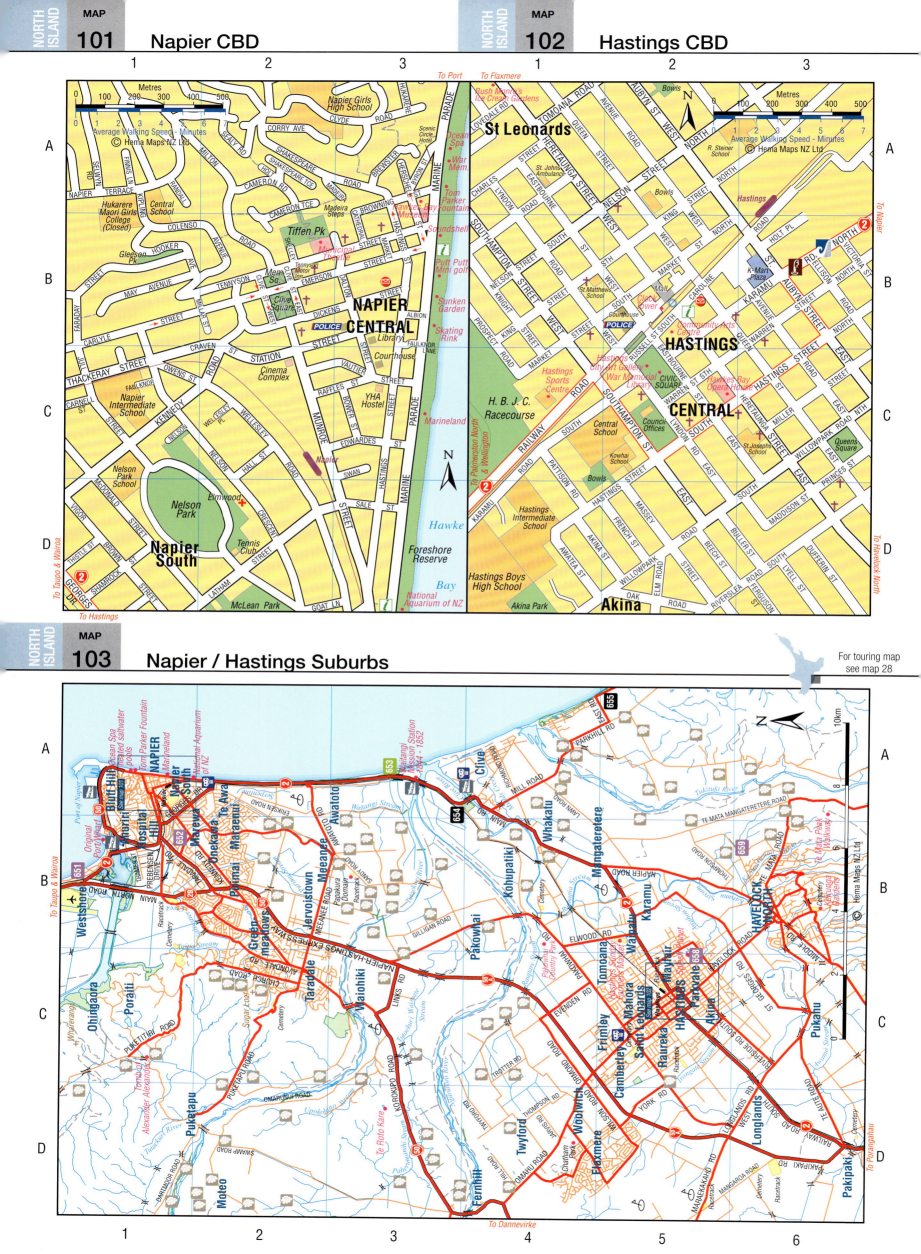

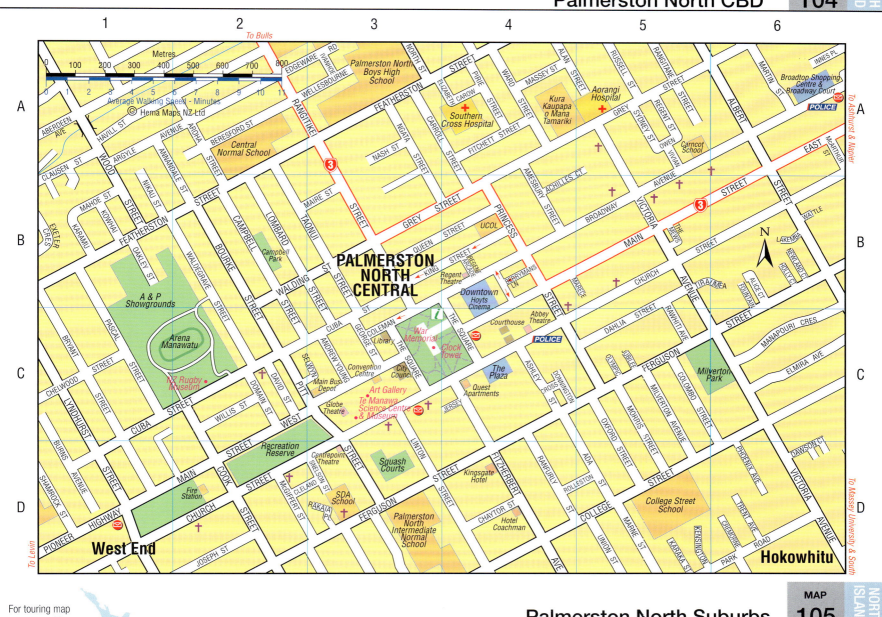

MAP 104 — Palmerston North CBD (North Island)

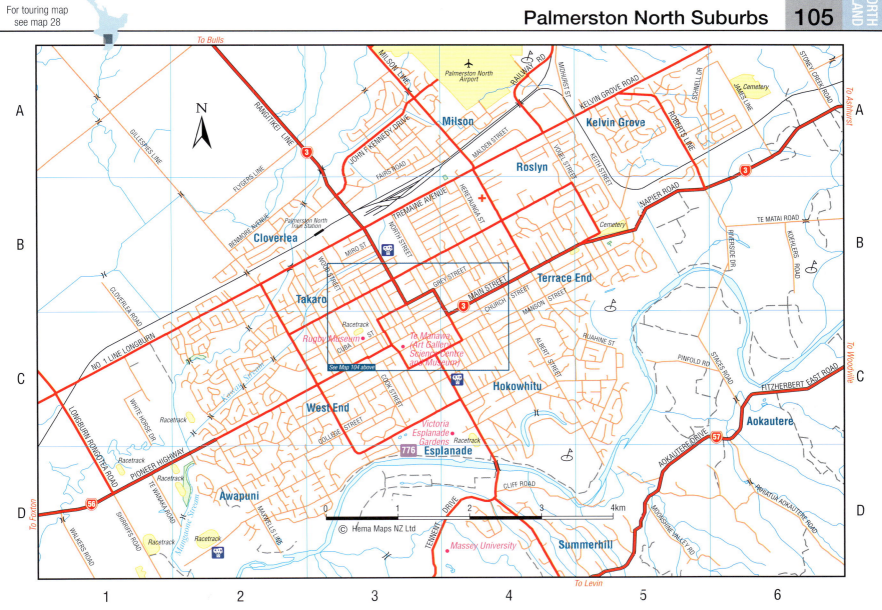

MAP 105 — Palmerston North Suburbs (North Island)

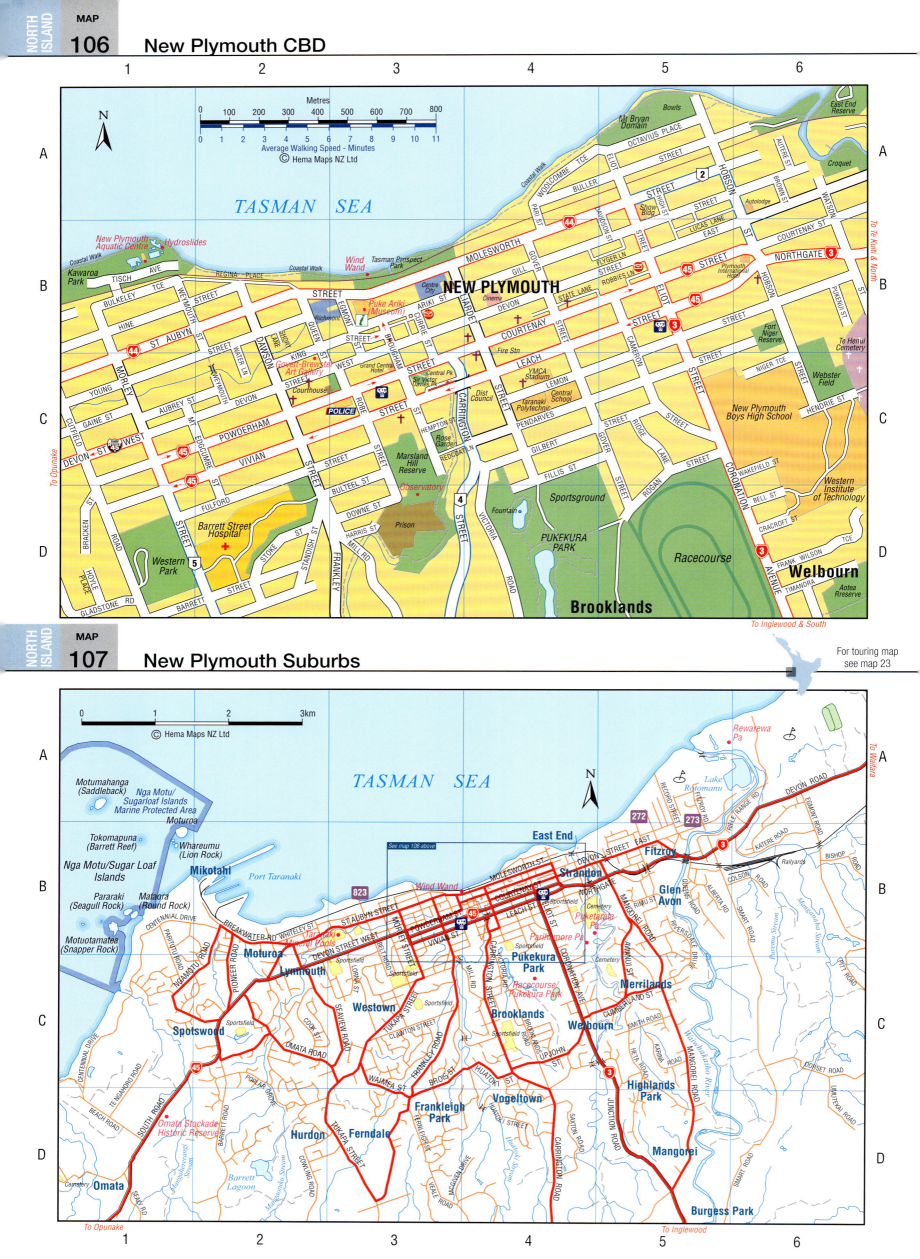

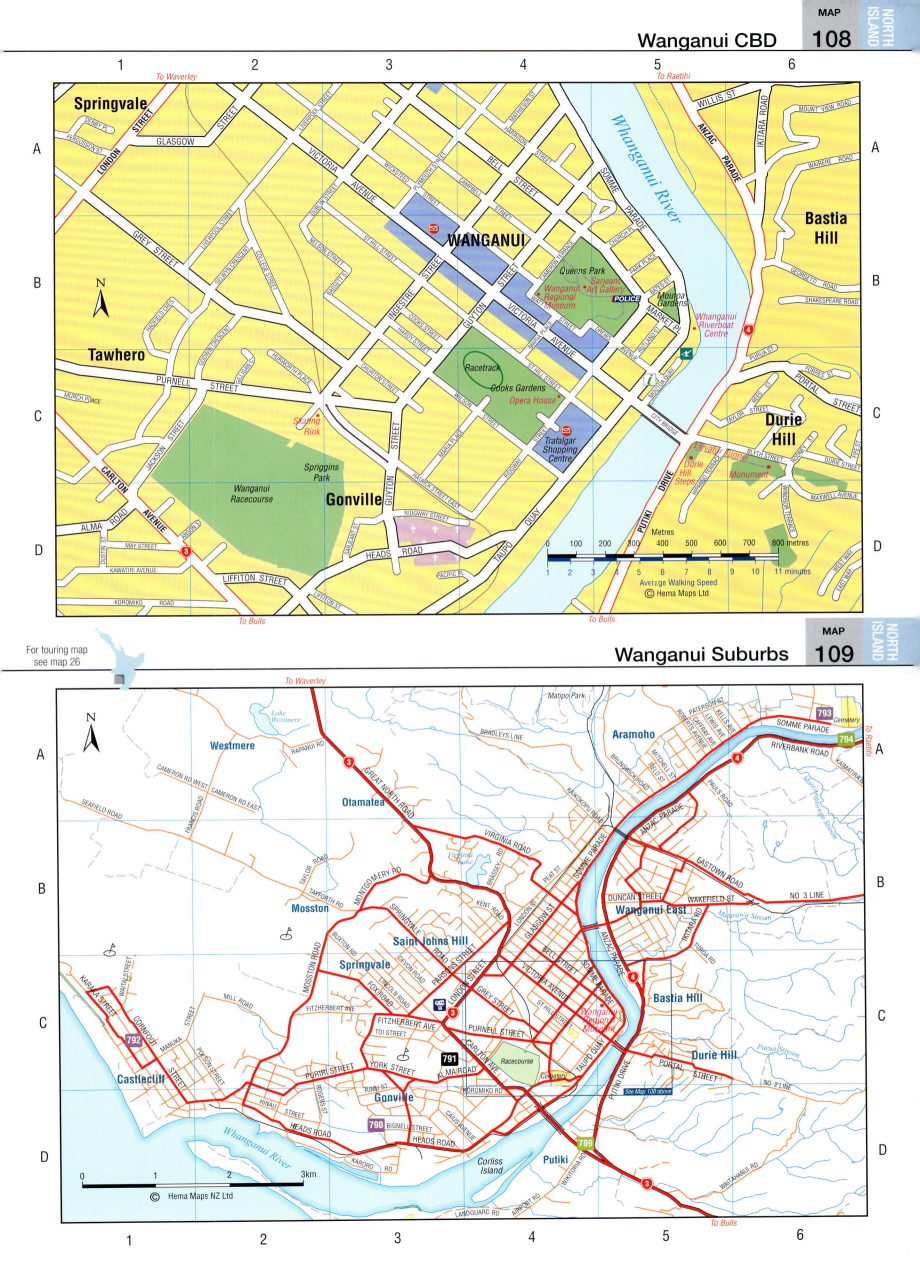

MAP 110 Wellington Suburbs

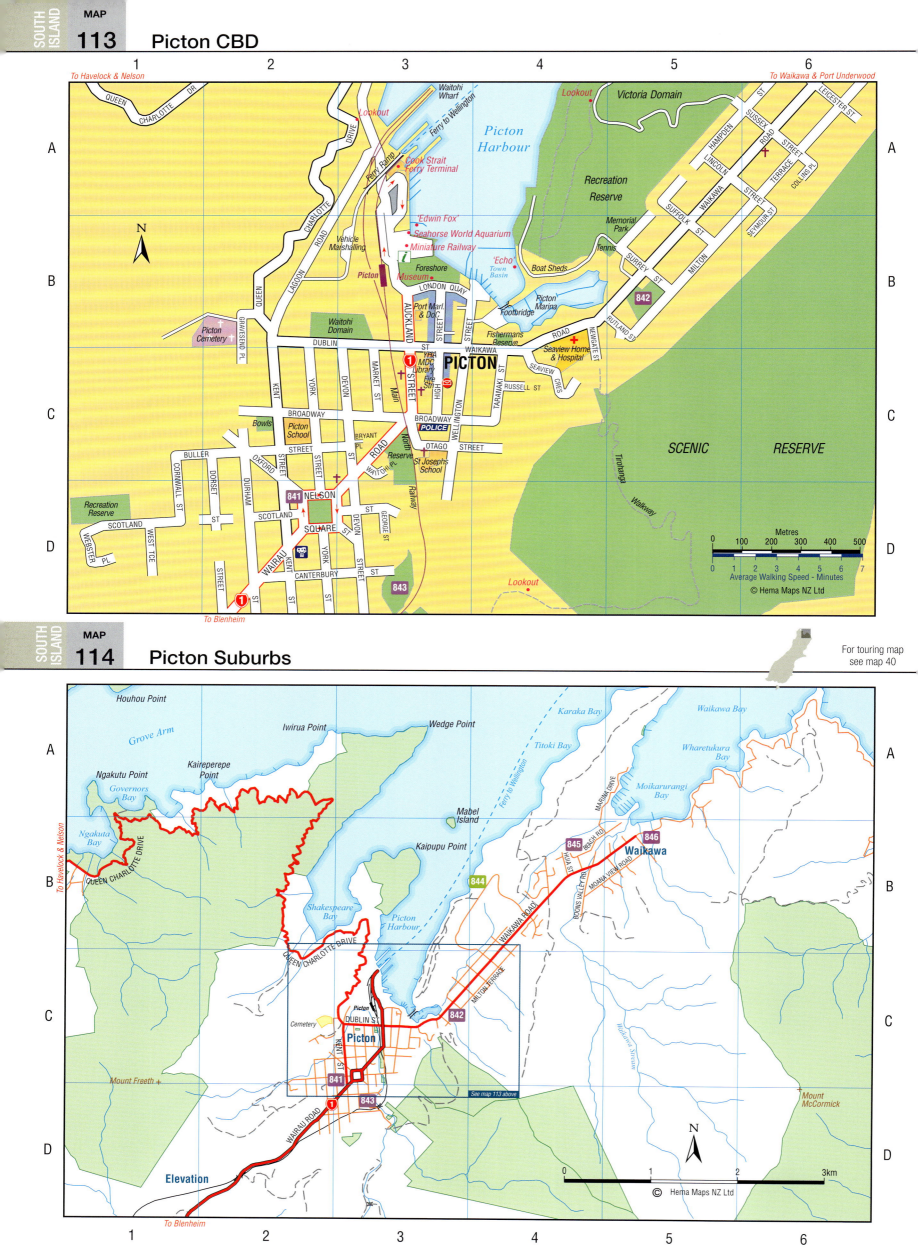

Nelson CBD

MAP 115

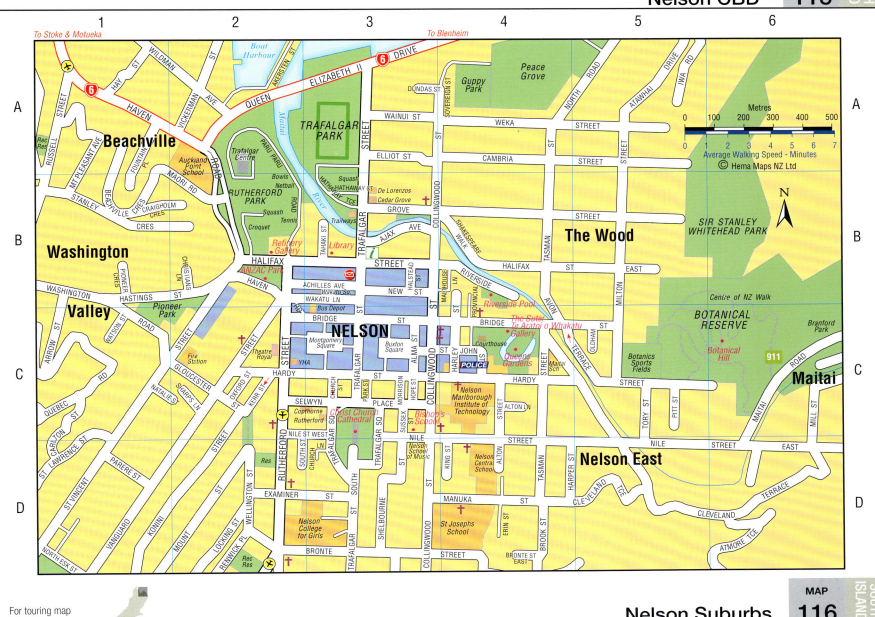

Nelson Suburbs

MAP 116

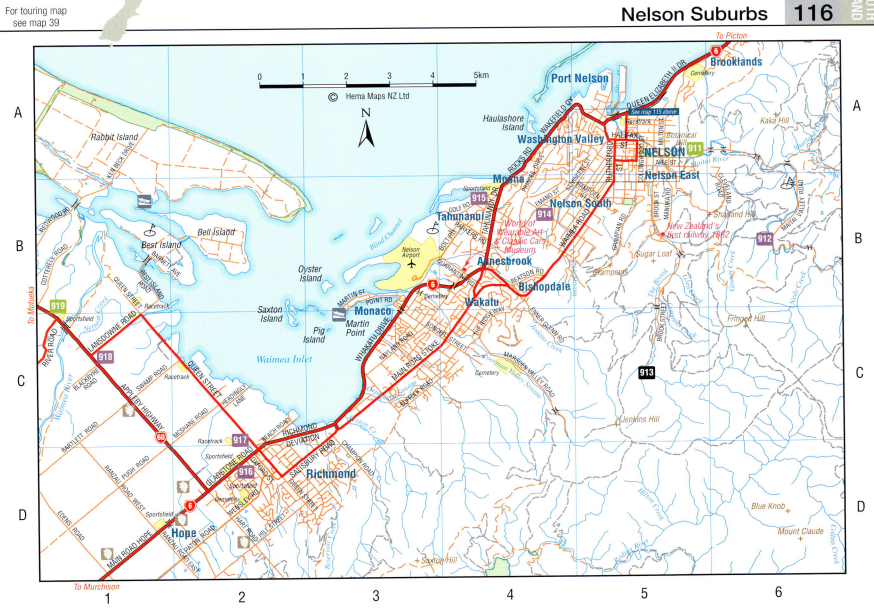

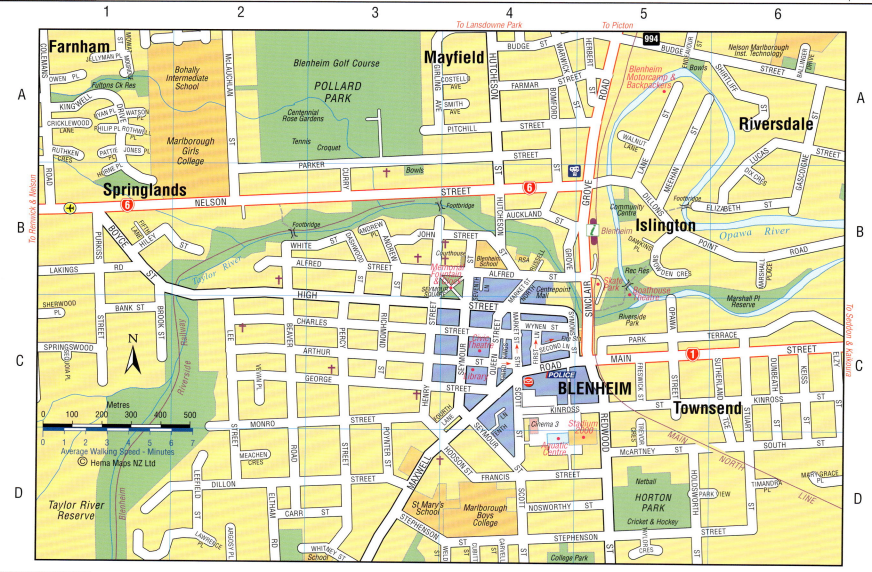

MAP 117 Blenheim CBD

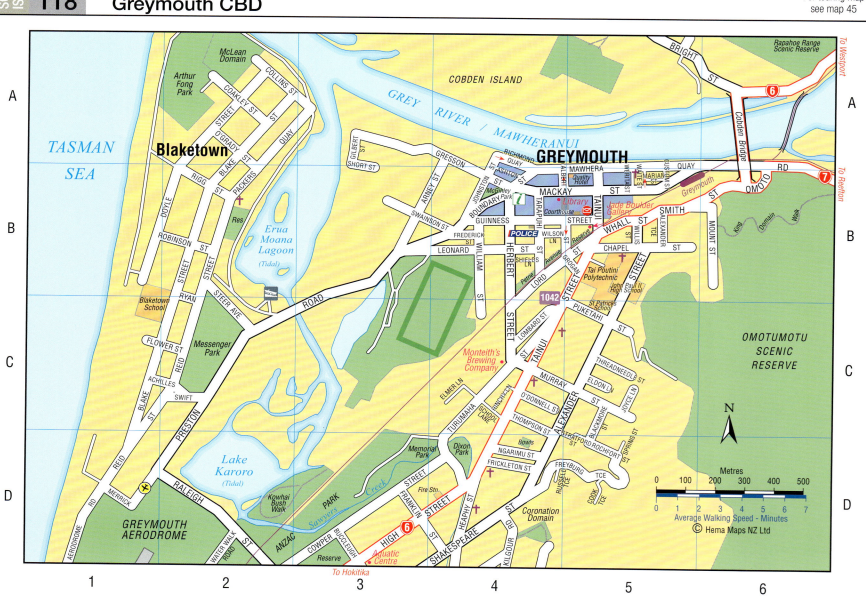

MAP 118 Greymouth CBD

MAP 120 Christchurch Suburbs

SOUTH ISLAND

For touring map see map 19

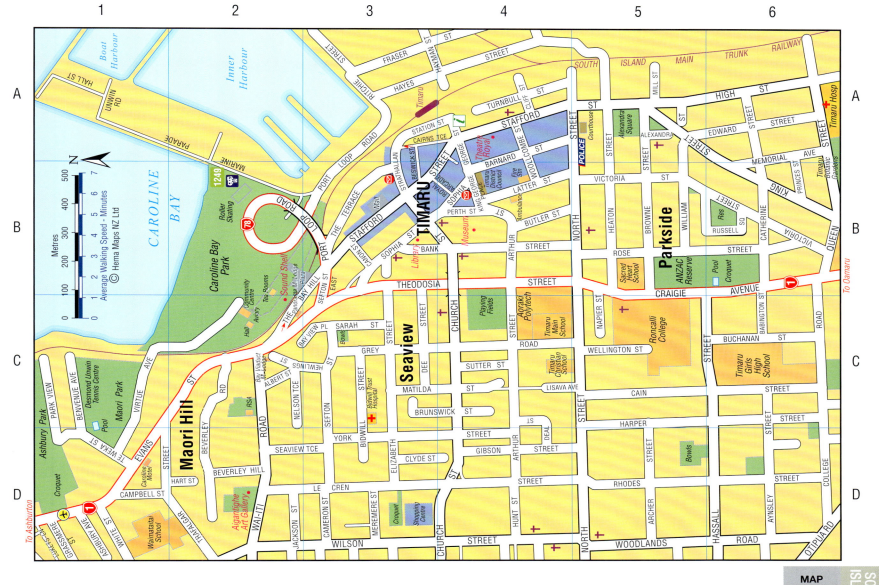

MAP 123 Dunedin CBD

MAP 124 — SOUTH ISLAND

Dunedin Suburbs

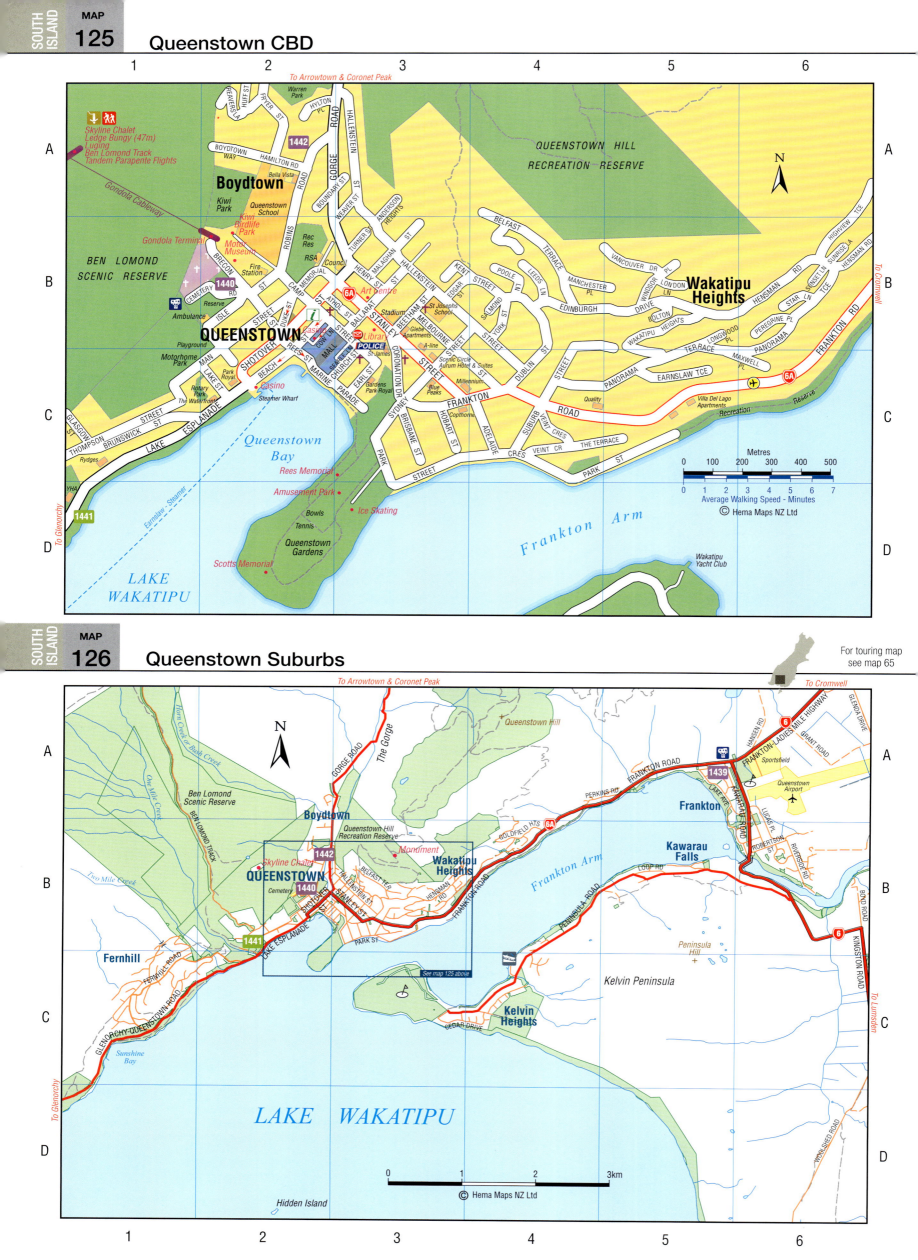

Invercargill CBD

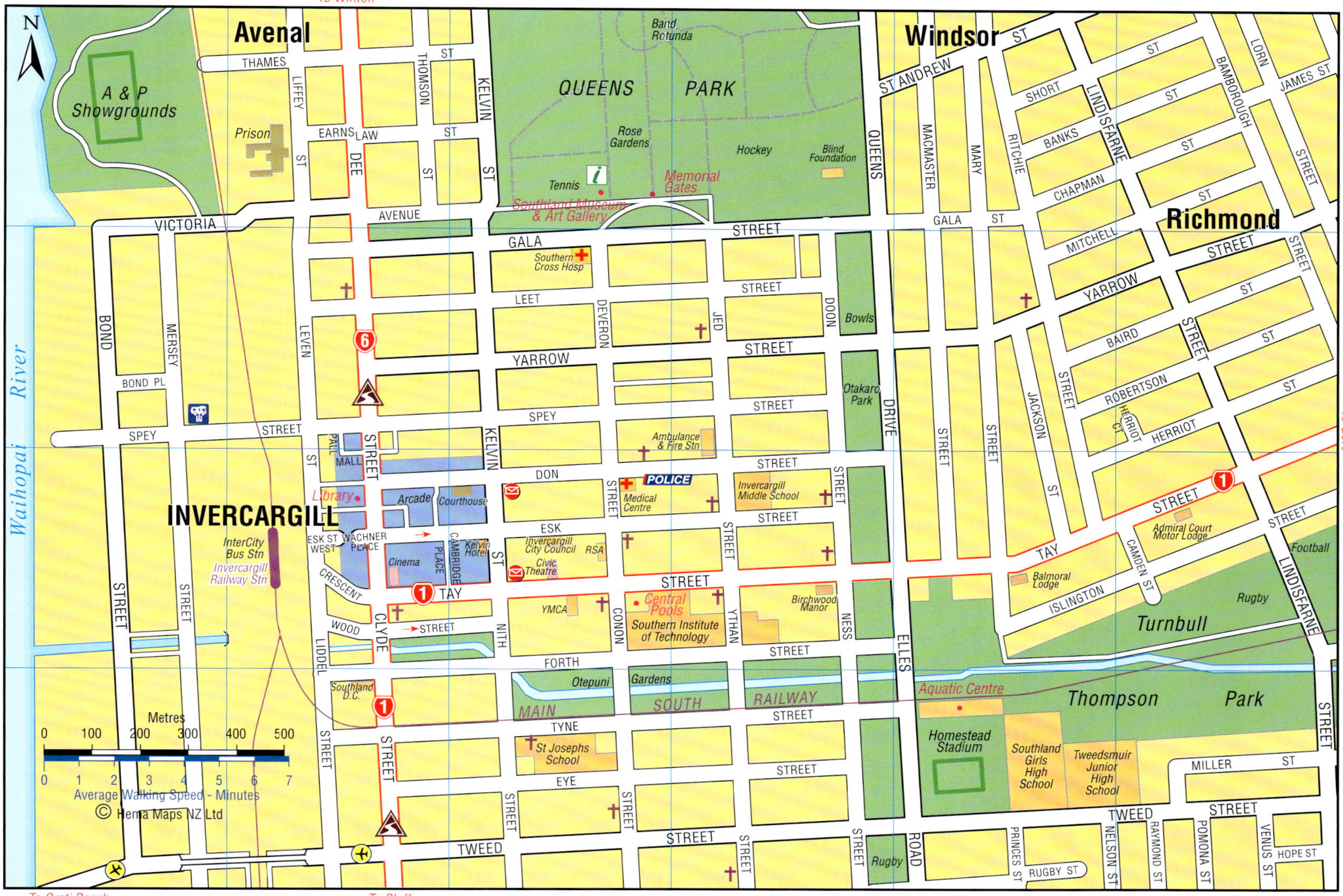

MAP 127 — SOUTH ISLAND

Invercargill Suburbs

MAP 128 — SOUTH ISLAND

For touring map see map 77

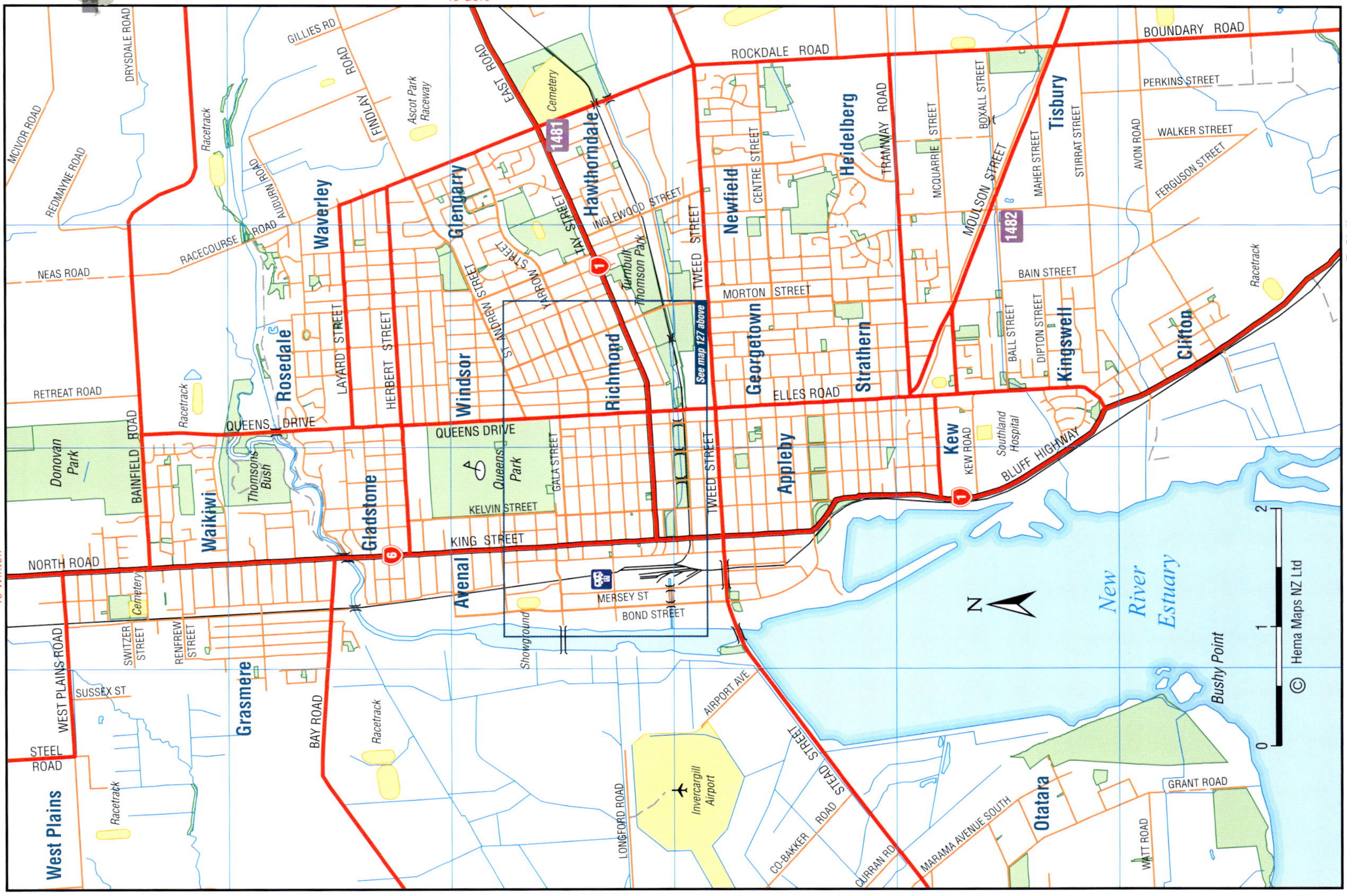

Motorhome Dump Stations

KINGSTON, SOUTH ISLAND PHOTO: MICHELLE BIGNELL

THE DISPOSAL OF WASTE from the sink, shower (grey) and toilet (black) is to be made at dump station/waste disposal sites. The locations listed here refer to most of the symbols shown on the maps. There may be a charge for using a dump station at some camping grounds, unless you are staying there. Some dump stations on septic tanks may limit their availability during peak times.

Under no circumstances is it acceptable to dispose of wastewater in rubbish disposal facilities.

International dump station/waste disposal signs for black and grey waste water.

  Motorhome Dump Station (Wastewater Disposal Site)

PUBLIC DUMP STATIONS – NORTH ISLAND

FAR NORTH

Kerikeri Public D/S (4 A8, 86 C2) – Cobham Rd, by memorial hall, Kerikeri
Gibby's Place (4 A8) – 331 Kerikeri Rd, Kerikeri
Mangonui Public D/S (2 H8) – Beach Road, next to public toilets, 400m from SH10, Kaitaia
Opononi Public D/S (3 E3) – SH12 on harbourside, old i-site car park.
Kawakawa Public D/S (4 C9) – Waimio St, off SH1, on the right hand side past entrance to bowling club, Kawakawa
Kaitaia Public D/S (1 J6) – A & P Showgrounds car park, South Rd, SH1 Kaitaia
Kaikohe Public D/S (3 C7) – Recreation Rd, Kaikohe; D/S on roadside at rear of Pioneer Village toilets

NORTHLAND

Dargaville Public D/S (3 J7) – Mobil Service Station on SH12 in town centre
Dargaville Public D/S (3 J7) – Caltex Service Station on SH12 in town centre
Dargaville Public D/S (3 J7) – Dargaville Museum, Harding Park, Mt Wesley Coast Rd; In public car park, Dargaville
Ngunguru Public D/S (4 F13) – Te Maika Rd, at North end of Ngunguru; Opposite the school, near public toilets
Caltex Star Mart (4 F11) – 15 Lower Tarewa Rd, Whangarei
Whangarei Public D/S (4 G12, 85 C2) – Outside the Council Waste Water Treatment Plant; Kioreroa Rd, Whangarei
Recreational Concepts (4 F11, 85 C1) – 6 South End Ave, Whangarei
Waipu Public D/S (6 A8) – Langs Beach, next to public toilet, Waipu
Warkworth Public D/S (6 E10) – Kowahi Park, cnr of SH1 & Sandspit, Warkworth

HIBISCUS COAST

Orewa Public D/S (6 G10) – South end of Orewa by KFC, Orewa
Whangaparaoa Public D/S (6 H10) – Gulf Harbour adjacent to public toilet by public boat ramp, Whangaparaoa

AUCKLAND

Shelly Beach (7 A1) – Kaipara Harbour, Helensville, beside public toilet
Waitakere Public D/S (7 D2) – McLeod Rd extension, Te Atatu South, fenced area in McLeod Pk opposite Riverglade Parkway road
Claris Landfill D/S (36 E5) – Gray Rd, Great Barrier Island
Manukau Mobil SS (7 F5, 90 E5) – Wiri Station Road, Manukau
Te Arai Point Public D/S (6 C9) – Beside public toilets, Te Arai
Wellsford Public D/S (6 D8) – Centenial Park, off SH1, Wellsford

COUNTIES

Waharau Public D/S (8 G9) – Opposite Waharau Regional Park, Kaiaua Coast
Pukekohe Public D/S (7 H5) – Franklin Rd, Pukekohe; 400m past sports stadium
Tuakau Public D/S (7 J6) – In St Stephens Drive, Tuakau, opposite Police Station
Drury Public D/S (7 H5) – Tui St, behind shops, Pukekohe
Waiuku Public D/S (7 J4) – Jane Gifford Reserve, on bypass road to Manukau Heads, on right

HAURAKI/COROMANDEL

Ngatea Public D/S (8 J11) – On SH2 in village centre near public hall
Stuart Moore Motors BP Service Station (8 H11) – Thames, turn into Bank Street opposite the Toyota factory, E corner of parking area
Coromandel Public Dump Station (8 C11) – Wharf Road Scenic Reserve, Coromandel; Turn left towards Long Bay, 300m over bridge, near public toilets
Whitianga Public D/S (8 D13) – At rubbish station at Tin Town opposite airport
Pauanui Public D/S (8 F14) – Pleasant Point Boat Ramp (off Vista Paku) –
Whangamata Public D/S (8 J14) – Whangamata Domain, Whangamata; Turn off Port Rd into Aicken Rd, at public toilets
Waihi Public D/S (10 F10) – In Victoria Park, Waihi on SH2, near public toilets in the park
Paeroa Public D/S (10 E9) – Marshall St, Paeroa, near public toilet and information centre
Paeroa RV Centre (10 E9) – Coronation Rd, Paeroa
Tairua Public D/S (10 A11) – 175 Beach Road, Tairua
Cooks Beach Public D/S (8 D13) – Next to public toilets, Cooks Beach

WAIKATO

Te Kauwhata Public D/S (9 F5) – Turn off Mahi Rd into Domain in township
Te Aroha Public D/S (10 G9) – Skate Park toilets on Terminus Street
Matamata Public D/S (12 C11) – On SH27, turn off Broadway into Hetana St, near public toilets
Ngaruawahia Public D/S (9 J4) – In Waikato Esplanade Domain (The Point), on riverbank between Rowing Club & Railway bridge
Tirau Public D/S (12 E11) – Near public toilets down service lane from SH1, behind OK Tirau Motel
Te Awamutu Public D/S (11 E7) – On SH3, at Mobil Service Station at north end of town
Hamilton Public D/S (11 C6) – SH1, Minogue Park, Tui Ave, Forest Lake
Raglan Public D/S (11 C3) – Raglan Club, 22 Bow St, Raglan
Mangakino Public D/S (12 J11) – 44 Wairenga Rd, Mangakino

ROTORUA

Rotorua Public D/S (13 G4) – Entrance to Wastewater Treatment Plant, Te Ngae Rd
Tokoroa Public D/S (12 H12) – Whakauru St, Tokoroa; Next to sewerage treatment station
Wairakei BP Service Station & Truck Stop (19 C5) – On SH1 opposite hotel; D/S in parking area at the rear on left side
Kinloch Marina D/S (19 D4) – In Marina Car Park, Kinloch
Taupo Public D/S (19 D5) – 2 Mile Bay Boat Ramp, Taupo; 5 km south on SH1, next to public toilet
Tokaanu Public D/S (19 G3) – At boat ramp
Putaruru Public D/S (12 F11) – Market St. Heading south on SH1, first left turn after roundabout
Boatshed Bay Wastewater D/S (13 H5) – Near Boatshed Bay boat ramp, Spencer Rd, Lake Tarawera
Glenholme Reserve Public D/S (13 G4) – Miller Street, Rotorua

BAY OF PLENTY

Katikati Public D/S (10 G11) – North side of Katikati shopping centre turn off SH2 into roadway beside the A&P showgrounds
Mt Maunganui Shell Service Station (13 B4) – Hewletts Rd, Mt Maunganui on main route to Tauranga via Harbour Bridge
Tauranga Public D/S – (13 B3, 93 C5) – Tauranga Domain, Cameron Rd, Tauranga
Te Puke Public D/S (13 C5) – Situated at public toilets
Tauranga Public D/S (10 J13, 94 D2) – Maleme Rd, can be reached from Oropi Rd or Cameron Rd, close to transfer station, Tauranga
Omokoroa Public D/S (10 H12) – Omokoroa Beach at west end of Peninsula in Omokoroa Domain Car and Trailer Park, Omokoroa
Omokoroa Public D/S (10 J12) – 1.9km from SH2 opposite Fire Station, turn left into road to main pump station 200m.
Mt Maunganui Public D/S (10 J14, 13 B4, 94 B3) – Seawind Lane, Tauranga Airport

EASTERN BAY OF PLENTY

Kawerau Public D/S (14 G8) – Behind Bowling Club opposite information centre, town centre
Whakatane Public D/S (14 E10) – Caltex Service Station, Commerce St, next to fire station
Ohope Public D/S (14 E11) – Situated at public toilets, half-way along beach before bridge, in Maraetotara Reserve with play equipment
Waiotahi Beach Public D/S (14 F13) – Waiotahi Beach Domain; On SH35 at public toilets
Opotiki BP Service Station (14 F13) – Cnr Bridges St & Church St, past the last diesel pump
Murupara Public D/S (20 B11) – Behind BP Station, Pine Dr; off SH38, Murupara
Omaio Public D/S (15 D5) – Omaio Domain, off SH35
Te Kaha School House Bay (15 C6) – New toilet block, Te Kaha

EASTLAND

Gisborne Mobil Service Station (22 D10, 99 C5) – 49 Wainui Rd, Gisborne; East end of main road across bridge
Gisborne BP Service Station (22 D10, 100 B3) – Corner Ormond Rd & Sheridan St, Gisborne
Te Araroa Public D/S (16 B12) – Transfer Stn, 26 Te Arawapaia Rd, Te Araroa
Gisborne Public D/S (22 D10, 100 C2) – Watson Park, Awapuni Rd, Gisborne

HAWKES BAY

Napier Public D/S (28 D12) – Marine Parade by Ellison
Napier Public D/S (28 D12) – 104 Latham St, Napier; Beside Council Sewerage Pump Station
Clive BP S/S (28 E12) – Main Rd, Clive
Hastings BP S/S (28 F11, 103 C5) – Stortford Lodge; Corner Maraekakaho Rd & Heretaunga St

Motorhome Dump Stations

Waipawa Public D/S, BP Service Station (28 J9) – 1 High St, Waipawa

Takapau Public D/S (16 F11) – 15 Nang St, Takapau

TARANAKI

New Plymouth Public D/S, Mobil Service Station (23 B5, 106 B5) – Corner Leach & Eliot Streets

New Plymouth Public D/S, BP Service Station (23 B5, 106 C3) – 71 Powderham St, New Plymouth

Opunake Public D/S (23 F3) – Beach Rd, Opunake

Whangamomona Domain (24 C11) – 32 Whangamomona Rd

Normanby Public D/S (25 D1) – On Main Hwy, North of Hawera, Normanby

Aotea Park Public D/S (25 F4) – Cnr of Chester St & SH3, Waverley

Opunake Public D/S (23 F3) – Corner Napier and King Sts, Opunake

Stratford Public D/S (25 B1) – Esk Road

WANGANUI

Taihape Public D/S (27 F2) – Linnet St, Taihape

Wanganui Public D/S (26 J8, 109 C3) – Springvale Park, London St, Wanganui

Ohakune Public D/S (26 C11) – Ohakune Club, 72 Goldfinch Ave, Ohakune

Taihape BP Connection (27 F2) – 80-88 Hautapu St, Taihape

MANAWATU

Feilding BP Express Service Station (29 C7) – Corner Kimbolton Rd & Aorangi St next to KFC

Feilding Sewerage Treatment Plant (29 C7) – Kawa Kawa Rd, Feilding, past abattoir and Manfield Racetrack, on LHS down long drive, turn right at end of drive

Ashhurst Public D/S (30 D9) – Ashhurst Domain, SH3, Ashhurst

Palmerston North Caltex Service Station (29 E7) – Cnr Fitzherbert Ave & College St

Palmerston North Public D/S, Totara Rd Wastewater Plant (29 E4, 105 D2) – Behind Racecourse, Palmerston North

Foxton Public D/S (29 E5) – Inside the entrance to Victoria Park off Victoria St

Levin Public D/S (29 G5) – Sheffield St, Levin

Otaki Public D/S (29 J4) – Riverbank Rd, Otaki; Off SH1 just north of the Otaki River bridge

WAIRARAPA

Pongaroa Public D/S (30 G13) – Behind public toilets on SH52; not good van access

Woodville Public D/S (30 D10) – Swimming pool area, Normanby Rd, Woodville

Greytown Public D/S (34 C7) – At Arbor Reserve, Greytown; Rest/picnic area on SH2 opposite Kuranui College

Martinborough Public D/S (34 E7) – West end of Dublin St, Martinborough, close to Motor Camp & swimming pool

Carterton Public D/S (34 C7) – Dalefield Rd, Carterton

WELLINGTON

Upper Hutt Public D/S (33 D4, 111 B5) – On SH2 (River Rd), Upper Hutt; 500m north of Moonshine Bridge at Rest Area sign, beside toilets on gravel road by river

Tawa Public D/S (33 D2) – Tawa Swimming Pool, Davis St; D/S opposite pool entrance

Wellington Public D/S (33 F1, 110 D2) – Ngauranga Gorge, Hutt Rd, Wellington

Paraparaumu Public D/S (33 B4) – Mobil Service Station, corner SH1 and Kapiti Rd, Paraparaumu

Porirua Public D/S (33 D2) – Prosser St, Porirua

Lower Hutt Public D/S (33 E3, 110 D3) – Seaview Marina, Port Road, Lower Hutt

PUBLIC DUMP STATIONS – SOUTH ISLAND

MARLBOROUGH

Blenheim Public D/S (44 C10) – Mobil Service Station, Cnr of Grove Rd and Nelson St, Blenheim

Picton D/S (35 J3, 40 G10, 44 A11, 113 C3) – Challenge Service Station, Corner Wairau Rd and Kent St, Picton

NELSON/TASMAN

Takaka Mobil Service Station (38 E8) – Cnr Commercial St & Motupipi Rd, Takaka

Takaka Public D/S (38 E8) – Golden Bay i-Site Visitor Centre in the car park, 8 Willow Street, Takaka

Motueka Public D/S (38 G10) – Follow sign from High St into Tudor St to Hickmott Pl

Richmond Public D/S (43 A4) – Jubilee Park, Gladstone Rd, Richmond

Nelson Public D/S (38 J11) – Mobil Tahunanui, 28 Tahunanui Dr, Nelson

Nelson Public D/S (38 J12) – BP Truck Stop, Hay St, Port Nelson

Murchison Public D/S (42 G9) – On SH6 by entry to TNL Freight Yard, between Mobil Service Station and Matakitaki Bridge

Murchison Public D/S (42 G9) – Mobil Service Station, 41 Waller St, Murchison; on back fence past the truck diesel pump

Seddon Auto Services D/S (44 E11) – 4 Clifford Street, Seddon

Tahunanui Mobil D/S (38 J11) – 28 Tahunanui Drive, Tahunanui

Uruwhenua Bridge D/S (38 F8) – East Takaka Road, Upper Takaka

WEST COAST

Greymouth Public D/S (45 F4) – Caltex S/S Tainui St, Greymouth

Hokitika Public D/S (45 H2) – SH6; north end of town, 1km from centre, adjacent to sewage ponds in large laybys on either side of road

Goldfields Tourist Centre (50 A11) – Ross; beside public toilet on roadside

Glacier Motors Mobil Service Station (49 G6) – Franz Josef, on SH6

Haast Public D/S (58 D9) – In front of public toilets on Marks Rd, Haast

DOC camp site, rest area (58 E12) – On SH6; 45km east of Haast beside the river, in front of toilet block, Pleasant Flat

Westport Public D/S (41 G3) – Countdown car park, 18 Fonblanque St, Westport. Enter via Russell St.

Westport Public D/S (41 G3) – New World car park, 244 Palmerston St, Westport

Nelson Creek Public D/S (45 E6) – Nelson Creek Domain, Nelson Creek

Blackball Public D/S (45 D5) – Adjacent to Sports Domain

Runanga Public D/S (45 E4) – Runanga Workingmen's Club, corner of Pitt and McGowan Sts, Runanga

Ross Information and Heritage Centre (50 B11, 51 B2) – 4 Aylmer St, Ross

Greymouth Public D/S (45 F3) – New World car park, cnr High and Marlborough St

Greymouth Public D/S (45 F3) – Cobden Bridge rest area, north side of bridge

Cheviot Public D/S (48 J9) – Centre of village, accessed from service lane (key at Mobil service station)

Waikari Public D/S (54 B8) – in domain, Princess St; signposted off SH7 at Waikari (Key held by Mary Booker, 20 Princes St or Roger Mander, 18 Princes St)

Oxford Public D/S (53 F4) – High St, Oxford; approximately 800m from the cnr of Oxford Rd & Main St

Amberley Public D/S (54 D8) – Mobil S/S Carters Rd, Amberley

Kaiapoi Public D/S (54 G8, 56 C10) – Charles St, Kaiapoi

Rangiora Public D/S (53 F7, 56 B9) – 22 Railway Rd, Rangiora

Kaikoura BP 2GO (48 E12) – 84 Beach Rd, north side of Kaikoura

Kaikoura Public D/S (48 E12) – South Bay Domain, Kaikoura

CHRISTCHURCH

Christchurch Public D/S (53 H7, 56 D9, 120 E5) – Styx Mill Road Eco Dept, off SH1 between Belfast and Redwood, Christchurch

Canterbury A&P Association D/S (120 C2) – 71 Wigram Road, Wigram Park, Christchurch

A & P Showgrounds (53 J6) – Curletts Rd, Christchurch; between motorway corridor and Lincoln/Halswell Rd intersection

Lincoln Club (53 J6) – 24 Edward St, Lincoln

Templeton Public D/S (56 D8, 120 A2) – at information kiosk; 784 Main South Road, Templeton

Rolleston BP Connect (56 E8) – Cnr Main South Rd & Tennyson St, Rolleston

SOUTH CANTERBURY

Washdyke Public D/S (61 J5) – Allied Truck Stop site, Sheffield St, Timaru

Fairlie Public D/S (60 F12, 61 F1) – Gladstone Grand Hotel, 43 Main St, Fairlie

Lake Tekapo Public D/S 1 (60 E9) – Tekapo village; on roadside, 400m from village centre on SH8 towards Fairlie

Lake Tekapo Public D/S 2 (60 E9) – On road in Lakeside Drive, follow Motor Camp sign for 200m.

Rakaia Public D/S (55 G5) – Rolleston St, Rakaia; off SH1, beside public toilet

Rakaia Gorge Public D/S (55 D2) – SH72; at public toilet, north side of river

Methven Public D/S (55 F1) – Mobil Service Station (Methven Motor Services), Hall St, Methven

Twizel Public D/S (59 H6) – Turn off SH8 to town centre, adjacent to Shell Service Station

Timaru Public D/S (61 J4) – Follow truck by-pass route off Marine Pde to Caroline Bay; adjacent to toilet and carpark by rollerskating rink

St Andrews Domain (68 B13) – Main South Rd, St Andrews; 250m south

Lake Benmore (67 C5) – At Otematata Boat Harbour Campground, and at Wildlife Camping Ground

Oamaru Public D/S (68 H12) – SH1 on northern boundary of town, outside Waitaki Transport yard

Wanaka Public D/S (66 D8) – Brownston St, S of McDougall St

OTAGO

DK Auto Services (74 E12) – 175 Main Rd, Waikouaiti, at rear

Warrington Public D/S (74 F12) – Warrington Domain; off SH1 at Evansdale, follow signs to beach, at public toilet

Mosgiel Public D/S (74 H10) – BP 2GO, Alco Motors, 77 Gordon Rd, Mosgiel

Dunedin North (74 H11) – BP 2GO, 867 Cumberland St North, one way system, south near gardens

Dunedin Shell Service Station (74 H11) – turn off SH1 for Andersons Bay Rd, adjacent to Old Gas Works between Hillside St & McBride St

Dunedin Shell Valley Service Station (74 H11, 124 E4) – 248 Kaikorai Valley Rd, Belleknowes; off SH1, 3km

Ranfurly Public D/S (67 H5) – Intersection of Northland and Charlemont St, off SH85, Ranfurly

Dunedin Public D/S (74 H11, 123 H3) – BP Connect Southern, 50 Cumberland St, Dunedin Central

CLUTHA VALLEY

Kidds Bush Reserve (DOC camp site) (66 A9) – Hunter Valley Rd, Lake Hawea

Arrowtown Public D/S (65 G6) – Behind the Lake Districts Museum at the public toilets, Ramshaw Lane

Queenstown BP Connect Public D/S (65 H4, 126 A5) – Cnr SH6 & Frankton Rd, Frankton

Caltex Cromwell (66 H8) – 9 Murray Tce, Cromwell

Caltex Alexandra (72 A13) – 50 Centennial Ave, Alexandra

Roxburgh Council Depot (72 D13) – Teviot St, close to motorcamp

Lawrence Public D/S (79 A3) – SH8; on west side of town beside rest area

Clinton Public D/S (78 C13) – On the roadside adjacent to park, from SH1 turn at BP Service Station and War Memorial

Albion Cricket Club (66 D9) – SH6, Main Rd, Luggate

Omakau Public D/S (66 H12, 67 H1) – Omakau Recreation Reserve, 13 Alton St, Omakau

Cromwell Public D/S (66 H9) – BP 2GO, Sargood Drive

Queenstown Public D/S (65 H5, 125 B2, 126 B2) – Cemetery Rd

Clyde (66 J10) – Clyde Recreation Reserve, 7 Whitby St

Tapanui Public D/S (73 J2) – Bushy Hill St

SOUTHLAND

Milford Sound Public D/S (64 D9) – In car park Milford Village

Knobs Flat Public D/S (64 H9) – SH 94, Te Anau, Council operated

Te Anau Public D/S (70 C11) – Lake Front Dr, Te Anau; at boat harbour, adjacent to public toilets

Manapouri Public D/S (70 E11) – 45 Hillside Rd, Manapouri

Otautau Public D/S (76 F14) – At public toilet, behind Plunket Rooms in Hulme St, just off Main St

Riverton BP Service Station (77 E2) – Bay Rd, towards Riverton Rocks

Riverton Race Course Public D/S (77 E2) – Bay Rd, towards Riverton Rocks

Invercargill Public D/S (77 E5, 128 C3) – Rockgas Invercargill, 20 Spey St, Invercargill

Riversdale Service Station (72 J9) – 92 Newcastle St, Riversdale

Gore Public D/S (78 B9) – Gore A&P Showgrounds; down first entry

Gore Public D/S (78 B9) – Richmond Rd, Gore; at kerbside, 750m upstream from SH1 Bridge and Trout Monument

Winton Public D/S (77 B4) – Great North Road; behind Mobil Service Station, Winton

Tokanui Shop (78 G9) – Southern Scenic Route through Catlins (old SH92), Tokanui

Anzac Oval Public D/S Winton (77 B4) – Park in the middle of town

1849 Dansey Pass Hotel – Butter Junction Hut

A

1849 Dansey Pass Hotel - Kyeburn Diggings 67 G2
Abbotsford 124 F5
Abbotslee Historic Home - Waipawa 28 J9
Abel Tasman Coastal Track - Great Walk 38 E10 39 C2
Abel Tasman Memorial 38 D9
Abel Tasman National Park 38 E9 39 C1
Acacia Bay 19 D5
Acheron Hut 43 J4 48 B8
Acheron Lakes 64 J10 70 A14 71 A3
Acland Falls 61 C5
Ada Pass Hut 46 D14 47 D2
Adair 61 J4 68 A13
Adams Flat 79 C4
Adams Wilderness Area 50 F9
Addington 53 H7 56 D9 119 G3 120 D2
Adelaide Tarn 37 F6
Adelaide Tarn Hut 37 F6
Adele Island 38 F10 39 D2
Agrodome - Rotorua 13 F4
Ahaura 45 D6
Ahikiwi 3 G6
Ahikouka 34 C7
Ahipara 1 J5 3 A1
Ahititi 17 F4
Ahuriri 103 B1
Ahuriri Base Hut 58 H13 59 H2
Ahuriri Conservation Park 58 H14 59 H3
Ahuriri Flat 79 G3
Ahuroa 6 F9
Aickens 45 J7
Aiguilles Island 36 B4
Airedale 68 G11
Airim Basin Hut 64 E14 65 E4
Aka Aka 7 J4 9 D1
Akaroa, NI 30 G13 31 G7
Akaroa, SI 56 G12
Akarua 111 D4
Akatere 2 G9
Akerama 4 D10
Akina 102 D2 103 C5
Akitio 32 G8
Albany Heights 6 J9 7 C3 88 F2
Albany Village 88 F2
Albert Town 66 D8
Albury 60 G13 61 G2
Aldermen Islands 10 A13
Alexandra 72 A13 73 A2
Alford Forest 51 J7
Alfred Track 23 D5
Alfredton 30 H10 31 H4
Alfriston 7 F6 9 A3 90 E6
Algies Bay 6 F10
Alicetown 110 C3
Allandale 60 F12 61 F1
Allanton 74 H9
Allendale 54 J8 56 F10
Allenton 55 H2 62 C8
Allports Island 35 J3 40 G10
Alma 68 H11
Almadale 30 B8 31 B2
Almer Hut 49 H6
Alpha Hut 33 B6
Alpine Lake / Ata Puai 49 F5
Alton 24 H8 25 E3
Amberley 54 D8
Amberley Beach 54 D9 56 A11
Amodeo Bay 8 B10 36 J4
Amuri Skifield 47 E4
Anakiwa 35 K3 40 G9
Anama 61 B6
Anatimo 38 D9 39 B1
Anatoki Forks Hut 37 F6
Anatoki Track 37 E6
Anawhata 7 E2
Anchor Island 69 H2 75 B2
Anchorage Hut 38 F10 39 D2
Anchorage Island 80 H2
Ancient Kauri Kingdom - Awanui 1 H6
Anderson Memorial Hut 33 A6
Andersons Bay 124 D4
Anderson's Hut 52 A13 53 A4
Andrews Track 52 B10 53 B1
Angelus Hut 42 H12
Aniwaniwa 21 E3
Annat 52 G11 53 G2 55 C4
Anne River Hut 47 D3
Annesbrook 116 B4
Ant Stream Hut 52 A12 53 A3
Anti Crow Hut 51 C7
Aokautere 30 D8 31 D2 105 C6
Aongatete 10 H12 12 A13 13 A2
Aoraki/Mt Cook 59 B6
Aoraki/Mt Cook National Park 49 J6 59 A7
Aorangi (East Cape, NI) 16 F10
Aorangi (Manawatu) 29 C7 31 C1
Aorangi Forest Park 33 G6
Aorere 37 C6
Aorere Historic Goldfields 37 C6
Aorere Hut 37 E5
Aoroa 4 J8 5 A3
Aotea 11 E2

Aotea – Wellington 110 B3
Aotuhia 24 D11 25 A6
Apanui 14 F13 15 F2
Aparima 76 E14 77 B2
Aparima Forks Hut 70 F13 71 F2 76 A13
Aparima Huts 70 G14 71 G3 76 A14
Apata 10 H12 12 A13 13 A2
Apiti 27 J3
Apiti Hut 14 J10
Aponga 4 F9
Apotu 4 F11
Appleby 128 C5
Apuerewa 2 H8
Aputerewa 2 H8
Arahiwi 12 F13 13 F2
Arahura 45 H2
Arakura 33 E3 35 A3
Aramiro 11 D4
Aramoana, NI 32 B12
Aramoana, SI 74 G13
Aramoho 26 H8 109 A5
Aranga 3 G5
Aranga Beach 3 G5
Aranui 54 H8 56 D10 120 G3
Arapae 18 A9
Arapaoa 2 C5
Araparera 6 F8 7 A2
Arapawa Island 35 G2 40 F12
Arapito 37 J2 41 A7
Arapohue 4 J8 5 A3
Arapuni 12 F10
Ararata 23 G7 25 D2
Ararimu 7 H7 9 C4
Ararua 5 A5
Aratapu 19 B3
Aratapu 5 A3
Aratiatia 19 C6
Aratika 45 G6
Aratoro 18 B10
Arawhata 57 F6
Arch Hill 87 H1 90 C4
Archway Islands 37 A7
Ardgour 66 F10
Ardgowan 68 H11
Ardkeen 21 G3
Ardlussa 72 G8
Ardmore 7 F6 9 A3
Ardmore Airport 7 F6 9 A3
Arero 16 J11
Arete Forks Hut 29 J6
Argyll East 28 H9
Aria 18 B8
Ariki 42 G8
Army Bay 88 B6
Arno 68 D12
Aroha Island 2 K13 4 A9
Arohena 12 G9
Around the Mount Circuit 23 E4
Arowhenua 61 H5
Arowhenua Pa 61 H5
Arrow Junction 65 G6
Arrowtown 65 G6
Arthur's Pass 52 B8
Arthur's Pass National Park 52 A10 53 A1
Arthurs Point 65 G4
Arthurstown 45 J2
Arthurton 78 B11
Arundel 61 D5
Asbestos Cottage 37 H7
Ashburton 55 H2 62 C8
Ashcott 27 J7
Ashers 77 F7
Ashhurst 30 D9 31 D3
Ashley 53 E7 56 A9
Ashley Clinton 27 J6 30 A13 31 A7
Ashley Downs 78 B13 79 D1
Ashley Gorge 52 E13 53 E4 55 A6
Ashton 62 E9
Ashton Hut 71 C4
Ashwick Flat 60 E12 61 E1
Aspiring Hut 64 B14 65 B4
Ataahua 56 G10
Atapo 42 E13
Atarau 45 D6
Atau Paparua 40 C9
Atawhai 38 J12 39 G4
Atea 29 G7 31 G1
Atene 31 A14 26 F9
Athenree 10 F12
Athenree Hot Springs 10 F12
Athol 71 D7
Atiamuri 19 A5
Atiwhakatu Hut 34 A7
Auckland 7 D4
Auckland City 87 D5
Auckland International Airport 7 F4 9 A1 90 E4
Auckland Zoo 7 D4
Aukopae 18 F9 24 A14
Aurere 2 G7
Auripo 66 H13 67 H2
Auroa 23 F4
Ava 110 C3
Avalon 33 E3 35 A3 111 C4
Avenal 127 A2 128 C3
Avenues 93 B1
Aviemore 67 C6

Avoca Hut 51 C7
Avoca, NI 4 H8
Avoca, SI 52 D10 53 D1
Avondale (Auckland) 89 C3
Avondale (Christchurch) 120 G4
Avondale (Southland) 71 H4
Avonhead 53 H7 56 D9 120 C3
Avonside 54 H8 56 D10 120 F3
Awahou 13 F4
Awahou North 30 B9 31 B3
Awahou South 30 C9 31 C3
Awahuri 29 C7 31 C1
Awaiti 10 E9
Awakaponga 14 E9
Awakeri 14 F10
Awakeri Hot Springs 14 F9
Awakeri Springs 14 F9
Awakino 17 C5
Awakino Point 4 J8
Awakino Ski Huts 67 E6
Awakino Skifield 67 E6
Awamangu 79 C3
Awamarino 11 H2
Awamoko 68 F11
Awanui (Bay of Plenty) 15 D6
Awanui (Northland) 1 H6
Awapoto Hut 38 E9 39 C1
Awapuni (Gisborne) 100 B2
Awapuni (Manawatu) 29 E7 31 E1
Awapuni (Palmerston North) 105 D2
Awariki 30 C13 31 C7
Awaroa 3 B2
Awaroa Creek 85 C3
Awaroa Hut 38 E10 39 C2
Awarua, NI 3 E7
Awarua, SI 77 F5
Awatane 11 G7
Awatea 78 D14 79 F2
Awatere 16 C12
Awatere Hut 27 J5
Awatoitoi 34 B11
Awatoto 28 E12 103 A3
Awatuna, NI 23 F5
Awatuna, SI 45 H3
Awhitu 7 G3
Awhitu Central 7 G3
Aylesbury 52 H14 53 H5 55 D7

B

Back Ridge Hut 27 B7
Back River 2 H8
Back Valley Hut 70 F10
Bainesse 29 E6
Bainham 37 D6
Balaclava 124 E4
Balcairn 54 E8 56 A10
Balclutha 79 E3
Balfour 71 H7
Ballance 30 E9 31 E3
Ballarat Hut 64 E14 65 E4
Ballard Hut 28 A8
Balloon Hut 37 H6
Balmoral 90 C4
Balmoral Hill 120 H1
Balmoral Huts 68 G8
Balmoral, SI 47 J4 54 A8
Bankside 55 F5 62 A11
Bannockburn 66 H8
Bare Island / Motu o Kura 28 H13
Bark Bay Hut 38 E10 39 C2
Barker Hut 51 B6
Barkes Corner 94 B1
Barlow Hut 27 F6
Barnego 79 E3
Barra Track 34 A7
Barrhill 55 F3 62 A9
Barron Saddle Hut 59 B5
Barrys Bay 56 G12
Barrytown 45 C5
Barryville 18 B13 19 B1
Bartletts 22 F9
Basins Hut 51 D7
Bastia Hill 108 B6 109 C5
Batley 5 C6
Battersea 33 D7
Bauza Island 69 C5
Bay of Islands Airport 4 A8
Bay View (Auckland) 88 H1
Bay View (Hawkes Bay) 28 C12
Baylys Beach 3 J6
Bayswater 90 B4
Bayswater, SI 77 B2
Beach Haven 88 J2
Beachlands 7 E6
Beachville 115 A1 116 A4
Beaconsfield 30 B8 31 B2
Bealey Hut 52 C8
Bealey Spur 52 C8
Bealey Spur Hut 52 C8
Beaumont 73 G4
Beautiful Valley 60 F14 61 F3
Beckenham 120 E1
Becketts Hut 70 F14 71 F3

Becks 66 G13 67 G2
Beebys Hut 42 F14 43 E2
Beerescourt 92 E3
Belfast 54 G8 56 C10 120 E6
Belfield 61 F5
Belgrove 39 J1 42 C14 43 B2
Bell Block 23 A5
Bell Hill 45 G7
Bell Island 38 J11 39 G3 43 A4
Belleknowes 124 E4
Bells Junction 26 D12
Bellvue 94 B1
Belmont (Auckland) 90 B4
Belmont (Wellington) 33 D3 35 A2 110 C3
Bench Island 80 E6
Bendigo 66 F10
Benhar 79 E4
Benio 78 A10
Benmore 71 J5 77 A4
Benmore Hut 52 G9 55 C2
Bennetts 52 F14 53 F5 55 B7
Bennetts Siding 27 F2
Benneydale 18 B11
Berhampore 110 E2
Berlins 41 H5
Berwick 74 J8 79 B6
Bethlehem 10 J13 12 B14 13 B3 94 C1
Bexley 52 F12 53 F3 55 B5 120 G3
Bideford 34 A11
Big Bay 7 F3
Big Bay Hut 57 J2
Big Hellfire Hut 80 D2
Big Island 80 H1
Big Lagoon 35 H6 44 C12
Big Manly 88 C5
Big Omaha 6 D10
Big River 46 C9
Big River Hut 46 C9
Billy Goat Track 8 G12 10 B10
Binser Saddle Track 52 C10 53 C1
Birch Hill 59 C6
Birchfield 41 F4
Birchville 33 C4
Birchwood 70 J13 71 J2 76 C13
Bird Island 77 J6
Birdlings Flat 56 H10
Birkdale 88 J2
Birkenhead 7 D4 6 J10 89 B3
Bishop and Clerks Islands 77 H1 80 B3
Bishopdale (Christchurch) 120 D4
Bishopdale (Nelson) 116 B4
Black Gully 72 H13 73 H2
Black Hill Hut 52 D11 53 D2 55 A4
Black Reef 41 F2
Black Rock 80 H4
Blackball 45 D5
Blackburn 27 H7
Blackhead, NI 32 C12
Blackhead, SI 74 H11 124 F5
Blackmans 72 A12 73 A1
Blackmount 70 H11 76 B11
Blacks Point 46 B9
Blackstone Hill 66 G13 67 G2
Blackwater 46 C8
Blackwater Lake 52 D11 53 D2
Blackwater River Ecological Area 41 H4
Blairlogie 34 B12
Blaketown 118 A2
Blandswood 61 D4
Blenheim 35 J6 44 C11 117 C4
Blind River 44 E12
Blockhouse Bay 7 E4 89 D3
Blowhard Track 52 D13 53 D4
Blue Cliffs 68 A11
Blue Lake Hut 47 A4
Blue Lake, NI 18 J14 19 J2
Blue Lake, SI 72 D10
Blue Lakes Walk 59 A7
Blue Range Hut 29 J7 31 J1
Blue River (Blowfly) Hut 58 C11
Blue Spur 45 H2
The Bluff/Motupohue 77 H5
Bluff Damp Hut 48 C10
Bluff Hill 103 A1
Bluff Hut 50 C13 51 C4
Blumine Island 35 G2 40 F12
Blyth Hut 26 B12
Blyth Track 26 B12
Blythe Valley 54 B12
Boat Group 80 H1
Bobs Hut 46 C14 47 C2
Boddytown 45 F4
Bog Inn Hut 18 C13 19 C1
Bog Lake 70 A12 71 A1
Bombay 7 H6 9 C3
Bonny Glen 29 A5
Bortons 71 E3
Botany Downs 90 D6
Bouldcott 111 C4
Boulder Lake 37 E6
Boundary Stream Track 20 J12
Bowen Falls 64 D8
Bowentown 10 F12
Bowlers Creek 73 H4 79 A2
Bowscale Tarn 47 B6

Boyd Hut 19 J6
Boydtown 125 A2 126 A2
Boyle Flat Hut 46 E14 47 E2
Boyle Village 46 F13 47 F1
Bradford 124 E4
Braeburn 38 H9 39 F1
Braigh 5 A7
Brames Falls Track 23 E4
Branch Creek Hut 42 D10
Branxholme 77 D4
Breaker Bay 110 E2
Breaksea Island 69 F3
Breaksea Islands (North Stewart Is) 77 J7
Breaksea Islands (South Stewart Is) 80 G6
Bream Islands 4 H14
Brewster Hut 58 F12 59 F1
Bridal Veil Falls, NI - Raglan 11 D3
Bridal Veil Falls, SI 65 F4
Bridge Hill 72 A13 73 A2
Bridge Pa 28 F11
Bridgend 120 F6
Brighton 74 J10 124 J6
Brightwater 39 H2 43 A3
Brixton 17 G1 23 A6
Broad Bay 74 G12
Broad Gully 68 E12
Broadfield 53 J6 56 E9
Broadlands 20 B8
Broadmeadows 110 D2
Broadway Park 90 C4
Broadwood 3 A3
Brockville 124 F3
Brodrick Hut 59 E3
Broken Hills 8 G13 10 B10
Broken Islands 36 E3
Broken River Hut 52 E10 53 E1 55 A3
Broken River Skifield 52 D9
Bromley 120 G2
Bronte 38 J10 39 G2
Brookby 7 F6 9 A3
Brookfield 94 B1
Brooklands (New Plymouth) 106 D4 107 C4
Brooklands Lagoon 54 G8 56 C10
Brooklands, SI (Christchurch) 54 G8 56 C10
Brooklands, SI (Nelson) 38 J12 39 G4 116 A6
Brooklyn 110 E1
Brooklyn, SI 38 G9 39 E1
Brookside 55 F7 62 A13
Broomfield 54 D8 120 B3
Brown Hut 37 E5
Brown Owl 33 D4 111 A4
Browne Island 57 G3
Browns 77 B5
Browns Bay 6 J10 7 C4
Browns Beach 61 G6
Browns Island 71 D5
Bruce Bay 58 A13 59 A2
Brunner 45 E5
Brunswick 26 H8
Bruntwood 12 C8
Bryant Park 92 D3
Brydone 78 C8
Brynavon 4 F13
Brynderwyn 5 B7
Brynderwyn Hills Walkway 6 B8
Bryndwr 53 H7 56 D9 120 D4
Buccleuch 61 A6
Buckland (Auckland) 7 J6 9 D3
Buckland (Waikato) 12 D10
Buckland Peaks Hut 41 H3
Bucklands Beach 7 D6 90 C6
Bucklands Crossing 74 E12
Buckleton Beach 6 E10
Bull Creek Hut 52 A11 53 A2
Bull Flat Hut 58 G13 59 G2
Bulls 29 B6
Bulwer 40 D9
Bungaree Hut 80 D5
Bungtown 73 H6 79 A4
Bunker Islets 80 D6
Bunnythorpe 30 D8 31 D2
Burgess Island 36 A2
Burgess Park 107 D5
Buried Village - Rotorua 13 H5
Burkes 124 C2
Burkes Pass 60 F11
Burn Creek Hut 58 B14 47 B2
Burn Hut 29 G7 31 G1
Burnbrae 46 A12
Burnetts Face 41 G5
Burnham 52 J14 53 J5 55 E7
Burnside (Christchurch) 53 H7 56 D9 120 C4
Burnside (Dunedin) 124 F5
Burnt Bush Hut 66 B11
Burswood 90 D6
Burwood 54 H8 56 D10 120 G4
Bush Hut 58 J12 59 J1 66 A10
Bush Siding 77 F7
Bushey 74 C13
Bushline Hut 42 H13 43 G1
Bushline Hut (Sylvester(37 G6
Bushside 51 J7 61 A6
Butchers Dam 72 B13 73 B2
Butchers Gully 72 B13 73 B2
Butler Junction Hut 50 G8

Caberfeidh – The Five Bridges

C

Caberfeidh 78 F13 79 H1
Cabin Hut 65 D5
Cable Bay 2 H8
Cable Bay Walkway 38 H13 39 F5
Cairnbrae 55 F2 62 A8
Caldervale 37 H2
Callaghans 45 H3
Camberley 103 C5
Camborne 33 C2
Cambrians 66 F13 67 F2
Cambridge 12 D8
Cameron Hut (Lake Sumner) 46 H10
Cameron Hut (Ruahine FP) 27 C7
Cameron Hut (Westland) 50 G12 51 G3
Camerons 45 G3
Camp Valley 60 G12 61 G1
Campbells Bay 88 G4
Candlesticks Bivvy 52 A12
Cannibal Gorge Hut 46 D14 47 D2
Cannington 60 J13 61 J2
Cannons Creek 110 B3
Canvastown 39 G7 44 A8
Cape Brett Track 4 A12
Cape Foulwind 41 G2
Cape Palliser Lighthouse 33 J6
Cape Reinga 1 A1
Cape Reinga Lighthouse 1 A1
Caples Track 64 F11 65 F1
Capleston 46 A10
Captains Creek Hut 39 H5 43 A6
Cardiff 23 E6 25 B1
Cardrona 65 F7
Cardrona Cromwell Pack Track 66 G8
Cardrona Hotel 65 F7
Cardrona Roaring Meg Pack Track 65 G7
Cardrona Skifield 65 F6
Carew 61 D5
Careys Bay 74 G12 124 A1
Carkeek Hut 29 J6
Carleton 52 F14 53 F5 55 B7
Carluke 39 G7
Carlyle Hut 47 F2
Carnarvon 29 D6
Caroline 71 H6
Caroline Creek Hut 47 B4
Caroline Hut 70 J8 76 D8
Carricktown 66 J8
Carrington 34 B8
Carrington Estate Golf Course 2 F7
Carrington Hut 51 B7
Carroll Hut 45 J7
Carswell 34 B11
Carters Beach 41 G3
Carterton 34 C8
Cascade Creek 64 G10
Cascade Hut (Kaimanawa FP) 19 H5
Cascade Hut (Mt Aspiring NP) 64 B14 65 B4
Cascade Saddle Route 65 B4
Cascade Track 42 H13
Casebrook 53 H7 56 D9 120 D5
Casey Hut 52 A10 53 A1
Cashmere (Christchurch) 120 E1
Cashmere (Wellington) 110 D2
Cashmere, SI 54 J8 56 E10
Casnell Island 6 F10
Cass 52 C9
Cass Bay 54 J8 56 E10
Cass Saddle Hut 52 D9
Cassel Flat Hut 59 A4
Castle Hill Village 52 E9 55 A2
Castle Rock Hut 38 F9 39 D1
Castle Rocks Hut 49 H6
Castlecliff 25 J7 109 C1
Castlehill 30 J10 31 J4
Castlepoint 34 B13
Castlerock 71 G6
Castor Bay 6 J10 7 C4 88 H5
Cathedral Caves 78 G13 79 J1
Cathedral Cliffs - Gore Bay 54 A13
Cathedral Cove - Haihei 8 D13
Catlins Forest Park 78 E12
Catlins Lake 79 H3
Catlins River Walk 78 E13 79 G1
Cattle Creek 68 A9
Cattle Creek Hut 30 A12 31 A6
Cattle Flat 71 F7
Cattle Ridge Hut 29 J7
Cattle Valley 60 E13 61 E2
Cavalli Islands 2 H12
Cave 60 H13 61 H2
Cavendish 61 B6
Caverhill 48 J9
Caversham 124 E4
Cayenne Hut 68 J8
Cecil Kings Hut 42 C10
Cedar Flat Hut 50 B13 51 B4
Centennial Hut 49 H6
Central Te Hoe Hut 20 F11
Central Waiau Hut 20 E12
Central Whirinaki Hut 20 E10
Centre Bush 77 A4
Centre Island 70 B11
Chain Hills 124 H4

Chalky Island 75 E2
Challis 124 C4
Chamberlain 60 G12
Chancellor Hut 49 H5
Chancet Rocks 44 G12
Chaneys 54 G8 56 C10 120 F6
Chapel Downs 90 E6
Charing Cross 52 H13 53 H4 55 D6
Charleston 41 H2
Charlestown 65 F4
Charlton 78 B9
Charming Creek Walkway 41 E6
Charteris Bay 54 J8 56 F10
Chartwell (Hamilton) 92 D3
Chartwell (Wellington) 110 D1
Chaslands 78 G12
Chasm Creek Walkway 41 D7
Chatswood 38 J3
Chatto Creek 66 J11
Chatton 72 J10 78 A9
Chatton North 72 J10
Cheddar Valley 14 F12
Chedworth Park 92 D4
Cheltenham (Auckland) 90 B4
Cheltenham (Manawatu) 30 B8 31 B2
Chertsey 55 G4 62 B10
Chesterfield 45 G3
Chetwode Islands 40 C10
Cheviot 48 J9 54 A13
Cheviot Museum 48 J9 54 A13
Chorlton 56 F13
Christchurch 54 H8 56 D10
Christchurch City 119 C5 120 E4
Christchurch International Airport 53 H7 56 D9
Christmas Village Hut 77 J2 80 C4
Christopher Hut 47 D3
Chrystalls Beach 79 D6
Chummies Track 42 C11
Churchill 9 F4
Churton Park 110 C2
Clandeboye 61 G6
Claremont 61 J3
Clarence 48 B14
Clarendon 79 C6
Clareville 34 C8
Claris 36 E5
Clark Hut 70 H8 76 B8
Clarks Beach 7 G4 9 B1
Clarks Junction 74 F8
Clarksville 79 D5
Clarkville 53 G7 56 C9
Claudelands 91 B6 92 E4
Claverley 48 G10
Clay Cliffs 36 A14 67 A3
Clendon House - Rawene 3 C4
Clevedon 7 F7 9 A4
Clifden 76 D12
Clifton (Christchurch) 120 H1
Clifton (Hawkes Bay) 28 F13
Clifton, SI (Clutha) 78 B14 79 D2
Clifton, SI (Invercargill) 77 F5 128 B6
Clifton, SI (Tasman) 38 D8
Clinton 78 C12
Clinton Forks Hut 64 G8
Clive 28 E12 103 A4
Cloustonville 33 B4
Clover Park 90 E6
Cloverlea 29 D7 31 D1 105 B2
Clyde 66 J10 72 A13 73 A2
Clydesdale 29 C5
Clydevale 78 A14 79 C2
Coal Creek Flat 72 D13 73 D2
Coal Island 75 F3
Coalgate 52 H11 53 H2 55 D4
Coatesville 6 J9 7 C3 88 F1
Cobb Hut 37 G6
Cobb Reservoir 37 H7
Cobb Track 37 G6
Cobden 45 E4
Codfish Is (Whenua Hou) Nature Res 80 D1
Codfish Island (Whenuahou) 80 D1
Colac Bay/Oraka (township) 76 H13 77 E1
Cold Stream Hut 46 J13 47 J1
Coldstream (Ashburton) 61 F7
Coldstream (Waimakariri) 53 F7 56 B9
Coldwater Hut 42 H13 43 G1
Colenso Hut 27 F5
Colin Todd Hut 57 J6 64 A14 65 A4
Colliers Junction 26 E13
Collingwood 37 C7
Collinswood 124 B4
Colonial Knob Walkway 33 D2 35 B2
Colville 8 B11 36 J5
Colyton 30 C8 31 C2
Comet Hut 27 D7
Company Bay 124 B3
Concord 124 F5
Cone Hut 33 B6
Conical Hill 78 A11
Conroys Gully 72 A13 73 A2
Conway Flat 48 G10
Cooks Beach 8 D13
Coombe Rocks 35 H4 40 H11 44 A12
Coonoor 30 E12 31 E6
Cooper Island 69 H5 75 B5

Coopers Beach 2 H8
Coopers Creek (Timaru) 61 E5
Coopers Creek (Waimakariri) 52 F12 53 F3 55 B5
Cooptown 56 G11
Copland Shelter 59 A6
Copland Track 49 J3 59 A4
Corbyvale 41 D7
Cormacks 68 H11
Cornwallis (Te Karanga-a-Hape) 7 F3 89 E2
Coroglen 8 E13
Coromandel 8 C11
Coromandel Forest Park 8 A10 36 H4 10 D10
Coromandel Walkway 8 A10 36 G4
Coronet Peak Skifield 65 G5
Corriedale 68 G10
Corstorphine 124 E5
Cosgrove Island 79 H3
Cosseys - Wairoa Track 7 G7 9 B4
Cosseys Reservoir 7 G7 9 B4
Cotters Hut 58 J13 59 J2
Courtenay 52 H13 53 H4 55 D6
Coutts Island 120 E6
Cove, The 74 H11 124 C4
Cow Creek Hut 29 J6
Cowes 8 D8
Cowins Track 37 J6 42 B11
Cracroft 120 D1
Craigellachie 73 H4 79 A2
Craigieburn (Buller) 45 D7
Craigieburn (Selwyn) 52 D10 53 D1
Craigieburn Conservation Park 52 C8
Craigieburn Skifield 52 D9
Crail Bay 35 J2 40 F10
Crater Lake 26 A13
Crawford Junction Huts 50 B14 51 B5
Crawfords 70 J14 71 J3 76 C14
Crichton 79 D4
Cricklewood 60 G12 61 G1
Crippletown 66 G9
Croesus Track 45 C5
Crofton 29 A6
Crofton Downs 110 D1
Cromel Base Hut 71 E5
Cromel Branch Hut 71 D5
Cromwell 66 H9
Cronadun 46 A9
Crookston 72 H13 73 H2
Crossans Corner 72 H12
Crow Hut (Arthur's Pass NP) 51 B7
Crow Hut (Kahurangi NP) 37 J5 42 A10
Crow Hut (Ruahine FP) 27 G5
Crown Hill 88 H4
Croydon 78 A9
Crucible Lake 58 G9
Crumb Hut 67 H7
Crushington 46 B9
Cullers Hut 59 D4
Culverden 47 J5
Cumbria Downs 90 D6
Cupola Hut 42 J12
Curio Bay 78 H11
Curtis Memorial Hut 50 H10 51 H1
Cust 53 F5 55 B7
Cuthill 6 J10 7 C4 88 G3

D

Dacre 77 D7
Dairy Flat 6 H9 7 B3 88 D1
Dairy Flat Airport 6 H9 7 B3
Dale, The 70 C13 71 C2
Dalefield 34 C7
Daleys Flat Hut 64 C12 65 C2
Dallington 120 F3
Dalmore 124 D3
Dannemora 90 D6
Dannevirke 30 C12 31 C6
Danseys Pass 68 G8
Daphne Hut 27 J5
Darfield 52 H12 53 H3 55 D5
Dargaville 4 J8
Dart Hut 64 B13 65 B3
Dashwood 44 D11
Davies Track 23 C4
Dawson Falls 23 E5
Days Bay 33 E2 35 B3 110 D3
Dead Dog Hut 27 E7
Deanwell 92 G3
Deas Cove Hut 69 A5
Deborah 68 H11
Deborah Bay 74 G12 124 A1
Deep Creek 68 C12
Demon Trail 64 B9
Demon Trail Hut 64 B9
Denniston 41 F5
Denniston Walkway 41 F4
Devonport 75 D9 90 B4
De La Beche Hut 49 J6
Diamond Harbour 54 J8 56 E10
Diamond Lake 64 E12 65 E2
Dianes Hut 27 E7
Dickie Spur Hut 50 C11 51 C2

Diggers Hut 30 B11 31 B5
Diggers Valley 1 K6 3 A2
Dillmanstown 45 H4
Dinsdale 92 F2
Dip Flat 42 H14 43 G2
Dipton 71 J6
Dipton West 71 J5
Dobson 45 E5
Dodger Hut 59 D4
Dodson Valley 38 J12 39 G4
Dog Island 77 H5
Dome Islands 70 C11
Dome Valley 6 E9
Dome Valley Forest Track 6 E9
Domett 54 A12
Donnellys Crossing 3 F5
Donoghues 50 A14 51 A1
Dora Track 29 J6
Dorie 55 H5 62 C11
Dorothy Falls 50 A14 51 A5
Dorset Ridge Hut 29 J6 33 A7
Doubtful Hut 46 F13
Doubtful Island 70 A11
Doubtful Sound 69 B4
Doubtless Hut 46 F12
Douglas Corner 13 D4
Douglas Rock Hut 59 A5
Douglas, NI 24 D8 25 A3
Douglas, SI 68 D11
Douglasvale 65 G5
Dovedale 38 J9 42 A14 43 A2
Dover Track 23 D4
Downes Hut 24 J14 26 F9
Downie Hut 47 B3
Doyleston 55 G7 62 B13
Dreyers Rock 30 J9 31 J3
Dromore 55 H3 62 C9
Drummond 77 B3
Drury 7 G6 9 B3
Drybread 66 G12 67 G1
Duckville Hut 14 J9 20 A12
Dumbarton 72 E13 73 E2
Dumpling Hut 63 E7
Dun Mountain Walkway 39 H4 43 A5
Dunback 74 B12
Dundas Hut 29 H6
Dunearn 77 A3
Dunedin 74 H11 124 D4
Dunedin Airport 74 H9 79 A7
Dunedin Central 123 F3
Dunganville 45 G5
Dunmore 9 H3 11 A4
Dunns Creek Hut 51 A7
Dunollie 45 E4
Dunolly 30 A8 31 A2
Dunrobin 72 G13 73 G2
Dunsandel 55 F6 62 A12
Duntroon 68 E9
Durie Hill 108 C6 109 C5
D'Urville Hut 42 H12
D'Urville Island / Rangitoto ki te Tonga 40 B8
D'Urville Track 42 J11 47 A3
Dusky Forest 72 H12
Dusky Sound 69 H1 75 B1
Dusky Track 69 F7
Duvauchelle 56 G12
Dyerville 33 E7

E

Eade Memorial Hut 50 H8
Ealing 61 E6
Earl Mountain Tracks 64 G9
Earnscleugh 72 A13 73 A2
Earnslaw Hut 64 C12 65 C2
Earthquake Flat 13 H5
Earthquake Lakes 37 H5 42 A10
Earthquakes 68 F9
East Cape Lighthouse 16 C13
East Chatton 72 J10 78 A9
East Egmont 23 D5
East End 107 B4
East Gore 78 B9
East Hawdon Bivvy 52 A10
East Island / Whangaokeno Island 16 C14
East Matakitaki Hut 47 B3
East Ruggedy Hut 80 C2
East Taieri 74 H10 124 H5
East Takaka 38 E8
East Tamaki 7 E5 90 D6
East Tamaki Industrial 90 D6
Eastbourne 33 F2 35 B4 110 E3
Eastern Beach 90 C6
Eastern Bush 76 D12
Echo Cliffs - Turangi 19 G3
Echolands 18 F11
Eden Terrace 87 J3 90 C4
Edendale 78 D8
Edgecumbe 14 E9
Edievale 72 G13 73 G2
Edwards Hut 52 B8
Edwards Island (Motunui) 80 D1
Egmont National Park 23 D5
Egmont Village 23 C5

F

Eiffelton 62 E8
Eight Mile Hut 65 F6
Eight Mile Junction 18 A9
Eketahuna 30 H8 31 H2
Elaine Bay 40 E8
Elcho Hut 59 D4
Elderslie 68 G10
Elephant Hill 68 E10
Elgin (Canterbury) 55 J3 62 D9
Elgin (Gisborne) 100 B2
Elizabeth Hut 46 H9
Ella Hut 47 A3
Ellerslie 90 C5
Ellesmere 55 F7 62 A13
Elletts Beach 7 G5 9 B2
Ellis Hut (Kahurangi NP) 37 J7 42 A12
Ellis Hut (Ruahine FP) 27 F7
Elsdon 110 B2
Elsthorpe 28 J11
Elstow 10 G9
Eltham 23 F7 25 C2
Empress Hut 49 J5 59 A6
Endeavour Inlet 35 H1 40 E11
Enderley 92 E4
Enfield 68 G11
Engineers Camp 46 G13 47 G1
Enner Glynn 38 J12 39 H4 43 A5
Entrance Island 63 J1 69 A5
Entry Island 69 H2 75 B2
Epsom 90 C4
Epuni 33 E3 35 A3 111 C4
Epworth 61 G5
Erceg Hut 59 C5
Ermedale 76 G14 77 D2
Ernest Island 80 J2
Ernest Islands 80 F2
Erua 26 A11
Esk Valley 68 B12
Eskdale 28 C11
Ettrick 72 E13 73 E2
Eureka 9 J7 12 B8
Evans Hut 50 E13 51 E4
Evansdale 74 F12
Eversley 60 F12 61 F1
Explorer Hut 50 C12 51 C3
Eyre Mountains/Taka Ra Haka Conservation Park 71 C5
Eyreton 53 G7 56 C9

F

Fairburn 2 J7
Fairdown 41 F4
Fairfax 77 C2
Fairfield (Dunedin) 74 H10 124 G4
Fairfield (Hamilton) 92 E3
Fairfield (Wellington) 111 C4
Fairhall 35 K6 44 C10
Fairlie 60 F12 61 F1
Fairlight 72 C8
Fairton 55 H3 62 C9
Fairview 61 J4
Fairview Downs 92 D4
Falls Dam 66 F14 67 F3
Fanal Island 36 A2
Farewell Spit Nature Reserve 38 A9
Farm Cove 90 C5
Farnham 117 A1
Favona 90 D4
Featherston 33 D6
Featherston Heritage Museum 33 D6
Feilding 29 C7 31 C1
Feldwick 76 D12
Fencourt 12 D8
Fendalton 120 D3
Fenella Hut 37 G6
Fenton Park 95 B6 96 D3
Ferguson Hut 58 F13 59 F2
Fergusons 50 B10 51 B1
Fern Flat, NI (Northland) 2 J8
Fern Flat, NI (Wanganui) 29 A6
Fern Flat, SI 42 G8
Ferndale (New Plymouth) 107 D3
Ferndale (Southland) 78 C9
Fernhill, NI 28 E11 103 B4
Fernhill, SI 64 H14 65 H4 126 C1
Ferniehurst 48 G9
Fernland Spa Mineral Pools - Tauranga 10 J13 12 B14 13 B3
Fernside, NI 33 C6
Fernside, SI 53 F7 56 B9
Ferntown 37 B7
Ferry landing 8 D13
Ferrymead 120 G1
Field Hut 33 A6
Fields Track 33 B6
Fife Rock 77 J5
Finegand 79 E3
Finlay Face Hut 50 H10 51 H1
Fiordland National Park 69 A7
Fisherman Island 38 F10 39 D2
Fitzroy (Hamilton) 92 G4
Fitzroy (New Plymouth) 23 A5 107 B5
Five Bridges, The 22 A12

Five Forks 68 G10
Five Mile Lagoon 49 F5
Five Rivers 71 F6
Five Roads 77 B4
Flag Swamp 74 D12
Flagstaff 92 C3
Flanagans Hut 37 J6 42 A11
Flat Bush 90 E6
Flat Island 2 G11
Flaxmere 28 F11 103 D5
Flaxton 53 F7 56 B9
Flemington, NI 32 B9
Flemington, SI 62 E8
Flora Hut 37 H7
Forbes Hut 58 F13 59 F2
Fordell 26 J9
Fordlands 96 C2
Forest Lake 91 B1 92 E2
Forks Hut 30 B11 31 B5
Forks, The 49 F6
Forsyth 73 J5 79 B3
Forsyth Island / Te Paruparu 40 D10
Fortification 78 F10
Fortrose 78 G8
Four Peaks 61 E3
Four Rivers Plain 42 G9
Fox Glacier 49 H4
Foxhill 39 J1 43 B2
Foxton 29 F5
Foxton Beach 29 E4
Frankleigh Park 107 D3
Frankton (Hamilton) 92 F3
Frankton (Queenstown) 65 H5 126 A5
Franz Josef Glacier 49 G6
Fraser Dam 66 J9 72 A12 73 A1
Frasertown 21 H5
Freds Camp Hut 80 E4
Freemans Bay 87 F2 90 C4
French Bay 89 D2
French Farm 56 G12
French Pass, SI 40 C9
French Pass, NI 12 D9
French Ridge Hut 64 A14 65 A4
Frenchmans Swamp 4 B10
Freshford 72 G9
Frews Hut 50 C13 51 C4
Frimley 103 C5
Frisco Hut 50 C13 51 C4
Fruitlands 72 B13 73 B2
Fuchsia Creek 68 H9

G

Gable Islet 22 C13
Gabriel Hut 46 H13
Gabriels Gully 73 H5 79 A3
Gair Loch 69 F7
Galatea 20 A11
Galloway 66 J11 72 A14 73 A3
Gammans Creek 52 F13 53 F4 55 B6
Gap Road 77 C4
Gapes Valley 61 F4
Gardens, The 90 E6
Gardiner Hut 59 A6
Garston 72 D8
Gate Pa 10 J13 94 C2 13 B3
Gebbies Valley 56 F9
George Lyon Hut 47 A3
George Sound Track 63 H5
Georgetown (Invercargill) 128 B4
Georgetown (Oamaru) 68 F10
Geraldine 61 F4
Geraldine Downs 61 F4
Geraldine Flat 61 F5
Gibbs Track 42 C11
Gibbston 65 H7
Gibbstown 37 C7
Gilbert Islands 69 F3
Gillespies Beach 49 H3
Gillows Dam 41 G3
Gimmerburn 67 J4
Gisborne 22 D10 99 B4 100 B3
Gisborne Point 13 F6
Gladfield 77 B3
Gladstone, NI (Manawatu) 29 H5
Gladstone, NI (Wellington) 34 C9
Gladstone, SI (Grey) 45 F3
Gladstone, SI (Invercargill) 128 C2
Gladstone, SI (Queenstown) 66 C9
Glasnevin 54 D8
Glen Afton 9 H3 11 A4
Glen Avon 107 B5
Glen Eden 7 E3 89 D2
Glen Eden South 89 D2
Glen Eden West 89 D2
Glen Innes 7 E5 90 C5
Glen Massey 9 H4 11 A5
Glen Murray 9 F3
Glen Oroua 29 D6
Glenavy 68 F13
Glenbervie 4 F12 85 A3
Glenbrook 7 H4 9 C1
Glenbrook Beach 7 H4 9 C1
Glencoe 77 C7
Glendale 111 D4
Glendene 89 C2
Glendhu 34 G9
Glendhu Bay 65 D7
Glendowie 90 C5
Glenduan 38 H13 39 F5
Glenfield 6 J10 7 C4 88 H3
Glengarry (Invercargill) 77 E5 128 B2
Glengarry (Tasman) 42 H8
Glenham 78 E9
Glenholme 95 D5 96 C3
Glenhope 42 E11
Gleniti 61 J4
Glenkenich 72 J12 73 J1
Glenleith 74 G11 124 E2
Glenomaru 79 G3
Glenorchy 64 F12 65 F2
Glenore 79 C4
Glenpark 74 C12
Glenrae Hut 46 J14 47 J2
Glenroy 52 H10 53 H1 55 D3
Glenside 33 E2 35 B3 110 C2
Glentui 52 E14 53 E5 55 A7
Glentunnel 52 H11 53 H2 55 D4
Glenure 71 H7
Glenvar 6 J10 7 C4 88 E3
Glenview 92 H4
Glinks Gully 5 B2
Glorit 6 F8
Goat Creek Hut 42 E8
Goat Island 6 D11
Goat Pass Hut 52 A8
Godley Hut 50 H8
Gold Creek Hut 27 G6
Golden Cross 10 E10
Golden Downs 42 D14 43 C2
Golden Springs 19 B7
Golden Stairs Walkway 3 C2
Golden Valley 10 E11
Goldsborough / Waimea 45 H3
Golflands 90 D6
Gomorrah Track 42 C11
Gonville 108 D3 109 D3
Goodwood 74 D13
Goodwood Heights 90 E6
Goose Bay 48 F10
Gordon 10 J10 12 B11
Gordons Valley 68 A12
Gordonton 9 J6 11 B7
Gore 78 B9
Gore Bay 54 A13
Gorge Creek 72 B12 73 B1
Gorge Islands 57 H2
Gorge Road 77 F7
Gouland Downs Hut 37 E4
Goulds Road 56 F8 62 A14
Governors Bay 54 J8 56 E10
Gowanbridge 42 F11
Gracefield 33 E3 35 A3 110 D3
Grafton 87 H5 90 C4
Grahams Beach 7 G3 9 B1
Granity 41 E5
Granity Pass Hut 42 D11
Grasmere 77 E5 128 D2
Grassy Flat Hut 51 A6
Grays Corner 68 E12
Grays Hut 68 J8
Great Barrier Island Aotea 36 D4
Great Island 75 E3
Great Mercury Island 8 B14
Greatford 29 B6
Green Bay 89 D3
Green Gate Huts 65 F5
Green Hills 68 E12
Green Island, SI (Dunedin) 74 H11 124 F4
Green Island, SI (Foveaux Strait) 77 J7
Green Island, SI (Pacific Ocean) 74 J10
Green Islets 75 G5
Green Lake 70 H9 76 B9
Green Lake Hut 70 H9 76 B9
Green Meadows 103 B2
Green Valley 74 A11
Greenacres 110 B2
Greendale 52 J12 53 J3 55 E5
Greenfield 78 A14 79 C2
Greenhills 77 G4 80 A6
Greenhithe 89 A2
Greenland Reservoir 73 C4
Greenlane 90 C4
Greenmount 90 D6
Greenpark 56 F9
Greenpark Huts 56 G9
Greenpoint 77 G4 80 A6
Greenstone / Pounamu 45 H4
Greenstreet 55 G2 62 B8
Greenvale 72 H11
Greerton 10 J13 12 B14 13 B3 94 D1
Greigs 45 D4
Grenada 110 C2
Grenada North 110 C2
Greneys Road 54 D8
Greta Valley 54 B10
Greta Valley Walkway 54 B10
Grey Group Islands 36 D3
Grey Lynn 7 D4 87 G1
Greymouth 45 F4 118 A4
Greys Hut 37 J3 42 A8
Greytown 33 C7
Griffin Creek Hut 45 J5
Groper Island 36 A1
Gropers Bush 77 D2
Grough Hut 59 D5
Grove Bush 77 D6
Grove, The 35 K3 40 G9
Grovetown 35 J6 40 J10 44 C11
Gulf Harbour 6 H11 7 B5
Gum Tree Flat 68 E12
Gumdiggers Park 1 G6
Gummies Bush 76 G14 77 D2
Gumtown 4 F10
Guthrie 12 J14 13 J3

H

Haast 58 D9
Haast Beach 58 D8
Haast Hut 49 J6
Haast Paringa Track 58 C10
Hackthorne 55 H1 61 C7
Hadlow 61 J4
Hagens Hut 58 G14 59 G3
Hahei 8 D14
Hairini (Bay of Plenty) 10 J13 13 B4
Hairini (Waikato) 11 E7
Hakarimata Walkway 9 H4 11 A5
Hakaru 6 B8
Hakataramea 68 D8
Hakatere Conservation Park 51 H3 51 H6 51 H7
Hakatere (Ashburton Coast) 62 E9
Hakatere (Ashburton) 50 J14 51 J5 61 A4
Haku 11 J3 17 A7
Halcombe 29 B7 31 B1
Haldane 78 G10
Half Moon Bay 7 E6 90 C6
Half Moon Hut 68 H8
Halfmoon Bay / Oban 80 E5
Halfway Bush 124 E3
Halfway Hut 69 H7 75 B7
Halkett 52 H14 53 H5 55 D7
Halswell 53 J7 56 E9 120 C1
Hamama 38 E8
Hamilton 9 J6 11 B7 92 E3
Hamilton Airport 11 D7
Hamilton Central 91 E5
Hamilton East 92 F4
Hamilton Gardens 11 C7
Hamilton Hut 52 D8
Hamilton North 91 D4 92 E3
Hamilton West 91 G4 92 F3
Hampden 74 A13
Hampstead 55 J3 62 D9
Hamua 30 G9 31 G3
Hamurana 13 F4
Hanamahihi Hut 20 A13 21 A1
Hangaroa 21 E7
Hangatiki 11 H6
Hanmer Conservation Park 47 F4
Hanmer Springs 47 F5
Hanmer Springs Thermal Resort 47 F5
Hannahs Bay 13 G5 96 B5
Hannahs Clearing 57 E7
Happy Daze Hut 27 J5 30 A12 31 A6
Happy Valley (Auckland) 7 H7 9 C4
Happy Valley (Wellington) 110 E1
Happy Valley, SI 76 E12
Hapuakohe Track 9 E6
Hapuku 48 D13
Harakeke 38 J10 39 G2
Harapepe 11 D5
Harbour View (Auckland) 89 B2
Harbour View (Wellington) 110 C3
Haretaunga 111 B5
Harewood 53 H7 56 D9 120 C4
Harihari 50 D9
Hariki Beach 15 C6
Harington Point 74 G13
Harini 94 D2
Harkness Hut 27 A6
Harman Hut 51 B6
Haroto Bay 11 C4
Harper Pass Bivvy 46 H9
Harper Pass Track 46 H11
Harrisville 7 J6 9 D3
Haruru 4 B9 81 B1
Haruru Falls - Paihia 4 B9
Harveys Flat 74 G9 79 A7
Harwood 74 G12
Hastings 28 F11 103 C5
Hastings Central 102 B2
Hastwell 30 H8 31 H2
Hataitai 110 E2
Hatepe 19 F5
Hatfield 55 G4 62 B10
Hatfields Beach 6 G10 7 A4
Hatuma 32 A9
Hatuma Lake 32 A10
Hauiti 22 A13
Haukawakawa 40 C9
Haumoana 28 E12
Haunui 30 G11 31 G5
Hauparu Bay 13 F5
Haupiri 46 G9
Hauraki 90 B4
Hautanoa 16 G11
Hautapu 12 D8
Hautu Village 19 G3
Hauturu 11 F3
Hauturu / Little Barrier Island 36 D1 6 C13
Hauwai 44 E12
Havelock 40 G8
Havelock North 28 F12 103 B6
Hawai 15 E4
Hawarden 54 B8
Hawdon Hut 52 B9
Hawea Conservation Park 58 H12 59 E3
Hawea Flat 66 C9
Hawera 23 H7 25 E2
Hawkes Bay Museum - Napier 28 D12
Hawkins 52 H12 53 H3 55 D5
Hawksbury Bush 74 D12
Hawkswood 48 H9
Hawthorndale 128 B3
Hays Gap 79 G4
Haystack Hut 42 D9
Haystack, The 40 C11
Haywards 33 D3 35 A2 111 B4
Hazletts 77 D3
Healey Creek Hut 50 C11 51 C2
Heao 18 G8 24 A13
Heaphy Hut 37 F2
Heaphy Track - Great Walk 37 E3
Heathcote Valley 54 J8 56 E10 120 G1
Heatherlea 29 G5
Hector 41 E5
Heddon Bush 77 B3
Hedgehope 77 C6
Heenans Corner 77 A3
Hei Hei 53 H7 56 D9 120 B2
Heidelberg 77 E5 128 B4
Heipipi 20 D12
Helena Bay 4 C12
Helensburgh 124 E3
Helensville 6 H8 7 B2
Helicopter Flat Hut 42 C9
Hells Gate - Rotorua 13 F5
Helvetia 7 H5 9 C2
Hen and Chickens Islands 6 A10
Hen and Chickens Islands Nature Reserve 6 A10
Henderson 7 E3 89 C2
Henderson Valley 89 C2
Henley 74 J9 79 B7
Hepburn Creek 6 F10
Herbert 68 J10 74 A13
Herbertville 32 F10
Herekino 3 B1
Herekino Forest 1 K6 3 A2
Herekopare Island / Te Marama 80 D6
Herepai Hut 29 H7 31 H1
Herepo 50 D9
Heriot 72 H13 73 H2
Herne Bay 89 B3
Herricks Hut 27 E7
Hexton 22 D10
Heyward Point 74 G12
Hicks Bay 16 B11
Hidden Falls Hut 64 D10
Highbank 52 J9 55 E2 62 A8
Highbury (Auckland) 88 J3
Highbury (Wellington) 110 E1
Highcliff 74 H12 124 B5
Highland Park 90 C6
Highland Park (Wellington) 110 D2
Highlands Park 107 C5
Hihi 2 G9
Hihitami 26 E14 27 E2
Hikawera 34 F8
Hikuai 8 G13 10 B10
Hikumutu 18 G10
Hikurangi 4 E11
Hikutaia 8 J12 10 D9
Hikuwai 16 H11
Hilderthorpe 68 G12
Hill Park 90 E6
Hillcrest (Auckland) 88 J3
Hillcrest (Hamilton) 92 F5
Hillcrest (Rotorua) 96 C5
Hillend 79 D3
Hillersden 43 D6
Hillgrove 74 B13
Hills Creek 66 F14 67 F3
Hillsborough (Auckland) 90 D4
Hillsborough (Christchurch) 120 F2
Hillsborough, NI (Taranaki) 23 B5
Hilltop 56 G11
Hilmorton 120 D2
Hilton 61 F4
Himatangi 29 E5
Himatangi Beach 29 D4
Hinakura 34 F9
Hinau, NI 27 H3
Hinau, SI 46 B8
Hindon 74 F10
Hinds 55 J1 61 E7
Hinehopu 13 F6
Hinemoa 30 G10 31 G4
Hinerua Hut 27 H6
Hinuera 12 D11
Hira 38 J13 39 G5
Hiruharama 16 E11
Hiwinui 30 C8 31 C2
Hiwipango 42 D14 43 C2
Hoanga 4 J8
Hobsonville 7 D3 88 J1
Hodderville 12 G11
Hoe-O-Tainui 9 G7
Hohonu 45 H4
Hokianga - Kai Iwi Coastal Track 3 E3
Hokio Beach 29 G4
Hokitika 45 H2
Hokonui 77 B6
Hokowhitu 104 D6 105 C4
Hokuri Hut 64 A9
Holborn 111 B4
Holdens Bay 13 G4 96 B5
Holly Hut 23 D5
Hollyford 64 E10
Hollyford Track 64 A9
Homai 90 E5
Home Point 4 H13
Homebush, NI 34 B9
Homebush, SI 52 H11 53 H2 55 D4
Homedale 111 D4
Homer Tunnel 64 E9
Hone Heke Monument - Kaikohe 3 C7
Honeymoon Valley 2 J8
Honikiwi 11 G5
Hook 68 C13
Hook Bush 68 C11
Hooker / Landsborough Wilderness Area 59 B4
Hooker Glacier Walk 59 A6
Hooker Hut 59 A6
Hoon Hay 53 J7 56 E9 120 D2
Hoopers Inlet 74 G12
Hope 39 H3 43 A4 116 D2
Hope Kiwi Hut 46 G12
Hope shelter 46 G13
Hopelands 30 D11 31 D5
Hopeless Hut 42 J12
Hopeone 21 A3
Hopuhopu 9 H5 11 A6
Horace Walker Hut 59 B5
Horahia 8 J11 10 D8
Horahora 85 C1
Horahora (Northland) 4 F13
Horahora (Waikato) 12 E10
Horeke 3 C5
Hornby 53 J7 56 E9 120 B2
Hornby Hut 44 J9 48 A13
Horoeka 30 F13 31 F7
Horoera 16 B13
Horohoro 12 H14 13 H3
Horokino 18 A12
Horokiwi 110 C3
Horomanga 14 J8 20 A11
Horopito 26 B11
Hororata 52 H11 53 H2 55 D4
Horotiu 9 J5 11 B6
Horrellville 52 F14 53 F5 55 B7
Horseshoe Flat Hut 58 C12
Horseshoe Lake 28 J11
Horsham Downs 9 J5 11 B6 92 A3
Horsley Down 54 A8
Hospital Hill (Napier) 103 B1
Hospital Hill (Opotiki) 14 F13 15 F2 103 B1
Hot Water Beach 8 E14
Hot Water Beach Hot Springs 8 E14
Hoteo 6 E8
Hoteo North 6 D8
Houghton Bay 110 E2
Houhora 1 E5
Houhora Heads 1 F5
Houhou 45 H2
Houipapa 78 F14 79 H2
Houpoto 15 E5
Houto 4 G9
Howard 42 G12
Howard Junction 42 F12
Howard Track 42 H12
Howick 7 E6 90 C6
Howletts Hut 27 J5
Huapai 6 J8 7 C2
Huarau 5 B6
Huia 7 F2 89 E1
Huiakama 24 D9 25 A4
Huiarua 16 G9
Huinga 24 E8 25 B3
Huirangi 17 H1 23 B6
Huiroa 24 D8 25 A3
Huka Falls - Taupo 19 D5
Huka Village 98 A4
Hukanui 30 G8 31 G2
Hukapapa 18 H11
Hukarere 46 C8
Hukatere (Northland - Far North) 1 F4
Hukatere (Northland) 5 C5
Hukawai 46 D8
Hukerenui 4 D10
Humphreys 45 J3

Hundalee – Lake Alice

Hundalee 48 G10
Hungahunga 10 J10 12 B11
Hunter 68 C12
Hunterville 26 J13
Huntingdon 55 J2 62 D8
Huntington Park 90 D6
Huntly 9 G5
Hunts Creek Hut 51 A7
Huntsbury 120 F1
Hunua 7 G7 9 B4
Hunua Falls - Auckland 7 G7 9 B4
Hunua Ranges Regional Park 8 G8 9 B5
Hupara 4 C9
Hurdon 107 D2
Hurford 23 B4
Hurleyville 24 H8 25 E3
Hurricane Hut 42 D9
Hurunui 54 A9
Hurunui Hot Springs 46 H11
Hurunui Hut 46 H11
Hurunui Mouth 54 A13
Hurworth 23 C5
Hutnters Hut 50 E10 51 E1
Hutxley Forks Hut 59 E3
Hyde 74 A9
Hyde Park 120 C3

I

Ice Lake 50 G8
Ida Valley 66 H14 67 H3
Idaburn 67 G4
Idaburn Dam 66 G14 67 G3
Ihaia Track 23 E4
Ihakara 29 G5
Ihumatao 90 E4
Ihungia 16 G10
Ihuraua 30 J9 31 J3
Ikamatua 46 C8
Ikawai 68 E11
Ikawatea Forks Hut 27 E6
Ilam 120 D3
Inaha 23 G6
Inangahua 41 H6
Inangahua Junction 41 H6
Inangahua Landing 41 H5
Inch Clutha 79 E4
Inch Valley 74 B12
Inchbonnie 45 H6
Incholme 68 H10
Indian Island 69 H3 75 B3
Inglewood 17 J1 23 C6
Inland Track 38 E9 39 C1
Invercargill 77 E5 127 C2
Invercargill Airport 77 E4
Irirangi 26 D14 27 D2
Iris Burn Hut 70 C10
Iron Bark Hut 27 F5
Iron Gate Hut 27 J5
Iron Whare Hut 28 A8
Irwell 55 F7 62 A13
Isla Bank 77 C3
Island Bay 33 F1 35 C4 110 E2
Island Block 7 J7 9 D4
Island Cliff 68 F9
Island Gully Hut 47 B5
Island Lake (Buller) 37 G5
Island Lake (Southland) 70 H9 76 B9
Island Lake (Tasman) 47 B6
Island Stream 68 J10
Island View 10 F12
Islands Hut 71 D5
Islington (Blenheim) 117 B5
Islington (Christchurch) 120 B2
Ivory Lake Hut 50 D12 51 D3
Ivydale 3 C5
Iwikau Village 26 A13
Iwitahi 19 F7

J

Jackett Island 38 H10 39 F2
Jacks Blowhole 79 H3
Jacks Island / Tuhawaiki 79 H3
Jackson Bay 57 E5
Jacksons 45 J6
Jacky Lee Island / Pukeokaoka 80 D6
Jacobs River 49 J2
Jam Hut 44 J8 48 A12
James Mackay Hut 37 E3
Jameson Ridge Track 42 J11
Janefield 74 H10 124 H4
Jerusalem 24 G13 26 D8
Jervois Hut 47 E3
Jervoistown 103 B2
John Coull Hut 24 D12 25 A7
John Reid Hut 42 C11
John Tait Hut 42 J13
Johnson Hut 42 C8
Johnson Track 42 C8
Johnsonville 33 E2 35 B3 110 C2
Johnstone 73 J5 79 B3
Jollie Brook Hut 46 H13 47 H1

Josephville 71 H6
Jubilee Hut 74 F11
Judea 94 C2
Judgeford 33 D3 35 A2 111 B4
Julia Hot Springs 51 A7
Julia Hut 51 A7
Jumbo Hut 34 A7
Junction Burn Hut 70 A9
Junction Hut 66 B10
Junction Islands 36 E3

K

Ka Whata Tu o Rakihouia
  Conservation Park 48 C11
Kaawa 9 G2
Kaeo 2 J11
Kaharoa 13 E4
Kahika 28 A12
Kahikatoa 3 B5
Kahoe 2 H10
Kahotea 11 G6
Kahui Hut 23 D4
Kahui Track 23 D4
Kahuika 78 F13 79 H1
Kahunui Hut 21 B4
Kahurangi National Park 37 F5
Kahutara 33 E6
Kai Iwi 25 H7
Kai Iwi Beach 25 H7
Kaiaka 2 J8
Kaiapoi 54 G8 56 C10
Kaiate Falls 13 C4
Kaiatea 4 F3
Kaiewe Junction 27 F3
Kaihere 9 E7
Kaihiku 78 C14 79 E2
Kaihinu 45 H2
Kaihu 3 G6
Kaihu Forest 3 G7
Kaiiwi Lakes 3 H6
Kaik 74 B14
Kaikarangi 26 H13
Kaikohe 3 C7
Kaikorai 123 D1 124 E3
Kaikou 4 E6
Kaikoura 48 E12
Kaikoura Island 36 D3
Kaikoura Peninsula Walkway 48 E12
Kaimai-Mamaku Conservation Park 10 G10
  12 E12 13 E1
Kaimamaku 4 D11
Kaimanawa Forest Park 19 H4 27 A3
Kaimarama 8 E12
Kaimata, NI 17 J2 23 C7
Kaimata, SI 45 F5
Kaimaumau 1 G6
Kaimiro 23 C5
Kainga 54 G8 56 C10
Kaingaroa 1 H7
Kaingaroa Forest 20 A10
Kainui 9 H5 11 A6
Kaipaki 11 D7
Kaipara Flats 6 E8
Kaipara Flats Airfield 6 E9
Kaipara Lighthouse 5 E5
Kaiparoro 30 H8 31 H2
Kaipikari 17 G3 24 A8
Kairakau Beach 28 J12
Kairaki 54 G8 56 C10
Kairanga 29 D7 31 D1
Kairangi 12 E9
Kairara 3 G7
Kairua 13 B4 94 C5
Kaitaia 1 J5
Kaitaia Airport - Awanui 1 H6
Kaitangata 79 E4
Kaitaratahi 22 C9
Kaitawa (Hawke's Bay) 21 F2
Kaitawa (Manawatu) 30 F10 31 F4
Kaite 100 C4
Kaitemako 13 C4
Kaiteriteri 38 G10 39 E2
Kaitieke 18 H10
Kaitoke (Manawatu) 30 C12 31 C6
Kaitoke (Waikato) 8 E13
Kaitoke (Wanganui) 26 J8
Kaitoke (Wellington) 33 C5
Kaitoke Hot Springs 36 D4
Kaitoke Lake 26 J8
Kaitui 3 F5
Kaituna Lagoon 56 G9
Kaituna Track 37 B6
Kaituna Valley 56 G10
Kaituna, NI 34 A8
Kaituna, SI 40 J8 44 B9
Kaiwaiwai 33 D7
Kaiwaka 6 C8
Kaiwera 78 B10
Kaiwhaiki 26 G8
Kaiwharawhara 110 D2
Kaka 42 D12

Kaka Point 79 G4
Kakahi 18 G11
Kakahu 60 F14 61 F3
Kakahu Bush 61 F3
Kakanui, NI 6 G8 7 A2
Kakanui, SI 68 J11
Kakapo Hut 42 B9
Kakapo Track 42 B8
Kakapotahi 50 B10
Kakapuaka 79 E3
Kakaramea 24 J8 25 F3
Kakariki (Gisborne) 16 D12
Kakariki (Manawatu) 30 G8 31 G2
Kakariki (Wanganui) 29 B6
Kakatahi 26 F11
Kamahi 78 D8
Kamaka 45 E5
Kambton 112 D5
Kamo 4 F11 85 A1
Kamo East 85 A1
Kanakanaia 22 B10
Kangaroo Lake 45 G7
Kaniere 45 J2
Kaniwhaniwha 11 D5
Kanohi 6 G8 7 A2
Kanohirua Hut 20 C14 21 C2
Kapakapanui Hut 33 A5
Kapenga 13 H4
Kapiro 2 K12 4 A8
Kapitea Reservoir 45 H4
Kapiti 79 C5
Kapiti Island 33 A3
Kapiti Island Nature Reserve 29 J2 33 A3
Kaponga 23 F5
Kapowairua 1 A2
Kapua 68 D11
Kapuka 77 F7
Kapuka South 77 F7
Kapuni 23 F5
Karahaki 24 J9 25 F4
Karaka 7 G5 9 B2
Karakariki 33 E1 35 C3 110 D2
Karamea / Red Island, NI 28 H13
Karamea Bend Hut 37 J5 42 A10
Karamea Centennial Museum 37 J2 42 A7
Karamea, SI 37 J2 41 A7
Karamu (Hawke's Bay) 28 F12 103 B5
Karamu (Waikato) 11 D5
Karangahake 10 F10
Karangahake Gorge 10 F10
Karangarua 49 J3
Karapiro 12 D9
Karatia (Thoms Landing) 1 C2
Karehana Bay 33 C2 35 B1
Karekare 7 F2
Karekare Falls 7 F2
Kareponia 1 H6
Karere 29 E7 31 E1
Karetu 4 C10
Karewarewa 27 H3
Karioi 26 C12
Karioitahi 7 J3 9 D1
Karitane 74 E12
Karori 33 F1 35 C4 110 D1
Karori West 110 D1
Karoro 45 F4
Karuhiruhi 3 D4
Katea 79 G2
Katikati 10 G11
Katiki 74 B14
Katipo Creek Shelter 37 G2
Kauaeranga 8 H12 10 C9
Kauana 77 A5
Kauangaroa 26 J10
Kaukapakapa 6 H8 7 B2
Kaupokonui 23 G5
Kauri 4 F11
Kauri Flat 9 J2 11 B3
Kaurilands 89 D2
Kauroa 11 C3
Kauru Hill 68 H10
Kauwhata 29 D7 31 D1
Kawa 36 C4
Kawaha Point 96 A3
Kawakawa (Northland - Far North) 1 G7
Kawakawa (Northland) 4 C9
Kawakawa Bay 8 E8 9 A5
Kawakawa Hut 33 H6
Kawarau Falls 65 H5 126 B5
Kawarau Gorge 66 H8
Kawatiri 42 F11
Kawatiri Walkway 42 F12
Kawau Island 6 F11
Kawautahi 18 H10
Kaweka Forest Park 19 J6 27 C7
Kaweka Hut 27 B7
Kawerau 14 G8
Kawerua 3 F4
Kawhia 11 F2
Kawhia Museum 11 F2
Kawiti 4 C8
Kawiti Caves - Kawakawa 4 C9
Kekerengu 44 H11
Kelburn 110 D1
Kelchers 68 D10

Kelly Knight Hut 27 H5
Kelly Tarltons Underwater World - Auckland
  7 D5 90 B4
Kellys Bay 5 D4
Kellyville 7 J7 9 D4
Kelman Hut 49 J7
Kelso 72 H12 73 H1
Kelson 33 D3 35 A2 111 C4
Kelston 89 C2
Kelvin Grove 30 D8 31 D2 105 A5
Kelvin Heights 65 H5
Kenana 2 H9
Kenepuru 110 B2
Kenepuru Head 35 H2 40 F11
Kenepuru Sound 35 K2 40 F9
Kenmure 124 E4
Kennedy Bay 8 C11 36 J5
Kennedy Memorial Hut 59 D5
Kennington 77 E5
Kensington 123 J2
Kensington (Dunedin) 124 E4
Kensington (Whangarei) 85 B1
Kepler Track - Great Walk 70 C10
Kereone 10 J9 12 B10
Kerepehi 8 J11 10 C8
Kereru 28 F8
Kererutahi 14 F12
Keretu 21 B6
Kerikeri 4 A8 86 B2
Kerikeri Inlet 2 K13 4 A9
Kerin Forks Hut 58 H9
Kerosene Creek Thermal Area - Waiotapu 13 J5
Kerrytown 61 H4
Ketetahi 18 H13
Ketetahi Hot Springs -
  Tongariro National Park 18 J13 19 J1
Ketetahi Hut 18 J13 19 J1
Kew (Dunedin) 124 E5
Kew (Invercargill) 128 B5
Key, The 70 E13 71 E2
Khandallah 33 E1 35 C3 110 D2
Kia Ora 68 H11
Kihikihi 11 F7
Kikiwa 42 F13 43 E1
Kilburnie 110 E2
Killinchy 55 G6 62 B12
Kimbell 60 E12
Kimberley 52 G12 53 G3 55 C5
Kimbolton 30 A9 31 A3
Kime Hut 33 B6
Kimihia 9 G5
Kina 38 H10 39 F2
Kings Creek Hut 42 C10
Kingsdown 68 A13
Kingseat 7 G5 9 B2
Kingsley Heights 111 B6
Kingsland 87 J1 89 C3 90 C4
Kingston (Wellington) 110 E1
Kingston Crossing 72 H8
Kingston, SI 72 B8
Kingswell 128 B5
Kinleith 12 H12 13 H1
Kinloch, NI 19 D4
Kinloch, SI 64 F12 65 F2
Kinohaku 11 G2
Kintail Hut 69 F7
Kiokio 11 G6
Kirikau 18 G9 24 A14
Kirikopuni 4 H9
Kirioke 3 D7
Kiripaka 4 F13
Kiritaki 30 C11 31 C5
Kiritaki Hut 30 C10 31 C4
Kiritehere 11 J2
Kiriwhakapapa 29 J7 31 J1 34 A8
Kirwans Track 46 A10
Kirwee 52 H13 53 H4 55 D6
Kiwi 42 D12
Kiwi Hut 46 J8
Kiwi Mouth Hut 27 B7
Kiwi Saddle Hut (Kahurangi FP) 42 C10
Kiwi Saddle Hut (Kaweka FP) 27 B7
Kiwi Track 42 C10
Kiwitahi 10 J8 12 B9
Kiwitahi Station 10 J8 12 B9
Kiwitea 30 B9 31 B3
Klondyke Track 46 C11
Knapdale 72 J10 78 A9
Knights Track 27 J4 30 A11 31 A5
Knobbies, The 80 C1
Knobs Flat 64 H9
Koaunui Hut 14 J12 15 J1 21 A3
Koeke Junction 26 F13
Kohaihai Shelter 37 G2
Kohatu 42 C13 43 B1
Kohe 3 B2
Kohekohe 7 H3
Kohi 24 J9 25 F4
Kohika 68 B12
Kohiku 30 G12 31 G6
Kohinui 30 E11 31 E5
Kohukohu 3 C5
Kohumaru 2 J9
Kohupatiki 103 B4

Kohuratahi 17 H6 24 B11
Koiro 18 G9 24 A14
Koitiata 29 A4
Kokako 21 F3
Kokatahi 50 A12 51 A3
Kokiri 45 F5
Kokoamo 68 F10
Kokonga 67 J6
Kokopu 4 G10
Kokowai Track 23 D5
Komako 30 B10 31 B4
Komakorau 9 H5 11 A6
Komata 10 E9
Komata Reefs 10 E10
Komokoriki 6 F8
Kongahu 37 J2 41 A7
Konini (Auckland) 89 D2
Konini (Manawatu) 30 F9 31 F3
Kononi 73 J4 79 B2
Kopaki 18 A10
Kopane 29 D7
Kopara 46 G8
Kopikopiko 30 F8 31 F2
Kopu 8 H11 10 C8
Kopuarahi 8 J11 10 D8
Kopuaranga 34 A9
Kopuaroa 16 F11
Kopuawhara 22 J8 22 AA1
Kopuku 8 J8 9 D5
Kopuriki 14 J9 20 A12
Koputaroa 29 G5
Korakonui 12 G8
Koranga 21 B5
Koranga Forks Hut 21 A4
Korapuki Island 8 B14
Koremoa 5 B3
Korere 42 D13 43 C1
Koriniti 24 J14 26 F9
Korito 23 C5
Korokoro 110 C3
Koromatua 11 C6 92 H1
Koromiko 35 J4 40 H10 44 A11
Koropuku Hut 46 J8 52 A9
Korora 30 F12 31 F6
Korowai/Torlesse Tussocklands Park
  52 E10 52 F9
Koru 23 B4
Kotare 17 F5
Kotemaori 20 J13 21 J1
Kotepato Hut 14 J13 15 J2 21 A4
Kotinga 38 E8
Kotuku 45 F6
Kourawhero 6 F9
Koutu (Kauri Coast) 3 D3
Koutu (Rotorua) 13 G4 96 B2
Kowai Bush 52 F11 53 F2 55 B4
Kowhai Park 110 E1
Kowhitirangi 50 A12 51 A3
Kuaotunu 8 C13
Kuku 29 H4
Kukumoa 14 F13 15 F2
Kukupa 56 F12
Kumara 45 G4
Kumara Junction 45 G3
Kumara Reservoir 45 H4
Kumeroa 30 D11 31 D5
Kumeti Hut 30 B11 31 B5
Kumeu 6 J8 7 C2
Kundy Island 80 H1
Kupe 23 D7 25 A2
Kuranui 10 H8 12 A9
Kuratau 19 F3
Kuratau Junction 18 F14 19 F2
Kuri Bush 74 J9 79 B7
Kuriheka 68 J10
Kuripapango 27 C7
Kuriwao 78 C13 79 E1
Kurow 67 D7
Kutarere 14 F12 15 F1
Kyeburn 67 J6
Kyeburn Diggings 67 G6
Kyle 55 J5 62 D11

L

Ladbrooks 53 J7 56 E9
Lady Barkly 77 B4
Lady Knox Geyser - Waiotapu 13 J5 20 A8
Lady Lake 45 G7
Lagmhor 55 H2 62 C8
Laingholm 7 F3 89 E2
Laingholm Central 89 D2
Lairdvale 18 F10
Lakehead Hut 42 H13
Lake Ada 64 E8
Lake Adelaide 64 E9
Lake Agnes 64 C9
Lake Ahaura 46 F8
Lake Alabaster/Wawahi Waka 64 B10
Lake Alabaster Hut 64 C10
Lake Alexandrina 60 D9
Lake Alice, NI 29 B5
Lake Alice, NI (locality) 29 B5

Lake Alice – Mairetahi

Lake Alice, SI 63 H5
Lake Angelus 42 H12
Lake Aniwhenua 14 J9
Lake Annie 70 C8
Lake Aorere 37 G4
Lake Arapuni 12 G10
Lake Aratiatia 19 C6
Lake Areare 9 H5 11 A6
Lake Atiamuri 12 J13 13 J2 19 A5
Lake Aviemore 67 C6
Lake Barfoot 37 H4
Lake Barra 58 E11
Lake Beattie 69 E4
Lake Beddoes 63 G5
Lake Benmore 67 A5
Lake Bernard, NI 29 B5
Lake Bernard, SI 63 G6
Lake Bloxham 70 A9
Lake Brown 64 E8
Lake Browne 69 D6
Lake Browning 51 B6
Lake Brownlee 63 G7
Lake Brunner 45 G6
Lake Brunton 78 H9
Lake Cadman 69 J4 75 C4
Lake Camp 50 J13 51 J4 60 A13 61 A3
Lake Carrick 69 J4 75 C4
Lake Catherine 52 E8 55 A1
Lake Chalice 43 D5
Lake Chalice Track 43 D4
Lake Christabel 46 E12
Lake Christabel Hut 46 E12
Lake Christabel Track 46 E12
Lake Clark 63 J5
Lake Clarke 57 G6
Lake Clearwater 50 J13 51 J4
Lake Cobb 37 G5
Lake Coleridge 51 F7
Lake Coleridge (locality) 52 G8
Lake Constance 47 A4
Lake Daniell 46 D13
Lake Dispute 64 H13 65 H3
Lake Dive Hut 23 E5
Lake Dive Track 23 E5
Lake Douglas 58 E9
Lake Dudding 29 A5
Lake Duncan 70 B8
Lake Dunstan 66 H9
Lake Ella 47 A3
Lake Ellery 57 F6
Lake Ellesmere / Te Waihora 56 G8
Lake Elmer 37 G4
Lake Elterwater 44 F12
Lake Emily 50 J14 51 J5
Lake Emma 50 J13 51 J4 60 A13 61 A3
Lake Erskine 64 F9
Lake Eyles 70 B9
Lake Fergus 64 F10
Lake Ferry 33 G4
Lake Forsyth 56 G10
Lake Fraser 69 J2 75 C2
Lake Gault 49 H4
Lake George 76 H13 77 E1
Lake Gow 72 D9
Lake Grasmere 52 C10
Lake Grassmere 44 E12
Lake Grassmere (locality) 44 E12
Lake Grave 63 F6
Lake Greaney 57 F7
Lake Gunn 64 F10
Lake Guyon 47 D4
Lake Guyon Hut 47 C4
Lake Hakanoa 9 G5
Lake Hakapoua 75 F6
Lake Half 1 E4
Lake Hall 70 B8
Lake Hankinson 63 J6
Lake Hankinson Hut 63 J6
Lake Hanlon 41 C7
Lake Harihari 11 G2
Lake Haupiri 46 G8
Lake Hauroko -
  New Zealand's deepest lake 76 D8
Lake Hawdon 52 D10 53 D1
Lake Hawea 66 A9
Lake Hawea (locality) 66 C9
Lake Hay 69 H6 75 B6
Lake Hayes 65 G5
Lake Head Hut 42 H13 43 G1
Lake Head Track 42 H13 43 G1
Lake Heaton 29 B5
Lake Hector 75 E2
Lake Herbert 29 B5
Lake Herengawe 25 G5
Lake Heron 50 H14 51 H5
Lake Herries 70 C9
Lake Hilda 70 B9
Lake Hochstetter 45 E7
Lake Hope 65 J6
Lake Horizon 69 G7 75 A7
Lake Horowhenua 29 G5
Lake Howden Hut 64 F10
Lake Humuhumu 5 D5
Lake Ianthe 50 C9
Lake Iceberg 64 F8

Lake Innes 75 F6
Lake Jasper 44 E11
Lake Jeanette 42 D9
Lake Jewell 37 H4
Lake Kaiiwi 3 H5
Lake Kaikokopu 29 E5
Lake Kakapo 69 J6 75 D6
Lake Kaniere 50 A13 51 A4
Lake Kaniere Walk 50 A13 51 A4
Lake Kanono 5 E5
Lake Karaka 5 D4
Lake Karapiro 12 E9
Lake Kaurapataka 46 J8
Lake Kereta 5 G6
Lake Kimihia 9 G5
Lake Kini 49 J1 58 A13 59 A2
Lake Kiwi 75 F5
Lake Koitiata 29 B4
Lake Koputara 29 E5
Lake Kuratau 18 F14 19 F2
Lake Kuwakatai 5 G6
Lake Leeb 57 G6
Lake Letitia 52 C11 53 C2
Lake Lockett 37 G6
Lake Lois 70 E8
Lake Luna 64 G13 65 G3
Lake Lyndon 52 F9 55 B2
Lake Macarthur 69 J3 75 D3
Lake Mackinnon 63 J4 70 A8
Lake Mahinapua 45 J1 50 A11 51 A2
Lake Mahinerangi 73 G7 79 A5
Lake Man 46 F12
Lake Mangakaware 11 D6
Lake Mangawhio 24 H11 25 E6
Lake Manuwai 2 K11 3 A7
Lake Mapourika 49 F6
Lake Maraetai 12 J11 19 A3
Lake Marahau 25 H6
Lake Maratoto 11 D7
Lake Marchant 63 J4
Lake Marian 64 E10
Lake Marina 42 C8
Lake Marion 46 H12
Lake Marymere 52 D10 53 D1
Lake Mason 46 J12
Lake Matahina 14 G9
Lake Matheson 49 H4
Lake Matiri 42 F9
Lake Matiri Hut 42 F9
Lake Maungarataiti 26 H12
Lake Maungaratanui 26 H12
Lake McIvor 63 J5
Lake McKellar 64 F10
Lake McKerrow 64 B9
Lake McRae 48 B9
Lake Middleton 59 H4
Lake Mike 69 J5 75 C5
Lake Minchin 46 J9 52 A10 53 A1
Lake Moananui 12 H11
Lake Moawhango 26 C14 27 C2
Lake Moeraki 58 B11
Lake Moeraki (locality) 58 B10
Lake Mokeno 5 E4
Lake Monk 75 E6
Lake Monowai 70 J9 76 C9
Lake Morehurehu 1 D4
Lake Moreton 63 E7
Lake Morgan 46 H8
Lake Mouat 75 E6
Lake Moumahaki 24 J10 25 F5
Lake Mudgie 45 H4
Lake Mueller 49 H4
Lake Namunamu 26 H12
Lake Never-never 64 C8
Lake Ngaroto 11 E7
Lake Ngaruru 26 H11
Lake Ngatu 1 H5
Lake Nigel 71 B6
Lake Nisson 57 F7
Lake Norwest 70 D8
Lake Ohakuri 19 A6
Lake Ohau 59 H4
Lake Ohau Alpine Village 59 H4
Lake Ohia (locality) 1 H7
Lake Okareka 13 G5
Lake Okareka (locality) 13 G5
Lake Okataina 13 G5
Lake Okoia 25 G5
Lake Omapere 3 B7
Lake Omapere (locality) 3 B7
Lake Onoke 33 G4
Lake Onslow 73 D4
Lake Orbell 70 B11
Lake Otamangakau 18 G13 19 G1
Lake Otamatearoa 7 J3 9 D1
Lake Ototoa 5 F6
Lake Otuhie 37 C5
Lake Oturi 25 G4
Lake Owhareiti 4 C8
Lake Papaitonga 29 G4
Lake Paradise 69 D4
Lake Parangi 11 E2
Lake Paringa 58 B11
Lake Paringa (locality) 58 B12 59 B1
Lake Pearson 52 D10

Lake Perrine 42 D8
Lake Phyllis 42 C8
Lake Poerua 45 H6
Lake Pokorua 7 H3
Lake Poteriteri 75 E7
Lake Poteriteri Hut 75 F7
Lake Pouarua 20 G8
Lake Poukawa 28 G10
Lake Pounu 33 F4
Lake Pukak 59 F7
Lake Pupuke 6 J10 7 D4
Lake Purser 69 J4 75 C4
Lake Quill 63 F7
Lake Rahui 41 G5
Lake Rakatu 70 F10
Lake Rasselas 58 B11
Lake Ratapiko 17 J2 23 C7 25 A2
Lake Reporoaere 22 D9
Lake Rerewhakaaitu 13 J6
Lake Roe Hut 69 G7 75 A7
Lake Ronald 63 D7
Lake Ross 64 G9
Lake Rotoaira 18 H14 19 H2
Lake Rotoehu 13 F7
Lake Rotoiti, NI 13 F6
Lake Rotoiti, SI 42 G13 43 F1
Lake Rotokakahi 13 H5
Lake Rotokare 24 F8 25 C3
Lake Rotokauri 9 J5 11 B6
Lake Rotokauwau 26 J9
Lake Rotokawa 19 C6
Lake Rotokawau (Northland - Far North) 1 F6
Lake Rotokawau (Northland) 5 E5
Lake Rotokino 50 B8
Lake Rotoma 13 F7
Lake Rotoma (locality) 13 F7
Lake Rotomahana 13 H6
Lake Rotongaro 9 F4
Lake Rotonuiaha 20 G14 21 G2
Lake Rotopounamu 19 H2
Lake Rotorangi 24 G9 25 D4
Lake Rotoroa, NI (Northland) 1 H5
Lake Rotoroa, NI (Waikato) 11 C7
Lake Rotoroa, SI 42 H12
Lake Rotorua, NI 13 F4
Lake Rotorua, SI 48 E11
Lake Rototuna 5 D4
Lake Roxburgh (Central Otago) 72 C13 73 C2
Lake Roxburgh (locality) 72 D13 73 D2
Lake Roxburgh (Southland) 63 H7
Lake Ruapapa 21 G3
Lake Ruataniwha 59 H6
Lake Sarah 52 C10
Lake Scott 72 D10
Lake Selfe 51 E7
Lake Serpentine 11 E7
Lake Sheila 80 D3
Lake Sheppard 46 J12
Lake Shirley 63 J3
Lake Stanley 37 F6
Lake Story 69 G7 75 A7
Lake Sumner 46 H12
Lake Sumner Conservation Park 46 F14 47 F2
Lake Sutherland 63 H6
Lake Swan 69 E4
Lake Sylvan 64 D11 65 D1
Lake Sylvester 37 G6
Lake Taeore 1 D4
Lake Taharoa (Northland) 3 H5
Lake Taharoa (Waikato) 11 G2
Lake Tarawera 13 H6
Lake Tauanui 3 D7
Lake Taupo / Taupomoana 19 E4
Lake Taylor 46 J12
Lake Te Anau 70 A11
Lake Te Au 70 B8
Lake Te Kahika 1 C4
Lake Tekapo 60 D10
Lake Tekapo (locality) 60 E9
Lake Tennyson 47 C4
Lake Thomas 75 E2
Lake Thompson (Southland) 63 H5
Lake Thompson (Tasman) 47 B4
Lake Tikitapu 13 H5
Lake Track 20 E13 21 E1
Lake Truth 64 C9
Lake Tuakitoto 79 E4
Lake Turner 64 D9
Lake Tutira 28 A12
Lake Unknown 64 D11 65 D1
Lake Victor 63 J4 75 D4
Lake Victoria 70 D9
Lake Vipan 29 A5
Lake Waahi 9 G4
Lake Wade 63 J5
Lake Wahakari 1 D3
Lake Wahapo 49 F6
Lake Waiau 25 G5
Lake Waihola 74 J8 79 B6
Lake Waikare (Taranaki) 24 J11 25 F6
Lake Waikare (Waikato) 9 F5
Lake Waikareiti 21 E3
Lake Waikareiti Track 21 D3
Lake Waikaremoana 20 E14 21 E2
Lake Waikere 3 G5

Lake Waimimiha 1 J5
Lake Waipapa 12 J10
Lake Waiparera 1 G5
Lake Waipori 74 J8 79 B6
Lake Waipu 29 A4
Lake Wairarapa 33 E5
Lake Waitaki 67 C7
Lake Waitaki (locality) 67 D7
Lake Waitawa 29 H4
Lake Wakatipu 64 H14 65 H4
Lake Wanaka 66 B8
Lake Wapiti 63 J5
Lake Whakamaru 19 A4
Lake Whakaneke 5 E4
Lake Whangape 9 F4
Lake Widgeon 69 J5 75 C5
Lake Williamson 64 A12 65 A2
Lake Wilmot 64 A10
Lake Wiritoa 26 J8
Lake Wisely 70 A9
Lakeside 55 G7 62 B13
Lakeside Track 42 H13 43 G1
Lame Duck Hut 59 B4
Langdale 34 B12
Langs Beach 6 A8
Lansdowne 53 J7 56 E9
Larrikin Creek Hut 42 D9
Larrys Creek 41 J5 46 A9
Lauder 66 H12 67 H1
Lauriston 55 G3 62 B9
Lawrence 73 H5 79 A3
Lawrence Hut 50 G11 51 G2
Lawyers Delight Hut 50 A13 51 A4
Le Bons Bay 56 G13
Le Crens Hut 59 E5
Leamington, NI 12 D8
Leamington, SI 48 J8
Lee Flat 73 G7
Lee Stream 74 G8
Lees Valley 52 D13 53 D4
Leeston 55 G7 62 B13
Leigh 6 D11
Leith Valley 74 G11 124 D2
Leithfield 54 E8 56 A10
Leithfield Beach 54 E8 56 A10
Leon Kinvig Hut 27 J5 30 A12 31 A6
Lepperton 17 H1 23 B6
Leslie - Karamea Track 37 J5 42 A10
Levels 61 H4
Levels Valley 61 H3
Levin 29 G5
Lewis Hut 37 F2
Lewis Pass Scenic Res 46 D13 47 D1
Liberton 124 D3
Lichfield 12 F11
Liebig Hut 60 A8
Limehills 77 A4
Limestone Downs 9 F1
Limestone Valley 60 G12 61 G1
Lincoln 89 C2
Lincoln University 53 J6 56 F8 62 A14
Lincoln, SI 53 J6 56 F8
Linden 33 D2 35 B2 110 B2
Lindenvale 110 B2
Lindis Crossing 66 F10
Lindis Hut 66 B11
Lindis Valley 66 D11
Linkwater 40 G9 44 A10
Lintley 71 G6
Linton 29 E7 31 E1
Linwood 54 H8 56 D10 120 F3
Lismore 61 D6
Little Akaloa 56 F12
Little Barrier Island 6 C13 36 D1
Little Barrier Island Nature Reserve
  6 C13 36 D1
Little Bay 8 B11 36 J5
Little Huia 7 F2 89 E1
Little Island 75 D3
Little Manly 88 C5
Little Rakaia 55 H6 62 C12
Little River 56 G11
Little Valley 72 B14 73 B3
Little Waihi 13 C6
Little Wanganui 41 B7
Littlebourne 123 D2
Liverpool Hut 64 A14 65 A4
Livingstone (Hamilton) 92 F2
Livingstone (Wanganui, NI) 26 J13 27 J1
Livingstone, SI 13 68 G8
Loburn 53 E7 56 A9
Loburn North 53 E7 56 A9
Loch Katrine 46 H12
Loch Loudon 73 H7 79 A5
Loch Luella 73 H7 79 A5
Loch Maree 69 G6 75 A6
Loch Maree Hut 69 G6 75 A6
Loch Norrie 6 H8 7 B2
Lochiel 77 C4
Lochindorb 78 D14 79 F2
Lochinvar Hut 52 B11 53 B2
Lochnagar 64 C14 65 C4
Locke Stream Hut 46 J9
Logantown 66 G10
Lonely Lake Hut 37 F6

Long Bay 6 H10 7 B4 88 E4
Long Beach 74 F12
Long Harry Hut 77 J1 80 C3
Long Island (Marlborough) 35 G2 40 F12
Long Island (Southland) 69 H3 75 B3
Long Range Lake 32 B12
Longbeach 62 F8
Longburn 29 E7 31 E1
Longbush, NI 34 D8
Longbush, SI 77 E6
Longford 42 G9
Longlands 28 F11 103 D6
Longridge 72 H8
Longridge North 71 G7
Longview Hut 27 J5
Longwood 76 H14 77 E2
Lorneville 77 E5
Lovells Flat 79 D4
Loveridge Hut 37 J6 42 A11
Lowburn 66 G9
Lowcliffe 61 F7
Lower Arahura Hut 51 A6
Lower Goulter Hut 43 D4
Lower Hutt 33 E3 35 A3 110 C3
Lower Kaimai 12 C13 13 C2
Lower Kawhatau 27 G3
Lower Matakuhia Hut 20 G10
Lower Moutere 38 H9 39 F1
Lower Nevis 72 A10
Lower Portobello 74 G12
Lower Princhester Hut 70 E13 71 E2
Lower Selwyn Huts 56 G8 62 B14
Lower Shotover 65 H5
Lower Tama Lake 19 J1 26 A13 27 A1
Lower Waihou 3 C3
Lower Waiohine Track 33 B7
Lower Wairaki Hut 70 H13 71 H2 76 B13
Lower Windley Hut 71 D4
Lowgarth 23 E6 25 B1
Lowry Bay 33 E3 35 A3 110 D3
Lowther 71 F6
Lucretia Hut 46 E13 47 E1
Luggate 66 D9
Lumsden 71 G6
Luna Hut 42 C9
Lupton Hut 26 B12
Luxmoore Hut 70 C10
Lyall Bay 33 F2 35 B4 110 E2
Lyalldale 68 A12
Lyell 41 G7
Lyell Hut 50 F12 51 F3
Lyell Walkway 41 G7
Lyndhurst 55 F2 62 A8
Lynfield 89 D3
Lynmore 13 G4 96 C5
Lynmouth 107 C2
Lynnford 61 E7
Lyttelton 54 J8 56 E10
Lyttelton Harbour/Whakaraupo 54 J9

M

Maata 23 F7 25 C2
Mabel Bush 77 D6
Macandrew Bay 74 H12 124 B3
Macetown 65 F5
Mackaytown 10 F10
Mackenzie Hut 46 H10
Mackford 17 D5
Mackintosh Hut 28 B8
Maclennan 78 F13 79 H1
Macraes Flat 74 B10
Maerewhenua 68 F9
Maeroa 91 C1 92 E2
Maewa 29 C7 31 C1
Magdalen Hut 46 F14 47 F2
Mahakirau 8 E12
Mahana 38 J10 39 G2
Mahanga 22 H9 22 AA2
Maharahara 30 C11 31 C5
Maharahara West 30 C10 31 C4
Maharakeke 32 A9
Maheno 68 J10
Mahia 22 J9 22 AA2
Mahia Beach 22 J9 22 AA2
Mahina Bay 110 D3
Mahinepua 2 H11
Mahitahi 58 A13 59 A2
Mahoe 23 E6
Mahoenui 17 B7
Mahora (Bay of Plenty) 16 E12
Mahora (Hastings) 103 C5
Mahurangi 6 F10
Mahurangi West 6 F10 7 A4
Mahuta (Northland) 5 A2
Mahuta (Waikato) 9 G4 11 A5
Maia 124 C3
Maihiihi 11 H7
Maimai 46 B8
Maioro 7 J4 9 D1
Maioro Sands 9 E1
Mairangi Bay 6 J10 7 C4
Mairehau 120 F1
Mairetahi 5 G7

Mairoa 11 J4
Mairtown 85 B2
Maitahi 3 H6
Maitai 115 C6
Maitai Dam 38 J13, 39 G5, 43 A6
Maitland 72 J11, 78 A10
Makahika 29 G6
Makahu 24 D10, 25 A5
Makahu Saddle Hut 28 B8
Makaka (Taranaki) 23 F5
Makaka (Waikato) 11 D2
Makakaho 24 G12, 25 D7
Makakaho Junction 24 H11, 25 E6
Makakoere Hut 21 B4
Makara 33 E1, 35 C3, 110 D1
Makara Beach 33 E1, 35 C3, 110 C1
Makaraka 22 D10, 100 A1
Makaranui 26 C11
Makarau 6 G8, 7 A2
Makareao 74 B12
Makaretu 27 J6, 30 A13, 31 A7
Makaretu Hut 27 J5, 30 A12, 31 A6
Makarewa 77 D5
Makarewa Junction 77 D5
Makaro / Ward Island 110 E3
Makarora 58 H10
Makarora Township 58 J10
Makarora Hut 58 G12, 59 G1
Makauri 22 D10
Makerua 29 F6
Maketawa Track 23 D5
Maketu 13 C6
Maketu Pa 11 F2
Makikihi 68 C13
Makino 30 B8, 31 B2
Makirikiri 30 C12, 31 C6
Makirikiri South 29 A5
Makohine Valley 26 G14, 27 G2
Makomako (Manawatu) 30 F9, 31 F3
Makomako (Waikato) 11 E3
Makomako Hut 21 C3
Makorori 22 D11
Makotuku 30 B13, 31 B7
Makuri 30 F11, 31 F5
Mamaku 12 F14, 13 F3
Mamaranui 3 H6
Mana 33 C2, 35 B1
Mana Island 33 C1, 35 C1
Manaia (Taranaki) 23 G5
Manaia (Waikato) 8 D11
Manakau 29 H4
Mananui 45 J1
Manaohau Right Branch Hut 20 A13
Manapouri 70 E10
Manaroa 35 J2, 40 F10
Manawahe 13 F7
Manawaora 4 B11
Manawaru 10 H10, 12 A11
Manawatawhi/Great Island (75 E3)
Manawatu River Estuary Wetland 29 F4
Mandeville 72 J9, 78 A8
Mandeville North 53 G7, 56 C9
Mangaehuehu Hut 26 B12
Mangaeturoa 26 C10
Mangahao 30 E9, 31 E3
Mangahao Flats Hut 29 H6
Mangahei 30 C13, 31 C7
Mangahouhou 18 G13, 19 G1
Mangaiti 10 G9
Mangakahika Hut 20 F11
Mangakahu Valley 18 D11
Mangakakakahi 96 C2
Mangakino 12 J11, 19 A3
Mangakino Track 10 G10
Mangakirikiri Hut 15 F6
Mangakura 6 F8
Mangakuri Beach 28 J12, 32 A13
Mangamahu 26 G11
Mangamaire 30 F9, 31 F3
Mangamako Hut 14 J9
Mangamate Hut 20 E11
Mangamaunu 48 D13
Mangamingi 24 F8, 25 C3
Mangamuka 2 K9, 3 A5
Mangamuka Bridge 3 A5
Mangamuka Gorge Walkway 2 K7, 3 A3
Mangamutu 30 E9, 31 E3
Manganui Skifield -
   Mt Taranaki / Mt Egmont 23 D5
Manganuku Hut 15 J3
Mangaohae 11 J3
Mangaokewa 18 A11
Mangaone Walkway 33 A5
Mangaonoho 26 H13, 31 H7
Mangaoranga 30 H9, 31 H3
Mangaorapa 32 D9
Mangaore 29 G6
Mangaorongo 11 G7
Mangaotaki 17 A7
Mangapa 2 J9, 3 A5
Mangapai 4 H11
Mangapakeha 34 B12
Mangapapa 100 A3
Mangaparo 18 F8
Mangapehi 18 B11

Mangapiko 11 E6
Mangapiko Valley 9 F6
Mangapouri Hut 20 C12
Mangarakau 37 B5
Mangarawa 30 D10, 31 D4
Mangarimu 27 J3
Mangaroa 33 D4
Mangaroa Valley 111 B6
Mangatainoka 30 E10, 31 E4
Mangatainoka Hot Springs -
   Tarawera 20 J8, 28 A8
Mangatainoka Hut 19 J7
Mangataiore 2 J8, 3 A4
Mangatangi 8 H8, 9 C5
Mangatangi Reservoir 8 G8, 9 B5
Mangatara 3 J7
Mangataraire 3 C6
Mangatarata 8 J10, 9 D7
Mangatawhiri 7 H7, 9 C4
Mangatea 11 J5
Mangateparu 10 H8, 12 A9
Mangatepopo Hut 18 J13, 19 J1
Mangatera 30 C12, 31 C6
Mangateretere 28 F12, 103 B4
Mangati 11 F5
Mangatiti 30 G12, 31 G6
Mangatoatoa Hut 21 C3
Mangatoetoe 2 J7
Mangatoetoe Hut 33 J5
Mangatoi 13 D4
Mangatoki 23 F6, 25 C1
Mangatoro 30 D13, 31 D7
Mangatu 3 F5
Mangatuna (Gisborne) 16 J11, 22 A13
Mangatuna (Manawatu) 30 D14, 32 D8
Mangatupoto 18 D10
Mangaturutu Hut 27 A7
Mangaturuturu Hut 26 B12
Mangatutara Hut 15 E7
Mangatutu 12 H8
Mangawara 9 G5
Mangaweka 27 G2
Mangawhai Cliffs Walkway 6 B9
Mangawhai Golf Course 6 B9
Mangawhai Heads 6 B9
Mangawhai Point 6 B9
Mangawhata 29 E6
Mangawhere 3 J7
Mangawhero (Northland) 3 D4
Mangawhero (Taranaki) 23 F5
Mangawhero (Waikato) 11 H6
Mangawhero Hut 20 A12
Mangawhio 24 J10, 25 F5
Mangere 7 F5, 9 A2, 90 E4
Mangere Bridge 90 D4
Mangere East 90 E5
Mangitaipa 3 A4
Mangles Valley 42 G9
Mangonui 2 H8
Mangonui Whaling Museum 2 G8
Mangorei 23 B5, 107 D5
Mangorei Track 23 C4
Mangungu 3 C5
Mangungu Mission House 3 C5
Maniatutu 13 D6
Manoeka 13 C5
Manor Park 33 D3, 35 A2, 111 B4
Manorburn Reservoir 73 B4
Mansion Hut 71 D6
Manson Hut 27 B7
Manson Nicholls Memorial Hut 46 D13
Mansons Siding 18 H11
Manui 27 G2
Manuka Creek 79 C4
Manuka Lake 51 H5
Manukau - Auckland 7 F5, 9 A2, 90 E5
Manukau - Northland 3 A2
Manukau Heights 90 E6
Manunui 18 F11
Manuoha Track 20 D14, 21 D2
Manurewa 7 F5, 9 A2
Manurewa East 90 E6
Manutahi 23 H7, 25 E2
Manutuke 22 E9
Many Islands 69 H2, 75 B2
Maori Hill (Dunedin) 123 B2, 124 D3
Maori Hill (Timaru) 121 D2
Maori Lakes 50 J14, 51 J5
Maori Rocks 36 A2
Maoribank 111 A6
Mapau 5 B4
Mapiu 18 C10
Mapua 38 J10, 39 G2
Mara 30 H13, 31 H7
Maraehara 16 D12
Maraekakaho 28 F10
Maraenui 103 B2
Maraeroa (Northland) 3 B5
Maraeroa (Waikato) 18 B13
Maraetaha 22 F9
Maraetai (Auckland) 7 E7
Maraetai (Waikato) 12 J10
Marahau 38 F10, 39 D2
Marakerake 68 H10
Maramarua 8 J8, 9 D5

Mararewa 42 C13, 43 B1
Maratoto 8 J13, 10 E10
Marauiti Hut 20 E13, 21 E1
Marawiti 55 F3, 62 A9
Marco 17 H6, 24 B11
Mareretu 5 A6
Marewa 28 D12, 103 B2
Marima 30 F8, 31 F2
Mariri 38 H10, 39 F2
Market Cross 37 J2, 41 A7
Marlborough 88 H3
Marlborough Forest 3 F6
Marlow 4 E10
Marohemo 5 B6
Marokopa 11 H2
Marokopa Falls 11 H3
Maromaku 4 D10
Maronan 55 J1, 61 D7
Maropea Forks Hut 27 G5
Maropiu 3 H6
Marsden 45 G4
Marsden Bay 4 H13
Marsden Point Oil Refinery 4 H13
Marshland 54 H6, 56 D10, 120 F5
Marshlands 35 J5, 40 J10, 44 B11
Martha Gold & Silver Mine - Waihi 10 E11
Martinborough 34 E7
Marton 29 A6
Marton Block 27 J4
Marua 4 E12
Maruakoa 68 G10
Maruia 46 B12
Maruia Springs 46 E13, 47 E1
Maruia Springs Thermal Resort 46 E13, 47 E1
Marumaru 21 G5
Mary Island 76 D9
Marybank, NI 26 J8
Marybank, SI 38 J12, 39 G4
Maryhill 15 E7
Masham 120 B3
Mason Bay Hut 80 E3
Masons Flat 53 A7
Massey 7 D3, 89 B2
Massey East 89 B2
Massey North 89 B2
Massey West 89 B2
Masterton 34 B9
Mata (Northland - Far North) 3 B4
Mata (Northland) 3 D4
Matahanea 14 G13, 15 G2
Matahapa 14 G12, 15 G1
Matahi 14 J11
Matahina 14 G9
Matahiwi (Wanganui) 24 H14, 26 E9
Matahiwi (Wellington) 34 A8
Matahuru 9 F6
Matai, NI 12 C11
Matai, SI 45 D6
Mataikona 30 J13, 31 J7
Matakana 6 E10
Matakana Island 10 H13, 12 A14, 13 A3, 94 A2
Matakanui 66 G11
Matakatia Bay 88 C5
Matakawau 7 G3
Matakitaki 42 J9
Matakohe 5 B5
Matamata 12 C11
Matamata Aerodrome 10 J10, 12 B11
Matamau 30 B12, 31 B6
Matangi 12 C8
Matangirau 2 H11
Matapihi 13 B4, 94 C3
Matapouri 4 E13
Matapu 23 F6, 25 C1
Matarae 74 E8
Matarangi 8 C12
Matarau 4 F11
Mataraua 5 H6
Mataraua Forest 3 E5
Matarawa 34 C7
Matariki 42 C12
Mataroa 26 F14, 27 F2
Matata 14 D9
Matatoki 8 H12, 10 C9
Matau, NI 17 J4, 24 C9
Matau, SI 79 F4
Mataura 78 C9
Mataura Island 78 E8
Matauri Bay 2 H12
Matawai 21 A6
Matawaia 4 D8
Matawhera 3 C4
Matawhero 22 D10
Matemateaonga 24 F9, 25 C4
Matemateaonga Track 24 E12, 25 B7
Matiere 18 E9
Matihetihe 3 C2
Matingarahi 8 F9, 9 A6
Matipo Heights 96 D2
Matira 9 G2, 11 A3
Matua 94 B1
Maud Island 35 K1, 40 E9
Maude Track 23 C5
Mauao/Mt Maunganui 94 A2

Mauku 7 H5, 9 C2
Maungahuka hut 33 A6
Maungakaramea 4 H10
Maungapohatu 20 C14, 21 C2
Maungapohatu Track 20 C14, 21 C2
Maungaraki 110 C3
Maungarau Hut 24 F12, 25 C7
Maungaroa 18 J9, 24 C14
Maungatapere 4 G10
Maungatapu 13 B4, 94 C3
Maungatautari 12 E9
Maungati 68 A11
Maungaturoto 5 B7
Maungatua 74 H8, 79 A6
Maungawera 66 C9
Maungawhio Lagoon 22 J9, 22 AA2
Maunu 4 G11
Maupuia 110 E2
Mauriceville 30 J8, 31 J2
Mauriceville West 30 J8, 31 J2
Mavora - Greenstone Track 64 G10
Mavora Walkway 64 J11, 65 J1
Mawaro 60 H13, 61 H2
Mawheraiti 46 C8
Maxwell 25 G6
Mayfair 103 C5
Mayfield 117 A3
Mayfield (Ashburton) 61 C6
Maymorn 33 D4, 111 A6
Mayor Island / Tuhua 10 E13
Maytown 68 D12
McConchies Hut 42 E9
McCoy Hut 50 G10, 51 G1
McKellar Hut 64 F10
McKerrow Island Hut 64 B9
McKerrow Track 33 F3, 35 A4
McKinnon Hut 27 G5
McLaren Falls - Tauranga 12 C13, 13 C2
McLaren Park 89 C2
McLean Falls (SI) 78 G12
McLeod Bay 4 H13
McNab 78 A9
Mead 55 F5, 62 A11
Meadowbank 90 C5
Meadowbank, SI 74 C12
Mechanics Bay 90 B4
Medbury 54 A8
Meeanee 28 E12, 103 B2
Meg Hut 65 F7
Mellons Bay 90 C6
Melrose 110 E2
Melville 91 J4, 92 G3
Menzies Ferry 78 D8
Mercer 7 J7, 9 D4
Mercury Islands / Iles d'Haussez 8 B13
Meremere (Taranaki) 24 G8, 25 D3
Meremere (Waikato) 7 J7, 9 E4
Meringa 18 F12
Merino Downs 72 J11
Merita 2 F7
Merivale 119 A1, 120 D3
Mermaid Pods - Matapouri 4 E13
Merrijigs 46 C9
Merrilands 107 C5
Merrivale 76 E13
Merton 74 E12
Methven 52 J9, 55 F2, 62 A8
Michies Crossing 74 F12
Mid Flat Hut 58 F13, 59 F2
Mid Glenroy Hut 46 B13, 47 B1
Mid Goulter Hut 43 D4
Mid Greenstone Hut 64 G11, 65 G1
Mid Okahu Hut 20 D12
Mid Pohangina Hut 30 A11, 31 A5
Mid Robinson Hut 46 F11
Mid Styx Hut 50 A14, 51 A5
Mid Taipo Hut 51 A7
Mid Trent Hut 46 H9
Mid Waiohine Hut 33 A7
Mid Wairoa Hut 43 D4
Middle Head Hut 58 C12, 59 C1
Middle Hill Hut 28 A8
Middle Hut 68 H8
Middle Stream Hut 27 H6
Middle Valley 60 F13, 61 F2
Middlemarch 74 D8
Middlemore 90 D5
Middleton 120 D2
Middy Creek Hut 39 J5, 43 B6
Midhirst 23 D6, 25 A1
Midway Hut 20 B12
Mihi 19 B7
Mihiwaka 74 G12
Mikimiki 34 A9
Miko 41 D5
Mikonui Flat Hut 50 C11, 51 C2
Mikotahi 107 B2
Milburn 79 C5
Milford Huts 61 H5
Milford Sound (Piopiotahi) 63 C7
Milford Sound (locality) 64 D8
Milford Track - Great Walk 64 E8
Milford, NI 6 J10, 7 C4
Milford, SI 61 G5
Mill Creek 8 E12

Mill Road 77 E5
Millers Flat 72 F14, 73 F3
Millerton 41 E5
Milltown (Selwyn) 55 H7, 62 C13
Milltown (Westland) 45 J4, 50 A14, 51 A5
Milnthorpe 37 C7
Milson 30 D8, 31 D2, 105 A4
Milton 79 C5
Mimihau 78 D9
Mina 48 J8
Minaret Bay 66 A8
Minchin Bivvy 46 J9
Minden 10 J12, 12 B13, 13 B2
Minehaha 42 H8
Mingha Bivvy 52 B8
Minginui 20 D11
Mintaro Hut 63 F7
Miramar 33 F2, 35 B4, 110 E2
Miranda 8 H9, 9 C6
Miranda Hot Springs 8 H9, 9 C6
Mirror Lakes 63 F8
Mission Bay 7 D5, 90 C5
Mission Bush 7 H4, 9 C1
Mistake Flats Hut 50 H10, 51 H1
Mitcham 55 G3, 62 B9
Mitchells 45 H5
Mitchells Hut 68 J8
Mitchelltown 110 E1
Mitikarukaru 40 C8
Mitimiti 3 C2
Mititai 5 A3
Mitre Flats Hut 29 J6, 34 A7
Moa Creek 66 J12, 67 J1, 73 A4
Moa Flat 72 F13, 73 F2
Moa Park Hut 38 F9, 39 D1
Moana (Nelson) 116 B4
Moana (Westland) 45 G6
Moana Roa Beach 29 C5
Moawhango 27 E3
Moeatoa 11 J2
Moeawatea 24 G10, 25 D5
Moehau 3 D5
Moengawahine 4 F9
Moenui 40 G8, 44 A9
Moera 110 C3
Moeraki 74 B14
Moeraki Boulders 74 B13
Moerangi (Waikato) 11 E4
Moerangi (Wanganui) 18 F13, 19 F1
Moerangi Hut 20 E11
Moerewa 4 C9
Moeroa 24 F10, 25 C5
Moewhare 4 H11
Mohaka 21 J3
Mohuiti 3 B4
Moirs Hill Walkway 6 F9
Mokai 19 B4
Mokaikai Scenic Reserve 1 B3
Mokau (Northland) 2 J11
Mokau (Waikato) 17 D5
Mokau Tarns Track 20 E14, 21 E2
Mokauiti 18 C9
Moke Lake 64 H14, 65 H4
Mokihinui 41 D6
Mokihinui Forks Ecological Area 42 E8
Mokihinui Forks Hut 42 D8
Mokohinau Islands (Flax Islands)
   Nature Reserve 36 A2
Mokohinau Islands / Flax Islands 36 A2
Mokoia 23 H7, 25 E2
Mokoia Island 13 F4
Mokoreta 78 E10
Mokotua 77 F7
Mole Hut 42 J11
Mole Track 42 J11
Molesworth Recreation Reserve 48 B8
Momona 74 H9, 79 A7
Monaco 116 C3
Monavale, NI 12 D8
Monavale, SI 60 H12, 61 H1
Moncks Bay 120 H1
Moncks Spur 120 H1
Moneymore 79 D5
Monowai 70 H11, 76 B11
Monowai Hut 70 H9, 76 B9
Montalto 61 B5
Montgomerie Hut 46 B10
Monument Hut 59 E4
Moonbeam Hut 50 D11, 51 D2
Moonlight 74 C10
Moonlight Hut 66 B10
Moonstone Lake 42 B10
Morere 22 H8
Morere Hot Springs 22 H8
Morgan Hut 42 J12
Morningside (Auckland) 89 C3
Morningside (Whangarei) 84 D5
Mornington 110 E1
Mornington (Dunedin) 74 H11, 124 E4
Morrinsville 10 H8, 12 A9
Morrisons 74 A11
Morrisons Bush 33 D7
Morton Mains 77 D7
Morven 68 E13
Mosgiel 74 H10, 124 J4

Mossburn 71 F4
Mosston 109 B2
Motairehe 36 C4
Motakotako 11 D3
Motatau 4 D9
Motea 30 D13 31 D7
Moteo 28 D11 103 D2
Motiti Island 13 A6
Motu 15 J4
Motu Rimu 77 F5
Motuanauri Island 39 E7
Motuara Island 35 G1 40 E12
Motuariki Island 60 D10
Motuarohia Island 4 A10
Motueka 38 G10 39 E2
Motueka Aerodrome 38 G9 39 E1
Motuhaku Island 13 A7
Motuhaku Island / Schooner Rocks 13 A7
Motuhina Island 16 J11
Motuihe Island 7 D6 90 B6
Motukahaua Island 8 B10 36 J4
Motukaika 60 J14 61 J3
Motukaraka 3 C4
Motukaramarama Island 8 C10 36 J4
Motukarara 56 G9
Motukauri 3 C3
Motukawaiti Island 2 H12
Motukawanui Island 2 H12
Motukawao Group 8 C10 36 J4
Motuketekete Island 6 F11
Motukiekie Island 4 A11
Motukiore 3 C5
Motumakareta Island 8 B10 36 J4
Motumaoho 10 J7 12 B8
Motunau Beach 54 C11
Motunau Island / Plate Island, NI 13 B7
Motunau Island, SI 54 C11
Motunui 17 G2 23 A7
Motuoapa 19 G3
Motuora Island 6 F11 7 A5
Motuoroi Island 16 J11
Motuoruhi Island 8 C10
Motupapa Island 2 K13 4 A9
Motupiko 42 C13 43 B1
Motupipi 38 E8
Moturau Hut 70 D10
Moturekareka Island 6 F11
Moturoa 107 B2
Moturoa Island (Northland - Far North) 1 E7
Moturoa Islands 1 E7
Moturua Island (Northland) 4 A10
Moturua Island (Waikato) 8 C10
Motutaiko Island (Auckland) 36 D3
Motutaiko Island (Taupo) 19 F4
Motutangi 1 F5
Motutangi Swamp 1 F5
Motutapere Island 8 D10
Motutapu Island 6 J12 7 C6 90 A6
Motutapu Island Recreation Reserve 6 J12 7 C6
Motutere 19 F4
Motuti 3 C3
Motutoa 3 D3
Motuwi Island 8 B10 36 J4
Mou Tapu 65 C7
Mou Waho 65 B7
Moumahaki 25 G5
Moumoukai 8 G8 9 B5
Mount Albert 7 E4
Mount Albert 89 C3
Mount Allan 74 F10
Mount Arthur Hut 37 H7 42 A12
Mount Aspiring National Park 57 H7
Mount Auckland Walkway 6 F8
Mount Barker 66 D8
Mount Bee Huts 71 D5
Mount Biggs 29 C7
Mount Brown Hut 50 A14 51 A5
Mount Bruce 29 J7 31 J1
Mount Bruce National Wildlife Centre
  - Eketahuna 30 H8 31 H2
Mount Cargill 74 G12 124 B1
Mount Cheeseman Skifield 52 D9
Mount Cook Village (The Hermitage) 59 B6
Mount Cook (Wellington) 110 E2 112 E5
Mount Cook / Aoraki, SI 59 B6
Mount Cook / Aoraki National Park 49 J6 59 A7
Mount Curl 26 J12
Mount Eden 7 E4 90 C4
Mount Eggeling 57 G4
Mount Herbert Walkway 56 F10
Mount Holdsworth Track 34 A7
Mount Hut 68 J9
Mount Hutt 52 H8 55 D1
Mount Hutt Methven Airfield 52 J8
Mount Hutt Skifield 52 H8
Mount Lyford Skifield 48 F8
Mount Marua 111 A6
Mount Matthews Track 33 F3
Mount Maunganui 13 A4 94 B3
Mount Misery Hut 42 J12
Mount Nessing 60 H12 61 H1
Mount Olympus 37 E5
Mount Olympus Skifield 52 E8 55 A1
Mount Owen 42 D11
Mount Parahaki 4 G12

Mount Pickering 70 C9
Mount Pisa 66 F9
Mount Pleasant 54 J8 56 E10 120 G1
Mount Pleasant (Marlborough) 35 J4
  40 H10 44 A11
Mount Pleasant (mountain) 54 J8 56 E10
Mount Potts 50 J12 51 J3
Mount Richards 30 B10 31 B4
Mount Richmond Conservation Park 39 F7
  40 H8 43 B7 44 A9
Mount Robert Skifield 42 H13 43 G1
Mount Roskill 7 E4
Mount Roskill 89 C3
Mount Somers 61 A6
Mount Stoker 74 E9
Mount Stuart 79 C4
Mount Tinsley 70 C10
Mount Victoria 33 F1 35 C4 110 E2 112 E6
Mount Wellington 7 E5 90 D5
Mount Wesley 3 J7
Mount William Walkway 7 H7 9 C4
Mountain House Hut 33 A7
Mourea 13 F5
Mouse Point 47 H5
Moutahiauru Island 16 G12
Moutoa 29 F6
Moutohora 15 J4
Moutohora Island 14 D10
Moutoki Island 14 D10
Mud Spa - Rotorua 13 F5
Mudflats Hut 51 A6
Mueller Hut 59 B6
Muhunoa 29 H4
Muhunoa East 29 H5
Mukahanga 40 B9
Mullins Hut 50 C13 51 C4
Mungo Hut 50 C14 51 C5
Mungoven Gardens - Marton 29 A6
Murchison 42 G9
Murchison Hut 49 H7
Muri 33 C2
Muritai 110 E3
Muriwai 22 E9
Muriwai Beach 7 D1
Murray Aynsley 120 F2
Murray Bay 88 F4
Murupara 20 B11
Musselburgh 124 D4
Muttontown 66 J10 72 A13 73 A2
Myross Bush 77 E5
Mystery Creek 11 D7
Myttons Hut 37 H6

N

Naenae 33 E3 35 A3 111 C4
Naike 9 G3
Napenape 54 B13
Napier 28 D12 103 A1
Napier Central 101 B3
Napier South 101 D1 103 A1
Nardoo Hut 47 A2
Narrow Neck 90 B4
Naseby 67 G5
National Aquarium - Napier 28 D12
National Park 18 J11
Native Island 80 E6
Naumai 5 B3
Nawton 92 E2
Nawton North 92 E2
Neave Hut 50 E12 51 E3
Neavesville 8 H13 10 C10
Nee Islets 69 B4
Neill Forks Hut 33 B6
Neils Beach 57 E6
Nelson 38 J12 39 G4 115 C3 116 A5
Nelson Airport 38 J11 39 H3 43 A4
Nelson Creek 45 E6
Nelson East 115 D5 116 B5
Nelson Island 36 D3
Nelson Lakes National Park 47 A3
Nelson South 38 J12 39 G4 43 A5 116 B4
Nenthorn 74 C10
Ness Valley 8 F8 9 A5
Netherby, NI 9 H6 11 A7
Netherby, SI 55 H3 62 C9
Netherton 10 E9
Nevis Crossing 65 J7 72 A10
New Brighton 54 H8 56 D10 120 H4
New Creek 41 G6
New Lynn 7 E4 89 D3
New Plymouth 23 B5 106 B3
New Windsor 89 C3
New Windsor, SI 76 H14 77 E2
Newall 23 D3
Newbury 29 D7 31 D1
Newfield 128 A4
Newland 55 H3 62 C9
Newlands 110 C2
Newman 30 G8 31 G2
Newmarket 87 H6 90 C4
Newstead 11 C7 92 E6
Newton 87 G4 90 C4
Newton Creek Hut 51 A6

Newton Flat 42 G8
Newtown 33 F1 35 C4 110 E2
Nga Kiore / Jag Rocks 40 B10
Nga Manu Wildlife Sanctuary - Waikanae 33 A4
Nga Motu/Sugar Loaf Islands 23 B5
Ngaawapurua Hut 27 A7
Ngaere 23 E7 25 B2
Ngahape (Waikato) 11 G7
Ngahape (Wellington) 34 D11
Ngaheramai Hut 20 B13 21 B1
Ngahere 45 E6
Ngahinapouri 11 D6
Ngaio 33 E1 35 C3 110 D2
Ngaiotonga 4 B11
Ngaiotonga - Russell Forest Track 4 C11
Ngakawau 41 E5
Ngakonui 18 E11
Ngakuru 13 J3
Ngamatapouri 24 H11 25 E6
Ngamoko 30 A12 31 A6
Ngamoko Hut 30 A12 31 A6
Ngamoko Track 21 E3
Ngapaenga 11 J3
Ngapaeruru 30 C13 31 C7
Ngapara 66 F10
Ngapeke 13 B4 94 D3
Ngapipito 4 C8
Ngapuhi 3 D7
Ngapuke 18 F11
Ngapuna (Otago) 74 C8
Ngapuna (Rotorua) 96 C4
Ngaputahi 20 C12
Ngararatunua 4 F11
Ngarimu Bay 8 G11 10 B8
Ngaroma 12 J9
Ngaroto 11 E7
Ngarua 10 J9 12 B10
Ngaruawahia 9 H5 11 A6
Ngataki 1 E4
Ngatamahine 18 B9
Ngatapa 22 D8
Ngatea 8 J11 10 D8
Ngatimoti 33 H9 42 A14
Ngatira 12 F12 13 F1
Ngatiwhetu 1 D3
Ngaturi 30 F10 31 F4
Ngauranga 33 E2 35 B3 110 D2
Ngawaka 27 E2
Ngawapurua 30 E10 31 E4
Ngawaro 12 E14 13 E3
Ngawha 3 C7
Ngawha Springs - Kaikohe 3 C7
Ngawi 33 J5
Ngongotaha 13 F4
Ngongotaha Valley 12 G14 13 G3
Ngunguru 4 F13
Ngutunui 11 F5
Ngutuwera 25 G5
Niagara 78 G11
Niagara Falls 78 G11
Nichols Hut 29 J6 33 A7
Nightcaps 70 J14 71 J3 76 D14 77 A2
Nihoniho 18 E8
Nikau Caves - Waikaretu 9 G2
Nikau Flat Hut 21 A4
Nikau, NI 30 F9 31 F3
Nikau, SI 41 D6
Nina Hut 46 E13 47 E1
Nireaha 30 C8 31 G2
Noble Island 80 J2
Nobles 46 D8
Nokomai 72 J8
Nolans Hut 50 G8
Nonoti 48 J8 54 A12
Nopera 35 J2 40 F10
Norfolk 17 J1 23 C6
Normanby (Dunedin) 124 C2
Normanby, NI 23 G6 25 D1
Normandale 33 E2 35 B3 110 C3
Norsewood 30 A13 31 A7
Norsewood Pioneer Museum 30 A13 31 A7
North Arm Hut 80 E5
North Cape -
  Northernmost point of New Zealand 1 A4
North Clyde 21 H5
North Dunedin 123 B4 124 D3
North East Valley 74 G11 124 D3
North Egmont 23 D5
North Harbour 88 G3
North Harbour Stadium 6 J10 7 C4
North Island 80 D6
North Linwood 120 F3
North Mavora Lake 71 A4
North New Brighton 120 H4
North River 4 J12 5 A7
North Taieri 74 G10 124 J2
Northcote (Auckland) 7 D4 88 J4
Northcote (Christchurch) 120 D4
Northcote Central 90 B4
Northcote Point 90 B4
Northcross 88 F3
Northland 33 E1 35 C3 110 D1
Northope 77 C4
Northpark 90 D6

North-west Nelson Conservation Park 37 C5
Northwood 120 D5
Norton Reserve 68 D12
Norwest Lakes 70 D8
Norwood 52 J13 53 J4 55 F6 62 A12
Notown 45 E6
Nuhaka 22 J8
Nukuhau 19 D5 97 A1 98 A3
Nukuhou North 14 G12
Nukumaru 25 G6
Nukuroa 68 D13
Nukutaunga Island 2 G12
Nukutawhiti 3 F7
Nukuwaiata Island 40 C11
Nydia Track 40 F8

O

Oaklands 53 J7 56 E9 120 C1
Oakleigh 4 H11
Oaks Hut 33 F3 35 A4
Oakura (Northland) 4 C12
Oakura (Taranaki) 23 B4
Oamaru 68 H12 122 B4
Oamaru Hut 19 H7
Oaonui 23 E2
Oaro 48 F11
Oban / Halfmoon Bay 80 E5
Ocean Beach, NI (Hawke's Bay) 28 G13
Ocean Beach, NI (Northland) 4 H14
Ocean Beach, SI 77 G5 80 A6
Ocean Grove 74 H11 124 C5
Ocean Spa heated saltwater pools -
  Napier 28 D12
Ocean View 74 H10 124 H6
Oeo 23 G4
Ohaaki 19 B7
Ohaeawai 4 C8
Ohai 70 J13 71 J2 76 C13
Ohakea Wing RNZAF Museum - Bulls 29 C6
Ohakune 26 C11
Ohakuri 19 A5
Ohana 40 D8
Ohane Hut 20 A14 21 A2
Ohangai 23 H7 25 E2
Ohapi 61 G5
Ohapuku 54 G8 56 C10
Ohariu Valley 110 C2
Ohau 29 H5
Ohau Skifield 59 G4
Ohaua 20 C13 21 C1
Ohauiti 13 C4
Ohaupo 11 D7
Ohautira 9 J3 11 C4
Ohawe 23 H6 25 E1
Ohineakai 16 F11
Ohinemutu 13 G4 96 B3
Ohinepaka 21 H4
Ohinepanea 13 D7
Ohinetahi 54 J8 56 E10
Ohinewai 9 F5
Ohingaiti 26 H14 27 H2
Ohingaroa 103 C1
Ohiwa 14 F12 15 F1
Ohiwa Oyster Farm 14 F11
Ohoka 53 F7 56 B9
Ohope 14 E11
Ohora Hut 14 J11
Ohotu 27 F3
Ohui 8 G14 10 B11
Ohura 18 F8
Ohurakura 28 A11
Ohuri 3 C4
Oingo Lake 28 E11
Oio 18 H11
Okaeria 9 E6
Okahu (Northland - Far North) 1 J6
Okahu (Northland) 5 A4
Okahu Island 4 A11
Okahukura 18 E10
Okaiawa 23 G6 25 D1
Okaihau 3 B7
Okains Bay 56 F13
Okaka 3 B6
Okapu 11 E3
Okarae 30 C13 31 C7
Okaramio 40 J8 44 B9
Okari Lagoon 41 H2
Okarito 49 E5
Okarito Lagoon 49 E6
Okato 23 C3
Okau 17 F5
Okauia 12 C12
Okauia Pa 12 C12 13 C1
Oke Island 69 G5 75 A5
Okere Falls 13 F5
Okete 11 C4
Okiato 81 C2 4 B10
Okiore 14 H13 15 H2
Okitu 22 E11 100 C6
Okiwa Bay 39 E7
Okoia 26 H9
Okokewa Island 36 D3

Okoki 17 G3 24 A8
Okoroire 12 E11
Okui Hut 20 B12
Okuku 53 E6 56 A8
Okuku Reservoir 45 J4
Okupu 36 E4
Okura 88 D3
Okura, NI 6 H10 7 B4
Okuru, SI 58 D8
Okuti Valley 56 G11
Old Man Rock 76 H12
Old Powell Hut 33 A7
Olivine Hut 64 B10
Omaha 6 E10
Omaha Flats 6 E10
Omahu (Hawke's Bay) 28 E11
Omahu (Waikato) 8 J12 10 D9
Omahuta Forest 2 K9 3 A5
Omaio 15 D5
Omakau 66 H12 67 H1
Omakere 32 A12
Omamari 3 H6
Omana 4 J9
Omana Beach 7 E7
Omanaia 3 D4
Omanawa 12 C14 13 C3
Omanawa Falls 12 D14 13 D3
Omanu 13 B4 92 B3
Omanu Beach 13 B4
Omanuka Lagoon 29 D5
Omapere 3 E3
Omarama 67 A3
Omaru Hut 24 D11 25 A6
Omarumutu 14 F14 15 F3
Omata 23 B4 107 D1
Omatane 27 F4
Omaui 77 G4 80 A6
Omaui Island 77 G4 80 A6
Omaunu 2 J10
Omiha 7 D7
Omihi 54 C9
Omimi 74 F12
Omoana 24 F9 25 C4
Omokoroa 10 J12 12 B13 13 B2
Omokoroa Beach 10 H12 12 A13 13 A2
Omori 19 F2
Omoto 45 F4
Onaero 17 G2 23 A7
One Tree Hill 7 E5 90 C4
Onehunga 7 E4 90 D4
Onekaka 37 D7
Onekawa 103 B2
Onemana 8 H14 10 C11
Onepoto 21 F2
Onepu 14 F8
Onepu Hut 14 J11
Onerahi 4 G12
Oneriri 5 D7
Oneroa 6 J13 7 D7
Onetangi 7 D7
Onewhero 7 J5 9 E2
Ongaonga 28 J8
Ongarue 18 D10
Ongaruru 16 H11
Onoke 3 C3
Onslow Hut 60 A8
Onuku 56 H12
Opaea 27 E3
Opaheke 7 G6 9 B3
Opahi 4 D9
Opakau Island 36 D3
Opaki 34 A9
Opaku 24 J9 25 F4
Opal Hot Springs - Matamata 12 C12
Opape 15 F3
Opara 3 C4
Oparara 37 J2 41 A7
Oparau 11 F3
Oparure 11 J5
Opatu 18 G8 24 A13
Opawa 54 J8 56 E10 120 F2
Opawe Hut 30 B10 31 B4
Open Bay Islands 57 D7
Ophir 66 H12 67 H1
Ophi 60 G14 61 G3
Opiki 29 E6
Opio 71 J3
Opito 8 C13
Opoho 124 D3
Oponae 14 J13 15 J2
Opononi 3 D3
Oporo 77 D4
Opotiki 14 F13 15 F2
Opou 37 B7
Opouriao 14 G11
Opoutama 22 J8 22 AA1
Opouteke 3 F7
Opoutere 8 G14 10 B11
Opua 4 B10 81 C3
Opuatia 9 J3
Opuawhanga 4 D12
Opuha 60 G14 61 G3
Opunake 23 F3
Opuha 60 G14 61 G3
Opunake 23 F3
Opureke Track 20 G9
Oraka Beach 22 J9 22 AA2

Orakau – Pukawa

Orakau 12 F8
Orakei 90 C5
Orakei Korako 19 B6
Orakipaoa 61 H5
Oranga 90 D4
Orangapai 67 J5 74 A8
Orangimea 24 J11 25 F6
Orangipongo 26 H13 27 H1
Oranoa 3 F5
Oraora 3 E4
Orapiu 8 D8
Orari 61 F5
Orari Bridge 61 E5
Oratia 7 E3 89 D2
Orauta 4 C8
Orautoha 26 B10
Orawau 3 B4
Orawia 76 E12
Oreore 26 D10
Orepuki 76 G12
Orere 8 F8 9 A5
Orere Point 8 F8 9 A5
Oreti Beach 77 F4
Oreti Plains 77 B4
Orewa 6 G10 7 A4 88 A3
Oriental Bay 110 E2 112 E6
Orikaka Ecological Area 41 F6
Oringi 30 C11 31 C5
Orini 9 G6
Orinoco 38 J9 42 A14
Orira 3 B5
Ormond 22 C9
Ormondville 30 B13 31 B7
Orokonui 74 F12
Oromahoe 4 B8
Orongo 8 H11 10 C8
Orongo Bay 4 B10 81 B3
Orongorongo Track 33 F3 35 A4
Oronui Hut 16 E8
Oropi 13 D3
Orotere 2 J11
Oroua Downs 29 D5
Orton, NI 9 E4
Orton, SI 61 F6
Orua Bay 7 G3
Oruaiti 2 H9
Oruaiti Beach 16 B8
Oruaiwi 18 E12
Oruanui 19 C5
Oruatua 19 F4
Oruawharo 5 D7
Oruhia 120 F6
Oruru 2 H8
Osborne 74 F12
Ostend 7 D7
Ota Creek 78 D8
Otago Central Rail Trail 66 H13 67 H2 74 C8
Otaha 2 J12
Otahu Flat 70 J11 76 D11
Otahuhu 7 E5 90 D5
Otahuti 77 C3
Otaihanga 33 A3
Otaika 4 G11
Otaika Valley 4 G11
Otaio 68 B13
Otaio Gorge 68 B11
Otaitai Bush 77 E2
Otakairangi 4 F10
Otakeho 23 G4
Otaki 29 J4
Otaki Beach 29 J3
Otaki Forks 33 A5
Otakiri 14 E9
Otakou 74 G13
Otama, NI 8 C13
Otama, SI 72 J9
Otamakapua 26 H14 27 H2
Otamaroa 16 B8
Otamatea 26 H8 109 A3
Otamatuna Ridge Track 14 J12 15 J1 21 A3
Otamauri 28 D9
Otamita 78 A8
Otane (Bay of Plenty) 21 A2
Otane (Wairarapa) 28 J10
Otanetea Hut 20 B14 21 B2
Otangarei 85 A2
Otangaroa 2 J9
Otangiwai 18 D9
Otanomomo 79 F3
Otao 4 B9
Otapiri 77 A5
Otapiri Gorge 77 A5
Otapukawa Hut 21 A3
Otara, NI 14 F13 15 F2
Otara, NI - Auckland 7 F5 9 A2 90 D5
Otara, SI 78 H9
Otaraia 78 C10
Otaramarae 13 F5
Otarawhata Island 16 A9
Otatara 77 F4
Otatara – Invercargill 128 D5
Otaua (Northland) 3 D6
Otaua (Waikato) 7 J4 9 D1
Otautau 76 F14 77 C2
Otawhao 30 A13 31 A7

Oteake Conservation Park 67 E4
Otehake Hut 52 A9
Otehirinaki 15 D5
Otekaieke 68 E8
Otekura 79 G3
Otematata 67 C5
Otepopo 68 J10 74 A13
Oteramika 77 E7
Otewa 11 H7
Otiake 68 E8
Otikerama 78 B10
Otipua 61 J4 68 A13
Otira 45 J7 52 A8
Otiria 4 C9
Otokia 74 J9 79 B7
Otoko 21 B7
Otoko Lake 58 C14 59 C3
Otonga 4 E11
Otoroa 2 H11
Otorohanga 11 G6
Otuhaereroa Island 39 E7
Otuhi 4 H10
Otukota Hut 27 F5
Otukou 18 H13 19 H1
Otumatu Rock 48 F11
Otumoetai 10 J13 13 B3 93 A6 94 B2
Otunui 18 F9
Oturehua 66 G14 67 G3
Oturere Hut 18 J14 19 J2
Oturoa 13 F3
Oturu 1 J6
Otutu Hut 27 B6
Otuwhare 15 D5
Otway 10 G9
Oueroa 32 B11
Ouruhia 54 J8 56 C10
Outer Island 38 G10 39 E2
Outer Kaiti 100 C5
Outram 74 H9 79 A7
Overdale 55 G4 62 B10
Owahanga 30 H14 32 H8
Owairaka 89 C3
Owairaka Valley 12 F8
Owaka 79 G3
Owaka Valley 78 E14 79 G2
Oware 78 D9
Oweka 41 H5
Owen Island 80 G6
Owen Junction 42 F10
Owen River 42 F10
Owhango 18 G11
Owhata, NI (Bay of Plenty) 13 G4 96 C5
Owhata, NI (Northland) 3 B1
Owhata, SI 40 C8
Owhiro Bay 110 E1
Owhiro, NI 11 G3
Owhiro, SI 74 H10 124 J5
Owhiwa 4 G13
Oxford 52 F13 53 F4 55 B6

P

Pa Island / Te puke-ki-wiataha 56 F13
Pack Horse Hut 56 F10
Paekakariki 33 B3
Paemako 18 B8
Paenga 42 J8
Paengaroa 13 D6
Paepaerahi 12 F8
Paerata 7 H5 9 C2
Paerata Ridge 14 F13 15 F2
Paerau 73 C7
Paeroa 10 E9
Paetawa Track 20 B14 21 B2
Paewhenua 12 H8
Pahaoa 34 G9
Pahau 47 J5
Pahautane 45 A5
Pahautea 33 E6
Pahi 5 C6
Pahia 76 H12
Pahiatua 30 F10 31 F4
Pahoia 10 H12 12 A13 13 A2
Pahou 14 F10
Paiaka 4 D10
Paihia 4 B10 81 B2
Pakanae 3 D3
Pakaraka 4 C8
Pakatoa Island 8 D8
Pakawau 37 B7
Pakiaka Hut (Parahaki) 20 E12
Pakihi Heads Hut 15 H4
Pakihi Hut 15 H4
Pakihi Island 8 E8
Pakihikura 26 J14 27 J2
Pakipaki 28 F11 103 D6
Pakiri 6 D10
Pakotai 4 F8
Pakowhai 28 E12 103 B4
Pakuranga 7 E5 90 D5
Pakuranga Heights 90 D6
Pakuratahi 33 C5
Palm Beach 6 J13 7 D7

Palm Heights 89 C2
Palmerston 74 C13
Palmerston North 30 D8 31 D2
Palmerston North Central 104 B3
Palmerston North International Airport 105 A4
Pamapuria 1 J7
Panaki Island 2 G12
Pancake Rocks & Blowhole - Punakaiki 45 B5
Pandora 1 B2
Panekiri Hut 20 F14 21 F2
Panetapu 12 G8
Pangatotara 38 H9 39 F1
Panguru 3 C3
Panmure 7 E5
Papaaroha 8 C10
Papakai 18 H13 19 H1
Papakaio 68 G12
Papakowhai 110 A3
Papakura 7 G6 9 B3
Papamoa 13 B5 94 B5
Papamoa Beach 13 B5 94 C5
Papanui 53 H7 56 D9 120 D4
Papanui Junction 26 F12
Paparangi - Wellington 33 E2 35 B3
Paparangi (Taranaki) 24 J12 25 F7
Paparangi (Wellington) 110 C2
Paparata 7 H7 9 C4
Paparimu 7 H7 9 C4
Paparoa 5 B6
Paparoa National Park 45 A6
Paparore 1 G6
Papatawa 30 D10 31 D4
Papatea 15 B7
Papatoetoe 7 F5 9 A2 90 E5
Papatotara 76 F11
Papatowai 78 G13 79 J1
Papawai 34 D7
Papawera 16 E11
Paponga 3 B4
Papua 3 C4
Papueru 20 D12
Para 35 K4 40 H9 44 A10
Paradise 64 D12 65 D2
Paradise Valley Springs - Rotorua 12 G14 13 G3
Parahaka 4 J11
Parahaki 85 C3
Parahi 5 A5
Parakai 5 H7 7 B1
Parakai Hot Springs 5 H7 7 B1
Parakao 4 G8
Parakiwai 8 J14 10 D11
Paranui 2 H8
Paraoanui Pa 14 J11
Parapara, NI 2 H7
Parapara, SI 37 C7
Paraparaumu 33 A3
Paraparaumu Beach 33 A3
Pararaki Hut 33 H6
Parau 7 F3 89 E2
Parawa 71 E7
Parawai 8 H11 10 C8
Parawera 12 F8
Parekarangi 19 A7
Parekura Bay 4 B11
Paremata (East Cape) 22 B12
Paremata (Wellington) 33 D2 35 B2
Paremoremo 6 J9 7 C3 88 G1
Pareora 68 A13
Pareora West 61 J4 68 A13
Paretai 79 F4
Parewanui 29 C5
Parihaka Pa (Cape Egmont) 23 D3
Parikino 26 G9
Parinui 24 E13 26 B8
Pariokara 15 D6
Park Hill 72 G12 73 G1
Park Morpeth Hut 51 B6
Parkhurst 5 H7 7 B1
Parklands 54 H8 56 D10 120 G5
Parks Peak Hut 27 F6
Parkside 121 B5
Parkvale 103 C5
Parkville 30 H8 31 H2
Parkway 111 D4
Parnassus 48 H9
Parnell 90 C4
Paroa Bay 4 B10
Paroa, NI 14 E10
Paroa, SI 45 F3
Paroanui 2 H9
Parore 3 J7
Parrot Island 69 G2 75 A2
Parua Bay 4 G13
Paske Hut 47 B4
Passage Islands 75 E3
Patangata 28 J10
Pataua 6 G13
Patea 24 J8 25 F3
Patearoa 73 A7
Paterangi 11 E6
Patetonga 10 F7
Patoka 28 B10
Patons Rock 37 D7
Patuki 40 A10
Patumahoe 7 H5 9 C2

Paturau River 37 B5
Patutahi 22 D9
Paua 1 C3
Pauanui 8 G14 10 B11
Pauatahanui 33 D3 35 A2 111 A4
Pauri Village 26 J8
Pawarenga 3 B2
Pea Viner Corner 38 J11 39 H3 43 A6
Peaks, The 47 J3 53 A7
Pearl Island 80 H2
Peats Hut 65 F5
Peebles 68 F11
Peel Forest 61 D5
Peel Forest Walks 61 C4
Peep-o-Day 27 J3
Pegasus Bay Walkway 54 F8 56 B10
Pehiri 21 D7
Pekerau 1 H7
Peketa 48 E11
Pelorus Bridge 39 H6 43 A7
Pelorus Sound 40 F9
Pelorus Track 39 H5 43 A6
Pemberton 27 H3
Pembroke 23 E6 25 B1
Pendarves 55 H4 62 C10
Penn Creek Hut 33 A6
Penn Creek Track 33 A6
Penrose 90 D5
Pentland Hills 68 C10
Pepepe 9 H3 11 A4
Pepin Island 38 H13 39 F5
Peria (Northland) 2 J8
Peria (Waikato) 12 C10
Perry Saddle Hut 37 E4
Petone 33 E2 35 B3 110 C3
Petrel Island 69 H2 75 B2
Pfeifer Bivvy 46 J8
Phillipstown 120 F2
Phoebe 48 J8
Piarere 12 E10
Pickersgill Island 35 G2 40 F12
Picton 35 J3 40 G10 44 A11 113 C3
Picton Museum & Historical Society 35 J4 40 H10 44 A11
Pig Island (Queenstown) 64 G12 65 G2
Pig Island / Matau (Southland) 76 H14 77 E2
Pigeon Bay 56 F12
Pigeon Bush 33 D6
Pigeon Flat 74 G11 124 D1
Pigeon Island (Queenstown) 64 G12 65 G2
Pigeon Island (Southland) 69 G2 75 A2
Piha 7 E2
Pihama 23 G4
Pikes Point 68 E12
Pikiwahine 4 J10
Piko Piko 76 E12
Pikowai 14 D8
Pine Bush 78 F8
Pine Hill (Auckland) 88 F3
Pine Hill (Dunedin) 124 D2
Pine Valley 88 C1
Pinedale 12 F11
Pinehaven 33 D3 111 B5
Pines Beach, The 54 G8 56 C10
Pioneer Hut 49 J6
Piopio 18 A8
Piopiotahi Marine Res 64 D8
Pios Beach 10 F12
Pipiriki 24 G13 26 D8
Pipiroa 8 J11 10 D8
Pipitea 35 J5 40 J10 44 B11
Pipiwai 4 F9
Piriaka 18 F11
Pirimai 103 B2
Pirinoa 33 F5
Piripai 14 E10
Piripaua 21 F3
Piripiri (Manawatu) 30 B12 31 B6
Piripiri (Waikato) 11 H3
Piripiri Caves 11 H3
Pirongia 11 E6
Pirongia Forest Park 11 E4
Piropiro 18 C11
Pitokuku Island 36 E5
Plateau Hut 49 J6
Plateau, The 33 C4
Pleasant Heights 96 B1
Pleasant Point 61 H4
Pleasant Point Museum & Railway 61 H4
Pleasant Valley 61 F4
Pleckville 30 H9 31 H3
Plimmerton 33 C2 35 B1
Poet Hut 50 C13 51 C4
Pohangina 30 B9 31 B3
Pohara 38 D8
Pohatu Marine Reserve 56 H13
Pohatukura 16 E11
Pohokura (Hawke's Bay) 20 G9
Pohokura (Taranaki) 17 J5 24 C10
Pohonui 29 J2
Pohuehue 6 F9
Point Chevalier 89 C3
Point Elizabeth Walkway 45 E4
Point England 90 C5

Point Howard 110 D3
Point View Park 90 D6
Point Wells 6 D10
Pokaka 26 B11
Pokapu 4 C8
Pokeno 7 J6 9 D3
Pokere 4 D9
Pokororo 38 J8 42 A13
Pokuru 11 F6
Pollock 7 G3
Polluck Creek Hut 50 C11 51 C2
Polnoon Hut 65 D5
Pomahaka 72 J12 73 J1 78 A11
Pomarangai 11 J2
Pomare (Rotorua) 96 C2
Pomare (Wellington) 33 D3 35 A2 111 B4
Pomona Island 70 E9
Pompeys Pillar 56 H13
Ponatahi 34 D8
Ponga 7 G6 9 B3
Pongakawa 13 D6
Pongakawa Valley 13 D6
Pongaroa 30 G13 31 G7
Ponsonby 87 E1
Ponui Island 8 E8
Poolburn 66 J13 67 J2
Poolburn Reservoir 73 B5
Poor Pete's Hut 42 E9
Popotunoa 78 A13
Poraiti 28 D12
Porangahau 32 D10
Porati 103 C1
Porewa 29 A7
Pori 30 G10 31 G4
Porirua 33 D2 35 B2 110 B2
Porootarao 18 B11
Poroporo 14 E10
Poroti 4 G10
Poroutawhao 29 F5
Port Albert 5 D7
Port Chalmers 74 G12
Port Charles 8 A11 36 H5
Port Craig School 76 G9
Port Fitzroy 36 D4
Port Jackson 8 A10 36 G4
Port Levy 54 J9 56 F11
Port Molyneux 79 F4
Port Motueka 38 H10 39 F2
Port Nelson 38 J12 39 G4 116 A5
Port Ohope 14 F12
Port Puponga 37 A7
Port Robinson 54 A13
Port Robinson Walkway 54 A13
Port Waikato 9 E1
Port Whangarei 4 G12 85 D2
Port William Hut 80 D5
Portage 35 J2 40 F10
Porter Heights Skifield 52 F9 55 B2
Porters Creek Hut 43 D2
Portland 4 H12
Portland Island 22 AC1
Portobello 74 G12 124 A2
Possum Hut 74 F11
Potaka 16 A10
Pouakai Hut 23 D4
Poukawa 28 G10
Poukiore 26 H13 27 H1
Poukura Pa 19 F3
Poulson's Hut 66 D12
Poulter Bivvy 46 J8
Poulter Hut 52 A10
Pounawea 79 H3
Pourakino Valley 76 F13 77 C1
Pourangaki Hut 27 H5
Pourerere 32 B12
Pourewa Island 22 B13
Pouri Hut 24 E11 25 B6
Pouto Point 5 E5
Pouwhakaura 26 H14 27 H2
Prebbleton 53 J7 56 E9
Prebelton 120 A2
Price Basin Hut 50 D12 51 D3
Price Flat Hut 50 D12 51 D3
Price Flat Hut (Old Hut) 50 D12 51 D3
Prices Corner 38 J10 39 G2
Progress Junction 46 B9
Progress Valley 78 G11
Providence Rocks 75 E2
Puaha 56 G11
Puahue 12 F8
Puangiangi Island 40 B10
Puari 54 J9 56 F11
Puau 24 J11 25 F6
Puerua 79 F3
Puha 22 B9
Puhata 3 B2
Puhinui 90 E5
Puhipuhi 4 D11
Puhoi 6 G9 7 A3
Puhuka 61 J4
Pukahu 28 F11 103 C6
Pukaki Aerodrome 59 H7
Pukapuka 6 F10
Pukororo Rock 48 F11
Pukawa 19 F2

Pukearuhe – Seaview

Pukearuhe 17 F4
Pukeatua 12 F9
Pukeawa 79 D2
Pukehangi 96 C1
Pukehiki 74 H12 124 A4
Pukehina 13 C7
Pukehou 28 H10
Pukeinoi 11 F3
Pukekapia 9 G4
Pukekaroro 5 B7
Pukekawa 9 E3
Pukekohe 7 H5 9 C2
Pukekohe East 7 H6 9 C3
Pukekoma 79 C3
Pukekura Park 107 B4
Pukekura, NI 12 D8
Pukekura, SI 50 C10
Pukemaori 76 E12
Pukemiro (Northland) 3 B3
Pukemiro (Waikato) 9 H3 11 A4
Pukemoremore 12 C8
Pukemutu 77 A3
Pukengahu 24 E8 25 B3
Pukenui 1 F5
Pukeokahu 27 E4
Pukeoware 7 J4 9 D1
Pukepito 79 D3
Pukepoto 1 J6
Pukepuke Lagoon 29 D5
Pukerangi 74 E9
Pukeraro 68 F8
Pukerau 78 B10
Pukerimu 12 D8
Pukeroro 12 D8
Pukerua Bay 33 C2 35 B1
Puketaha 9 J6 11 B7 92 C5
Puketapu 28 D11 103 D1
Pukete 92 D2
Puketeraki 74 E12
Puketi Forest 2 K10 3 A6
Puketi, NI 3 A7
Puketi, SI 78 A14 79 C2
Puketiro 78 F13 79 H1
Puketitiri 28 B9
Puketoi 30 F12 31 F6
Puketona 4 B8
Puketotara 11 F6
Puketotara Hut 24 E13 26 B8
Puketui 8 G13 10 B10
Puketurua 12 F10
Puketurua Track 29 G7
Puketutu 18 A10
Puketutu Island 7 F4 9 A1
Pukeuri 68 G12
Pukio 33 E6
Punakaiki 45 B5
Punakitere 3 D6
Punakitere Valley 4 D8
Punaromia 13 H5
Punaruku 4 C12
Punawai 61 B7
Punehu 3 C3
Pungaere 2 K11 3 A7
Pungapunga 18 F11
Pungarehu (Taranaki) 23 D2
Pungarehu (Wanganui) 26 G9
Pungataua 27 E3
Puni 7 J5 9 D2
Puniho 23 C3
Puniho Track 23 D4
Puniwhakau 24 E9 25 B4
Puponga 37 A7
Pupu Springs Walking Track 37 E7
Pupuke 2 J10
Purakauiti 78 F14 79 H2
Purakanui (Dunedin) 74 F12
Purakanui Bay 74 F12
Purakaunui (Clutha) 78 F14 79 H2
Purakaunui Bay 79 H2
Purakaunui Falls 79 H2
Puramahoi 37 D7
Purangi (Taranaki) 17 J4 24 C9
Purangi (Waikato) 8 E13
Purau 54 J8 56 F10
Purekireki 78 D13 79 F1
Pureora 18 B13 19 B1
Pureora Forest Park 12 J9 18 A13 19 A1
Purerua 2 J13 4 A9
Purimu Lake 32 B9
Puriri 8 J12 10 D9
Purity Hut 27 H5
Purua 4 F10
Pururu 11 J7
Putangirua Pinnacles -
  Aorangi Forest Park 33 G5
Putara 29 H7 31 H1
Putaruru 12 F11
Puteore Hut 24 E11 25 B6
Putiki 26 J8
Putorino (Hawke's Bay) 20 J13 21 J1
Putorino (Wanganui) 26 J13
Puwera 4 H11
Pyes Pa 12 C14 13 C3
Pyke Big Bay Track 57 J2
Pyramid Valley 53 B7

Q

Quail Island 54 J8 56 E10
Quail Island Walkway 54 J8 56 E10
Quarry Hills 78 G10
Queen Charlotte Sound 35 J3 40 G10
Queen Charlotte Walking Track 35 H2 40 F11
Queens Flat 68 F10
Queensberry 66 F9
Queenstown 65 H4 125 B2 126 B2
Queenstown Airport 65 H5
Queenwood 92 D3
Quigleys Track 46 C9

R

Rabbit Island 38 J11 39 G3
Racecourse Hill 52 G12 53 G3 55 C5
Raekohua Falls - Tahora 17 G6 24 A11
Raes Junction 72 G14 73 G3
Raetea Forest 2 K7 3 A3
Raetihi 26 C10
Raglan 11 C3
Rahanui 11 D2
Rahiri 3 B6
Rahotu 23 E2
Rai Valley 39 G6
Rainbow Falls - Kerikeri 2 K12 4 A8
Rainbow Hut 43 J1 47 A5
Rainbow Isles 78 G13 79 J1
Rainbow Point 98 C4
Rainbow Springs 96 A2
Rainbow Springs & Farm - Rotorua 13 G4 96 A2
Rainbow Valley Skifield 42 H13 43 G1
Rainbow Warrior wreck - Cavalli Islands 2 G12
Rainbows End Adventure Park -
  Auckland 7 F5 9 A2
Raio 1 F5
Rakahouka 77 D6
Rakaia 55 G5 62 B11
Rakaia Gorge Walkway 52 H9 55 D2
Rakaia Huts 55 H6 62 C12
Rakaia Lagoon 55 H6 62 C12
Rakau 42 C13 43 B1
Rakaumanga 9 G4
Rakaunui (Manawatu) 30 G12 31 G6
Rakaunui (Waikato) 11 F3
Rakauroa 21 B6
Rakautao 3 D7
Rakautara 48 C13
Rakautatahi 30 A13 31 A7
Rakino Island 6 J12 7 C6
Rakitu Island 36 C5
Rakiura National Park 80 D3
Rakiura Track - Great Walk 80 D5
Ramanui 24 E13 26 B8
Ramarama 7 H6 9 C3
Rameka Track 38 E8
Ranana 24 H14 26 E9
Ranfurly 67 H5
Rangaiika 28 F14
Rangataua 26 C12
Rangatira Beach 5 G5
Rangatira Valley 61 G4
Ranger Bivvy 52 A10
Rangi Point 3 D3
Rangiahua (Hawke's Bay) 21 G4
Rangiahua (Northland) 3 B5
Rangiahua Island 36 D3
Rangiaowhia 11 E7
Rangiatea 11 H7
Rangihaeata 38 D8
Rangiora, NI 3 C4
Rangiora, SI 53 F7 56 B9
Rangiotu 29 E6
Rangipo 19 H3
Rangipo Hut 26 B13 27 B1
Rangipu 11 C3
Rangipukea Island 8 D10
Rangiputa 1 F6
Rangiriri 9 F4
Rangitaiki 20 F8
Rangitata 61 E5
Rangitata Island 61 F6
Rangitatau 25 G6
Rangitihi 1 J7
Rangitoto 11 J6
Rangitoto Island 6 J11 7 D5 90 A5
Rangitoto Island Scenic Reserve 6 J11 7 C5
Rangitoto Islands 40 B10
Rangitoto ki te Tonga / D'Urville Island 40 B8
Rangitukia 16 D13
Rangitumau 34 A9
Rangiuru 13 C5
Rangiwaea Island 10 H13 12 A14 13 A3
Rangiwaea Junction 26 D13
Rangiwahia 27 H3
Rangiwahia Hut 27 H4
Rangoon Heights 110 D2
Rankleburn 78 A12
Ranui 11 C4 89 C2
Ranui - Auckland 7 D3
Ranui - Wellington 110 B3
Rapahoe 45 E4

Rapaki 54 J8 56 E10
Rapanui 25 H7
Rapaura 35 K5 40 J9 44 B10
Rapid Creek Hut 50 C12 51 C3
Rapuwai 60 F14 61 F3
Rarangi 35 J5 40 J10 44 B11
Raroa 110 C2
Raroa Track 14 H11
Rarotoka Island / Centre Island 76 J13 77 F1
Raspberry Creek Hut 65 B5
Rata 26 J12 29 A7 31 A1
Rataiti 26 H12
Ratana 29 A4
Ratanui 79 H3
Ratapiko 17 J2 23 C7
Raukawa Falls 26 E10
Raukawa Rock 35 F3 40 G13
Raukokore 16 B8
Raukumara Forest Park 16 E8
Raumai 30 C9 31 C3
Raumanga 85 C1
Raumati 30 C12 31 C6
Raumati Beach 33 A3
Raumati South 33 B3
Raupo, NI 5 B3
Raupo, SI 45 D7
Raupunga 21 J2
Raureka 103 C5
Raurimu 18 J11
Ravensbourne 74 H12 124 C3
Rawene 3 C4
Rawhia 3 B5
Rawhiti 4 A11
Rawhitiroa 23 F7 25 C2
Raymonds Gap 76 E13 77 B1
Reardon Hut 59 C5
Red Beach 5 H10 7 B4
Red Hill 7 G6 9 B3
Red Hills Hut 43 E2
Red Hut 59 E4
Red Jacks 45 E6
Red Stag Hut 50 J8
Redan 78 E9
Redcliffs 54 J8 56 E10 120 H2
Redhill 5 A2
Redruth 61 J4 68 A13
Redvale 6 H10 7 B4 88 E2
Redwood Valley 38 J10 39 H2 43 A3
Redwood, NI 33 D2 35 B2 110 C2
Redwood, SI 53 H7 56 D9 120 E5
Redwoodtown 35 K6 44 C10
Reefton 46 B9
Reena 3 C3
Rees - Dart Track 64 B12 65 B2
Rees Valley 54 E12 65 E2
Regent 84 A4
Rehia 5 A4
Rehutai 3 J7 5 A2
Reidston 68 H11
Reikorangi 33 A4
Reischek Hut 50 F12 51 F3
Remarkables Skifield 65 H6
Remarkables, The 65 J5
Remuera 7 E5 90 C4
Renata Hut 33 B5
Renown 9 G4
Reotahi Bay 4 H13
Repia 5 B3
Reporoa 20 A8
Reporua 16 E12
Rere 21 C7
Rere Falls - Bay of Plenty 21 C7
Rerekapa Falls 17 G6 24 A11
Rerekapa Track 17 F5 24 A10
Rerewhakaaitu 13 J6
Reservoir, The 78 H10
Resolution Island 69 G3 75 A3
Retaruke 18 J9 24 C14
Retaruke Upper 18 J10
Rewa 26 J13 27 J1
Rewanui 45 E5
Rewarewa 1 H7
Rewiti 5 J7 7 C2
Riamaki (Upper Ruatiti) 18 J10 26 A10
Riccarton 53 H7 56 D9 120 D3
Riccarton Park 120 C3
Richard Pearse Airport - near Timaru 61 H4
Richardson Track 52 E13 53 E4 55 A6
Richmond (Christchurch) 120 F3
Richmond (Invercargill) 68 G12 127 A5 128 B3
Richmond (Tasman) 39 H3 43 A4 116 D3
Richmond Downs 12 C10
Richmond Heights 98 C5
Richmond Hill 120 H1
Richmond Hut 66 E12 67 E1
Right Branch Wairoa Hut 43 C3
Rigney 72 F14 73 F3
Rileys Lookout - Panau Island 48 E11
Rimarik Island 4 C13
Rimu (Southland) 77 E6
Rimu (Westland) 45 J2
Rimutaka Forest Park 33 E5 33 F3 33 A1
Ringway 76 F14 77 C2
Riordons Hut 37 G7

Ripiro Beach 3 H5
Riponui 4 E10
Ripponvale 66 H8
Rissington 28 D10
Riverdale 100 A2
Riverhead 6 J9 7 C3
Riverlands 35 J6 44 C11
Riverlea 23 F5
Riversdale (Blenheim) 117 A6
Riversdale (Central Otago) 72 J8
Riversdale Beach 34 D12
Riverside 84 B5
Riverside, SI 62 E9
Riverstone Terraces 111 A5
Riverton 76 H14 77 E2
Riwaka 38 G9 39 E1
Roa 45 D5
Roaring Lion Hut 37 H5 42 A10
Roaseneath 110 E2
Robinsons Bay 56 G12
Rock and Pillar 74 B9
Rockdale 128 A4
Rockford 52 F12 53 F3 55 B5
Rocks Ahead Hut 27 B7
Rocks Hut 39 H4 43 A5
Rocks, The 77 E2
Rockville 37 C6
Rocky Creek Hut 45 J5
Rodedale 128 B2
Rodgers Inlet Hut 70 J9 76 C9
Rogers Hut (Te Wairoa) 20 E11
Rokeby 55 G4 62 B10
Rokeby Hut 46 E14 47 E2
Rolleston 53 J6 56 E8
Rolling Junction Hut 42 C11
Romahapa 79 F3
Rona Bay 110 D3
Rona Island 70 E10
Rongahere 72 J14 73 J3 79 B1
Rongoiti Junction 26 F14 27 F2
Rongomai 30 G9 31 G3
Rongotai 110 E2
Rongotea 29 D6
Rosebank Road 89 C3
Rosebery 68 G11
Roseneath (Dunedin) 74 G12 124 B2
Rosewill 61 H4
Roslyn (Dunedin) 124 E3
Roslyn (Palmerston North) 30 D8 31 D2 105 A4
Roslyn Bush 77 E6
Ross 50 B11 51 B2
Rosvalls Track 27 H5
Rotherham 47 H6
Rothesay Bay 88 F4
Rotoehu 13 F6
Rotokakahi 3 B2
Rotokare Walkway 24 F8 25 C3
Rotokauri 9 J5 11 C6 92 E1
Rotokautuku 16 E11
Rotokawa (Bay of Plenty) 13 G5 96 A6
Rotokawa (Waikato) 19 C7
Rotokino 49 E7
Rotokohu 41 J5
Rotomahana 13 J5
Rotomanu 45 H7
Rotongaro 9 G4
Rotongata (Bay of Plenty) 13 E4
Rotongata (Waikato) 12 G9
Rotoorangi 12 E8
Rotoroa 42 G11
Rotoroa Island 8 D8
Rotoroa Track 42 H12
Rotorua 13 G4
Rotorua Airport 13 G5 96 B6
Rotorua Central 95 D3
Rotorua Museum 13 G4 96 C3
Rototuna (Northland) 5 D4
Rototuna (Waikato) 9 J6 11 B7 92 C3
Rotowaro 9 H4
Round Hill (Clutha) 73 J6 79 C4
Round Hill (Southland) 76 H13
Round Hill Skifield 50 G10
Round the Island Track North West Circuit
  77 J2 80 C4
Round the Mountain Track 26 A13 27 A1
Routeburn Falls 64 E10
Routeburn Flats Hut 64 E11
Routeburn Track - Great Walk 64 D11 65 D1
Rowan 23 E5
Roxburgh 72 D13 73 D2
Roxburgh East 72 D13 73 D2
Royal Oak 90 D4
Ruahine Corner Hut 27 E6
Ruahine Forest Park 27 F5 30 A11 31 A5
Ruahine Hut 27 E7
Ruahine, NI 27 H3
Ruahine, SI 76 H12
Ruakaka 4 J13
Ruakituri 21 E5
Ruakiwi 9 J2 11 B3
Ruakokoputuna 33 F7
Ruamahunga 8 F11 10 A8
Ruanui 26 E13 27 E1

Ruapani Track 21 E2
Ruapekapeka 4 D10
Ruapuke 11 D2
Ruapuke Island 77 J6
Ruapuna 61 C5
Ruarangi 4 J11
Ruaroa (Manawatu) 30 B11 31 B5
Ruaroa (Northland) 1 J7
Ruas Track 21 C3
Ruatahuna 20 C13 21 C1
Ruatangata West 4 F10
Ruataniwha 28 J8
Ruataniwha Conservation Park 59 F6
Ruatapu 45 J1 50 A11 51 A2
Ruatiti 26 A9
Ruato 13 F6
Ruatoki North 14 G11
Ruatoria 16 E11
Ruawai 5 B4
Ruawaro 9 G4
Ruawhata 30 E10 31 E4
Rugged Islands 80 C2
Rukuhia 11 D7 92 J5
Rukuwai 4 G13
Runanga 45 E4
Runanga Lake 28 E10
Runaruna 3 B3
Runciman 7 G6 9 B3
Rurima Island 14 D10
Ruru 45 G6
Russell 4 B10 81 A3
Russell Forest 4 C11
Russells Flat 52 G11 53 G2 55 C4
Russley 120 C3
Rutherglen 45 F3
Ryal Bush 77 D4

S

Sabine Hut 42 H12
Sabine Track 42 J12
Saddle Hill 74 H10 124 H5
Saddle Hut 65 C6
Saddle Rocks 40 A10
Saies 2 H10
Sainsburys Hut 65 F4
Saint Albans 54 H8 56 D10 120 E4
Saint Andrews 68 B13
St Andrews 92 D3
St Andrews Hill 120 G2
Saint Arnaud 42 G13 43 F1
Saint Arnaud Track 42 G13 43 F1
Saint Bathans 66 F13 67 F2
Saint Clair 74 H11 124 E5
St Heliers 90 C5
St Jacob's Hut 46 G12
Saint James Walkway 46 D14 47 D2
St Johns 90 C5
Saint Johns Hill 26 H8 109 B3
St Johns Park 90 C5
Saint Kilda 74 H11 124 D5
Saint Leonards 103 C5 102 A1
Saint Leonards, SI 74 G12
St Lukes 89 C3
St Martins 120 F2
St Marys Bay 87 C1
Saint Patricks 71 H7
St Winifred Hut 50 G10
Salisbury 61 J4 68 A13
Saltwater Creek 54 E8 56 A10
Saltwater Lagoon 49 D7
Sandringham 89 C3
Sandspit 6 E10
Sandstone 71 H7
Sandy Bay Hut 21 E3
Sandy Knolls 52 J14 53 J5 55 E7
Sandymount 74 H12 124 A3
Sanson 29 C6
Santoft 29 B5
Sapphire Springs - Katikati 10 H11
  12 A12 13 A1
Sawyers Bay 74 G12 124 B2
Saxon Hut 37 E4
Sayers Hut 33 B7
Scarborough (Christchurch) 120 J1
Scarborough (Timaru) 61 J5 68 A14
Scargill 54 D8
Scone Hut 50 G9
Scotsman Valley 12 C8
Scotts Gap 76 E13 77 B1
Scow Landing 4 F13
Scroggs Hill 74 H10 124 J5
Seacliff 74 E12
Seadown 61 H5
Seafield 55 J4 62 D10
Seaford 37 E7
Seaforth 61 H5
Seagrove 7 G4 9 B1
Seagull Lake 51 H5
Seal Island 45 A5
Seal Islands 69 H2 75 B2
Seal Rocks 77 J7
Seatoun 33 F2 35 B4
Seaview (Timaru) 121 C3

Seaview (Wellington) 110 D3
Seaward Downs 78 E8
Secretary Island 69 B5
Seddon 44 E11
Seddonville 41 D6
Sedgemere 55 H7 62 C13
Sefton 54 E8 56 A10
Sefton Bivvy 59 A6
Selwyn Heights 96 B2
Selwyn Huts 56 F8 62 A14
Selwyn, NI 12 D12
Selwyn, SI 52 J13 53 J4 55 F6 62 A12
Sentry Box Hut 27 F7
Sentry Hill 17 H1 23 B6
Sergeants Hill 41 G3
Serpentine Hut 50 C13 51 C4
Shaftesbury 10 H10 12 A11
Shag Lake 3 G5
Shag Point 74 C13
Shag Rock 48 J9 54 A13
Shamrock Park 90 D6
Shamrock Park 58 G14 59 G3
Shannon, NI 29 F6
Shannon, SI 74 E8
Shantytown 45 F4
Sharks Tooth Hut 65 C5
Sheffield 52 G12 53 G3 55 C5
Shelly Beach 5 G7 7 A1
Shelly Park 90 D6
Shelter Islands 69 B5
Shelter Rock Hut 64 C13 65 C3
Shenandoah 42 H8
Sherenden 28 D9
Sherwood 55 G3 62 B9
Shiel Burn Hut 65 D5
Shiel Hill 124 D4
Shingle Creek 72 C12 73 C1
Shirley 54 H8 56 D10 120 F4
Shoe Island / Motuhoa 10 A11
Shorts Track 30 A11 31 A5
Shutes Hut 27 D7
Shy Lake 69 F5
Siberia Hut 58 H9
Silver Island 66 A9
Silver Peaks Route 74 F11
Silverdale 88 B2
Silverdale (Auckland) 6 H10 7 B4
Silverdale (Hamilton) 92 F5
Silverhope 26 J12
Silverstream 111 B5
Simmonds Islands 1 E5
Sir Robert Hut 50 C13 51 C4
Sisters, The 80 H1
Six Foot Track 21 B2
Six Mile 42 H9
Six Mile Walkway & Track 42 H9
Skippers 65 F4
Skippers Canyon 65 F4
Skyline Track 24 J14 26 F9
Slaty Creek 45 D6
Slipper Island 10 B12
Slyburn Hut 64 G11 65 G1
Smithfield 61 J5
Smiths Ponds 57 G5
Smiths Stream Hut 27 H6
Snells Beach 6 F10
Sockburn 53 H7 56 D9 120 C2
Somerfield 120 E2
Somerton 55 G4 62 B10
Somerville 90 D6
Somes Island 33 E2 35 B3
South Bay 48 E12
South Beach 45 F4
South Dunedin 124 E4
South Head 5 F6
South Hill 122 D5
South Hillend 77 A4
South Malvern 52 H11 53 H2 55 D4
South Mavora Lake 71 B4
South New Brighton 120 H3
South Oamaru 122 D6
South Ohau Hut 29 H6
South Temple Hut 59 G4
Southbridge 55 G6 62 B12
Southburn 68 A12
Southdown 90 D5
Southern Alps / Ka Tiritiri o te Moana 58 J8
Southern Coastal Track 76 F9
Southshore 54 H8 56 D10 120 H2
Spar Bush 77 D4
Speargrass Hut 42 H12
Speargrass Track 42 G13
Spectacle Lake 6 C9
Spence Hut 70 G13 71 G2 76 A13
Spencerville 54 G8 56 C10 120 G6
Sphinx Lake 69 J7 75 C7
Sportswood 107 C2
Spotswood, NI 23 B4
Spotswood, SI 48 J9
Spreydon 53 J7 56 E9 120 D2
Spring Creek 35 J5 40 J10 44 B11
Spring Grove 39 H2 43 A3
Springbank 53 F6 56 B8

Springbrook 68 A13
Springburn 61 A6
Springdale 10 G8
Springfield (Rotorua) 96 D2
Springfield, NI 4 H12
Springfield, SI 52 F11 53 F2 55 B4
Springhill 27 H7
Springhills 77 C6
Springlands 35 K6 44 C10 117 B1
Springs Flat 4 F11
Springs Junction 46 D12
Springston 53 J6 56 F8 62 A14
Springston South 56 F8 62 A14
Springvale (Otago) 66 J10 72 A13 73 A2
Springvale (Wanganui) 108 A1 109 C3
Spye 54 B10
Square Top Island 36 G4
Stafford 45 H3
Stafford Hut 57 E5
Stag Flat Shelter 42 C9
Staglands Wildlife Park - Cloustonville 33 B4
Staircase 52 E11 53 E2 55 A4
Stanfield Hut 30 B11 31 B5
Stanley Bay 90 B4
Stanley Brook 42 B13 43 A1
Stanley Point 90 B4
Stanmore Bay 88 B3
Stanway 29 B7 31 B1
Station Hut 59 E5
Staveley 61 A6
Stephens Island / Takapourewa 40 A10
Stephenson Island 2 G11
Stevensons Island 66 C8
Stewart Island / Rakiura 77 J1 80 C3
Stewarts Gully 54 G8 56 C10
Steyning Hut 47 F3
Stillwater 88 C3
Stillwater, NI 6 H10 7 B4
Stillwater, SI 45 E5
Stirling 79 E4
Stirling Falls, The 64 D8
Stockton 41 E5
Stodys Hut 56 B10
Stoke 39 H3 43 A4
Stokes Valley 33 D3 111 C4
Stone Hut 42 C10
Stoneburn 74 C11
Stony Creek 79 D3
Stony River Walk 23 C3
Stony Stream Hut 46 J11
Strandon 107 B4
Stratford 23 E7 25 B2
Strathern 128 B4
Strathmore 24 D9 25 A4
Strathmore Park 110 E2
Streamlands 6 E9
Stronvar 34 C11
Stuarts 78 F13 79 H1
Studholme 68 D13
Studholme Saddle Hut 28 B8
Styx 120 D5
Subritsky Homestead 1 F5
Sudden Valley Bivvy 52 B9
Sugar Loaf Islands / Nga Motu 23 B5
Summer Hill 79 F4
Summerhill (Canterbury) 52 E14 53 E5 55 A7
Summerhill (Palmerston North) 105 D4
Summerlea 41 D6
Sumner 54 J9 56 E11 120 J1
Sundale 110 C2
Sunnybrook 96 C2
Sunnyhills 90 C5
Sunnynook 88 H4
Sunnyvale (Auckland) 89 C2
Sunnyvale (Dunedin) 124 G5
Sunrise Hut 27 G6
Supper Cove Hut 69 G5 75 A5
Surfdale 7 D7
Sutherland Falls 63 F7
Sutherlands 60 H14 61 H3
Sutton 74 D8
Swan Lagoon 59 H5
Swannanoa 53 G6 56 C8
Swanson 7 D3 89 C1
Sweetwater 1 H6
Sydenham 119 G6 120 D2
Sylvia Flat Hot Springs 46 F13 47 F1

T

Tablelands (Bay of Plenty) 14 F13 15 F2
Tablelands (Wellington) 34 E8
Tadmor 42 C12
Taemaro 2 G9
Tahaia 11 H6
Tahakopa 78 F13 79 H1
Taharoa 11 G2
Tahatika 78 E14 79 G2
Tahawai 10 G11
Taheke 3 D5
Tahekeroa 6 G9 7 A3
Tahere 4 F13
Tahora (Bay of Plenty) 14 J12
Tahora (Taranaki) 17 H6 24 B11

Tahoraiti 30 C12 31 C6
Tahorakuri 19 C7
Tahuna 10 G8
Tahunanui 38 J12 39 G4 43 A5 116 B4
Tahunga 21 D6
Tahuroa 10 J8 12 B9
Taieri Beach 79 C7
Taieri Island / Moturata 79 C7
Taieri Mouth 79 C7
Taihape 27 F2
Taiharuru 4 G14
Taihoa 12 C11
Taikirau 4 D9
Taiko 60 J14 61 J3
Taikorea 29 D6
Taingaehe 5 C4
Tainui 124 D5
Taipa 2 H8
Taipo Hut 42 C9
Taipoiti 46 B9
Taipuha 5 A6
Tairua 8 F14 10 A11
Taita 33 D3 35 A2 111 C4
Tai Tapu 56 F9
Taitville 110 E1
Taka Ra Haka Conservation Park 71 C5
Takahiwai 4 H12
Takahue 1 K7 3 A3
Takaka 38 E8
Takaka Hill 38 F8
Takamatua 56 G12
Takamore 16 E11
Takanini 7 F6 9 A3
Takapau (East Cape, NI) 16 F11
Takapau (Gisborne) 22 A12
Takapau (Manawatu) 30 A14 32 A3
Takapou 38 D9 39 B1
Takapu Rd 110 C2
Takapu Valley 110 B3
Takapuna 7 D5 90 A4
Takaputahi 15 G5
Takapuwahia 110 B2
Takaro 29 D7 31 D1 105 B3
Takarua Hut 20 B13 21 B1
Takatu 6 E10
Takou 24 F10 25 C5
Takou Bay 2 J12
Takutai 45 J2
Tamahere 11 C7 92 H6
Tamaki 7 E5 90 C5
Tamaki Maori Village - Rotorua 13 H4
Tamarau 100 D5
Tamaterau 4 G12
Tamihana 10 J10 12 B11
Tanatana 14 H11
Tane 30 G10 31 G4
Taneatua 14 F11
Tanehopuwai 11 J5 18 A9
Tanekaha 4 E11
Tangahoe 24 E12 25 B7
Tangarakau 17 G7 24 A12
Tangarakau Gorge 17 G6 24 A11
Tangihua 4 H10
Tangihua Forest 4 H10
Tangimoana 29 D5
Tangiteroria 4 H9
Tangitu 18 C10
Tangiwai 26 C13 27 C1
Tangoake 1 C3
Tangoio 28 B12
Tangowahine 4 H8
Taniwha 9 F6
Tanoa 5 C7
Tanupara 26 D10
Taonui 30 C8 31 C2
Taoroa Junction 27 F4
Taotaoroa 12 D10
Tapanui 72 J13 73 J2
Tapapa 12 E11
Tapawera 42 C13 43 B1
Tapora 5 E6
Tapu 8 F11 10 A8
Tapuhi 4 D11
Tapui 68 G9
Tapuiwahine 18 C10
Taputeranga Island 33 F1 35 C4
Tapuwae (Northland) 3 B7
Tapuwae (Waikato) 18 B11
Tara 6 B8
Tara Hills 74 G10 124 J1
Taradale 28 E12 103 C2
Tarakohe 38 D9
Taramakau 45 H4
Taramea Bay 76 H14 77 E2
Taramoa 77 E4
Taranga Island 6 A10
Taranui 68 J11
Tarara 78 F14 79 H2
Tararu 8 G11 10 B8
Tararua Forest Park 29 H7 29 J5 31 H1 33 A6
Tarata 17 J2 23 C7
Taraunui 4 G13
Tarawera 20 H9
Tarawera Hot Springs 20 H9
Tariki 23 D6 25 A1

Taringamotu 18 F10
Taringamotu Valley 18 E11
Tarn Hut (Canterbury) 52 C13 53 C4
Tarn Hut (Mt Richmond CP) 43 C4
Tarn Ridge Hut 29 J6
Taronui Bay 2 J13
Tarras 66 E10
Taruheru 100 A1
Tarukenga 12 F14 13 F3
Tarurutangi 23 B6
Tasman 38 H10 39 F2
Tasman Lake 59 B7
Tasman Saddle Hut 49 H7
Tata Islands 38 D9 39 B1
Tataiahapi Pa 14 H12
Tatapouri 22 D11
Tataraimaka 23 C3
Tataramoa 30 B12 31 B6
Tatarariki 5 A3
Tatare 49 G6
Tataweka Hut 21 B3
Tatu 17 F7 24 A12
Tatuanui 10 H8 12 A9
Tauanui Hut 33 G6
Tauhara 98 B5
Tauhei 9 H7 12 A8
Tauherenikau 33 D6
Tauhoa 6 E8
Taumaka Island 57 D7
Taumarere 4 C9
Taumariti 18 F10
Taumarunui 18 F10
Taumata 78 B13 79 D1
Taumatatahi 24 G11 25 D6
Taumatawhakatangihangakoauauotamatea-
  pokaiwhenuakitanatahu - New Zealand's
  longest place name 32 E10
Taumutu 55 H7 62 C13
Taungatara 23 F4
Taungatara Track 23 E4
Taunoka 24 G12 25 D7
Taupaki 7 D2
Taupo 19 D5 97 B3 98 B4
Taupo Airport 19 E5 98 D4
Taupo Bay 2 H10
Taupo Hot Springs 19 D5
Tauranga 10 J13 13 B3 94 B2
Tauranga Bay 2 H11
Tauranga Central 93 D5
Tauranga Mission House 13 C4
Tauranga Valley 2 H11
Tauranganui 7 J5 9 E2
Taurangaruru 7 J3 9 D1
Tauraroa (Northland) 4 H11
Tauraroa (Waikato) 12 H8
Taurawharana Hut 20 B14 21 B2
Taurewa 18 H3
Tauriko 10 J13 12 B14 13 B3 94 D1
Taurikura 4 H13
Tautoro 3 D7
Tautuku 78 G13 79 J1
Tauweru 34 B10
Tauwhare (Bay of Plenty) 14 J11
Tauwhare Pa 12 C8
Tauwharemanuka 21 A2
Tauwhareparae 16 J9
Tawa 33 D2 35 B2 110 B2
Tawa Hut 21 B4
Tawai 68 F12
Tawanui 78 E14 79 G2
Tawataia 30 G9 31 G3
Tawhana 21 B2
Tawharanui 6 E11
Tawharekiri Lakes 58 C9
Tawhata 18 H8 24 B13
Tawhero 108 C1
Tawhiti, NI 23 G7 25 D2
Tawhiti, SI 72 C12 73 C1
Tawhiwhi 24 H11 25 E6
Tawhiwhi Hut 20 B13 21 B1
Taylor Dam 35 K6 44 D10
Taylors Mistake 54 J9 56 E11 120 J1
Taylorville 45 E5
Te Ahuahu 3 B7
Te Akatea 9 H4 11 A5
Te Akau 9 J2 11 B3
Te Akau South 9 J2 11 B3
Te Anau 70 D11
Te Anau Downs 70 A12 71 A1
Te Anga 11 H3
Te Angiangi Marine Reserve 32 C12
Te Aputa 18 E14 19 E2
Te Arai 6 C9
Te Arai Point 6 C9
Te Arakura 29 C7 31 C1
Te Araroa 16 B12
Te Ariruru 16 H11
Te Aro 110 E2 112 E5
Te Aroha 10 G9
Te Aroha Aerodrome 10 F9
Te Aroha West 10 H10 12 A11
Te Atatu North 7 D3
Te Atatu Peninsula 89 B2
Te Atatu South 89 C2

Te Awa (Canterbury) 61 G5
Te Awa (Napier) 103 A2
Te Awaatu Channel Marine Reserve 69 C5
Te Awamutu 11 E7
Te Awanga 28 F13
Te Ekaou Hut 30 B10 31 B4
Te Hana 6 D8
Te Hapara 100 B2
Te Hapua 1 B3
Te Haroto 20 J10
Te Hauke 28 G10
Te Haumi 81 C2
Te Henga / Bethells Beach 7 E1
Te Henga Goldie Bush Walkway 7 D1
Te Henui 23 C5
Te Hihi 7 G5 9 B2
Te Hoe 9 G6
Te Horo 29 J3
Te Horo Beach 29 J3
Te Horoa 26 E13 27 E1
Te Houka 79 E3
Te Huahua 3 B4
Te Hue Track 20 C13 21 C1
Te Huia 2 J11
Te Hutewai 11 D3
Te Iringa 3 D7
Te Kaha 15 C6
Te Kahui Kaupeka Conservation Park 60 A11
Te Kainga 110 D2
Te Kakaho Island 40 C11
Te Kao 1 D3
Te Karae 3 B4
Te Karaka (Gisborne) 22 B9
Te Karaka (Northland) 3 C3
Te Karanga-a-Hape (Cornwallis) 7 F3 89 E2
Te Kauri 9 G4
Te Kauwhata 9 E5
Te Kawa 11 F7
Te Kawa West 11 F6
Te Kinga 45 G6
Te Kiri 23 F4
Te Kiteroa 72 J11
Te Kohanga 7 J5 9 D2
Te Kopua (Bay of Plenty) 15 C6
Te Kopua (Waikato) 11 F6
Te Kopuru 5 A3
Te Koraha 11 G3
Te Kouma 8 D11
Te Koura 18 E10
Te Kowhai (Northland) 5 B4
Te Kowhai (Waikato) 9 J5 11 B6
Te Kuha 41 G3
Te Kuiti 11 J5
Te Kumi 11 J5
Te Mahia 35 J3 40 G10
Te Mahoe 14 G9
Te Maika 11 F2
Te Maire 18 G9
Te Mapara 18 A9
Te Marua, NI 33 C4
Te Marua, SI 40 B10
Te Mata (Waikato - Coromandel) 8 F11 10 A8
Te Mata (Waikato) 11 D3
Te Mata Peak Walkway 28 F12
Te Matai 13 C5
Te Matawai Hut 29 J6
Te Maunga 13 B4
Te Mawhai 11 F7
Te Miko 45 A5
Te Miro 12 C9
Te Moana 61 E3
Te Moananui 10 F9
Te Moehau Junction 27 E3
Te Motu Island 11 F2
Te Mutu Kairangi / Miramar Peninsula 110 E2
Te Namu 41 B7
Te Ngae 13 F5
Te Ngaire 2 H11
Te Ngaru 74 G12
Te Ohaki Pa 12 C12
Te Oneone Rangatira Beach 5 G5
Te Opai Lagoon 33 F5
Te Ore Ore 34 B9
Te Pahu 11 D5
Te Paki 1 B2
Te Paki Recreation Reserve 1 B1
Te Panaa Hut 21 B2
Te Papa Museum - Wellington 33 F1 35 C4
Te Papanui Conservation Park 73 F5
Te Papapa 90 D4
Te Papatapu 11 D3
Te Peka 78 F9
Te Pirita 52 J11 53 J2 55 F4 62 A10
Te Pohue 28 A10
Te Poi 12 D12
Te Popo 23 D7 25 A2
Te Pourewa Hut 21 A2
Te Pouwhakatutu 19 C5
Te Pu 13 E4
Te Pua 5 H7 7 B1
Te Pua Hut 21 B3
Te Puhi 2 J8
Te Puia Hut 28 A8
Te Puia Lodge 20 J8 28 A8
Te Puia Springs 16 G11

Te Puia Springs – Waingaro

Te Puia Springs - Kawhia 11 F2
Te Puia Springs Hot Pools - East Cape 16 G11
Te Puka 16 H11
Te Puke 13 C5
Te Puna 10 J13 12 B14 13 B3
Te Puninga 10 G8 12 A9
Te Puru 8 G11 10 B8
Te Rae 37 A7
Te Rahu 11 E7
Te Raina 18 E14 19 E2
Te Ranga (Bay of Plenty) 12 C14 13 D4 13 C3 94 D1
Te Rangiita 19 F4
Te Rapa 9 J5 11 B6 92 D2
Te Rauamoa 11 F5
Te Raumauku 11 G5
Te Raupo 1 E5
Te Reinga 21 F6
Te Rerenga 8 C12
Te Rerepahupahu Falls 17 F7
Te Rore (Northland) 2 K7 3 A3
Te Rore (Waikato) 11 D6
Te Roti 23 G6 25 D1
Te Rou 43 C6
Te Tahi 11 E5
Te Taho 50 E8
Te Teko 14 F9
Te Tii 2 J13
Te Tipua 78 C8
Te Toro 7 H3 9 C1
Te Totara Hut 20 E12
Te Tua 76 F11
Te Tuhi Junction 24 H12 25 E7
Te Tumu 13 C5
Te Uku 11 C4
Te Uku Landing 11 C4
Te Urewera National Park 14 H10 20 A13 21 A1
Te Uri 32 C8
Te Waewae 76 F11
Te Waiiti 20 D13 21 D1
Te Waikoropupu Springs / Pupu Springs 38 E8
Te Waimate Mission 4 B8
Te Waiotukapiti Hut 20 F12
Te Wairoa 13 H5
Te Waitere 11 G2
Te Waiti Hut 14 H14 15 H3
Te Wakatehaua Island 1 D3
Te Wera 24 D9 25 A4
Te Whaiti 20 C11
Te Whakarae 18 F10
Te Whanga 34 C9
Te Wharau (Northland) 4 J8
Te Wharau (Wellington) 34 E10
Te Whau 2 J12 4 A8
Teal Bay Hut 76 E8
Teardrop Lake 69 B7
Teddington 56 F10
Telford Hut 70 G12 71 G1 76 A12
Temple Basin Skifield 52 A8
Temple View 11 C6 92 G2
Templeton 53 J6 56 E8 120 A2
Temuka 61 G5
Tennyson Inlet 40 F8
Tentpoles Hut 48 D10
Tepene 2 H12
Terrace End 30 D8 31 D2 105 B4
Teschemakers 68 J11
Teviot 72 E13 73 E2
Thames 8 H11 10 C8
Thames North 8 H11 10 C8
The Brothers (Marlborough) 35 E2 40 F14
The Brothers (Stewart Island) 80 H3
The Hermitage 59 B6
Theta Tarn 57 H4
Third House Hut 39 H4 43 A5
Thomsons Crossing 77 C4
Thor Hut 42 B10
Thornbury 77 D3
Thorndon 110 D2 112 C5
Thornton 14 E10
Thornton Bay 8 G11 10 B8
Thorpe 38 J8 42 A13
Three Bridges 3 E6
Three Kings 90 C4
Three Mile Bush 85 B1
Three Mile Lagoon 49 F5
Three Mile Stream Hut 46 H12
Three Steeples 41 F2
Three Streams 11 C3
Thrillseekers Canyon 47 G5
Ti Point 6 D11
Ti Tree Point 32 F8
Tia Island 80 G6
Tiakitahuna 29 E7
Tihaka 76 H14 77 E2
Tihiroa 11 F6
Tihoi 18 C14 19 C2
Tikinui 5 B3
Tikipunga 4 F12
Tikitere 13 F5
Tikitiki 16 D12
Tikokino 28 H8
Tikorangi 17 G2 23 A7
Tikotiko 9 F3

Timaru 61 J5 121 B3
Timber Bay 30 C12 31 C6
Timberlea 111 A6
Timpanys 77 F6
Tindalls Beach 88 B4
Tiniroto 21 F6
Tinkertown 70 J14 71 J3 76 C14 77 A2
Tinopai 5 D6
Tinui 34 A12
Tinui Island 40 B10
Tinwald 55 J2 62 D8
Tipapakuru 30 C12 31 C6
Tipunga 85 A2
Tiratu 30 C13 31 C7
Tirau 12 E11
Tiraumea 30 H11 31 H5
Tiraumea Hut 42 H11
Tiraumea Track 42 H11
Tiriraukawa 26 G13 27 G1
Tiritiri Matangi Island 6 H11 7 B5
Tiroa 18 B12
Tirohanga (Bay of Plenty) 14 F14 15 F3
Tirohanga (Wellington) 110 C3
Tirohanga, SI 79 G4
Tirohia 10 F9
Tiroiti 74 A9
Tiromoana 45 A5
Tiroroa 41 H4
Tisbury 128 B5
Titahi Bay 33 D2 35 B2 110 A2
Titi Island 40 D11
Titirangi 7 E3 89 D2
Titirangi Beach 89 D2
Titirangi North 89 D2
Titirangi Park 100 C4
Titirangi South 89 D2
Titiroa 78 F8
Titoki 4 G9
Toa Bridge 11 H7
Toatoa (Bay of Plenty) 15 G4
Toatoa (Northland) 2 H8
Todds Valley 38 J12 39 G4
Toetoe 4 G11 85 D2
Tohunga Junction 26 B11
Toi Flat 30 D13 31 D7
Tokaanu 19 G2
Tokanui, NI 11 F7
Tokanui, SI 78 G9
Tokaora 23 G6 25 D1
Tokarahi 68 F9
Tokata 16 B12
Tokata Island 14 D10
Tokatoka 5 A3
Tokerau 13 E5
Tokerau Beach 1 F7
Tokirima 18 G8 24 A13
Toko 24 E8 25 B3
Toko Mouth 79 E6
Tokoiti 79 D5
Tokomaru 29 F7 31 F1
Tokomaru Bay 16 H11
Tokomaru Steam Engine Museum 29 F7 31 F1
Tokorangi 29 A7
Tokoroa 12 H12
Tolaga Bay 22 A13
Tomarata 6 C9
Tomarata Lake 6 C9
Tomoana 103 C5
Tonga Island 38 E10 39 C2
Tonga Island Marine Res 38 E10 39 C2
Tongaporutu 17 E4
Tongariro 18 H13 19 H1
Tongariro Crossing 18 H13 19 H1
Tongariro National Park 18 H13 19 H1 26 A13 27 A1
Tongariro Northern Circuit 18 J14 19 J2 26 A14 27 A2
Top Branch Hut 43 H3
Top Butler Hut 50 G8
Top Crawford Hut 51 B5
Top Dingle Burn Hut 58 H13 59 H2
Top Forks Hut 58 H8
Top Gorge Hut 27 J5
Top Hope Hut 46 G12
Top Hut 58 F14 59 F3
Top Kokatahi Hut 50 B14 51 B5
Top Maropea Hut 27 G6
Top Robinson Hut 46 F12
Top Timaru Ck Hut 66 A11
Top Toaroha Hut 50 C13 51 C4
Top Trent Hut / Lagoon Hut 46 H9
Top Tuke Hut 50 D11 51 D2
Top Wairoa Hut 43 D3
Top Waitaha Hut 50 D11 51 D2
Tophouse 42 G14 43 F2
Topuni 6 C8
Torbay 6 J10 7 C4 88 F4
Torehape 9 E7
Torere 15 E4
Torlesse Tussocklands Park 52 E10 52 F9
Totara Flat 45 D7
Totara Heights 90 E6
Totara North 2 H10
Totara Park 33 D4 111 A6
Totara Valley 60 G14 61 G2

Totara, NI 8 H11 10 C8
Totara, SI 68 H11
Totaranui 38 D10 39 B2
Towai 4 D10
Town Basin - Whangarei 4 G12
Townsend 117 C5
Townsend Hut 46 J9
Townsend Huts 52 B12 53 B3
Travers - Sabine Track 42 J13
Traverse Hut 30 B11 31 B5
Treaty House - Waitangi 4 B9
Treble Cone Skifield 65 C6
Trentham, NI 33 D4 111 B5
Trentham, SI 60 E13 61 E2
Trevor Carter Hut 42 C9
Triangle Hut 27 H5
Trilobite Hut 37 H6
Trinity Lakes 70 E9
Trio Islands / Kuru Pongi 40 B10
Triplex Hut 27 G6
Tripp Settlement 61 E4
Trotters Gorge 74 B13
Trust/Poulter Hut 52 A10 53 A1
Tryphena 36 E5
Tuai 21 F3
Tuakau 7 J6 9 D3
Tuamarina 35 J5 40 J10 44 B11
Tuapeka Flat 73 J4 79 B2
Tuapeka Mouth 73 J4 78 A14 79 C2
Tuapeka West 73 J4 79 B2
Tuatapere 76 F11
Tuatapere Hump Ridge Track 76 E9
Tuateawa 8 B12 36 J6
Tuatini 16 H11
Tuhara 21 F6
Tuhikaramea 11 D6
Tuhipa 4 C8
Tuhitarata 33 F6
Tuhua 18 E9
Tui 42 D12
Tui Brewery Tower - Pahiatua 30 E10 31 E4
Tui Glen 38 J12 39 G4
Tukaki Marae - Te Kaha 15 C6
Tukemokihi 21 G6
Tukino Skifield - Mt Ruapehu 26 B13 27 B1
Tumahu 23 D3
Tumai 74 D12
Tumunui 13 H5
Tuna 23 D7 25 A2
Tunakotekote 18 F10
Tunnel Creek Hut 58 C13 59 C2
Tuparehuia 4 C12
Tuparoa 16 E12
Turakina 29 A4
Turangaomoana 10 J10 12 C11
Turangarere 26 E14 27 E2
Turangi 19 C3
Turitea 30 E8 31 E2
Turiwhate 45 J5
Turiwiri 4 J8
Turoa Skifield - Mt Ruapehu 26 B12
Turua 8 J11 10 D8
Tussock Creek 77 D5
Tussock Hut 19 J6
Tutaematai 4 B11
Tutaenui 26 J11 29 A6
Tutaki 42 G13
Tutamoe 3 F6
Tutekehua 3 B4
Tutira 28 A12
Tutu Hut 47 F3
Tutukaka 4 E13
Tuturau 78 C3
Tuturumuri 34 G7
Tututawa 24 E9 25 B4
Tutuwai Hut 33 C6
Tuwhakairiora Marae - Hicks Bay 16 B11
Twelve Mile Delta 64 H13 65 H3
Twin Bridges 3 F7
Twizel 59 H6
Twyford 28 E11 103 D3

U

Ulva Island 80 E5
Umawera 3 B5
Umere 37 J3 42 A8
Umutaoroa 30 B12 31 B6
Umutoi 27 J4 30 A11 31 A5
Unahi 1 H6
Underwood 77 E4
Unwin Hut 59 B6
Upokongaro 26 H9
Upokorau 2 J11
Upper Atiamuri 12 J13 13 J2
Upper Atiamuri Hot Pools 12 J13 13 J2
Upper Charlton 78 B8
Upper Deception Hut 52 A8
Upper D'Urville Hut 42 F11
Upper Hutt 33 D4 111 B6
Upper Junction 74 G12 124 C2
Upper Kawhatau 27 G4
Upper Makaroro Hut 27 F6
Upper Mangatawhiri Reservoir 8 G8 9 B5

Upper Matakitaki 42 J9 46 A13 47 A1
Upper Matakuhia Hut 20 F10
Upper Moutere 38 J10 39 G2
Upper Princhester Hut 70 F13 71 F2
Upper Riccarton 120 D2
Upper South Branch Hut 46 J10
Upper Spey Hut 69 F7
Upper Takaka 38 G8
Upper Tama Lake 18 J13 19 J1 26 A13 27 A1
Upper Te Hoe Hut 20 F11
Upper Travers Hut 42 J12 47 A4
Upper Wairaki Hut 70 G13 71 G2 76 A13
Upper Waitati 74 F11
Upper Waitohi 61 G3
Upper Whirinaki Hut 20 F10
Upper Windley Hut 71 D4
Urenui 17 G3 24 A8
Uretane 68 D12
Uretara Island 14 F12
Urquharts Bay 4 H13
Urquhart's Hut 51 C6
Urrall 55 F2 62 A8
Urungaio 3 B4
Urupukapuka Island 4 A11
Uruti 17 G4 24 A9
Uruwhenua 38 F8
Utakura 3 C6
Utiku 27 G3
Utuhina 96 C2
Utuwai 30 A11 31 A5

V

Valetta 61 B6
Vauxhall (Auckland) 90 B4
Vauxhall (Dunedin) 123 J6 124 D4
Venison Tops Hut 27 A7
Venus Hut 42 B10
Victoria 100 C3
Victoria Conservation Park 46 A12
Victoria Valley 2 J7
Victory Island / Moutiti 40 A9
View Hill 52 F12 53 F3 55 B5
Vinegar Hill 26 J13 27 J1
Vinetown 84 C3
Virginia 52 A14 53 A5
Vogeltown (New Plymouth) 23 B5 107 C4
Vogeltown (Wellington) 110 E1

W

Waddington 52 G12 53 G3 55 C5
Wade Heads 88 C4
Wadestown 33 E1 35 C3 110 D2
Waenga 66 H9
Waerenga 9 E5
Waerengaahika 22 D9
Waerengaokuri 22 E8
Waewaetorea Island 4 A11
Waharoa 10 J10 12 C11
Wai O Taiki Bay 90 C5
Waiake 88 F3
Waianakarua 74 A13
Waianiwa 77 D4
Waiapi 61 G4
Waiare 2 J11
Waiareka Junction 68 H11
Waiarikiki 78 D10
Waiaro 8 B10 36 J4
Waiaruhe 30 D11 31 D5
Waiatarua 7 E3 89 D1
Waiatoto 57 E7
Waiau Beach 7 H4 9 C1
Waiau Falls - Coromandel 8 D11
Waiau Pa 7 G4 9 B1
Waiau, NI 8 D11
Waiau, SI 47 H7
Waiaua 14 F14 15 F3
Waiaua Gorge Hut 23 E4
Waiawa Hut 20 C14 21 C2
Waihaha (Northland) 4 B11
Waihaha (Waikato) 19 D2
Waihaha Hut 18 D13 19 D1
Waihao Downs 68 E11
Waihao Forks 68 D11
Waihaorunga 68 D10
Waihapa 2 J10
Waiharakeke (Waikato - Coromandel) 8 J14 10 D11
Waiharakeke (Waikato) 11 G3
Waiharara 1 G5
Waiharuru Hut 20 E14
Waihau Bay 16 B8
Waiheke Island 8 D8 6 J13
Waihemo 74 B11
Waihi (Bay of Plenty) 10 F11
Waihi (Waikato) 19 G2
Waihi Beach 10 F12
Waihi Falls 30 E13 31 E7
Waihi Hot Springs 18 G14 19 G2
Waihirere 22 D10
Waihoaka 76 G12
Waihohonu Hut 18 J14 19 J2 26 A14 27 A2

Waihohonu Track 18 J13 27 A1 26 A13 27 A1
Waihoki 30 G13 31 G7
Waihoki Valley 30 H12 31 H6
Waihola 74 J8 79 B6
Waihopai 128 B2
Waihopo 1 E4
Waihou 10 H9 12 A10
Waihou Valley 3 B6
Waihua 21 J4
Waihua Hut 14 J10
Waihuahua Swamp 1 F6
Waihue 3 H7
Waihuka 2 J11
Waiinu Beach 25 H5
Wai-iti 39 J1 43 B2
Waikaia 72 G9
Waikaka 72 J11
Waikaka Valley 78 A10
Waikakahi 68 E12
Waikakaho - Cullen Creek Track 40 H9 44 A10
Waikamaka Hut 27 G5
Waikana 78 C9
Waikanae 33 A4
Waikanae Beach 33 A4
Waikaraka 4 G12 85 D3
Waikare 4 B11
Waikare Junction Hut 20 A13 21 A1
Waikaremoana 21 E3
Waikaretu 9 G2
Waikari (Canterbury) 54 B8
Waikari (Dunedin) 124 E3
Waikato 37 B7
Waikaura 68 E9
Waikawa (Marlborough) 35 J3 40 G10
Waikawa (Southland) 78 G11
Waikawa Beach 29 H4
Waikawa Museum 78 G11
Waikawa Valley 78 F11
Waikawau (Waikato - Coromandel Coast) 8 E11 10 A8
Waikawau (Waikato - Coromandel) 8 B11 36 J5
Waikawau (Waikato) 17 A5
Waikeria 11 G7
Waikiekie 4 J11
Waikino 10 F10
Waikirikiri 14 H11
Waikite Valley 13 J4
Waikite Valley Hot Pools & Thermal Area 13 J4
Waikiwi 77 E5 128 C1
Waikoau 28 A11
Waikoikoi 72 J12 78 A11
Waikokopu 22 J8 22 AA1
Waikokowai 9 G4 11 A5
Waikorea 9 G2
Waikouaiti 74 E12
Waikoukou Valley 6 J8 7 C2
Waikouro 76 E14 77 B2
Waikowhai 89 D3
Waikuku 54 F8 56 B10
Waikuku Beach 54 F8 56 B10
Waikune 18 J1 26 A11
Waima 89 D2
Waima (East Cape, NI) 16 G11
Waima (Northland) 3 D5
Waima Forest 3 D4
Waima Main Range Track 3 E5
Waima Valley 3 D5
Waimahaka 78 F8
Waimahora 19 B7
Waimahora 11 H7
Waimairi Beach 54 H8 56 D10
Waimakariri Falls Hut 51 B7
Waimamaku 3 E4
Waimana 14 G11
Waimangaroa 41 F4
Waimangu 13 J5
Waimangu Volcanic Valley 13 J5
Waimanoni 1 H6
Waimanu Bay 89 B2
Waimapo 10 J13 94 D1 13 C3
Waimarama 28 H13
Waimari Beach 120 H4
Waimarie 41 D6
Waimata (Bay of Plenty) 10 F11
Waimata (Gisborne) 22 C11
Waimate 68 D12
Waimate Aerodrome 68 D12
Waimate Historical Museum 68 D12
Waimate Island 8 C10
Waimate North 4 B8
Waimate Walkway 68 D12
Waimatenui 3 E6
Waimatua 77 F6
Waimatuku 77 D3
Waimauku 6 J8 7 C2
Waimaunga 46 C8
Waimea 72 H8
Waimiha 18 C11
Waimihia 19 E7
Waimiro 30 F13 31 F7
Waimotu 68 J10
Waimumu 78 B8
Waingake 22 F8
Waingaro 9 J3 11 B4

Waingaro Forks Hut – Yourk Bay 233

Waingaro Forks Hut 37 G7
Waingaro Hot Springs 9 J3 11 B4
Waingaro Track 37 F7
Waingawa 34 B8
Wainihinihi 45 J5
Wainoni (Auckland) 88 H2
Wainoni (Christchurch) 120 G3
Wainono Lagoon 68 C13
Wainui Falls - Abel Tasman National Park 38 E9 39 C1
Wainui Hut 38 E9 39 C1
Wainui Junction (Manawatu) 27 E3
Wainui Junction (Northland) 1 J5 3 A1
Wainui Track 38 E9
Wainui, NI (Bay of Plenty) 14 F11
Wainui, NI (Gisborne) 22 E11 100 D6
Wainui, NI (Northland - Far North) 2 H11
Wainui, NI (Northland) 6 H9 7 B3
Wainui, SI 56 G12
Wainuiomata 33 E3 35 A3 111 D4
Wainuioru (Wellington) 34 C10 34 E9
Waioeka Gorge Scenic Reserve 14 H13 15 H2
Waioeka Pa 14 G13 15 G2
Waiohau 14 H9
Waiohiki 28 E11 103 C3
Waiomatatini 16 D12
Waiomio 4 C9
Waiomu 8 F11 10 A8
Waione 30 F13 31 F7
Waioneke 5 G6
Waiopaoa Hut 20 F13 21 F1
Waiopehu Hut 29 H5
Waiopehu Track 29 H5
Waiorongomai 10 G10 12 A11
Waiorore 15 C6
Waiotahi 14 F12 15 F1
Waiotahi Beach 14 F13 15 F2
Waiotahi Marae 14 F12 15 F1
Waiotahi Valley 14 G12 15 G1
Waiotama 4 H9
Waiotapu 13 J5
Wai-o-tapu Thermal Area 13 J5 20 A8
Waiotauru Hut 33 B5
Waiotehue 3 A2
Waiotemarama 3 E4
Waiotira 4 J10
Waiotu 4 E11
Waiouru 26 D14 27 D2
Waipa Valley 18 A11
Waipa Village 13 G4
Waipahi 78 B11
Waipahihi 19 D5 98 C4
Waipaipai 4 E13
Waipakihi Hut 19 J4
Waipango 76 G14 77 D2
Waipaoa 22 C9
Waipapa (Northland) 2 K12 4 A8
Waipapa (Waikato) 12 J10
Waipapakauri 1 H6
Waipapakauri Beach 1 H5
Waipara 54 C9
Waiparera 3 D3 4 G13
Waiparu 72 G9
Waipatiki 30 E13 31 E7
Waipatiki Beach 28 B13
Waipatu 103 B5
Waipawa 28 J9
Waipiata 67 J5
Waipipi 7 H3 9 C1
Waipiro Bay 16 G11
Waipopo 61 H5
Waipori Falls 73 H7 79 A5
Waipoua Forest 3 F5
Waipoua Forest (locality) 3 F5
Waipoua Settlement 3 F4
Waipounamu 72 H9
Waipu 4 J13 6 A8
Waipu Caves 4 J12
Waipu Cove 6 A8
Waipuku 23 D6 25 A1
Waipukurau 28 J9 32 A10
Waipuna, NI 26 D9
Waipuna, SI 46 D8
Waipunga Falls 20 G9
Waipuru 26 H14 27 H2
Wairakau 10 H10 12 A11
Wairakei 19 C5
Wairakei Village 19 C6
Wairamarama 9 F2
Wairapukao 20 B10
Wairata 14 J14 15 J3
Wairau Bar 35 J6 44 C11
Wairau Pa 35 J5 40 J10 44 B11
Wairau Park 88 H3
Wairau Valley 43 C7
Wairaurahiri Hut 76 G8
Waireia 3 C3
Waireka 12 H14 13 H3
Wairere (Northland - Far North) 3 C5
Wairere (Northland) 5 B6
Wairere Boulders Nature Park 3 C5
Wairere Waterfall - Whakatane 14 E11
Wairio 76 D14 77 A2
Wairoa (Bay of Plenty) 10 J13 12 B14 13 B3
Wairoa (Dunedin) 124 G2

Wairoa (Gisborne) 16 D12
Wairoa (Hawke's Bay) 21 H5
Wairoa Pa 10 J13 12 B14 13 B3 94 C1
Wairoa Reservoir 7 G7 9 B4
Wairua Falls - Whangarei 4 G9
Wairuna 78 B12
Wairunga 74 D13
Waitaanga 17 E6
Waitaha 50 C10 51 C1
Waitahanui 19 E5
Waitahora 30 D13 31 D7
Waitahu 46 A9
Waitahuna 73 J5 79 B3
Waitahuna Gully 73 J6 79 B4
Waitahuna West 73 J4 79 B2
Waitakaruru 8 J10 9 D7
Waitakere 7 D2 89 B1
Waitakere Regional Park 7 E2
Waitakere Reservoir 7 E2
Waitaki Bridge 68 F12
Waitane 78 C8
Waitangi 4 B9 81 A2
Waitangirua 110 B3
Waitanguru 11 J3 17 A7
Waitao 13 B4 94 D3
Waitapu, NI 3 D3
Waitapu, SI 38 D8
Waitara 17 G1 23 A6
Waitarere 29 F4
Waitaria Bay 35 J2 40 F10
Waitaruke 2 H10
Waitati 74 F12
Waitawa 61 H4
Waitawheta 10 F10
Waiteitei 6 D9
Waitekauri 10 E10
Waitepeka 79 E3
Waiterimu 9 F6
Waiteti (Bay of Plenty) 13 F4
Waiteti (Waikato) 11 J6 18 A10
Waitetoki 2 G8
Waitetoko 19 F4
Waitetuna 11 C4
Waitewaewae Hut 29 J5 33 A6
Waiti 10 G7
Waitiki Landing 1 B2
Waitoa 10 H9 12 A10
Waitohi, NI 29 C6
Waitohi, SI 61 G4
Waitoki 6 H8 7 B2
Waitomo Caves (locality) 11 H5
Waitotara 25 G5
Waituhi 22 D9
Waituna (Invercargill) 77 E7
Waituna (Waimate) 68 D12
Waituna Lagoon 77 G7
Waituna West 30 A8 31 A2
Waitutu Hut 75 G7
Waitutu Track 75 G7
Waiuku 7 J4 9 D1
Waiuna Lagoon 57 J2
Waiuta 46 D9
Waiuta - Big River Track 46 C9
Waiwaka 30 H8 31 H2
Waiwera (Auckland) 6 G10 7 A4
Waiwera (Manawatu) 30 G8 31 G2
Waiwera Hot Springs 6 G10 7 A4
Waiwera South 78 C13 79 E1
Waiwhetu 111 C4
Waiwhiu 6 E9
Wakamarina - Onamalutu Track 39 J7 44 B8
Wakanui 55 J3 62 D9
Wakapatu 76 H13
Wakapuaka 38 H13 39 F5
Wakarara 27 G6
Wakari 74 G11
Wakatipu Heights 125 B5 126 B3
Wakatu 116 B4
Wakefield 39 J2 43 B3
Wakelings Hut 27 G5
Waldronville 74 H10 124 G6
Walker Island 1 G6
Wall Island 41 G2
Wallacetown 77 D4
Wallaceville 111 B5
Wallingford 32 C10
Waltham 120 F2
Walton 10 J9 12 B10
Wanaka 35 C6
Wangaloa 79 E5
Wanganui 26 J8 108 B4
Wanganui East 26 H8 109 B5
Wangapeka Track 42 C9
Wanstead 32 B10
Waoku Coach Road Walk 3 E5
Waotu 12 G10
Warawara Forest 3 C3
Ward 44 F12
Ward / Makaro Island 110 D3
Wardville 10 J10 12 B11
Warea 23 D3
Warepa 79 E2
Warkworth 6 E9
Warkworth District Museum 6 E10
Waro 4 E11

Warren, The 52 F13 53 F4 55 B6
Warrington 74 F12
Warwick Junction 46 B12
Washdyke 61 J5
Washdyke Lagoon 61 J5
Washington Valley 115 B1
Washpool Hut 33 H6
Watchdog Hut 50 G11 51 G2
Waterfall Hut (Mackenzie Region) 59 C5
Waterfall Hut (Mt Cook) 50 J9 60 A10
Waterfall Hut (Ruahine FP) 27 H5
Waterloo 33 E3 35 A3 111 C4
Waterton 62 E8
Waterview 89 C3
Watlington 61 J4
Wattle Bay 7 F3
Wattle Downs 7 F5 9 A2
Waverley, NI 24 J9 25 G4
Waverley, SI (Dunedin) 74 H11 124 D4
Waverley, SI (Invercargill) 128 B2
Wawa 12 J12 13 J1
Wayby 6 D8
Wayby Valley 6 D9
Waynes 74 B12
Weavers Crossing 9 G4
Weber 30 E14 32 E8
Wedderburn 67 G4
Weedons 53 J6 56 E8
Weka Pass 54 C8
Wekaweka 3 E4
Welbourn 106 D6 107 C4
Welcome Bay 10 J13 13 B4 94 D2
Welcome Flat Hot Pools 59 A5
Welcome Flat Hut 59 A5
Wellington 33 F1 35 C4 110 D2 112 D5
Wellington Zoo 33 F1 35 C4
Wellsford 6 D8
Wendon 72 H9
Wendon Valley 72 H10
Wendonside 72 G8
Wentworth Falls - Whangamata 8 J13 10 D10
Weraroa 29 G5
Wesley 89 C3
West End 104 D1 105 C3
West Eweburn Dam 67 G4
West Eyreton 53 F5 55 B7
West Harbour 89 B2
West Harper Hut 52 D8
West Melton 53 H5 55 D7
West Plains 77 E4 128 D1
West Sabine Hut 42 J12 47 A4
Westerfield 55 H1 61 C7
Western Heights (Auckland) 89 C2
Western Heights (Rotorua) 96 B2
Western Springs 89 C3
Westfield 90 D5
Westhaven (Christchurch) 120 F4
Westhaven (Te Tai Tapu) Marine Reserve 37 B5
Westhaven (Wellington) 110 B2
Westlake (Auckland) 88 H4
Westlake (Christchurch) 120 C1
Westland Tai Poutini National Park 49 F6
Westmere (Auckland) 89 C3
Westmere (Waikato) 9 G4 11 A5
Westmere (Wanganui) 26 H8 109 A2
Westmere (Wellington) 34 C10
Westmorland 120 D1
Weston 68 H11
Westown 23 B5 107 C3
Westport 41 G3
Westshore 28 D12 103 B1
Westwood 74 H10 124 H6
Wetheral 53 G7 56 C9
Wetherstons 73 H5 79 A3
Weymouth 7 F5 9 A2
Whakaari/White Island 14 A13
Whakahoro 18 B8 24 B13
Whakahoro Hut 18 H8 24 B13
Whakaki 21 H6
Whakaki Lagoon 21 J6
Whakamara 24 H8 25 E3
Whakamarama 10 J12 12 B13 13 B2
Whakamaru 19 A3
Whakanui Track 33 F3
Whakapapa Skifield - Mt Ruapehu 26 A13
Whakapapa Village 18 J12 26 A12
Whakapapaiti Hut 26 A12
Whakapapaiti Hut Track 18 J12 26 A12
Whakapara 4 E11
Whakapirau 5 C6
Whakapourangi 16 E11
Whakarae 14 J11
Whakarewarewa 13 G4 96 D3
Whakarewarewa Thermal Valley - Rotorua 13 G4 96 D3
Whakarongo 30 D8 31 D2
Whakataki Hut 20 D13 21 D1
Whakataki 34 A13
Whakatane 14 E11
Whakaterepapanui Island 40 B10
Whakatete Bay 8 G11 10 B8
Whakatina 24 E13 26 B8
Whakatiwai 8 G9 9 B6
Whakatu 28 E12 103 B4
Whakawhitira 16 D11

Whale Stream Hut 59 D6
Whananaki 4 D13
Whananaki South 4 D13
Whanarua Bay 15 B7
Whangaahei 8 B11 36 J5
Whangae 4 B9
Whangaehu Hut 26 A13
Whangaehu (Wanganui) 26 J9 29 A4
Whangaehu (Wellington) 34 B10
Whangaimoana 33 G5
Whangamarino (Bay of Plenty) 13 F5
Whangamarino (Waikato) 9 E4
Whangamata 8 J14 10 D11
Whangamomona 17 J6 24 C11
Whanganui 18 E14 19 E2
Whanganui Hut 20 E14 21 E2
Whanganui Island 8 D10
Whanganui National Park 18 J8 24 D12 25 A7
Whangaparaoa (Auckland) 6 H10 7 B4
Whangaparaoa (East Cape, NI) 16 A9
Whangaparapara 36 E4
Whangape 3 B2
Whangapoua 8 C12
Whangara 22 D12
Whangara Island (Auckland) 36 E4
Whangara Island (Gisborne) 22 D12
Whangarata 7 J6 9 D3
Whangarei 4 G11 84 B4
Whangarei Airport 4 G12
Whangarei Falls 4 F12
Whangarei Heads 4 H13
Whangaripo 6 D9
Whangaroa 2 H10
Whangaruru 4 C12
Whangaruru South 4 C12
Whangateau 6 D10
Wharanui 44 H12
Whare Creek Hut 70 F12 71 F1
Whare Flat 74 G11 124 F1
Whareama 34 B12
Wharehine 5 D7
Wharehuanui 65 G5
Wharehuia 23 D7 25 A2
Wharekahika Hut 14 H11
Wharekaho Beach / Simpsons Beach 8 D13
Wharekaka 22 A13
Wharekakahu Island 74 H13
Wharekauhau 33 G4
Wharekawa (Auckland) 8 G9 9 B6
Wharekawa (Waikato) 8 H14 10 C11
Wharekohe 4 G10
Wharekopae 21 C6
Wharepaina 20 A8
Wharepapa 5 J7 7 C1
Wharepapa South 12 G9
Wharepoa 8 J12 10 D9
Wharepoga 16 F12
Wharepuhunga 12 H8
Wharereoa 23 H7 25 E2
Wharetoa 78 A13 79 C1
Wharewaka 19 D5 98 D4
Wharfedale Hut 52 E12 53 E3 55 A5
Wharfedale Track 52 E12 53 E3 55 A5
Whariwharangi Hut 38 D9 39 B1
Whataroa 49 F7
Whatatutu 22 A9
Whataupoko 100 B4
Whatawhata 11 C5
Whatipu 7 F2
Whatipu Caves 7 F2
Whatitiri 4 G10
Whatoro 3 G6
Whatuwhiwhi 2 F7
Whau Valley 85 B1
Whawharua 11 H6
Wheatstone 62 E9
Wheki Valley 4 H10
Whenuahou 30 A14 32 A8
Whenuakite 8 E13
Whenuakura 24 J9 25 F4
Whenuanui 5 B4
Whenuapai 6 J9 7 C3 89 A2
Whenuapai Airforce Base 6 J9 7 D3
Whetukura 30 B14 32 B8
Whirinaki (Hawke's Bay) 28 C12
Whirinaki (Northland) 3 D4
Whirinaki Forest Park 20 D10
Whiritoa 8 J14 10 D11
Whiriwhiri 7 J4 9 D1
Whitby 110 A3
White Hut 50 B14 51 B5
White Island 14 A13
White Pine Bush 14 F10
White Rock 80 G5
White Rocks 35 F1 40 E13
Whitecliffs 52 H11 53 H2 55 D4
Whitecliffs Walkway 17 F4
Whitecraig 68 H11
Whitehall 12 D9
Whitemans Valley 33 D4
Whiterigg 78 A9
Whiterock 53 D6
Whitford 7 E6 9 A3
Whitiaga Airfield 8 D12
Whitianga (Bay of Plenty) 15 D5

Whitianga (Waikato) 8 D13
Whitikahu 9 H6 11 A7
Whitikau 15 H4
Whitiroa 91 C3 92 E3
Whitstone 68 H11
Whymper Hut 49 H7
Wigram Aerodrome - Christchurch 53 J7 56 E9 120 C2
Wigram Park 120 V2
Wilden 72 G13 73 G2
Wilder Settlement 32 D9
Wilkinson Hut 50 D12 51 D3
Willowbank 78 A10
Willowbridge 68 D13
Willowby 55 J2 62 D8
Willowford 28 C8
Willows Hut 48 C9
Wills Hut 58 F12 59 F1
Wilsons Crossing 77 D5
Wilsons Siding 53 G7 56 C9
Wilsonville 4 E11
Wilton 110 D1
Wiltsdown 12 G11
Wimbledon 32 F9
Winchester 61 G5
Winchmore 55 H2 62 C8
Windermere 55 J1 61 D7
Windsor (Invercargill) 68 G10 127 A5 128 B2
Windsor Park 68 G11
Windwhistle 52 H9 55 D2
Windy Hill 4 J8
Windy Ridge 88 J3
Wingate 33 E3 35 A3 111 C4
Wingatui 74 H10 124 G4
Winiata 27 F3
Winscombe 60 F12 61 F1
Winslow 55 J2 62 D8
Winton 77 B4
Wiri 7 F5 9 A2 90 E5
Wither Hills Walkway 35 K6 44 C10
Woburn 110 C3
Womens Island 80 D6
Wood Bay 89 D2
Wood, The 115 B5
Woodaugh 123 A4 124 D3
Woodbourne 44 C10
Woodbury 61 E4
Woodcocks 6 F9
Woodend (Invercargill) 77 F5
Woodend (Waimakariri) 54 F8 56 B10
Woodend Beach 54 F8 56 B10
Woodhill 5 J7 7 C1 84 C2
Woodlands Park 89 D2
Woodlands, NI (Bay of Plenty) 10 G11 14 F13 15 F2
Woodlands, SI 77 E6
Woodlaw 76 D14 77 A2
Woodleigh 9 G2
Woodridge 110 C2
Woodside, NI 33 C7
Woodside, SI 74 H9 79 A7
Woodstock (Tasman) 38 J8 42 A13
Woodstock (Westland) 45 J2
Woodville 30 D10 31 D4
Woolleys Bay 4 E13
Woolston 54 J8 56 E10 120 F2
Woolwich 103 D4
Worsley Bivvy 52 A10
Wreys Bush 77 A3
Wrights Bush 77 D4
Wyllies Crossing 74 H10 124 J3
Wyndham 78 D9

Y

Yaldhurst 53 H7 56 D9 120 A3
Yaldhurst Museum of Transport & Science - Christchurch 53 H7 56 D9
Yankee River Hut 77 J1 80 C3
Yeates Track 29 H6
Yeats Ridge Hut 50 B13 51 B4
Yellow Hut 74 F11
Yeoman Track 27 G6
York Track 23 D5
Young Hut 58 G9
Youngman Stream Hut 52 C13 53 C4
Yourk Bay 110 D3

Camping sites index

- (bracketed) numbers – site number
- normal numbers – map references, specified by map number followed by grid reference
- **bold** page numbers – the page number containing the site's information

219 on Johns' Motel & Holiday Park (1157) 120 D5 56 C9 **87**
252 Beachside Motels & Holiday Park (1051) 45 H2 **82**
3 Mile Hill Rest Area & View Point (1323) 124 F3 74 G11 **97**
5 Mile Bay Rest Area (328) 98 D4 19 E5 **40**

A

A1 Kaikoura Motels & Holiday Park (1103) 48 E12 **85**
Aaron Lodge Top 10 Holiday Park (1328) 124 E3 74 H11 **97**
Aberfeldy Hill North Side Rest Area (796) 26 G10 **66**
Abisko Lodge & Apartment (& Campground) (1231) 52 J9 55 F2 **92**
Accommodation at Te Puna (367) 10 J13 **41**
Acheron Accommodation House (1139) 47 E6 **87**
Acre Creek Rest Area (1047) 45 G3 **81**
Addington Accommodation Park (1172) 120 D2 56 D9 **88**
Affordable Westshore Holiday Park (651) 103 B1 28 D12 **57**
Ahipara Holiday Park (92) 1 J5 **26**
Ahuriri Bridge (1399) 67 A4 **100**
Ahuriri Motels (1398) 67 A3 **100**
Airport Information Roadside Rest Area (271) 23 A6 **36**
Airport Road Rest Area (455) 92 H6 11 C7 **46**
Akapoua Bay (134) 36 D4 **29**
Akaroa Domain Rest Area (1221) 56 G12 **91**
Akaroa Top 10 Holiday Park (1220) 56 G12 **91**
Akitio Beach Camping Ground (761) 32 G8 **64**
Albert Town Tavern (1415) 66 D8 **101**
Alec McKenzie Arboretum (1477) 77 C2 **105**
Alexanders Holiday Park (843) 113 D3 114 D3 40 H10 **70**
Alexandra Holiday Park (1318) 73 A2 **96**
Alexandra Tourist Park (1317) 73 A2 **96**
Alfredton Domain Rest Area (746) 31 H4 **63**
All Day Bay Recreation Reserve (1296) 68 J11 **95**
All Seasons Holiday Park Hannahs Bay (533) 96 B5 13 G5 **51**
All Seasons Holiday Park Christchurch (1206) 120 G2 56 D10 **90**
Allendale Reserve (1211) 56 E10 **90**
Alpha Motel & Holiday Park (13) 84 D2 85 C1 4 G11 **21**
Alpine Adventure Holiday Park (1138) 47 F5 **87**
Alpine View Holiday Park (1223) 120 A2 56 D8 **91**
Alpine-Pacific Holiday Park (1101) 48 E12 **85**
Amber Holiday Park (1173) 120 D2 56 D9 **88**
Amberley Beach Reserve (1171) 54 D9 **88**
Amble on Inn Holiday Park (1482) 128 B5 77 F5 **105**
Ambury Regional Park (207) 90 D4 7 E4 **33**
Anaura Bay Motor Camp (602) 16 J11 **54**
Anaura Bay Waipare Scenic Reserve (603) 16 J11 **55**
Andrews Shelter Arthur's Pass National Park (1190) 52 B10 **89**
Anglers Lodge Motels & Holiday Park (408) 8 B10 **44**
Aotea Camping Ground (667) 110 B3 33 D2 **59**
Aramoana Beach (774) 32 B12 **64**
Arataki Motels & Holiday Park (659) 103 B6 28 F12 **58**
Arataki Visitors Centre (186) 89 D2 7 E3 **32**
Army Road Kaimanawa Forest Park (646) 19 G6 **57**
Arnold Park Rest Area (985) 41 G7 **78**
Arrowtown 'Born of Gold' Holiday Park (1436) 65 G6 **102**
Arundel Bridge Reserve (1238) 61 D5 **92**
Ashburton Holiday Park (1234) 62 D8 **92**
Ashhurst Domain (751) 31 D3 **63**
Ashley Gorge Holiday Park (1179) 55 A6 **89**
Ashley Park Campground (808) 25 G6 **66**
Aspiring Campervan Park (1413) 66 D8 **101**
Athenree Hot Springs & Holiday Park (357) 10 F12 **41**
Athenree Lavender Holiday Park (360) 10 F11 **41**
Athol Roadside Rest Area (1458) 71 D7 **104**
Auckland North Shore Motels & Holiday Park (137) 88 J4 90 A4 7 D4 **29**
Aussie Bay Queen Charlotte Sound (851) 40 G9 **70**
Avalanche Creek (Arthur's Pass) Arthur's Pass National Park (1194) 52 B8 **90**
Avondale Motor Park (182) 89 C3 7 E4 **31**
Avro Motel & Caravan Park (791) 109 C3 26 J8 **66**
Awakeri Hot Springs (523) 14 F9 **50**
Awakino Bridges (Ladies Mile) Rest Area (249) 17 C5 **35**
Awana Beach (132) 36 D5 **28**
Awatere Motor Camp (1086) 44 E11 **84**
Awatere Rest Area (1088) 44 E12 **84**
Awhitu Regional Park (Brook Homestead and Peninsula Campground) (213) 7 G3 **33**

B

Back Country Accommodation (835) 17 H6 **68**
Bakers Creek Rest Areas (2) (1017) 45 D4 **80**
Balclutha Motor Camp (1343) 79 E3 **98**
Balfour Roadside Rest Area (1466) 71 H7 **104**
Bannockburn Domain Motorcamp (1403) 66 H8 **101**
Barn (The) Cabins Camping & Backpackers (935) 38 F10 **75**
Barneys Point Rest Area (757) 31 D3 **63**
Bay of Islands Holiday Park (Lily-Pond) (57) 4 B9 **24**
Bay of Islands RV Park (53) 4 B9 **24**
Bay of Many Coves (868) 40 F11 **71**
Bay View Snapper Holiday Park (649) 28 C12 **57**
Bay View Van Park (65C) 28 D12 **57**
Baylys Beach Holiday Park (115) 3 J6 **27**
Bazil's Hostel (1023) 41 G3 **80**
Beach Grove Holiday Park (490) 94 C5 13 B4 **48**
Beach Haven Holiday Camp (354) 10 F12 **41**
Beach Holiday Park (496) 13 C6 **49**
Beach Road Holiday Park (769) 32 D11 **64**
Beach Road Motor Camp (1484) 77 F4 **105**
Beach Road Rest Area (14) 85 D3 4 G12 **21**
Beachfront Reserve (501) 13 D7 **49**
Beachfront Reserve Picnic Area (359) 10 F12 **41**
Beachside Holiday Park (49) 81 C2 4 B10 **23**
Beachwalk Motor Camp (1049) 45 H2 **82**
Belt Road Seaside Holiday Park (823) 107 B3 23 B5 **68**
Bendigo Rest Area (1389) 66 G9 **100**
Bendrose Creek Rest Area (1262) 59 H6 **93**
Benmore Dam Recreation Reserve (1290) 67 C5 **95**
Big Bay Motor Camp (214) 7 F3 **33**
Bignell St Motel & Caravan Park (790) 109 D3 26 J8 **65**
Birch Park Rest Area (814) 25 G6 **67**
Black Gully Retreat (1369) 72 H13 **99**
Black Rock (867) 40 F10 **71**
Blackhead Beach Camping Ground (771) 32 C12 **64**
Blackwater Creek Rest Area (1036) 46 C8 **81**
Blairich Bridge Rest Area and Camping Ground (1087) 44 E10 **84**
Bland Bay Motor Camp (40) 4 B12 **23**
Bland Bay Reserve (39) 4 B12 **23**
Bledisloe Holiday Park (497) 13 C6 **49**
Blenheim Backpackers and Motorcamp (994) 44 C10 117 A5 **78**
Blenheim Top 10 Holiday Park (995) 44 C11 **78**
Blind Billy's Holiday Camp & Middlemarch Motels (1331) 74 D8 **97**
Blue Heron Holiday Park (17) 4 G12 **22**
Blue Lake Recreation Reserve (1312) 66 F13 67 F2 **96**
Blue Lake Top 10 Holiday Park (536) 13 G5 **51**
Blue Pools Roadside Rest Area (1424) 58 G11 **102**
Blue Skies (1162) 56 C10 **88**
Blue Waters (605) 22 A13 **55**
Bluff Camping Ground (1483) 77 G5 **105**
Blumine Island (881) 40 F12 **72**
Boat Ramp Roadside Rest Area (219) 9 G5 **34**
Bob's Bay Roadside Rest Area (844) 114 B4 **70**
Booms Flat (383) 8 G12 **42**
Boulders (616) 15 G3 **55**
Boundary Creek (1421) 58 J10 **102**
Bowentown Beach Holiday Park (358) 10 F12 **41**
Bridge Lodge (682) 29 J4 **59**
Bridge Motor Lodge (781) 29 B6 **65**
Brighton Domain (1333) 124 J6 74 J10 **97**
Brighton Motor Camp & Boat Hire (1332) 124 J6 74 H10 **97**
Broken Hills (447) 8 G13 **46**
Brook Valley Holiday Park (913) 116 C5 39 H4 **74**
Bucks Road (729) 33 C6 **62**
Bulls by Rangitikei River Bridge Rest Area 3.3 (782) 29 B6 **65**
Butchers Dam Reserve (1378) 73 B2 **99**
Butchers Flat Mt Richmond Conservation Park (884) 39 H6 **72**
Byron's Resort (684) 29 J3 **59**

C

Cable Bay (48) 4 A11 **23**
Cable Bay Holiday Park (909) 39 F5 **74**
Cairnmuir Camping Ground (1402) 66 H8 **101**
Cairnmuir Lakeside Reserve (1401) 66 H8 **101**
Cambridge Motor Park (456) 12 D8 **47**
Cameron Creek Rest Area (1426) 58 G11 **102**
Cameron Flat Mount Aspiring National Park (1425) 58 G11 **102**
Camp Bay Queen Charlotte Sound (878) 40 F11 **72**
Camp Elsdon (666) 110 B2 33 D2 **58**
Camp Kiwi (235) 11 G6 **35**
Camp Waipu Cove (6) 6 A8 **21**
Canaan Downs (940) 38 F9 **75**
Cannibal Cove (880) 40 E12 **72**
Cape Reinga Roadside Rest Area (91) 1 A1 **26**
Capital Gateway Motor Inn (665) 110 C2 33 E2 **58**
Carlyle Beach Motor Camp (811) 25 G3 **67**
Carnival Park Campground (749) 31 F3 **63**
Caroline Bay Beach Rest Area (1249) 121 B2 61 J5 **92**
Carterton Holiday Park (737) 34 C8 **62**
Cascade Creek (1521) 64 G10 **108**
Castlecliff Seaside Holiday Park (792) 109 C1 25 J7 **66**
Castlepoint Holiday Park & Motels (740) 34 A13 **63**
Catchpool Valley Rimutaka Forest Park (722) 33 F3 **62**
Catleys (382) 8 G12 **42**
Catlins Woodstock Lodge & Camping Ground (1353) 78 E14 79 G2 **98**
Cave Rest Area (1251) 61 H2 **93**
Cave Stream Scenic Reserve (1187) 52 E9 **89**
Central Motor Home Park (1042) 118 B4 45 E4 **81**
Chalets The Holiday Park (1400) 66 H8 **101**
Champagne Creek Reserve (1382) 66 J10 **100**
Charleston Motor Camp (1012) 41 H1 **80**
Charteris Bay Reserve (1212) 56 F10 **91**
Chartridge Park (859) 40 H8 **71**
Chasm The (1526) 64 E8 **108**
Cheltenham Rest Area 54.3 (779) 30 B8 **65**
Cheviot Motel & Holiday Park (1117) 48 J9 **85**
Christchurch Top 10 Meadow Park Holiday Park (1156) 120 E4 56 D9 **87**
Clarkes Bluff (1433) 58 E12 **102**
Clarks Beach Holiday Park (210) 7 H4 **33**
Clements Clearing Kaimanawa Forest Park (644) 19 G6 **57**
Clements Roadend Kaimanawa Forest Park (645) 19 G6 **57**
Clifden Historic Bridge Reserve (1494) 76 D12 **106**
Clifton Beach Reserve Motor Camp (657) 28 F13 **58**
Clifton Road Reserve (655) 103 A5 28 F13 **58**
Clive Motor Camp & Chalets (654) 103 A4 28 E12 **57**
Club Habitat (309) 19 G3 **39**
Club Waimea Waimea Town & Country Club (917) 116 C2 39 H3 **74**
Clutha River Rest Area (1375) 73 E2 **99**
Clyde Dam Recreation Reserve (1381) 66 J10 **100**
Clyde Holiday & Sporting Complex (1380) 66 J10 **100**
Coachman's Inn Motor Lodge (1481) 128 A3 77 E5 **105**
Cobb River Kahurangi National Park (944) 37 H6 **76**
Colac Bay Boat Ramp (1489) 76 H13 77 E1 **105**
Colac Bay Tavern & Camping Ground (1488) 76 H13 **105**
Colac Bay/Oraka Township Camping Area (1487) 76 H13 **105**
Coldwater (1003) 43 J2 **79**
Collingwood Motor Camp (957) 37 C7 **76**
Collins Memorial Reserve (987) 40 H10 **78**
Colville Bay Motel & Motor Camp (410) 8 B11 **44**
Colville Bay Roadside Rest Area (411) 8 B11 **44**
Colville Farm Holidays (409) 8 B11 **44**
Corner Creek (724) 33 G4 **62**
Coromandel Motels & Holiday Park (403) 8 C11 **44**
Coronation Hill Reserve/Sign of the Kiwi Rest Area (1210) 56 E10 **90**
Coronation Holiday Park (1228) 55 J3 **91**

Camping sites index

Cosy Corner Holiday Park (488) 94 B3 13 B4 **48**
Cosy Cottage International Holiday Park (542) 96 B3 13 G4 **51**
Courthouse Flat Kahurangi National Park (965) 42 C11 **77**
Cowshed Bay Pelorus Sound (865) 40 G10 **71**
Craigieburn Craigieburn Conservation Park (1188) 52 D9 **89**
Cromwell Roadside Rest Area (1386) 66 H9 **100**
Cromwell Top 10 Holiday Park (1385) 66 H9 **100**
Cullen Point Lookout (857) 40 G8 **71**
Curio Bay Camping Ground (1359) 78 H11 **99**

D

Dannevirke Holiday Park (760) 31 C6 **64**
Dansey Pass Hotel (1307) 67 G6 **96**
Dansey's Pass Holiday Park (1280) 68 F8 **94**
Dargaville Campervan Park & Cabins (117) 3 J7 **27**
Dargaville Holiday Park (116) 3 J7 **27**
Dargaville North Rest Area (119) 3 J7 **28**
Davies Bay (853) 40 G9 **70**
Davis Flat Roadside Rest Area (1427) 58 G11 **102**
Deer Flat (1515) 64 H9 **107**
Deer Hunters Flat (1147) 47 F1 **87**
Deer Valley (1148) 46 E13 **87**
Delhaven Motels & Camping Ground (1170) 54 D8 **88**
Devils Creek Rest Area (1388) 66 G9 **100**
Dickey Flat (350) 10 F10 **41**
Dickson Holiday Park (390) 8 G11 **43**
Dipton Roadside Rest Area (1465) 71 J6 **104**
Discovery Lodge (289) 18 J12 **38**
Divide The & Routeburn Track Base (1523) 64 F10 **108**
Dolamore Park Scenic Reserve (1470) 78 A8 **104**
Donneraille Park (584) 21 E6 **53**
Donovan Park Entrance (495) 13 C5 **49**
Double Bay (861) 40 G9 **71**

Douglas Domain Rest Area (829) 24 E8 **68**
Duddings Lake Motorcamp (783) 29 A5 **65**
Dunedin Holiday Park (1325) 124 D5 74 H11 **97**
Dunham Point Reserve (475) 19 A4 **47**
Dunsdale Recreation Reserve (1473) 77 B6 **105**
Duvauchelle Bay Rest Area (1218) 56 G12 **91**
Duvauchelle Holiday Park (1219) 56 G12 **91**

E

East Taieri Roadside Rest Area (1335) 74 H9 **97**
Edwards Stream Rest Area (1257) 60 F10 **93**
Eight Mile Rest Area (983) 41 G7 **78**
Ekatahuna North Roadside Rest Area (747) 31 G3 **63**
Eketahuna Camping (745) 31 H2 **63**
El Rancho (680) 33 A4 **59**
Elaine Bay Pelorus Sound (896) 40 E8 **73**
Elterwater Rest and Camping Area (1090) 44 F12 **84**
Emery Store Entry (531) 13 F6 **50**
Eskdale Caravan Park (640) 28 C12 **56**
Ettrick Holiday Park (1373) 73 E2 **99**
Everetts Mohaka River (642) 20 J11 **57**

F

Fairlie Gateway Top 10 Holiday Park (1254) 61 F1 **93**
Falls Motel & Waterfront Campground (56) 81 B1 4 B9 **24**
Fantail Bay (413) 8 A9 **44**
Fantail Falls Roadside Rest Area (1429) 58 F12 **102**
Farewell Gardens Motor Camp & Holiday Accommodation (958) 37 A7 **76**
Feilding Holiday Park (777) 29 C7 **65**
Ferndale Pelorus Sound (876) 40 F10 **72**
Fernland Spa Thermal Mineral Springs (372) 94 C1 10 J13 **42**

Fernwood Holiday Park (927) 39 F2 **75**
Fiordland Great Views Holiday Park (1506) 70 C11 **106**
Fiordland National Park Lodge Te Anau Downs (1508) 70 A12 **107**
Fisherman's Bend Lake Aviemore (1285) 67 C7 **95**
Fitzgerald Glade (468) 12 E12 **47**
Fitzroy Beach Holiday Park (272) 107 A5 23 B5 **36**
Flat Ford Rest Area (982) 41 G7 **78**
Flaxmill Bay Hideaway (436) 8 D13 **45**
Fletcher Bay (415) 8 A10 **44**
Forest Pools Puketi Forest (99) 3 B6 **26**
Forest View Motor Camp (237) 11 F2 **35**
Forest View Rest Area (95) 2 K8 **26**
Fortrose Area B (1362) 78 G8 **99**
Fortrose Domain (1361) 78 G8 **99**
Four Brothers Roadside Rest Area (227) 11 C5 **34**
Fox Glacier Holiday Park & Motels (1071) 49 H4 **83**
Fox Glacier Lodge & Campervan Park (1069) 49 H4 **83**
Fox Glacier Viewpoint (1070) 49 H5 **83**
Foxton Beach Motor Camp (696) 29 F4 **60**
Foxton North Roadside Rest Area (697) 29 E5 **60**
Foxton Straights Roadside Rest Area (698) 29 E5 **60**
Frankton Motor Camp (1439) 126 A5 65 H5 **102**
Franz Josef Mountain View Top 10 Holiday Park (1066) 49 G6 **83**
French Farm Rest Area (1215) 56 G12 **91**
French Pass Pelorus Sound (899) 40 C9 **73**

G

Gates of Haast Bridge (1430) 58 F12 **102**
Gebbies Pass Summit (1213) 56 F10 **91**
Gentle Annie Point Camp & Cafe (1027) 41 D6 **80**
Geraldine Kiwi Holiday Park (1242) 61 F4 **92**

TAUPUTAPUTA, NORTHLAND

Camping sites index

Gibby's Place (60) 86 C1 4 A8 **24**
Gillespies Beach (1074) 49 G3 **83**
Gisborne Showgrounds Park Motorcamp (626) 100 A2 22 D10 **56**
Glacier Country Campervan Park (1068) 49 G6 **83**
Glade The Holiday Park (443) 8 G14 **46**
Glen Esk Road (177) 7 E2 **31**
Glen Innis Farmstay (585) 21 E7 **53**
Glencoe Reserve (1297) 68 J10 74 A13 **95**
Glendhu Bay Motor Camp (1414) 65 D7 **101**
Glenfalls Mohaka River (641) 20 J10 **57**
Glenmark Holiday Park (1250) 61 J4 **93**
Glenorchy Holiday Park (1448) 65 F2 **103**
Glenorchy Lakeside Reserve (1447) 65 F2 **103**
Glenquoich Caravan Park (1457) 71 D7 **104**
Glentanner Park (1260) 59 D6 **93**
Glentunnel Holiday Park (1175) 55 D4 **89**
Goat Island Camping & Accommodation (167) 6 D11 **31**
Gold Park Motor Camp (1366) 79 A3 **99**
Golden Bay Holiday Park (956) 37 C7 **76**
Golden Grove Holiday Park (489) 94 B4 13 B4 **48**
Golden Springs Motel Holiday Park & Restaurant (557) 19 B7 **52**
Goldsborough (1048) 45 H3 **82**
Gore Bay & Buxton Campgrounds (1118) 54 A13 **85**
Gore Motor Camp (1471) 78 B9 **104**
Gorge Creek Miners Monument & Picnic Area (1377) 73 B1 **99**
Goudies Road Rest Area (565) 20 A9 **52**
Governors Bay Scenic Reserve (848) 114 A1 40 G10 **70**
Graces Stream (723) 33 F3 **62**
Great Lake Holiday Park (332) 98 B3 19 D5 **40**
Green The (135) 36 E4 **29**
Greenwood Park (918) 116 C1 39 H3 **74**
Greta Valley Camping Ground (1121) 54 B10 **86**
Greta Valley Rest Area (1120) 54 B10 **86**
Grey River (1180) 53 D7 **89**
Greymouth Seaside Top 10 Holiday Park (1043) 45 F4 **81**
Greyneys Arthur's Pass National Park (1193) 52 B8 **90**
Greytown Camp Ground (735) 34 C7 **62**
Grumpys Retreat N' Holiday Park (1237) 61 E5 **92**
Guy Roe Reserve (Homestead Arm) (560) 13 J6 **52**

H

Haast Beach Holiday Park (1085) 58 D8 **84**
Haast Lodge (1084) 58 D9 **84**
Hahei Holiday Resort (437) 8 D14 **46**
Hakataramea Rest Area (1282) 68 D8 **94**
Halfway Hill Roadside Rest Area (222) 9 J5 **34**
Halletts Bay Picnic Area (320) 19 F5 **39**
Hamilton City Holiday Park (231) 92 E4 11 C7 **35**
Hangdog Camp (947) 38 E8 **76**
Hanmer River Holiday Park (1133) 47 G5 **86**
Hanmer River Rest Areas (1130) 47 G5 **86**
Hanmer Springs Alpine Holiday Apartments & Campground (1135) 47 F5 **86**
Hanmer Springs Forest Camp (1134) 47 F5 **86**
Hans Bay-Lake Kaniere (1053) 45 J3 **82**
Harataonga (133) 36 D5 **29**
Harbourside Holiday Park (431) 8 D13 **45**
Harcourt Holiday Park (726) 33 C4 **62**
Harihari Motor Inn (1059) 50 D9 **82**
Haruru Falls Resort (55) 81 B1 4 B9 **24**
Harvey Bay Pelorus Sound (891) 40 E8 **73**
Hastings Top 10 Holiday Park (658) 103 C5 28 F12 **58**
Hautapu River Bridge Rest Area 1.2 (715) 26 E14 **61**
Havelock Motor Camp (858) 40 G8 **71**
Hawai Bay Camping Ground (588) 15 E4 **54**
Hawdon Shelter Arthur's Pass National Park (1191) 52 B9 **89**
Helme Holiday Park (926) 39 F2 **75**
Henry Creek (1507) 70 B12 **107**
Herbertville Motor Camp (762) 32 F10 **64**
Hideaway Lodge (59) 4 B8 **24**
Hihi Beach Holiday Camp (74) 2 G9 **25**
Hikurangi Roadside Rest Area (23) 4 E11 **22**
Himatangi Beach Holiday Park (699) 29 D4 **60**
Himatangi North Roadside Rest Area (700) 29 D5 **60**
Hinemaiaia River Access (322) 19 F5 **39**
Hinemaiaia Scenic Reserve Access (321) 19 F5 **39**

Hiwi Hills Rest Area (243) 18 C10 **35**
Hokitika Holiday Park (1052) 45 H2 **82**
Holdens Bay Top 10 Holiday Park (534) 96 B5 13 G4 **51**
Holdsworth Tararua Forest Park (738) 34 B7 **62**
Home Bay (128) 7 C6 **28**
Homestead (1314) 66 E14 67 E3 **96**
Hope River Rest Area (1142) 47 G2 **87**
Horopito Rest Area 4.6 (293) 26 B11 **38**
Horseshoe Creek Rest Area (1141) 47 G3 **87**
Hot Water Beach (539) 13 H6 **51**
Hot Water Beach Holiday Park (438) 8 E14 **46**
Hotoritori (385) 8 G12 **43**
Huia – Karamatura Valley & Barn Paddock Campgrounds (189) 89 E1 7 F2 **32**
Huiarau Summit Roadside Rest Area (574) 20 C14 **53**
Huka Falls Scenic Reserve (485) 19 D6 **48**
Hunterville Rest Area 1 7 (702) 26 J12 **60**
Hydrabad Holiday Park (693) 29 G4 **60**

I

Ikamatua Holiday Park (1037) 46 C8 **81**
Info/Rest Area (444) 8 G13 **46**
Invercargill Top 10 Holiday Park (Gum Tree Farm) (1479) 77 E5 **105**
Island View Family Holiday Park (514) 14 F13 **50**

J

Jack's Gasthof Camping & Accommodation Bar & Pizzeria (1011) 41 H2 **79**
Jacksons Retreat (1202) 45 J6 **90**
Jerusalem Rest Area (799) 26 D8 **66**
Jim Currie Reserve (473) 12 H12 **47**
John Coull (282) 25 A7 **37**

K

Kaiaua Beach (604) 22 A13 **55**
Kaiaua Motor Camp (201) 8 G9 **33**
Kaikoura Coastal Campgrounds Goose Bay (1107) 48 F11 **85**
Kaikoura Peketa Beach Holiday Park (1105) 48 E11 **85**
Kaikoura Top 10 Holiday Park (1102) 48 E12 **85**
Kaimai Watering Hole Rest Area (467) 12 D12 **47**
Kaimanawa Road (302) 19 J3 **38**
Kaipawa Trig Lookout (418) 8 C11 **45**
Kairakau Beach (775) 28 J12 **65**
Kairaki Beach Motor Camp (1163) 56 C10 **88**
Kaitangata Riverside Motor Camp (1347) 79 E4 **98**
Kaitarakiri Walking Track (377) 10 C9 **42**
Kaiteriteri Beach Motor Camp (933) 39 E2 **75**
Kaiwaka North Roadside Rest Area (2) 6 B8 **21**
Kaka Point Camping Ground (1348) 79 G4 **98**
Kakaho (482) 19 C2 **48**
Kakahu Rest Area (1256) 61 F3 **93**
Kakanui Camping Ground (1295) 68 J11 **95**
Kakapo Kaimanawa Forest Park (647) 19 G6 **57**
Kamo Springs Holiday Park (21) 85 A1 4 F11 **22**
Kapiti Holiday Resort (679) 33 A3 **59**
Kapowairua (Spirits Bay) Te Paki Recreation Area (89) 1 A2 **26**
Karaka & Scorching Bay Reserves (663) 110 E2 33 F2 **58**
Karamea Domain Camping Ground (1030) 41 A7 **80**
Karamea Holiday Park (1029) 41 A7 **80**
Katikati Naturist Park (364) 10 G11 **41**
Kauaeranga Christian Camp (387) 8 H11 **43**
Kauauroa Bay Pelorus Sound (894) 40 E10 **73**
Kauika Campsite (798) 26 E9 **66**
Kaupokonui Beach Motorcamp (816) 23 G5 **67**
Kauri Coast Top 10 Holiday Park (112) 3 G6 **27**
Kauri Grove Lookout & Scenic Reserve (439) 8 F14 **46**
Kauri Grove Track/Lynch Stream Coast Track (440) 8 F14 **46**
Kawakawa Roadside Rest Area (42) 4 C9 **23**
Kawatiri Junction Kahurangi National Park (969) 42 F11 **77**
Kawhatau (711) 27 G5 **61**
Kawhia Beachside S-Cape/Kawhia Harbourview Cottages (236) 11 F3 **35**
Kawhia Camping Ground (238) 11 F2 **35**

Kea Motel & Holiday Park (470) 12 F11 **47**
Kelcey's Bush Farmyard Holiday Park (1274) 68 C11 **94**
Kellys Bay Reserve (121) 5 D4 **28**
Kenepuru Head Pelorus Sound (874) 40 F11 **72**
Kennedy Park Top 10 Resort (652) 103 B1 28 D12 **57**
Kerikeri River Rest Area (64) 4 A8 **24**
Kerikeri Stone House DOC Reserve (65) 86 B2 4 A8 **24**
Kerikeri Top 10 Holiday Park (61) 86 C1 4 A8 **24**
Kerr Bay Nelson Lakes National Park (1005) 42 G13 **79**
Keswick Park Camping Ground (1350) 79 H3 **98**
Kidds Bush Reserve (1419) 66 A9 **102**
Kina Beach Camping Ground (925) 39 F2 38 H10 **75**
King Edward Park Motor Camp (824) 25 E2 **68**
Kingston Flyer Northern Railway Terminal & Reserve (1456) 72 B8 **104**
Kingston Flyer Southern Railway Terminal (1455) 72 C8 **104**
Kingston Motels & Holiday Park (1454) 72 B8 **104**
Kinloch (1449) 64 F12 65 F2 **103**
Kiosk Creek (1518) 64 H10 **108**
Kiriwhakapapa Tararua Forest Park (743) 34 A8 **63**
Kiwi Park Motels & Holiday Park (979) 42 G9 **78**
KJ's Accommodation & Camping (1046) 45 G3 **81**
Klondyke Corner Arthur's Pass National Park (1192) 52 B8 **90**
Knobs Flat (1517) 64 H9 **108**
Knobs Flat Rest Area (1516) 64 H9 **108**
Knottingley Park Motor Camp (1273) 68 D12 **94**
Kohaihai Kahurangi National Park (1032) 37 H2 **81**
Koitiata Camping Ground (785) 29 A4 **65**
Kopaki Rest Area (242) 18 B10 **35**
Kowai Pass Domain Camp (1182) 55 B4 **89**
Kowhai Point (1002) 43 E3 **79**
Kuaotunu Motor Camp (419) 8 C13 **45**
Kumeti Ruahine Forest Park (759) 31 B5 **64**
Kumutoto Bay (866) 40 G10 **71**
Kuranui Bay Reserve (388) 8 G11 **43**
Kuripapango (Ox Bow) (719) 27 C7 **61**
Kurow Holiday Park (1281) 67 D7 **94**

L

Lake Access and Rest Areas (2) (472) 19 A4 **47**
Lake Benmore Holiday Park (1293) 67 B4 **95**
Lake Brunner Country Motel Holiday Park (1040) 45 G6 **81**
Lake Brunner Motor Camp (1041) 45 G6 **81**
Lake Ferry Holiday Park (732) 33 G4 **62**
Lake Gunn (1522) 64 F10 **108**
Lake Hawea Holiday Park (1416) 66 C9 **101**
Lake Hawea Lookout (1417) 66 B9 **101**
Lake Ianthe Matahi (1058) 50 C9 **82**
Lake Karapiro Camping & Pursuits Centre (459) 12 D9 **47**
Lake Lyndon Rest Area (1185) 55 B2 **89**
Lake Mahinapua (1054) 45 J1 **82**
Lake Matheson Roadside Rest Area (1072) 49 H4 **83**
Lake Ohau and Lake Middleton Recreation Reserves (1267) 59 H4 **93**
Lake Okareka (537) 13 G5 **51**
Lake Outlet Holiday Park (1410) 66 D8 **101**
Lake Paringa (1078) 58 B12 **83**
Lake Pearson (Moana Rua) (1189) 52 C10 **89**
Lake Pukaki Rest Area & Viewpoint (1259) 59 G7 **93**
Lake Rotoiti Holiday Park (551) 13 F5 **52**
Lake Rotoroa Nelson Lakes National Park (972) 42 G11 **77**
Lake Ruataniwha Holiday Park (1264) 59 H6 **93**
Lake Ruataniwha Recreation Reserve (1265) 59 H6 **93**
Lake Sumner Forest Park Rest Area (1143) 47 G1 **87**
Lake Tarawera Outlet (538) 13 H6 **51**
Lake Taupo Top 10 Holiday Resort (333) 98 A5 19 D5 **40**
Lake Taylor (1124) 46 J12 **86**
Lake Tekapo Holiday Park (1258) 60 E9 **93**
Lake Tennyson (1004) 47 C4 **79**
Lake Tutira Hawke's Bay (637) 28 A12 **56**
Lake View Rest Area (306) 19 G2 **39**
Lake Waihola Holiday Park & Recreation Reserve (1336) 79 B6 **97**
Lake Wairepo Rest Area (1266) 59 H6 **93**
Lakeside Rest Area Waitahanui (324) 19 E5 **39**
Lakeside Rest Area Lake Wakatipu (1451) 72 B8 **103**
Lakeside South Rest Area (1452) 72 B8 **103**
Landing Road (478) 12 G10 **47**

Camping sites index

Larchview Holiday Park (1309) 67 G5 **96**
Last Light Lodge (1492) 76 E11 **106**
Last Spike Obelisk Rest Area 4.7 (292) 26 A11 **38**
Lauder Roadside Rest Area (1315) 66 H12 67 H1 **96**
Lawrence Rest Area (east) (1365) 79 A3 **99**
Lawrence Rest Area (west) (1367) 79 A3 **99**
Lawrence Kaweka Forest Park (720) 28 C8 **61**
Leith Valley Touring Park (1322) 124 D3 74 G11 **97**
Leithfield Beach Motor Camp (1169) 56 A11 **88**
Levin Motorcamp (689) 29 G5 **60**
Lindale Motor Park (678) 33 A3 **59**
Little Wanganui Hotel & Camping Ground (1028) 41 B7 **80**
Loch Katrine (1125) 46 H12 **86**
Loch Laird Recreation Reserve (1291) 67 B4 **95**
Log Jam Road (180) 7 F2 **31**
Loisel's Beach Waihau Bay (608) 22 B13 **55**
Long Bay Motor Camp (404) 8 C11 **44**
Longwood Holiday Park (1485) 76 H14 77 E2 **105**
Lookout Hill Roadside Rest Area (11) 85 D1 4 G11 **21**
Lookout Rest Area (229) 11 F4 **34**
Lorneville Holiday Park (1480) 77 E5 **105**
Lowburn Rest Area (1405) 66 G9 **101**
Lower Mangatawhiri Campground (203) 8 G8 **33**
Lucky Bay Rangitoto Kite tonga/D'Urville Island (900) 40 C9 **73**
Lucys Gully Rest Area (821) 23 C4 **67**
Luggate Cricket Club Camping Ground (1407) 66 D9 **101**
Lyell Rest Area (986) 41 G7 **78**

M

Macandrew Bay Rest Area & Reserve (1326) 124 B3 74 H12 **97**
Macetown (1437) 65 F6 **102**
Mackay Creek (1513) 64 J9 **107**
Maharanui (279) 18 H8 **37**
Mahia Beach Motels & Holiday Park (630) 22 J9 **56**
Mahurangi Regional Park (153) 6 F10 **30**
Maitai Bay (81) 2 F7 **25**
Maitai Valley Motor Camp (912) 116 B6 39 G4 **74**
Makarora Wilderness Resort (1422) 58 H11 **102**
Makatote Gorge Rest Area 4.8 (291) 26 A11 **38**
Makerua Rest Area (692) 29 F6 **60**
Maketu Hilltop Holiday Park (498) 13 C6 **49**
Makorori Beach Rest Area (613) 22 D11 **55**
Manapouri Lakeside Reserve (1497) 70 E10 **106**
Manapouri Motels & Holiday Park (1499) 70 E10 **106**
Mangahuia (288) 18 J12 **38**
Mangamate (568) 20 D11 **53**

Manganuku (620) 15 J3 **56**
Manganuku Roadside Rest Area (619) 15 J3 **55**
Mangaotaki Rest Area (248) 17 B7 **35**
Mangapapa (280) 18 J8 **37**
Mangapurua (284) 25 A7 **37**
Mangaturuturu Roadside Rest Area (294) 26 B11 **38**
Mangatutu Hot Springs Kaweka Forest Park (643) 28 A8 **57**
Mangawaiiti (283) 25 A7 **37**
Mangaweka Campgrounds (710) 27 G3 **61**
Mangaweka North Roadside Rest Area (712) 27 G2 **61**
Mangaweka South Rest Area 1.5 (709) 27 G2 **61**
Mangawhai Heads Motor Camp (4) 6 B9 **21**
Mangawhero (297) 26 C11 **38**
Mangawhiri Bridge Roadside Rest Area (564) 20 B11 **52**
Mangorei Road Information Area (266) 23 B5 **36**
Manuka Gorge Tunnel Rest Area (1364) 79 C4 **99**
Manukau Top 10 Holiday Park (208) 90 E5 7 F5 **33**
Maori Beach (1528) 80 D5 **108**
Mapua Leisure Park (921) 39 G2 **74**
Maraehako Camping Ground (593) 15 B7 **54**
Maraetai Beach Reserve (194) 7 E7 **32**
Marahau Beach Camp (934) 39 D2 **75**
Marble Hill (1152) 46 D12 **87**
Marchwood Park (928) 39 E2 **75**
Marfells Beach (1089) 44 E13 **84**
Marine Park Motor Camp (269) 17 G1 **36**
Martinborough Village Camping (731) 33 E7 **62**
Martins Bay Holiday Park (160) 6 F10 **30**
Marton Motor Camp (701) 29 A6 **60**
Maruia Falls Roadside Rest Area (980) 42 H8 **78**
Maruia Springs Thermal Resort (1149) 46 D13 **87**
Matahi Spit Reserve (524) 13 F7 **50**
Matakohe Top 10 Holiday Park (124) 5 B5 **28**
Matata Recreation Reserve (508) 14 D9 **49**
Matauri Bay Holiday Park Ltd (66) 2 H12 **24**
Maungaongaonga Scenic Reserve (554) 13 J5 **52**
Maungaroa Station (590) 15 C7 **54**
Maunu Hill Roadside Rest Area (27) 85 C1 **22**
Mavora Lakes (1505) 71 B4 **106**
Mawley Park Motor Camp (739) 34 B9 **63**
Mayfair Camping Ground & Cabins (601) 16 H11 **54**
McGregor Park (1476) 77 A2 **105**
McKee Recreation Reserve (923) 39 G2 **75**
McLean Falls Holiday Park (1357) 78 G12 **98**
McLeod Bay Roadside Rest Area (18) 4 H13 **22**
Medlands Beach (131) 36 E5 **28**
Memorial Lookout Rest Area 3.4 (778) 29 C6 **65**
Mercury Bay Motor Camp & Holiday Park (430) 8 D13 **45**

Methven Camping Grounds (1230) 52 J9 55 E2 **91**
Mihi Bridge Rest Area (558) 19 C7 **52**
Milford Sound Lodge (1527) 64 D9 **108**
Mill Arm Rangitoto Kite tonga/D'Urville Island (902) 40 B9 **73**
Mill Creek Bird & Campervan Park (432) 8 E12 **45**
Mill Flat (1000) 43 C7 **79**
Miller's Reserve Roadside Rest Area (744) 31 H2 **63**
Millers Flat Holiday Park (1372) 73 F3 **99**
Mimiha Roadside Rest Area (572) 20 D12 **53**
Miranda Holiday Park (206) 8 H9 **33**
Mirror Lakes DOC Reserve (1514) 64 H9 **107**
Mission Bay Reserve (316) 19 F4 **39**
Mission Bay Rest Area (317) 19 F4 **39**
Mistletoe Bay (864) 40 G10 **71**
Moawhango Lookout (300) 27 C2 **38**
Moawhitu (903) 40 B8 **73**
Moeraki Boulders Holiday Park (1299) 74 B13 **95**
Moeraki Village Holiday Park (1300) 74 B14 **95**
Moetapu Bay Pelorus Sound (860) 40 G9 **71**
Mohakatino Rest Area (255) 17 D5 **36**
Moirs Hill Walkway Rest Area (155) 6 F9 **30**
Mokau Landing Te Urewera National Park (578) 20 E14 21 E2 **53**
Moke Lake (1445) 65 H4 64 H14 **103**
Molesworth Cobb Cottage (1140) 43 J5 **87**
Momorangi Bay Holiday Park Queen Charlotte Sound (850) 40 G9 **70**
Monkey Island (1490) 76 G12 **106**
Monowai (1496) 70 H10 76 B10 **106**
Monument Lookout Rest Area (984) 41 G7 **78**
Morere Hot Springs Camping Ground (627) 22 H8 **56**
Mororimu Rest Area (1094) 48 C14 **84**
Morrison Memorial Bridge (1201) 45 J6 **90**
Mosgiel Motor Camp (1329) 124 J3 74 H10 **97**
Mossburn Country Park (1460) 71 F5 **104**
Mossburn Roadside Rest Area (1461) 71 F4 **104**
Motueka Top 10 Holiday Park (Fearons Bush) (929) 39 E2 **75**
Motuihe (129) 90 B6 7 D6 **28**
Motukaraka Point Reserve (670) 33 C2 **59**
Motunau Beach Camping Ground (1122) 54 C11 **86**
Motuoapa Motor Camp (313) 19 G3 **39**
Motuora Island (159) 6 F11 **30**
Motutere Bay Holiday Park (318) 19 F4 **39**
Mount Somers Holiday Park (1233) 61 A5 **92**
Mountain View Top 10 Holiday Park (1136) 47 F5 **86**
Mowhanau Holiday Park (807) 25 H7 **66**
Mt Cavendish Scenic Reserve (1209) 56 E10 **90**
Mt Lyford Lodge (1129) 48 F8 **86**

WAITANGI, OVERLOOKING THE BAY OF ISLANDS

PHOTO: DONNA BLABER

Camping sites index

Mt Maunganui Beachside Holiday Park (487) 94 A3 13 A4 **48**
Mt Nimrod (1252) 60 J13 **93**
Munro Beach Track Roadside Rest Area (1080) 58 B11 **83**
Murchison Motorhome Park (975) 42 F10 **77**
Muriwai Beach Motor Camp (176) 7 D1 **31**
Murphy's Holiday Camp (507) 14 D8 **49**

N

Nelson City Holiday Park & Motels (914) 116 B4 39 G4 **74**
Nelson Creek Reserve (1038) 45 E6 **81**
Nevans Lookout Rest Area (837) 18 F8 **68**
New Plymouth Top 10 Holiday Park (273) 107 A5 23 B5 **37**
Newhaven Holiday Park (1352) 79 H3 **98**
Ngaere Overbridge Rest Area (827) 23 E7 **68**
Ngaherenga (481) 18 B13 **48**
Ngakuna Bay Rest Area (849) 40 G10 **70**
Ngaporo (286) 26 C8 **38**
Ngaruawahia Roadside Rest Area (220) 9 J5 **34**
Ngaruru Bay (869) 40 G12 **71**
Nikau Cove Pelorus Sound (872) 40 F10 **72**
Nine Mile Creek Reserve (1383) 66 H9 **100**
Norfolk Motel & Campervan Park (82) 1 H6 **25**
Normanby Rest Area (825) 23 G6 **68**
Norsewood South Rest Area 2.1 (765) 31 B7 **64**
North South Holiday Park (1158) 120 C5 56 D9 **88**
Nydia (892) 40 F8 **73**

O

Oakura Beach Holiday Park (822) 23 B4 **68**
Oakura Motels & Holiday Park (37) 4 C12 **23**
Oamaru Bay Motor Camp (406) 8 C11 **44**
Oamaru Top 10 Holiday Park (1294) 68 H11 **95**
Oasis Motel & Caravan Park (307) 19 G2 **39**
Ocean Beach Camping Ground (660) 28 G13 **58**
Ohakune Top 10 Holiday Park (296) 26 C11 **38**
Ohau Point Lookout Rest Area (1096) 48 C13 **84**
Ohauora (281) 17 J7 **37**
Ohauparuparu Bay (875) 40 F11 **72**
Ohawe Beach Motor Camp (815) 23 H6 **67**
Ohikanui Rest Area (1009) 41 H4 **79**
Ohinepane (838) 18 G9 **68**
Ohingaiti Rest Area 1.6 (706) 26 H13 **61**
Ohingaroa Bay (862) 40 G9 **71**
Ohiwa Family Holiday Park (511) 14 F12 **49**
Ohope Beach Picnic Areas (521) 14 F12 **50**
Ohope Beach Top 10 Holiday Park (520) 14 E12 **50**
Okahu Roadend (570) 20 D12 **53**
Okahukura Rest Area (245) 18 E10 **35**
Okains Bay Camping Ground (1222) 56 F13 **91**
Okarito Camping Ground (1062) 49 E5 **82**
Okarito Car Park (1063) 49 E5 **82**
Okiwi Bay (1093) 48 C14 **84**
Okiwi Bay Holiday Park and Lodge (895) 39 E7 **73**
Old McDonald's Farm & Holiday Park (936) 38 F9 **75**
Old Steam Engine Roadside Rest Area (1039) 45 E5 **81**
Olive Grove Lodge and Holiday Park (1298) 68 J10 74 A13 **95**
Omahuru (Ogilvies) (510) 14 J12 **49**
Omakau Recreation Reserve Camping Ground (1316) 66 H12 **96**
Omana Regional Park (193) 7 E7 **32**
Omarama Top 10 Holiday Park (1397) 67 A3 **100**
Omokoroa Thermal Holiday Park (366) 10 H12 **41**
Onaero Bay Holiday Park (264) 17 G2 **36**
Onamalutu (999) 44 C9 40 J8 **79**
Onepoto Caves Walk Rest Area (582) 21 F2 **53**
Opal Hot Springs & Holiday Park (464) 12 C11 **47**
Opape Motor Camp (587) 15 F3 **54**
Oparara Basin Kahurangi National Park (1031) 37 H3 **81**
Opepe Historic Graves Carpark (327) 19 E6 **40**
Opononi Beach Holiday Park (102) 3 D3 **27**
Opotiki Holiday Park (515) 14 F13 **50**
Opoutere Coastal Camping (448) 8 G14 **46**
Opunake Beach Holiday Park (817) 23 F3 **67**
Orangihikoia Te Urewera National Park (576) 20 D14 21 D2 **53**
Orari Gorge (1240) 61 E4 **92**

Orari River Rest Area (1243) 61 H5 **92**
Ore Ore Rest Area 4.4 (804) 26 D10 **66**
Orere Point Top 10 Holiday Park (196) 8 F9 **32**
Orewa Beach Top 10 Holiday Park (146) 88 A3 7 A4 **29**
Orewa Lookout Rest Area (150) 7 A4 **30**
Orongo Bay Holiday Park (44) 81 B3 4 B10 **23**
Orua Bay Beach Motor Camp & Accommodation (215) 7 F3 **34**
Otago Central Rail Trail Memorial Rest Area (1306) 74 B9 **96**
Otaio Gorge (1270) 68 B11 **94**
Otaki Forks (681) 33 A5 **59**
Otama Beach Camp (426) 8 C13 **45**
Otama Beach Reserve Picnic Area (425) 8 C13 **45**
Otamure Beach (35) 4 D13 **23**
Otautu Bay Motor Camps (412) 8 B10 **44**
Otematata Holiday Park (1289) 67 C5 **95**
Otira Hotel Campsite (1200) 52 A8 **90**
Otira Viaduct Lookout (1199) 52 A8 **90**
Otorohanga Holiday Park (234) 11 G6 **35**
Otto/MacDonalds (1064) 49 F6 **82**
Otunui Stream Rest Area (839) 18 G9 **68**
Outram Glen Picnic Area (1330) 74 G9 **97**
Owen River Recreation Reserve (974) 42 F10 **77**
Owhango Rest Area 4.9 (277) 18 G11 **37**

P

Pacific Park Christian Holiday Camp (493) 94 C6 13 B5 **48**
Paddys Lookout Rest Area (941) 38 F9 **75**
Paekakariki Holiday Park (676) 33 B3 **59**
Paengaroa Domain Entrance (503) 13 D6 **49**
Paengaroa Motor Lodge (499) 13 C6 **49**
Pagoda Lodge (62) 86 B3 4 A8 **24**
Pahi Beach Motor Camp (125) 5 B6 **28**
Pahiatua South Rest Area 2.4 (748) 31 F3 **63**
Pakiri Beach Holiday Park (169) 6 D10 **31**
Palmerston North Holiday Park (776) 105 C3 30 E8 **65**
Papa Aroha Holiday park (407) 8 C10 **44**
Papamoa Beach Top 10 Holiday Resort (491) 94 C5 13 B5 **48**
Papamoa Village Park (492) 94 D5 13 B5 **48**
Paparoa Motor Camp (127) 5 B6 **28**
Paradise Springs Motor Camp (173) 5 H7 **31**
Park The Top 10 Ninety Mile Beach (84) 1 H5 **25**
Parikarangaranga Scenic Reserve (314) 19 G3 **39**
Parklands Marina Holiday Park (845) 114 B4 40 G10 **70**
Parklands Motor Lodge (310) 19 G3 **39**
Parklands Tourist Park (1263) 59 H6 **93**
Parsons Creek Recreation Reserve (1287) 67 C6 **95**
Passing Bay (341) 10 F10 **40**
Patea Dam (812) 25 F3 **67**
Peak Lookout Roadside Rest Area (1073) 49 H4 **83**
Peel Forest (1239) 61 C5 **92**
Peg Leg Hill Rest Area (1197) 52 A8 **90**
Pelorus Bridge (885) 39 H6 **72**
Penguin Bay Rangitoto Kite (901) 40 B9 **73**
Piano Flat (1469) 72 E11 **104**
Picnic Bay Pelorus Sound (871) 40 F10 **71**
Picnic Reserves (664) 110 E2 33 F2 **58**
Picton Campervan Park (841) 113 D2 114 C3 40 G10 **70**
Picton Top 10 Holiday Park (842) 113 B5 114 C3 40 G10 **70**
Piggotts Campground (204) 8 G8 **33**
Piha Domain Motor Camp (178) 7 E2 **31**
Pikowai Reserve Camping Ground (504) 14 D8 **49**
Pine Beach Campground Kaiiwi Lakes (113) 3 H6 **27**
Pineacres Holiday Park (1166) 56 B10 **88**
Pinedale Motor Camp (683) 39 H7 **72**
Pines Holiday Park (1137) 47 F5 **86**
Pinewoods Motor Park (145) 88 B3 7 B4 **29**
Pioneer Park (1255) 61 F2 **93**
Pipi Beach (893) 40 F9 **73**
Pipiriki Rest Area (800) 26 C8 **66**
Piriaka Lookout Rest Area 4.10 (274) 18 F10 **37**
Piripiri (753) 30 A11 **63**
Piropiro (480) 18 C12 **48**
Pleasant Flat (1432) 58 E12 **102**
Pohara Beach Top 10 Holiday Park (949) 38 D8 **76**
Pokaka Mill (305) 18 H12 **39**
Port Jackson (414) 8 A9 **44**
Port Waikato Holiday Park (223) 9 E1 **34**
Port William (1529) 80 D5 **108**

Portobello Village Tourist Park (1327) 124 A2 74 G12 **97**
Possum Lodge Motel & Holiday Park (1498) 70 E10 **106**
Pouawa Beach (609) 22 D12 **55**
Poukaria (278) 18 G9 **37**
Pounawea Motor Camp (1351) 79 H3 **98**
Pourerere Beach (773) 32 B13 **64**
Pouto Point Motor Camp (122) 5 E5 **28**
Promenade Point Campground Kaiiwi Lakes (114) 3 H5 **27**
Pudding Hill Lodge (1232) 52 J8 **92**
Puhi Puhi (1100) 48 C13 **85**
Pukehina Motor Camp (500) 13 C7 **49**
Pukekura Lodge (The Bushman's Centre) (1057) 50 C10 **82**
Pukenui Holiday Park (86) 1 F5 **26**
Puketi Recreation Area (100) 3 A7 **26**
Punakaiki Beach Camp (1015) 45 B5 **80**
Punakaiki Bridge Rest Area (1016) 45 B5 **80**
Purakaunui Bay (1354) 79 H2 **98**
Puriri Bay Whangaruru Scenic Reserve (41) 4 C12 **23**
Putangirua Pinnacles (733) 33 G5 **62**
Putanui Point (854) 40 G9 **71**
Puti Bluffs Rest Area (228) 11 F3 **34**
Putiki Rest Area (789) 26 J8 **65**

Q

Queenstown Lake View Holiday Park (1440) 125 B2 126 B2 65 H4 **103**
Queenstown Rest Area (1441) 125 D1 126 B2 65 H4 **103**
Queenstown Top 10 Holiday Park 'Creeksyde' (1442) 125 A2 126 B2 65 H4 **103**
Quinney's Bush Camp and Caravan Park (962) 42 C13 **77**

R

Raetea North Side (97) 2 K8 **26**
Raetihi Holiday Park (802) 26 C10 **66**
Raetihi North Roadside Rest Area (801) 26 C10 **66**
Raetihi South Roadside Rest Area (803) 26 C10 **66**
Raglan Kopua Holiday Park (225) 11 C3 **34**
Rainbow Falls Scenic Reserve Rest Area (63) 86 B1 4 A8 **24**
Rainforest Retreat & Holiday Park (1067) 49 G6 **83**
Rakaia Huts Camping Area (1226) 55 H6 **91**
Rakaia River Holiday Park & Motels (1225) 55 G5 **91**
Ranfurly Holiday Park (1308) 67 H5 **96**
Rangiora Holiday Park (1164) 56 B9 **88**
Rangiora Leigh Camp & Holiday Park (1165) 56 A9 **88**
Rangitaiki Bridge Roadside Rest Area (563) 20 B11 **52**
Rangitata Rest Area (1235) 61 E5 **92**
Rapahoe Beach Motor Camp (1021) 45 E4 **80**
Rapurapu Reserve (465) 12 D12 **47**
Rarangi (990) 40 J10 **78**
Rarawa (87) 1 E4 **26**
Ratimera Bay Queen Charlotte Sound (873) 40 G11 **72**
Raukawa Falls & YMCA Raukawa (806) 26 E10 **66**
Raukawa Falls Rest Area 4.3 (805) 26 E10 **66**
Rawene Holiday Park (101) 3 C4 **27**
Rays Rest Roadside Rest Area (205) 8 H9 **33**
Redwood Holiday Park (535) 96 C4 13 G4 **51**
Reefton Motor Camp (1033) 46 B9 **81**
Reids Farm Recreation Reserve (486) 19 D5 **48**
Remuera Motor Lodge & Inner City Camping Ground (192) 90 C5 7 E5 **32**
Rerewhakaaitu - Ashpit Road (Ash Pit Bay) (561) 13 J6 **52**
Rerewhakaaitu - Brett Road (Awaatua Bay) (562) 13 J6 **52**
Riccarton Park Holiday Park (1174) 120 C2 56 D9 **89**
Richmond Top 10 Holiday Park (916) 116 D2 39 H3 **74**
Rimutaka Summit Rest Area (727) 33 D5 **62**
River's Edge Holiday Park (772) 28 J9 **64**
Riverglen Holiday Park (433) 8 E13 **45**
Riverhaven Roadside Rest Area (218) 9 G5 **34**
Riverlands Holiday Park (1161) 56 C10 **88**
Riverlands Roadhouse (996) 44 C11 **78**
Riversdale Rest Area (1467) 72 J8 **104**
Riverside Holiday Park (3) 6 B9 **21**
Riverside Motor Camp (631) 21 H5 **56**
Riverside Rest Area Lewis Pass (1146) 47 F1 **87**
Riverside Rest Area Temuka (1247) 61 F5 **92**
Riverton Rocks Scenic Reserve (1486) 77 E2 **105**

Camping sites index

Riverview Holiday Park (978) 42 G9 **77**
Riverwalk Way Roadside Rest Area (221) 9 J5 **34**
Riwaka Domain Rest Area (931) 39 E1 **75**
Roadrunner Motel and Holiday Park (232) 11 E7 **35**
Roaring Billy Falls Reserve (1434) 58 D11 **102**
Roaring Meg Viewpoint and Picnic Area (1435) 66 G8 **102**
Robin Hood Bay (988) 40 H11 **78**
Rocky Angle Rest Area (943) 38 G8 **76**
Rosie Bay (581) 21 E2 **53**
Ross Historic Goldfields Reserve (1055) 50 B11 **82**
Rotoma Holiday Park (527) 13 F7 **50**
Rotorua Family Holiday Park (544) 13 F4 **51**
Rotorua Thermal Holiday Park (540) 96 D3 13 G4 **51**
Rotorua Top 10 Holiday Park (541) 96 C3 13 G4 **51**
Rough Creek Rest Area (1150) 46 E12 **87**
Roxburgh Rest Area (1376) 73 D2 **99**
Ruakaka Reserve Motor Camp (10) 4 J13 **21**
Ruatahuna Road Rest Area (571) 20 C12 **53**
Russell Top 10 Holiday Park (45) 82 A5 81 A3 4 B10 **23**

S

Sailors Cutting Recreation Reserve (1292) 67 B4 **95**
Sanctuary (569) 20 D11 **53**
Sanctuary Point (373) 94 D2 10 J13 **42**
Sandspit Holiday Park (164) 6 E10 **30**
Sandspit Motor Camp (212) 7 J4 **33**
Sapphire Springs Motor Camp (365) 10 H11 **41**
Sawdust Bay (1530) 80 E5 **108**
Scandrett Regional Park (162) 6 F10 **30**
Schoolhouse Bay (879) 40 F12 **72**
Scoutlands (788) 26 J8 **65**
Sea Air Motel & Holiday Park (356) 10 F12 **41**
Seabreeze Holiday Park (434) 8 E13 **45**
Seal Colony Top 10 Holiday Park (1025) 41 G2 **80**

Seaview Holiday Park (250) 17 D5 **36**
Seddonville Holiday Park (1026) 41 D6 **80**
Sentry Hill Motel & Roadhouse (270) 23 A6 **36**
Settlers Motor Camp (450) 8 J14 **46**
Shag Stream (386) 8 H12 **43**
Shakespear Regional Park (144) 88 B6 7 B5 **29**
Shakespeare's Scenic Reserve (435) 8 D13 **45**
Sheepworld Caravan Park (157) 6 E9 **30**
Shelly Beach Camping Ground (175) 5 G7 **31**
Shelly Beach Top 10 Holiday Park (405) 8 C11 **44**
Shining Star Beachfront Accommodation (1050) 45 H2 **82**
Shotover Top 10 Holiday Park (1443) 65 G4 **103**
Siberia Flat Kahurangi National Park (964) 42 C11 **77**
Silver Birch Family Holiday Park (371) 94 C2 10 J13 **42**
Sinclair Wetlands Camp (1337) 79 B6 **97**
Skippers-Mt Aurum (1444) 65 F4 **103**
Slab Hut Creek (1035) 46 B9 **81**
Smiths Farm Holiday Park (855) 40 G9 **71**
Smithy Creek (1519) 64 G9 **108**
Solscape Eco Retreat (230) 11 C2 **35**
South Arm Rangitoto Kite tonga/D'Urville Island (904) 40 B9 **73**
South Auckland Caravan Park (209) 7 H6 **33**
South Beach Motel & Motor Park (1044) 45 F3 **81**
South Brighton Motor Camp (1207) 120 H2 56 D10 **90**
South Westland Salmon Farm & (1077) 58 B12 **83**
Speechleys Bridge Rest Area (1244) 61 F4 **92**
Spencer Beach Holiday Park (1159) 56 C10 120 G6 **88**
Spring Creek Holiday Park (992) 44 B10 **78**
St Andrews Recreation Reserve & Camping Ground (1271) 68 B13 **94**
St Bathans Domain (1313) 66 F13 67 F2 **96**
St James Walkway Rest Area (1145) 47 F1 **87**
Staging Post The (1115) 48 H9 **85**
Stony Bay (416) 8 A10 **44**
Stormy Point Lookout Rest Area 54.2 (780) 30 A8 **65**

Stratford Top Town Holiday Park (828) 25 B1 **68**
Summit Rest Area (549) 13 F5 **52**
Sumner Beach Reserve (1208) 120 H1 56 E11 **90**
Sumner Road Rest Area (1045) 45 F3 **81**
Sunset Bay (46) 4 A11 **23**
Sutherland Stream Picnic Area (997) 44 C10 **78**
Sylvan (1450) 64 E11 65 E1 **103**

T

Taahunaatara Rest Area (553) 13 J3 **52**
Taheke Rest Area (104) 3 C7 **27**
Tahorakuri Forest Roadside Rest Area (559) 19 C7 **52**
Tahuna Beach Holiday Park (915) 116 B4 39 G3 **74**
Taieri River Scenic Reserve (AKA Kaarston Park) (1334) 79 C7 **97**
Taihape Riverview Holiday Park (714) 27 F2 **61**
Tainui Scenic Reserve (252) 17 D5 **36**
Tainui Wetere Domain (254) 17 D5 **36**
Takaka Camping Ground (948) 38 E8 **76**
Takapuna Beach Holiday Park (138) 88 H5 90 A4 7 D4 **29**
Tamahere Wayside Stop (454) 92 G6 11 C7 **46**
Tane Mahuta Reserve and Rest Area (109) 3 E4 **27**
Tapanui Motor Camp (1371) 72 J13 **99**
Tapapakanga Regional Park (Sea View & Beachfront Campgrounds) (198) 8 F9 **32**
Tapawera Settle (963) 42 B13 **77**
Tapotupotu (90) 1 A1 **26**
Tapu Camp (394) 8 F11 **43**
Tapu Creek Campervan Park (393) 8 F11 **43**
Tapu Reserve (399) 8 F11 **43**
Tarewa Park Roadside Rest Area (12) 85 C1 4 G11 **21**
Tariki Subway Roadside Rest Area (268) 23 C6 **36**
Tarukenga Rest Area (547) 13 F3 **51**
Tasman Motor Camp (924) 39 G2 **75**

LAKE PEARSON, NEAR ARTHUR'S PASS
PHOTO: DONNA BLABER

Camping sites index

Tatapouri By the Sea (612) 22 D11 **55**
Tatum Park (688) 29 H4 **60**
Taumarunui Holiday Park (275) 18 F11 **37**
Taupo All Seasons Holiday Park (331) 98 B4 19 D5 **40**
Taupo Bay Holiday Park (72) 2 G10 **25**
Taupo De Bretts Spa Resort (330) 98 B5 19 D5 **40**
Tauranga Bay Holiday Park (70) 2 H11 **25**
Tauranga Tourist Park (370) 94 C2 10 J13 **42**
Tautuku Beach Scenic Reserve (1356) 79 J1 **98**
Tawa Bay (897) 40 E8 **73**
Tawanui (1355) 78 E13 79 G1 **98**
Tawharanui Regional Park (165) 6 E11 **30**
Taylor Dam Rest Area (998) 44 D10 **79**
Taylor Park Motor Camp (1338) 79 C5 **98**
Te Anau Downs Rest Area (1509) 70 A12 **107**
Te Anau Great Lakes Holiday Park (1504) 70 D11 **106**
Te Anau Lakeview Holiday Park (1502) 70 D11 **106**
Te Anau Top 10 Holiday Park (1503) 70 D11 **106**
Te Araroa Holiday Park (595) 16 B11 **54**
Te Aroha Holiday Park (344) 10 G10 **40**
Te Awanga Holiday Park (656) 28 F13 **58**
Te Haumi Rest Area (51) 4 B10 81 B2 **23**
Te Iringa Kaimanawa Forest Park (648) 19 G6 **57**
Te Kaha Holiday Park (589) 15 C6 **54**
Te Kohania Camping Ground (93) 1 J5 **26**
Te Mata Reserve (396) 8 F11 **43**
Te Ngutu-O-Te Manu Historic Reserve Campground (826) 23 F6 **68**
Te Ora Farm (967) 42 A13 38 J8 **77**
Te Paerahi Beach (770) 32 D11 **64**
Te Pakau (Eight Acre) (509) 14 H12 **49**
Te Puke Holiday Park (494) 13 C5 **49**
Te Puru Holiday Park (391) 8 G11 **43**
Te Taita O Makora Te Urewera National Park (577) 20 D14 21 D2 **53**
Te Wera Valley Lodge (831) 25 A4 **68**
Te Whaiti Roadside Rest Area (567) 20 C11 **52**
Temple (1269) 59 F4 **93**
Temuka Holiday Park (1246) 61 G5 **92**
The Barn Cabins Camping & Backpackers (935) 38 F10 **75**
The Chalets Holiday Park (1400) 66 H8 **101**
The Chasm (1526) 64 E8 **108**
The Divide & Routeburn Track Base (1523) 64 F10 **108**
The Glade Holiday Park (443) 8 G14 **46**
The Green (135) 36 E4 **29**
The Old Steam Engine Roadside Rest Area (1039) 45 E5 **81**
The Park Top 10 Ninety Mile Beach (84) 1 H5 **25**
The Staging Post (1115) 48 H9 **85**
The Tree House (98) 3 C4 **26**
The Trout Hotel (882) 39 G7 **72**
Thicket Burn (1495) 76 D10 **106**
Thomas's Lodge & Holiday Park (1349) 79 G3 **98**
Thornbury Aparima Bridge (1478) 77 D3 **105**
Thornton Beach Holiday Park (517) 14 E10 **50**
Thunder Creek Falls & Forest Walk (1431) 58 F11 **102**
Tidewater Tourist Park (401) 8 D11 **43**
Tieke Kainga (285) 26 B8 **37**
Timaru Top 10 Holiday Park (1248) 61 J4 **92**
Tiniroto Lakes and Community Centre Campground (583) 21 E6 **53**
Tirohanga Beach Motor Camp (586) 15 F3 **54**
Tokamariro River Picnic Area (1363) 79 C4 **99**
Tokerau Beach Motor Camp (79) 1 F7 **25**
Tokomaru Bay (599) 16 H11 **54**
Tokoroa Motor Camp (471) 12 H12 **47**
Tolaga Bay Holiday Park (607) 22 B13 **55**
Tongariro Family Holiday Park (304) 19 H1 **39**
Totara (1512) 64 J9 **107**
Totara Flat (380) 8 G12 **42**
Totara Flat Picnic Area (887) 39 H6 **72**
Totara Reserve/Camp Rangi Woods (752) 31 B4 **63**
Totaranui Abel Tasman National Park (953) 38 D9 **76**
Treasure Island (19) 4 G13 **22**
Tree House The (98) 3 C4 **26**
Trestle View (379) 8 G12 **42**
Trotters Gorge (1301) 74 B13 **95**
Trounson Kauri Park (111) 3 G5 **27**
Trout Hotel The (882) 39 G7 **72**
Tuatapere Domain Reserve (1493) 76 E11 **106**
Tuatapere Motel (1491) 76 F12 **106**
Tui Lodge (402) 8 C11 **43**
Tumunui (555) 13 H4 **52**
Turakina Rest Area 3.2 (784) 29 A4 **65**
Turangi Holiday Park (311) 19 G3 **39**
Turihaua Beach (610) 22 D11 **55**
Turihaua Point (611) 22 D11 **55**
Tutukaka Holiday Park (30) 4 E13 **22**
Twelve Mile Delta (1446) 64 H13 65 H3 **103**
Twin Kauri Walking Track (441) 8 F14 **46**
Twin Pines Tourist Park (54) 81 B1 4 B9 **24**

U

Upper Eglinton (1520) 64 G9 **108**
Upper Mangatawhiri Campground (202) 8 G8 **33**
Upper Orari Rest Area (1236) 61 E5 **92**
Urchin (303) 19 J3 **38**
Urenui Beach Camp Ground (263) 17 G3 **36**
Uretiti (9) 4 J13 **21**
Uretiti Fatigue Stop (8) 4 J13 **21**
Urupukapuka Bay (47) 4 A11 **23**

V

Vauxhall Reserve (1324) 124 D4 74 H11 **97**
Viaduct Lookout Rest Area (1196) 52 A8 **90**
Victoria Park Camp & Cabins (1272) 68 D12 **94**
Vinegar Hill (Putai Ngahere Reserve) (704) 27 J1 **60**
Vinegar Hill Rest Area 54.1 (705) 27 J1 **61**

W

Wagener Holiday Park (85) 1 F5 **25**
Wagon Train RV Park (58) 4 B8 **24**
Waharau Regional Park (Blackberry Flats & Tainui) (199) 8 F9 **32**
Wahi Pai Reserve North Entrance (763) 31 C6 **64**
Wahine Bay (662) 110 E2 33 F2 **58**
Wai-inu Beach Camp (809) 25 H5 **67**
Wai-iti Beach Retreat (262) 17 F3 **36**
Waiau Motor Camp (1127) 47 H7 **86**
Waihau Bay Holiday Park (594) 16 B8 **54**
Waihi Beach Top 10 Holiday Park (355) 10 F12 **41**
Waihi Gorge (1241) 61 E4 **92**
Waihi Motor Camp (351) 10 F10 **41**
Waikahoa Bay Mimiwhangata Coastal Park (36) 4 D12 **23**
Waikaia Domain Motor Camp (1468) 72 F9 **104**
Waikanae Beach Holiday Park (615) 99 C2 100 C3 22 E10 **55**
Waikare River Mouth (634) 28 A13 **56**
Waikaremoana Motor Camp Te Urewera National Park (579) 21 E2 **53**
Waikawa (687) 29 H5 **60**
Waikawa Bay Holiday Park (846) 114 B5 40 G10 **70**
Waikawa Point Roadside Rest Area (592) 15 B6 **54**
Waikawa Recreation Reserve (1358) 78 G11 **99**
Waikawau Bay (417) 8 B11 **44**
Waikite Valley Thermal Pools (556) 13 J4 **52**
Waikouaiti Beach Motor Camp (1319) 74 E12 **96**
Waikuku Beach Holiday Park (1168) 56 B10 **88**
Waimakariri River Rest Area (1177) 55 B5 **89**
Waimakariri River Rest Areas (1160) 56 C10 **88**
Waimarama Seaside Resort (661) 28 H13 **58**
Waimaru Pelorus Sound (877) 40 E10 **72**
Waimiha/Ongarue Rest Area (244) 18 D10 **35**
Waingaro Hot Springs Caravan Park & Hot Pools (224) 9 J3 **34**
Wainora (381) 8 G12 **42**
Wainui Beach Reserve (226) 11 C3 **34**
Waiohine Gorge Tararua Forest Park (736) 33 B7 **62**
Waiomu Domain Rest Area (392) 8 G11 **43**
Waiona Bay Pelorus Sound (898) 40 D9 **73**
Waiongana Hill Roadside Rest Area (267) 23 B6 **36**
Waipapa Bay Camping Ground (1092) 48 C14 **84**
Waipapa Road Rest Area (477) 12 J10 **47**
Waipara Sleepers Motor Camp (1123) 54 C8 **86**
Waipatiki Beach Farm Park (639) 28 B13 **56**
Waipehu Reserve & Picnic Area (319) 19 F4 **39**
Waipiro Bay (597) 16 G11 **54**
Waipoua Forest Campsite (110) 3 F5 **27**

Waipu Cove Cottages & Camping (7) 6 A8 **21**
Waipu Cove Roadside Rest Area (5) 6 A8 **21**
Waipukurau Holiday Park (768) 32 A10 **64**
Wairakei Thermal Valley (484) 19 C5 **48**
Wairau Incident Rest Area (991) 44 B11 **78**
Wairau Valley Tavern (1001) 43 C7 **79**
Waitaki River Rest Area (1276) 68 F13 **94**
Waitaki Waters Holiday Park (1277) 68 F13 **94**
Waitangi Holiday Park (52) 81 B1 4 B9 **24**
Waitarere Beach Motor Camp (694) 29 F4 **60**
Waiteti Trout Stream Holiday Park (545) 13 F4 **51**
Waitiki Holiday Park (88) 1 B2 **26**
Waitomo Top 10 Holiday Park (240) 11 H5 **35**
Waiwera Holiday Park (151) 7 A4 **30**
Walker Creek (1511) 64 J9 **107**
Wanaka Lakeview Holiday Park (1408) 66 D8 **101**
Wanaka Top 10 Holiday Park (1412) 66 D8 **101**
Waterfront Rest Area (600) 16 H11 **54**
Watters Cottage Rest Area (1126) 47 H6 **86**
Waverley Beach Domain (810) 25 G4 **67**
Wayside Road Roadside Rest Area (217) 9 E4 **34**
Wedderburn Roadside Rest Area (1310) 67 G4 **96**
Welcome Bay Hot Pools & Campground (374) 94 D3 13 B4 **42**
Wellington Top 10 Holiday Park (721) 110 D3 33 E3 **61**
Wenderholm Regional Park (152) 7 A4 **30**
Wentworth (451) 8 J14 **46**
West Bay Nelson Lakes National Park (1006) 43 F1 **79**
Westport Holiday Park & Motel (1024) 41 G3 **80**
Whaitiri Point Rest Area (580) 21 E2 **53**
Whakahoro (287) 18 H9 **38**
Whakamaru Recreation Reserve (476) 19 A3 **47**
Whakanewha Regional Park (130) 7 D7 **28**
Whakapapa Holiday Park (290) 18 J12 **38**
Whakatane Holiday park (516) 14 E11 **50**
Whananaki North Motel & Holiday Park (34) 4 D13 **22**
Whangaehu Hill Rest Area 3.1 (786) 26 J9 **65**
Whangaiterenga (384) 8 G12 **42**
Whangamata Motor Camp (449) 8 H14 **46**
Whangamomona (834) 17 J6 **68**
Whangamomona Saddle Rest Area (833) 24 C11 **68**
Whanganui River Top 10 Holiday Park (793) 109 A6 26 H8 **66**
Whangapoua (136) 36 C4 **29**
Whangarei Falls Holiday Park & Backpackers (28) 85 A2 4 F12 **22**
Whangarei Top 10 Holiday Park (20) 85 B2 4 G11 **22**
Whangaroa Harbour Holiday Park (71) 2 H10 **25**
Whangaruru Beachfront Camp (38) 4 C12 **23**
Whangateau Holiday Park (166) 6 D10 **30**
Wharariki Beach Holiday Park (960) 37 A7 **76**
Wharehunga Bay (870) 40 F12 **71**
Whatamango Bay Queen Charlotte Sound (847) 40 G11 **70**
Whatuwhiwhi Top 10 Holiday Park (80) 2 F7 **25**
White Horse Hill (1261) 59 B6 **93**
Whitebait Inn Cabins & Motor Camp (253) 17 D5 **36**
Whites Bay (989) 40 J10 **78**
Whitestone Stream Bridge (1500) 70 E12 **106**
Whitianga Campground & Beach Motel & Cabins (429) 8 D13 **45**
Whitikau (621) 15 G5 **56**
Wiers Beach Reserve (1360) 78 H10 **99**
Willowhaven Holiday Park (543) 13 F4 **51**
Winchester Motor Camp (1245) 61 G5 **92**
Windsor Lodge Motel & Caravan Park (323) 19 E5 **39**
Winton Golf Course & Camp (1474) 77 B4 **105**
Wiritoa Lake Reserve Rest Area (787) 26 J8 **65**
Wooded Gully (1181) 53 E5 55 A7 **89**
Woodend Beach Holiday Park (1167) 56 B10 **88**
Woodville Domain Camping Area (750) 31 D4 **63**
Wyndham Camping Ground (1472) 78 D9 **104**

Y

YMCA Wainui Park Campground (1216) 56 G12 **91**